Remembering Tomorrow

Remembering Tomorrow

From SDS To Life After Capitalism

By Michael Albert

SEVEN STORIES PRESS

NEW YORK

LONDON

TORONTO

MELBOURNE

Seven Stories Press
140 Watts Street
New York, NY 10013
http://www.sevenstories.com

In Canada:
Publishers Group Canada
250A Carlton Street
Toronto, ON M5A-2L1

In the UK:
Turnaround Publisher Services Ltd.
Unit 3, Olympia Trading Estate, Coburg Road
Wood Green, London N22 6TZ

In Australia:
Palgrave Macmillan
627 Chapel Street
South Yarra VIC 3141

Library of Congress Cataloging-in-Publication Data
Albert, Michael, 1947- Remembering tomorrow: from SDS to life after capitalism / Michael Albert.
p. cm.
ISBN-13: 978-1-58322-742-8 (hardcover : alk. paper)
ISBN-10: 1-58322-742-3 (hardcover : alk. paper)
1. Liberalism. 2. Albert, Michael, 1947- 3. Economists–Biography. I. Title.

JC574.A43 2006
322.4'2092–dc22
[B]
2006013635

College professors may order examination copies of Seven Stories Press titles for a free six-month trial period. To order, visit www.sevenstories.com/textbook or fax on school letterhead to (212) 226-1411.

Book design by Michael Albert
Printed in Canada

9 8 7 6 5 4 3 2 1

REMEMBERING TOMORROW

REMEMBERING TOMORROW

Acknowledgments

All memoirs depend on people and events populating their pages. In this particular memoir, various social movements and projects wrote the reality.

Thanks also to Lydia and Andrea Sargent who each painstakingly edited the whole book, giving it whatever stylistic merit it may display. Likewise, parts of the book were read and edited by friends who especially commented on interpretations and remembrances, including Stephen Shalom, Justin Poder, Peter Bohmer, Cynthia Peters, and Andrej Grubacic. A number of people mentioned in *Remembering Tomorrow* were sent the manuscript in advance and made suggestions to correct errors or clarify intent. These included Anita Albert, Arthur MacEwan, Sam Bowles, Herb Gintis, Michael Ansara, Ivy Hahnel, and Robin Hahnel. Hopefully, *Remembering Tomorrow* is true to our collective experience.

Finally, thanks also to Dan Simon and Ria Julien at Seven Stories Press, Dan for taking an interest and championing the book and Ria for editorial help with the final manuscript.

Wheel of Law

By Ho Chi Minh

The wheel of the law turns
without pause.
After the rain, good weather.
In the wink of an eye
the universe throws off
its muddy clothes.
For ten thousand miles
the land
spreads out like a beautiful brocade.
Light breezes. Smiling flowers.
High in the trees, among
the sparkling leaves
all the birds sing at once.
People and animals rise up reborn.

What could be more natural?
After sorrow, comes joy.

Table of Contents

INTRODUCTION

Bang, Bang Goes
The Beat Of My Drum

What's In a Memoir

*If you really want to hear about it, the first thing you'll probably want to know
is where I was born, and what my lousy childhood was like, and how my parents
were occupied and all before they had me, and all that David Copperfield kind
of crap, but I don't feel like going into it, if you want to know the truth.*
— *J. D. Salinger*

A memoir recounts events, explicates a life, explores history, and draws lessons. A memoir should excite, tell truth, affront, and reveal. No preaching allowed. A memoir should be an honest novel.

My father, Melvin Albert, advised, cajoled, defended, and supported. He was a liberal corporate lawyer. Alzheimer's killed him before he died. My mother, Pearl Fleischman, taught kindergarten and fourth grade and labored over house, home, and health. Mom was appreciated by all. A few weeks before her 91st birthday she died. Relentless cancer was her Armageddon. The ocean became her cemetery.

I was told my early family lived in the same building as the great comedian Milton Berle. Uncle Miltie reputedly said, "If opportunity doesn't knock, build a door." Did I get my door-building predilections from Miltie?

My sister is nine years my senior. When I was five Anita was fourteen. She was a girl, then a woman. I was a boy, then whatever. Young, we barely crossed paths. Anita went to Cornell, in Ithaca, New York. I saw Cornell while visiting Anita and liked Ithaca's natural gorges. As a high school junior, I summered at Cornell in a science program for budding Stephen Hawkings. Anita married Jack Karasu, from Turkey, whom she met at Cornell. Jack's business took Anita to Spain. When Anita returned to the U.S., an artist and teacher, she and I lived far apart. Years later, Anita moved nearer and we are now sister and brother sharing life's circumstances. Anita's son, my nephew Marc, works in New York City in advertising. At Marc's Bar Mitzvah I gave him a copy of Che's writings. For his last fifteen years, Seymour Melman was Anita's partner. Seymour was a teacher/activist who spent his life fighting for peace and against military economy.

To assess family influences is perhaps a fool's errand. My brother Eddie and I had the same parents and sister, lived in the same places, and had similar mental faculties. But rather than becoming two peas in a pod, we became an apple and an kumquat or a tuna and a turtle. Eddie was eight years my senior. We both liked sports, TV, and boy things. As a preteen I always sought Eddie's company. This annoyed him and I remember Eddie would make me say uncle while I held out against submission. Did lopsided familial fighting produce insecurities? Or did withstanding big brother's bullying produce a strong will?

Eddie was smart and congenial but his life pirouetted from a typical suburban trajectory into callous, near-suicidal gambling. Contingent choices of whom to befriend steered Eddie's options. With a little twist, perhaps Eddie would have had radical social concerns. Perhaps I would have suffered consumptive addictions.

As a young kid I watched Eddie's continuous heated conflicts with my parents. Did a soap-opera youth make me too timid or did it make me properly cautious? Either way, I decided in ninth grade that whatever I would do in life, I would reject subservience to parents, teachers, and siblings. I would respect reason, but not take orders. I became my own person. No big catharsis. No tumultuous introspection. I just found my own drum and started banging. Bang, bang, here is a memoir.

Me as Memoirist

> *Outside of a dog, a book is man's best friend.*
> *Inside of a dog it's too dark to read.*
> —Groucho Marx

My writing a memoir is like a sumo wrestler ballet dancing. First, my recollection of the past is not eidetic. Cramming high school facts was torture. Names, places, and dates eluded me. Asked to cough up sequence and pattern, I reconstructed them from foundations as if doing mathematical deductions. Experiences implant in the sinews of my mind as they do for everyone else, but I have a defective playback mechanism.

My dad was older than the average father. He had me at 43. My mom was older than average too. She had me at 32. Mom got sick in her fourth month post-conception. Vacationing away from home, she was advised by a friend's doctor that I was dead. Flush me out, he urged. Mother instead went home to check with her own specialist. I was doing just fine, he reported. Ping, ping. Mom's stubbornness started my little drum.

I had a childhood disease, Celiac. Eating nearly anything wrenched my stomach. My staying-alive diet was bananas, chopped hamburger, and cottage cheese. Family lore says I often begged food from strangers and looted garbage cans. Did youthful scrounging affect my maturity? Today, I can't eat bananas. I can beg and steal. Did my early days template my later life?

In grade school I was a math whiz, but horrible in spelling, penmanship, and writing. I received extra math books to keep me busy from first grade through high school, where, in addition to accelerated classes, my friend Irwin Gaines and I left school twice a week to travel about a mile to a local college, Iona. There we took a course in differential equations with college upperclassmen. Irwin and I were the two best differentiators. Irwin went to Harvard when I went to MIT. Irwin became a physicist, following a path Vietnam pushed me off.

In ninth grade, I suffered through Latin. It was incredibly shaming. Our octogenarian teacher would spend most classes making students read out loud, one after another. The text was in Latin and when called on you had to translate and recite the appropriate English. I failed every time. I looked a fool, but never walked out of class. This type submissive obedience later wore off. What did my classmates look like? How did my teacher dress? What did I say when shamed? Some memoirists include in their books descriptions of decades-old dress, dialogue, weather, and feelings. They fill up pages with "then I blushed and said 'what's up with that.'" They remember details, get them from journals, or just make them up like books about writing memoirs advocate.

Not me. What I can't remember generally includes who said what to whom, when, wearing what clothes, in what mood, with what facial expression, during what weather pattern. And I kept no journals. But it isn't just bad memory that makes me an odd memoirist. I also don't introspect. Corralling inner motivations, much less inner demons, doesn't excite me. Looking inward would preclude looking outward, even if just for a minute. My visiting a psychiatrist would generate a cacophony of silence.

Another memoir obstructing trait of mine is that though I am intellectually pugnacious, I have little interest in revisiting combats. What benefit could that bring? I avoid ad hominem history.

I don't remember my father coming home from work and my rushing to greet him, jumping into his arms from the porch outside our house, and accidentally blasting him in the head with a rock I had cradled in my hand. Did forgetting this teach me to censor my memories? Did trauma from this shape my whole life? Does it matter? I can't see how.

I do remember the big house I inhabited through the sixth grade. But did the house's large size, varied rooms, great comforts, and intriguing crannies help shape me? Why should anyone care?

Were there politically relevant events at a young age? Maybe, but how could anyone decide what qualifies? I remember getting in a fight in fifth grade with a bully over his picking on someone else. Did that make me a lifelong defender of the oppressed? Suppose he had beat me up. Would that have soured me to defending the oppressed? Do I owe my life path to the bully's weakness?

I also remember getting in a fight with my then-best friend, Donald Pearlman. We were in third grade and I chipped his front tooth. Donald was back playing after a couple of hours. I was depressed for days. Did this give me savage solidarity for others? Maybe. Maybe not. Donald and I lived next door to one another all through primary school. When we were ten, or thereabouts, a large house across the street was sold to Liberia's U.S. ambassador. Though I never met or even saw the ambassador himself, not long after his family moved in, and not long before his family moved out, Donald and I played one day with the ambassador's super prissy son. The three of us were on the ambassador's front lawn, across the street from my and Donald's neighboring houses, playing a game called "let's see who can hit the softest." The Liberian lad, I can't remember his name for the life of me, hit Donald in the accepted target in this game, his arm. Liberia did it very softly. Donald then hit my arm softer still, as per the logic of the game. I hauled off and blasted his Liberian Lordship's arm as hard as I could and said, "Whoops, I lose." It was cruel, and he ran off crying. Was it that I didn't like him? Was it a turf war? Was it racism? Since I remember the event, and since I still feel guilty over it, I have to assume the worst. Bang, bang, it was a bad beat.

Another damning deed from that time happened when Donald and I were sitting by the roadside, and saw a big nail there, almost a spike. I picked it up and carefully balanced it in the roadway on its flat hammer-hitting zone with the point facing upward. Before long a multiaxle truck plowed down our street, leaving behind no nail. It had to have been the only such truck to ever get so lost as to mistakenly go through our leafy suburb. Five minutes later a human mountain comes marching down the street asking if we saw anyone put something in the road. He had a destroyed tire and he waved about our missing nail. We said "no." I later suffered unsettling guilt and it didn't take Aristotle to realize this condition was better avoided. Perhaps my undying inclination to avoid guilt-inducing acts was part innate and part early experience. Perhaps different early experiences could have undone rather than enhanced the innateness. Life is largely unfathomable. It is better to focus on the occasional simple parts we can learn from than to drown in the complicated minutiae beyond our ken.

I ran for student body president of the ninth grade and lost. In high school I ran for treasurer of the school and won. In high school, too, I had my first love, Nancy Shapiro. My interest in physics grew. I met Bob Dylan's music—and Dylan rebuilt me with a little help from the Beatles, the Stones, and all the rest. My high school years were idyllic. They had no personal pain to rebel against or escape. Saturdays I went to Columbia University for a morning class with Irwin Gaines, Linda Lurie, and a few other aspiring Isaac Newtons, including Larry Seidman. Larry, a year ahead of me in high school, became my closest friend and raised the bar for maturity and integrity in my life. There was a lot of softball, touch football, and tennis. Good friends are a blessing. Everyone knows that.

I remember sitting in a car, in a train station parking lot, waiting for my father who each day commuted from New Rochelle to New York City and back. It was January 1959. I was twelve. On the radio was a story about Cuba. It mentioned a guy named Castro. It mentioned a guy called Che. Dad arrived. Off went the radio. He was tired from work. I guess I turned it on again, metaphorically, years later.

My high school yearbook proclaimed I would be a physicist. No one would have guessed I would write piles of books about revolution. But while I wasn't remotely literary, nonetheless, in high school music lyrics conquered my mind. I dissected songs for hours with Larry Seidman. I remember "Johnnie's in the basement mixing up the medicine, I'm on the pavement, thinking about the government" and I especially remember the second verse:

Ah get born, keep warm
Short pants, romance
Learn to dance, get dressed, get blessed
Try to be a success
Please her, please him,
Don't steal, don't lift
Twenty years of schooling and they put you on the day shift

I got born. I kept warm. I wore short pants. I romanced. I barely danced. Few would emulate my dress. My blessings ran perpendicular to those Dylan's "Subterranean" lyric rejected. My successes inverted those Dylan rhymed. I pleased some people. I stole. I lifted. I got the 20 years. I work days, but nights too.

Emulating My Muse

> *Some editors are failed writers, but so are most writers.*
> *—T. S. Eliot*

So what's the point of a memoir from someone with a poor memory, without introspection, who rejects personal fireworks, and who avoids personal revelation? Moving from draft one of *Remembering Tomorrow* through draft two and on toward draft 37, I found that pressures mounted from readers for greater personal revelation. "It isn't just the political experiences, thoughts, books, institutions, and movements that matter," people advised me. "You have to include life lived by real people in real times. Use personal context to familiarize and humanize broader stories." Okay, I let these critics bang on my drum one time. I inserted some personal stuff.

As I began writing *Remembering Tomorrow*, I devoured a couple of books on writing memoirs. They urged revelation, novelist style, and pugnacity. I examined memoirs to emulate. Tom Hayden's *Rebel* told about the New Left. Dave Dellinger's incredibly inspiring *From Yale to Jail*, Bill Ayers's ultimately overwritten *Fugitive Days*, and Jane Fonda's very personal *My Life So Far,* all covered parts of those times. Bertrand Russell's, Simone de Beauvoir's, Malcolm X's, and Gandhi's autobiographies provided examples of style and content. I read some less memorable shorter works, too, and finally, I also read the first volume of Bob Dylan's memoir, *Chronicles*. Despite its being socially detached, *Chronicles* most affected my plans.

Chronicles jumps all over Dylan's timeline. Thematic flow facilitates comprehension despite chronological chaos. Emotional, intuitive, and musical links, not sequential causality, connect paragraphs. I assumed *Chronicles'* disorganization reflected Dylan's artistic genius. I guessed Dylan wrote a chronologically ordered draft and found nonlinear ways to reorganize it. I figured he had future volumes finished, awaiting their release date. But however Dylan did his *Chronicles*, I learned from reading him that writing meanderingly respected that a memoir should circle the narrator, the narrator's life, and even the narrator's experiences, but should be about perceptions, insights, and lessons that the narrator happened to be positioned to relay. I liked temporal chaos and have tried to modestly mimic Dylan's method.

The last memoir I read was very short, Kurt Vonnegut's, while rewriting this one. Kurt's the master. His words are depressing, every time he writes. Yet the damn thing made me laugh, tear up, and inspired me. That's a hell of a talent. Chomsky does that too, differently. With these guys I cry, I laugh, the message is a real downer in so many ways, but I am inspired. I can't do what they do. To inspire I will have to include hopeful content.

Remembering Tomorrow

> *Any reviewer who expresses rage and loathing for a novel*
> *is preposterous. He or she is like a person who has put on full*
> *armor and attacked a hot fudge sundae.*
> —*Kurt Vonnegut, Jr.*

Remembering *Tomorrow* is about the sixties, activism, institutions, and ideas. Part One has nine chapters, largely about attending a peculiar college located in Cambridge, Massachusetts. It introduces the civil rights movement and the New Left, recounts fraternity rush through tumultuous expulsion, includes science, sniffing glue, designing corridors, chutzpah, burning draft cards, creating sanctuaries, attending finishing schools, career planning, elections, and riots. We meet Marxism, Abbie Hoffman, the Living Theater, drugs, Hubert Humphrey, the Grateful Dead, Muhammad Ali, and Mr. Basketball, Bill Bradley, and we consider tennis, intellectual chasms, mathematician's proofs, and human capacities. We meet Noam Chomsky and consider torching libraries, provost propositions, corporate seduction, paths bypassed, Dow Chemical, academic channeling, the calculus of dissent, and the contours of cynicism. I get elected, stand eyeball to gun barrel, and begin considering tomorrows.

Part Two has ten chapters about organizing. Dreams of bombs lead from grassroots media to street rioting. Washington warfare leads from the Pentagon through CIA illogic and Mayday mayhem to Polish lessons. Dirty stories segue into Bread and Roses. Women and revolution fire up. We visit gender from the sadomasochistic to the masochistic-sadistic. I find sexism damaging, learn love, meet Lydia for life, assess marriage, examine women's intuition, and consider aging. Socializing or not—that is the question. Seattle Liberation macho, Weather storms, and planned mayhem. The Black Panthers rise, fall, and shine a light. I get mugged on Halloween. Lydia gets mugged on our steps. *Between Labor and Capital* highlights Ehrenreich, antagonizes Aronowitz, and inspires Albert and Hahnel. *No Nukes* illuminates class. Sixties books highlight Dellinger and Hayden. I learn fishing on Golden Pond. The ringing of revolution grows quiet.

Part Three has four chapters about higher education and teaching. MIT and Harvard reveal educational inadequacy. Is economics astrology? Odd byways illuminate academia. Cheating disciplines life. I test well but obey poorly. I teach with Chomsky, but get fired from U. Mass Boston. I avoid a slippery slope, and learn from prison. Walking butterflies convey a key life lesson.

Part Four has six chapters about alternative media. South End Press is born, foreshadows participatory economics, survives capitalism, endures ambition, and succeeds. We visit books from sexual revolution through friendly fascism. Herman and Chomsky uplift us. Toffler surprises us. We pass on fat. Small is our bugaboo. Seas aren't friendly. South End Press biases persist and what the hell is going on in a Left less diverse than the mainstream? We entice money from a clothing entrepreneur, a Rockefeller, and Hunter the headliner. House sales resuscitate us. Investment packages preserve us. Printer profusion and staring down the IRS protect us. *Z Magazine* spins off and beats bad odds. An NFL owner provides plenty of pain and no gain. *Z Papers* is prescient but disastrous for Albert and Hahnel. ZMI rocks. LBBS drains life and just misses generating big bucks becoming Left On Line, which morphs into Shareworld, which just misses generating even bigger bucks and morphs into ZNet, which makes okay bucks and becomes an international phenomenon. The megaphone problem leads to what makes alternative media alternative, keeping on keeping on, media and democracy, donor delusions, funding fiascos, and media politics writ larger.

Part Five, basically about ideas, has six chapters. Ideas transcend postmodernism. Kayaking teaches persistence. Marxism morphs into liberating theory with a major in economics that detours into class or multitude. Vision overcomes resistance via pop culture. Parecon leads through The Award of The President of the Italian Republic toward a participatory society. Sammy Reshevsky and Bobby Fischer beget strategy. Strategy traverses Egypt, addresses stickiness and class, unfolds the umbrella problem, revisits lifestyle, visits Australia, Turkey, and India, and considers elections. The Organization to Liberate Society and We Stand try to extend the lessons of the past into the future. I rant about Left defeatism, assess Life After Capitalism, seek serious intellectual engagement, visit Venezuela, and address my generation.

In today's world social structures saddle us. Freedom flaunts us. Information inebriates us. Water wastes us. Climate crashes us. Images insulate us. Prisons parole us. Complacency constrains us. Doubt deadens us. Stomachs staunch us. Backs break us. Eyes blind us. Bombs burst us. Repression, inequality, and corpses curse us. False graveyards gnaw us. Should we revolt? To get where? How? Accomplishing what? Remember Tomorrow.

PART 1

The Old Folks' Home At MIT

I went to college at the Massachusetts Institute of Technology. While I entered MIT all eyes, ears, and interest, within three years I called the place "Dachau on the Charles." MIT's victims burned in the fields of Vietnam but MIT's administration and faculty didn't like my nickname for their institution, and even most MIT students thought it excessive. Still, my calling MIT "Dachau on the Charles" said volumes about my college days. I'd certainly have lit a match, if I thought it would have done any good.

Chapter 1

Too Young to Notice

Civil Rights and the New Left

> *The past is not dead. In fact, it's not even past.*
> *—William Faulkner*

From September 1962 when I was fifteen to June 1965 when I was eighteen, the struggling civil rights movement and emerging New Left were born in Mississippi, Alabama, Georgia, Michigan, New York, California, and New Jersey. I was playing tennis and touch football and learning modest night moves.

It's February 1960. Four black students seek service at a lunch counter in Greensboro, North Carolina, and refuse to leave without a meal. SNCC, the Student Nonviolent Coordinating Committee, and SDS, the Students for a Democratic Society, are soon born, quickly becoming organizational beachheads for making America better. SNCC and SDS said society must honor its description of itself as free, equal, and democratic. They confronted white Southern racism. They rejected recalcitrant bureaucratic politics. They had little to say about underlying social organization. They had a lot to say about its most egregious surface manifestations. Mainly, they pumped the blood that sustained subsequent activism—and that determined my future.

The 1962 Port Huron Statement was the proximate work of Tom Hayden though it derived from the practices of many mentors and students alike. The Statement birthed the New Left. It called the American experience "contentment amidst prosperity" and "a glaze above deeply felt anxieties." Port Huron argued that people wanted to see how to "change circumstances in the schools, the workplaces, the bureaucracies, the government."

SDS and SNCC directed their appeals to this yearning, calling it "the spark and engine of change." The Port Huron Statement supported a "search for truly democratic alternatives." This search moved early radicals, who offered their document "as an effort in understanding and changing the conditions of humanity" and devoted themselves to its realization.

Some SNCC and early SDS members were more radical, which tended to mean they were more militant and more skeptical of the federal government and the racist sheriffs and judges of the South. Many members identified with Albert Camus saying that on this earth, where there are pestilences and there are victims, "it is up to us, so far as possible, not to join forces with the pestilences."

The battle for civil rights was waged largely in the South. The summer of 1964 saw over a thousand civil rights arrests. Thirty buildings were bombed and thirty-six churches burned down by the KKK. The guiding recipe was to root out old, moribund features of society. It was to elevate humane officials. It was to demand better outcomes. Bad officials were the problem, not bad institutions.

Early SNCC and SDS thought that virtually all social ills were rooted in anachronisms that could be extirpated without fundamental institutional change. After JFK was murdered, the key SDS slogan was "Part of the way with LBJ," and many SDS members expected much more than partial gains from Democrats. But the early belief that individual office holders could be corrupt but the structures were okay began to unravel when the Mississippi Freedom Democratic Party was denied seating at the 1964 Democratic presidential convention. Naive hope devolved further when the federal government dragged its heels on protecting dissent in the South. It collapsed completely with the deaths of Malcolm X (1965), the Watts rebellion (1965), the Newark and Detroit rebellions (1967), and the death of Martin Luther King Jr. (1968), and most of all, with the lessons of Vietnam. Advanced thinking transcended bemoaning bad leaders. We began to realize that it wasn't just bad people. It was bad institutions.

I was particularly affected, I remember, by reading a path breaking speech SDS president Carl Oglesby gave at a 1965 Washington antiwar rally. What Oglesby said then, which I read a couple of years later, was at the heart of my political emergence and that of the New Left more widely. Picture this young fellow speaking from the Capitol Building in Washington DC, to thousands of angry young people. Envision him offering views his audience had never heard before. "The original commitment in Vietnam was made by President Truman, a mainstream liberal. It was seconded by President Eisenhower, a moderate liberal. It was intensified by the late President Kennedy, a flaming liberal." Oglesby asked us to "think of the men who now engineer that war—those who study the maps, give the commands, push the buttons, and tally the dead: Bundy, McNamara, Rusk, Lodge, Goldberg, the president himself." He highlighted the obvious. "They are not moral monsters. They are all honorable men. They are all liberals."

Oglesby told us that the U.S. aim in Vietnam was

...to safeguard what they take to be American interests around the world against revolution or revolutionary change...never mind that for two-thirds of

11

the world's people the twentieth century might as well be the Stone Age; never mind the melting poverty and hopelessness that are the basic facts of life for most modern men; and never mind that for these millions there is now an increasingly perceptible relationship between their sorrow and our contentment.

Making linkages that fueled a turn from dissent to revolution, Oglesby asked, "Can we understand why the Negroes of Watts rebelled? Then why do we need a devil theory to explain the rebellion of the South Vietnamese?" Oglesby got gritty. "We have become a nation of young, bright-eyed, hard-hearted, slim-waisted, bullet-headed, make-out artists. A nation—may I say it?—of beardless liberals." The contrast was to Castro and Guevara. I loved the image. After a bit, Oglesby offered a run of paragraphs that bent my mind:

In 1953 our Central Intelligence Agency managed to overthrow Mossadegh in Iran, the complaint being his neutralism in the Cold War and his plans to nationalize the country's oil resources to improve his people's lives. Most evil aims, most evil man. In his place we put in General Zahedi, a World War II Nazi collaborator. New arrangements on Iran's oil gave 25 year leases on 40 percent of it to 3 U.S. firms, one of which was Gulf Oil. The CIA's leader for this coup was Kermit Roosevelt. In 1960, Kermit Roosevelt became a VP of Gulf Oil.

In 1954, the democratically elected Arbenz of Guatemala wanted to nationalize a portion of United Fruit Company's plantations in his country, land he needed badly for a modest program of agrarian reform. His government was overthrown in a CIA-supported rightwing coup. The following year, Gen. Walter Bedell Smith, director of the CIA when the Guatemala venture was being planned, joined the board of directors of the United Fruit Company.

Comes 1960 and Castro cries we are about to invade Cuba. The Administration sneers, 'poppycock,' and we Americans believe it. Comes 1961 and the invasion. Comes with it the awful realization that the United States Government had lied.

Comes 1962 and the missile crisis, and our administration stands prepared to fight global atomic war on the curious principle that another state does not have the right to its own foreign policy.

Comes 1963 and British Guiana where Cheddi Jagan wants independence from England and a labor law modeled on the Wagner Act. And Jay Lovestone, the AFL-CIO foreign policy chief, acting, as always, quite independently of labor's rank and file, arranges with our government to finance an 11-week dock strike that brings Jagan down, ensuring that the state will remain British Guiana, and that any workingman who wants a wage better than 50 cents a day is a dupe of communism.

Comes 1964. Two weeks after undersecretary Thomas Mann announces that we have abandoned the Alianza's principle of no aid to tyrants, Brazil's Goulart is overthrown by the vicious right-winger, Ademar Barros, supported by a show of American gunboats at Rio de Janeiro. Within twenty-four hours, the new head of state, Mazzilli, receives a congratulatory wire from our president.

Comes 1965. The Dominican Republic. Rebellion in the streets. We scurry to the spot with twenty thousand neutral Marines and our neutral peacemakers— like Ellsworth Bunker Jr., Ambassador to the Organization of American States. Most of us know that our neutral Marines fought openly on the side of the junta, a fact that the Administration still denies. But how many also know that what was at stake was our new Caribbean Sugar Bowl? That this same neutral peacemaking Bunker is a board member and stock owner of the National Sugar Refining Company, a firm his father founded in the good old days, and one which has a major interest in maintaining the status quo in the Dominican Republic? Or that the President's close personal friend and advisor, our new Supreme Court Justice Abe Fortas, has sat for the past 19 years on the board of the Sucrest Company, which imports blackstrap molasses from the Dominican Republic? Or that the rhetorician of corporate liberalism and the late President Kennedy's close friend Adolf Berle, was chairman of that same board? Or that our roving ambassador Averill Harriman's brother Roland is on the board of National Sugar? Or that our former ambassador to the Dominican Republic, Joseph Farland, is a board member of the South Puerto Rico Sugar Co., which owns two hundred and seventy-five thousand acres of rich land in the Dominican Republic and is the largest employer on the island–at about one dollar a day?

Oglesby was outraged. Me too. "Neutralists!" he bellowed:

God save the hungry people of the world from such neutralists! We do not say these men are evil. We say, rather, that good men can be divided from their compassion by the institutional system that inherits us all. ...Generals do not hear the screams of the bombed; sugar executives do not see the misery of the cane cutters: for to do so is to be that much less the general, that much less the executive.

Stage Three, Please

Woe betide those who seek to save themselves
the pain of mental building by inhabiting dead men's minds.
—*G.D.H Cole*

SNCC and SDS leapt into action in the Southern countryside and Northern inner cities a half-decade before my time. Their goal was to make the American dream universal. By the time I followed their lead American dreaming was over. I saw only nightmares from Watts to Wall Street, from Birmingham to Boise, and from the White House to Seattle. Early New Left idealism recapitulated cornfield college homecomings. That was SNCC's time. Later New Left idealism recapitulated smoldering cities. That was my time. Early activists looked back. Later activists looked forward. Early anger passionately rejected the worst of America. Later anger passionately added the best of America to the reject pile.

Stage one of the New Left was fueled by commitment to current American society. It was in some ways the most courageous moment of the Sixties. I missed stage one. I was born a day too late. But stage one didn't miss me. Political and social events often meanderingly affect people. My life was incubated in the early New Left, even as I was playing high school tennis and touch football. My formative years occurred before I knew politics at all, and before politics knew me. The New Left's inception was a roadmap to my future. Its explorers were my tutors.

Michael Schwerner was born in New York City but lived for a time in my home town, New Rochelle, a suburb of New York. Schwerner's online web biography tells us that at twenty-four, Schwerner went to Mississippi. That was January 1964. Schwerner was seven years my senior, more my brother's and sister's age than mine. He hired on as a Congress of Racial Equality (CORE) field worker. In his application to CORE, Schwerner wrote, "I have an emotional need to offer my services in the South." He hoped to spend "the rest of his life" working for an "integrated society." He did.

On January 15, 1964, Schwerner and his wife Rita went to Mississippi. Schwerner met the well-known and highly admired civil rights leader Bob Moses in Jackson and from there went to Meridian to organize a community center. Schwerner received $9.80 a week working for CORE. Once in Meridian, Schwerner organized a boycott of a variety store, forcing it to hire its first African American. He wrote "Mississippi is the decisive battleground for America. Nowhere in the world is the idea of white supremacy more firmly entrenched, or more cancerous, than in Mississippi." The KKK raised their crosshairs.

On Memorial Day 1964, Schwerner and his equally young, black friend James Chaney went to Longdale in Neshoba County, where Schwerner asked a black congregation at Mount Zion Church if CORE could use their church as the site for a new "freedom school." On June 16, while Schwerner was north in Ohio attending a training session for Freedom Summer volunteers, Mount Zion was burned to the ground by the Mississippi KKK. The first thing Schwerner did when he returned a week later from Ohio with Chaney and Andrew Goodman was to go back to Longdale and meet with those who had lost their church. After visiting Longdale, while driving back to Meridian, Schwerner was pulled over in his blue CORE station wagon by Deputy Cecil Price, and the three civil rights workers fell into the Klan's fatal trap.

Schwerner was the second of two sons. His father operated a wig manufacturing plant. His mother taught high-school biology. Schwerner was described as friendly, good-natured, gentle, mischievous, and "full of life and ideas." He believed people were essentially good. He named his cocker spaniel Gandhi. Schwerner enrolled at Michigan State and transferred after a year to Cornell, where he campaigned successfully to have a black student accepted to his fraternity. Following graduation, Schwerner enrolled in Columbia's graduate sociology department, but later dropped out to take a job as social worker on New York's Lower East Side. Schwerner's commitment to civil rights was deepened by watching the Birmingham riots of 1963 and so Schwerner applied to CORE, seeking to devote his life to attaining an "integrated society." I don't remember any discussion of Michael Schwerner in my hometown, New Rochelle, but there must have been some—and somehow, some way, it probably helped to make me who I am.

Stage two of the New Left, 1966–1975, was fueled by steadfast hatred for the inherent structural inadequacies of society. It retained only threadbare sympathy for the devils that inhabited the details. It had all kinds of courageous and cowardly, caring and callous, exceptionally smart and also incredibly dumb moments. I became who I am in the midst of stage two. Its glory days inspired my future. Its crashing but sometimes meaningless blows set my life agenda.

Stage three of the New Left is still being born. I am trying to contribute to stage three, including by writing this memoir. Stage three pays tribute to, and derives from, early SNCC and SDS. The future will later be present.

Chapter 2

Dachau on the Charles

Fraternity Rush Riot

> *I have always regarded myself as the pillar of my life.*
> —*Meryl Streep*

In high school, in 1964–65, I applied to five colleges and got in everywhere except Harvard. I wanted to go to Harvard because I wanted to be in the same school as my best friend Larry Seidman, who was a Harvard freshman during my senior year in high school, and to be near my girlfriend Nancy Shapiro, who was going to Simmons College in Boston. All was not lost, however. I chose to go to MIT, just down the river from Harvard and a few miles from Simmons, instead of going to Yale, Princeton, Columbia, or Cornell. I was only a fraction as good at humanities as I was at physics. I would have been only a fraction as able to excel as a speaker or even to feel comfortable as a person at an Ivy League school as I was at socially-backward MIT. MIT inflated my confidence.

In July 1965, following my senior year at New Rochelle High, MIT upper classmen visited and befriended me. One of these campus suitors was a pre-med student two years older and wiser than me. He patiently helped me consider my future academic options and urged that I join his fraternity, Alpha Epsilon Pi. We spent considerable time at the beach that summer—he, me, and Nancy, listening to the Rolling Stones bemoaning getting no "Satisfaction," and to the Temptations celebrating "My Girl," among other classics.

I arrived for MIT's Rush Week just before the official school semester began, as did about a third of my classmates. We were all seeking to join a fraternity. Physics was on my mind, not politics. I went to fraternity houses and was wined, dined, and often invited to stay for the evening. Some fraternities were more party oriented. "Wooly Bully" was the big dance hit. Some favored athletics. Go Celtics, though I favored the Knicks. Some emphasized academics, and a few were havens for all-around achievement. The differences could affect your days and nights at MIT. I was shopping for a home. The fraternities were shopping for freshmen. It was advanced living group matchmaking. I became a brother at Alpha Epsilon Pi, one of MIT's four Jewish fraternities. My pre-med emissary had recruited better than emissaries from Sigma Alpha Mu and other fraternities.

Rush Week preceded five months of pledging. Since MIT outlawed dangerous hazing, pledging involved having to light cigarettes for upper classmen, to learn everyone's name and hometown, to do push-ups whenever we forgot some required fact, and "pantsing"—we were tackled by numerous upper classmen, throttled to exhaustion, and stripped. Among those treating me to such indignities was a sophomore named Robert Horvitz. He was a good guy, and quite bright. In 2002 he shared with two others the Nobel Prize in Biology "for their discoveries concerning 'genetic regulation of organ development and programmed cell death.'" The opening sentence of his acceptance speech was "I never expected to spend the rest of my life studying worms." Pretty cool. Go AEPi, go.

On Friday nights, the AEPi pledge class rigorously cleaned the fraternity. Partly the sessions were a rational way to thoroughly clean, polish, and sometimes restore broken or worn items. It kept a large pair of four-story brownstones comfortable. Partly the sessions entailed washing a floor, and then washing it again, two, three, or even four times, as hazing. Cleaning would extend from immediately after dinner to as late as four in the morning, depending on what screwups occurred while we waxed on and waxed off. Upperclass authority eradicated our Friday nights and even exhausted us so we couldn't enjoy our Saturdays. Since personal time at MIT was slim, saying goodbye to Friday nights and many Saturdays was a considerable sacrifice.

About twenty Fridays later, AEPi held for its freshman a melodramatic induction ceremony. Amidst candles and pomp, we were declared brothers. After the ceremony, our new brothers told us how Rush Week had been organized. We learned that the fraternities had carefully researched lists of all incoming freshmen well in advance of our arrival. It was like NBA basketball teams researching prospective recruits before a player draft. MIT had few women in those days but only men chose between various all-male dorms and a couple of dozen all-male fraternities. Our choosing fraternities and them choosing us was a male ritual.

When a freshman arrived at AEPi, he either got the bum's rush—a quick walk out the back door into an alley—or he got the Prospect's Perusal, for which he'd be taken upstairs, introduced around, and offered information and snacks. If the freshman impressed the brothers, he'd be enticed to stay for elaborate dinners and perhaps overnight and throughout the week. Contenders were closely evaluated at late-night sessions during which brothers sat around judging each prospective inductee for how he would fit the fraternity's ethos. After we heard the above, we heard the big news. The rooms in the fraternity that we had inhabited overnight had been tapped. The phones we had used to make outgoing calls had been bugged. Big brothers told us they used information gleaned from wiretapping and bugging to judge our thoughts and, for those whom they sought, to offer us our preferred inducements to join.

For example, when I privately mentioned to a friend in a shared room or to my lover Nancy over the phone that I liked what I saw at AEPi but would prefer a bit more emphasis on physics and would enjoy it if some AEPiers were into playing tennis and participating in campus politics, the next morning, bright and early, I was nonchalantly welcomed into a bull session on physics. Later, I was casually invited for a game of tennis. In the evening I was given a tour of the campus student-committee rooms. Of course, if I had mentioned other preferences to my girlfriend, those desires too would have been met. Had I said disturbing things or indicated questionable tastes or inclinations, this too would have been conveyed to the brothers and affected their votes on me.

If I had discovered these wildly intrusive policies during Rush Week I would have gone berserk. You did what? But having given up six months of Friday nights, made new friends, and acclimated to a new and very comfortable home, on learning of these policies I felt only momentary anger. Similarly, after induction, no one in the fraternity's past had ever been pissed for long. Beyond a disconcerted day or two, life continued without a hitch. Mine, too. Malleable humanity. The excuse offered by our upperclass brothers for AEPi's duplicitous manipulations convinced everyone, including me, that in context, the brothers' actions had been wise. The upperclassmen had researched us. They had taken long hours to carefully assess our personalities. They had determined where we would best fit on campus. In Rush Week we had only a week to make life-affecting decisions. Because everyone was trying to rush us, we had no honest information to guide our choices. How could AEPi's brothers trust us to decide for ourselves? The big brothers, therefore, told us they decided for us, and then, for those they wanted to rush, they used whatever wiles they could muster to get us to join their house, lest we mistakenly end up somewhere else.

What is perhaps most instructive about all this is that we MIT freshmen, with half a year of college under our belts, smug as all get out about our wisdom, all accepted this explanation, as did midyear freshmen in other houses. We welcomed the pebble of caring that resided in the upperclassmen's revelations. We ignored the boulder of elitist, paternalist, deception that also resided there. We were living where we wanted to be. We were happy. Our home away from home was good. Anger would rock everyone's boat. Selection worked. Why question success?

For the rest of the second semester, life at AEPi proceeded as in past years. Our little community was academically serious but we enjoyed ourselves, too. We competed but also mutual-aided. AEPi pressured excellence. We had privacy, but we also had nearby friends for advice and support. Did Barry need help with classes? It was there. Did Steve need help with meeting people, dating, or personal angst? It was there. AEPi offered communal rewards made even more attractive by the exigencies of dreaded dorm life.

AEPiers were serious about campus politics and particularly the position and influence of their fraternity. For each new member, upperclassmen would envision plausible futures and then help to make them happen. One or perhaps two people in each new class, unbeknownst to them, would be selected for special grooming to become campus stars. So it was that within days of Rush Week, I was picked out by my big brothers for a prominent future.

My upperclass handlers envisioned me becoming undergraduate association president of the whole student body, or UAP, by my senior year. Within days of the end of Rush Week, they charted me through running for freshman class president and through a number of other steps, including using contacts of AEPi upperclassmen to participate in various campus activities devoted to assessing campus teaching and academics. Upperclassmen didn't discuss these plans with me until a half year later, after my induction. At first they simply planned my future and projected me in the directions they chose.

Oblivious to all that, for my first half year at MIT I enjoyed having my girlfriend Nancy Shapiro close to me at nearby Simmons. I aced my classes and enjoyed playing touch football and then softball in campus athletic leagues. I had a happy freshman year, nearly perfect from AEPi's perspective, and from mine too.

Nancy and I were very close, even thinking about future marriage. We regularly studied together in the MIT libraries, went out every weekend, and slept together via a system where fraternity roommates would vacate space for one another before women's curfews. Sometime in the late winter, however, Nancy and I fought, pretty seriously, and I feared our relationship was over. I was despondent and I milked the situation for a week or so.

I remember sitting in a downstairs living area at AEPi listening to Paul McCartney repeatedly sing "Yesterday," me singing along under my breath, as maudlin as one can get. I remember walking across what was called the Harvard Bridge—which links Cambridge, where the main MIT campus was, to Boston, where AEPi was—over the Charles River. I remember looking over and thinking about jumping. But I wasn't really thinking about suicide. I was trying to make myself that forlorn in order to experience that state of mind. Wasn't it the condition I was supposed to be in? So the one depressed part of my opening year at MIT wasn't even depression. It was me exploring myself through a technique I never employed again. Nancy and I didn't break up then. It was just an argument. But that summer, college contentment collapsed.

Summer Job, Something for Nothing

A fashion is nothing but an induced epidemic.
–George Bernard Shaw

I spent that summer in the city. My father got me a job in a hospital for which he was doing legal work. I went in, met my boss, and was put in a very small office. I was supposed to help the hospital staff with medical programming. I knew nothing about programming or about anything medical. The first day on the job I spent eight hours alone, bored silly, doing nothing. The second day replicated the first. On the third day I smuggled a book to work. I read the book all day in my little office and no one cared. I formed a hypothesis: the hospital gave me the job as a favor to my father but actually had nothing for me to do and would very much prefer that I was silent and invisible than that I constantly sought assignments. I tested the hypothesis by hiding out and ignoring the whole place, doing my thing, alone in my hospital office, reading. No problem. My first brush with wage slavery was delightful. I was paid to read whatever I liked with no boss in sight.

I didn't only read, however. I also wrote letters back and forth with one of my fraternity mates, Bob Barr. Bob left AEPi, as did some others in my class, about six months after I did. In fact, most of my class left, and much of it joined Students for a Democratic Society at MIT, which in turn became the most effective student organization in the Boston-Cambridge area. Like me, Bob was very into Bob Dylan and music generally, and we became close friends. Bouncing my concerns about AEPi off him was very helpful to my finally deciding to leave the fraternity.

Early in my freshman year, my AEPi classmate Larry White, who was from San Francisco, told Bob and me that he knew who the next big band would be: The Jefferson Airplane. We said no way—how could a group with such a stupid name get anywhere?—and we bet him a tidy sum, which he, of course, won. My father used to tell me if someone wants to bet you that a camel can fit through the eye of a needle, don't take the bet: it will happen. It was good advice. Later, Larry left AEPi and became radical. One of our early protests was to disrupt a talk by Walt Rostow, who was Lyndon Johnson's national security adviser and an architect of the Indochina war. I remember Larry hopping onto a stage where Rostow was talking and throwing dollar bills at him. Larry joined a Marxist-Leninist sect called the Progressive Labor Party (PLP). I learned that good people could get drawn into idiotic projects, and that there but for fortune I might have gone. I should note that there are those who would say that there but for fortune I went, one cubicle over.

By the way, the evil Walt Rostow's parents were socialist. Walt's older brother, Eugene Victor, was named for the socialist Eugene V. Debs and became dean of the Yale Law School and Lyndon Johnson's undersecretary of defense for political affairs. A third brother, Ralph Waldo Rostow, was named for Ralph

Waldo Emerson. As reported in a Texas obituary, Walt Rostow expressed no public regrets about the war. "I'm not obsessed with Vietnam, and I never was," he said in 1986. "I don't spend much time worrying about that period." Larry and I differed with Walt on the matter. So did a classmate of Walt's at Yale, Dave Dellinger, whom we'll meet soon.

Leaving AEPi

One can never consent to creep when one feels an impulse to soar.
—Helen Keller

After my summer of letters at the hospital job, I returned to MIT. It turned out that the psychic investment of pledging hadn't permanently exterminated my common sense. During my hospital stint, my brains and scruples made a comeback and I became outraged at my fraternity brothers' manipulations. Earlier I had ignored the debits of Rush Week to cling to a nice new home. Now I ignored the benefits of my nice home to jettison its duplicity. I quit AEPi during its pre-Rush Week cleanup period. When Rush Week started and the brothers were enticing new freshman into earshot of AEPi's tapped phones and bugged rooms, I sat on the fender of a car directly outside AEPi's front door and called over incoming freshmen as they were about to enter the house. I told them exactly what was going on.

Sitting on that car and telling the truth to those freshman was my first overtly political act, though at the time I had not a political thought in my head. There was a street brawl. Some of my AEPi ex-brothers sought to forcefully silence me. Others sought to limit the carnage for fear of repercussions for AEPi's campus credentials. A few sought to save my hide.

The school administration acted quickly. Removed by campus police, I was banned from returning to the corner. The MIT administration opened private discussions of Rush Week reform. Lacking political motivation, however, my public dissent didn't last. I wanted no part of AEPi's mini-pestilence, but I wasn't yet actively focused on the broader pestilence that was MIT itself, not to mention U.S. society.

Within a few days of the curbside fracas, my father arrived in Cambridge. Dad was welcomed by AEPi upperclassmen, who rented a nearby motel room for a daylong meeting. First, junior and senior AEPi brothers urged me to stay in the fold. My sophomore classmates were kept away, lest my example spread. In the afternoon came AEPi's officers. Toward evening, highly successful alumni and the current fraternity president arrived.

With the elite's arrival, the day's rhetoric became blatantly disgusting. The fraternity's leaders, unlike the younger brothers who had filed through earlier, admitted to my father that my accusations were correct. Of course the fraternity pried and lied, but why couldn't I see that I would benefit from the lying and prying? I was headed for the top of the heap. I would be an AEPi success story. "It works for us," they told my father, "and since Mike's going to be one of us, he shouldn't give it up."

At this point, my father changed sides. He was sad about having to ratify my moving off-campus, a prospect he dreaded, but he was sickened more by the fraternity's arrogance. Dad and I saw true elitism that didn't even rationalize itself to itself. The elitism that infected society's boardrooms also infected first-rank campuses. AEPi's big shots paraded it.

The upperclassmen told Dad and me that tapping phones was justified. Freshmen were ignorant. All the living groups lied. Should AEPi forego practices that would attract desirable recruits? No, AEPi should manipulate better than other houses to ensure that incoming freshmen wound up where they would be best off rather than elsewhere. AEPi's duplicity worked, my ex-brothers argued.

I had two grounds to reject AEPi's hypocrisy. First, I could let principle trump practicality. You can't lie like that. You can't manipulate like that. You can't call lying befriending even to people who are, in all other respects, your friends. But this approach had a problem. In fact, morals are often contextual. Situations arise in which, if you meet a high burden of proof, it can be right to lie. Even forty years later, while my deeply held feeling is that "the truth is always revolutionary," I also know there are exceptions. So I wanted a second reason. I wanted to judge AEPi's manipulations for their implications. I wanted to decide that contrary to the AEPi analysis of it, manipulative recruitment was destructive.

During AEPi's ceremony of our new brotherhood, all the implications looked positive, and I later realized that this is precisely how most corruption looks to its advocates. Someone benefits. A supporting argument claims that the situation's persistence would be superior to its termination. If AEPi didn't manipulate us, we would have wound up no less manipulated by others, but we would have settled on living units less suited to our tastes and potentials. What would be gained by that?

But the fraternity leaders' argument on behalf of lying, even granting their assumption that manipulation yielded locally happy outcomes, failed to take into account that yearly submission to the fraternity process replicated the rationale for even worse social behavior. The manipulative rush process had some good outcomes: there was no other living option that could confidently achieve better residences for us. The problem was that that same logic on a larger scale would forever preserve all kinds of injustice. There was also the issue of the impact, which I sadly admit I never researched, on those who got the bum's rush.

I rejected AEPi viscerally on account of my feeling that you just can't act that way. That propelled me out. Later I found a more systemic argument against the fraternities. The key was the mindset of the last few power-broker fraternity brothers who urged me to stay, as well as the subordinate mindsets that accepted unquestioningly the boss's smiling dominance. AEPi was part of how the whole country continually replicated hypocritical domination by a few over many, saying it was the only viable option, especially when undertaken with a friendly face.

Anyhow, in the ensuing months about half my class left AEPi. This was unprecedented at MIT, but even more interesting was that a number of these folks became a working core of what we later called Rosa Luxemburg SDS. What distinguished the ex-AEPi-ers who helped turn MIT upside down from any random group of students at MIT was only our implicit rejection of benefits that rested on and rationalized duplicity and elitism. That my friends and I increased SDS's ranks was, in that sense, largely contingent. If whatever caused me to leave AEPi had not done so, all our lives would have been different. Contingent history.

And here is a final wrinkle to the story. When first inducted into AEPi, I was told there was a moment in the nightly sessions that evaluated contenders for admission when there was doubt about my acceptance. Someone was reporting on my day's interactions and noted that late in the evening, in a bull session in one of the AEPi rooms with a couple of other freshman guests and a few upperclass brothers, I had sat on a bed that wasn't mine, with my bare feet bent under me, on a pillow, talking. The brothers listening were appalled that I had sat on someone else's pillow—and the room of brothers, hearing the report, feared that I was about to get negative votes. Then those present at the bull session reported that when it ended for the night I noticed I had been sitting on someone's pillow, picked it up, went to the room I would be staying in, and replaced the pillow I had been sitting on with my own pillow, which hadn't been sat on. Everyone relaxed. My acceptance was certain.

Here's the craziness. These guys were sitting around comparing notes about freshman candidates to live with, including using data secretly culled from our private conversations. They were manipulatively deciding our futures, lying and deceiving, and yet they were simultaneously concerned that I might be a bad bet as a brother due to my having sat on someone's pillow. I remember being profoundly moved when I first read a particular passage in Kurt Vonnegut's novel *Mother Night* addressing the complexities of human diversity in cases of great evil. It was about prison camp guards during the Holocaust. It went like this:

> I have never seen a more sublime demonstration of the totalitarian mind, a mind which might be likened unto a system of gears whose teeth have been filed at random. Such a snaggle toothed thought machine, driven by a standard or even substandard libido whirls with the jerky, gaudy, pointlessness, of a cuckoo clock in Hell.

Jones wasn't completely crazy. The dismaying thing about the classic totalitarian mind is that any given gear, though mutilated, will have at its circumference unbroken sequences of teeth that are immaculately maintained, that are exquisitely machined.

Hence the cuckoo clock in Hell—keeping perfect time for eight minutes and thirty three seconds, jumping ahead fourteen minutes, keeping perfect time for six seconds, jumping ahead two seconds, keeping perfect time for two hours and one second, then jumping ahead a year.

The missing teeth of course are simple, obvious truths, truths available and comprehensible even to ten year olds, in most cases. The willful filing off of gear teeth, the willful doing without certain obvious pieces of information. That was how my father-in-law could contain in one mind an indifference toward slave women and a love for a blue vase. That was how Rudolf Hoess, Commandant of Auschwitz, could alternate over the loudspeakers of Auschwitz great music and calls for corpse carriers. That was how Germany could see no important differences between civilization and hydrophobia.

My fraternity life ran from 1965 into 1966. For Frank Sinatra, "It Was A Very Good Year." For James Brown, "Papa Got A Brand New Bag." The Animals better communicated my sentiments: "We've Gotta Get Out of This Place."

MIT Teaches, Too

A fool's brain digests philosophy into folly, science into superstition, and art into pedantry. Hence university education.
—*George Bernard Shaw*

At MIT, you get a faculty advisor right off. Mine was Rainer Weiss, an experimental physicist. He focused on detecting gravity waves, a goal that only now, forty years later, is first becoming possible, and he is right in the thick of it, still. Gravity is a spatial distortion that emanates from mass. If a mass is large and dense and if it is in great turmoil, its motion can yield ripples in space, a bit like sound waves but much harder to notice. Weiss was intent on finding these ripples. He took a shine to me as a potential protégé and not only advised me about course selection, but personally designed a one-on-one course for me at his lab once a week for a few hours. Weiss would push and prod me, not so much about textbook learning as about the thinking that goes into doing real physics. As a freshman I took Weiss's special course, as well as an overload of normal courses.

MIT is supposed to be very tough. In truth it is and it isn't. There is a lot of work. The courses cover considerable ground and quickly reach far into their respective fields. But if you are highly confident and you are taking courses you have good facility for, then MIT isn't all that hard. When I took courses that I had no real talent for, however—one in philosophy, another in computer science, and a third in economics—MIT was murder. In physics and math, however, I most often ignored the classes and just crammed for finals and got my As. In the first two years I spent very little time in classrooms because most classes were actually quite boring. You could read the texts, ignore lectures, and miss little. Later, politics took me away even from the classes I liked, including some graduate ones.

MIT was full of highly proficient scientists. They might have come to class and told us what it meant to be a physicist, chemist, biologist, or whatever, including the social, personal, and intellectual ins and outs of being in their field. They might have conveyed information about pursuing careers, including insights that few books even try to communicate. But with few exceptions, my MIT professors didn't do that. Weiss tried, in our special sessions, and I looked forward to those until politics pulled me entirely out of physics. But Weiss was an exception. Most MIT classes conveyed only textbook knowledge. Often professors literally read a text aloud, or summarized one working from notes, conveying little that wasn't book-based. Nonetheless, I did learn a lot at MIT. Books matter. Partly it was classical mechanics, electromagnetic theory, relativity, and quantum mechanics. For purposes of lasting value, however, what I most learned was what an argument is, how to test a hypothesis, how to determine the implications of an assumption or claim, and when and how to employ thought experiments.

Of course, everyone knows how to do these things in a few realms. Many people never become comfortable and confident, however, using evidence and logic and paying attention to consistency across all realms, much less ubiquitously using thought experiments to seek truthful positions and insights. Instead, people sometimes forego logic and evidence due to habit, or whenever these contradict other priorities. This occurs most dramatically with fundamentalist or sectarian communities and, ironically, among the most highly educated sectors. The more mainstream training people have, I discovered in time, the more capacities they have for rationalizing falsehoods and the more they can prosper by deviating from truthfulness.

Marxism Afternoon

Workers of the world, unite.
—Karl Marx

The ins and outs of some physics theories, the methods and content of various mathematical frameworks, and the art of paying attention to evidence, logic, and consistency, as well as to employing many associated techniques, weren't all I learned at MIT. I learned Marxism, too. We had just had an activist meeting in a lounge room in the MIT student center. There had been some discussion of campus organizing and the war and some mention of related Marxist analysis. The meeting ended and Robin Hahnel and I were sitting and chatting after everyone else had left. Robin was in SDS at MIT, despite his being a student at Harvard, because Robin preferred our organizing group at MIT to the one at Harvard. I had met Robin because in freshman year he was Larry Seidman's roommate, and Larry was my best friend from high school whom I had visited a couple of times the prior year. If not for that link through Larry, Robin and I would likely never have known each other. When I came back to Cambridge for my sophomore year and left AEPi, I moved off campus with another MIT student, Andy Pearlman. For the second semester, Robin joined us in a Cambridge apartment. This was 1967.

At any rate, in the MIT student center, I suddenly asked Robin, as the meeting was breaking up, can you teach me Marxism? Robin was majoring in economics, reading it voraciously, and my structured learning up to that time had had zero to do with politics or economics. I assumed Robin was much more familiar with Marxism than I was, and I hoped I could learn from him.

We spent the next few hours with him presenting Marxist concepts and answering my questions. This was eye-opening in two main ways, and highly fortunate in a third. First, I learned much about Marxist economics. Second, and this didn't percolate into awareness until much later, there was the astounding reality that the core of this famous intellectual framework had been conveyed to me in a single long sitting. It didn't take thousands of pages of reading and years of study. Yes, before Robin and I talked I already had a vague familiarity with the Marxist framework from my sophomore year of fledgling activism, but this session demonstrated that if clearly instructed, a person could become broadly and usefully knowledgeable in a subject to the point of being able to ask cutting-edge questions in hours or days, not years.

Third, I think Robin teaching me Marxism that afternoon was the beginning of the two of us working together as a kind of intellectual team. The dynamic employed that day became typical. Robin would sit while I would pace around asking questions. I played devil's advocate, spouting idea after idea. He brought to bear evidence and careful analysis. In this way, we'd push lines of thought in directions that we would likely each ignore working alone.

Many Marxists would reply to all this by saying, "Albert, oh yes, he thinks he knows what we Marxists are about, but it is mere hubris. He understands the most mechanical Marxism, but he doesn't understand the rich framework we employ." Here is a rejoinder I almost got to offer. Not long after our book *Unorthodox Marxism* was published, about ten years after the sessions described above, Robin and I got a message from a British economist, the world-famous Marxist Ronald Meek. Meek liked our book. Indeed, he found it very convincing. Meek agreed that we understood Marxism. More important, and rather astoundingly, he agreed with our critique of Marxism. This was incredibly good news. Meek was arguably the dean of international Marxist economic scholarship, and a Meek review saying *Unorthodox Marxism* was compelling, much less that he agreed with it, would have profoundly boosted our arguments. Meek died, however, before he wrote the review. Robin and I greatly mourned his passing even though we had never met the man.

Here is the rejoinder I have offered, in lieu of quoting Meek, who died too soon to go public, in reply to the many Marxists who question my comprehension. When I went to the University of Massachusetts in Amherst, some years after MIT, I studied with prominent adherents of two different schools of Marxism. I never had to learn new basic core concepts to successfully participate in their classes and debates. None of them found fault with my comprehension. Likewise, when Robin and I published the book *Unorthodox Marxism*, no Marxist even claimed that it demonstrated a lack of comprehension. In fact, quite to our surprise, Part One of the book, which presented Marxism, was used in a considerable number of Marxism courses. Could I have written Part One the day after our initial session in the MIT student union? Probably not, but certainly it wouldn't have taken much additional effort to be ready to do so. Part Two of *Unorthodox Marxism* critiqued the Marxist framework presented in Part One. When we wrote *Unorthodox Marxism*, Robin and I saw ourselves as extending the Marxist heritage, which is why the book wasn't called *Anti-Marxism* or *Beyond Marxism* or *After Marxism*, but was called instead *Unorthodox Marxism*.

Chapter 3

Yesterday's Papers

The Glue That Binds Us All

> *The most potent weapon in the hands*
> *of the oppressor is the mind of the oppressed.*
> —*Steve Biko*

A year out of AEPi, 1967–68, I lived with Robin Hahnel and Larry Seidman in an apartment in a relatively depressed working-class neighborhood in Somerville, Massachusetts, just north of Cambridge where MIT was located. Across the street another friend, John Adler, lived in a smaller place, making four of us on the block. Among other activities, we used to play touch football with the local high school kids.

We got along well with our neighborhood friends and enjoyed our games together. But a few months into the semester, we noticed a drift in their play. Quality went down. Attention went down. Soon our neighbors wouldn't play at all. We'd see them spaced out. They'd barely notice us. Our VW van was frequently occupied in the cold winter evenings. Before long, we knew our friends had taken to sniffing glue in the backseat of our van.

Glue sniffing was popular in many working-class communities. Glue was easy and cheap and provided an escapist trip. Where marijuana heightened the senses, glue dulled them. Glue fumes destroyed brain cells. Feed your head, indeed. Glue manufacturers noticed the inflated demand. Being market-wise, scuttlebutt had it that manufacturers increased the glue's deadly ingredients to attract additional users. If so, no doubt they told themselves that if they didn't do it, someone else would. Shocking? Think cigarettes and nicotine.

Anyhow, we got our neighbors together and tried to talk them out of their new pastime. They told us that they liked sniffing glue because doing so temporarily wiped away their problems. We told them sniffing glue was also wiping away their lives. They laughed and told us their lives were already wiped clean. How much of a brain did it take to be a box boy? Why should they worry about cutting off an already dead-end future? In their other worldly wisdom, early death was no biggie. First you forget, then you die.

These young friends were killing themselves and we were powerless to stop it. Finally, we told them sniffing glue would make them impotent and destroy their sex lives. This shook them. They saw sexual inadequacy as a real danger, so they gave up sniffing. In hindsight, this lie—for we had no idea what effect glue sniffing had on sexual performance—was not entirely different from the lies AEPI brothers told me to prevent me from doing what they thought wasn't in my interest. This is the upside and the downside of contextual morals. Was our manipulation regarding their gonads to curtail glue sniffing morally warranted because as a result some of these kids lived longer? Or was it morally wrong because we were exploiting our authority as elite students to pull it off? In the same situation I would do it again, but that may say more about me than about right and wrong. Mostly, this deadly experience made me realize that the kids had a point. In context, seemingly insane behavior often has logical justification.

Paint that Slogan

A witty saying proves nothing.
—Voltaire

Like most of my peers who trod roughly the same path I did, my slip-slide toward revolution was quick. Social concern begets social involvement begets social revolutionary. I can't detail every step of this progression but I can describe parts. For example, when students started each new year at MIT there was an initial regimen of registering for classes in a gymnasium with everyone entering, dealing with the bureaucracy, and moving on. Everyone therefore knew that on a particular morning, let's say it was a Tuesday, starting just after breakfast, there would be an immense flow of students through the prescribed room. Opportunity knocked.

It was the outset of my junior or perhaps senior year. It was certainly not my first act at MIT, and also not my last. We positioned ourselves at various locales on campus and in each of these one or more of us spray-painted slogans onto prominent walls. George Katsiaficas and I had the plum assignment: the registration hall. George was president of the intrafraternity conference. I had recruited him to the movement and to SDS, picking him out for his prominent position—like the fraternity picking me out—and had befriended and talked with him, helping him extricate himself from his prior life as I had been helped to extricate myself from mine. At any rate, late on Monday night George and I turned up at the registration hall and were about to go in—but, sitting in the middle of the hall on a small chair near the entry door was a guard reading a book. We reversed course. Outside again, I was ready to pick a lesser target, but George was undeterred. I had hubris enough for most situations, but George was healthily over the top with it and led me around the side of the building, near the back of the outside of the hall. We boosted up to a ledge, pried open a window, and snuck into the room. We were in the same big area with the guard, but we were behind the guard's back and separated from him by a stretch of open space. The guard was nodding off while reading and we painted slogans about the war, capitalism, and MIT all around the big hall. We did it quickly, all over the room. At times George moved within twenty feet of the guard. Luckily, we got out unscathed. The next day course registration occurred as scheduled. The walls had been whitewashed. Audacity sometimes had limited impact despite considerable risk.

Chutzpah Lessons & Results

> *Every child is an artist. The problem is how*
> *to remain an artist once he grows up.*
> *—Pablo Picasso*

Eddie, my older brother, the gambler, may have provided me my first lessons in chutzpah, the only Yiddish word I know, which means, more or less, gumption plus cleverness. When I was about ten, for my birthday, Eddie took me to a professional wrestling match in Madison Square Garden. It was the nicest thing Eddie ever did for me, save for letting me use his Chevy convertible on my high school prom night.

Eddie and I both loved professional wrestling, perhaps due to our grandfather's passion for it. Antonino Rocca, a good-guy master of flying dropkicks, was one of my favorite stars and so was the strongman Bruno Sammartino, both on the card that night. Eddie preferred the more thugish Johnny Valentine with his Atomic Skull Crusher and Jerry Graham, whose best move was smashing an opponent in the head with a chair. We got to the Garden and it was toe-to-toe outside the arena. We had no tickets and the scalpers were asking way beyond our budget. It looked futile and I was resigned to leaving. Eddie took me to a lamppost and told me to wrap my arms around it and stay attached. He was then away awhile. Crowds jammed, including mounted police to clear people out, but Eddie came back just in time, smiling like crazy. He took me to the door where we were joined by a uniformed employee who escorted us past the ticket taker, through the entry, up an elevator, up some stairs, then up a ladder, until we wound up looking down from an impossibly high balcony, off by ourselves, above all the crowds, and just barely able to make out the mayhem below.

After a few minutes of getting used to our unique seats, I turned to Eddie and asked how he did it. It turned out he had wheedled his way in to see the guard and told him he had his little brother along and that it was my birthday and that I had leukemia and this was my last chance to see pro wrestling, and could they please make an exception and let us in. Eddie combined an infinite capacity to lie with a high degree of cleverness.

Another foray into chutzpah occurred much later, well after MIT, around the mid-1970s. It perhaps reflects the kind of confidence that rebellion often requires. One night around midnight, when we were graduate students at the University of Massachusetts economics department, I was staying at my friend Peter Bohmer's apartment in Northampton, Massachusetts. We were chatting and somehow it came up that Peter's apartment needed a new chair. Why not get one from the department, someone suggested. Off we went, four of us. About fifteen minutes later we reached the campus and brazenly drove up to the social sciences building. We went up the elevator to the economics department and found a very nice chair. With nary a thought to consequences or morality, we rolled it out to the elevator, took it down, and carried it out to the car. We stuffed it in, and off we went. The department exploited us through the work we did teaching. It provided us a marginally acceptable educational experience. It had way too many chairs for its needs. Redistributing was, as later generations would say, a no-brainer.

Then came the memorable part. We had barely gotten the car in motion when a police light flashed in our rearview mirror. We stopped and a campus patrolman—one of two present—came to the window, leaned in, and asked, "What the hell do you think you're doing with that chair?" Schooled by prior experiences, I went into chutzpah mode. I said "We are taking the chair home to Northampton." "You must be kidding," the cop said. I said "No, it's authorized, what's the problem? We teach in the economics department. The department has a surplus chair. We are borrowing it. You can call the department head if you like, no problem, though I think it may be a bit late to wake him. You want to see ID? You want something else? Whatever, but let's get this done." I went on like that, belligerently, as in, what can you possibly think you are doing, stopping us? Of course the reality was that we were in deep trouble and who knows what action the economics department might have taken had the cops detained us or followed through the next day. Worse, Peter was on felony probation from having been the target of political repression in San Diego, where he had lived before coming to Amherst, and he might well have gone back to prison had it gone further. But the cops begged off. My seemingly righteous anger convinced them we were legit. The upshot is that there are contexts in which believing you are above the law can put you there. This knowledge usually works, however, to increase injustice and inequity, rarely so benignly as in getting Peter another chair for his home.

Finally, still on this chutzpah topic, while at MIT, in the summer between my sophomore and junior year, I was a house painter with Robin Hahnel. We did only outdoor painting. There was sun, good pay, and no boss. We could talk while we worked. Many of the ideas of my first book, *What Is To Be Undone*, were discussed while standing on ladders painting the sides of houses.

We were not only unalienated, but also daredevilish about our craft. Way up ladders, even hanging from the side like lunatics, we could only reach so much area. To reach more, the ladder had to be moved. A sane person would climb down, shift the ladder, climb back up, and paint again. But you go up and down ladders often enough and you begin to feel quite at home. We brought donuts up and jumped the ladders over, a little at a time, literally getting them to hop up off the ground and slide either to the right or the left. It was crazy, of course, as was hanging off them, one hand holding a brush, the other holding the edge of the ladder, our bodies floating in space, but the fearful becomes mundane with enough practice. More revealingly, in tumultuous times, political issues are so paramount that they become what one talks about while hanging off ladders painting houses.

Interior Design

> *There's something happening here / What it is ain't exactly clear.*
> —*Stephen Stills*

Returning to MIT protest, a related and more successful organizing endeavor than spray-painting walls involved building design. Not all politics is leaflets, speeches, chants, and rallies. MIT was incredibly gray. Regimentation reigned supreme. MIT students were called "tech tools" and our disparaging nickname was often depressingly apt. To transform student complacency, we decided to give MIT a jolt of intellectual adrenaline.

One option was to make a visible statement about MIT's long, dreary corridors. We didn't think MIT's design was random and it certainly wasn't aesthetic artistry. Harvard, just up the Charles River, looked in many of its corridors like a corporate boardroom or a fancy law firm—or even like a rich person's home. MIT, just down the Charles River, lacked color, lacked wall hangings, and indeed lacked anything resembling assertive aesthetic human presence. It wasn't that Harvard's prettier design was admirable. Harvard trained the masters of the universe, and everything about Harvard provided a master's finishing school. Harvard graduates had to be confident and have the clothes, manners, and verbal intonations of leadership even while being hell-bent on personal advance. MIT graduates had to be tech tools available for the Harvard types to utilize. The design of MIT was utilitarian. MIT graduates were supposed to sell our minds to the Harvard-bred masters of the universe. Asked to profit them, we should have no qualms about purpose, motives, and implications. Our task, should we accept it, was only to seek good pay for solving interesting problems.

I also spent some time across the Charles River at Boston University. BU had huge classes, lots of noise, and little participation. When I went to visit a junior college I found students taking classes in corners of large halls sheltered from one another by hanging drapes. Such students were learning to operate under the conditions not of laboratories (as at MIT), or of boardrooms (as at Harvard), but of wide open, corporate-style work areas and factory floors.

The graphic differences between colleges were unmistakable when I was comparatively looking at many of them but were invisible to students enduring only one environment. Colleges turned out different products to fill different social slots. Differences between departments were similarly utilitarian. The humanities building at MIT was more artistic and social than the utilitarian but comfy physics building which was different from the austere chemical engineering building. We called all this "tracking," and it continued what began in high school, where students were divided into college-bound and vocational. I remember in my high school not knowing many people beyond the borders of my advanced placement classes even though I ran for and won student office.

In any case, the goal for MIT graduates was that we would unquestioningly perform any interesting tasks that the powers that be from Harvard, Princeton, and Yale proposed for us. If the masters of the universe wanted us to produce a mechanism of corporate control over workers, or a mechanism of government oversight over citizens, or a reentry system for multiple nuclear warheads delivered by one missile, or a stabilization system so that helicopter guns could more reliably shoot water buffalo and Vietnamese peasants, or, for that matter, if the masters of the universe unexpectedly asked us to design a handgun so that those same peasants could shoot down B52s, we tech tools from MIT should meet the master's challenge. We should leave calculating the social worth of the product to the masters, their having been propitiously prepared for that at Harvard finishing school. The masters would get the social calculation right. They would ask for smart bombs, not B52-threatening handguns. Our expertise was bordered by MIT's long, gray corridors. We would deliver the goods.

So it wasn't a magic cure-all, but it was nonetheless quite effective when in the dead of night we moved couches and chairs from offices out into MIT's long corridors and gray gathering places so that students could sit and talk. Redecorating was incredibly shocking to the MIT community. It wasn't just the disobedience, though that was important. It was the redesign. The new furniture in MIT's corridors messed with people's minds. More, shortly later, and even more successfully, we hung posters all over the walls of the famous long corridors of MIT. These were slabs of construction paper, affixed to the walls and adorned with a magic marker hanging for public use. The top third of the oversize posters that we hung throughout MIT's long corridors had some provocative claim, quotation, or fact neatly written in large letters. Our idea was for students to write below our entry their reactions, reviews, rebuttals, or rethinkings of the imprinted claims. One day the corridors were bare. The next day they were full of posters with people hunched around reading and adding their own comments. It was excerpts from noted social critics or revolutionaries that adorned MIT's walls. I remember one poster had a favorite poem of mine from Langston Hughes:

What happens to a dream deferred?
Does it dry up
Like a raisin in the sun?
Or fester like a sore—
And then run?
Does it stink like rotten meat?
Or crust and sugar over—
like a syrupy sweet?
Maybe it just sags
like a heavy load.
Or does it explode?

Another had the last paragraph of James Baldwin's *The Fire Next Time*: "If we do not now dare everything, the fulfillment of that prophecy, recreated from the Bible in song by a slave, is upon us: God gave Noah the rainbow sign, No more water, the fire next time!" Some had statistics about bombs falling in Vietnam or wages falling in the U.S. Some had provocative song lyrics, quotations, or questions. It turned out MIT students could vigorously engage in public discussion. Political activism, we learned by this action, shouldn't be a cookie cutter process with the same templates endlessly employed. What awakens insight and activity in one place might be inappropriate elsewhere.

Church Service

The struggle is eternal. The tribe increases. Somebody else carries on.
—*Ella J. Baker*

Much opposition to ongoing Indochina massacres involved GIs. Indeed, the first demanding political context I experienced occurred in downtown Boston at a church during my sophomore year before all the above took place. It was an antiwar gathering and four of us, including myself, Robin Hahnel, Larry Seidman, and John Adler, went to the event and ended up sitting in a balcony overlooking the sanctuary of the Arlington Street Church.

Speakers described the U.S. role in bombing the people of Indochina and urged the audience to act. It wasn't donations that the organizers, pastors, and speakers were eliciting, but lasting antiwar opposition. Students went forward, shook hands, and burned their draft cards. One after another, students and some Boston citizens marched up, flicked a Bic, and to raucous applause set a draft card alight. The four of us sat and applauded from upstairs. The event ended, we left, and I was greatly troubled. Something was happening here, and, indeed, watching the protest helped awaken my understanding of the war, but mostly it affected my personal view of responsibility. If the card-burning warranted my applauding, why didn't it warrant my participating? I think the way this church protest got me to applaud direct action by others and to then consider why I wasn't more directly active myself was pivotal in making me who I am today.

Decades later, while reading Dave Dellinger's autobiography, *From Yale to Jail*, I discovered that Dave had been at that service, acting as a master of ceremony, and that his son had been one of the students who burned a draft card. I didn't know Dave then and I don't explicitly remember him being there. But I wouldn't be surprised if Dave's style and grace, unbeknownst to him and to me, helped precipitate my reaction that day, which was precisely the reaction that he was no doubt seeking, and precisely the reaction civil disobedience aims for.

Chapter 4

Spiritual Crossroads

Sanctuaries

For my part I would as soon be descended from a baboon...as from a savage who delights to torture his enemies...treats his wives like slaves...and is haunted by the grossest superstitions.
—Charles Darwin

During my years at MIT, military disobedience became a central part of the antiwar movement. To get out of going to Vietnam, some people would fail their physical by making themselves unhealthy or by appearing ill-suited to making war. People gorged on coffee or went to the induction centers stoned or even tripped out on LSD. People went in comatose from sleep deprivation or displaying (what was then) outlandishly homosexual behavior. Many people soberly sought religious or philosophical exemptions. Other people fled to Canada. It was often argued that all these folks were cowardly for defying the draft. What a silly claim that was.

A young man ignorant of the world and spurred on by recruiters, friends, and parents could easily feel that joining the war effort was a patriotic, mature, and wise choice. People would celebrate a son becoming a GI. While you might think there was a major element of bravery in agreeing to serve despite the palpable risk of death or debilitation, recruitment and induction hid those worrisome aspects and promoted the idea that going to war was doing one's duty. Young men going off to war felt not so much fear plus courage as pride plus responsibility. To succumb to the pressure to become a GI was natural. It happened fluidly, nearly inevitably, without angst. On the other hand, to resist war often meant defying not only history and social expectations but family and friends. When a draft resister fled to Canada, it often meant breaking with home and family and losing one's future prospects. Resistance required courage.

Other people became soldiers and rejected the war only after seeing Vietnam and experiencing blind obedience, unrestrained killing, and horrific dying. Less frequently, some people who hated the war actually joined the army to resist from within. These enlistees knew the emotional costs, physical travail, and psychic trauma that Vietnam implied and they enlisted anyhow. These were the bravest and most effective organizers, since in many respects, it was the dissolution of the army, abetted by these activist recruits, that ended the Indochina War.

GI organizing took many forms. Young people in considerable numbers leafleted and otherwise sought to talk with potential recruits as they approached a draft board or enlistment office. Other activists provided counseling, helping people understand their options and pursue their choices. Many organizers created media projects around military bases to provide to soldiers in training information and support. These organizers tried to hook up with GIs who got leave to go off base. The projects were often coffeehouses or hole-in-the-wall meeting places offering antiwar newspapers, leaflets, and handouts. When the soldiers would visit, activists were there to talk. On the other hand, most antiwar activists weren't against the draft per se. The draft was horrible because the war was horrible. No one should have to serve because the war shouldn't be waged. Resisting the draft was warranted, because the war was unwarranted. But surely a draft system was more equitable than people being able to buy their way out of service.

Sometimes coffee-shop socializing yielded a GI who wanted to desert the army. There was an underground railroad to help these deserters escape the country. Other soldiers wanted to go AWOL, or "absent without leave," to defy the war and help organize against it. The movement created public sanctuaries for these GIs. A soldier would leave his base and be surreptitiously driven to the venue where he (there were at that time few women soldiers) would publicly announce his resistance and actively await arrest. Supporters would join the AWOL GI to ensure that his arrest educated others.

I went to three of these sanctuaries. The first was at Brandeis University, the second at Boston University, and the third at MIT. The Brandeis event lasted about a week. I knew some of the organizers and went there to lend my support. I met but didn't get to know the AWOL GI. I remember the arrest, including cops throwing those of us who were trying to block their access out of the way. And I especially remember one particular person who attended the Brandeis sanctuary and whom at one point I had a memorable conversation with.

The fellow at Brandeis was a black man, unconnected to the student organizers, but attending as a photojournalist, hoping to place his work in radical outlets. I am about five-foot nine, and he was a bit shorter than I, but he was stocky and very self-confident. Based on his Southern civil rights experiences, he told me the best ways to deal with police busts. He also told me that, being small, he learned early that in confrontations where you were willing to fight, nothing was more important than the appearance of absolute confidence. Bravado tipped the odds. If you weren't willing to fight, then you should appear insane. On the streets, if you were afraid some thugs were going to molest you, you should appear utterly demented and out of control, talking to yourself, exhibiting odd movements. Very few people, he reported, liked to mess with someone who has no sense of proportion, whether it's from confidence or craziness. Abbie Hoffman, just weeks later when he was visiting MIT, told me the same thing. Confidence is everything. Exuding the aura that you are oblivious to any pain that you might have to endure and that you are intent on doling out pain that others would certainly not want to endure, conveyed, they said, a tremendous advantage in conflicts.

At the Brandeis sanctuary, the exchange I most remember was about the photojournalist's camera. We were sitting and talking, and he was holding it close. The camera was a large, expensive, professional one of a sort that I had never seen. So I asked him how he could afford it since it was clear that he was not rolling in money. He told me the camera was a Leica and that it cost a couple of thousand dollars, which was then a whole lot of money. He also told me that if you are going to undertake any kind of project one thing you need to understand is that you should not save pennies on the tools of your trade. In the long run, penny-pinching would cost way more than it would save. Somehow that advice stuck with me, and I noticed over the years endless instances of people squandering money over and over on numerous small items and on endless little outlays and then saying that they couldn't afford more expensive but also far more critical one-time items.

Of course, this pattern is most debilitating if the expensive items are, as the photojournalist pointed out, part and parcel of your work. And, indeed, later, I was always intent that in publishing we should not spite ourselves regarding the tools of our trade. But even in other realms, I have found that the advice makes sense. For example, most leftists think that large consumer expenditures reveal either greed or having been tricked by media and what they call consumerism. Of course, both can be true, but why always assume the worst? This photographer made me realize the opposite might be true too.

Indeed, my life partner Lydia Sargent and I have a very large TV and live quite comfortably, nowadays. This wasn't always so. In college and for about ten years afterward I lived in deadbeat apartments, sometimes without heat, owning nothing. Cheerios were a staple. I remember ice inside windows and even on the floors of one Somerville apartment, sleeping through winter under multiple blankets and piles of clothing. Even in the early days of the publishing house we helped to found, South End Press, beginning in 1979, Lydia and I and all other employees received only room and board and contributed endless work. Over time, however, some clever machinations centering on buying and selling homes and living and working in the same place enabled Lydia and me to steadily improve our living conditions.

When Lydia and I finally left Boston, moving to Woods Hole in Cape Cod, at age fifty-one and forty-five, respectively, we finessed purchasing a house on a pond that was in turn connected under a drawbridge to the ocean. I had to hassle about twenty banks to elicit a mortgage, and even then we had to have three cosigners beyond the two of us, but, after all that, we had a new home. Until then we never owned anything and rarely had disposable income at all, much less savings. Suddenly, having finessed a house, it was good-bye discomfort, hello American capitalist logic: not much saving, but way more comfort.

Once we had the house, credit was no problem. More, the resale value climbed as if the house were on steroids. Exploiting the house's escalating value, we have periodically refinanced the place, each time winding up with the same monthly payments but with considerable cash in hand, which has in turn helped us to live far more comfortably than we ever had in the past, including building an addition to the house fit for handling grandchildren and other guests, which of course further escalated the house's already escalating value, allowing the house to become our ace in the hole asset should our political projects ever need a last-ditch bailout. In fact, the plot of land and home we own have earned more in fifteen years than Lydia and I combined, working like maniacs, have together earned in thirty years. So I learned from the photographer not only that it was economical to spend large sums for fine tools of one's trade, but at times for items to enjoy.

Getting back on track, my second sanctuary was at Boston University. It was held in a large chapel, called Morse Hall. There was a similar pattern of GI arrival, AWOL celebrations, and closing arrest. Boston University was home to Howard Zinn, an inspiring figure. He had a kind of calm about him, and a friendliness, that together uplifted virtually everyone in his vicinity. Howard's *People's History of the United States* has not only analytical brilliance, evidentiary originality, and stylistic eloquence, but a human touch. I came to know Howard, never as a close friend but enough to be confident that his appearance isn't false. Howard was and is special. Howard has good karma.

But what I most remember of the BU sanctuary was more personal. I was in the chapel with lots of other students, and suddenly, out of nowhere, walking toward me across the floor, was my father. We went outside and he told me that he and my mother had seen a news report about antiwar conflict at BU on TV and were convinced that they had seen me in the image. They got worried. What was I doing away from MIT at BU at an illegal event? My father, remember, was a lawyer, and abhorred lawbreaking, not to mention that he was very protective of me.

Dad and my mom had certainly already gotten the message that I was not going to be the prominent senator, big-time lawyer, or Nobel Prize scientist they'd hoped. But even with that realism, they hadn't contemplated that I might wind up in jail. Like other parents, they heard what I said but they projected their own pasts onto my present, deducing that my words were youthful bravado. The possibility of imminent arrest shocked them, and so here was dad, having flown up on a moment's notice to extricate me from the muddy waters I was apparently sinking in. We talked, and to Dad's credit, while he thought my risking a legal blot on my record for a GI I didn't know was lunacy, he left Boston saying that whatever happened of course he and Mom would support me. I knew his word was good, and, indeed, I knew my parents were never deeply hostile to my views, as right-wing parents or even middle-of-the-road parents might have been. Mom and Dad generally agreed with the broad critical substance, though not the details or deeper commitments of my beliefs, fearing the implications.

It was ironic and prescient, I suppose, that amid all the chaos then and with quite a bit more to come, to assuage one of their prime worries, I told my parents that I was no martyr. I had no inclination to suffer purely for the sake of suffering. I might spend time in jail, I told them, but if I did, it would not mean I wanted to suffer out of guilt or out of a desire to celebrate being jailed.

But there was more to it. When my generation rebelled, we meant to escape the whole damn existence around us. We grew our hair. We changed our wardrobes. We moved our mattresses to the floors. We did drugs. We spoke a new language. And this was all a gigantic break from anything anyone was remotely familiar with. We did all this, plus we developed new political awareness and views.

To our parents, it was as if we had transformed into aliens. But they were far more outraged by our lifestyle choices than our political ones. When they saw mattresses on the floor they went ballistic. When they saw a copy of Marx or Mao on someone's desk, it was no big deal. Changes in lifestyle, in sexual openness, and even in musical tastes tore them up. Intellectual experiments didn't bother them nearly as much. I think this was because our parents were reacting based on their own pasts. They knew young people dabbled in dissident ideas because they had done the same thing. They expected as much from us and anticipated that it would last a few years and would then disappear, as it had for them. But they feared our lifestyle changes more, on two counts. First, our lifestyle choices called into question what they valued and were struggling to give us, and even their identities. They slaved to buy us a life we now dismissed. Second, our lifestyle choices had an aura of possible permanence about them, if not intentionally, then by default. If we lived in groups of like-minded folks practicing a whole new way of being, our deviance might persist too long to later be thrown off for the American dream. Our parents were pretty smart, I think, worrying more about long hair and mattresses than about the manifestos we read or wrote. The famous sixties musical was named *Hair*, not *Manifesto*, for a reason.

Nowadays I suspect things have reversed. Dabbling in dissident culture is now familiar. Lifestyle experiments are expected and seen as transitory. Today body piercing, for example, is more extreme than long hair was in the Sixties, but not as socially disruptive. It is students carrying around the wrong books, I suspect, that might make today's parents nervous.

At any rate, the third sanctuary I was involved with was one of the most successful political actions I ever encountered. Due to draft resistance connections, MIT was in the line of march for GI dissent. So when another GI decided he wanted to make a statement, MIT became his sanctuary.

Mike O'Connor arrived at MIT surreptitiously in November 1968 and we set him up in a room in our student center. In one day the event was big. In two days it was huge. In a week it was gargantuan. It isn't clear why the MIT sanctuary escalated so greatly. In the planning stages, only Noam Chomsky and I—he was teaching at MIT at the time—had felt that perhaps MIT wasn't ready for this kind of action. To do a successful sanctuary we would have to attract a large number of folks ready to devote full attention to the event. I worried, as did Chomsky—more about him soon—that there wouldn't be enough MIT support to sustain a sanctuary. We were outvoted in our efforts to hold off the project and we wholeheartedly joined the effort. Instead of our fears coming true, interest and support exceeded anyone's expectations. The sanctuary had to move from a modest room to the main hall of the student center, and then take over the entire building with spillover crowds clogging numerous other campus sites. Friendly faculty would come to give their classes either in the student center sanctuary or outdoors in the vicinity. There was constant music, talks, and open microphones. Dialogs would flourish late into the night. There were suddenly two MITs: the drab one and ours. Each night hundreds of people would bring sleeping bags to stay with our AWOL GI. At the height of the event I guess as many as six hundred people stayed late or overnight, with thousands in and out during the day, including people from Cambridge, Boston, and beyond.

To call the sanctuary a culture shock for MIT would immensely understate its impact. People came from near and far to experience the unfolding event. The culture was Woodstockish, but with radical politics, innovative courses, teach-ins, music, theater, constant consciousness raising, and debate. Dialogs were about the war, economy, society, and MIT's campus life and courses. People argued both for and against turning everything upside down. "Mr. Jones" met the "White Rabbit." It was ten days that shook my campus that made me a full-time social activist.

The sanctuary ended with a negotiated arrest. Mike O'Conner was taken to a military stockade. He could choose two visitors outside his immediate family. One was a woman he had met during the sanctuary and had a relationship with; the other was me. Visiting Mike each week in the stockade during his incarceration

41

was my first serious experience with jail. Mike handled his stockade time well, later emerging and joining the area's antiwar movement. I rolled along too.

Antiwar work by GIs yielded Vietnam Veterans Against the War. I remember one testimony by an ex-GI, a Native American. He told how we would fight against the powers of war until the rivers stopped flowing and grass stopped growing. I wept at his commitment. I desired to win well before his deadline.

Meeting Tactics

*One cannot in the nature of things expect a little
tree that has been turned into a club to put forth leaves.*
—*Martin Buber*

One evening I was chairing from the sanctuary stage, handling the throng's choices, which bounced between entertainment and politics. We were in a big hall, called the Sala de Puerto Rico. The hour was getting late. Hundreds of people were there. Most wanted to sleep but some were still eager to talk or hear music. Should we have a speech? Should we listen to the Jefferson Airplane (for the youth) or Beethoven (for the older folks)? Finally I had to calm the room into a willingness to drift off quietly for the night. Somehow, in doing so, I learned to relate effectively to large audiences.

Many years later at a Socialist Scholars Conference in NYC, I similarly calmed a fractious and large setting, Steve Shalom, a close friend from MIT, tells me. A major hall was crammed to capacity for a debate among Noam Chomsky, Paul Berman, and Ellen Willis about anti-Semitism and the Left. I was moderating. The speakers presented, but then an issue arose. Some audience members wanted the panelists to respond to each other. Others wanted to ask questions. The two groups started yelling at each other, and dissolution loomed. As Steve reminded me, at that time I said, "Hold on. I'm going to call on people from the floor. If you want to ask a question, ask a question. If you want panelist A to reply to something panelist B said, ask that." The audience sat in stunned amazement at this solution, or at least Steve did, and we continued the session without further rancor.

At a national antiwar meeting debating when to hold demonstrations in the upcoming season, I was again chairing, which is why I particularly remember what followed. There was a hot debate, but clearly leaning toward a majority viewpoint. I knew some of the movement leaders had a different desire than the agenda that was gaining ground, but it seemed the rank and file was going to opt for its own preference. I didn't think much was at stake, but regardless, whatever the assemblage decided, so be it. I was there to facilitate, not to channel. Suddenly, Rennie Davis, a major and very charismatic antiwar organizer, with prior history in the civil rights and local organizing realms, barged into the hall from the rear, shouting that he needed to be heard immediately. He spoke on behalf of the minority position and in just a few minutes he won the day. Why did he get the floor? How did he swing everyone? He did it by yelling out that he had just gotten off the phone with the Vietnamese chief negotiator, Madame Binh, who had personally asked him to argue on behalf of the minority's preferred dates for the events, not the popularly preferred dates. People urged that he be permitted to speak immediately. How convenient. To this day, I think Rennie made it all up.

U.S. radicals at various moments went to Cuba on what were called Venceremous Brigades to participate in sugarcane cutting and learn about the revolution. I remember hearing of one meeting in particular in Havana. There were Vietnamese officials, the U.S. delegation, and various Cubans. A film was shown of the Vietnam War that had a scene of Vietnamese shooting down an American plane seemingly with a hand weapon. The U.S. delegation cheered. At the end of the film the Vietnamese representative spoke, shocked, emotional, asking how these young militants possibly dreamed they could organize change in the United States if they could cheer the deaths of their fellow citizens. I never forgot that story. The Vietnamese built movements intending to win massive, overwhelming, undying popular support. What were we building?

Rennie Davis was at times the most inspirational speaker I ever heard. He used to talk on behalf of going to a demonstration by combining long but incredibly vivid and provocative descriptions of Vietnamese resilience in struggle with powerful, stunning condemnations of the war. Rennie's talks, or at least the couple that I remember hearing, were theatrical events, yet also totally natural. He moved crowds, and me too, the couple of times I heard him. Maybe it was the context. Maybe it was him. Probably both. Rennie had won a 4H chicken-judging contest at age sixteen in 1956. Ironically, he won it in Chicago, where he would later be tried as one of the Chicago Eight. Graduating from Oberlin, getting a masters at the University of Illinois, joining early SDS and then the antiwar movement, Rennie later became an insurance salesman, a venture capitalist, and a meditation lecturer. It was sad that someone lucky enough to have had many radical experiences and lessons, and to have thereby amassed considerable political insights and wisdom, cast it all aside to become what he had previously fought against.

Abbie Hoffman

Sacred cows make the tastiest hamburger.
—*Abbie Hoffman*

I met Abbie Hoffman at the MIT sanctuary. Like many other people, he had come to see what was going on. I remember standing with Hoffman on a second-floor balcony overlooking the large quadrangle outside the student center hall where the sanctuary was held. Abbie suddenly went down the stairs and started marching around the public area, with students passing by in the sun. Abbie had a make-believe rifle over his shoulder. The rifle was the cross that marked the MIT chapel. Abbie Hoffman was born in Worcester, Massachusetts, on November 30, 1936. He graduated from Brandeis in 1959. He earned a master's degree at Berkeley. In the early 1960s, he worked as a psychologist in a state hospital in Worcester. He joined SNCC in the South, but gained much wider notoriety when he turned on to drugs and began the loosely organized Yippies with Jerry Rubin.

After the Chicago Conspiracy trial in 1974 and up until 1980, Abbie lived underground, avoiding arrest for, ironically, an unrelated drug charge. Incredibly, while hiding from the law, he became the local organizer Barry Freed in upstate New York. He was often involved in demonstrations and events, all while wanted by the police. Abbie later turned himself in and did a work-release program in 1981–82, resuming political activism thereafter. He was brilliant, outrageous, courageous, and provocative. Few have ever had as much moxie as Abbie. At a 1988 reunion of the Chicago Eight, Abbie described himself as "an American dissident. I don't think my goals have changed since I was four and I fought schoolyard bullies." Hoffman was found dead at his home in New Hope, Pennsylvania, April 12, 1989. The death was ruled suicide. It was a very sad loss.

The whole hippie phenomenon, which Abbie was central to, has often been horribly misunderstood. Usually countercultures operate on the fringe, oppose their surroundings, and are somewhat cultish because their small size divorces them from wider realities beyond and causes them to become insular and defensive. The whole hippie phenomenon was huge, however, and penetrated not just elite campuses or urban avant-garde centers, but all campuses, and pretty nearly all cities and towns too. Hippies, and to this extent I was one too, weren't saying no to injustice, poverty, or pain so much as rejecting the wealth and status that injustices convey to social winners. Hippies said no to success. They said no to comfort and wealth. They rejected the upside, not the downside, of contemporary life. Hippies didn't want to be on top. It wasn't just wrong, it was boring and lifeless. Hippies said no to education, careers, and the accouterments of success in dress, housing, and even dialect. And hippies began to replace all that with communes, shared possessions, being on the road, and being alive now rather than only in some distant envisioned life. There was a whole lot to admire in the hippie movements and also a whole lot of excess and confusion. Sexism was intense. Returning to the land was ignorant. Rejecting success lost its allure when families were at stake. But all that said, the driving personal desires of hippie life were far healthier than the driving personal desires routinely inculcated by law schools, medical schools, or management programs. And the cultural commitments of hippies were a powerful defining and solidifying aspect of sixties activism.

Theater Lives

All the world's a stage,
And all the men and women merely players.
—Shakespeare

The Living Theatre with Julian Beck and Judith Malina also came to Cambridge for the MIT Sanctuary. They were given the stage at MIT's main theater, called Kresge Auditorium, which was a rather remarkable freestanding building able to house a few thousand people, a large stage, a big backstage area, a basement, some utility rooms, and a smaller gathering area. The Living Theatre not only performed at Kresge, but also trooped around campus making a visual statement with their dress and behavior.

The sanctuary scene was beyond hip, but even amidst its outrageousness, the members of the Living Theatre cast an indelible aura. I do not remember the play they performed, though I do remember that to me it seemed excessively affected though others were greatly moved by the performance. The period of resistance to the war in Indochina may have been the high point of the Living Theatre's near-lifetime of theatrical activism that took them all over the globe, from large to small venues.

Interestingly, much later, Lydia Sargent, my life partner, created a local theater group in Boston and Cambridge called The Living Newspaper. The name came from an earlier New Deal program, not from the Beck/Malina experience, but it always reminded me of the more famous project. The irony was that for me, Lydia's group—which was entirely amateur and which did its short plays and vignettes almost spontaneously based on the news of the day, often on the street, at a strike, at a demonstration, or in the basement of a local left bookstore called the Red Book—said more and was also more engaging and moving than the seriously financed productions of the more famous troop.

Lydia herself would most likely have been a professional actress in a better world. Even in this world, Lydia has through the years created and maintained theater groups for which she has repeatedly acted in starring roles, and directed as well as written plays. She does it all brilliantly. I remember the first play of Lydia's that my father went to see in a little but amazingly central theater space for her then-current group called the Newbury Street Theater, in Boston. My dad was astounded by the performance and particularly, but not solely, by Lydia's acting. The play was a kind of montage of vignettes drawn from Studs Terkel's book *Working* and it made a big impression on my father, not least because of his inclination, like many people's, to doubt that volunteers could sometimes be better than people getting paid. In truth, in the case of Lydia's group, they did vastly better than professional shows in content and often did comparably in staging and acting, their political motivations being powerful enough to elicit the hard work involved. What the Living Newspaper lacked was the historic times the Living Theater enjoyed.

Getting High

We are what we repeatedly do.
—Aristotle

Given that Abbie Hoffman and the Living Theatre were strong advocates of its use, this is a good place to mention marijuana. There is no denying that for many people, marijuana was liberating. Smoking grass was rebellious and could change one's pace of life and foster perceptions leading to different attitudes. I first encountered marijuana one night in an apartment I shared in Cambridge with Robin Hahnel and a friend named Andy Pearlman. This was my sophomore year, ditto for Andy, and it was Robin's junior year. Robin was not new to marijuana, but nor was he a well-traveled tutor. We had a joint. It was late. We sat together in the living room and puffed it to extinction. Nothing happened for me or Andy, though Robin claimed to be pleasantly high. We all retired. The place had two bedrooms and I was sleeping in its living room where there was a stereo turned on to nod off to.

After a bit, I realized that I was high. I not only had not previously had a joint, I also didn't drink other than an occasional beer. The clue to my doped state was the music. It was sharper, clearer, and more exact than normal. Each note was so special that a whole song was hard to notice. The notes drew my attention from the song, as if I was looking at individual trees so intently that I didn't notice they were part of a huge forest. I stayed awake for quite a while, coming to grips with heightened perception.

I used marijuana many times thereafter, for many years, maybe two or three times a week, diminishing as the years wore on. I lessened my use not so much because I lost a taste for being high but because it became more difficult to safely procure marijuana. I was and am more susceptible to getting high than most people. A contact high, which is when someone else smokes and you get high from what is floating in the air, was easy for me. Like a cheap drunk, I got high with less. I could never understand people smoking a joint and driving a car, reading a book, taking a test, or even just having a conversation. But many people certainly did all this, and more, without any discernible variation from typical behavior. Robin could do much of it, for example. And I later had a friend named Skip Asheim, a Go playing partner, who could play stoned, talk stoned, write stoned, drive stoned, do anything at all stoned, and you wouldn't know he was stoned. Stomach cancer got him, though.

I have known potheads—a person who smokes so much or is so susceptible that it alters his or her personality and capacities. I have also known people affected by other imbibed materials. Media portrayals of potheads are pretty accurate, if exaggerated. It wasn't just the volume smoked that did it, however. Skip, for example, smoked as much or more than most potheads, and certainly wasn't one. I suspect if I smoked even a fifth as much as Skip did, I might have wound up other than who I am. But pothead or not, I don't think I ever knew anyone who was addicted to marijuana. I never saw anyone suffer withdrawal symptoms, even when heavy users were denied access.

My one experience driving stoned was on the West Side Drive leaving New York City. I had earlier had only a few puffs and I thought I wasn't high by the time I took the wheel. I was fine for a bit, and then, off to the left, out over the Hudson River, there loomed the George Washington Bridge. How pretty it was, how entrancing. It was a miracle that I didn't drive off into nothingness. I managed to get off the road and survive. It is interesting to think that if I had crashed into a car I would probably have gone to jail for a long time for vehicular homicide. Am I less guilty for having been lucky enough to not crash? If not, then should I go to jail for a long spell for what I did?

Another time I went bike riding stoned. I wanted to see what it would be like. I rode for what seemed a huge distance without my hands touching the steering wheel, feeling the road flowing under me, even cornering by the weight of my torso and pressure of my legs. Then there was a moment of entrancement with something that caught my eye. Suffering flying-over-the-handlebar bruises, I didn't try riding stoned again. Marijuana was intense and enjoyable. But I don't think it had much to do with who I am.

My generation, at least the relevant, roused, sixties part of it, all had at least some politics. We all also smoked at least some dope. When the politics were dominant the drugs were nice, but peripheral, or in some cases, even rejected outright. When the drugs were dominant, the politics were nice, but peripheral, or in some cases, even rejected outright. Sex and rock and roll were prominent on both sides of this divide.

One of the more notable and recurrent features of being stoned is that being high changes your sense of time. You can listen to a three-minute song for what seems like eternity. You can kiss for a millennium in a minute. The clock on the mantle is still ticking as usual, even if it feels like an hour for each jump of the minute hand. I suspect that when stoned we perceive a long period passing even in brief spans because our perceptions accrue more inputs per minute. If we weren't stoned, accumulating so much sensory input would have required much longer, and that's precisely how much more time seems to us to have passed. We cram more sense data into less time, and we feel like it is, therefore, more time. That was my guess about doped time thirty-five years ago, at any rate, and it rings true to me as I recall it now too, so I suspect it is probably at least part of the story. But now I know as you get older, time seems to pass faster. I suspect this is because a week or a month or a year is a smaller percentage of what you have lived so far. At any rate, it seems like you are speeding up your life trajectory even as you are slowing down your actions within it and even as there is less of it left.

The upshot about marijuana is that I wouldn't pressure anyone to get stoned. I don't think getting stoned is mandatory for being a full person, accruing diverse experiences, or attaining wisdom. But I would recommend marijuana. Of course, I had the white suburban elite university privilege of knowing I wasn't likely to be jailed and that the person I bought my stuff from wasn't likely to be armed and dangerous.

Stoned Cold Picnic

It's all right letting yourself go as long as you can let yourself back.
—Mick Jagger

My personal experience with drugs was overwhelmingly confined to marijuana. Out in the youth culture, however, LSD also had a prime place. Infinitely more powerful, LSD really did take many users to different worlds, contributing to the ideas and lifestyles of the time, and blasting many people into psychic oblivion as well. My one experience with LSD occurred one day in Somerville, Massachusetts. It was a Saturday and I went to visit Robin Hahnel and Ivy Leichman, who at the time lived together there, doing community organizing. They had another local friend or two visiting, and also Ivy's brother, Larry, and his wife, Gail. I was without a partner for the day, the rest were coupled up. This occurred a couple of years, maybe three, after MIT, but since drugs were part of my generation's college experience, the story fits nicely here.

Like many important events in many people's lives, my LSD experience wasn't planned. The day's agenda, which I heard only upon arrival, was to go to a local park, picnic for the day, and return home. On the trip by car to the park, we all took LSD tabs. This was my first time, while the rest had tripped before. We ate the tabs, a little spot of LSD on paper, timed, according to the experts, so that we would drive to the area and walk the half mile or so to the idyllic picnic spot before we started to feel the effects.

We got there. We parked. We began walking to the picnic spot, feeling the effects a bit early. Robin gets energized even by marijuana. This stuff made him incredibly hyper, to the point that he was literally swinging from tree branches. Gail and I dragged to the rear of the procession, the rest of the group moving faster and I guess not realizing that we were separated and slower. Before long, I was struggling mightily just to stay on the path. It was like trying to run a race while exhausted and disoriented, except I wasn't exhausted, I was mildly dissociated, or whatever one calls it. Proceeding to the picnic spot was a giant challenge and burden. How to move at all? How to not wander off into the woods? Why not just sit? Which direction was forward? I had to concentrate for what seemed forever on only the path and my feet and the distance of one step, and then another, and another, with each foot, each time, landing on the path in front of the other foot, while aggressively avoiding noticing anything else. To step off would be disaster, was my only thought.

We got to the picnic site to much relief from others that Gail and I had finally arrived. Everyone assumed we had simply been enjoying the trees and flowers. That's when my situation nosedived. I am not a painter, a dramatist, a novelist, or a wordsmith. I fear I can't compellingly convey passing through the doors of perception into the wilds of delusion. I quickly went from way more out of it than dope ever remotely induced to completely psychotic. In between there were hallucinations of the pond being a swirling ocean, of a nearby hill being a live mountain, of massive animals all around, and of tumultuous earth bubbling. But that was only transitional. For that stuff, I was still there, even if amidst a lot of swirling, roiling, sometimes magnificent, other times unpleasant hallucination. After that point, however, I was no longer there. There was no self to me. No mind inhabited my body. The boundary between me and not me was gone. My hand was no more me than was a plant I would stare at, and my hand and the plant were each also no less me than the surrounding trees. There was no me staring, or if there was a me staring, then I was staring out and staring back too. Others questioning me weren't questioning a sentient entity that could reply.

I think maybe I could have taken LSD less traumatically. Maybe I could even have taken it and gone nearly as far as I did and enjoyed or even been enriched by the experience, though that is a bit less plausible. But to go as far as I did with no forethought, and to that point no aid, was skirting disaster. I might not have returned from wherever I had gone, though this wasn't a thought I could have had at the time, because at that point, there was no I having thoughts.

Others took note. All but one, I later found out, thought I was joking with them. Larry, Ivy's brother, was a doctor. So was Gail, though she was in no shape to worry about me. Larry found nothing to be concerned about. Robin, however, I was told later, decided my behavior was no joke. I suspect this was because he knew that I wouldn't joke in this manner and that I couldn't act so convincingly, in any case. For hours, I am told, Robin, while high on acid himself, and restraining all the wild energy it induced in him, settled me and talked with me and tried to entertain me, calmly, to take my mind off being mindless and to prevent hysteria or catatonia or whatever.

One trick he used after considerable time had passed and I was somewhat better was to pull out a chess set and induce me to play. I was still incoherent and unable to speak, but we apparently played many games. I remember a little of it, toward when the therapy was bringing me back through those doors of perception. I saw the pieces animate. I saw my moves as patterns of plans. I saw others walking over, laughing at Robin and me sitting there playing chess, denying what was occurring. I suspect Robin has never really understood that he may well have saved the life I have lived that day. No memoir without Robin the drug escort.

Well, I did return to normal existence, and but for a few nightmares in subsequent weeks, and the occasional flashback to the bucking mountain hills and tumultuous ocean pond, there was no harm done. Did I take a lesson? It all made me of two minds about drugs. On the one hand, in one mood, it seemed clear to me that consciousness-altering drugs transformed us from who we were into someone else, and that disturbed me. On the other hand, I saw another sense in which all that was ridiculous. Whoever drugs made us, after all, that's who we were. Why were drugs different than air, water, food, or anything else we imbibed? But abstract similarity or not, I realized after LSD that I wouldn't have arsenic as a snack to experience its effects. I wouldn't eat arsenic to have a richer and more diverse arsenal of personal memories. Comparing arsenic to a chocolate bar in that both are imbibed and both impact our chemistry, and asserting that on basis we are who we are whichever we eat, wouldn't convince me to take arsenic. After LSD, the same held for some drugs, or at least for some drugs in some circumstances. I had LSD only once and wouldn't recommend even a single try to anyone else.

Musical Interlude and Some Films Too

> *I don't know anything about music. In my line you don't have to.*
> —Elvis Presley

Drugs arose from and fed into the musical tides of the sixties. Unlike the drugs, rock and roll was, for me, a very powerful influence. I remember seeing the Rolling Stones at Forest Hills Tennis Stadium on Long Island as a senior in high school. What had me pondering that event for days wasn't their lyrics, though those weren't to be lightly dismissed, nor was it the Stones' beat and style, which certainly got under my skin even if Mick Jagger was actually London School of Economics-bred and not street smart like, ironically, the clean-cut Beatles. What got me thinking that day, instead, were Mick's fans in the stands.

As the Stones entered and later left the stadium by helicopter, I remember the girls in the stands, literally standing on their seats, reaching out their hands toward the craft as if to hang on for dear life, exhibiting a sort of passionate desire I had not seen before. I was deeply unsettled. I loved the Stones, but this was psychotic.

There was so much of it, however, that it had to reflect society's character and not just personal idiosyncrasies. I didn't know what it meant until much later, when the women's movement discovered and reported the ubiquitous depths of female oppression and male macho.

Along with the Rolling Stones event, some others stand out. I didn't get to see the Beatles in Shea Stadium. Nancy Shapiro and I missed that, my having bollixed the tickets, whereas Larry Seidman and his lady friend Jane Schur and some other friends went. Nancy and I listened on the radio, in her den. In person the event was a cacophony of adulation. To hear the Beatles it was better to use a stereo. To feel the passion and be part of the tribe, you had to go, and we didn't.

I was, however, at Dylan's famous concert at Forest Hills. This was the second of the three famous concerts in which Dylan first unveiled his electric rock future. Amazingly, I also saw Dylan at Newport, the first of those three. At Newport I didn't understand what was going on. Why the booing? The first half of his longer show at Forest Hills was familiar Dylan, with guitar, harmonica, and otherworldly lyrics. The second half of the show, he was backed by an electric band. This brought out taunts, catcalls, and even serious hatred. How could Dylan deface his own material, even the whole folk canon? purists bellowed. How could the purists not hear what was in the wind? I wondered. And Bob played on, not entirely oblivious, but certainly not bending. No puppet strings for Bob. If you can listen to "I ride on a mail train baby, can't buy a thrill," and not resonate to the sound, you aren't busy dying, you are already dead.

Still, I didn't appreciate Dylan right out of the gate. At first I heard only irritating noise. Larry Seidman made me listen again, and then again, and it still wasn't coming through. The Byrds rendition of "Mr. Tambourine Man" opened the door to my appreciating Dylan's voice. Thereafter, I heard his words in my gut and soul as much as in my ears and mind. Dylan pulled out of the times tones that conveyed its mood and meaning better, by far, than others. This was true not only when Dylan was speaking in the tongues of dissent, but also when he was extricating himself from militant movement identification. In a short time he went from activist anger "Masters of War":

And I hope that you die
And your death'll come soon
I will follow your casket
In the pale afternoon
And I'll watch while you're lowered
Down to your deathbed
And I'll stand o'er your grave
Til I'm sure that you're dead

to disengaged pathos as revealed in *"Farewell Angelina,"* which to me was Dylan saying good-bye to the Left via a song to Joan Baez:

> The machine guns are roaring
> The puppets heave rocks
> The fiends nail time bombs
> To the hands of the clocks
> Call me any name you like
> I will never deny it
> Farewell Angelina
> The sky is erupting
> I must go where it's quiet.

It is hard to convey how much rock and roll meant to me and my peers. It opened our hearts, eyes, and minds. From "Satisfaction" to "Help" to "California Dreaming" to "Hey Joe" to "Saturday Afternoon" to "The Gates of Eden," popular music was our literature. Dylan was an emotional and intellectual jungle gym. I was a kid, climbing.

The best concerts I ever saw were one by The Band, due to the shock of watching them shuffle their instruments from member to member as well as the rave-up joy of a long medley of rock and roll screamers they did; one by the Chambers Brothers in Harvard Stadium, shaking the place with a very long rendition of "Time Has Come Today;" and more than one by Bruce Springsteen, of which the most soul-shaking was the first, in Harvard Square, which Jon Landau saw and said, afterward, "I have seen the future of rock and roll and his name is Bruce Springsteen." I was at that historic performance with Lydia Sargent. We went to it, Lydia tells me, based on my hearing Bruce's first album and wanting to see him in person. Like everyone else, Lydia and I were flabbergasted by his energy, spirit, talent, and plain old joyousness.

Springsteen is the only performer I have heard since the sixties who got under the popular skin and into the popular mind the way a whole panoply of fifties and sixties rockers did, but uniquely Bruce spoke seriously and with substance to the white male working class and in turn was passionately heard by them. This fact, so evident at Bruce's concerts, made me realize that no one else did that for white working class guys in a liberating way that spoke to and from their experiences. Maybe if John Lennon had lived and delved further into his own roots as he began to do on "Working Class Hero" it might have happened, but, bang bang, some wrong drumming, and John died.

Then there was Woodstock. As a concert and as music from stage, Woodstock had its great moments. Most particularly, I remember waking up to the Jefferson Airplane, with the sun rising and a few hundred thousand fists waving. The Who had been the closing act the night before. Pete Townshend had whacked Abbie Hoffman of New Left hippie/yippie notoriety (and, implicitly, whacked revolution itself) over the head for trying to get up on stage during The Who's set. Abbie wanted to inject politics. Pete wanted to bash and burn his guitar. The two are not the same thing. It had to be 3 in the morning when that happened, or thereabouts. And then the next morning, probably about 7 or maybe 8, we're all singing along with the Jefferson Airplane:

Look what's happening out in the streets
Got a revolution got to revolution
Hey I'm dancing down the streets
Got a revolution got to revolution.

At Yasgur's farm, we were all "Volunteers of America" and Woodstock wasn't really a concert. Yes, it was a weekend of nonstop music, but it was mainly a generational gathering. It was not a politics pinnacle—there was little overt politics present—but it was a youth-culture pinnacle. We came from far and wide and spent a few days camped in proximity, sharing vibes. Woodstock was sex, drugs, and rock and roll, but it was mainly solidarity.

Did Woodstock have vendors trying to make a buck? Did it have cruisers trying to make a score? Did it have posers trying to make reputations? It had all that, of course, and it had worse, too—can you imagine bad LSD, given my description of the good stuff?—but mostly it was just honest people briefly celebrating outside society's pliers, in the sunny rain. The problem with Woodstock wasn't that it was too big or that it went on too long. The problem with Woodstock was that it was too small and it didn't last long enough.

I am not a literary guy. I haven't been educated in the length and breadth of human artistry. Whether innately or by contingent personal history, my eyes are not artistic. In Florence, Italy, seeing the paintings and statues was nice but not profoundly memorable. In Egypt, Greece, London, and New York, seeing statues and hangings and all manner of artistic miracles has barely moved me. I have enjoyed a small share of great literature, but great literature hasn't contoured my life. Hesse's *The Glass Bead Game,* Melville's *Moby Dick,* and Dostoevsky's *Crime and Punishment* mattered to me, but if I hadn't read them I would still be who I am. Likewise, if I never saw the *Mona Lisa* I'd still be me. But without Buddy Holly, I wonder. And without the British Invasion, the Doors, Jimi Hendrix, Motown, and the "Dock of the Bay," and certainly without the Beatles, Stones, Dylan, and long hair and joints, forget about it. Without all that, I would simply not be me. Woodstock was a moment in our lives, a big and important moment, no more, and no less. But what Woodstock stood for, that was much more.

I remember trying to explain my musical ties to Eric, Andrew, and Andrea, Lydia's children. I have been a friend to them, and vice versa, for thirty years. I was no doubt paternalistic and they had justifiably little patience for my pleading, just as I had had little patience for my father telling me about Al Jolson, or about some song about not having bananas, or some singer crooning about a Depression and a Great War. When I told Lydia's kids that it was too bad their joy in music couldn't give them for the rest of their lives what my joy in music gave me over the course of my life, I am sure my words fell on deaf ears.

Was I repeating my father's error in thinking that my generation was special in this regard? As much as reason says that's probably the case, my experience makes me feel it is unlikely that later generations will remember the words and melodies they danced to in high school and college five or seven decades later the way that my generation remembers the original musical scores of our youth. I suspect the music of Eric, Andrea, and Andrew's youth will not be for them a time machine that goes both forward and backward during all their days, as the music of my youth is for me. Andrew is an accomplished drummer. As time passes, he seems to grow steadily more attached to the Beatles and less to performers of his own times. One of his children, Owen, has taken up the bass. He seems most attached to Cream, Led Zeppelin, and Jimi Hendrix, all sixties rockers. Regardless of its affect on others, the music that I loved and learned from will always have awesome impact on me. It was entirely integrated with who we were and it remains soul deep for at least a good number of us. And, of course, it wasn't just genius or muse that tied rock and roll to my generation's souls. It was how the songs, the beat, and the melodies meshed with the times. A tumultuous world propelled sixties songs into our personalities and cemented their lyrics and sound into our consciousness. All day and all of the night, those times rocked. My generation's signature was, at least in part, rock and roll that never forgets.

Likewise, there is a sense in which many people in my generation are still eighteen or twenty. That's part music, part politics. For us, for me, some kind of rite of aging didn't happen as it usually does, even if biology proceeded as always. We, or I, identify more as peers with people much younger than with people my age. Put in a room with people who could be my kids, I feel like I am in among my own kind. Put in a room with people my own age, I feel like I am a youngster caught in an old folks home. And this will be true at sixty-four, too.

In that vein, one of the rudest awakenings of my life came when around 1995 I realized that it had been as many years since the Vietnam War as it had been years from World War II to the mid-sixties. I remembered that when I was in high school and even in college, when I heard tales of World War II, the stories seemed to me to be from a time out of mind. World War II was before the past; it was prehistoric. World War II was, for me, irrelevant. It was other people's glory days. And suddenly I saw that for young people around me, a past that for me was in many respects closer than last week was not just the old days, but was never. Vietnam was, for them, prehistoric. I was getting old.

I should perhaps say that my interface with rock and roll wasn't always pure delight. At one point I met The Grateful Dead who were in Boston for a show. Some of us went to their hotel to ask them to do a concert for the antiwar movement. The Dead heard our appeal for a few seconds and then verbally berated us, almost assaulted us, and had us thrown out of their hotel room. Who the hell did we think we were? It was a rude awakening.

I understood stars feeling bombarded by fans. It was no fun for Jerry Garcia to never know if someone seeking him out was a starfucker or sincere. It was no fun to not know whether someone cared about you or cared only about benefits they could cajole from you. It was no fun to have no privacy. But being tongue-lashed by Jerry was not much fun either. Thinking through this, I decided that stars are famous not just by dint of talent, but also by lucky circumstance. The excessive and often obscene wealth that stars garner has no legitimate moral sanction. Applause for The Grateful Dead was appropriate. Massive payments to The Grateful Dead were not. The wealth of stars like The Dead, I realized, ought to have found its way back, at least in considerable degree, into social good. That's why we asked them to help.

I didn't much care for the early Grateful Dead and cared only somewhat more when they got more melodic. I preferred the Jefferson Airplane, The Doors, Janis Joplin, Hendrix, and The Beatles, Stones, Band, and Dylan. I mention the exchange with The Dead because it was emblematic of the barely civil relations between serious activists and entertainment stars. There were exceptions, such as Leonard Bernstein relating to the Black Panthers, Jane Fonda relating to GIs dissenters, and Bonnie Raitt and Jackson Browne relating to the antiwar movement, or later Bruce Springsteen relating to the No Nukes movement and GI organizations.

Rock and roll isn't easy. Little Feat was incredible. Lowell George died. The Clash was incomparable. Joe Strummer died. So did Jim Morrison, Janis Joplin, Buddy Holly, Jimi Hendrix, and John Lennon. Rock and roll was dangerous.

While I am at it, there were a bunch of films that mattered greatly too, to the sixties. In 1962, there was *Birdman of Alcatraz*. I remember being powerfully moved by Burt Lancaster's highly fictional portrayal of Robert Stroud's time in prison. In 1963, there was *Lord of the Flies* and *The Great Escape*. Steve McQueen was us, and the collective project of the escape had a loud resonance. In 1964, there was *Dr. Strangelove, A Hard Day's Night, The Pawnbroker*. and *Zorba the Greek*. Dance beneath the diamond skies. In 1965, there was the *Battle of Algiers*—movie as education—*Help*, and *A Thousand Clowns*. Jason Robards affected me greatly. *Clowns* didn't birth the hippie explosion but it definitely contributed to it. In 1966, there was *Blow Up* and *Fahrenheit 451*. In 1967, there was *Bonnie and Clyde, Cool Hand Luke, Don't Look Back*, and *The Graduate*. These films all said you couldn't win but somehow we ignored that, censored it, reworked it. We came away raring to fight. In 1968, there was nothing. The world sufficed. And in 1969, there was *Butch Cassidy and the Sundance Kid, Easy Rider, Midnight Cowboy, They Shoot Horses Don't They*, and, of course, *Z*. Finally, 1970 gave the world my favorite political movie, *Burn*. Whether it was films or sounds, sixties culture had a way about it.

Chapter 5

Stargazing

Debating Hump

And I'll stand o'er your grave
Til I'm sure that you're dead.
—*Bob Dylan*

MIT is one of the most famous and prominent institutions of higher learning in the world. Famous people come and go. The major MIT auditorium, Kresge, where the Living Theatre performed, was also for me the scene of a far more personally demanding experience. I had been elected president of the MIT student body and Hubert Humphrey, Vice President of the U.S., was coming to town. It was arranged that he would debate three students in Kresge. We all were to appear on stage, but the others agreed it was to be a showdown between myself, representing the local movement, and the Hump, which was my name for Hubert, representing the devil as incarnated in Lyndon Johnson and U.S. imperialism.

Before the debate I was alone in a room behind the Kresge stage. Humphrey, with his impeccable liberal credentials, was in another room, probably with his bodyguards and aides-de-camp, also behind the Kresge stage. This wasn't Ali versus Frasier, but still I sat in a chair with my hands grasping the arms feeling like they were digging into the wood. I don't know what to call the emotions I felt. Fury, fear, rage, catatonia. It was a little bit of everything. The Hump was probably next door having a drink.

I often speak publicly nowadays, sometimes to ten, fifty, or a hundred people, sometimes to a few thousand. I always feel a little squeamish before starting a talk, though after I start the nervousness and stage fright quickly recede. But for the Humphrey debate I was completely wired and scared silly. I had prepared by researching a bunch of case-study examples of international events and conditions, choosing them to rebut anything that Humphrey might bring up while we debated. So I had lots of facts and connections about Vietnam and the war, but also about India, Latin America, the U.S., and so on. As it turned out, the debate was a massacre. When I got on stage and saw Humphrey, I was ready to rumble. Humphrey wasn't. Hubert underestimated the situation, and got beat down.

I was dumbfounded. I could not understand how the vice president of the U.S. could be so intellectually empty, verbally slow, and unprepared. No doubt Humphrey wasn't as mentally moribund as I took him to be—and maybe I was better at this sort of exchange than I gave myself credit for—but HH certainly wasn't the massive intellect and cruel soul I had anticipated. I wrote that it was like debating a talking marshmallow. How could the U.S. imperial juggernaut proceed with people as mushy as Humphrey at the helm? I later decided there were two main answers to that question. The first was that people like Humphrey weren't at the top levels of power. The second was that even mush-heads, when they command an imperial juggernaut against meager opposition, win most battles.

Fearing Killian

> *With his businesslike anger and his bloodhounds that kneel*
> *If he needs a third eye he just grows it.*
> *—Bob Dylan*

On another occasion, I encountered in the main hallway of MIT James Killian, who was not only chairman of the MIT Board of Overseers but also director of the Ford Motor Company and of numerous other Fortune 500 corporations. Killian was a living, breathing, ruling-class actor who played starring roles in the long-running drama "Empires Are Us."

Humphrey played at vice president. Killian was full of vice and was also a president. In just a few minutes of chatting with Killian I was chilled to the bone. It wasn't his words—it was that this guy was the *Bold Marauder*. Killian seemed to me violent, amoral, and pathological, but also competent. He was like Hannibal Lector. Perhaps it was an artifact of the preconceptions of capitalists that I carried in my own mind, but while I saw civility in Killian, I didn't see a soul. What I decided is that there are people up top who lack moral character and have sufficient amoral mind to get hierarchy's dirty jobs done. I realized they were more present at the heights of corporate rule than at the heights of political rule because if you didn't have a quick mind plus steel nerves plus uncaring blood in the corporate world, you lost. In corporate institutions, more or less equally armed people struggle for market share and pathology triumphs. In the political hierarchy, while there are some Killians prowling the corridors, there are apparently also many Humphreys.

When I asked Noam Chomsky how people as dimwitted as the Hump could make pressure-laden decisions that were horribly effective at attaining elite ends, Chomsky's answer was that when an elephant fights fleas almost any decisions the elephant makes wind up looking like brilliant strategy. The elephant tends to trounce fleas regardless of which way the elephant flounces. The limits of elephant strategy become evident only when flea opposition sufficiently escapes conformity and submission to mount a real threat. At such times elephants can look exceedingly stupid.

There Ain't Nothing Like Ali

Power never takes a back step—only in the face of more power.
—*Malcolm X*

As undergraduate association president I met Muhammad Ali when he came to MIT to speak. Given the brevity of the exchange, even Ali's aura could barely make the event memorable. But I do remember listening on the radio to Cassius Clay's fights, and sometimes seeing them on TV. Before Clay, I barely knew boxing, and I never before gave a damn about it. I never understood it until talking with a friend, Sandy Carter, decades later, who had fought Golden Gloves and explained the sport to me. But Clay's Olympic exploits in 1960 made me, like millions of others, a staunch fan.

Cassius Clay exuded charisma. Clay was so flamboyant, playful, clever, intensely confident, and outrageously irreverent that his excitement boosted you up a notch, and that notch Clay boosted us up helped lead to a mid-century cultural, political, and social explosion. Indeed, I was so vested in Cassius Clay's success, and then in Muhammad Ali's success, that to listen to his fights was a kind of joyous but incredibly intense torture. If Clay didn't win all his early fights, if he lost even one, I think I would have been devastated.

When Clay beat the incredibly frightening Sonny Liston in 1964, going in as a 19-and-0 underdog and coming out as a 20-and-0 World Champion, it was like lightning flashing on behalf of liberty. When Clay immediately thereafter became a Muslim, changing his name to Mohammed Ali, a good part of the U.S. was culturally expanded. When the world heavyweight champion, the most famous person on the face of the planet, a person who could have anything or do anything he wanted, later said, "I ain't got no quarrel with those Vietcong" and refused induction and got stripped of his title and his license to fight and sentenced to jail, that was a great historical moment.

Clay came back from his gold medal Olympics in love with America, with boxing, and with his medal. He went to eat a cheeseburger in a Louisville restaurant. The restaurant wouldn't serve him. Clay threw his medal into the Ohio River. Bang, bang, Clay was marching into history.

Years later, out on bail from refusing the draft, Ali joined Martin Luther King Jr. at a rally for fair housing in Louisville. Ali said, "In your struggle for freedom, justice, and equality I am with you. I came to Louisville because I could not remain silent while my own people, many I grew up with, many I went to school with, many my blood relatives, were being beaten, stomped, and kicked in the streets simply because they want freedom and justice and equality in housing." Later the same day, in front of cameras, Ali continued:

Why should they ask me to put on a uniform and go 10,000 miles from home and drop bombs and bullets on Brown people in Vietnam while so-called Negro people in Louisville are treated like dogs and denied simple human rights? No I'm not going 10,000 miles from home to help murder and burn another poor nation simply to continue the domination of white slave masters of the darker people the world over. This is the day when such evils must come to an end. I have been warned that to take such a stand would cost me millions of dollars. But I have said it once and I will say it again. The real enemy of my people is here. I will not disgrace my religion, my people, or myself by becoming a tool to enslave those who are fighting for their own justice, freedom, and equality.

The fact that Ali is now celebrated and revered in the U.S. is not a sign of societal health, but is, instead, a sign of societal hypocrisy and, regrettably, also a sign of his own ill health. The spirit of Ali has absolutely nothing in common with the corporate hacks who today laud him, just as the spirit of Martin Luther King Jr. is routinely violated by many who now celebrate him.

Stars Are Us

"Incapacity of the masses." What a tool for all exploiters and dominators,
past present and future, and especially for the modern
aspiring enslavers, whatever their insignia.
—Volin

One of the central themes running through hippie movements during my MIT days was excellence. What was it? What did it mean? Where did it come from? What did it warrant? Were stars excellent? My own lessons in understanding excellence, and even genius, occurred largely in daily life, not in the movement.

Go is an ancient Asian board game just as chess is, but in Go you place identical stones on the board. They are ideally made of slate and shell and are always shaped like M&M's, so they make a nice "plunk" when you slap them down. One player has white stones and the other has black ones. The board is a 19x19 intersection grid that looks like graph paper. You put your stones, turn by turn, on the intersections. You try to cordon off areas and also to capture groups of the opponent's stones. You can't change the position of a stone once you place it on the board, but even so, because there are so many intersections, the game involves a stupendous array of possibilities.

Go has helped me pass a lot of time pleasurably, but my biggest lesson came in my earliest playing days. I had been playing friends, including a physics faculty member at MIT for about a year. I heard about a club, and went to try it out. I entered and was promptly asked my rank. Rank? I just said that I thought I was pretty good. Okay, play that fellow over there. He will give you a nice handicap that will make the game interesting. He let me put nine stones at designated spots on the board before we even moved. I thought this was ridiculous. How could anyone at some local club, or maybe anywhere in the world, give me such a huge advantage? It was tantamount, I learned later, to giving me a queen in chess.

He proceeded not to just win, but to humiliate me. After mulling over this seeming miracle, I saw the guy who played me start playing another fellow. My torturer was now playing with the advantage of a nine-stone handicap. I watched him lose, badly, and I was now well beyond surprise. I asked the winner just how good he was—at least eighteen handicap stones better than me—compared to, say, the best player in the world. He said real masters could give him nine stones and still beat him soundly. I not only had no idea what Go was about, but, more important, I had no idea how gigantic the gap was between being truly accomplished at something and being an okay amateur.

I learned the same lesson somewhat earlier, by a physical example. When applying for colleges I visited Princeton University for an interview. I arrived on a horribly gloomy day that soured me to the school. I went to the Princeton gym, however, hoping to see Bill Bradley work out. I didn't know what Dollar Bill (that was his nickname) looked like, but I knew that he was touted as being the greatest college basketball player of all time. So I weaseled my way into the gym and sat on the floor near the court, as if I belonged there. After a while some team members came out of the locker room to practice. One guy seemed phenomenal and I decided he must be Dollar Bill. After watching the phenom for awhile, another team member came onto the floor and started shooting and then this second guy played my phenom one-on-one. The first guy was in fact Geoff Petrie, who later also had an NBA career. But watching the real Bill Bradley, the second guy, make mincemeat of the phenom in their little competition, and just seeing Bradley's absolute confidence and the beauty of his movement, I saw, as later with Go, the gigantic range of human capacity.

Even from a great distance you can see this range in athletics. I used to see it watching my idol (Say Hey) Willie Mays run out from under his hat. Willie was not only exciting, but just plain phenomenal, a hero of my youth. Or I saw it much later in life, watching Torvill and Dean synchronously slide across the ice to Bolero, chilling my spine. When watching such exceptional displays nowadays, I wonder why human excellence threatens many egos or makes people despair for equity. Exceptional excellence should inspire and glorify everyone. It certainly shouldn't endanger equity.

The same lesson recurred much later, involving a tennis pro at a center where I played near Woods Hole, Massachusetts. The local pro I took lessons from and became friends with was a good club pro. We would play sometimes in an unusual manner, a tennis version of taking a multi-stone Go handicap. The pro got one serve for each point instead of two. I got three serves instead of two. Moreover, every game started 30-love in my favor, and I could hit my shots as wide as the doubles lines, whereas he had to hit his in the singles court. We called my shots generously. We called his shots close. It was fun, exciting, and with this handicap I could compete. So one day we were talking and I asked how he would do at Wimbledon. He said that he would get annihilated in the first round. Again, the vast range from an okay amateur (me), up to a club pro (him), and then to a top pro (winning Wimbledon), was evident. Some people find this mountainous difference off-putting. Some deny that it exists. I have always found the difference a joy to behold—even when being bashed over the board or on the court. And brains show range, too.

At MIT, in one math course we had a take-home final exam. Take-home final exams are notoriously the most difficult challenges MIT students ever face. After all, you can take the test home and use any source you want, and it is just some problems, so how can you miss? The take-home test has to be awfully hard or the methodology makes no sense. In this case, it was ten true/false questions, but when you put true or false, you had to explain why. You ought to be able to guess fifty percent, except that you can't get credit for your guess unless you explain your reasoning. I think I got a 50 on the test, maybe less. At any rate, there was this one student who got it all right, and who got an extra credit question to boot. And in the few class sessions I had attended, this student had always stood out in a way I had never seen from any other student in any class. I was very good at test-taking and at math, but this fellow was mathematically Martian. We were never friends, but I bet he is a prominent mathematician now, probably among the top few in the world.

At MIT, I also encountered a physicist, this time faculty, named Steven Weinberg. He too was, even to my not-so-tutored eyes, special. Later, he got a Nobel Prize for work he was doing roughly at the time I first encountered him. I also attended some lectures by Julian Schwinger once, and he was clearly incredibly smart as well, but I didn't get quite the same feeling from him as from Weinberg. With Weinberg it was like watching Willie Mays. He had the means to arrive at answers, always.

And then there has been knowing Noam Chomsky, which is a bit like knowing Newton. Noam told me once he had been awed a bit by a biologist friend named Salvador Luria, another Nobel prize winner, who was quite political. Noam said Luria would arrive at conclusions without seeming to traverse intermediate ground. He just got there. This used to be said about the famous physicist Richard Feynman too. For some especially talented people what they do, in other words, is like what everyone else does, only better. They use the same data, manipulate it into the same arguments, but faster or deeper. I think this is true of Noam, but with him the added power is really quite incredible, like it was, say, for Von Neumann in mathematics, who was famously noted for his calculating capacity. In contrast, there are other especially talented people who can certainly think in a world-class way, though perhaps not supremely (Einstein, for example, was only a creditable mathematician), but can also get to the end point by what seems to be magic. They leap over what the rest of us do, and use completely inexplicable pathways.

The Zone

> *You have to believe in yourself, that's the secret...*
> *Without it, you go down to defeat.*
> *—Charlie Chaplin*

Having celebrated exceptional range of achievement, I should say that in my experience the range that each typical individual has personal access to is often more than the range that each such individual actually traverses. Of course we don't each pursue most avenues of human excellence that we could, not having time for it, and we never learn what we might have attained in areas we didn't pursue. But beyond that, even in areas we do pursue, often we don't tap our fullest potentials. This accounts, to a considerable degree, for the gap between very accomplished and more run-of-the-mill performance, I think, and sometimes perhaps even for the gap between genius and everything else. The geniuses reach their potential. The rest of us don't.

I first learned about the gap between what we do and what we are capable of doing in an odd adventure not long out of high school. My then-best friend Larry Seidman and I went across the country in an old VW bus. There were all kinds of high points, naturally. I like to tell about arriving on the West Coast at about two in the morning. I was driving and I couldn't find San Francisco. I have always been notorious for getting lost, but this was an extreme instance and I certainly wasn't senile or jaded way back then. In more recent times, I have gone out of a hotel, circled to the reverse side of the block, bought a toothbrush, circled back, and been unable to find my hotel. But not finding San Francisco perhaps takes the cake. Larry slept through it, only to laugh later.

But the story at hand isn't about that. We stopped over at the Grand Canyon. We decided to go down to the Colorado River and Larry did it sensibly, strolling down the path at a leisurely pace. I did it more or less like a lunatic who had just escaped an asylum, running off the path, climbing things, overjoyed and uplifted by the environment.

The Grand Canyon is deep. Its sun is hot. By the time we got to the bottom, I was well beyond exhausted. We had to sleep there and then sit and soak in a public shower they had down there until mid-afternoon the next day to avoid the heat of the day before trying to climb out. And even all that wasn't enough. About three-quarters of the way up, I was zombified. My parched mouth felt like sandpaper. It was no longer animate. I have never been in such a condition before or since. I could barely move, even with Larry cajoling me, fearing he would have to try to carry me if we were to get out of the canyon. Just as I went to make another of what seemed likely to be my last few self-propelled steps, a large rattlesnake rattled under my foot and took off like a rocket into the surrounding bushes. Simultaneously, I reflexively jumped back about five feet. Adrenaline put me in overdrive. From being roughly in the shape people who die in the desert are in right before they sit down to wait for the end, I became unable to not run the rest of the way home. Larry had a hard time keeping up. My reserve capacities were suddenly accessible. I decided a lot of great performance is due to people learning to utilize full capacities.

I learned that the human body, and I suspect also the human mind, is capable of much more than most of us ever get from them. Differences in our accomplishments, it followed, owe not only to different inborn talents, which are certainly real enough, and to different training and learned skills, which are also real, but to different ability to tap the roots of our potentials, which talent is probably part learned, part stumbled on, and part persevered to. When I look at professional athletes, for example, I take it for granted that what they are doing that I can't do is, at least in part, getting the most out of themselves.

As long as we are taking this side trip into sports, have you ever watched an athletic contest and heard the announcer say about one athlete or another that "he's in the zone?" The phrase communicates that the athlete is functioning at a level that comes only very rarely, that isn't invited, that can't be made to stay, but that is truly phenomenal. In basketball, almost all players believe in being in the zone and talk about how, in the zone, they see the basket much wider across than normal. In other sports, athletes say everything slows down, that they are more in touch, or that things come automatically. Mathematicians have considered these claims, however, and have decided that they have no reality but are only how we explain random variations to ourselves—though it must be admitted that mathematicians also talk about singular times when ideas just bubble up incredibly and they can't seem to stop the flow of insights.

Take shooting baskets. The mathematicians say that if you look at the shooting percentage of a player at any level, and you then look at its day-to-day composition and see how many times and with what regularity the player strung together a spell of significantly more baskets made per shot taken, it turns out to be exactly as often as we would expect him or her to do if we assumed no variation in underlying probability of hitting shots from shot to shot. In other words, you get the patterns of great achievement even if you assume the player isn't fluctuating in the actual quality of their play, just like if you flip a coin a thousand times every so often you will get a long run of heads (a hot streak) and of tales (a cold streak) even though your flipping ability and the odds on each toss never vary. There is no such thing, in other words, as being in the zone. There is only the statistical happenstance of sometimes getting a good run though your shooting quality is constant. The zone is like throwing a bunch of sequential winners when playing dice. You may think you were throwing the dice better, but you weren't. Chance gave you a good run.

I usually side with mathematicians when they make a case based on sound logic and evidence, and I have a hard time not doing so in this case, too. Their argument is very strong. But, I have a few experiences that make me wonder, nonetheless, about being in the zone.

There was a young woman named Gerry Satenstein, the daughter of a friend of my mother's, who I was friends with in grade school. I remember one time we were playing hockey on a lake in our neighborhood with some other folks, no doubt including my then-best friend Donald Pearlman, who later played on the high school hockey team, and others, too. Gerry might have played on the high school team too, but for sexism. She was an excellent athlete. I was, however, not much for the ice, having trouble even keeping upright. I remember Gerry coming alongside and taking my hand and scooting with me over the ice, then letting go but talking with me, while we flew. She got me to skate faster and with better balance than I ever had before, showing me that it was possible, mostly by preventing my fear of falling from interfering with my staying up, by keeping me distracted by our talk so my feet could do much better than otherwise. I would be flabbergasted if Gerry remembers any of this, but it was very similar to how my father taught me how to ride a bike. We were having difficulty and Dad stood in front of me, holding the bike with me on it, and we talked. He got me focused on something, let go of the bike, and I was balancing even without moving. I noticed that I was balancing after a time, held it a bit longer, and knew I could ride. Once you see that you can do something, skating or biking or anything else, you can do it thereafter much more easily than otherwise. If you feel, however, that you can't do something, skating or biking or anything else, odds are very good that you will be right, you won't be able to do it.

If you think this observation is inflated, consider how athletic accomplishments occur. Someone like Roger Bannister achieves some previously unheard of goal, say a four-minute mile, and suddenly others follow suit. The goal enters human range. Thanks for the insight, and for skating and biking, go to Gerry and Dad. It is related to being in the zone, but not quite the same.

In high school, one summer vacation, I was playing tennis one evening at the Beach and Tennis Club with a fellow I didn't even much like. It was getting dark, but we both entered a groove. We were rallying, not playing, but the quality kept climbing. For maybe an hour, finally cut off by darkness, I played way over my head and so did he. I don't believe it was typical play made to appear atypical by lots of lucky bounces. It was actually, in fact, atypical. If I could have attained the same level of play, the same quality of swing, the same speed and smoothness of motion and quickness afoot all the time, I might have played competitively in college and who knows what else. The play that night indicated ultimate capacity. Even at this level I was no Rod Laver, but it was a capacity I very rarely approached again. I think I was in the zone, such as mine was.

Similarly, in my freshman year at MIT, AEPi had a softball team that played in intramurals. Surprisingly, MIT at the time had more campus intramural sports than any college but the Naval Academy. We were practicing in an indoor gym, a "cage" it was called. I wanted to play third base and the brothers were essentially trying me out for that position. One was hitting me grounders, hard, that I had to field and throw across to first base. I got in a groove. He just kept hitting, harder, with less time between each ground ball. And I just kept scooping them up and throwing strikes across the infield. I wasn't Brooks Robinson, but neither was I me. I was in the zone, fielding like I never had before and never did again.

My head tells me the mathematicians are onto something when talking about night-to-night variations in professional basketball. But my experiences tell me there is also something to being in the zone. Can we usher ourselves into the zone? Can we get into the zone mentally, physically, emotionally?

The Incongruous Star: Noam Chomsky

A habit of basing convictions upon evidence, and of giving to them only that degree or certainty which the evidence warrants.
—Bertrand Russell

For all the famous people who passed through MIT during my stay, or whom I have known in any other capacity since, for all the great achievers, to me the most important has been Noam Chomsky. His example has illuminated many paths I have followed. I met Chomsky when taking his course "Intellectuals and Social Change." We became friends, he a mentor, me a student, and we have stayed close for decades.

Chomsky is often asked what makes him so productive. He flusters and says the only thing he can see in his makeup that seems different from most other people is that he can sit down at a project after having been away for a time and pick it back up instantly, getting immediately back in gear. Noam is right. Other writers typically waste time rereading what we have written and reintegrating ourselves when we return from time off. He is wrong, however, in believing that this is the main thing that differentiates him from the rest of us.

I have been Noam's publisher for nearly forty years and talked with him many hundreds of times. I have regularly had his input on my work and occasionally offered my input on his. I have seen him in all kinds of interactions and shared all kinds of moments with him, personal and political, social and private, on stage and off. It has been a highlight of my life to not only have Noam as a friend and guide, but also to learn from and enjoy so many of his engagements and undertakings. It hasn't even been annoying that whenever I go someplace to speak, from Florida to Ohio, New York to Alaska, Greece to Brazil, England to India, Poland to Australia, invariably considerable time goes to answering questions about Chomsky. How is Noam doing? What does Noam think about the invasion? Why did Noam say that stuff about Cambodia? How does Noam do it? And even, can you explain Noam's linguistics to me? So here are some answers.

Lydia Sargent and I went to Poland in 1980. The trip occurred because South End Press had published young Polish writer Slawomir Magala's book on the uprisings in that country and the emergence of the Polish Workers' Party led by Lech Walesa. Lydia and I went to Frankfurt for the International Book Fair, and continued on to meet Magala in Warsaw and to see events in Poland. I remember being in an apartment talking with Swavek—the author's nickname—and with a number of his friends as well. At one point, as I was replying to questions about America, the subject of Chomsky's political writings came up. Later, after a break, there was more general discussion, and as there was a biologist and a linguist present, Chomsky's linguistic theories came up for some airing. As I was telling my hosts about Chomsky's views on linguistics, just as I had relayed information about his views about Poland and Russia shortly before, someone interrupted and said, "Wait a minute, how could you know both Chomskys personally? That's quite a coincidence."

I had heard right. It turned out these Poles, who were certainly among the most cosmopolitan people in Poland, all thought that there was one Chomsky who was political and who wrote the books about Vietnam, and another who was a linguist and wrote about grammar and human nature. On reflection, I realized it was a far more likely explanation that there were two special people with one name than that there was one person with two incredibly stellar but thoroughly unconnected professions. So what does make Chomsky special? First, what makes Chomsky so insightful and productive? Second, what makes Chomsky someone worth admiring and emulating?

Partly what makes Chomsky insightful and productive is inborn. Genetic endowment, obviously desirable, isn't something we should praise, and can't be emulated. I can be awed by attributes someone was born with, even if the capacities had to be nurtured to emerge, whether we are talking about Jackie Robinson's speed, Fyodor Dostoevsky's prose, Bob Dylan's song, Emmy Noether's mathematical creativity, or Barbra Streisand's voice. I can enjoy seeing these traits at work. I can be wowed by them. I can be fascinated and enlightened by them. But it doesn't make sense that the owner is worthy of special respect, admiration, or emulation based simply on being born with special abilities.

Noam's inborn abilities include an incredible memory that retains both broad strokes and also fine detail with computer-like recall. Memory declines with age, but even at seventy five Noam's remains formidable. In the 1960s, Noam would routinely give references from books he'd read referencing a page, or even a part of a page. But Noam's memory was by no means photographic, just profound, at least for things he found important. Even now, at speaking engagements, people will query all manner of topics, completely off the assigned agenda, and Noam will reply with singular information in a field other than his own that even experts in that subject can only marvel at.

Second, Noam can think rapidly and clearly. If he was in physics, say, or math, I would have a better feeling for whether this part of his capacity is just incredibly substantial, like von Neumann, or phenomenal, like Feynman. But there is another trait Noam has for which I suspect there are both inborn and also trained aspects that involve effort and discipline.

Noam can, and routinely does, extricate himself from habit and familiarity to consider possibilities that are strikingly different than most people contemplate. It isn't only that there is a wealth of data at hand, or that he can make connections and test logical possibilities that would try another person's capacity. Others who have these talents mostly just collect, enumerate, and detail what is known, or maybe discover some new facts, but don't repeatedly generate dramatically new insights. Noam asks the unexpected question. He raises the odd possibility. He sees the hidden connection.

Think of Einstein. What Einstein did that was phenomenal was to extract general physical truths from snippets of physical reality, generating previously untried insights. To think about what would happen if someone ran alongside a light ray, or to think through the dynamics of a falling elevator, two of Einstein's guiding thought experiments, didn't require tremendous calculating capacity or following a logical train of thought through endless byways. The genius Einstein exhibited was not in the number of steps in his deductions, or in their technical difficulty, but in undertaking the key steps at all and following them down paths that others would habitually avoid. The genius was in the innovation. It was in his leaps off the beaten path. Einstein often leaped, and his main catapult was what scientists call thought experiments. His mental gymnastics pared away reality's inessentials and highlighted its key aspects. To do this, Einstein envisioned unattainable contexts, rendered pure and pristine, ready for him to turn inside out.

I think one of the ways Noam innovates is by employing analogies far more often and far more effectively than other people do. Noam takes a familiar situation—and this is a trait that we can learn from and try to emulate—and finds another that is structurally like it, regarding which, however, his (and our) habits and biases operate less powerfully or not at all. He uses this technique both to try to communicate to reticent audiences views that affront their prejudices or expectations, and, I believe, to discover new views for himself as well. He does this magic by analyzing the less-controversial and less-familiar situation that he invents or sometimes remembers in analogy, and then demonstrating the possible meaning it holds for the situation that is under discussion and obstructed by preconceptions.

Physicists do something similar, which is what may have attuned me to the importance of this trait in Noam, when they abstract away countless details, assume all kinds of features that are unattainable, and view in their mind's eye what occurs in the imagined world to discern innermost dynamics without endless cluttering facts and personal prejudices interfering. Noam's analogy trick is quite similar, but is more suited to the realm of worldly affairs, though I would guess that regarding linguistics he probably uses both analogies and thought experiments, or a cross between the two.

The analogy technique Noam uses can be found all through his writings. Thus he switches from talking about the U.S. in Vietnam (fraught with preconception and prejudice) to the role of Russia in Eastern Europe (where an American sees more clearly). He switches from discussing the possibility of a U.S. invasion of Afghanistan (biased for someone from the U.S.) to the possibility of Iran invading Afghanistan (clearer for someone from the U.S.). He switches from assessing the possibility of the U.S. punishing Syria for housing terrorists who attack the U.S. (confused) to Britain punishing the U.S. for housing and financing IRA acts in Britain (clearer). Or he switches from talking about the media emphasizing 9/11 as terrorism to the rest of the world seeing the U.S. embargo of Iraq as chemical and biological terror waged on civilians, or from comparing U.S. and old Soviet media dynamics, or U.S. foreign policy and the behavior of Mafia dons, and so on.

Noam also works hard. Is he driven, compulsive, and even over the top when it comes to work? If you named twenty prominent athletes, actors, and musicians over the past thirty years, Noam would probably have heard of two or three, or maybe five at most, but he would be able to offer essentially zero information about any of them. Noam sees maybe two or three movies a year. He sees a few hours of TV a year. He listens to almost no radio.

Carol Chomsky and Noam have a summer home in Wellfleet, Massachusetts. They have a motor boat and a small sailboat and they live on a lake in the summers and in a home in Lexington, Massachusetts, the rest of the year. Over the course of each summer they probably get out on the water in either boat three or four times. They visit the beach more often, walking down to the lake and sitting for a time, often with guests, and Lydia and I have been there many times. Mostly, though, Noam is ensconced in his study, writing, in the summer just like during the rest of the year. Hour upon hour he reads and writes. Combine this diligence with the quick start and with very little editing, since the writing winds up pretty much the way it first comes out, and you get a lot of output, and actually way more output than most people realize.

Noam often answers short letters from unknown folks with long letters back, to the tune of a small book's worth of correspondence each month. Noam revolutionizes an intellectual discipline—linguistics and what is called cognitive science—not once, but every few years. He teaches a seminar each Friday, or did so for decades, and people came from all over the planet just to attend. Why? Each week Noam presented new, original material. This alone is an unfathomable pace of production.

Meanwhile, another Noam churns out scathing denunciations of U.S. foreign policy, media machinations, and other political phenomena, speaks dozens of times a year, each time for hours, does many interviews each week, travels the globe giving talks, and wherever he goes he addresses that place's history and context with the same incredible precision and innovation he offers about the U.S.

Anyone's hard work is worthy of admiration but maybe in a desirable world not everyone should be so driven as Noam. Indeed, I suspect in a desirable world, while Noam would still have worked tirelessly on his science out of the joy and accomplishment of it, he would also have been out sailing on the water, weeding in the garden, and even laughing at movies considerably more often than he does in our current world. So his sacrifice for justice also merits admiration. But what is really most admirable about Noam, it seems to me, is he is scrupulously honest. He has the thing we call integrity in large supply. He respects but does not condescend to others. And he cares.

Honesty is easy to understand. Noam says what is on his mind, sometimes at a cost. Indeed, bad comes with good. Noam's death grip on the truth can interfere, at times, with other virtues, such as sensitivity to the impact words may have on others. Assessing someone in Noam's position, my tendency is to think truth-telling should take precedence over sensitivity, though others might disagree, and it certainly isn't one size fits all.

Integrity is harder to pin down. It means being true to one's values, when one has values that one can be true to. Noam does have values and is true to them. This too can reach levels that cause problems. Noam eschews people affecting the choices of other people by anything other than logic and evidence. This causes Noam to be tremendously wary of his notoriety, worrying that his words will be overweighted by his listeners. It makes Noam loathe giving advice, to the point that quite often he will withhold words that might usefully have been heard.

Respecting others is tricky for Noam. He is constantly queried by people who are relatively ignorant of what they ask about. A person in a position like his gets used to these kinds of questions. Respecting the people involved means taking them seriously and answering honestly with patience and attention to communicating clearly. Noam does that. But he also quite reasonably wants such exchanges to move along and a problem arises because Noam is a quick study.

When someone starts to ask Noam something familiar, Noam tends to fill in the blanks, deducing the person's real intent, and interrupting to begin answering sometimes well before the person finishes their question. This can sidetrack Noam's hearing what is actually being said in the interests of saving time and even imposing accuracy. Experience counts and often Noam helps the questioner by making the question more precise and complete. Other times, however, Noam jumps too quickly and misrepresents the questioner, due to thinking he recognizes the questioner when in fact he doesn't. In other words, sometimes a person accosting Noam or disagreeing with him knows more than those who typically use essentially the same initial words. Noam may miss this difference, thereby seeming to be oblivious to the person's true intents and insights. It is not pleasant when it happens to you, and I have undergone it plenty of times, but it is not ill motivated, either.

To understand caring is hard. There are people who routinely evidence extreme sympathy and concern for others, but who, in my view, don't really give a damn. Something that looks and sounds like caring is present, to be sure, and many people are very impressed by its symptoms, but minutes or even seconds later the seeming concern is gone. It has no staying power and few implications beyond appearances. With Noam the caring is less evident, less demonstrative, and less of a show, but it lasts and it has implications.

Noam believes strongly in civility, though I think many people who have gotten into debates with him and had their views dismissed or even annihilated—sometimes with words like "stupid" and "trivial" punctuating the dissection—would find that hard to believe. But for Noam, calling an idea stupid or calling a claim trivial is not uncivil but truthful. In this, he is a scientist in the sense that scientists routinely debate and skewer one another in no uncertain terms. Finding the truth and escaping falsehoods, which is the scientist's reason for being, demands this behavior.

But Noam does not denigrate others to build himself up. Likewise, Noam does not evidence the kind of condescending and self-promoting or guilt-salving concern for others that is all too frequent in many circles, particularly, I hate to say it, in progressive (politically correct) circles. Noam's caring is real. There is no pomp or circumstance. He does not weep wildly or gush effusively. But Noam remembers people's needs. He fulfills requests. He notices pain and tries to do real things to alleviate it. He is quite civil. You could even call Noam very conservative in daily life characteristics. If there is a sign to stay off a lawn, Noam obeys. Noam routinely abides almost all rules unless higher values take precedence.

For Noam's seventieth birthday, as a present, I oversaw a kind of testimonial tribute. I put on the Internet a means by which people could write a message that he would see on his birthday. About two thousand people entered messages and the results went online. Most of these folks were people who Noam had never closely met but who had read his work, or heard him speak, and had been dramatically affected and wanted to register their thanks. Many other people who contributed did know Noam, but also wanted to say their piece to their friend, ally, teacher, coworker, or what have you.

The entry I was most moved by was written by Fred Branfman, who was himself a very effective advocate of human rights and supporter of the Indochinese people against U.S. violence.

When you visited me in Laos in 1970, I was at a real low point, anguished by the bombing and feeling almost totally isolated. Your passion, commitment and shared pain about the need to stop the bombing, and warm, personal support and caring, meant more to me than you will ever know. It also meant a lot to me for reasons I can't quite explain that of the dozens and dozens of people I took out to the camps to interview the refugees from the bombing you were the only one, besides myself, to cry. Your subsequent article for the *New York Review of Books* and all the other writing and speaking you did on Laos, was also the only body of work that got it absolutely right. It has given me a little more faith in the species ever since to know that it has produced a being of so much integrity, passion and intellect. I feel a lot of love for you on your birthday—and shake my head in amazement knowing that you'll never stop.

Noam and I have had plenty of arguments over the years. Noam can be a very ornery fellow, and he is world-class stubborn, even if not demonstrative or flailing about it. He expects to be right, since he most often is, and he doesn't like to lose an argument—ever.

This may be a bit like someone not liking to fall down when crossing the room, or to slip in the tub—in other words, not liking to do something that is highly unfamiliar and which has a negative aspect. Still, it is an unendearing trait that makes Noam the human he is. It can be and has been for numerous people immensely annoying, frustrating, and even hurtful. All in all, though, I have never known anyone smarter, with a better memory, with a greater facility for creatively escaping the bounds of acceptable thought, or, more admirably, a person with more honesty, integrity, respect, and real universal concern. Noam is a package deal. As with everyone, Noam travels through life warts and all. It is just that in Noam's journey there are few warts, and the "and all" is a big deal.

Oftentimes Noam and I will see what's out in the world a bit differently or feel responses ought to have slightly different aspects. Sometimes we have larger disagreements. Here are two such disputes, each important, I think.

The first was about what I call the crowding-out effect, borrowing the label from economists. Noam goes out and speaks a huge amount to very large audiences. Everyone wants Noam to come and talk. Very few people want any of the many others who, while perhaps not as excellent as Noam, would be much more than ample. The result is that Noam talks a huge volume but even with his great industry, many places, settling for no one other than Noam, have no speaker. Other undeniably worthy speakers, lacking fame, won't fill the bill because they won't attract sufficient audience. What to do?

Over the years, I urged Noam to tell those asking him to come speak that he would not do so unless there could be a second speaker on the bill with him whom he would select. Each time he would go out, in that scenario, so too would Steve Shalom go, or Holly Sklar, Cynthia Peters, or Clarence Lusane, and so on. In this way, others would be seen, word of mouth about the quality of their talks would spread, and in time these people would get more invitations. Then these additional people, becoming better known, could themselves do the same thing, bringing along still another generation. After a bit, many more people, steadily more diverse in background and experience, would be going around speaking and many more talks would be given and heard.

Noam never did this and we argued about it quite a few times. His resistance was partly ideological and partly personal. He didn't want to use his "bargaining power" to impose conditions—he would also deny that he could get a positive response by making such demands, which was of course false—and he also, I am sure, didn't want to share the stage with a co-speaker, since that would mean traveling just as far, taking as much time away from other work, but speaking and dealing with questions for a lot less time, not to mention having to listen to the other speaker. I speak publicly recently much more than earlier, though still only a fraction as often as Noam does, and I now understand better his side of this dispute. I now think what's needed is not largesse by prominent speakers placing demands on hosts, but for speakers' bureaus to impose the condition for us.

A second disagreement has been over matters of vision, economic mostly, but otherwise as well. This is a far more important debate, I think, and one where I have to say, years passing or not, I haven't given an inch. Noam feels that trying to describe a future society can overstep existing bounds of knowledge, crowd out creativity by establishing aims prematurely, and tend toward sectarianism. He feels broad values are what we need, plus practice, practice, and more practice that in turn yields day-to-day innovations that in turn lead to people experimenting with and implementing new ways of being from the bottom up. I feel this is all well and good, true on every count, but after a couple of hundred years of it we should have something more to show. How do the lessons of thinking hard, analyzing, and experimenting become part of the general popular movement if they are not presented, debated, refined, and finally advocated?

To me, it seems obvious that we need answers to the question "what do you want" that can provide hope, direction, and a positive tone able to inform both analysis and strategy. This entails more than a list of broad values and aspirations. It requires institutional pictures. Noam's concern is to ensure participation and avoid elites imposing a view on movements. My answer is that I agree with this priority but I feel we will get what Noam fears if we don't have movements full of participants who understand, advocate, and continually refine a full vision able to motivate and orient participation. The alternative to elitist vision isn't having no vision, but having the most accessible, widely shared, compelling, and substantial vision we can write up, debate, refine, and advocate.

Our differences aside, I once wrote a piece built around the experience of reading Chomsky and its impact on people and also around how Noam manages to constantly immerse himself in so much data about pain without becoming jaded himself. It isn't that his burrowing in the tombs of injustice doesn't take a toll—it does. There are times when Noam is brought down low by the news he wades through, and times when he is wired tight and becomes difficult. How Carol Chomsky gets through all that may be as amazing as some of Noam's accomplishments. At any rate, the essay I wrote with these personal dimensions and of course also the problem of changing the world in mind was called "Stop the Killing Train." For me, this was an infrequent attempt at being poetic and it later became the lead essay of a book going by the same name. Over a decade old, written in the lead-up to the first Gulf War, I think the essay is no less timely now than when it was written, and perhaps it is a good way to move on from Noam—so here is the key part.

Suppose a hypothetical god got tired of what we humans do to one another and decided that from January 1, 1991 onward all corpses unnaturally created anywhere in the "free world" would cease to decompose. Anyone dying for want of food or medicine, anyone hung or garroted to death, shot or beaten to death, raped or bombed to death, anyone dying unjustly and inhumanely would, as a corpse, persist without decomposing. And the permanent corpse would then automatically enter a glass-walled cattle car attached to an ethereal train traveling monotonously across the U.S., state by state, never stopping. One by one the corpses would be loaded onto the cattle cars and after every thousand corpses piled in, higgeldy piggeldy, a new car would hitch up and begin filling too. Mile after mile the killing train would roll along, each corpse viewed through its transparent walls, 200 new corpses a minute, one new car every five minutes, day and night, without pause.

By the end of 1991, on its first birthday, the killing train would measure over 2,000 miles long. Traveling at 20 miles an hour it would take about five days to pass any intersection. By the year 2000, assuming no dramatic change in institutions and behavior in the interim, the train would stretch from coast to coast about seven times. It would take about six weeks from the time its engine passed the Statue of Liberty to when its caboose would go by, God still wondering when pitiful, aspiring humanity would get the message.

Think how a young child sometimes points to a picture in a book or magazine and asks for an explanation, "Tell me about a tree?" A car? A boat? A train? A big train? The killing train? Go ahead, answer that.

If the ecologists are right that this planet is a single super-organism, they are wrong that pollution, toxic waste, and other human-created garbage is the most deadly virus attacking it. The killing train is worse.

Think about the pain that radiates from the Vietnam War monument with its 50,000 names in Washington, D.C. Imagine the lost opportunity and lost love and the network of negative influences that radiate from the unnecessary deaths enumerated on that monument. Now think about the killing train stretching from coast to coast and back and forth and back and forth and back and forth. Consider its impact, not only on those on board, but on every person that any of those corpses ever loved or would have loved, fed or would have fed, taught or would have taught.

Who rides the killing train? Citizens of the "Third World," selling their organs for food, selling their babies to save their families, suffering disappearances and starvation. They live in Brazil, the Philippines, El Salvador, and New York. They are headed for the killing train. Every day. Millions.

Is this exaggerated? When 10 million children die yearly for lack of basic medical aid that the U.S. could provide at almost no cost in countries whose economies Exxon and the Bank of America have looted, what can you call it other than mass murder? Bloated diseased bodies are victims of murder just as surely as bullet-riddled bodies tossed into rivers by death squads. Denying medicine is no less criminal than supplying torture racks or stealing resources.

Evolution has given humans the capacity to perceive, think, feel, imagine. At a time of war—as now in the Gulf—if we get aroused to action we begin to see the whole train as it persists day in and day out. When this happens, what do we do about it. Become depressed? Cynical? Anguished? Cry? Daydream of Armageddon? Daydream of justice? Hand out a leaflet?

Once we begin to see it, how do we face the killing train? Part of me says these crimes are so grotesque, so inhumane, that the perpetrators deserve to die. A little tiny killing train for the killers and no more big killing train for everyone else. An eye for a million eyes. What other step makes more sense?

But that's not the way the world works. People give the orders, wield the axes, withhold the food, pay the pitiful salaries, but institutions create the pressures that mold these people. When an institutional cancer consumes the human patient, what kind of surgeon can cut it all away? Is the weight of repression so intense it can never be lifted?

At first, becoming attuned to our country's responsibility for the corpses the hypothetical God stacked behind transparent cattle-car walls makes handing out leaflets, or arguing for peace with a co-worker, or urging a relative to think twice about paying taxes, or going to a demonstration, or sitting in, or even doing civil disobedience seem insignificant. But the fact is, these are the acts that the hypothetical God, tired of our behavior, would be calling for if she were to actually parade the "free world's" corpses down our main streets in killing trains. These are the acts that can accumulate into a firestorm of informed protest that raises the cost of profiteering and domination so high that the institutions breeding such behavior start to buckle.

"You lose, you lose, you lose, and then you win." Every loss is part of the process that leads to transforming institutions so that there can be no people as vile as Hussein or Bush. No more "Good Germans" or "Good Americans," cremated Jews or decapitated peasants.

Finally, about knowing Noam, I might echo what Bob Dylan had to say about Dave Van Ronk: "No puppet strings on him, ever. He was big, sky high, and I looked up to him. He came from the land of giants."

Chapter 6

Why Do It?

Would You Torch a Library?

> *Hungry man, reach for the book: it is a weapon.*
> *—Bertolt Brecht*

W hen I was giving speeches at MIT, I was repeatedly asked, would you burn down a library to end the war? I would say, of course I would burn down a library to end the war, wouldn't you? A library has books. A war destroys not only books, but authors and readers. If I could end the war by burning down all the libraries in this city, I would do it in a heartbeat. And so would you, unless you are callous. But in the real world burning libraries won't end wars. What will help end the war has none of the onus of burning books. You can educate. You can demonstrate. Will you do that? That's the real question. In the documentary *The Sixties*, Henry Kissinger describes how Nixon was preparing to use nuclear weapons. He had to back off, however, due to immense dissent throughout the country. It wasn't burning a library that ended a war, it was amassing gigantic opposition that threatened policies held even more dear.

The Provost's Proposition

> *It ain't me, it ain't me, I ain't no fortunate one.*
> *—John Fogerty*

S hortly after the 1968–69 undergraduate association presidential (UAP) election, I was sitting in my new office when MIT's provost, Jerome Wiesner, second in command at MIT, knocked on the door and entered. Wiesner had been science advisor to John Kennedy. He was a Humphrey supporter and had been, and still was, a civil rights advocate. Wiesner had a sense of humor, too, being known, for example, for saying that "getting an education from MIT is like taking a drink from a fire hose." He wasn't all bad politically, either, saying, "It is no longer a question of controlling a military-industrial complex, but rather, of keeping the United States from becoming a totally military culture." Still, we both knew that Wiesner had actively assisted my opponents in the UAP election and had been miserable when I won. My campaign planks included no war research, open admissions, and indemnities to the Black Panther Party. Nonetheless, Wiesner came to make peace. Wiesner was a good liberal put out by his inability to relate to student radicals more positively. He thought we ought to appreciate him and his accomplishments and respect his advice. I thought that Wiesner was buffoonish and unworthy of respect, though I do remember how in meetings he used to deploy his pipe as a prop people's eyes would gravitate to, giving him prominence in the room, and added power. Others do the same trick by where they sit at a table, hand motions, clothes, etc.

Anyway, I remember three parts to our discussion in my campus student government office. In the first part, after some chatting, I asked Wiesner something that I had been wondering for some time. This was the first era of antimissile missiles and I had a strong suspicion that work on them was entirely a boondoggle in addition to being politically destabilizing. So I asked about this, and Wiesner took a pencil, stood it point upward, and said, "This pencil has as much chance of shooting down an incoming Intercontinental Ballistic Missile as any antimissile missile we could conceivably deploy." Wiesner knew that the antimissile program was a massive sop to high-tech industry. I asked how he could know that and not trumpet the truth. Wiesner shrugged. Interestingly, decades later, new efforts at antimissile programs that were promulgated by the Bush regime, and before Bush by Clinton, have had as an opponent a fellow named Theodore Postal. Ted was a year ahead of me at MIT and a fraternity brother during my year at AEPi. Now he is employed by MIT but causing trouble for militarists. Ripples persist.

My second memory of the Wiesner meeting was of Wiesner's prime purpose in coming to my office. He invited me to spend a weekend with him at the Kennedy compound in Hyannis on Cape Cod. He jovially told me how I would have a great time and I would meet Teddy Kennedy and others and develop friendships that would be valuable later in life. Wiesner was, in short, brazenly seducing me with an offer of entry into the young people's branch of the Kennedy mystique. I dismissed the invitation without a thought. Wiesner was flustered. How could I reject such an obvious invitation to power, relevance, and wealth? I tried to convey to him just how unattractive his offer was. "Would you consider an invitation to visit a mass murderer a perk? Would you consider it seductive? Or would you find it obscene? For me this decision is trivial," I told him. "I am not giving up something I would want to have."

The third item on Wiesner's agenda, after I rejected his invitation, was a promise. Preparatory to leaving my UAP office and our having no further communications other than on opposite sides of police lines, Wiesner told me that he would never allow me to be thrown out of MIT unless I did something utterly insane or horribly destructive. He didn't like my priorities, he admitted, and he knew we would always be at loggerheads, but, Wiesner said, "I will defend your right to pursue your goals." I think Wiesner probably meant it, but only because he couldn't envision what was to come. MIT had never thrown out any students for political activism, and he didn't see any reason to think it would start with me. I replied that, in fact, he would indeed throw me out of MIT, despite there being no just cause. It would be for being effective at opposing the MIT administration and the war. He would do it because he would be desperate to get rid of me. He laughed and said, "Not a chance, I'll take the bet." I laughed and said, "We'll see." Ha ha, about a year later, expelled, I won.

Chemicals, Son?

> *I'd rather be living a free man in my grave*
> *Than as a puppet or a slave.*
> —*Jimmy Cliff*

Wiesner dangling Kennedy's Camelot to induce me to leave the movement wasn't even the oddest or most brazen offer I got. Protocol requires that the undergraduate association president of MIT's student body give a yearly speech to notable alumni. So I had that honor, my year as UAP. Obviously, this was quite a lark. My audience was a group of successful graduates returning for a kind of power reunion. Corporate executives, politicos, and media types, as well as scientists and engineers all assembled in a large lecture hall to hear the student president, me, pontificate on matters of the day. Isn't protocol silly? At any rate, I gave one of the more militant speeches I ever delivered. I had no misgivings about convincing the power alumni, so I decided, what the hell, I would say exactly what I felt and let the chips fall however fate decreed. The speech was peppered with vulgar assaults on U.S. elites, including MIT's administration, the government, corporate America, and my audience. I explained my values and those of the movements I supported. I finished to dead silence, stepped down, and strode down the aisle to leave the hall. Make my day, why don't ya?

As I got near the door, an elegantly dressed man, probably in his forties, but maybe younger, blocked my path. I braced myself expecting to get assaulted. Instead, he held out his hand to shake, and once he got mine, he hung on, leaned in, and said in a low voice, "Chemicals." Yes, it was like the scene from *The Graduate*, except in the movie the industry proposed was "plastics." I looked askance at my suitor and said, roughly, "What the fuck are you talking about?" He said "Listen, you are wasting your time here. You can come with me right now. You don't even have to graduate from MIT; you can pick up a degree anytime. We'll go back to my firm in Germany"—it was some chemical company that he named—"and we will make you a vice president right off." His manner said, let's get cracking, this is an offer you can't possibly refuse.

I had just savaged capitalism, corporations, his whole world, and yet all this chemical entrepreneur saw was that I was smart, confident, and a good speaker, and therefore a good profit-making prospect. He thought if he made a sufficiently lucrative offer I would dispense with all I had said and sign on with his gray-flannel operations. My contrary allegiances would melt into nothingness. Wiesner too had heard me swear my revolutionary allegiances before he sat in my office and held out his arms hoping I would plop into them as his protégé. He too thought my commitments would disintegrate upon my hearing about a Kennedy-benighted future. Who could refuse Camelot? Corporate America was worried about sixties dissent sweeping the country. Simultaneously, however, for a given individual, corporate Americans were confident offers of big-time power would easily buy allegiance.

Reasons for Rejecting Lucre

The heart has its reasons which reason knows nothing of.
—Blaise Pascal

The arrogance of these co-opters, in my eyes, was incredible. But it was also daunting because I could see that offerings by the powerful most often must have successfully ensnared young souls. Otherwise my suitors would not have been so confident. What they couldn't understand about me, however, and what was perhaps most important for me to realize about myself, wasn't that I was displaying some kind of great discipline in turning them down. That kind of rejection of desirable lucre is indeed rare, and I didn't display any more of it than the next person. It was, instead, trivial for me to reject Wiesner and Mr. Chemical because what they offered repulsed me. I didn't desire their bounty. In fact, you couldn't force me to go with either of them on grounds of personal fulfillment, much less on moral grounds. Their offers, even if I had nothing on my plate in their place, morals aside, were repulsive. That's what the hippies begot.

Three decades later Barbara Ehrenreich taught at the summer school called Z Media Institute. I had known Barbara intermittently for many years, but she had since gained considerable stature and was now not only a quite successful leftist author, but also a sometime columnist for *Time*. At a session with the ZMI students one asked Barbara, a bit incredulously, how she avoided selling out. Weren't the temptations great? Barbara said she couldn't speak for others, but in her case it wasn't a matter of great discipline or anything worthy of admiration. She just found people's sellout offers repugnant. "A future of power lunches and stressful competitive bidding in a world of pretense, even if studded with financial largesse, isn't very attractive. The people aren't interesting. The glitter isn't pretty. The power is to do only what the more powerful deem desirable. What's hard about saying no to that? It's easy." Well, that was my situation with the alumni's chemical vice presidency and the provost's Camelot. The offers were easy to reject.

When I became a professional activist—a person going from project to project always aiming at social change—it meant not becoming a physicist, which had been my prior life aim. That was a real sacrifice, letting go of something in my blood, but, honestly, I just slid into activism and thus out of physics. I never sat down and said, okay, is it graduate school and physics, or is it rioting and politics? I just did steadily more rioting and politics, and in time there was no more room for graduate school and physics.

So, suppose Wiesner had sat in my office and said, "Here, come with me to visit with Richard Feynman (one of the world's finest physicists). Feynman wants to take you on as his private student. You will later easily get a powerful position in physics, whether here at MIT or with Feynman out at Caltech. You will have the best conditions available. Feynman and I both think you will be very successful, perhaps all the way to Stockholm. What do you say?" Now that would have been an offer it would have been hard to refuse. I like to think I would have said no, but like Barbara, I don't know for sure.

Chomsky and My Career

Well I try my best to be just like I am
But everybody wants you to be just like them.
—Bob Dylan

Interestingly, there was one conversation that almost derailed my leftward drift. It was with Noam Chomsky. I sat in his office one day and asked him about his own choices. Why did he do linguistics as compared to doing only radical politics? Chomsky said there were three reasons. One was political. His achievements in linguistics gave him security and freedom that facilitated his political involvements and made his words more likely to be noticed. Second, though, Chomsky said he felt that he would dry up and decay if he didn't do creative intellectual work in his discipline, and would then likely be good for nothing in any realm. Third, he just plain loved it—and life was a mix of choices, some undertaken for principle, others undertaken out of taste and preference.

Noam rarely advises anyone about anything. But Noam did suggest that I should think hard about staying in physics. Victor Weisskopf, who was then the head of the MIT physics department, who was reasonably progressive, and whom Noam later told me was quite moved by some of my speeches, was sure I could be excellent in the field and had asked Noam to try to reel me back in. But Noam's entreaty came too late to affect my choice. I had already drifted too far to return, and at the time I didn't put much thought into it. I was primarily a political being, already. Noam was right though, in various respects. I have spent a whole lot of time doing things because they were needed and right, despite a relative lack of personal inclination. That I would write and publish really has no relation to my own innate preferences or talents. But I also speak a lot, and that is up my talent alley. I work on economic vision, which has at least some intellectual components that I enjoy, however far it is from my real strengths. I still spend a lot of time, it turns out, reading physics and other science books, keeping that part of me alive, if not nourished and blossoming.

Had I done physics, would my mix have been ideal? Would I have had a more worthy and perhaps also a more fulfilling life? I don't know. I suppose it is possible. Who can say? But as far as aiding political pursuits, I have doubts that I could have pursued physics with the kind of intensity necessary to gain major credibility (how many physicists' names do you know?) and even if I had beaten the odds, while it might have meant I could write politically with a larger audience, or write more authoritatively about nuclear power, for example, it would also have meant I wouldn't have worked on all the various projects and organizations I have, and likely would not have had the same things to say. The trade-off seems a bad one to me, however much I might sometimes miss the ins and outs of what I imagine to be the physicist's life.

The odd thing is, I was recently lucky enough to get a chance to see at least a glimpse of what a physicist's life for me might have included. I had a high school friend named Irwin Gaines. Irwin and I were pretty comparable in our mental faculties. He had a far better memory than I did, making school much easier for him, but that doesn't bear too much on physics. He was intellectually faster than me, too. I think my advantage relative to Irwin for a physics career would have been that it helps to believe you can conquer all obstacles so you can tackle large questions. That was more me than Irwin. At any rate, Irwin became an accomplished experimentalist, where I had wanted to be a theorist. I visited Irwin for the first time in about thirty years a few years ago, at Fermi Lab in Illinois, where he works facilitating experiments in high-energy particle physics. Linda Lurie, another very smart student in our high school, was still married to Irwin all these years later. It was a pleasant trip, but mainly I did not get jealous for a lost life path as I feared I might. Even considering only daily qualities and direct personal characteristics, I preferred my life situation to Irwin's, and I think that would probably remain so for all but the very top-ranking theoretical physicists, of which the number is tiny. Could I have been one of them? There is a lot of luck involved in such success even if I had sufficient qualities, which is far from certain.

Of course, I could have wound up on other paths too, such as that of my brother Eddie, the gambler. I think the biggest meaning of my brother Eddie's life for me was that it convincingly demonstrated how being on a particular social path could constrict one's personality, change one's values, warp one's aspirations, and delimit one's capacities. This insight was to continually inform my understanding of events and prospects. When I am feeling generous about Eddie, I believe he became an antisocial gambler to rebel against the same constricting and alienating world that I later rebelled against as a social revolutionary. Being a gambler is not being a wage slave, whatever ill effects it embodies. Eddie loved the lifestyle, relative to other available possibilities. There but for fortune, and seeing what it did to him, went I, I guess.

Chapter 7

Campus Organizing

Damning Dow

It is necessary, with bold spirit and in good conscience, to save civilization. The bare and barren tree can be made green again. Are we not ready?
—*Antonio Gramsci*

One of the first militant demonstrations at MIT occurred in 1967. Dow Chemical Company was coming to recruit students to their firm. Recruitment by corporations on campuses was typical, and involved a few people setting up a temporary office to interview prospective applicants. Part of the problem was having corporations of any type at all on campus, at least for many activists. More specifically, however, the issue was Dow.

Dow manufactured napalm, which was a chemical mixture dropped from planes that burned skin even when doused with water. It was a heinous weapon, widely opposed as inhumane, and widely used by the U.S. against the Vietnamese. I vaguely remember meetings planning for the Dow recruiters. The meetings were called by SDS and MIT Resist. The protest was part of an SDS national campaign against recruiting on campus. Phil Raup, an MIT graduate student, was an active national SDS member and brought the idea to our campus. I was just getting into the Left. MIT SDS was not yet Rosa Luxemburg SDS.

We decided to block entry to the placement offices with our bodies. I got to the event early, before breakfast, and so did Peter Bohmer, who was three years older than me, a graduate student in economics, and became a close friend, to remain so for decades. Peter and I were packed in next to each other and talked a lot during the day. Peter had more developed politics, and I mostly tried to soak up his knowledge and experience. We blocked the entire floor for many hours. There was no real violence, but I remember a young MIT administrator, highly belligerent, a big guy with intimidating, confident manners who gave off vibes that if he had the

84

authority he would vamp us into oblivion. His name was Paul Gray. In the 1980s he rose, as one might expect, watching garbage rise, to become president of MIT.

The logic of the Dow demonstration, which we wrote up in leaflets and distributed all over campus, was that since we wouldn't let the Mafia recruit at MIT, why should we let Dow Chemical do so? Dow produced napalm, which was more overtly destructive than anything the Mafia did.

We also argued that students should not have the right to work for Dow Chemical just like community members should not have the right to join the Mafia. Overt membership in criminal institutions should confer guilt by mutual association, a view that arguably went a bit too far, not least because we were all students at MIT, which was itself a criminal institution in the same respects as Dow Chemical was, contributing in various ways to the war.

We had many discussions and arguments with students who had appointments and wanted to get in to see the recruiters, as well as with MIT officials and employees. No one got through, and even with the administration the discussions, while sometimes heated, never crossed the line to outright physical conflict. The ensuing debate (except with Paul Gray) was at this early date in MIT activism, quite civil. Eventually, the Dow recruiters gave up on-campus recruiting, though it is certainly possible they made secret appointments off campus.

The Calculus of Dissent

> *Strong reasons make strong actions.*
> *—William Shakespeare*

Many people celebrated the Dow action on the grounds that we had successfully disrupted recruitment, but I thought that was completely beside the point. Yes, we had to disrupt the meetings if we were to address Dow effectively. But disrupting meetings was a means to an end. Raising consciousness and laying the seeds for more future involvement by more people was the aim. I think we succeeded on those grounds, too, but it was a very different criterion.

Here's how I thought about it. Suppose we had been cleared out of the hall and the recruitment had continued as planned but the act of clearing us had been widely discussed on campus and had aroused more people's interest and affected more people's ideas. Assuming it aided movement building, would that have been less of an achievement? Would getting routed have made us less successful? I didn't think so. Suppose we had found a way to prevent the recruitment of MIT students by Dow but our approach had less effect on people's future views and contributed less to building antiwar activism. Imagine we surreptitiously blackmailed Wiesner into calling it off. Would that have been better? Not to my thinking.

In the heat of social conflict, the above calculus wasn't always obvious to everyone. Many of my friends, for example, focused on the proximate details of obstruction, not on broader movement building. Indeed, throughout the sixties, people frequently lost track of the logic of their own actions and evaluated them by self-denying criteria imposed by media. We struck a university or tried to shut down a building or stop a meeting and looked only at the scorecard of the confrontation itself. In our confrontational posture, bent by media machinations, we judged the day and all the efforts leading up to it, and all the follow-up efforts, in terms of whether the opposed meeting occurred or not. How we assessed our actions, in other words, was sometimes incredibly self-defeating and confused, missing the real point.

The day of the demo against Dow, and all the work leading up to and following that day, should have been judged, some of us argued then and later, not on the basis of narrow, proximate, tactical details, but on the basis of movement building. One reason activists frequently focused on proximate details rather than the larger picture was that we vested the proximate with so much tactical attention that it crowded out the real prize. We got caught up in it like in a prizefight or ball game. Another reason we often lost track of the larger picture, however, was that some people really did care only about the proximate issue and nothing more. They were not confused but only wanted Dow out. For example, at MIT there was tension between those caring only about MIT complicity, and those caring about ending the war in Vietnam, or even ending imperialism. Similarly, at strikes, there was tension between those wanting to win a higher local wage and those wanting to increase the bargaining power of labor more widely, or even to replace capitalism. And at women's health clinics there was tension between those wanting to supply medical care locally, those wanting to gain reproductive rights and to smash the glass ceiling obstructing women from management socially, and those wanting to end patriarchy globally. All over the sixties, this divide existed.

At MIT, my friends and I used to constantly hassle over what to do and how to do it. If we wanted new campus rules, higher pay in a workplace, a new affirmative action law, pollution controls, or the end of a war, we knew that we had to force authorities to submit. Activism from Selma through Cambridge by way of Indochina taught that those who had power would meet demands only when they decided that refusing demands would cost them more than granting them. Those of us attuned to this logic realized that to win battles we must raise costs that elites refused to bear. We had to convince elites that the only way to eliminate the threat we created was to meet our demands. That was the first half of the logic of dissent that some of us were learning. The second half had to do with focus. As with building an antiwar movement beyond ending recruitment on campus, or as with building an anti-imperialist movement beyond ending a particular war, or as with

86

building a movement to win new defining social institutions beyond ending imperial policies, the additional logic was that you must contribute to a continuing process. What you did should affect immediate activists and people viewing activism in ways that increased the prospects for future successes. Each act of dissent, from painting walls and holding rallies to marching, sitting in, or burning draft cards or buildings, should increase the numbers of committed activists and their organizational wherewithal, as well as move the larger public into being more supportive of our long-term goals. The Dow demo made all this clear. That's what dissent should do, for those who participate.

Cynicism 101

> *No matter how cynical you get, it is impossible to keep up.*
>
> *—Lily Tomlin*

When I would talk with MIT students about obstructing Dow, ending war research, ending the war, or ending poverty, racism, or capitalism, underneath people's confusion there was always another obstacle. Sessions would last hours. Concerns and doubts would surface. I would begin such talks offering evidence about the war's horrors. But most of the serious discussion that followed wasn't about U.S. motives, it was about whether people should resist or not. And the reason many of my fellow students repeatedly offered not to resist was because "people suck."

What these MIT students would say was that there was ultimately no point to resistance regardless of my facts, which they agreed were right, and regardless of the war's immorality, which they also admitted. The reason they gave to not demonstrate, organize, or even learn about the facts and conditions of the people we were murdering overseas was that all people are greedy, nasty, and brutish, so nothing positive was possible. These MIT classmates told me that human nature leads to war and injustice. There is no way to prevent this trajectory. You can't stop war, these classmates asserted, in the same way you can't make trees talk or make stones cry. There is no more point opposing war's trajectory, they concluded, than blowing into the wind. If we don't fight wars, someone else will. So we should do nothing.

The second most prevalent reason MIT students gave against resisting was that it was impossible to fight City Hall. You may have good goals and intentions. You may even come up with a way of seeking your preferences that wouldn't create a new mess just as bad as what you are battling against. Nonetheless, you can't win. This was the old folk's home at the college mustering defeatism on behalf of inaction. You can't stop the war, my classmates asserted, in the same way that a kid can't outbox Muhammad Ali. The state and corporations are too powerful.

Even if people could live better lives in a better world, humanity is too entangled in this world to reach a better one. The obstacles are insurmountable. We are condemned. And these views are also common now, in the U.S. and probably everywhere else in the world too. Belief that there is no alternative and that you can't win change is a straitjacket preventing opposition to oppression.

I remember a related phenomenon that always simultaneously amused and depressed me. I'd be handing out antiwar leaflets, and those who didn't eagerly take the antiwar leaflet would brush it away like it was infected with deadly germs. Sometimes the person despised us but often it was clear that that wasn't the root of it. I would walk along with such people, going backward, facing them from in front, as they moved forward, and I repeatedly offered them the leaflet. They would keep refusing and I would keep thrusting it at them. They could easily take the leaflet and then throw it out, or they could shout or threaten me off, but few who avidly didn't want it did that. The leaflets were indeed germ-infected. The disease was antiwar activism. The leaflets sat atop a slippery slope. If you took a leaflet, you might read it. If you read it, you might accept its message. If you accepted its message, you might demonstrate. The leaflet was dangerous because it might hook you into something you wanted to avoid. Better to avoid seeing it.

People who actively resisted communication sometimes explicitly hated us and our views, of course. But more often their resistance stemmed either from doubting the efficacy of activism for reasons noted above, or from wishing to avoid dangerous involvement. It was important to understand this because it meant organizing was not just a matter of conveying previously unfamiliar truths, however important that aspect was. I began to realize that reaching people often entailed overcoming not only ignorance, but also fear of failure.

Organizing Mechanics

First of all two people get together
an' they want their doors enlarged
—Bob Dylan

In the early 1960s and right up to 1965, there were occasional, quite small antiwar demonstrations on the Boston Common. MIT students who went to these demonstrations were generally not protestors but instead part of a large crowd of sometimes-violent hecklers. Campus antiwar activity was almost nonexistent, particularly at MIT, right through my first year there. But from my sophomore through my senior year the situation went ballistic. Antiwar rallies on the Boston Common regularly exceeded 100,000 people, with only a handful of hecklers. MIT students poured out of dorms and fraternities to join marches. In 1968 and 1969, we had not only massive but also very militant demonstrations.

When I ran for office at MIT, I would go into a dorm to speak and the entire dorm would turn out to listen and then discuss the issues. These sessions would last a few hours and many folks would continue talking afterward. What happened? What induced such a change in consciousness and activism in just a few years?

Partly, events happened all over the country and around the world, and each one prodded others. There was a sequence of campus activities from the Berkeley free speech movement in the early sixties through rallies and demonstrations, to the sanctuaries, and finally the massive building occupations at many schools, including Harvard, just up the river from MIT. There were constant rallies and actions at MIT, too, continually growing in scale, but what I want to highlight here is different.

At MIT, a relatively small group of people—at first, about 15 or so—organized the campus. We redesigned corridors, put up posters, and sponsored educational events. We held rallies and teach-ins. We talked to fellow students, over and over, at every opportunity. We went door to door in dorms and fraternities night after night. We stuck leaflets under people's doors, mimeographing them all one night and then distributing them all the next night, going around to talk about reactions thereafter. We sat and talked to folks in the eating areas. We brought up the war and many other issues in classes. We continually urged new people to address their often-incredible ignorance or conservatism.

The thing about movements in the sixties is that people discovered that their pains were not due to personal inadequacies. People got angry at newly unveiled culprits. Lies were uncovered and the lies made people indignant.

The civil rights movement highlighted racism and repression in the restaurants, bus stations, and streets of the south, and then also in northern ghettos. It painted before people's eyes stark images revealing that the horrendous situation of blacks in the U.S. was systemic. Legal lynching and all manner of economic and social indignities came into bright light due to the public actions of the bus boycotters, the lunch counter sitters, the vote registrars, and the rest of civil rights activists risking and sometimes losing their lives to turn racism around. We saw that. We became angry.

The antiwar movement offered a second revelation. The U.S. was engaged in a vicious war against peasants half a world away, not for a good cause, but for power and wealth. The U.S. brought mayhem on a poor peasant land. Images of assassination and destroyed towns accompanied claims that power and greed were the cause. The more we brought human carnage to light, the more we unveiled corporate motives, the more people got angry and considered systemic issues. Movement focus went from dissociating from right wingers, to dissociating from liberals, to dissociating from the underlying institutions of corporate capitalism and bourgeois democracy.

The women's movement provided the most explicit case of mind-changing, soul-transforming revelation. Women began to gather in one another's homes to discuss their life situations. They spoke about their experiences more openly than ever before and discovered that the rapes, brutalities, denials of dignity, and depredations of intelligence that they all daily endured were not unique. The oppressive patterns were so common from one woman to the next that once women's private stories were made public, one woman after another realized that their seemingly private situations couldn't be due to personal preferences, nor even due to a particular man or a few men they just happened to have unluckily hooked up with. It was systemic. The system could be fought. Up burst the energy of struggle.

And finally, or in some ways firstly, the hippie, youth, antiauthoritarian cultural movement was similarly revelatory. Now it was boredom, irrelevance, ageism, and alienation that were shown to be not personal infections but social impositions. Hippies rebelled at suburban plasticity. Hippies rejected daily life and all its accouterments, not just the most oppressive features, but even those indicating success. Hippies found suburbia and the American dream obscene. Hippies created alternative lifestyles. It wasn't just our hair growing.

The sixties I participated in erupted over anger at promises unmet and ubiquitous lies and hypocrisy. A big part of our sixties emergence was people receiving honest, accurate information. A smaller though also necessary part was people overcoming cynicism. At MIT we had to bring the truth about Vietnam into every dorm room, fact by precious fact, and then, after getting antiwar revelations across against student incredulity, we had to overcome cynicism too. I suspect that the situation has reversed in the decades since. I suspect the biggest issue now is overcoming cynicism, while providing honest, accurate information is a smaller—though still necessary—part of developing movement support. I believe, in other words, that 40 years ago when people heard things were broken and realized that many citizens were suffering who didn't have to, they got angry. Today, however, I suspect that everyone knows more or less who and what is at fault regarding poverty, health care, and war, and who is suffering. The problem today is that while consciousness of injustice is more advanced, cynicism—the view that nothing better is possible and that the enemy is all powerful—has become far more prevalent and powerful.

Still, beyond these contextual changes, which bear on what needs doing now, there is the issue of organizing and just what it is. In the sixties, organizing was face-to-face talk with everyone we could corner. Now organizing is often sending e-mails. Whereas in the sixties I would stay up all night mimeographing a leaflet, looking at the end of the night as if I had rolled in ink, and then stay up the next night with many others taking the leaflets to room after room, perhaps getting as many as 1,000 of them under people's doorjambs via two full nights of work by a bunch of people, now, in a click of a mouse, I can send 200,000 e-mails each containing the equivalent of a long leaflet, right to people's desks.

This is luxurious efficiency. E-mail is cheap and labor-saving. The international ties that e-mail has facilitated are enormous. The galvanizing of quick responses and gatherings is a blessing. But, as an organizer's tool, e-mail also has a dangerous flaw. We can only send e-mail to addresses that we have. On campuses all over the U.S., for example, student activists e-mail to their lists with ease and regularity. For those who are on the lists, information flies. Wisdom accrues. But most students aren't on the lists. They get no e-mail. They hear of no evil. The point is, it is one thing to use new technologies to augment the essential task of constantly reaching out to talk with more and more people in steadily deeper ways. It is another thing for the dynamics of using new technologies to crowd out time given to talking to new people. Talking matters. Reaching new people matters. Leafletting, in the old days, facilitated both talking and reaching new people. E-mailing, efficacious for some purposes, nonetheless nowadays often has a tendency to crowd out both talking and reaching new people.

Chapter 8

Big Man on Campus

UAP: To Win or to Educate, That's the Wrong Question

I'll be a different kind of congressman than most. I don't care if I am never elected again if winning an election means compromising my principles.
                                                                            —*Ron Dellums*

A year after the glue-sniffing shock therapy in Somerville, Massachusetts, I ran for what is called undergraduate association president at MIT. Ironically, my fraternity brothers' prognostications about my campus future were fulfilled, though not as they had intended.

Running for office had a simple logic. Why couldn't we utilize campus politics to reach out even more widely than when we redesigned halls, postered walls, held rallies, blocked recruiters, and hosted sanctuaries? Why not run for campus government, advocating our views in every cranny of campus life? Most organizers thought campus elections were a silly diversion from real dissent, but we all found attractive the prospect of using the process to speak and organize. But we should not become electoral panderers. Our goal had to be to organize, not to amass votes.

Ordinarily I might have spearheaded this position, but on the MIT campus I saw things a little differently. I believed we should seek votes with full disclosure, not deceit. I think this, plus the fact that I was our best public speaker and had endless energy, was why people settled on me as candidate. In my view not only were our politics what had to be conveyed to build our movement, but they were also our best chance to win lots of votes. More, I didn't just think we could get more votes being absolutely forthright than any other way; I thought we could win.

The campaign had to be waged against other candidates as well as against the MIT administration and many faculty members, all of whom realized that we needed to be stopped. The campaign included among its programmatic goals: no more war research—which was like running for president of a religious organization on the platform of no more prayer—a $100,000 indemnity payment to the Black Panther Party to redress historical grievances of racism, no more grades or requirements, and a redistribution of MIT's resources to upgrade nearby community colleges. For a few weeks all I did, 18 hours a day, was campaign. I would talk in dorms and fraternities, to clubs, and even to sports teams, and of course at candidate debates, but I would also just roam the corridors striking up conversations wherever I happened to be.

People came out of MIT's woodwork to vote either for or against me. My program, if fully implemented, would have meant the dissolution of the university. While our efforts at MIT had turned many heads, it was certain that there was not a majority of revolutionaries on campus. So why did I win? Beyond those who were fully in our camp, a great many students respected what we were trying to do and thought, okay, let's see what they can muster. Curiosity helped us. So did thrill seeking. Running gave our movement more supporters. Winning gave us furnished offices, equipment, rights of access all over campus, and a budget. We used all this to resist and dissent, of course.

Traditionally, the UAP and MIT's president gave welcoming speeches to an opening day assembly of incoming freshmen. The UAP and the university president would each pat the other on the back, welcome the new class, tell them how momentous their opportunities were, and how hard they needed to work. Howard Johnson was the president of MIT and a typical bureaucratic CEO-type, who had risen up from being a professor of management at MIT to being its president. During his tenure he created the Undergraduate Research Opportunities Program, the Independent Activities Period, freshmen pass/fail, and the Wellesley Exchange Program. All were sops to the left, to ward off dissent with humane alterations. Johnson's legacy was forced on him. He never said thank you.

After Johnson welcomed the incoming Freshmen, it was my turn. I comprehensively rejected the war, excoriated MIT's war research, advocated liberation on campus and in society, and indicated that all this was to be pursued full time by campus movements that were going to be as important to the lives of incoming freshmen as any faculty person, administrator, or friend. They should look up RL-SDS, even as they signed up for courses. Many did. Interestingly, I got no flack for this. It was within MIT's rules and MIT mostly abided its rules.

A second quite odd result of being UAP was that MIT had a longstanding club called Osiris. Osiris's membership included each year's UAP as an automatic student member, a few faculty, some administrators, the provost, president, etc. Osiris was secret. The membership was self-selecting and supposed to comprise the key people on campus. Osiris's mandate was to develop plans for the community. It was MIT's version of Yale's Skull and Bones, I guess, but more secret and smaller, and concerned not just with mutual preening, but with defining ongoing MIT relations. So as UAP I was invited to attend. It really is amazing that instead of changing the rules, they followed them even in that regard. Maybe the Osiris members thought this one last temptation would get me back on board the gravy train. I not only didn't go to Osiris, I promptly made known their existence all over the campus. Good-bye, secrecy. Good-bye, Osiris. Do you know the expression "boys with their toys"? How about "men with their secrets"? How about "elitists with their delusions"? How about "regimenters with their regimentations"?

The Fame Factor and Snowballing Individualism

I am somehow less interested in the weight and convolutions of Einstein's brain than in the near certainty that people of equal talent have lived and died in cotton fields and sweatshops.
—Stephen Jay Gould

My winning as campus president made me a campus star. The *Boston Globe* did a big spread and interview. *The Tech* and *Thursday*, the two campus papers, frequently had pictures of me on the front page, reports about me, and talks with me. People would walk up with or mail me questions, praise, criticism, curses, death threats, and what have you. I didn't have Tom Cruise notoriety, of course, but I did experience something of what it means to be a celebrity, at least in a tiny corner of the U.S. Celebrity boosts ego, conveys confidence, and enlarges influence, but obliterates privacy.

People generally try to make the best of their circumstances. The natural and easiest option for me, as UAP, was to change myself to maximally enjoy my new situation. There was huge pressure to reconstruct myself to actually like people attending to my every word. There was pressure to agree with the surrounding chorus that I was special and deserved elite perks. Fame involved a snowballing dynamic that could move anyone who, for whatever odd combination of reasons, was selected for even just modest fame, toward being a fame-lover, which might in turn lead toward being an authoritarian egomaniac, and, in our society, winning more fame as a result.

This picture might strike you as obvious, but it is the kind of personal pattern, rather than detailed psychological mumbo jumbo, we ought to take account of in social relations. This is what the idea that power tends to corrupt and absolute power corrupts absolutely means. External stimuli transform the internal person.

Maybe Gandhi wasn't susceptible to this. Who knows? My impression was that Dave Dellinger, a central figure of protest in the U.S. and himself a kind of

American Gandhi, wasn't susceptible. Maybe they retained their own inner preferences and never rationalized their fame. Maybe they never saw themselves as superior. Maybe they never inflated their view of themselves and never deflated their view of others. Maybe they never acclimated to unequal treatment. I think it is most likely, however, that if this was true for them, then they had to work hard at avoiding these problems. At any rate, I had to work hard at it in a much less corrupting situation.

I thought about what had happened to make me such a special figure on campus and decided that the whole thing was luck, chance, and circumstance, and not moral, social, or any other kind of superiority. Almost daily, I lectured myself on this matter. I decided that true success had nothing to do with endearing myself to others, climbing ever higher in other people's eyes, or with anything pandering or manipulative, but rather that true success for me depended on using my situation to benefit the movement while also constantly rejecting its tendency to co-opt me.

That's a feature that a radical needs, or anyone needs, to safely navigate even modest fame. But keeping perspective shouldn't be a purely personal task. Those who attract fame need other people to keep them honest. But there is a Catch-22 to friends safeguarding one against power corrupting. Unless structural pressure precludes it, growing fame lets a person change who is around him or her to accord with a steadily inflating self-image. I saw similar dynamics and had my feelings reinforced about their meaning when I much later witnessed Jesse Jackson in the Rainbow campaigns and Ralph Nader in the Green campaigns. The two candidates worked admirably hard and lived lives of great struggle. But they were also propelled by circumstance, happenstance, and luck, into their prominence, and in my view suffered the snowballing dynamics accruing to fame.

I watched Jackson and Nader, interacting with their efforts and at times very briefly with them. They both rose rapidly in esteem and power. It quickly got so the only real obstacle to power corrupting them into believing that their will was so superior that it should be implemented above the will of their whole supporting organizations and movements was themselves. No institutional restraints were put in place to forcefully corral them. To remain rooted they had to willingly subject themselves to participatory influences rather than subordinate such influences to their preferences. But, instead, Jackson and Nader elevated their own preferences above all others. Jesse destroyed the Rainbow. Ralph squandered the immense potentials of his 2000 campaign. Call it the fame dynamic or anything else you want, it works at diverse levels, whether on a campus or in a country, to distort interpersonal relations and, in the worst cases, to produce leaders with inflated power and ego who in turn almost always make critically wrong choices. The point is, no one should assume personal goodness will ensure integrity against the dynamics of fame and power.

Chapter 9

Heating Up and Melting Down

Divesting or Transforming

If we don't stand for something, we may fall for anything.
—Malcolm X

One of the campus activist approaches that garnered lots of sixties energy went under the label of divestment. The issue was campus involvement in war recruiting and research. One impetus for some was simply to wash their hands. MIT should not be involved in war-making. Put it somewhere else. Be pure. A second motive was resistance. Proponents of this view felt that nowhere should be involved. We ought to get rid of war accommodations at MIT, and throughout society as well. There was a different calculus to the two approaches. The first approach could accept war, but not academic involvement. Campus activism was self-contained. The second approach rejected war entirely. Campus activism contributed to larger activism. It was like the two sides of ecology activism later: pursuit of sustainability and ecological sanity throughout society on the one hand, or the myopic "not in my backyard" approach, on the other hand.

In efforts to build sixties movements, these two orientations often clashed. The Dow recruitment demonstration described earlier provided one example. Our movement against Dow gained strength from people's narrow "get it out of here" involvement, but our movement would also have had its integrity and longevity undermined if people's involvement remained narrow.

University administrations sometimes understood these issues better than activists. In the late sixties, Princeton University students waged a campaign against a war-related research center. Princeton said it surrendered. The building remained active, its tasks and procedures unchanged. The university redrew Princeton's boundaries so that the building was no longer part of the campus. The center was spun off. The movement declared victory and largely went home. The war research continued largely unchanged. This wasn't even co-option. It was sleight-of-hand manipulating moral minimalism. At MIT, similarly, its Instrumentation Labs were made into the private Draper Labs—but our movement was not confused by gerrymandered labels.

A huge portion of the MIT budget came from the Pentagon. While I sometimes called MIT "Dachau on the Charles," stretching a point, almost everyone called MIT "The Pentagon on the Charles," barely stretching the truth at all. We knew MIT war research was developing multiple-entry nuclear warheads and we opposed that. Given a vote in the matter, however, I would happily have shifted more military money to missiles that would never be fired, and probably didn't even work, and away from weapons actually used on real people. After a time we also discovered that the MIT labs were working on helicopters. Public relations claimed MIT was trying to better stabilize helicopters for traffic coverage in windy cities like Chicago. We intuitively knew better, but it wasn't until some activists snuck onto the fields and photographed the helicopters that the truth became undeniable. The helicopters were gunships from Vietnam, and MIT's technical task was to stabilize their flight so they could fire more effectively at peasants below. What we didn't discover until considerably later was MIT's effort to generate radar-related tools suitable for guiding smart bombs directly to predetermined targets. The MIT smart bomb succeeded in changing bombing tactics in the last stages of the Vietnam War by making the bombing of dikes and dams far more damaging. It came to full fruition later in the Gulf wars.

During World War II, MIT's radiation labs, in buildings that later housed academics like Noam Chomsky, were the center of radar research that was critical to the air war against Hitler. The radar studies were universally celebrated, like the WWII code-breaking work centered in England. The difference between the radar work for World War II and the guidance-system work for Vietnam was the nature of the war.

The smart bomb research undertaken at MIT was the only example I personally encountered where even a small-scale action could have saved many lives. Suppose we had known about that smart bomb research. Suppose we had found a way to terminate it by blowing up the labs in which it was occurring. The research was occurring only there and could not have been replicated elsewhere fast enough to become operative in Vietnam. Sabotage, in this one case, would have prevented the last stages of the bombing in Indochina, particularly the bombing of dikes, from being as devastating as it was, thereby saving many lives. It is personally lucky that I didn't know these things at the time. I think there is a good chance that if I had known that truth I would have acted with others on the knowledge and probably bollixed the effort, either blowing my friends and myself up or rotting in jail ever since. This happened to good people of my generation, who, elsewhere in the country, thought that they were in clear-cut situations and as a result had precisely those misfortunes. If I would have done something similar believing I was in that clear-cut situation, am I as guilty as they are for their having been in what they thought was that situation and having gone ahead and done it? Or are they as innocent as I am, despite their having done such things?

At any rate, some people, including Chomsky, felt that we were wrong to try to banish MIT's ties to the Pentagon. His argument was odd, in my view, but it had some weight. If the work was done in secret private firms, there could be no visible counterpressure. If it was done on campuses, at least it might be known and kept in check. My counterposition was that building movements isn't a matter of ideal conceptualization. We have to make do, at times, with what we can actually achieve, particularly regarding what appeals to people. We can't always get what we want. Given attitudes at MIT, we could successfully organize around closing down research on helicopter stabilization. We could not develop support for preserving war research with modest amendments. I learned you operate partly based on what you desire and partly based on what conditions permit.

In any case, many of the most militant and massive struggles at MIT involved confronting war research. I can remember having huge shouting matches with faculty at MIT about science and its use and misuse. I would rail against doing the bidding of war, the bidding of capital, the bidding of profit. And they would rail back against anti-intellectualism. For intellectuals, they seemed remarkably obtuse. I wasn't against knowledge. I was against the way they perverted knowledge's use. Activities stemming from this motivation at MIT led to commissions investigating MIT's science ties, to a new program at MIT on social relations and technology, to various lasting movement projects, including the periodical *Science for the People*, and later, coupled with other causative factors, to massive campaigns about nuclear missiles, the rebirth of the nuclear freeze, and arguably even the emergence of the No Nukes movement. But the biggest, most important project undertaken at the time at MIT was called the November Action Coalition, or NAC.

Human Donuts

Those who profess to favor freedom and yet deprecate agitation, are people who want crops without plowing the ground. Power concedes nothing without a demand; it never has and it never will.
—Frederick Douglass

The NAC idea was that we would build a coalition of campus movements and groups from all over the Boston area and bring it to bear on the chief target: MIT's war research. NAC wasn't, however, solely focused on war or science. The NAC buildup involved numerous actions, events, talks, etc., relating to local strikes and issues of campus policies in other areas as well as war. NAC was anti-imperialist, anticapitalist, antipatriarchal, and antiracist. Name your injustice, NAC was its enemy.

I remember one trip out to Boston College to give a talk there. I knew nothing about the place. The talk was outdoors, in a kind of commons area. As I walked up to speak I saw some nuns, of whom I took no special notice. I gave my speech, liberally peppered with expletives, railing at U.S. imperialism and capitalism, but also addressing patriarchy, sexism, and racism, and calling aggressively for support for the ongoing NAC campaigns. At the end I got less applause than I was used to, or was it less than I was addicted to? Boston College was a Catholic school and had never been treated to a talk like mine. I probably would have cursed just as much had I known where I was, and perhaps more. Would it have been better, however, to speak more in BC's language than in mine? I think the answer is that sometimes modifying our language is a slippery slope to conformity. Molding self to meet others' preferences is tricky. Other times, modifying our language is as sensible as speaking French in Paris and Italian in Rome.

One of the actions of NAC was a one-day takeover of the Center for International Studies (CIS) at MIT. This was a warmup event to the main engagement at MIT's war labs. We wanted not only to highlight the CIS and its war complicity, but to make some material gains as well. The former point was simple. In our view, whether segregated or not, war research was vile. But there was an additional truth to be told. War blood ran through MIT's veins. It flooded the research facilities and seeped even into the classrooms. In the halls of the CIS, for example, war criminals mentored students. The president of the CIS was Max Millikan, a former executive officer of the CIA. Down the hall was Ithiel de Sola Pool, who periodically would disappear from campus, taking trips to Vietnam to help interrogate prisoners as part of the Phoenix Program assassination campaign to wipe out local resistance. Imagine reading your professor's comments that "In the Congo, in Vietnam, in the Dominican Republic, it is clear that order depends on somehow compelling newly mobilized strata to return to a measure of passivity and defeatism from which they have recently been aroused by the process of modernization." Imagine realizing that your professor felt that "the maintenance of order requires a lowering of newly acquired aspirations and levels of political activity." Imagine realizing that ratified acting on the insight that there is nothing like a bullet in your head, or in your brother's or sister's or friend's or parent's or child's head to "lower newly acquired aspirations" and induce "a measure of passivity and defeatism." Our reaction was to realize that Vietnam had nothing to do with "building democracy." And that's why fervor, outrage, and even hatred animated our relationship with the CIS, Millikan, and Pool.

Discussions about how to undertake our CIS protest were otherworldly. We wanted to hold the offices for a day to pilfer the place. We hoped to find useful materials, and emerge triumphant. Only one aspect was problematic. How could we avoid disastrous conflicts with staff? The problem involved not only Millikan and Pool, but also less-vile or even quite humane faculty—there were a few in the CIS—as well as secretaries, custodians, and others. Some of those discussing what to do—Weatherman, the most militant SDS-related group at the time—advocated booting everyone out with whatever level of force that entailed, including beating up war criminals, or, in some moments of heightened rhetoric, tossing them out windows. There was a lot of testosterone bluster in this, of course. There was also, however, a considerable amount of honest, informed passion. We were, after all, dealing with war criminals of the most odious sort.

Other people present for the discussion, including nearly all RL-SDSers, thought that using violence would be immoral for the innocent folks inside the CIS as well as strategically disastrous for our message and image. We didn't want to spend weeks talking about a secretary or custodian who got pushed and hurt, or even about Pool or Millikan being hurt. We wanted the focus to be war crimes and their place in American institutional priorities.

Once that view prevailed, a new problem arose: how do we get people out without hurting anyone? We would enter in large numbers and ask folks to leave. Those who refused we would urge, cajole, and give more chances to go. Some suggested blasting them with really loud music. Those who still refused we would escort out or, if that was too difficult, escort into unoccupied rooms. We would not permit them to mill about and hector us, not only to avoid the diversion, distraction, and demoralization their presence would impose, but to avoid the danger someone would haul off and slug one of them.

Now another problem demanded attention: how do we escort them out when they are yelling at us, or even slapping at us or hurling things at us, and otherwise ignoring our wishes? Our answer was that we would become human conveyors. We called it the "donut strategy." We would link arms and form a circle around each person in turn—creating a human donut with the adversary in the center—and then we would walk the person out, or to another room. Of course it would have been a complete fiasco the minute the person sat down. But, with some self-delusion, we made this our plan and, luckily, the building's inhabitants were far less interested in confrontation than in rapid escape. They left of their own accord before we even got there. The place was ours and we stayed for the day and then left as planned. There was no intervention by police and no immediate repression of any kind. MIT tried to avoid cops and conflict on campus—but not from largesse. They knew from Berkeley and Columbia University's experiences that bringing cops on campus to remove students would only provoke mayhem.

The MIT yearbook for 1970 has a full-page picture of me leaning over Max Millikan's desk, taking a folder off it. We were trying to find incriminating materials, not just good photo ops, but we pretty much failed in that respect. Since we had given plenty of warning that the CIS was a target, all the damning materials had been cleared out. By way of capturing incriminating material, an earlier Harvard strike and building occupation had been far more successful. At that event, a key presidential office was being trashed when friends of mine, including Mike Ansara and Danny Schechter (who was later the news dissector on Boston WBCN radio and has for decades been a conspicuously effective media activist on the Left), and others urged people to leave the elite room and stop damaging it lest the message of the occupation be lost. While everyone else filed out, Mike and Danny stayed. They uncovered documents damning to Harvard. The building was surrounded by cops. Arrests were imminent. How would Mike and Danny get the documents out?

Danny was less well-known so he stuffed the files under his clothes, stumbled up to the supposedly uncrossable police lines surrounding the building, wept that he was a loyal right-wing Harvard-loving student who had gotten inadvertently caught in the fray and pleaded, couldn't he please get out of the building and away from these maniac demonstrators before the police arrested everyone. Some caring campus cop let him through, thereby freeing the files. Later, the documents were displayed in a special edition of *The Old Mole*, our local radical underground newspaper, and then in a more complete study called *Who Rules Harvard?*, which later spawned similar studies of other universities.

In any case—returning to MIT—the climax of the NAC campaign was to be an assault on MIT's instrumentation labs, where much of MIT's war research was conducted. We intended to barricade the lab to prevent workers from going in. One notable lead-up event was a mass meeting of employees and NAC organizers a few days before the assault. We made a case for our right to shut down their workplace. They made a case for their right to work.

I had one of my worst political moments at that meeting. In the midst of speaking to the group, getting heckled somewhat and not gaining much agreement, I blurted out something about our being their future bosses. This was incredibly obnoxious. I don't know the extent of damage it did, but probably not very much. Engineers aren't particularly affronted by elitism. But it was a perfect example of the typical elitism of a lawyer, doctor, or manager toward an assembly worker. My frustrated utterance was comparable to an avowed antiracist, for whatever reason, calling a group of blacks he was negotiating with "niggers." Of course the reaction wasn't remotely that strong, but that's because class consciousness was far less advanced than race consciousness, not to mention that my audience were mostly elite managers and engineers and not assemblers and custodians.

My outburst aside, our written demands for NAC had no class problems. We demanded an end to imperialist research at MIT, in particular regarding anti missile missiles (the kind used for shooting other missiles down), multiple warhead nuclear missiles, and helicopter stabilization. We didn't know they were developing smart bombs or we would have addressed those as well. We demanded that no worker lose pay or employment due to conversion or the NAC action. We signed off, as always, by demanding immediate withdrawal of all U.S. forces from Vietnam, victory to the NLF, and support for women's liberation.

Leading up to NAC, the MIT administration tried everything to dissuade us. Finally, despite negative repercussions for their liberal image, they got a restraining order to keep us off campus. For the record, those named on the restraining order were Robin Hahnel, George Katsiaficas, Philip Raup, Stephen Shalom, Peggy Hopper, Stephen Krasner, Michael O'Connor, Peter Bohmer, Owen Franken, Michael Ansara, Abraham Igelfeld, Jeffrey Mermelstein, Stephen Soldz, and me. Our reaction was to mount the main steps of MIT, face Massachusetts Avenue, give fiery speeches, and rip up the restraining order. Clearly, we could have been arrested, though in time, the order was actually defeated in court, I believe. When I stood on MIT's front steps and publicly ripped up the restraining order, however, I knew there wasn't a prayer the police would grab me and the others and haul us off, whether the order was valid or not. Actually, we hoped they would do so, which is precisely why they didn't.

It was one thing for MIT to make a threat. It would be quite another thing for them to haul off various students and townsfolk, including the very well-known president of the student body, on grounds that we had violated an order demanding that we not set foot on our own campus. Support for us would have grown rather than waned. Helping us grow was, of course, the opposite of MIT's intent. If we had been in Texas, Iowa, or South Carolina and had lacked wider community support and had blatantly violated an injunction, the restraining order would likely have been enforced. But in Cambridge, Massachusetts, in 1969, our level of support in the community and on neighboring campuses prevented such an act.

This lesson is easily generalized, and it was important for me then and has been ever since. In the U.S. and in any industrialized country, the forces of the police and the army cannot be physically beaten. I knew then with absolute certainty, and have never seen any reason to think differently since, that we could not have successfully resisted arrest had the powers that be wished to corral us. If they had wanted to kill us, we would be dead. In response to any offensive stance we adopted, they could up the ante by an order of magnitude. On the other hand, the police and the army in industrialized countries are not without fracture lines, and likewise the public. Repression can only be beaten by creating a context in which its implementation would be more costly to elites than letting the matter drop. MIT and the City of Cambridge didn't ignore our violation of their injunction out of concern for us or moral scruples; they ignored it out of fear that arresting us would have doubled, tripled, or, even more dramatically raised the turnout of the NAC events. They weren't stupid. They chose not to help us.

I realized from all this that, ultimately, the same holds for overcoming police and military repression more generally. I saw that to win change we must make military actions by authorities counterproductive. The first level of achieving this was creating a context in which elite repression would provoke more response than it would deter. The ultimate way to utterly defeat repression was to organize within repressive forces and cause their members to resist their own orders. Of course, none of this was a new idea. Armies do collapse. We all knew our army in Indochina was well on the way to dissolution by the time of NAC. Elites understood the problem. This was hammered home to many of us, as well, when we witnessed the inner city rebellions in Watts (1965), Detroit (1967), Newark (1967), and in many other places as well. We saw how elites realized that there was a very real danger that police would decide that they did not want to repress rioters. We saw that to avoid this system-threatening calamity, elites brought in National Guard units from distant, hostile places. Units from the deep South patrolled California ghettos. Young recruits were scared and angry and by design knew no one in the neighborhoods they entered. Local units would have been unreliable.

The lesson I took was that winning change means not only reaching the broad public, but also the part of the public that carries guns and is nominally the bulwark of reaction. I decided—contrary to many of my comrades in action at the time—that dehumanizing police with chants like "today's pig is tomorrow's bacon," was politically suicidal, especially as compared to understanding the situation of soldiers and police and trying to organize them to become a central part of resistance rather than viewing them as intractable enemies.

So the main NAC event neared. It turned out that the MIT labs were full of classified projects. They were designated as U.S. military institutions. To obstruct them was to commit treason. Legally, when we went to obstruct them, the surrounding forces could not only club us, they could shoot us. This wasn't going to happen, however, and we knew it for the reason noted above: it would hurt rather than benefit them to escalate so viciously.

The day came. A few hundred core activists gathered at the campus center a few blocks from the labs, with many people sleeping there overnight and others assembling in the morning. The idea was to march to the labs to obstruct them. We woke to an unexpected sight. The streets outside were lined with jeeps and military transports. There were snipers on rooftops. This was all meant to scare us off, like the prior injunction. We knew it wouldn't be used. We marched to the destination, tried to obstruct it, and all hell broke loose. Well, not really. The shooters were gone. Now the local police were the opposition. They clearly wanted to bust heads, to give us a working over, as well as to prevent our disrupting the labs. Without firing a shot, they easily won the physical day, though there was plenty of skirmishing in the streets for a few hours. All the physical conflict, however, was a sideshow. It was necessary as a focus that we organized around, geared up for, undertook, and then evaluated. But the heart of the matter for all actions, all projects, all constructions, and all demolitions was always the lasting effect on how many activists we have, the depth of our commitment, and our organizational wherewithal. It was never the size of the clouds of tear gas or the lumps, bruises, broken bones, or even busted bodies that provides the measure of a struggle. It was never what is finished and over that matters most. It was what follows.

About a year later there was another action in pretty much the same area. It was again an area-wide project, but now the focus was a train track right near MIT, in Cambridge. We planned to rip up the tracks to protest against the bombing of supply trains in North Vietnam. The demonstrators would surround the area. Some people would actually rip up the tracks. Other people would surround and protect the rippers long enough to get the job done. My arrest at this event is the only personal arrest where I graphically remember the act itself because I had so clearly been targeted even though I was long gone from MIT. I had avoided arrest at most other conflicts, such as NAC, May Day in Washington, DC, a riot in Harvard Square, and others. My general feeling was that—with the exception of civil disobedience where getting arrested was intended—being arrested drains time and energy. Being captured wasn't a virtue, unless it was your goal. Civil disobedience arrests were generally a cop pulling you off, more or less harshly. They weren't personally memorable, though they could be collectively profound.

The police had broken up the crowds at this demo, spreading us over a wide area. Lydia Sargent and I headed down a street that ran down one side of the MIT main campus area. Further up that street was a modest lab building that housed a small cyclotron, a tool that physicists use for experimental work. Someone broke some windows and ran off. Suddenly I was staring into the barrel of a revolver pointed at my head and was being accused of having broken those windows, which was in fact, false. In truth I never got into window breaking, though I wasn't against it in principle, only by temperament. At the grip end of the revolver was an MIT campus cop. He knew me and I could easily see his MIT campus cop uniform. He had me and he wasn't going to let me go, that much was clear.

The danger of getting shot at by police at an antiwar demonstration was probably nonexistent in Cambridge. The danger of getting panic-shot by this barely trained, horribly scared campus cop was momentarily real. Once I said, "Okay, you got me, now what?" the MIT cop quickly cooled down and took me calmly into custody. At that point, my situation ironically went from risky to beneficial. Had I been taken into police custody with no one from MIT around, I would probably have been dragged to the station and, once there, badly beaten like numbers of my friends who were less known than I was. But since I was picked up by liberal, lawsuit-averse MIT, I got no beating, and was later released. I even suspect, in retrospect, that MIT administrators had put the campus patrol on the streets in part to arrest me and get me out of the way of city police. This wasn't out of humanity, of course. They would have been quite happy to see me pummeled. Actually some of them would have loved to take part in that. They just knew the police were going to jump upside as many heads as possible, particularly folks whose names they had. MIT was fine with that, in general, probably providing some of those names. But messing up a notable alumnus would get wide coverage and might provoke sympathy for the devil. I had to be escorted out of the line of fire. How ignominious.

That's the only time, I think, I have ever been close to getting seriously mauled by the law. I have been hit and jostled, held and fought, and arrested and dragged, but nothing else has ever approached a fine line between living and dying. At the time I didn't even register the danger. For whatever idiotic reasons, mostly youth, no doubt, I felt I was fine. There was no way this guy was going to shoot me.

Strategic Options

In case of doubt, attack.
—George S. Patton

All our varied acts at MIT and around the country at other schools did not bring down the empire. But we did transform the mood and often the rules of higher education. We opened the minds of millions of people, sometimes for the long haul. We turned topsy-turvy many norms of the whole society. The ripples still spread. For now, though, there is one last aspect to the life and times of the November Action Coalition I would be remiss to ignore.

In the early stages of conceiving NAC, a clear division of opinion arose. We were going to bring together movements and organizations across as many campuses as possible in the Boston area. These ranged from Northeastern, Boston University, and Boston College, through MIT, Harvard, Wellesley, and Brandeis, on to an almost uncountable number of smaller campuses. They all had substantial activism. It was time to unite. But to what ends? One group said, "Let's create an area-wide student movement that by its weight and breadth can galvanize continuing development." We would unite the movements from all schools to gain weight across campuses and in turn spur campus chapters into majority movements. With that mass base, we would then achieve lasting renovations that would not only provide a model to emulate elsewhere in the country, but would create an infrastructure able to help off-campus activism. It would be slow, hard work, but the gains would be durable. Steve Shalom was in this camp.

The second group said, "That sounds great, but what about the war? We should use what we have already attained to generate a visible sign of our power." Movements that aren't visible don't raise social costs for elites. They don't inspire people elsewhere. I was in this camp and we understood that jumping into militant conflict would pretty much explode away the slow and patient building of a really lasting area-wide student movement, but we thought it would create sparks that would be seen from coast to coast. We were moving faster than people in most of the U.S. If the future potential in Cambridge had to be sacrificed somewhat to provide visible inspiration elsewhere, so be it. This side won. But we were wrong.

Neither argument always totally trumps the other. Sometimes creating fireworks is better than creating infrastructure. But I now think that Cambridge in 1969 wasn't one of those times. Our fireworks had modest inspirational effects elsewhere. The creation of a lasting, institutional, democratic, participatory, and radicalized student movement would have charted a durable path into directions people were as yet overlooking. I count our decision as a major mistake, with costly repercussions. I can't remember the extent to which I was really, honestly, soberly weighing the relative merits of slow but steady local growth versus a big blast to incite wider growth, or just personally eager to fight the bastards and letting that desire trump good sense. It was probably some of both.

Exiting MIT

Cannibals prefer those who have no spines.
—Stanislaw Lem

My promise to MIT's then-provost and later president Jerome Wiesner trumped Wiesner's promise to me. I was indeed thrown out of MIT. The school had a rule, however, that you had to have three major violations to get the axe. My first two violations were attending demonstrations where violence occurred. My third violation was disrupting my own trial, which was being held on account of the other two violations. I forcefully pointed out at that trial that each time I had been at a demonstration where violence was perpetrated, the campus police were also there, the provost and many deans were there, the faculty judge of my tribunal was there, and at least hundreds of other students were there. Since I was accused of nothing that all those others weren't identically guilty of, which was being at the scene, how was it that I alone was on trial? Of course, in truth I was guilty of all manner of violations that MIT didn't know about. But then again, they were guilty of complicity with U.S. imperialism. In any case, MIT was hell-bent on decorum and would not throw me out without abiding their own rules of proving three violations. Thus, they found this sequence of rather idiotic violations to pin on me, and then ushered me out the door.

My final trial was held deep in the bowels of MIT. When it concluded, I walked through the long corridors toward the front exit at 66 Massachusetts Avenue. There was a campus bank along the way. I got to it and went in to cash a check. I was refused. It was perhaps fifteen minutes after the official expulsion and already I was off the roles in the campus bank. I passed custodians wallpapering over pictures of me that were embedded in large murals and in other spots along the main corridor. I was treated to a complete, drastic, and immediate flush. They were expelling a virus. These weren't vindictive people, of course. They were civilized. I returned to my apartment to find that my draft board had already called me. I had been changed from student-deferred to 1A after a call from MIT reporting my expulsion and urging reclassification. Okay, perhaps they weren't so civilized, but they were efficient. In those days the draft operated based on a lottery, and my number was absurdly high, so my new status had no impact. But you had to hand it to MIT. When they finally moved against me, they did it with vigor.

What would have happened if my draft number had been lower? I don't know. I didn't think about it then. I certainly wouldn't have heeded the call up, but how would I have resisted? I don't think I could have gone to the draft board and feigned craziness or otherwise lied my way out. I doubt I could have been convincing, but more, I don't think I would have been emotionally able to do it. It isn't that I think lying to a draft board is wrong; it is that my personal constitution, for better or, more likely in this case, for worse, would have gotten in the way. One of my role models, Dave Dellinger, had chosen jail during World War II, due to his being a political resister. Other people were at the time doing likewise, or were joining up to organize on army bases and even to frag their officers in a slowly crumbling line of fire. And many others left for Canada. I doubt I would have become an exile. It was too foreign an idea. So it probably would have come down to a few years of jail or a few years of hell in the army. And it likely would have meant a very different life, if any life at all, thereafter. I was lucky in that lottery, but at the time I was truly oblivious to the situation. Youth and the assumptions of inviolable safety do that to you.

The follow-up to my expulsion was another demonstration, this time an occupation of the president's office. A few masked marauders went into the main MIT building with a large core of accompanying occupiers. The masks were for those who used a homemade battering ram to break in the doors to the president's suite. The occupation wasn't a particularly memorable event, just another day at the office—or a bunch of days there. One person, however, Stephen Krasner, did a year's jail time for the ramming and I always felt guilty that someone else should have suffered more than I did from my trial and expulsion. For that matter, earlier,

Peter Bohmer and George Katsiaficas also did time—sixty days—for disrupting classes at MIT during organizing for the NAC events, but they served their sentences later. In fact, in a surreal set of events, George's mother, distraught at his trial, was arrested for disturbing the peace, and she served ten days. I think those are all the actual jail terms that were done, however, for actions at MIT. We were pretty good about avoiding repression and Massachusetts was certainly not Texas.

Some years later, MIT decided that I should graduate. Big-time schools with a liberal inclination do not like to have political expulsions on their record. MIT wanted to be able to say that they traversed the sixties without student casualties, just as they could say that they had earlier traversed McCarthyism without casualties. But to be able to claim they had been above the sixties fray, MIT had to give me a degree, erasing the blot of my expulsion from their records. So they contacted my parents and urged a meeting at which an arrangement could be made permitting me to complete my undergraduate requirements. Dad came to town and we went to the MIT offices together. He was elated. I was bored and very irritated, but it was the least I could do to show up. So we arrived and the then-assistant provost hosted us, and he was quite cordial. He reported how MIT would love to see me graduate. He noted that by the time of my expulsion I had already completed virtually all my requirements, except for gym classes and a physics lab, and I think there was one other course, too. So he said if you will just finish out the requirements, you can have your degree, and bygones will be gone by.

Now for me, of course, this was obscene. I was not interested in "Dachau on the Charles" becoming a more pleasant perch for pundits by virtue of giving me a degree. Still, I was willing to go along for family stability as Dad luxuriated in the offer, but I would only do it, I said, without conditions. The offer was explained to Dad as if I had said nothing. I had to take the lab and the other course off campus. I was not to set foot on the main campus and in the main corridors of MIT. You see, the MIT officials told dad, they feared for my safety. There were some faculty who upon seeing me could easily get violent and the officials wanted to avoid that. Dad was a bit incredulous, needless to say, but I took the warning as a compliment, and I knew it was true, and so I also saw it as a way out. I said I would take the degree, for my father and against my own preferences, but that I would do it only if I didn't have to take the courses. There was no way I was enrolling at some school miles away. Back and forth we went and finally MIT caved. But what about gym, you must do that, they said. We can't compromise there.

Not only do we have the hypocrisy of them giving me a degree—in their view it was like giving Satan a certificate of family merit—and of me taking it (which was even worse), but they were willing to forego a lab and an academic course but not gym as a requirement for my graduation. The idea that I was going to take four missed gym courses was even more absurd than that I would take a lab across town. They gave in a little. How about if you demonstrate that you are athletically competent? I said how do I do that and do it off campus, no less? And how do I do it in one afternoon, which is the most I am willing to give? MIT proposed that I swim laps in the MIT pool, far away from the main class areas. Bingo. Negotiation completed. I got my post-expulsion MIT degree by swimming a few laps. My father got what he paid for, sort of, and officialdom got to watch me swim to prove my worthiness.

About the swimming, maybe they were right. Years later, Lydia had become a staff person for The Medical Committee for Human Rights. MCHR held a picnic for lots of people working with it and their families. Somehow during this, Lydia's daughter Andrea, then about ten years old, found her way into a canoe—actually, she says I put her in it—and drifted off. There was a prevailing wind, and by the time anyone spotted her, she was well out, and there was no other boat. I dove in and swam after her, which may not have been genius at work because, despite my MIT training, I wasn't the world's best swimmer and my having done it, no one else was going to follow up. I managed to catch up to Andrea a few hundred yards into the lake before losing what little energy I had. I got in the canoe and we went back to shore. Andrea grew up to work in publishing, among other pursuits, and she edited my last two books, and this one, too. I wasn't being Darwinian that day, however. There were no Albert genes preserved for posterity.

Yearbook Time Machine

You miss 100 percent of the shots you never take.
—Wayne Gretzky

Once I had officially seen the last of MIT, I was asked by students to write a piece for the 1970 MIT yearbook. Interestingly, I wrote it in part for myself. I figured, who is going to read an essay stuck in a yearbook? Maybe I will read it decades from now, looking back on my past. Would my early life be familiar? Would I be on the same road in the future as I was in the past? If so, would it be tenacity or inflexibility that held me so long? It is now decades later and I just reread my yearbook essay. It shows pretty well where I was at and the tone of the times. Here are some excerpts.

A million words read, coups here, wars there, always our corporations, always our financial interests at stake. I began to understand that something about our economy necessitated the depravity that we committed in the name of democracy. The process they call capital accumulation and the free unfettered pursuit of profit, I began to call imperialism. Imperialism, the highest stage of injustice, assumed for me the character of an all pervasive reality.

"I became committed to destroying imperialism and profit no matter what the cost." I tried to describe my step into full time political struggle:

The words and ideas all become a part of our being. Every act is related to every other: a rent strike, a car passing a hitchhiker, robbery, a nasty salesman, planes over Vietnam, mixers in dorms, maids in suburbia, Coca Cola in Bolivia, cosmetics, crowded streets, advertising, authority, alienation from school or work, casual conversation, and on and on. It seems so pat but it's so real–all the bad things that we try to make believe aren't there become related to one another and they all rest on a mutable set of relations and institutions, and so I read Marx and Che and became, at least in the mirror, an American Revolutionary.

I told of "one critical lesson I have learned" that "the movement for achieving [a better world] is itself the embryo of the new society. Any defects that it might have will appear in full grown horror in the world we are to build." I urged that "Revolutionary violence must be self conscious and seek its own dissolution. Revolutionary leadership must be antiauthoritarian, it must come from the initiative of the people. Revolutionary discipline must be offered and not demanded. Revolutionaries must always struggle against their own tendencies toward racism, chauvinism, and the accumulation of the power of privilege" and that "our movement must be as humane as the society we seek to create." I said that as graduates "we face the society characterized by fear, hatred, and greed. Every activity is marked by competition and the national character is molded around the influence of racism and male supremacy. When we look beyond our national boundaries or into the ghettos of our own cities, we see the other side of 'capitalist prosperity.' For a few to be prosperous and powerful, our present system demands that the many submit to human degradation, misery, and even death."

The choice, as I presented it, was simple:

It's graduation time and our choice is not that complicated. We can admit that our lives are a mass of contradictions–we can admit that the bourgeois existence is the existence of the living dead–we can confront our societally imposed inhibitions about using force and confronting authority, and we can recognize our responsibility to humankind. Indeed we can join the struggle or we can cast our lot with the other side. We can run with the movement or against it. We can try to destroy imperialism or we can implicitly work toward destroying the revolution, but the middle ground never was and never will be habitable.

Vietnamese are dying. Latin Americans are dying. Africans are dying. Black Americans are dying—revolutionaries throughout the world are struggling against imperialism, colonialism, capitalism, and the totalitarian bureaucracy that goes under the name of socialism in Russia. Revolutionaries are dying and we are still scabbing. At every stage in our development they will attempt to hand us the maudlin grey gowns of the aggressor. We must be strong and direct and we must choose instead the Black and Red of revolution.

The person with those views, remember, was a student at MIT in those years, prominent and respected precisely because of the views summarized above and the militancy with which they were espoused and acted on. That says nothing much about me, but it says a ton about the times. The article that immediately followed my essay in the yearbook was, ironically, one by James Killian projecting his expectations for the next fifty years. Later in the yearbook is an article about student government. The page before the student government article is the full-page photo of me reaching to pick up a folder from Max Millikan's desk in the Center for International Studies, which we were occupying at the time. Yet, in the section for head shots of the graduating class I am missing. I didn't graduate then, remember, I was thrown out. The yearbook folks snubbed the administration, though, by including the full-page photo instead, among several other photos of me throughout the volume.

Fred Hoyle was a very capable physicist who, when told as a child that the law required him to attend school, said of his experience, "I concluded that, unhappily, I had been born into a world dominated by a rampaging monster called 'law' that was both all powerful and all stupid." That's a fitting epitaph for my time at MIT.

PART 2

The Ringing Of Revolution

In the 1960s, we believed we were revolutionaries winning a new society. There was evidence all around, from Berkeley to Boston, New York to Prague, and Washington, DC to Mexico City. It didn't happen that way. The chimes of freedom rang, but with steadily diminishing tone and timbre in subsequent years. Only the most attuned ears continued to hear revolution's message.

Great symphonies rise and fall in volume. When decibels are highest, symphonies are not always greatest. In fact, often, it is precisely when they are least audible that symphonies are laying their groundwork and gathering steam. Similarly, social projects sometimes hang on, reentrench, and get set to climax during calm passages. The low decibel times are often the hard part. They are often the critical part. Nonetheless, Part 2 of *Remembering Tomorrow* continues exploring high decibel times. Here is a poem, "Wheel of Law," from Ho Chi Minh that meant a lot to me in 1969 and still does.

> After the rain, good weather.
> In the wink of an eye
> the universe throws off its muddy clothes.
> For ten thousand miles the land
> spreads out like a beautiful brocade.
> Light breezes. Smiling flowers.
> High in the trees, among the sparkling leaves
> all the birds sing at once.
> People and animals rise up reborn.
>
> What could be more natural?
> After sorrow, comes joy.

Chapter 10

Bean Town

The Old Mole Forever Surfacing

> *Revolution is not a onetime event.*
> *—Audre Lorde*

The "Old Mole" was Karl Marx's metaphor for revolution. It would burrow below ground, coming up to undermine capitalism's foundations. It would show up uninvited. It would sully the polite gardens of the ruling class. It would ring in a new world. The *Old Mole* in Boston, circa 1968, however, was an underground newspaper. So was the *Berkeley Barb, The Great Speckled Bird* from Atlanta, New York's *East Village Other,* and the *Chicago Seed*, for that matter, among many others.

Boston's *Old Mole* operated out of a storefront on Brookline Street running off Massachusetts Avenue, which, in turn, was Cambridge's main street, running from MIT through Central Square to Harvard University and beyond. Each week for a couple of years numerous folks helped produce the *Old Mole*. We didn't consciously work to create innovative divisions of labor, but *Old Mole* work was mostly volunteer and largely collective, and made at least some inroads against sexism, as well. Issues were sold or given away throughout Cambridge and Boston. Each time there was a crisis there would be a special issue of the *Old Mole*, so there was one for the Harvard strike, one for the November Action Coalition, and so on. Many people typed and laid out each issue. Many wrote content, and many more handed out issues or sold them. There were two communities—one that worked on and distributed the *Old Mole* and one that "consumed it"—and the ties were close. The *Old Mole* served the local left and with the network of associated similar weekly papers around the country was a powerful part of our growing movement. These papers incorporated lots of people's labor, including people learning to work together in new ways. They generated a product that could

113

be utilized for consciousness raising, morale boosting, agenda setting, and as an organizing tool providing information useful to undertaking actions including relevant timetables, addresses, etc.

The contemporary counterpart of the sixties underground press is partly local print papers, and partly the network that is called IndyMedia and Web sites more generally, including ZNet, the Web site I work on. Together, all this may well be larger than sixties alternative media. The internal clarity about values and social relations is often stronger now, too, due to lessons we have learned over the years. The general political awareness of editorial policy may be greater now as well. But there is also unquestionably something missing. The *Old Mole* and other underground papers were a kind of cultural meeting ground. People identified with these projects and were excited about and personally involved with them. The office of an underground paper like the *Old Mole* was always alive and bustling. The announcements in the paper were grist for people's weekly agendas much like TV listings currently organize many people's evenings. The lifestyles and culture of people at the *Old Mole* and similar institutions weren't contrary to those of the public that the papers appealed to, but instead grew from that public. If you looked at the way *Old Mole*-ers dressed, ate, talked, played, celebrated, and thought, and then did the same for their immediate audience of readers, and then did the same for a much wider pool of people beyond that reading audience, differences would be minor. The sixties counterculture was much bigger than the Left. The counterculture recruited from mass society. The Left recruited from the counterculture. The Left, in that sense, swam in a congenial sea. *Old Mole* writers and readers had a very large community in which we looked, talked, and celebrated like everyone else, just having somewhat more radical politics. The problematic interface was between that substantial sea of folks—the whole counterculture, which was considerably bigger than the Left—and the rest of society.

Nowadays, the Left has no massive surrounding congenial counterculture. We are no longer swimming in a much larger sea that we communicate well with. We are today right smack dab in society. There is no buffer between us and them, and our engagements with them are uncongenial not least because the gap is so large between how we look, talk, celebrate, and think, and how everyone else looks, talks, celebrates, and thinks. In the heady days of the sixties, in other words, we leftists didn't have nearly as much need to deal with the mainstream. We could grow our movement without learning how to address people of wildly different style, manner, and commitment. We could venture into the nearby friendly and relatively massive counterculture to enlarge our size. Nowadays, to grow, the Left has to recruit among people very different not just in politics, but in tastes and preferences too.

CD Too

Imagine all the people sharing all the world.
—*John Lennon*

The People's Coalition for Peace and Justice (PCPJ) was analogous, thirty years ago, to the coalition named United for Peace and Justice (UFPJ) that is a key organizational locus of widespread U.S. dissent in 2006. There are people, indeed, who were involved then and are still involved now, for example, Leslie Cagan. She has been a key figure in holding UFPJ together and she was active, as well, in PCPJ. For that matter, Cagan, a friend for decades, has been in that position over and over, from coalition and project to coalition and project.

PCPJ came together by way of an intersection of religious, secular, welfare, and campus-based organizing. It had New Left and Old Left components. The American Friends Service Committee was prominent. The National Welfare Rights Organization was prominent. I worked mostly in the Boston branch of PCPJ, as did Sid Peck, one of the organization's key conveners, and Dave Dellinger, one of its most prominent members. I attended national meetings as a youthful representative from our area.

PCPJ formed to oppose the war and also to try to broaden the then-surging antiwar opposition into fighting racism, poverty, sexism, and other foreign policy injustices, giving rise to the "J" in PCPJ. There was a second key coalition at the time also planning national events. It was a creation of the Socialist Workers Party, colloquially called the Trots. It had less local infrastructure and wasn't as multi-issue. This parallelism of old style and new style interestingly still exists thirty-five years later, with today's UFPJ paralleled by an outfit called ANSWER, which fronts for the Workers World Party. Whereas I think UFPJ is more politically sophisticated in diverse ways than PCPJ was, having progressed over the years, ANSWER is arguably worse than its counterpart from the past, having devolved politically.

At any rate, PCPJ meetings that I attended could be characterized as having three main dimensions. The first was for members to report the day-to-day achievements of local chapters and member organizations, including their staffs and affiliated organizers. Local venues were where the actual work got done: preparing materials, arranging for and sending out speakers to all manner of sites; welcoming and initiating new participants to ongoing activity in the local offices, at vigils and at places where materials were handed out, and so on; and holding smaller events that fed into larger regional or national ones. Second, we heard about finances, which were handled by committees I wasn't privy to. Financial reports would affect the budgets of national and local events and therefore what staffs and organizers could hope to spend. Third, we would decide matters such as dates of activities and their broad tactical definitions. PCPJ was a coalition of member organizations. Meetings were of representatives from those organizations.

I didn't change my actions much as a result of the birth and growth of PCPJ, other than attending meetings, offering opinions, voting, and so on. I was a kind of roving PCPJ speaker, mostly to student groups, but at times, also to labor gatherings or community groups, which is pretty much what I was doing before working with PCPJ, too. Lydia Sargent and I met through PCPJ, and became interested in each other while attending a national conference. She became a staff person for the organization, handling schedules, literature, timing, and pretty much everything that made PCPJ go. This was when Lydia was first becoming politically knowledgeable. Even before that had fully occurred, however, she was helping make the office more effective, often contributing more than those who'd been involved longer in political activism.

Perhaps the major achievement of the local Boston PCPJ chapter was the work involved in carrying out a key local action timed as a close follow-up to the May Day demonstrations in Washington, DC. May Day was wild in the streets. We went, we dispersed, and we tried to shut down the city. Because of the action's character, even though it was national, my guess would be that only three or four thousand people participated. We were young, highly mobile, and ready to rumble. The Boston follow-up was quite different.

Boston's event was to be a day of highly organized civil disobedience. The target was Boston's Federal Building. The proximate goal was to keep everyone out for the day. In that sense, it was like Seattle's later anticorporate globalization demonstration, though this was local and therefore not as large. About 5,000 Bostonians participated. We surrounded the Federal Building, packing ourselves in, sitting in the streets and on the sidewalks and paths right outside, to block all axis routes. We surrounded the building from well before nine in the morning until four in the afternoon. Periodically some intrepid government worker, or perhaps a police agent masquerading as a worker, would seek to enter the building. The person would have to wade through rows of demonstrators, packed like sardines, with aggressive aid from a phalanx of police. Sometimes there was pushing and shoving. Other times, people were clubbed aside.

The human barrier took different forms and was differently effective at different doors. In some places people blocking paths were older and less physical. At the more active main doors, younger and more militant elements blocked access. Students from different schools arrived early and had different rendezvous and gathering points, as did members of organizations. So, at each site, all around the Federal Building, there were well-prepared contingents who knew how to handle whatever might arise, and how to help others who were less prepared.

There were also people to educate and agitate, and to try to enlist new participants into ongoing involvement. We also brought medics and lawyers, well organized and carefully situated. All this was courtesy of the groundwork done by PCPJ staff and main volunteers. Of course, the real measure of the day was not how many times the government could talk a civil servant into being escorted through our ranks by club-wielding cops. It was, instead, what changes occurred in people's minds and in our organizational infrastructure by virtue of all the work leading to, involved in, and following upon, the events.

How many previously pro war people were shook up a bit? How many new people were, for the first time, willing to talk about issues with others? How many people became dissenters? How many people had their commitment increased (or decreased) and their understanding enhanced (or diminished)? What was the residual gain or loss in ties and organizational infrastructure that would facilitate organizing new talks, rallies, and confrontations leading in turn to a larger and more effective activism? When I went home from the demonstration, thinking through these questions was how I evaluated what had gone on. Many others went home tallying tactical trends, as in "how many people got in" or "did the war end." As a result, I saw events as victories that they saw as defeats. I maintained morale where they felt shattered.

Regarding major decisions in PCPJ, there were always a few prominent fault lines. First was the issue of militancy and tactics. Some favored more aggressive or violent options. Others favored avoiding anything aggressive or violent. Obeying or disobeying the law was another divide. Sometimes an advocate, on either side, felt allegiance to a tactic, per se. Such a person might say let's kick ass, because they liked kicking ass or at least they liked talking about kicking ass. Someone else might say, no, we can't obstruct or maybe we can't even march because obstructing or marching could lead to confrontations in which people might engage in violent acts—because they liked nonviolence, per se. Others of us weren't always for passive nonviolence, active nonviolence, aggressive confrontations, or all-out ass-kicking, but were, instead, intent on choosing tactics that led to desirable outcomes case-by-case.

Other issues that were also nearly always debated included geography, as in doing things locally or centrally. For some people this, too, was a case-by-case matter. Would a greater local or national emphasis yield better results? Was a mix best? For other people, one position or the other was deemed always right.

Likewise, small is beautiful meant for some PCPJers that you didn't have to evaluate the actual situation, you just always knew you wanted local and smaller, not national and larger. Other PCPJers always felt the opposite. They always wanted more people centrally together, period. Neither side needed to think through each specific case. Their allegiances were for them *a priori* true. For me, tactical allegiances about locale, scale, or tone that considered themselves immune to context were incredibly frustrating.

I remember, for example, being in way too many excessively long meetings listening to people argue for big demonstrations in Washington, DC, on the one hand, or for never going to Washington, DC and always having only local demonstrations all over the country, on the other hand. The problem was that people often acted as if opting for one or the other choice was a matter of principle. They thought favoring one or the other option marked a moral divide. In fact, of course, the matter was contextual. We should have always asked what choice, given where we were at, would best propel us forward.

In these engagements, I came to realize that reasonable people could certainly disagree about all these matters, but that it was not reasonable to think tactics were anything other than a contextual matter. To me, then as now, whether we want to have sexism in a better world is a matter of principle. Whether we want popular control over social life is a matter of principle. Whether we want wage slavery is a matter of principle. The decision as to whether movements should embody these dreaded features, or even celebrate them, could by extension also be called principled. But choices of what to do in a particular context, for a particular demonstration, I considered contextual and tactical, not principled. Of course, my not being a pacifist, or much worse, law abiding, was a factor. If I felt that to ever lift my hand, or even my voice, against some target, was simply and irretrievably wrong, then, yes, some tactical decisions might have seemed to me principled. But that was never my situation.

To me, it became clear that whether a movement should be very passive or very militant, abide all laws or go out of its way to break some, seek only to construct or also to destroy, and, finally, whether it should wage violent assaults, even—or war—were all a matter of careful case-by-case judgment. There was a higher burden of proof for some behaviors than for others, certainly, but it was precisely because those approaches risked undermining lasting change.

In the sixties, sometimes I was dead set against aggressive marching, much less civil disobedience. Mostly, though, I favored such things, and even at times favored great militancy and disruption, including rioting. It depended on context. I thought ripping up a legal injunction might help us in one place and be disastrous in another. We had to weigh off implications. I thought moving from peaceful legal marches to civil disobedience might enrich our internal growth and spread our appeal, or maybe not, depending on the time and place. For me, the same held for sitting in, striking, occupying a building, trashing a building, or rioting. The principle was to enlarge, deepen, broaden, and intensify movement opposition to injustice and, in time, movement advocacy of positive goals. The tactic was to accomplish those ends rather than, hands waving and voices soaring, to do something that felt or looked good, but obstructed gains.

Another key fault line in the sixties was activists having various attitudes to the question of representation. There were meetings in which someone would talk or vote who responsibly represented a large organization's members. Then someone else would talk or vote representing no one. Obviously, these should not have been treated alike, yet often they were. This was unsolvable, I think, short of having a much more participatory structure than was typical in the sixties.

Regarding discussion and work, there were fault lines about political differences that existed beyond coalition agreements. How would we deal with the fact that one PCPJ member organization thought x, and another thought y, where x and y were contradictory? Should we just not allow either position in the coalition and not talk about it? Should we recognize and try to address the divide? This was a conundrum, over and over. Later, I came to feel that solving this problem of solidarity along with autonomy was central to making practical progress and that we had never even properly taken up the matter in the sixties.

Another issue was race and gender. Everyone claimed, at least once the women's movement and the Black Power movement had been around awhile, to understand the need for organizational congeniality to and empowerment of women and minorities. But accomplishing this aim wasn't straightforward. Likewise, many times in PCPJ the face-off was between those who were young and those who were older, and between those aligned to old politics and those aligned to new politics. It seemed to me, then, that the young and the new were more often right. We brought a multi-issue tone into the movement, as well as militancy, dynamism, and civil disobedience. We rejected old-style Leninist organizational hierarchy and sectarianism, even sectarianism toward sectarians. We rejected timid movement legalisms and primness. We asserted self-management, popular participation, militancy, and daily-life innovation. By and large, this made the young better than the old as sources of movement policy. But, there were also serious exceptions.

We young folks often made huge errors and took our insights distressingly too far. We disparaged many people for ignorant reasons. We celebrated ourselves too much, often mistaking bravado for serious achievement. There were older folks we could have learned from, had we listened more closely and had they managed to convey their lessons more adroitly. Abbie Hoffman, Rennie Davis, and Tom Hayden, for example, were very impressive young people, and were right about a great many things. But Dave Dellinger, old in age though young at heart, would have been a far better role model. The point is, I only later realized, the issue in these disputes isn't age. The issue isn't duration. Among those with a lot of age and duration there will be fools as well as wise and effective activists, just as there will be fools and wise and effective activists among the young. The trick is to find insight and wisdom, whatever package it comes in.

That said, there is no doubt that in the sixties the lifeblood of left enthusiasm, innovation, and membership was youth. At a big meeting, if someone over thirty entered the room, it was reason to look up and smile, maybe even applaud. Nowadays, in 2006, almost the reverse imbalance obtains. For example, at an April 2005 conference in NYC called the Left Forum, opening night had a big panel discussion and a large proportion of the weekend's attendees were there. I looked around and felt the average age might have been fifty, or perhaps older. This is a huge difference between forty years ago and now. It isn't that there are too many old people now—it is that there are too few young people.

White Rioting

> *Now at midnight all the agents*
> *And the superhuman crew*
> *Come out and round up everyone*
> *That knows more than they do.*
> *—Bob Dylan*

One demonstration during the years of siege in Boston and Cambridge was aimed at Harvard's Center for International Affairs (CFIA). It was a three-pronged event. First there was to be a large antiwar rally at the Boston Common. This would be entirely peaceful, with no confrontation and no laws broken. It would have speakers, fanfare, and the usual rally protocol. Then there would be a march down Commonwealth Avenue through Boston, over the Massachusetts Avenue Bridge past MIT, and on toward Harvard. This would arrive at a target for a militant demonstration.

It was not pre-announced where we were going or what we were going to do there. The idea was to not let the authorities know in advance. There was what we called, in those days, a tactical leadership committee. The same thing had existed for NAC and other events that required secrecy. Usually our movement operated entirely openly, ratifying and carrying out details of broadly agreed plans in public. In this case, though, the tactical leadership was given leeway. And leeway it took. We picked a real target, Harvard's CFIA, but we discretely leaked through various channels that the target was, instead, Cambridge City Hall, about two-thirds of the way from MIT to where the CFIA sat on the outskirts of Harvard Square. The ploy worked. The Cambridge police were squeezed into City Hall waiting for our arrival. They expected to surprise us and quickly squelch our efforts.

I remember the large march crossing the Harvard Bridge. Few of us knew exactly where we were going. About half roughly knew what kind of mayhem was coming. The rest knew only vaguely that something was afoot. There were people rolling baby carriages. There were older folks who would be quite out of place. Some of us circulated in the jolly crowd telling people they should peel off just after Central Square. The message was received. We got about a block from City Hall and the remaining march, now just a few hundred strong, broke into a run right past City Hall and on to the CFIA, our real target.

When the running crowd got to the CFIA, entry was gained after Lydia went around back, found an open door, came to the front, and opened the doors for us all. One group then ran right into the building and trashed it from within, tossing stuff out. The other contingent ran around the building and started trashing it from without, tossing stuff in. It was amazing that there were no serious accidents due to those outside hitting those within or vice versa. There was bedlam and much damage quickly done, but the cops, though initially outwitted, were not resigned to utter failure. They trucked on up from City Hall even as we left the CFIA to avoid a fight with them.

A somewhat similar prior demonstration occurred in 1970, a day after a national Free Bobby Seale demo (he was the head of the Black Panthers and incarcerated at the time). First we held an antiwar rally at Boston Common. Then, as in the CFIA case, a march went to Cambridge, thinning along the way, leading into Harvard Square. At the Square there ensued one of the few organized, rather than spontaneous, sessions of mayhem and destruction that we had in those days.

Mostly the attacks were against large chain stores, luxury designer-type stores, and every bank and office that anyone could find. Bookstores and small restaurants and newsstands, and even small clothing or specialty stores, were spared. Everything else in range was a target for hundreds of stones and bricks. At night, street fighting continued, and considerable looting as well. But this was the sixties and the other side wasn't comatose. I remember not only running around dodging police, but also standing and watching people trying without the slightest success to break massive windows in banks and in one particularly hated upscale clothing store. The owners of these establishments were not fools. They saw the sixties like some Floridians see hurricanes, and they had prepared with seriously shatterproof windowpanes.

The festivities—and these types of events did have a festival atmosphere—went on late into the night. I had an apartment at the time above some stores in Harvard Square and my friends and I were in and out for hours. Was there any point to rioting? Did it matter? Was there a downside? I felt at the time that the rally had the virtues of displaying our numbers, incorporating new people, and developing our capacities. The same was true of the march. The same held, also, for the later CFIA event, though, of course, it had its problematic aspects. But what about the riot itself?

My criteria then, as now, for judging this weren't much different than my criteria for judging anything else. Did it help those involved to arrive at a higher level of comprehension and commitment? (I doubt it.) Did it convey an image to people not involved that prodded them to think about society in ways that increased their likelihood of moving left? (For some yes, for others no.) Were those involved made more likely to stay active due to their involvement? (For some probably yes, for others no.) Were those who viewed the events or heard about them given reason to turn away from the Left rather than toward it? (Again, some yes, some no.) You have to remember, this was an action on top of lots of other actions, leading in turn to more, with recurring opportunity to convey counterimages to the worst that the media presented.

For me, the issue, then as now, wasn't how many windows were broken, how many laws were violated, how many knees were bruised, or how many heads were busted. It was the impact our acts had on the internal and outreach attributes of the movement and on the audience it sought to organize. I don't know the answer. My guess is we could have done better.

Chapter 11

Washington Bullets

Hard Rain

And I'll tell it and think it and speak it and breathe it,
And reflect it from the mountain so all souls can see it.
—Bob Dylan

In my life I have had one recurring nightmare. It was in my teen years. Planes flew over and dropped packages held by parachutes. The packages, floating gently down, contained nukes. Next, rockets blasted the world. Then I'd wake up. I didn't want to let anyone into that dream.

At the Z Media Institute summer school, in the mid-1990s, Stephen Shalom taught sessions on U.S. foreign policy, including addressing the Cuban Missile Crisis. This crisis was a time when our planet came closer than ever before, and probably than ever since, to nuclear war. It had inspired my nightmare. I went to hear Steve's session. He recounted how U.S. officials slept in bomb shelters throughout the crisis, how the CIA told Kennedy that they estimated a one-third to one-half chance of all-out nuclear war if he was belligerent, and Kennedy went ahead anyway. That was, the media told us, Kennedy at his finest—and that's my image of Washington, DC.

The United States and the Soviet Union had nuclear weapons and long-range missiles. In the 1960 presidential election between Nixon and Kennedy, Steve recounted, the hawk in that campaign—the more militaristic candidate—was the Democrat, John Kennedy. Kennedy said that a missile gap had opened under the do-nothing Republicans. He insisted that we hadn't built enough missiles to stay even with the Soviet Union. Using this scare tactic, among other means, Kennedy got elected.

In truth, there was indeed a missile gap, but contrary to Kennedy's claims, it was a gap of about 100 to 1 in the U.S.'s favor, as U.S. spy satellites confirmed.

U.S. officials decided they would tell the Soviet Union that we knew the gap was in our favor, while they told the American people the opposite. Shalom continued:

> You see Khrushchev, the Soviet leader, was a bit of a cheapskate. He thought that although the Soviet Union knew how to build missiles, they cost a lot of money. So he'd talk a big game and make a lot of threats and pretend he had a lot of missiles, but wouldn't build them. On May Day, he would have military parades in Red Square and he would have the Soviet Air Force fly over Red Square and they would go around behind some clouds and come back and fly over again and you would see more and more waves of planes and you would say, wow, look at that! It's all very impressive, but Khrushchev in fact didn't build any significant number of ICBMs.

So the United States, led by Kennedy, said to Khrushchev, we know you're bluffing. You can't push us around. In fact, we're going to push you around now because we're the ones who've got the advantage. In addition to its ICBMs, intercontinental-range ballistic missiles, the U.S. also had shorter range nuclear missiles in Turkey, right on the Soviet border.

Shalom recounted how the Soviet Union decided to respond to this nuclear imbalance by putting Soviet missiles in Cuba, ninety miles from the United States. They did so, secretly, but U.S. spy planes saw the missile sites being constructed, and Kennedy had to decide how to respond to this. One option, Shalom told the ZMIers, was to do nothing. After all, the Soviet Union could, in any event, deploy missiles in the Soviet Union. (Whether you're hit by a missile from Cuba or from Russia doesn't matter much, admitted Defense Secretary Robert McNamara.) Neither side was planning to launch a sneak attack on the other, so what's the big deal? A second option was to use this opportunity to do some disarming. We could say to the Soviet Union, hey, we'll trade our missiles in Turkey for your missiles in Cuba. While we're at it, let's get rid of some intercontinental-range ballistic missiles, too. Those two approaches were rejected by the Kennedy administration. They didn't advance militarism, imperialism, and U.S. war-making capability. Instead, the debate within the administration centered on three other options: (1) invade Cuba; (2) launch air strikes to take out the Soviet missile sites; and (3) put a blockade around Cuba to prevent remaining missiles from reaching the island.

The Air Force thought the air strike was the best strategy and Kennedy said to them, well, what happens when we knock out those missile sites, would we kill any Russians? The Air Force replied that we'd probably kill a few thousand Russians. Kennedy asked what happens if the Soviets respond by attacking West Berlin? That will start a nuclear war, remarked the Air Force. Kennedy was not that rash, and said he'd go with the blockade. But of course the problem with the blockade was that there was still enough equipment in Cuba that they could build from what they had, and how would a blockade stop that? Kennedy went on television and said that he was putting a blockade around Cuba. Any Soviet ship heading to Cuba would be stopped and searched. If it had military equipment, it would not be let in. Now, this was an act of war. Countries are allowed to trade with whomever they want. The United States didn't ask Soviet permission before sending its missiles to Turkey. Countries send weapons as their sovereign right to other countries.

Anyway, Kennedy announced the blockade. Khrushchev responded that he was not backing down. He was sending ships through. The U.S. Navy said it would sink any ships that tried to get through. The Soviet Union said they had submarines in the area and would sink us back, and the U.S. built up its force, and a Soviet ship got steadily closer to the U.S. blockade and it was a very scary 24 hours. Ultimately, Khrushchev turned his ships around and Dean Rusk, the U.S. Secretary of State, said it was a "game of chicken." "We were eyeball to eyeball, and they blinked first." The survival of the human race—a game of chicken.

Khrushchev offered Kennedy to trade the missiles in Cuba for the missiles in Turkey. Kennedy said that was unacceptable. You must grovel. You must surrender. There are some analysts who now say that privately Kennedy had decided that before he started a nuclear war he would have been willing to trade the missiles, but what's interesting is that for many, many years, even supposing that claim is true, it wasn't known. All the members of the Kennedy administration and all those writing about the Cuban missile crisis who said this was Kennedy's greatest hour thought that one of the great things about it was that Kennedy was willing to risk nuclear war in order to enforce the principle that the United States is allowed to put missiles in Turkey, next to Russia, and the Soviet Union is not allowed to have some missiles in Cuba, next to Florida.

Moreover, the U.S. missiles in Turkey were obsolete. The United States had already decided to remove the missiles in Turkey, not because the Soviet Union wanted them out, but for other reasons. The United States had recently developed submarine-launched missiles and thought it would be better to put submarines in the Mediterranean that could hit the Soviet Union with nuclear weapons. There was no need to retain vulnerable land-based missiles in Turkey. The missiles in Turkey were precarious. They were aboveground and a terrorist driving by could shoot a bullet through one of them. Thus, the United States was willing to risk nuclear war rather than trade off obsolete missiles for Soviet missiles. This was what has become known as Kennedy's greatest moment—the greatest victory of the Cold War. And it gave me nightmares. And those nightmares, apolitical, prepolitical, during my late high school and early college days, no doubt fueled my passions about the government in Washington, DC, and still do.

Of course, beyond the missile crisis and the Cold War, the main impetus for my own radicalization was Vietnam. It made my life what it is, even as it corrupted, curtailed, made courageous, or terminated millions of other lives, at that time and ever since. I remember a waking dream. I was in the TV room of a house I had lived in through high school. There was a woman with me, someone I had met at the sanctuary at Brandeis. Suddenly, I guess it was a psychosis of a kind, I was in Vietnam, a place I had never seen and still haven't visited. It was as if the TV room was the jungle. The warmth we had was suddenly for survival and not for pleasure. The sky was falling. The daydream lasted only a few minutes, though it was very vivid. Dreams aside, for me Vietnam will last forever, vividly. Imagine what Vietnam is for those who directly suffered its falling skies.

In Vietnam, the United States set numerous records for military malice. World War II was the Good War, Vietnam was the Bad War, and today very few Americans will say the Vietnam War was not a mistake. In Jane Fonda's autobiography, *My Life So Far*, she wrote that Vietnam persisted because bad presidents wanted to win elections and not seem wimpy. Bad persons were Jane's enemy. Other New Leftists, including myself, became more institution-oriented. The difference wasn't energy, commitment, or militancy. Jane gave her all. Who could ask for more? The difference was perspective. Heart matters, but so does mind. Even gung-ho military types agree that something went wrong. And yes, there were mistakes involved, and human venality, but of course, the sadder truth is that the Vietnam War wasn't a mistake at all, but a logical outgrowth of U.S. foreign policy.

The argument against Vietnam being an imperialist war goes, as Shalom told his ZMI students: "Look, we spent more in Vietnam than any possible estimates of the total value of any investments then or in the future in Vietnam. So how could finances have been the motivation?" Shalom answered his own question.

There's a bank down the street. Let's say the bank is robbed and the robbers take $5,000. The police will chase these robbers. They will chase them across state borders. They will spend great amounts to catch them, put them on trial, and put them in prison. And if you add up that total cost–of the police work, the courts, and the prison—it will be incredibly beyond $5,000, and so you might say, well, what's the logic of that? Well, the logic of it is—as any public official will readily tell you—that if you don't stop this bank robber—if you let this bank robber get away with it—if you let bank robbers know they can get away with this kind of thing, there will be bank robberies all over the place. And so the purpose of catching and punishing this bank robber, whatever the cost, is not just to punish this one but to deter others, and that's the way one needs to look at U.S. foreign policy.

The U.S. position in the sixties, until the nineties when it began to look at literally everything greedily, was that the entire world except for China and the

Soviet Union was part of the American capitalist system. As Shalom put it, against China and the Soviet Union Washington would try subversive actions, but it wasn't going to pursue an all-out war. The rest of the world, however, was going to be subordinated to the United States, and so Washington had to deliver an uncompromising message to third-world revolutionaries everywhere: If you try to break out, we will smash you. The benefit U.S. policy makers expected to get from defeating the Vietnamese was not that this one piece of territory would be added to the U.S. empire instead of extricated from it, but rather that everyone would understand that you don't leave the U.S. empire when the United States doesn't want you to leave it.

United States officials talked about the domino theory and claimed that if Vietnam falls, Laos will fall, Cambodia will fall, Thailand will fall, all like a stack of dominos. That's why we're in Vietnam, said Eisenhower, Kennedy, Johnson, and Nixon. What they meant was that subversives were going to come in from outside and hop from place to place and overthrow otherwise stable systems. The claim was ridiculous. There were no hoppers and there were no otherwise stable systems. But there was a sensible version of their theory, which was that if revolution succeeded in Vietnam, revolutionaries in other countries would say, hey, we could have better lives too. We don't have to accept U.S. domination. To prevent that lesson from spreading, what Chomsky called "the threat of a good example," it was crucial for the United States to make sure the Vietnamese revolution failed. The Vietnamese couldn't be allowed to become free and prosperous, not because we were sadists, but because our elites wanted to maintain their world dominance.

For the United States, Vietnam was a war to prevent the spread of a good example. It was a war to demonstrate U.S. might and resolve. It was a war to teach that resistance is futile and costly. It was a war to drop bombs, bombs, and more bombs. Millions died. For the Vietnamese, Vietnam was resistance to win independence and freedom. It was resistance to demonstrate that the power of the people is greater than the man's technology. It was resistance to inspire, inform, and motivate. It was resistance to fight, fight, and fight—to win a new world. Washington was the architect of Vietnam, Laos, and Cambodia's destruction. It was a giant axe mercilessly beheading nations. Washington won the proximate war. Freedom-inspired dominos did not fall. At the same time, Vietnam not only repelled our troops—its aspirations will win in the end. And I sure as hell hated Washington. And I sure as hell loved the spirit of the Vietnamese resistance. Vietnam was for me a parent, a brother, a sister, a life guide. Vietnam was and still is everything for me. But then again, so is Nicaragua, El Salvador, Iraq, and so are Watts and Seattle, and every employee punching every clock, waiting for, and at some deep level, however unknowingly, getting ready to fight for, liberation.

Pentagon Demo

I don't care what others say
They say we don't listen anyway.
—Lester Chambers

T he 1967 Pentagon demonstration kicked off the massive period of the national antiwar era. Roughly 200,000 of us assembled in DC and marched to the Pentagon. There were Yippees trying to levitate the place, militants hoping to rumble, organizers celebrating the turnout and energizing themselves for more to come, and attendees mostly moving further leftward. The event was a great success. The Pentagon was ringed with young soldiers standing at attention, holding rifles with bayonets. This was the home of the masters of war, after all. But the Pentagon's guards could be dealt with. Organizers talked to them. Hippies put flowers into the barrels of their guns. The soldiers were a captive audience, at least until the final stages over thirty hours later. They had to stand. They had to hear us out. Every so often one would break down, drop his weapon and walk off, sick at the position he was in. Whoever defended the citadel of violence was assaulted by men, women, girls, and boys all exuding peace and calmly presenting stomach-turning facts about the military's behavior.

Only a small number of soldiers broke ranks, but you could easily see harbingers of the dissolution that was to come in the forests of Vietnam. Most of the impact was on us and on the country. But on the other side, it wasn't just the soldiers who had their consciousness jolted and went AWOL. Daniel Ellsberg later reported that on the day of the demonstration he had been in Robert McNamara's office, helping draft plans to invade North Vietnam. Hearing noises, Ellsberg and McNamara went to a window and saw demonstrators being clubbed. Ellsberg reports looking on and saying to himself, "They are putting their bodies where their hearts and minds are. What would happen if I did that?" Just as watching card-burnings in the Arlington Street Church changed me, Ellsberg was changed by watching our collective resistance to the Pentagon. He followed suit in his own way, surreptitiously releasing the aptly titled *Pentagon Papers*. That is a real profile in courage.

I could also see at that time the tremendous power of a movement that was only a little bit beyond its audience in the broader society, a movement that didn't appear so different, so otherworldly, as to seem crazy or alien. This is precisely what was lost to our movement as time passed. The movement began to separate itself in its internal manners, tone, style, and appearance from its potential audience. This was largely, I think, an identity problem, but it caused a communication problem. At first we were Americans, concerned about our country's misadventure. Then we were hippies, with confrontational cultural consciousness. Then we were outlaws situating ourselves as far from the mainstream as we could take up residence. Had we been able to remain concerned Americans but with more and more consciousness, our ability to reach others might have been greater. We were too insecure for that, though. Politics had come into our lives too quickly. From school to mayhem, from the constitution to anarchist manifestoes, from Jefferson to Che—we transformed overnight. Our commitments were often tenuous and we protected ourselves against backsliding by going further and further from our past as forcefully as we could. It's easy to see in hindsight that aggressively differentiating ourselves was self-defeating. But we faced a Catch-22. Those who didn't escalatingly rebel almost universally slid back toward the mainstream.

How do I put this? We went from doubting deceit, to doubting everyone over thirty, and from doubting everyone over thirty to decrying everyone over twenty-five. Smash patriarchy became smash monogamy, and for some, it even became smash your parents. Rejection of the war, racism, and later sexism was paramount, to be sure, but personal devolution pursuing independence sometimes warped its potentials. In hindsight, we could have achieved more had we avoided overplaying our hands. But it could be that as we thought then, had we not overplayed our hands our hands would have overplayed us.

Looking back, I can see that it was hard, especially when young and surrounded by deceit, to not put up barriers to separate ourself from the rot. And the easiest barrier to erect was a wall of difference and denigration. Instead of being organizers rooted in new insights as well as in respect for and communication with the broad population we needed to reach, we let the allure of our new insights drag us away from continuing connection to that broad population. This distancing of ourselves from the lives lived all around us, plus our inability to move from fighting for ideas and lifestyles to fighting for lasting institutional gains, were two of the key reasons our sixties movements accomplished less than we might have. These same factors diminished movement achievement in the seventies, eighties, and nineties, too.

Mr. CIA

> *The other day upon the stair, I saw a man who wasn't there.*
> *He wasn't there again today, I think he's with the CIA.*
> *—Anonymous*

Years later, Lydia and I were in Washington for a very different, but also massive, antiwar event, and on the way to it we visited our then-South End Press coworker Cynthia Peters at her home. Cynthia came aboard SEP at a very young age, but right from the start was not only a full contributor but a leading light and tireless and innovative builder of alternative institutions as well as an innovative community organizer. Cynthia's father—Cynthia fell far from the family tree—worked for the CIA his whole adult life. He climbed the infrastructure and for many administrations briefed presidents on CIA news and projects. The presidents came and went. Cynthia's dad remained. He was part of the permanent government. Cynthia's dad was serious business and during my brief time at Cynthia's house, her dad, Mr. CIA, and I got into an interesting discussion. It was not long after the United States had invaded the tiny island of Grenada to further U.S. aims there, eliminating any chance for there to be a government that might nationalistically pursue the well-being of the tiny island's citizens even against U.S. desires. Possible extrication from what was called the "Free World" to pursue domestic development in their own style was, of course, also the sin of the Vietnamese, the Nicaraguans, the Salvadorans, and so on.

Grenada's entire military establishment could have been quickly defeated, I would wager, by the police force of Phoenix, Arizona, or certainly by the campus police of the University of Chicago, which was the fourth-largest military force in Illinois after the Illinois National Guard, the Illinois state police, and the city of Chicago's police force. This latter fact I learned when speaking at that campus. I heard about how freshmen would have an opening indoctrination session in which they were told that if they strayed off campus they were on their own, and that the campus police were there to prevent that disastrous possibility and to protect them while they were on campus. The University of Chicago, you see, was on the edge of Chicago's black side of town, and the line between town and campus was a serious matter. Cross at your own risk. Think about a country with such an internal divide needing such a force to patrol its centers of higher learning. Well, that was the country that wreaked havoc upon the tiny little island of Grenada.

The CIA Web site tells us, in 2005, that Grenada's population is just under 90,000 people. It is "about twice the size of Washington DC," the CIA site reports. Under "Background," the site has this to say, and only this: "One of the smallest independent countries in the western hemisphere, Grenada was seized by a Marxist military council on 19 October 1983. Six days later the island was invaded by US forces and those of six other Caribbean nations, which quickly captured the ringleaders and their hundreds of Cuban advisers. Free elections were reinstituted the following year." Without belaboring the point, what really happened was the United States trounced the widely-backed domestic preferences of the people of Grenada into oblivion.

So, at Cynthia's house, her dad and I got into a discussion of the events. I was condemning, of course, what my country had done, and while Cynthia's dad was generally completely closemouthed about politics—not just with guests but also with Cynthia and her whole family and all their friends, as a good career CIA officer should be—with me, for some completely unfathomable reason, he momentarily loosened up just a tiny bit.

He asked me why I thought the U.S. did it. I said I believed it was to punish even the prospect of another country, no matter how tiny, escaping from subordination to U.S. dictates, and in particular, to prevent the spread of such behavior. In Chomsky's words, I said, it was to curb the threat of a good example. Mr. CIA said, but how could such a small place matter? I said, if this minute speck in the ocean could extricate itself from subservience to our international priorities, then other countries would think they could do so too—such as Brazil, not having sufficient foresight to suggest Venezuela.

I added that this was also my view about the motives driving the Indochina War. I thought it was ridiculous to think it was a war for tungsten or for some other resource found in Indochina. There was nothing Vietnamese so needed by the U.S. that even megamaniacs would risk the U.S. economy's stability to fight for it. Rather, the domino theory, just as Kissinger claimed, was the real explanation. But it was not Kissinger's stated domino dynamic at work. Kissinger didn't really think that if we didn't intervene and kill the communist parasite, marauding commies from outside would infect, subvert, and topple country after country. That was nonsense promulgated only to rationalize our actions. Kissinger worried instead about a "good example" domino dynamic: that is, the idea that if Vietnam could extricate itself and use its national resources and assets for the well-being of its own people, so too might Thailand, Malaysia, or even India. We had to nip nationalism that ran contrary to Americanism in the bud. Nationalism that supported Americanism was fine, of course, as in our later supporting Saddam Hussein, the Taliban, and so on, until they violated our instructions and we crushed them. The domino-toppling that we feared after Vietnam, and that we worked to prevent by unleashing unholy combustion on Vietnam, was based on internal nationalist and progressive trends, not on external coercion. As far as externalities, we were the mother of all external pressures and have been ever since, all over the world.

Well, Mr. CIA just laughed at all this and said he didn't know anyone in government who could come up with, and very few who would even understand, a rationale so subtle and clever. So I said, okay then, what's your explanation for the U.S. role in subverting nationalist and socialist trends in the tiny economically imperceptible island of Grenada? And he said his explanation was easy. If Grenada became an ally of the Soviet Union instead of the U.S., it might house some Soviet missiles. If that happened, we would have to retarget some of our missiles to take out Grenada in the event of war. I looked at him and wondered to myself, is Mr. CIA trying to make me believe this, or is he tacitly admitting that I am right in what I have been saying?

I said, you seriously want me to believe that we trounced these people and denied them their dignity and their preferred future not to prevent a trend that could seriously undermine U.S. economic and social control internationally, but, instead, because we didn't want to have to change the programming of two or three missiles to point at Grenada rather than at their current destinations?

Could it be that Mr. CIA's explanation was really the thinking behind U.S. policy, and that it was only by chance that the choices fit my explanation? Did he believe what he offered? I didn't think either could be the case. There are people, even highly placed, who believe the lunatic rationales that media offer to explain U.S. policymaking, but not Mr. CIA. On the other hand, Mr. CIA fathered Cynthia Peters, who spent a decade at SEP, making it better than it would otherwise have been, and who has been an activist organizer with extraordinary commitment, talent, and insight ever since. Strange tree.

May Day

Tell no lies, claim no easy victories.
—Amilcar Cabral

Getting back to the sixties, looking at all the Washington gatherings and events from on high, you could see a clear progression. At first our gatherings were only massive rallies. Then they were marches with a rally. Then we leapt to acts of civil disobedience that we appended onto the march/rally foundation. And then we leapt to May Day 1971. For May Day we said, let's forego the rally. Let's have the civil disobedience only. And let's make it memorable.

The logic was sound. The powers that be were pursuing the war to prevent the Vietnamese from gaining control over their own country, resources, and labor and utilizing it in ways that weren't dictated by U.S. corporate interests, but that instead sprung from Vietnamese national concerns. The danger was "the spread of a good example." If Vietnam could extricate itself from U.S. domination, so could Thailand, Laos, and maybe even India. Vietnam itself mattered marginally. Vietnam as an example mattered immensely.

The way I first grasped the point was to conduct a dreadful thought experiment. I imagined that a meteor hit Vietnam and wiped it off the face of the globe. I realized the geopolitical and economic loss to the United States would have been barely discernable. Returning to the real universe, if by its active and courageous resistance Vietnam removed itself from the international circuits of U.S. capital and took over its own destiny, I realized the demonstration effect would cost a lot. My deduction was that the war was not to prevent "the loss of Vietnam," but to prevent Vietnam's extricating itself teaching others that they could extricate themselves too. The war in Indochina sought to teach that if you try to escape us, if you violate us in any way, you will not only fail, you will go backwards, bombed, if necessary, back to the Stone Age. As far as I can tell, the same logic has informed U.S. policy ever since.

As we saw it, from the president on up to the heads of major corporations, U.S. elites were intent on pursuing the war to defend corporate and geopolitical interests. We in the antiwar movement, in contrast, wanted to stop it. We send, say, 200,000 people to the Pentagon to protest. Later we send, say, 400,000 and then more. So what? Why would this matter to DC's elites? For me, the answer was that our acts would only cause elites to reconsider Vietnam policy if they raised a specter of cost greater than the costs that elites felt losing the war entailed. Elites had to feel that pursuing the war was going to diminish their interests more than stopping the war would diminish their interests. They had to feel that the disruptions wrought by the movement were more dangerous to their power and wealth than Vietnam going its own way.

In that light, our assembling lots of people in DC over and over, but having the actions and numbers stabilize at some high level, would be irrelevant. Even if we put half a million people outside the White House every month, if the number of people stayed the same every time, the crowd's threat would diminish to zero because its trajectory would lead nowhere. As long as the numbers of demonstrators weren't steadily growing and their demeanor wasn't steadily becoming more militant, the White House could endure the annoyance of having to clean up after us. The powers that be would not have to worry about dissent unless dissent threatened their most basic interests.

The logic of going to Washington first with a rally, then with a march and a rally, then with a rally and civil disobedience, and then with just plain old disruption, was to convey that the movement was getting bigger and stronger and, moreover, that its focus was broadening from just this war to all war, and from war to capitalism. Our escalation said to elites, if you keep on with Vietnam, you may encounter problems at home that are too big to endure. It was the same logic as having demos in DC, and then, later, all over the country. We had to diversify, multiply, and intensify. If we weren't growing, we weren't threatening.

When elite individuals changed from advocating the war to opposing it, they would often hold press conferences announcing their decisions. They wouldn't say, I have discovered that dropping bombs and napalm on illiterate peasants to defend U.S. power is immoral. They wouldn't say I have discovered that the men from Detroit and Dallas and Des Moines sent to Indochina who come home in coffins or without limbs don't deserve that fate. They would instead say that our streets are in turmoil. We are losing the next generation. The fabric of society is being torn asunder. I can no longer in good conscience abide the war. In other words, they told us that continuing to pursue the war threatened their profits and power more than it advanced them. So, damn it all, against their inclinations, they had to change sides. You can judge for yourself what kind of conscience, what kind of personal and moral calculus that choice revealed. But the point for activists was that our demonstrations had to raise social costs beyond what elites would willingly bear. That's why it made sense to bring increasing numbers of people to each new demonstration. It's why it made sense to diversify tactics. It's why it made sense to continually broaden the scope of opposition. What elites feared sufficiently to surrender to was a movement that began to question their very right to exist. It wasn't enough to be more angry or more militant but with fewer numbers. It wasn't enough to have deeper analysis and broader focus, without having more support and militancy. A movement trying to win major gains had to manage all the variables at once.

May Day 1971 was a leap. The movement was going to try to move not just secondary numbers at a big peaceful demonstration to do civil disobedience in DC, it was going to try to bring out only folks committed to civil disobedience, and not just to moderate civil disobedience, but to shutting the city down. The slogan was, "If the government doesn't stop the war, we're going to stop the government." The plan was to occupy the streets, block traffic, and halt the city. This was not insurrection, but neither was it peaceful picnic-style dissent. I remember the organizing to assemble people to go to May Day. My friends and I organized in the Boston area. Others did it in other cities. Rennie Davis and Tom Hayden, in particular, went from place to place, across the country, to help.

This is one of those times when I heard Rennie speak. He made me cry, as he recounted Vietnamese history and bravery. He made me cheer, as he got us to shout how we were going to shut down DC and end the war. What he did was fantastically effective agitprop and education, at least for some of us. What he did was also horribly ill-conceived.

The problem was that you can't judge methods and actions by only short-term results if you have long-term desires. That many who he harangued went to DC was a plus for Rennie's methodology. But people believed Rennie. Rennie Davis knew we weren't going to shut down the government. Tom Hayden knew we weren't going to shut down the government. But their organizing approach was to rile up the audience, and probably themselves too, and excite people with the possibility of shutting down the government. Surely it was worth going to DC, occupying the streets, risking getting beaten and arrested, if it was going to end the war on the spot. It was like revving up for a big game, or for a kamikaze attack. You envision immense success and you go for it. You don't go for it if you envision losing.

So the day came, and we ran through DC's streets, pretty much shutting down the city and provoking the biggest mass arrest in U.S. history. But the next day, it was back to business as usual for DC, the government, and the B-52s pummeling the life out of Vietnamese peasants. May Day's demonstrators watched TV and got the wind knocked out of them. They felt defeated, even doomed. We had gone to DC. We had shut down the city. But the war raged on. Failure. Many gave up. Not Tom and Rennie. Also, not me and many others who thought in terms of a long-haul struggle. We didn't make apocalyptic judgments. But the predominant style of organizing often led others who were newer to activism to think in terms of immediate tallies and to crumple rather than continue when the immediate results weren't optimal. Whatever anyone thought about May Day, serious thoughts about the war and about strategy needed to be tied to reality. Of course May Day didn't end the war. Of course the White House opened for business Monday morning. But was the movement stronger, wiser, better organized, and eager to come back for more, or did May Day reduce prospects? Hearing that the war was still raging should not have caused any activist to think we failed. But it did.

Looking back, my guess is that May Day was at best much less successful than it should have been, and at worst counterproductive. What would have made it better was to get everyone there for the same reasons why Tom, Rennie, and many local organizers like myself went to DC—to build a movement. It was wrong to get people there in the expectation that being there would quickly end the war. Actually, Rennie himself did pretty much give up, not too long thereafter. Maybe he succumbed to his own eloquence, distraught that his extravagant promises weren't met.

Poland No Joke

> *Being one of the world's big vampires,*
> *Why don't you come on out and say so*
> *Like Japan, and England, and France,*
> *And all the other nymphomaniacs of power.*
> *—Langston Hughes*

Lydia Sargent and I went to Poland to see Slawomir Magala at the time that South End Press published his book, *Class Struggle in Classless Poland*. Ahh, you may be wondering, what's Poland got to do with a chapter on Washington? What logic can this have? Has the nontemporal approach strayed beyond any plausible motive? Let's see.

The trip to Poland was eventful in many ways. I will never forget coming around a corner and seeing a shrine in the street, with some flowers, artifacts, and pictures celebrating a famous victim of a nefarious crime, a person that the local people admired and wished to honor. No, it wasn't Lenin or Stalin. It wasn't Marx or Trotsky. It wasn't a Polish freedom fighter from any time or any place. It was instead the main mop-top, John Lennon. The shrine was moving in its simplicity, accurate in its homage, and somehow it made very real to me the interconnectedness of nations, people, and history.

While in Poland, Lydia and I toured a few cities, attended some meetings, met some organizers, and generally got a first-hand account of the unfolding workers' movements—remember Lech Walesa and Polish Solidarinosc?—and their organizations. What I heard contoured my ensuing understanding of what will be needed to carry off a fully liberating transformation of Poland or the U.S.

In Poland, under the heel of the Soviet Union, a group of young people—probably in part due to the delayed, reflected, percolating impact of the Sixties, including John Lennon's lyrics and much more—became politicized and deeply aroused. They decided they would try to prod Polish events—not to lead much less to dominate them. The idea was to become a social detonator. These young people would spread out in Polish society and use street theater, café meetings, underground newspapers, wall posters, and provocative rallies and demonstrations to detonate hope and desire in the populace. They were anti-Leninist and anti-elitist in much the same way as our movements had been at MIT. In fact, I think they were very much a Polish version of the tide of activism in the U.S. that went to the South and onto campuses in the earliest years of the sixties. But the Polish activists were even more aggressive and more productive than we had been, and at any rate had tremendous success.

I don't remember the Polish name for their project, but their acronym was KOR. And they did their job well. Polish society began to shake from their actions and the ensuing vibrations aroused a gigantic restiveness, and, in particular, a renewed workers' movement called Solidarity—which was Solidarnosc in Polish. This was the outpouring of dissent and resistance that swept Poland years before the demise of the Soviet Union. It generated strikes and factory occupations all over Poland. KOR agitated for self-management and for participation and the workers in turn sought, both by taking over their factories and shipyards in many parts of the country, not least Gdansk, to run them outside the strictures of the Leninist state. This was the movement Lech Walesa came from and, in time, led.

What Lydia and I saw in Poland was the tension between the truly sincere desires of people in KOR to only detonate a mass movement and then merge into it with no special status, and the countervailing tendency for them to find themselves writing leaflets, giving speeches, undertaking negotiations, and otherwise playing increasingly leading roles until, in the end, the new Polish government was full of earlier KOR members who wound up enacting continued Soviet-style rule in the aftermath of struggles that fell short.

The young KOR activists weren't just good guys pissed off at capitalism or, in this case, at Soviet-style authoritarianism. They were self-consciously and very explicitly guarding against precisely what finally unfolded. So how did hierarchy arise even in their own ranks and even against their concerted efforts? For Lydia and I, the Polish experience provided the best evidence for the view that while personal tendencies to elitism certainly play a role in the emergence of new elites, the central problem is instead structural. The workers of Poland were rebelling. Crises were unfolding. Conflict was erupting. Lives and history resonated risk and possibility. In each new exchange there was great pressure to excel. When a leaflet needed writing, activists looked for the person who had the most stylish verbal cadence and most information. When a speech had to be given, it sought the person who could string together the needed words, humor, and drama most confidently. When negotiations had to be undertaken, it followed the person who was most practiced at legal wrangling and fact bending.

The pressure of the moment continually and repeatedly conspired to elevate the highly educated and self-confident members of KOR into ever more prominent positions. Their initial advantages in skills, confidence, and knowledge were enlarged daily as they did the most skill-enlarging, confidence-inducing, and knowledge-increasing tasks while others in the wider movement looked on in appreciation. When a report was needed, ask the KOR person. He could do most quickly. She could do it most eloquently. It would be inefficient not to use him or her. Over time, everyone grew dependent on a relatively few KOR contributors. KOR members monopolized the slots in the movement that conveyed visibility, notoriety, and the confidence and cadence to dominate outcomes. The monopolizers, just trying to contribute to the struggle, began to dominate the struggle. And try as they might to not succumb to the inducements, they also began to see themselves as more worthy and better than others. They led events. Others followed.

It wasn't the genetic code of the new leaders at fault. Nor was it their personalities. In the case of KOR, their personal inclinations were about as good as activists can have. If these people's inner wiring or predispositions were the problem, then there was no solution and likely wouldn't be any solution in a future situation either. But, in fact, the problem was not in the members of KOR. It was in the lack of institutional dynamics able to ensure participation and self management. And if I had to condemn a problem inside people's minds, too, then it seemed to me the problem was a confusion about what efficiency was and about what quality outcomes were.

The Polish movement, like others before and after, simply did not have a wide enough or wise enough view of itself. To produce a good leaflet or speech or even negotiation while undercutting the underlying values of the movement was not, in fact, efficient, though everyone thought it was. Efficiency should have meant attaining desired ends without wasting—or destroying—valued assets. Elevating KOR members accomplished desired short-term ends, yes, but it did so at the cost of obstructing and finally obliterating not only self-management and participation in that moment, but also aspirations and prospects for the long run.

This was the lesson of Poland that Lydia and I learned from talking to our hosts there. It doesn't do to win the wrong goal. It doesn't do to lose completely, either. So the trick is, how do you undertake worthy and effective practice that can win desired goals without slip-sliding away your guiding values? Good aspirations and commitments are necessary but not sufficient. Imagine KOR operating with a rule that regardless of losses in time or quality of output every speech had to be made by someone who had made no more than three other speeches before, though accompanied and helped by a person with more experience. And likewise, imagine there having been similar rules for writing leaflets and conducting negotiations. Perhaps this suggestion is simplistic, but what was truly simpleminded was to seek self-management by means that failed to produce self-management.

Poland is in this Washington chapter because the lessons of Poland are apt for Washington too. And perhaps I should mention, as well, another insight from the Polish trip. While there, Lydia and I were saddened and astounded to encounter a widespread confusion. If another country was seen as in any way allied to Russia, it was deemed an enemy of the Polish movement. If another country was seen as in any way contrary to Russia, it was deemed to be an ally of the Polish movement. We had to work hard to dispel the view that the CIA would aid and nurture a Polish workers' movement into an equitable future. The problem was belief in a familiar mental gymnastic: "My enemy's enemy is my friend." This logic rears up all too often, not least in the U.S. Left. The most recent gyrations include the deductions that since Milosevic and even Hussein and bin Laden are the empire's enemy, they must be the anti-empire's friend. It was a lot easier to empathize with the Poles' confusions of this sort than with those of fellow American leftists.

Chapter 12

Bread and Roses

Dirty Stories

It starts when you sink in his arms and ends with your arms in his sink.
—Anonymous

Being in the movement doesn't eliminate typical day-to-day concerns. For one thing, gender dynamics are often personal—ranging from divisions of household labor and attitudes, through daily tasks, on to assumptions and methods of interpersonal behavior—as well as being about institutional patriarchy and collective feminist action.

I never got even an inkling of an inclination from my upbringing that I ought to clean anything, and I have always been, as a result, both a slob and disinclined to do anything about it. Obviously, being a slob isn't even a significant portion of what it means to be male chauvinist, but it is often part of the picture. I am not sure if my slovenliness is my father reborn in me, or is due to a household that required no chores of me, or both. Dad was even more hopeless than I am in a kitchen or facing a pile of dirt. My mother, on the other hand, was close to nutty about cleanliness. Our living room has been, in all her homes, more like a museum than a place lived in, which didn't crowd out living, but did sequester it into other spaces. My allergy to cleaning is a constant bane for my partner Lydia, who, as a result, spends more than her fair share of time reminding and battling with me to do my share. But I have seen worse days than my current incarnation. Much worse.

It isn't that I self-consciously rely on others to clean up for me. I am bad, but not that bad. Mostly, I just don't give a damn about cleanliness or even notice dirtiness unless it interferes with my productivity. My desks tend to be quite neat. Surely the worst messes I have created, by far, have been while living alone, and have oppressed only me, except that I rarely if ever noticed there was something there to be oppressed about. Of course, for Lydia, and for feminists generally for that matter, cleanliness isn't actually about clean things. It is about gender roles. To be left with the cleaning task is to be left with a role that in a sexist world is deemed to be women's labor. My aversion to cleaning is no doubt a product of the sexual division of labor manifested in me, via my mom and dad and TV-defined youth, and transported through millennia. But it isn't me wanting to preserve male dominance, a sexist division of labor, I tell myself, or of course that would manifest in my attitudes in other dimensions of life too, and it doesn't. Uncleanliness is a cruddy imposition from the past, hard for me to escape, or even to want to escape.

The most extreme instance was an apartment I had in Harvard Square in Cambridge. In that second-story apartment, there was a refrigerator. At some point I put stuff in it and left it for a time. It began to smell so that opening the refrigerator door was unpleasant. My solution, not really a conscious plan but just what I did, was simple. I didn't open the door again. I just forgot the rotting stuff was there and carried on without ever reopening the refrigerator.

I left the apartment to a friend, months later, who moved in when I was off on a cross-country journey. Later I heard that he and a bunch of other friends had to clean the refrigerator. It had become a bacteria-ridden jungle. The stench was incredible. It was one of the more onerous tasks a human being had ever undertaken, at least in their eyes, they later told me.

Another time, I lived off campus with Jeffrey Mermelstein, a political friend from MIT, who later became a psychologist. Jeff was a bit like me on the cleanliness axis, and we allotted one room of our shared apartment to house garbage. We would just open the door and throw garbage in, close the door and go on about our business. It was highly efficient. Unsurprisingly, I don't remember what became of that room.

When my father was alive and we would argue and I would urge him in this or that new direction, he would often say that "you can't teach an old dog new tricks." I would get furious. I thought it was a pathetic excuse for stasis. When Dylan sang "he not busy being born is busy dying" it resonated greatly with me and seemed a far more cogent and exemplary maxim to live by than "you can't teach an old dog new tricks." Be born over and over. Don't snooze like a schnauzer. Well it turns out that it is very hard, and perhaps even impossible, to be changing every facet of one's life, in every single year of one's life. In fact, far-reaching self-change can be great but it can also be a fool's errand. It can swamp doing very important tasks that are far more manageable. Even just being born in enough facets to be not overall dying is a tiring task that we all, eventually, let's face it, finally lose. Or maybe that is just my pathetic excuse for not doing better on the cleanliness axis. Either way, I have more sympathy for my father's doggie claim as I get older. Nowadays, I like snoozing like a schnauzer every now and then.

Partly my not cleaning is a matter of my just being a lazy old exploitative dog taking advantage of millennia of sexism. Just ask Lydia. Partly it is a matter of picking where to rebuild myself given the prospects of even minimal success. Just ask me. Of course, in the end Lydia wins this argument because she needs only to point out the larger implications of unchanging role definitions to retain high ground no matter what machinations I toss up. But, even if only to understand the abstract point, consider another domain.

Consider eating cows or chickens or what have you. I do it. Lydia does it too. Others, generally much younger, especially a few years back, used to tell us, clean up your act. They said eating meat is a vile behavior pattern induced historically, not biologically, and that it is morally reprehensible (which is what is analogous to what feminists rightly say about sexism, which is that it is induced historically and is morally reprehensible). Are the veggies and vegans like the abolitionists once were, or like feminists now are, urging on us a stance that will in the future be second-nature and morally utterly undeniable? And are we who eat meat hanging onto habitual behavior that will one day be considered subhuman, like lazy dogs who are not being born but are dying, because while we fight for justice for women, minorities, workers, and citizens of weak countries, we do not fight for chickens and cows?

Don't misread the above. I see no comparison in importance between seeking to eliminate the roots and branches of sexism, and seeking to eliminate the roots and branches of violence against animals. I see no comparison in importance between how chickens are treated and how women or any humans are treated. In fact, for me the animal rights agenda resonates barely at all, and the antisexism agenda is part of my life. The message of the little story is, instead, that life is not always easy or optimal. We have to pick and choose our battles, sometimes even setting aside parts of a whole that are worth affecting, but, at least for a time, are beyond our means. It is better to be somewhat sloppy while otherwise respecting women's full and equal rights and responsibilities than it is to focus on a minimal personal lifestyle innovation while violating women's larger rights.

Women in the Movement

When someone with the authority of a teacher, say, describes the world and you are not in it, there is a moment of psychic disequilibrium, as if you looked into a mirror and saw nothing.
—Adrienne Rich

Every day in the sixties, before the women's movement cleaned the movement house—at least somewhat—there were big gold men, big silver men, big steel men, and big lead men, and then there were little tin women. That was about the size of it. Women were pedestaled or damned. Women did tons of onerous work without which nothing useful would have happened. Women spoke but weren't heard. Women created, amazingly, given their exclusion from most centers of dispute and debate, but weren't respected. Women were seen but not seen. Of course nothing is universal, but this almost was.

But starting in 1967, groups of newly politicized women in Boston began to discuss women's issues. Within two years they organized a conference at Emmanuel College. Partly, women had been inspired by the civil rights struggles at the beginning of the decade. Partly, participating in those struggles and in antiwar movements, women had been forced to ward off sexism in the movement. The energy of over 500 attendees birthed new women's organizations in Boston, including Bread and Roses, which was one of the first New Left-style feminist women's organizations in the post-World War II United States. Bread and Roses addressed reproductive rights, child care, equal employment, gender discrimination, and violence against women. The organization seized an unoccupied building owned by Harvard University in 1971 and held it for ten days. At their building they offered free classes and childcare. Bread and Roses later bought a house in Cambridge and opened a women's center in 1972, now the longest-running women's center in the United States.

As the women's center advertised, "The struggle to gain control of all aspects of our lives—our bodies, our jobs, our social roles, and our creativity—is the struggle of every woman." The center provided reproductive counseling and housed groups fighting against rape or violence against women, discussion groups for lesbians and others for women dealing with incest, and informational resources for welfare, career placement, and women's issues. Diverse other projects followed in later years.

The women of Bread and Roses were committed to fighting all manifestations of sexism, both personal and institutional. They were militant and angry and often saw instances of sexism where others tended to see only commonplace circumstances. For this they were regularly called "hysterical," "knee-jerk," "frigid," and "maniacal," not only by the media, but by many leftist men. An irony of such criticism was that it was sometimes self-fulfilling. Call someone nasty names long enough and they sometimes began to act in the manner they were labeled. The condemner then took pride in being able to offer evidence of being right. This was a sad victory. Relatedly, sometimes women hid behind accusations of sexism, as blacks sometimes hid behind accusations of racism, pursuing not feminism or national liberation but personal advance or just vengeance. This did happen; to say it didn't would be silly. But such ills were a minor sidebar to resisting ubiquitous oppressive dynamics.

Another problem in all kinds of political struggle, but particularly where such intimate features were involved, was the possibility of taking rightful insights into wrongful postures. From rightfully rejecting subordination one could move toward rejectionist behavior that contradicted movement building. Bread and Roses as an organization was autonomous but not separatist. In other words, it did not argue that women should ignore issues men related to. It did not argue that women should avoid working with men. It did not avoid struggles along with men or refuse male support. But it did argue that Bread and Roses itself was a space for women to operate free of the need to constantly deal with male sexist attitudes. But, despite Bread and Roses' influence, in Boston, women with consciousness were sometimes hostile toward women without consciousness and lesbians were sometimes hostile to straight women as if being ignorant were a sin and as if having sex with men was itself part of the problem. The upside of this news is that if Bread and Roses and all other organizations of the sixties and early seventies were without flaws, we would have very bad prospects for future victory. After all, all these movements fell way short of achieving their aspirations and the world we live in still needs a gigantic revolutionary overhaul. That the movements of the sixties and early seventies were fraught with problems is good news in that it says we can do better and gives insight into how to do so.

Mostly, however, I remember good things such as how Bread and Roses would confront institutions and movements demanding that men "respect women and incorporate women at every level of leadership and participation and eliminate gender hierarchy, or we will disrupt your operations until you do." Bread and Roses confronted local radio stations, entertainment clubs, and cultural institutions, as well as groups in the New Left. They were ecumenical in choosing targets. "Women are everywhere. They are affected by everything. Therefore no institution, no project, and no person is exempt from the demand to respect women." To call "shit-work" "women's work" does not make it conceptual, adventuresome, or engaging, nor does it justify men not doing it or women doing nothing else. To portray women in a derogatory, sexist manner was to invite unremitting criticism. To ignore women's opinions, relegate women to lowly tasks, or visually or verbally objectify women was to invite harsh censure and disruption of operations. To structure gender inequality into organizations was to invite militant critique.

Marriage was called into question as a patriarchal institution. The basic structure of the family was called into question. Roles associated with dating were called into question. Macho posturing, male competitiveness, and sexual objectification were called into question. Opposition to pornography (with no accompanying censoring mind-set) was part and parcel of opposition to anything that manipulated, maligned, or mistreated women's minds or bodies or that perpetuated male behaviors that oppressed women. Child care was no longer seen as "women's work," and mothering and fathering were replaced, at least in some people's hopes and sometimes in some people's lives, with parenting. What was good in familiar male and female roles was merged to become part of women's and men's joint agendas. What was bad was rejected. Actions were direct and clear.

Bread and Roses was a local organization, but even in Boston its outreach was limited. It was far from the only militant feminist organization in the U.S., but others like it also had limited resources and range. The National Organization for Women (NOW), a much wealthier project, never became a larger example of this sort of committed, militant, multi-focused women's organization. NOW had its virtues, but it was far less politically promising even in its best moments than Bread and Roses was at its worst. Nor has any other national women's movement achieved such insight as Bread and Roses since then, I think. This absence may help explain why many women are once again emotionally and intellectually isolated from one another and why many accept that the pains they suffer arise from personal inadequacy or biological inevitability rather than from sexism. It may explain why, despite all of feminism's gains, we are currently, it seems, not only stalled in going forward after those many major gains, but perhaps even beginning to creep backward.

Women Readjust the Left

[History is the] quarrels of popes and kings, with wars or pestilences in every page; the men all so good for nothing, and hardly any women at all.
—*Jane Austen*

The antiwar movement of the sixties had the same modus operandi as the later anticorporate globalization movement. We held large open meetings to make plans for major events. At one particular meeting I happened to be chairing, about 200 people were planning an antiwar rally and march. I was at the front of the room when suddenly the door opened, a bit to my rear and right—yes, this detail I remember—and in marched about thirty women. They spread out across the front of the room and told me to sit down. I sat. The interlopers announced to the room that henceforth the movement in Boston was going to be antisexist or it wasn't going to be anything at all. If we didn't comply with their demands they would boycott our antiwar efforts and soon other women would, too. It was right to meet their demands, they said, and in any event, to do otherwise would be disastrous.

The demands were straightforward and immensely important. All decision-making bodies in the Boston movement would henceforth be comprised of at least fifty percent women. All meetings would have women chairs, or cochairs, or rotating chairs with women half the time. Whenever movement members went out to give talks or make presentations, women would fill at least fifty percent of the visible and empowering positions. Finally, in all public statements and political presentations, feminist content would be included at the core. This would not be done mechanically, but with thoughtful, caring precision.

Most men in the room felt that a major antiwar session was no place for women to exert feminist pressure, since opposition to the war was too important to interrupt. Others felt there was nowhere this should be done; the demands were nonsense. Some of us were, however, prodded to realize that there would be no successful opposition to the war, much less to sexism, unless women were respected and won their equal place. But before praising male supporters of Bread and Roses for holding this worthy view, it is critical to understand that the men who realized the importance and legitimacy of Bread and Roses' demands did so because we were forced to. Our awareness didn't come spontaneously. Carrying through the demands was far from easy and never perfect, for that matter.

Bread and Roses told those listening that they intended to form local and regional women's movements that would pressure all kinds of institutions by threatening to disrupt their operations unless they incorporated respect for the rights and capacities of women. Bread and Roses wanted a national women's movement that was militant, aggressive, multifocused, and sensitive to feminist concerns. They wanted feminists playing leading roles around matters of race, class, foreign policy, government policy, and ecological preservation. Bread and Roses sought all this, and made considerable gains on many fronts in subsequent years, sometimes against staunch male resistance, more often against recalcitrant habits and expectations.

At the time, movement men realized that we obviously had no right telling women what they should be doing about sexism, but we did have a responsibility to address other men and male-dominated institutions. We had to make known our desire to support militant feminism. Even more important, we had to compel the still male-dominated institutions we were part of to incorporate at least an equal share of women's leadership and to offer both material and organizational support for national and local women's organizing. This was never easy. Whatever other impediments obstructed the re-emergence of militant feminism on a national scale, surely the biggest obstacle was the continuing intransigence and outright sexism of men. For example, to choose women ahead of men who were by appearance more confident, better trained, more knowledgeable, more skilled at their tasks, and, were mostly just implicitly assumed superior required a broader understanding of what it meant to make progress. A guy didn't have to say women belong under his thumb to oppose change. He could just say, "Tom would be a better speaker, leader, chair, decision maker, than Mary. Keep Tom. Mary can wait." To defeat the less-obnoxious claims, you had to bring up the big picture of attaining gender balance, not just the narrow immediate productivity that Tom might, in fact, enlarge more than Mary. More, even regarding immediate competence, we had to realize as well that the highly trained and confident and often in many ways capable men such as Tom had some horrible baggage that often compromised our seeming competency, while the less trained and confident women such as Mary brought insights and commitments about a wider range of issues that augmented their competency.

Bread and Roses was a women's organization for women's rights and justice more broadly. It was a powerful product of the initiative of women seeking to overcome the sexist behavior of the New Left and society. To try and explain how much was accomplished, I often suggest that if you took a young woman from Boston in 2006 and sent her in a time machine back to 1960 or even 1965 or 1968, the day-to-day experience from that time would be unbearable for her. Literally, I think young women today would be unable to bear for hours, much less for lifetimes, conditions that existed then. To have eliminated that much rot marks great progress. At the same time, the sixties rarely institutionalized its feminist gains in new modes of child rearing, family structure, and schooling, and never really had that as a prime priority. As a result, from the close of the sixties, let's say 1975, to now, the right wing in the United States and around the world, fueled and abetted by persisting underlying patriarchal institutions, have been fighting a multi-front battle to put women back in the home, back under male thumbs.

Curious Courtship

To raise new questions, new possibilities, to regard old problems from a new angle requires creative imagination and marks real advances.
—Albert Einstein

One day a controversial and important book came to South End Press, by a writer named Batya Weinbaum, titled *The Curious Courtship of Women's Liberation and Socialism*. *Curious Courtship* and Weinbaum's other SEP book, *Pictures of Patriarchy*, offered an original thesis. They argued that if you look at workplaces and at the economy more generally you can see the imprint of gender dynamics in its defining structural relations. Weinbaum looked into factories and saw there the imprint and even replication of the roles typical of mothers, fathers, sisters, and brothers. Similarly, she looked into families and saw in them not only kin and gender relations, but also class dynamics.

The overarching idea that I took from publishing Batya's work matched and propelled where my own thoughts were going. I thought Marxism had many useful insights, but, among other damning problems, it was too economics focused.

Marxism asserted, sometimes explicitly and sometimes just by how its practitioners approached reality, that a society's economy emanated a field of force that critically imprinted how things occurred not only in workplaces but in households, churches, and schools. This seemed obviously true, but reciprocally, it also seemed to me that what I called the kinship sphere of social life, and the cultural sphere, and the political sphere, likewise emanated fields of force that also percolated into all sides of life, including the economy. Batya Weinbaum made a specific case about kinship affecting economy, and I found it very convincing and still refer to it when making related claims.

Women and Revolution

> *In my heart, I think a woman has two choices:*
> *either she's a feminist or a masochist.*
> *—Gloria Steinem*

About ten years after the heyday of Bread and Roses, Lydia Sargent, then at South End Press, edited another centrally important South End Press book about feminism titled *Women and Revolution*. Lydia invited the participants, prodded their submissions, and did the introduction and editing. In the book, a controversial essay by Heidi Hartmann titled "The Unhappy Marriage of Women's Liberation and Socialism" was the centerpiece, followed by reactions from various respondents and concluding with Hartmann's reply.

Women and Revolution explored the centrality of gender for social change, arguing the need to transcend struggle that highlighted only economics and class. For the most part its insights have successfully become part of Left consciousness in the years since its publication, but the battle against sexism and patriarchy is a long way from won. We are certainly far advanced from where we were thirty or forty years ago, but if you look at popular culture, ads, and patterns of increasing objectification in 2006, not to mention possible assaults on past gains like Roe v. Wade, it is clear that a great deal that the women's movement has won, in social organization, in laws, and even in the ideas and aspirations that reside inside people's minds, is now under attack.

Experience has taught me that gender hierarchies have to literally be extirpated to disappear. If they persist even a little, they attempt to reinvigorate themselves at the expense of women. Part of moving forward from the present is curtailing a sexist resurgence, enlarging feminist gains, and ultimately making the world a truly feminist place to live.

Chapter 13

Lydia and Life

Dates and Lovers

*I would venture to guess that Anon, who wrote
so many poems without signing them, was often a woman.*
—*Virginia Woolf*

In fifth and sixth grade, people's birthday parties often included dancing. I hated these parties. I vaguely remember dancing very poorly. I remember dancing with girls a foot taller than me who were my age, but were easily a year or two more mature than me. I took no joy in that. These parties were, however, how boys, or at least many boys, were personally introduced to girls. It didn't do much for future respect. The fact that we more familiarly met girls much earlier in our homes, in daily life, and through the media, always in patterns enforcing degradation rather than mutual respect, was an even larger problem.

Girls didn't do what we did. We didn't do what girls did. What boys did mattered. What girls did didn't matter. I don't remember the details, but they are well known from diverse accounts. I was a little boy, not a little girl. Different play, different talk, different clothes, different expectations—everything different—with every little thing stamped with a social imprint that was designed to produce men and women, two socially separated species with the former dominating the latter. That's it. That's young people's gender relations in the fifties—and for many men and women even now.

Matthew was one of my best friends from grade school through high school. He was a tall, broad, handsome guy, who looked way beyond his years. He would tell me, in junior high school, of his assignations at beach clubs with married women. Matthew was a fount of gender knowledge. In high school he had a girlfriend, actually quite a few, but he and this particular one broke up after a time, and later I wanted to go out with her. Matt helped set it up. She was a year younger

148

than Matt and I, and was a bit beyond her years physically, emotionally, and no doubt sexually, not least from having gone out with Matt. With me sixteen or maybe seventeen, and her I guess fifteen or sixteen, she turned me down after going out once and told me why. She liked me fine and thought I was a nice, smart fellow, but I didn't get excited enough about day-to-day life to sustain her interest. I was surprised, but I remembered this years later and decided she was right.

I don't get excited about most things other people find engaging. My small talk is unanimated. I am boring, at many times, in many places, for many people. I am far from being the life of a party, unless it is a political party, sometimes. This young woman wasn't interested in my interest in science, and I had only tangential interest in the day-to-day world that excited her. Right up to the present, while I can be animated about intellectual matters and issues of social change, I often have little patience for talking about the rest of daily life. I am not an optimal social package, or an optimal boyfriend or life-mate package, either.

What about sex? I remember in fifth grade, maybe fourth, Donald and I, he being my then-best friend, would be playing war or cowboys and Indians, or whatever. In the throes of creeping around, or making believe we were in quicksand, I would rub against the floor, a lot. I never thought about what I was doing. I just did it, for a while, and then didn't do it—that way—anymore. I remember, for that matter, no talks with anyone older about sex. I don't remember learning about it, so I have no idea how learning occurred, except by social osmosis, I guess, from friends, and practice.

Sex was everywhere in media and in life, but almost nowhere in conscious discussion. It was not noted, admitted, or openly explored, at least in my circles. This was not universal for high school, but typical for my friends. From Matthew I heard lurid stories of lonely older women. But this was not typical talk. I had no conscious calculated understanding of any of it, or of anything broader regarding gender or sex roles.

Nancy Shapiro was my first love. What picked her out for me or picked me out for her, I don't know. It happened, that's all. I suspect when people explain such things they just pick attributes to apply so the stories are more or less applicable. I don't know what the conclusion of our relationship was, either. I don't remember breaking up. My guess is it went on for one too many mornings and she went her way and I went mine.

If you go back and listen to the music of the times or view the movies or TV or read the books, you will know that we all then inhabited a world of much greater hurt for women than the one we inhabit now, which is certainly still piss-poor on that account. I have no doubt that I contributed to the injustices Nancy had to endure, and I am sorry for that, though I also know that I was never one of the boys who denigrated or tried to trick and exploit and later dump women. In fact, I tended to get into fights about such behavior. My sins were more subtle, whatever precisely they may have been.

High school was only Nancy as far as serious dating went, and then Nancy and I extended our relationship into college, too. During my freshman year at MIT, AEPi guys routinely tried to meet, impress, screw, and jettison women. They joked about and planned it endlessly. At the same time, some brothers, like me, had serious relationships, which put us largely above the wild fray. Such relationships were highly respected and even envied. Nancy was treated like royalty, as were other female partners, during that year at AEPi. This royal treatment hid the more generalized disgust involved in all our relationships in those times. Such civility has always made me uncomfortable. Royal treatment was form without substance and I like to think that it is these kinds of "sympathetic" human interactions that are missing from my life that people are referring to who call me uncivil, cold, or uncaring. I avoid sentimental displays that are, in my view, form without substance. Then again, perhaps obliterating my own elaborately constructed defense, it is said that you are what you do.

At any rate, I shared rock and roll with Nancy and we also shared my entry into MIT and hers into Simmons. But from then on we shared steadily less. For example, I can't remember talking with her about the feelings I developed toward AEPi and my decision to leave it. That would accord with my not properly respecting her and her views, wouldn't it? Sadly so, though I don't remember having anything but respect. And we also never shared the politics I began to hold, which is likely why we stopped sharing everything else, too. Our ways diverged. And I guess as far as politics was concerned, it was my way or the highway. This explained, as well, the end of my ties with my best friend, Larry Seidman. He became liberal. I became revolutionary. Good-bye.

In college, after Nancy, I went out with many women, sometimes sharing only one night, other times sharing a few weeks but not longer. What I saw and learned, mostly, is that sexism did unbearably profound damage, even in its most subtle forms. Yet against this observation, there were many people in the sixties who wanted to say that sexism was horrific, racism was horrific, classism was horrific, and yet also argue that the constituencies under the stamping boot of these phenomena showed no signs of degradation. I encountered this inclination often, but I never understood it, neither then nor later.

I certainly understood that women, blacks, and working people didn't want to be seen as terminally less than they should be. But I didn't understand why people felt a need to deny lasting ill effects entirely. It implied that these oppressions weren't so bad after all, if they had no lasting impact. In truth, of course, these oppressions did have very profound and painful lasting effects. People could be fighters, not victims, and still suffer the crippling effects of injustice. And if someone attained those heights, and claimed there was no great hurdle for others to overcome to do likewise, it seemed to me she was implicitly saying that others failed, rather than that they were beaten down by oppression's residues.

I saw some extreme examples of the overt agony of sexism. A woman I went out with was sadomasochistic. She wanted me to hurt her and she wanted to hurt me. She warned me away before these traits surfaced, and then urged me away, after they defined the scene. She did not want her traits. The personal inclinations she endured that obstructed her having humane relations weren't wired into her womanhood; they were forcefully imprinted on her. Her traits were an extreme example, but I was staggered by the insecurities and fears harbored by pretty much every woman I encountered. It wasn't just that they were continually trampled and violated. It was also that lifelong trampling and violating induced a lack of confidence, and in some cases even an expressed desire for male assertiveness to usurp the need for their own leadership. I learned the importance of creating conditions that no longer had these results. When I recently read Jane Fonda's autobiography, seeing the imprints in her life, even with all her incredible advantages and accomplishments, it only made the same point more forcefully.

A second major relationship followed with a woman named Holly. On the day of the election for MIT president, I met Holly in the corridors. She was incredibly beautiful, and I was, remember, a campus star. Given the sick norms of the times, this was a perfect match. We spent the night, and were coupled for about two years. I loved her, but I have to admit it would be incredible if there wasn't also an element of trophy-hunting involved. My guess is that Holly was probably manhandled all her life by eyes and thoughts and likely by hands and bodies, too. It was certainly constant while I knew her. Everywhere she went, she was undressed by eyes. Holly had an army of suitors, each made to feel ignorant of the rest. Election night, our first time together, she warned me that I shouldn't see her again. I would suffer if I did. I don't know if she warned everyone she took up with, but, if so, I doubt that many paid attention. Blinded by the beautiful light, they, and I, jumped aboard. I think maybe the warning was truth in advertising. Anyhow, I ignored it.

Over our time together, I learned what Holly was talking about. She had a lot of secrets. Once I was up to speed, I would sometimes follow her to verify who the other guys were and that I wasn't manufacturing my doubts. I couldn't believe she didn't know I knew, but we acted as if that were the case. She'd say she had an appointment, and I would take it at face value. I was Galahad. I would show her a man could love her, avoid abusing or misusing her, and this revelation would cure her of having to trap and leave man after man. I have no idea if my egomaniacal aims were met. We split, without a momentous breakup.

I remember cruising the Radcliffe library, sophomore year, after Nancy but before Holly, with Larry Seidman and Robin Hahnel. Robin had a girlfriend,

Jackie, from before college, with whom he was as close as the rest of us thought any two people could get. So Robin wasn't cruising, or not much, anyhow. Larry and I weren't good at it. No one should have been good at it, of course, but that wasn't our view at the time. The practice was sick, and yet, like so many other sick things, in context it was sensible. Should people not meet? Was failing to meet girls a better option than cruising? Was it better for girls not to meet boys than to be cruised? An alternative to habituating libraries was mixers. Young men and women went but the women were on display and the men were choosing. Until the women's movement offered a whole new spectrum of options, bad options were the only options and when young women of today think nothing has been won by feminism, they should consider the indignity of being implicitly auctioned off, not to mention gains in education, jobs, income, voting rights, and legal rights.

Lydia for Life

> *I ain't lookin' to compete with you,*
> *Beat or cheat or mistreat you,*
> *—Bob Dylan*

Lydia Sargent and I met through our political involvements. Lydia was a housewife, six years older than me, who had three young children. She was working for the People's Coalition for Peace and Justice (PCPJ). I was the MIT wunderkind, sloppy and unkempt, a youth about town, with unlimited confidence and able to give good talk. Lydia was quickly moving left from a background different than most people in activist circles. She was raised upper-class WASP, expelled from her family for marrying outside the tribe beyond her father's control, had given birth three times, and was mired in suburban life but trying to escape it. Lydia, in other words, had a lot more at stake than most people frequenting antiwar rallies. Lydia was initially horrified by me. I didn't notice her. She was married, had kids, and was older than me. She was sensible. I was a dunce.

As representatives to the national PCPJ, Lydia and I later went to a conference in Washington DC, in her VW van, with Henry Norr. Henry was a very nice guy who decades later wound up writing about the high-tech industry for the *San Francisco Chronicle* and was fired for attending an anti-Iraq war demonstration, an act that allegedly violated his journalistic neutrality. Lydia berated both Henry and me for ignoring her, which we did, no doubt, because being married, she was off-limits. For the rest of the trip, after she put us in our place, our discussion involved all three of us. I began to notice Lydia, and she began to find some redeeming features in me. Just over thirty years later, at a Z Media Institute (summer school) session, Barbara Ehrenreich was sitting next to me in the Woods Hole Theater where Lydia and her theater group were putting on a show for all the students and staff. At the end of the show, Barbara said, "Do you understand how lucky you are to be with her?" I said yes, and Barbara looked more closely to make sure I was being honest—sisterly solidarity.

I have been romantically and politically partnered with Lydia, mostly living together but not always, for about thirty years. Virtually everything I have gone through she has either gone through too, or at least been there. She was at the first Springsteen concert with me. She was next to me when I was arrested a block from the MIT cyclotron. We were arrested together at the mass civil disobedience events in Boston. She helped me make *What Is To Be Undone* happen, and likewise helped with every book I have authored since that first one, including helping edit most of them into whatever semblance of literacy they have had. Lydia gets no recognition of her insight and relevance, at least outside our network of two. The same goes, it should be said, for most of the projects we have done together. Lydia's writing style is vastly better than mine. Lydia directly helped build South End Press, *Z Magazine*, ZMI, and Z Video. If not for her, ZNet wouldn't have happened either. Lydia was often the moving force behind our endeavors and is always a tireless, amazingly swift, and accurate worker. Her comprehension of political possibilities is peerless, but she gets little legitimacy, respect, or stature for it. Being a political couple is tricky. Many times people don't know our relationship. We are not very affectionate or possessive in public. But when they do find out we're a couple, there is a tendency to assume that I am the initiator of all our joint achievements.

People can't easily accept that a woman is responsible, creator, designer, architect. Okay, I know it is more subtle. People know women can initiate, they just most often assume this possibility away. What's denied is that Lydia can produce, organize, and be a driving force. In those dimensions, often even feminists doubt women. But I have seen all Lydia's theater productions, read all her articles, and been there, for better or worse, during her thirty years too. There have been difficult times. There have been excellent times. Some of the ups and downs we endure are due to residual scars she bears from being a woman in a patriarchal world. Many are due to residues left on me from growing up a man in that same world. Lydia and I are not married. We never will be.

Marriage Madness

If divorce has increased by one thousand percent, don't blame the women's movement. Blame the obsolete sex roles on which marriages were based.
—*Betty Friedan*

Marriage for Lydia, and for me too, though I have never directly experienced the condition, is an institution that is part and parcel of patriarchal hierarchy. Men own women, at least metaphorically and often overtly. What my eyes have told me over the years, from Matthew's stories onward, is that there were better and worse plantations in the Old South and so, too, there are better and worse marriages throughout suburbia. If your only horizon was plantations, you would call some plantations bad and some good, not bothering to notice the norms by which they are all execrable. The same seems to hold for people assessing marriages. We call some bad. We call some good. We fail to notice that the whole idea is execrable.

Marriage, when I began to read feminists on the topic, was revealed to me to be state sanctioned and religion ordained, but neither Lydia nor I ever look to either the state or to organized religion for meaning. Why not just petition the devil for solace and guidance? Marriage, I read and saw, is a priori hypocritical. Everyone says "until death do us part" and everyone knows that more likely other factors than death will do you part. Marriage, I couldn't deny, defines behavioral expectations, personality traits, and social responsibilities that become very hard to resist and in turn continually reproduce sexism. In high school and through perhaps two years of college, I would have said sure, I will get married. By junior year, I had doubts. After a little Bread and Roses, marriage was a lost concept.

Lydia's and my attitudes toward marriage have at times created difficulties for us. It is hard to get people to understand that for us going to a wedding is like attending a dance at an overtly racist club. And it is hard to get ourselves to realize that, of course, people marry not to reproduce sexism, but to share their lives. To go to a wedding and celebrate, even if we think the bride and groom are great people and that their relationship is wonderful, is for us to celebrate something we find profoundly disturbing. On the other hand, it isn't the people. It is the institution.

By the same logic, then, why don't Lydia and I refuse to see someone at their capitalist-defined workplace, or to celebrate someone getting a new job? A site of wage slavery—why not boycott it? Why don't Lydia and I refuse to go to the local bank and deposit our paycheck or later write checks on it? The bank, after all, is a site of imperial domination. Why tell Lydia's children that we'd rather they not marry, and we would prefer not to attend any weddings, but not tell them to never work for a boss or to never use banks? For Lydia, as for me, marriage is not entirely coerced and, more so, is often welcomed and celebrated as a virtue rather than being merely put up with as an imposition.

When I thought closely about this, before talking about it to Lydia's kids, I realized it is one thing to marry because you believe it is a more wise and safe choice for socially imposed material and legal reasons. I understood that, though I thought the insight often underestimated the downside of marriage. But I also realized one could marry for that reason without making believe what had happened was an outgrowth of one's deepest longings, and without acting as though the wedding day was the most important day of one's life. I decided that when you spend a half a year's income on a wedding, when you think your wedding day is the most important day of your life, when you see the wedding as the lynchpin of all potential happiness and as a key determinant of mortal and moral success, that's a slippery slope toward gender hierarchy. Deciding to marry, celebrate, etc. is not a sign you are sexist; it is a step that tends to lead toward sexism even against one's better aspirations. Thus, Lydia and I resist celebrating marriage per se. The bigger the day is made, the worse we expect a marriage to be. It is one thing to suffer the limitations of society. It is another thing to search out limitations and savor them as windfalls. Why partake of a gigantic Stockholm Syndrome? But trying to explain all this to other people, including relatives, is not so easy. As to Lydia's children, Andrew, with three children of his own, married Sarah, with two of her own, not long ago, for legal reasons. Eric is not married but lives with Maureen and they have three children. Andrea, living with Joey and his son from a prior marriage, is also not married.

On what people think is the flip side of this issue, during my thirty-odd years with Lydia I have had women friends but no other lover. Is that due to loyalty or to morality? It is due to neither. I do not advocate monogamy in principle. I wouldn't bet that monogamy will be a majority lifestyle in a desirable future society—but I also wouldn't bet against it. Back in the early days of my personal relations with women, there were a couple of periods when I seriously dated two women at once. The dynamics were debilitating. It involved duplicity or, if not duplicity, tension. I didn't like it so I didn't repeat it. I didn't veto affairs on grounds of principle—save for the honesty part. I just vetoed them as a lasting preference.

Women Know More: Yes and No

A woman without a man is like a fish without a bicycle.
—Gloria Steinem

Sometimes uncanny predictive accuracy is a selection effect. We live in a world where a lot of bad shit happens. If you always predict bad shit happening, you will have a very high batting average. That kind of predictive success is not very useful, nor does it indicate cognitive talent. What is useful in a nasty world is to predict not the bad shit, but when worthy stuff will or could happen, and to help make it so.

Some people refer to "women's intuition." Obviously, there is no such thing, yet what people are referring to is a capacity that I have certainly encountered often over the years, including Lydia having it in great abundance. She says this is what's going to happen. She has no sequence of reasons to offer. She just concludes. But she is very often right. This makes people talk about "women's intuition" when the conclusion is about social relations. People talk about genius, when the conclusion is about anything else.

Even very young, I knew the capacity had nothing to do with female genes. There was no women's gene for leaping to correct conclusions about social relations. I knew we all had what is called women's intuition, male and female alike. I knew it was a capacity to feel evidence and indicators and to tease out a prediction without a sequence of logical steps and without even consciously knowing what the hell we were doing. As I got older, I realized scientists did this all the time to propose a hypothesis about natural patterns and sometimes even to describe the result of a calculation before grinding through it.

Still, try as I might, when Lydia's social prediction goes against my calculations, I just can't seem to say to myself—hey, there is another piece of evidence that ought to enter my logic before I assess Lydia's outrageous prediction. Her batting average is so high that I should count what she predicts as highly probable even if it is different than what I otherwise expect. So what are women doing when they exert what many people call women's intuition? They are doing the same thing men do, but perhaps with a socially conditioned radar more sensitive to subtle indicators in words and demeanor. That's it, but the attentiveness of women to social cues seems uncanny to men who have had the capacity largely wiped out as part of becoming sexist.

Children

> *When we consider that women have been treated as property,*
> *it is degrading to women that we should treat our own children*
> *as property to be disposed of as we see fit.*
> *—Elizabeth Cady Stanton*

When Lydia and I were first going out, her then-husband Gary didn't know about me. The kids didn't understand who I was. They were quite young. I went once or twice to Lydia's house and played with them, waiting to leave for some event or other. Later, Lydia moved out. A little later, Lydia and I moved in together.

At some point I sat in a room, I remember, on a bed, with Andrew, Andrea, and Eric, and tried to establish with them who I was for them and vice versa. I can still see the scene, unlike nearly all the rest of the past. I made no claims then, nor since, to be a parent. I don't think I ever acted like a parent, either, or even like an uncle, say, or like a relative at all. Rather, I told them I loved their mother, Lydia, and that Lydia and I were going to be together for a long time which meant I was going to see a whole lot them, too.

I told them I wanted to be their older friend. I wanted them to feel they could talk with me about anything, though I was not another parent. They had parents, and now they also had a good friend who lived with their mom. The boys got a new rough-and-ready playmate, which they seemed to feel good about, though I am sure the divorce downside was difficult even though Lydia and Gary remain friends. About half the time marriage fails, divorce occurs, and the condition of kids is complexified if not made horrible. I was certainly not what Lydia's kids were used to, since I often wound up being about as silly as them, having to be berated for food fights with them, etc. Andrea was more distant toward me than Eric and Andrew, and remained that way for a long time, but, I think, no longer.

I don't think I affected Lydia's kids as much as I might have affected children of my own for whom I had greater responsibility and toward whom I had no feelings of restraint, but who is to say? I might have bollixed my own. In any event, I am happy to report that Andrew, Andrea, and Eric are very progressive and humane. Eric works with Z full-time. Andrea edited my most successful book, another book that followed after that, and now has edited this one, too. Andrew has had more travail in his life than Eric or Andrea, including a debilitating separation from the mother of his first two children. He has had more ups and downs with Lydia and I, too, but all three of Lydia's children, I think, are closer to me in many respects than I was to my own father, and are closer to Lydia, in many respects, than any older kids I have ever seen are with their mothers. So I guess Lydia's divorce and my presence wasn't a debacle and can arguably be called a success.

Andrew, in turn, is the birth parent to three boys, and parent, by his marriage to Sarah, to two other boys. Eric is birth parent to two boys and a girl with Maureen. Andrea is, by partnership with Joey, a parent to one boy. The grandkids are delightful and show all kinds of inclinations, but their lives are ahead and essentially unknown. Divorce and disruption aside, Andrew, Andrea, and Eric, and their spouses, have emerged as wonderful parents. It is a big family. I am privileged to enjoy it.

Here is another oddity. I do not remember making a self-conscious decision about all this. I never sat down, looked in a mirror, and said to myself, do you really want to take up with a woman who is six years older than you and who has three children? Can you handle hearing about their birth and their early childhood—they were six, eight, and nine when I met them—over and over, for a lifetime, having not been a part of any of that, which has indeed been a real cost of the choice? Can you handle not passing on genes—which hasn't been a real cost, since I find that concern sort of silly. Can you handle being friend, not dad? The point is, like becoming an activist rather than remaining an academic, like becoming a media worker rather than becoming a physicist, for this decision too, the result just happened. I didn't second-guess myself. I didn't even first-guess myself. I just followed my instincts when logic wasn't definitive. I hate brainstorming about things that brains can't elucidate. I don't know if that is typical or not.

Aging

The first half of our lives is ruined by our parents
and the second half by our children.
—Clarence Darrow

I am fifty-nine, which is not seriously old. Maybe I will write another memoir sometime down the road and lay claim to being more expert in elderliness. But even in the late prime of life, I know that confusion about aging is rampant. My father, for example, used to love a poem by Rupert Brooke that I would hear him recite periodically. The key lines were, "Grow old along with me, the best is yet to be." This was self-delusion or, more gently, perhaps it was trying to make the best of a bad situation with a big fib. More years, I have found, can bring greater wisdom, skill, and opportunities, but aging also dissolves one's physical and mental faculties, and that's not good. To lose hearing, to creak, to have less motion, to not remember, to calculate less quickly—it's a drag. Sclerotic synapses. Fixed ways. We can mitigate losses, sure, but years per se don't convey wisdom. Experiences, well considered, convey wisdom. Plenty of lessons we accumulate turn out to have been wrong. Also, lessons can stop accumulating due to no more room or no more flexibility, and can be greatly missed. I doubt that I will be a better person, morally, socially, intellectually, or physically twenty years from now than I am right at this moment. I may be, and I hope I will be, but if I am it will be a rare accomplishment, not a typical byproduct of the normal attributes of aging.

Even at fifty-nine, I am less flexible and jovial than I was earlier. I have less mental might than earlier. I can't run as fast as earlier. I get immobilized by back spasms now, not earlier. My digestion isn't as robust. There are cracks in the crannies. Yes, I know many things that I didn't know years ago. But for many purposes, I'd take the younger me, not the current me, as an ally. Growing old is a mixed bag, and only with a whole lot of effort and considerable luck do we go out of adulthood more worthy, worldly, and productive than we entered it. "Grow old along with me," is fine. "The best is yet to be," is wishful thinking.

Living Radical and Socializing

Don't ask me nothin' about nothin',
I just might tell you the truth.
—Bob Dylan

One of the personal problems of being on the Left is living life. Different people conduct their social lives differently in different times. When I was in high school and college, and for some years thereafter, I had a lot of people to socialize with whose values and inclinations were congenial to me and vice versa. That's what we usually find in a community of friends. But for a revolutionary in the United States, this often doesn't exist.

There are some venues, I suppose we might call them, where a person with revolutionary beliefs and commitments can operate without undue derision and discomfort. I used to play Go at a club in Boston. Interactions there overwhelmingly centered around the game. If the topic turned to events of the day, there were a couple of people in the club I could relate to, more or less, but not the rest. Most of the people there had unadmirable views and I would either have to accept hearing them without commenting, or I would have to rebut them. I didn't want to be constantly educating people. It certainly isn't what I mean by socializing. It isn't congenial. It's organizing. There is nothing wrong with organizing, of course, but there is no point calling it a social life.

In Woods Hole, Massachusetts, where I have lived since 1992, I am basically a hermit. To be friends with lots of local people, for me, would mean having to dispute, debate, and otherwise interact about people's conservative, or, often worse, liberal, comments. Soon I would be either an oddity or a lecturer, and neither is my idea of a relaxing time. It is one thing to organize while organizing. It is another thing to organize while trying to be friends. It might be different if I worked with local folks. But I work at my desk, alone.

What makes me hermitic in Woods Hole is part of what causes the Left to become insular. We, like everyone else, want to spend time among people who we like and who we can talk to without worrying about offending them or being offended. But in that case, how do you reach out?

My main income-generating and political work is ZNet, along with a lot of speaking and writing. All that is no problem, because the people involved, who I mostly interact with at a distance, regrettably, are like me. I can socialize in those realms, or I could if the people I work with lived where I do, that is. In my off time, however, what little off time I have, I don't want to be teaching, organizing, or defending my views. So other than socializing with family and far away friends, I watch TV, read novels, play Go online, and kayak, but I avoid sustained contact with people from the local community. TV doesn't talk back. TV doesn't get offended. And TV doesn't offend me, or rather, when it does, I change the station. And the same goes for books that I choose to read, or for playing Go, or for kayaking, or eating, for that matter.

Lydia, in contrast, loves acting, writing, and directing theater. In Boston, years back, she produced and acted in shows with political content. In Woods Hole, however, she pretty much has to work with a little group that is mostly caring liberals. The people, in other words, are in no sense radical, much less closely similar to Lydia in views. In such a group, as compared to a Go Club, it is harder to avoid stressful differences. Things that offend Lydia while meeting with fellow theater folks can be completely imperceptible to others in the group. For example, when Lydia's theater group wants to accept funds from a consortium of companies that are seeking, in return, ads and sponsorship rights for theater events, for Lydia it is a horrendous situation but for the other theater members, her concerns appear outlandish and she seems to be from Neptune.

Smaller examples happen weekly. This is not pleasant on one's off hours, when one is trying to relax, or to be creative. And, of course, Lydia's theater buddies don't want to be organized while trying to enjoy theater in their leisure. Nor does Lydia want to organize them while trying to enjoy theater in her leisure. But the differences that exist aren't the kind that friends have that spice up life. These differences are instead immense, fundamental, life-defining, morals-upholding, cutting-edge, in-your-face, in-your-soul, chasms—at least for Lydia. Lydia struggles, often with huge personal dislocation and pain. I avoid the whole problem.Vive hermitude. Both approaches debilitate. Revolution is the only complete solution, as usual.

I suspect the above-described dynamics may have a good deal to do with why so many people enter but later leave the Left. If I go to a party and someone expresses views that horrify me, do I tell the person that what they are saying is tantamount to fascist violence and brutality? Do I let them know I think their morality has disappeared and their stance is, however far from their intentions, objectively barbaric? Do I let them know what I really think about their words and beliefs? Do I try to break through their smug complacency that the war is far away and who gives a damn? Or do I just say, hey, how's the weather, please pass the chips, how'd the Red Sox do yesterday?

I used to confront differences, but it was when I was attending parties where the chasms in beliefs were only gaps and lots of folks were traversing the same broad path I was. I tried to ignore differences at parties where I was traversing a path far removed from others. I didn't like either option. So now I just don't go. I am not saying this is ideal. I am not recommending it. There are better compromises, I am sure, and ones that are more productive, too, if one can hack them. I am just reporting the facts.

Lydia in contrast, goes to parties, and talks about all kinds of popular culture that deflects away from problem areas, and every once in awhile, makes some headway, even at parties, regarding things that matter, and of course, also, now and then, all hell breaks loose. Lydia grins or frowns and bears it. I neither grin nor bear it. The personal dimensions of political life are multifold. Navigating such matters gets easier, however, like many other complexities, when there are more revolutionaries and we are doing better.

There is another side to this: what it looks like to people outside. In short, to many, my life and the lives of people like me look demented. We should realize that it seems to many who view us that we are addicted to a cause and blind to all else. But I know a little about addictions. My brother Eddie stuck with his early-life gambling, becoming mostly a professional poker player, but also a world-class gin player. As a pro, Eddie played in Las Vegas as well as other casino towns, and finally in Florida. He frequently depended on parental help and married and divorced repeatedly.

My parents' great hope was to break Eddie of his gambling addiction. I think my mother was more accepting of it than my father, and also more aware that the battle against it was hopeless. First they tried unrelenting support, which was their most natural approach, year in and year out. Then they tried tough love, though they weren't as good at that. I still don't understand gambling as an addiction. Eddie doesn't get withdrawal symptoms when he can't gamble, even for months on end. How can gambling be an addiction like heroin, cigarettes, or alcohol, if withdrawal has no physical impact? In his more recent days, Eddie was, however, addicted to painkillers. Take those away and anyone could easily see the physical withdrawal he endured.

It seems to me, then, that Eddie was no more or less addicted to gambling than I am to reading mysteries, keeping up with popular science, or watching favorite TV shows, much less than I am to revolutionary involvement—or than my sister Anita is to art, say, or than Lydia is to theater or revolutionary involvement. But people look at Eddie, and because he gambles so much, and they don't get it, they call it addiction. Well, people look at me, and because I work all hours and am singularly focused on political calculations, and they don't get it, they think I am addicted.

What is wrong with gambling, I think, is not that it is addictive, whatever precisely that might mean, but that it destroys social solidarity, induces dependency, and makes catastrophe likely. When you gamble and you win, things move along swimmingly and you start to spend effusively. You throw around money as part of the gambling lifestyle. But if you have a losing spell (and the vagaries of statistics make that very hard to avoid) you may get all the way down to zero and even into debt. This makes gambling a fragile career. Eddie was very talented, ingratiating, and social, and even capable of generosity and kindness, but all this is now buried under the hide he has needed to develop for his craft, and under the impositions of real addictions.

Being a revolutionary, regrettably, has some things in common with being a gambler, and of course some things quite different, depending on the person and the societal context. For me, being a revolutionary means being committed to working to replace oppressive defining institutions of social life with new ones that meet far higher moral standards. In being a revolutionary, among so many people who are not, I find I have developed a thick and often bristly hide, but not, I hope, a callous or uncaring one.

Chapter 14

The Action Faction

SLF Booted Out

The big thieves hang the little ones.
—Czech Prover

On one trip across country, after graduating from MIT, I arrived in Seattle with my MIT friends Peter Bohmer and George Katsiaficas. There we met a group that called itself the Seattle Liberation Front (SLF). These guys had gone to Seattle in 1970 largely from upstate New York, where some had been students. They were intent on making waves and chose Seattle for their contribution. Their idea was to create a gigantic stir, galvanizing rebellion. The people in the SLF weren't stupid or malevolent, but nonetheless they instructively crystallized misconceived sixties macho madness, of which, it has to be acknowledged, there was way too much.

I remember arriving, chatting, and then going out with a member of the SLF to get some food for a meal. We went to a supermarket, him dressed in pants that were falling off—he was way ahead of his time on that score—and he promptly stuffed some steaks into his clothes (the actual reason they were so loose) and strutted out safely. Now, I have stolen, in that era in particular, but his approach felt more like bravado undertaken for show than something he needed to do to survive or improve his circumstances. He looked like a child doing something naughty in plain sight, expecting by sheer will to back down his parents.

Is that what someone else would have seen, had they been along on my chair-stealing episode in Amherst? Perhaps so. Which makes me wonder, as well, about my own mix of confidence and bravado. You see, the Seattle Seven, or whatever it was, turned out to be a disaster for Seattle. They did stir the kettle with their shenanigans. But the resulting chaos wasn't a positive inducement to activism. Instead, it sowed seeds of enmity and hostility, and, as I heard the stories, the group was finally thoroughly delegitimated in 1971 by Seattle's women's movement, which accused the SLF of violent, macho behavior.

Theft, however, wasn't just SLF posturing, but became part of the Left lifestyle for a few years in the late 1960s and early 1970s. I once took-off across the country with some friends, with only $5 in hand. I got out West and still had the $5. In those days we routinely stole our food, or scrounged it. We would go into a restaurant and eat off people's plates, sitting down for our meal in seats others had vacated, and eating the rest of the meals they had left on their plates. Alternatively, we would order and eat full meals, and then all but one of us at the table would leave the restaurant, while the one left would go to the bathroom. When that last person left the bathroom, he would leave the restaurant as well. If he was stopped, he pretended to believe his friends already paid. You could only pull off this trick safely if you had enough money on you to pay off the tab if you were stopped. Having the funds made the scam believable. Moreover, to do it morally we had to ask the waitress whether she would get stuck for the tab if we didn't pay. If she said yes, we would go somewhere else. The waitresses never ratted on us—they had no love, of course, for their employers. What was the difference between good stealing and bad stealing? A fine line.

While we are at it, there is also the opposite side of the coin: being ripped off. I lived for a time in a small apartment in Harvard Square above some stores. You could not only go down the front stairs and out into the Square, you could also go out a back window and climb down to an alley and from there go out to the Square. I had my stereo ripped off a couple of times from this place, via that rear window. My reaction was another of my not-proudest moments.

Each time my stereo was ripped off, maybe four times in six or eight years, here and at other apartments too, I would tell my father, who, in turn, reported it to his insurance company to get funds for a replacement. Each time I would go to the stereo store and let them know I was getting a new system and that it would cost whatever the insurance company felt the last one was worth, and that's how much I would have to spend on it. Each time the store would vouch for my having had a prior system that cost more than it really had. In this way, I kept upgrading my stereo. Stephen Shalom finally pointed out to me what I conveniently hadn't considered for myself. I assumed I was not only improving my listening experience but was also striking a blow against the corporate insurance business. Steve noted that what probably happened due to thefts was that the insurance outfits raised their rates, so I was really redistributing wealth from the rate-paying public to myself. In retrospect, it is likely a bit more complex. For example, if there was less theft could the insurance companies bargain as much from the public? Would their rates drop if theft dropped? If not, if the theft didn't increase their power to extract fees, then theft really did reduce what they accumulated without raising what the public paid. If the theft did enable them to charge more by the same volume than in its absence, then Steve was right.

I should note in passing that this reasoning might well have been the origin in me of what I think is an important insight about capitalist economy. Prices move with bargaining power. Who gets what is determined by a clash and jangle of countless interactions. You can't look at only one or two to predict outcomes. You can, however, predict large-scale market biases if you pay attention to overarching power relations. Powerful actors dump pain onto weak actors and retain gains for themselves. The insurance companies have a lot of power, way more than thieves or consumers, so insurance companies are rarely victimized.

While living in Cambridge, I had a Chevrolet Camaro that my parents had gotten me. I was the youngest child and got the most goodies because of it. It was the early years of that Chevy model and the car was sporty and got ripped off often. Cambridge was the car-theft capital of the country at the time, but this was actually people taking cars to joyride, not to paint and sell. The Camaro would turn up a day or two after being taken and the police would return it barely worse for wear. This got so predictable that I used to leave a note in the windshield when I particularly needed the car the next day. I would tell the thieves please to not take it that night. I only left the notes sometimes, and it was never taken on those nights. The joyriders and I had a thing going.

Weather Forecast

It was the best of times, it was the worst of times, it was the age of wisdom, it was the age of foolishness, it was the epoch of belief, it was the epoch of incredulity, it was the season of Light, it was the season of Darkness, it was the spring of hope, it was the winter of despair.
—Charles Dickens

In my opinion, the New Left represented an immense outpouring of solidarity, humanity, and creativity, with some rough edges, of course. The amazing and hard-to-comprehend feature of the rough edges is that by and large they weren't due to disturbed souls, ne'er-do-well personalities, moral misfits, or even just average folk. They arose from some of the most exemplary people in my generation. I am talking about people who went down self-destructive and otherwise harmful byways but who certainly were not pursuing wealth or power despite having plenty of means to do so.

For example, the organization named Weatherman, after the Dylan line "you don't need a weatherman to know which way the wind blows," was an outgrowth of some foolish differences within the major student and youth movements of the time. The Progressive Labor Party (PLP), a Maoist spinoff from the Communist

Party, started joining SDS in 1966—infiltrating so as to overcome. The PLPers pushed old-style Marxism, wore suspenders to look like workers, and had old-style mannerisms. These guys not only sounded like textbooks, they didn't even like rock and roll. SDS polarized, and finally split. At MIT, for example, PLP had its own ridiculously out-of-touch SDS chapter, alongside our hip one. The Weather people, going another step, decided that the population of the U.S., in particular the workers who PLPers celebrated, were a moral and social basket case. It would be hard to convey the anger that could arise, breaking into serious fights, between these scuffling sectarian trends. PLP disappeared as a relevant factor, especially for me, but not Weatherman.

With the exception of some more enlightened elements of the black and other minority communities, and of course also excepting the occasional white traitor to the U.S. who signed up to join Weatherman, the Weather people considered the U.S. population too bought off to see its own subjugation, much less to feel solidarity with people in Indochina and elsewhere. Weatherman thus came to the conclusion that a revolution in the U.S. depended overwhelmingly on the fighting tenacity of people in other countries. What did that leave for Weatherman to do? They could extend Third-World movements into the U.S. as a fifth column. They saw no hope of building massive movements here, but felt they could be a domestic thorn in the side of imperialism, helping the rest of the world bring imperialism down.

I first heard all this when the Boston chapter of Weatherman was trying to recruit me. You have to understand, again, these were highly educated, well-spoken, and, in virtually every case, highly committed folks. They also packed a wallop when it came to guilt-tripping and they asked me and Robin Hahnel to come along on a modest action, to see how they operated. So Robin and I went with a few Weather friends, including one who is now an organizer in LA, one who is an elected political official in Connecticut, and one who is a historian in New York. About ten of us, or thereabouts, piled into a subway car heading for the stop nearest a large dorm at Boston University. While in the subway car, trundling along underground, one of the Weather people, according to prearranged agreement, stood up on his seat to give a speech to his captive audience of other subway riders. He nervously yelled out "Country sucks, kick ass," and promptly sat down. That was his whole speech, and their whole message. It was their entire case. It was their whole damn enchilada. No wonder you don't need a Weatherman to know which way the wind blows. They had nothing useful to say about the wind or anything else. Robin and I weren't impressed. It didn't seem likely to go down in history as comparably eloquent to Martin Luther King's "I Have a Dream" speech or Fidel Castro's "History Will Absolve Me" speech. This wasn't a historic "Sermon in the Subway."

At any rate, we got to our stop and piled out. We were led into a BU dorm hosting a freshman mixer—or market, more aptly. The girls were meat. The boys were shopping. Weatherman, particularly in Boston, was significantly affected by the women's movement. It was not only out to end imperialism, but also to end patriarchy. So far so good, you might reasonably think. The plan for that evening, however, which Robin and I got to see unfold due to Weatherman's efforts to use this event to convince us that we should join their organization, was to teach the BU freshmen a thing or two about tactics and goals. The slogan of the day was "smash monogamy." The Weather people, older, more confident, and often larger than the freshmen, shuffled out into the mixer and broke up dancing couples, demanding, instead, that all dancing be singular or done in groups. Couples were called monogamous and disallowed. Brilliant! Recruitment didn't exactly break records that night. By the way, "smash monogamy" became a catch phrase, meaning sleep with anyone for any reason—dignity, much less honesty and mutual respect, be damned.

This was one of a string of masterpieces of organizing acumen that the best minds of my generation, stuck in a collective project that subverted their common sense, dreamed up. For example, there was the idea for what Weatherman called jailbreaks. Reveling revolutionaries would go to a public school and hand out leaflets urging the students to escape their jail cells and break free into society by walking out. This had a semblance of (vastly exaggerated) sanity to it, save for the idea that college kids were going to, in ten minutes, organize massive breakdowns in high schools. Worse than this effort, however, was Weatherman's beachhead ploy.

Weatherman, remember, felt that there were only going to be a small number of people operating in a fifth column, pro-Third World movement creating mayhem in the U.S. Some would be white and working class, so that was one place to recruit. However, the wisest Weather wizards pointed out that white working-class guys viewed radicals as whining pansies without substance. Weatherman couldn't befriend salt-of-the-earth workers, this argument ran, until Weatherman disabused working-class kids of thinking that revolutionaries were beneath contempt due to being soft and cowardly. From wherever they got this analysis, Weatherman managed to hatch an associated strategy.

One fine summer Saturday, a troop of about twenty Weather people went to a working-class beach in the Dorchester section of Boston. They strutted out onto the beach, en masse, and stuck a pole in the ground, flying the NLF (Vietcong) flag from it. Now this beach, of course, was full of relatives of boys in Indochina, not to mention boys buried from having been in Indochina. As expected, crowds surrounded the Weather people. The courageous revolutionaries didn't try to communicate rationally. Instead, they belligerently ratcheted up the tension. Their strategy was to provoke a fight and then show in the ensuing melee that they could dish it out, and they could take it, too. Then everyone would go off to a bar, tend wounds, and respectfully talk real substance. Of course, the plan was nonsense in every facet. Most disruptive of Weather intentions, the local Dorchester lads quickly routed the Weather warriors, probably thinking, for the first time in their lives, gee, how wimpy these folks are in battle.

While thinking about how to relate to the invitation to join Weatherman, I consulted two people. When I asked Michael Ansara, a very knowledgeable movement friend from the time, about Weatherman—and he had quite a few friends from Harvard who were in the group (whereas, to my knowledge, no one from MIT ever joined)—he said, look, even Weatherman's seemingly most solid claims don't hold up. The Vietnamese resistance came into being over decades and employed weapons left over from World War II and/or supplied over channels that don't exist in most Third World countries. The idea that this revolt against the U.S. will be repeated throughout the Third World, or, for that matter, that it will win really new relations in even Vietnam, all without massive movements inside the U.S. to restrain our government from annihilating Vietnamese aspirations, is comforting claptrap. The truth is, if we can't build huge movements in the U.S., people in the Third World can't win, no matter their heroism. Yes, the power of the people is greater than the man's technology—a slogan we all found appealing at the time—but the people have to be in position to constrain the technology. Ansara was convincing in his claims, but the allure of Weather militancy wasn't easy to overcome. So I went to Chomsky to ask him, too, about the choice.

Noam hates to give advice. He doesn't want people doing what he says because he says it, which is admirable, for the most part. But sometimes he thinks the way to avoid currying blind followers is not to say anything, as compared to relying on the person being addressed to weigh what he says carefully. Noam also has an aversion to addressing strategy on grounds that, since so little is known about social dynamics, and since conditions are so context specific, the only reliable arbiter is to try things. But when I asked Noam about Weatherman, he was willing to give advice. I think his worries for my future overrode his reticence to provide advice about life paths. I don't remember what he said about the relations of the U.S. and Vietnam, though I am guessing it was similar to what Ansara said, but with more evidence. But I do remember his conclusion. This old-timer (he was then just over forty, an old-timer to me) said to me, roughly, the bottom line is that a bunch of young people are going to go off hand in hand and alienate many others, and, finally, go to jail or otherwise horribly hurt themselves to no useful gain. This was before the Weather people began alienating people widely, getting uselessly arrested, and finally in a few cases even blowing themselves up. Noam, however sadly, was on target. I didn't join Weatherman, nor did Robin.

I remember going to demonstrations and on several occasions watching Weather people provoke cops into confrontations. They got good at doing that and also good at knowing when to run away to avoid getting busted or beaten, leaving others to suffer those fates. I also remember one night, around midnight, in my apartment, hearing a knock on the door. I opened and in came five or six Weather people. They were very quiet and stooped over, as if hiding from being seen. The local Weather leader asked me in hushed tones if they could stay the night. They were on the run from imperialism. In fact, they could have slept anywhere in the city, including in their own rooms, totally safely. But they were practicing for hard times to come. I let them stay and they were gone in the morning.

Others in my generation—it wasn't only Weatherman, though it was only a very small minority—routinely went off a few miles from their cities to practice rifle-shooting at tin cans, also for hard times to come. Some would cut themselves and then suture the cuts, learning minor self-surgery, again for hard times to come. Meanwhile, they would give speeches like, "country sucks, kick ass," setting themselves up for hard times to come.

I know I am being harsh, but it is all true. If piled up like this it gives a damning impression, that's because it was pretty damning. But where does the blame lie? As I look back on it, many of the best minds and hearts of my generation got caught up in spirals of anger that took them far from relevance. Revolution is not a tea party. We were very young. We had few models to consult. We had few reliable and caring elders to learn from. We were polarized into paranoia regarding everyone and everything—"paranoia runs deep, into your life it will creep." Throw in as-yet-unchallenged oppressive tendencies built into society and, via society, built into us, add macho personas and anti-intellectual leanings— and it isn't surprising we got what we got.

Weatherman's heritage, in my view, was a bunch of blown-up bathrooms, a few blown-up halls, and a few blown-up people, the latter within Weatherman itself. The ideas that fueled Weatherman, as distinguished from those fueling the broader Left, weren't worthy. It is not true that people in industrialized countries cannot create huge movements able to change their societies. It is not true that movements based elsewhere are the only hope. Blowing up bathrooms or picking fights with community people won't build movements, ever, anywhere.

To resist, and to do it well, honestly, and with real and lasting commitment— which is what Weatherman wanted to achieve—is still most certainly a goal to pursue. As but one indicator, there are 191 member states in the United Nations. There is a U.S. military presence in 141 of these member states. Weatherman, and the New Left more broadly, weren't wrong about the scale or the tenacity of imperial injustice. They were only wrong about how best to uproot it, about what was necessary to win lasting change.

My Adventurism

Fervor is the weapon of choice for the impotent.
—Franz Fanon

Memoirs entail personal revelations and this one may help convey a bit more about how good people can get caught up in odd thoughts. Robin and I entertained pursuing our own personal escapades at two different times. One plan was to go to a local war-related company—Dow or Raytheon or something of that ilk—with a large barrel of gasoline. We would sneak in and the two of us would be there, with this big barrel full of gasoline, with a short fuse attached. We would announce that unless we were given media coverage to state our case publicly, we would set it off. The second brainstorm was to go to Logan Airport, get on a plane on the ground, and hold it ransom with the same kind of demand. In hindsight I imagine we were playing out our frustration in daydreams that we would never implement. At the time, however, we thought we were seriously assessing these options. Given what I know about what I myself and lots of other people did in those days, I am not sure there is much difference between those two conditions. My guess would be that most odd things that get done are posturing that escapes the restraints of common sense and becomes real. In our case, saner heads, which meant Lydia, reeled us in. Two lives saved.

Timeline Confusions

First they ignore you. Then they laugh at you.
Then they fight you. Then you win.
—Mohandas Gandhi

Martin Luther King, near the end of his life, said, "For years I labored with the idea of reforming the existing institutions, a little change here, a little change there. Now I feel quite differently. I think you've got to have a reconstruction of the entire society, a revolution of values."

There was considerable confusion on the Left in the sixties associated with whether to fight day to day, as Rosa Luxemburg put it, for "reform or revolution," and about what each meant. I believed it was a false dichotomy. I thought you could fight for a revolution and also little changes here and little changes there. The trick was to have the little changes benefit future aims as well as current needs.

There is a different side of the same confusion. Martin Luther King might have said it earlier in his life but, instead, it was Hugo Chavez, as relayed by Tariq Ali in his book, *Street Fighting Years*. Chavez would not express his thoughts identically today, I believe, as he is now, at least as of this writing, unequivocally revulutionary, but here he is, talking to Ali in summer, 2004:

169

I don't believe in the dogmatic postulates of Marxist revolution. I don't accept that we are living in a period of proletarian revolution. All that must be revisited. Reality is telling us that every day. Are we aiming in Venezuela today for the abolition of private property or a classless society? I don't think so. But if I'm told that because of that reality you can't do anything to help the poor, the people who have made this country rich through their labor—and never forget that some of it was slave labor—then I say 'We part company.' I will never accept that there can be no redistribution of wealth in society. Our upper classes don't even like paying taxes. That's one reason they hate me. We said 'You must pay taxes.' I believe it's better to die in battle, rather than hold aloft a very revolutionary and very pure banner, and do nothing. That position often strikes me as very convenient, a good excuse. Try and make your revolution, go into combat, advance a little, even it it's only a millimeter, in the right direction, instead of dreaming about utopia.

Again there is a polarization: do something modest, or seek revolution. But for me the big problem with Chavez's advisory is, how does he know what the right direction is? How does he fulfill King's admonition while also delivering greater benefits now? Chavez rejecting idle dreaming is correct. I had no patience in the sixties for people who bull-sessioned nights away but never organized during the days. Idle dreaming is idle. King rejecting social democratic pragmatism is also correct. Seeking worthy but limited gains as ends in themselves will never transform deep sources of suffering. It is fatalist to think so. So how do we dream about tomorrow for benefit today? How do we act today to attain tomorrow? How do we connect the two inclinations without violating the logic of either?

I am a revolutionary, like King, and like Chavez in 2006, as I write, too. Our defining institutions need transcending and I want to help accomplish that. I can't abide capitalism, patriarchy, racism, or authoritarianism. We need innovation from top to bottom, and from skin to core and back again. In the sixties we rejected as insufficient a reformism that sought only "a little change here, a little change there," with each little change seen as an end in itself. We sought revolution, meaning systemic change of defining institutions, but I didn't believe that being revolutionary required that I reject little changes per se. Little changes could be the heart and soul of big ones.

For the reformist, the whole enchilada is tweaking the system via little changes. In the sixties, the reformist seeking to end the war saw the war's conclusion as the whole goal. You ended it and you went home. For the revolutionary, while little changes could be tasty, the full meal was revolution. In the sixties, the revolutionary seeking to end the war sought the war's end, but also sought to end imperialism, to end capitalism, and to usher in a better world.

Like reformists, I certainly believed that we should fight for little changes. In fact, I think that to denigrate fighting for little changes subverts prospects of revolutionary changes, and even of basic solidarity. How could I claim to be a revolutionary and also reject reforms? Imagine a revolutionary in the sixties rejecting as misguided work against the war, or against poverty, or against Jim Crow racism in the South. Not an appealing picture, is it? But there were some who did that on grounds that improving people's lives would diminish the likelihood they would rebel. How cynical, how crass, and how uncaring well-meaning strategy can be.

In the sixties popular slogans included "You are either part of the problem or part of the solution" and "Revolution is the only solution." I proclaimed both slogans often and loud. And I still like them, but I have learned that I have to be careful about what these slogans mean to others. I realized I could devote my life to revolutionary changes of basic underlying structures and seek surface reforms over and over too because there was nothing nonrevolutionary about surface reforms. I realized I fought for a new world, a revolution, and to end the war in Vietnam, a reform, and that the two were compatible. Worthy reforms, like ending wars, winning higher wages, and affirmative action, save and enrich people's lives. That is good, not bad.

Ending a war is a reform. Winning higher wages via a strike is a reform. Affirmative action is a reform. Shutting down the IMF would be a reform. Winning instant runoff voting, partial public control over government budgets, and public oversight of corporate production processes would be winning reforms. Reforms are good unless we think the quality of people's lives doesn't matter.

The thing that wasn't revolutionary, and that King was trying to transcend, was fighting for "little changes" as ends unto themselves and particularly in ways that presupposed or even ratified existing defining conditions. What wasn't revolutionary was fighting for little changes in ways that presupposed that those little changes were all there was and in ways that solidified society's underlying logic. Reforms were band-aids on a sick system. Using a band-aid is not a bad idea to stem bleeding and, indeed, we needed to stem the bleeding of Indochina in the sixties. Ignoring the underlying cause of bleeding—imperialism and capitalism—however, would not have been a good idea.

How did we fight for worthy gains in the present without falling into the trap of presupposing that a new system was impossible and that only limited gains were ever attainable? We had an analysis and understood our efforts in context. If this couldn't be done, we would have had to choose between fighting for reforms and forgoing revolution, or fighting for revolution and forgoing reforms. Luckily, the reality was and still is that we can seek revolution and also fight for reforms—both as part of the means of attaining revolution and on their own merits as well.

Those in the sixties who argued against seeking reforms worried about a slippery slope. The May 1968 France slogan was indicative: "No replastering, the structure is rotten." Such revolutionaries often thought that fighting for higher wages meant accepting capitalism since fighting for higher wages didn't immediately eliminate capitalism and even assumed it was persisting longer. They often thought fighting for an end to a war meant accepting imperialism since ending one war wasn't ending all wars.

More complexly, it wasn't that anti-reformers thought fighting against a war or for higher wages, by that fact alone, precluded more comprehensive change. It was that they thought that every advocate of reforms was on a slippery slope where the skidding involved calculating the mood of centers of power, petitioning centers of power, negotiating with centers of power, dressing for and talking like functionaries of centers of power, legitimating the rules proposed by centers of power, and ultimately slipping into accepting the permanent inevitability of centers of power. What's odd is that these opponents of reform, so attuned to the very real dynamics of these particular slippery slopes, didn't fear another slippery slope, easily as evident, which they themselves typically slid down.

Deriding reforms led via a most slippery path to callous arrogance and sectarian aloofness most often expressed as dismissing or even deriding other people's short-term well-being. This engendered a slip-slide into what is called ultra leftism. One slipped out of touch with the travails and aims of people. One viewed distant liberation as if it were imminent, simultaneously ignoring immediate pain.

Did the two slippery slopes, one leading into reformism and the other into ultra leftism—both of which really did exist—mean that we couldn't seek reforms and we also couldn't seek revolution, so the only solution was private—as in going to the beach or living in a commune? Did it mean that we had to give up social change lest we become disconnected and sectarian as well as callous to pain on the one hand, or become supporters of the status quo on the other hand? I think this conundrum caused many people to give up their sixties activism. I think today, too, it is why many young people reject "being political."

The resolution was made explicit by a French revolutionary from the era of the sixties, Andre Gorz. I remember being powerfully affected by Gorz's book, *Strategy for Labor*. Gorz suggested that the route bypassing the Scylla of reformism and the Charybdis of ultra leftism was to seek reforms in a manner that also sought revolution. He called doing this "fighting for nonreformist reforms." It wasn't that the reforms themselves were necessarily different in the two approaches. It wasn't, most often, the demands we made that made us nonreformist. It was our process of fighting for demands. The reformist might seek higher wages or affirmative action or to end a war, and so might the nonreformist revolutionary. The same demand, therefore, could be reformist or nonreformist. What mattered to Gorz was how we talked about our demands, how we created movements to win them, and what we sought to do in the aftermath of winning them. Gorz's idea of nonreformist reforms was to seek changes in the present that improved people's lives with rhetoric, organizations, and tactics, all of which contributed to people wanting still more gains, people being more aroused and conscious, and people being empowered and eager. The idea was to win reforms, organizational gains, and consciousness, all in a trajectory leading to sufficient power, clarity, and commitment to win new institutions.

The antidote to reformism for Gorz, which convinced me, too, was not to decry reforms (as in telling antiwar protesters they were misguided because they weren't saying revolution now), but to win reforms in ways that moved continually forward and presupposed system replacement. What some of us realized in the sixties, trying to avoid the slippery slopes of reformism and ultra leftism, was that we had to pay attention to both reforms and revolution and that the concept of nonreformist reforms was a convincing way to do it.

What about the personal tension between the reformist individual and the revolutionary individual? We saw plenty of that between sixties barricades and bookstalls. Most destructively, mutual respect was often destroyed by disdain. The sixties reformist who honestly believed that no new world was possible found the sixties revolutionary to be delusionally compromising people's realistic prospects in the pursuit of false dreams. Such a reformist, I came to realize, could be as committed as any revolutionary to justice, peace, and equity. Such a reformist could be as courageous, honest, and hardworking. But most revolutionaries had a hard time seeing those possibilities. Revolutionaries assumed reformist rejection of transformation stemmed from allegiance to one or another aspect of oppression. Assuming that motive, the revolutionary felt hostile to all reformists and often to all reforms. A degree of humility could—and when it occasionally surfaced did—do wonders for the effectiveness of both sides.

Chapter 15

The Black Panthers

From Smack to the Little Red Book

The walls, the bars, the guns and the guards
can never encircle or hold down the idea of the people.
—Huey Newton

In October of 1966, in Oakland, California, Huey Newton and Bobby Seale founded the Black Panther Party for Self-Defense. The Black Panther Party was, in its public persona, an armed organization that mainly (a) stood up to police repression, (b) engaged in social programs for community members, and (c) sought to raise community consciousness by distributing a newspaper, leafleting, etc., which (d) devolved into having to protect itself against constant violent attack that over time shattered its wherewithal.

The heart of the Black Panther Party's official self-definition was their ten-point program. They wanted "freedom," "power to determine the destiny of our black community," "full employment," "decent housing," honest, critical education, an end to "police brutality," military exemption, release of blacks from prisons, trial by peers, and "land, bread, housing, education, clothing, justice and peace."

The Panthers picked up the gun to demonstrate black unwillingness to succumb to force. They provided free breakfasts to poor kids from the community to serve the people. They lacked sufficient support in their own community, and beyond, to withstand the assaults hurled at them. They were hounded, harassed, manipulated, jailed, and murdered into oblivion.

My direct interactions with the Black Panthers were relatively few. I remember a private talk with Doug Miranda, who was then the head of the Boston chapter of the Panthers and who later moved on to become a southern coordinator of the party. We sat in a diner, eating a bit, and chatting. Partly we were talking about ongoing events of the time and partly I was asking Miranda about the Panthers. Most people in major projects for which they are taking great risks, even risking their lives, have a tendency to see what they are doing through filters that remove the flaws and highlight the gems. Doug Miranda, however, saw things more as they were. He explained to me, after our getting acclimated with one another, why the Panthers, despite their admirable commitments, nonetheless had such a horribly limited way of communicating and even comprehending reality—which was regrettably garnering them much visibility and notoriety but only modest gains in membership. He told me that many Panthers effectively went from dealing heroin to dealing Mao's Little Red Book overnight, and that the mind sets and habits of the former were only repackaged—not replaced—during the switch.

This was more than a telling revelation of what should have been obvious to everyone watching. And it also wasn't, if one was careful in thinking about what Miranda was saying, a total condemnation. Miranda was simply telling the truth. It was not meant to condemn or to propose elimination or enshrinement of the Panthers. It was meant to explain their less admirable traits and provide insight that might lead to improvements.

Social change, Miranda was implicitly noting, was not something that springs from elysian fields. It rises from the bedrock of real circumstances. Worse, the conditions of oppression imposed on people by real circumstances often lead to jaundiced behaviors, and those can be carried over, as well, into resistance. My lunch with Miranda taught me that even as one can't reject this truth about inadequacies, one must also not make believe it isn't so. One must see the truth, and act on it, working to correct problems.

My reading of Panther history is that the first generation of Panther leadership and prominent activists—such as Eldridge Cleaver, Huey Newton, and perhaps Bobby Seale, too—never fully transcended their ways of thinking from the past. They augmented them, yes, but not enough. They created a thuggish party, truth be told, not a party nourishing the seeds of a better future in the present. Perhaps Doug Miranda was different, and surely the key Panther from Chicago, Fred Hampton, who was massacred in his bed by police, was dramatically different, and one can see quite easily the trajectory between the early founders and these people. I am here praising what's special in Malcolm X's history, I think, and in Stokely Carmichael's, too.

Transcending one's past, I realized in those days, may sometimes mean transcending drug-dealing habits and mind-sets, both commercial and violent. Other times it might mean transcending elitism, prejudice, or, alternatively, feelings of subordination and inferiority. Odds are that none of the past's imprints on us can be completely undone in the lives of single individuals, much less over the course of just a few frenetic years of crisis. Personality is usually rooted deeper. Movements must patiently help people change without making people miserable. Panther history showed me that movements must adopt collective norms and structures that militate against negative features dominating outcomes, rather than opting, as the Panthers did, for practices that elevate negative traits. If your rhetoric emphasizes that "today's pig (cop) is tomorrow's bacon," you are unlikely to develop a caring, calm, sober, serious, and steadfast demeanor.

When Eldridge Cleaver went to Vietnam, he came back and announced that the Vietnamese had told him that thereafter all proposals for trips had to go through him, with him passing judgment on who should go or not. It was a lie. The Vietnamese never imbued him with such responsibility, much less power. That individuals lied and aggrandized, however, was not the biggest problem. Of course that happened. When Panther leadership engaged in horribly violent behavior inside their own organization, when they demeaned opponents as vermin, that wasn't the biggest problem, either. People in our movements, no less than in society, carry bad baggage. The biggest problem was when movements lacked means to readily discern and reject such behavior or, even worse, when they propelled and celebrated it.

There is another variant of this experience that I only read about that played a comparable role in my thinking. In the Bolshevik revolution there was a need to collect money that transcended the capacities the movement had for attracting donations. Bank and train theft was adopted as a major source of funds. In charge of this branch of operations, the Bolsheviks put a young man with well-suited personality and disposition. His name was Josef Stalin.

Assume the robberies were essential to movement success. One can predict many likely implications for the people engaging in violent and surreptitious theft. So when it was all over and the new government was being established, why of all people would one want to begin elevating the head bank robber to great authority? As a hedge against the probability that such a person adopted inclinations to put himself above all else, not to mention tendencies toward paranoia and violence, bank robbers should have been reserved for collective activities, not for activities where they might ride their self-centered identifications to problematic outcomes. The Bolsheviks, however, not only didn't hold authoritarian tendencies in ill repute, they admired them, a bit like the Panthers, and the results were horrendous.

The upshot I took from all this was that the problem of holding in abeyance or overcoming our own elitism—sexism, racism, authoritarianism, classism, or other harmful and even brutal tendencies—depended partly on seeing them and self-consciously orienting ourselves away from them, but also partly on creating circumstances of equality that raised checks against them. Possible strategies were multiple and context dependent. They could involve a person constantly reminding himself that his advantages owe to history, luck, and injustice and not to superiority, and forcing herself to behave contrary to expectations and patterns in those regards. But mitigating strategies could and should also involve changing the relations that pertain among activists and especially their standards and methods of decision making.

As RL-SDS tried to do, at least in some respects, I came to realize that a movement should change the roles of actors in ways that diminish race, gender, and class-based differentials, and that redress social differences to remove the imbalances that these nasty ideologies promoted. To demand only that people individually wage a psychological battle against the ideologies while maintaining the material conditions of their origination wasn't completely impossible, but over the long haul it was unlikely to succeed. That was the lesson of ills like those in Weatherman and the Black Panther Party. Bad conditions in the movement aggravated bad behavioral outcomes. Remember KOR in Poland. The Panthers were much worse in respect to internal structure and style than KOR, and so got less far, but in the end KOR succumbed too.

Intercommunalism

I swear to the Lord
I still can't see
Why Democracy means
Everybody but me.
—*Langston Hughes*

My second memorable interaction with the Panthers was at a conference in part about Huey Newton's incarceration and in part about positive developments in the Party's program. Many things happened at the conference. For example, there was a bomb threat and we all had to exit, watch the bomb squad search the place—imagine the ignominy of all these revolutionaries depending on the police—and then settle back into our agenda. One speaker gave a talk announcing a new program called intercommunalism. He was trying to identify a pattern of relations commensurate to vastly improving interracial, religious, and ethnic relations in the U.S.

Many Leninists, which the Panthers rhetorically were, had historically seen this problem as relatively simple. There ultimately needed to be unification of communities. We shouldn't have blacks, Latinos, Jews, Catholics, and so on and so forth, at each other's throats, and the easiest way to undo such conflicts was to undo such differences. Let's have one religion, nation, ethnicity, race—which is to say, let's have one culture. Over time, let's have the rest fade away, like a bad dream, leaving universality.

The Panthers, though they were Leninist in many respects—it being a simple leap from violent authoritarian drug-dealing gangs to violent authoritarian Leninist party-building—saw through this aspect of some Leninists' agendas. They realized that while having one universal culture would by definition mean an end to cultural and community hostilities, it was an impossible dream, or, more accurately, an impossible nightmare. Human conditions were too diverse, the Panthers understood, to permit only one culture. And once different cultures existed, nearly all cultures were far too serviceable and meaningful to people to be easily jettisoned. A truly domineering political project might impose on everyone a single culture, but it would be the culture of the dominant groups in the project even if it called itself something new and superior—like say "revolutionary culture," "humane culture," or "socialist culture," as opposed to more honestly calling itself "white" or "Christian" or "Russian culture"—but the subterranean reality would be that other patterns would live on and seek to revive. The imposition of a single dominant culture would be felt by most as a horribly oppressive denial and not as transcendence and liberation. This was the prior history of Leninist interaction with indigenous cultural communities, however well-motivated the choices were for many adherents, and it went far toward explaining not only the emergence of national conflict's role in the elimination of the Soviet regime, but perhaps even more the abiding hatred for Marxism Leninism among many indigenous communities. While resistance to Marxist cultural norms would often get mixed up with reactionary agendas, as in the case of the Miskito Indians' opposition to the Sandinistas in Nicaragua, for example, the indigenous core rejection of Marxism Leninism's rejection of religion and imposition of monolithic cultural values was quite legitimate.

At any rate, the Panthers, or some of them, saw through all this and were struggling to find a formulation that fought against all kinds of cultural subjugation and hierarchy while elevating cultural diversity as a primary value. They called their fledgling notions "intercommunalism" way before anyone came up with the label "multiculturalism," and I actually think intercommunalism is both a better name, and, more important, had lurking within it insights that were more serious in various regards. Later Robin Hahnel and I adopted that label, intercommunalism, for ideas we thought ought to be developed into a set of goals for cultural relations in a better world.

For all their faults, the Panthers were a heroic attempt and their destruction by a vicious state, not to mention taking the lives of so many leaders, paved the way for decades of despair and pain that black communities are still seeking in diverse ways to transcend back onto a path labeled liberation. King's mountain is still in our future.

Chapter 16

Black Like Who?

Bar Mitzvahed into Radicalism?

*It is not by confining one's neighbor that
one is convinced of one's own sanity.*
—*Fyodor Dostoevsky*

Religion has had a lot do with cultural politics throughout history, as it does today. My own religious encounters weren't particularly significant in my life, save for two. I am Jewish, just barely, I guess. I went to Jewish Sunday school until my Bar Mitzvah, which meant going to classes one day a week after regular school was out for a year or so. In Hebrew school I rebelled twice, and I think these acts may have primed what came later.

My religious school required us to write a book review to pass. I had one, from public school, on *Moby Dick*. So I handed that in, ignoring that it wasn't on the list of (in my view) ridiculous religious books we were supposed to choose from. The teacher wouldn't take my report, which meant I would be the first person in the history of the temple to be left back from Bar Mitzvah. I refused to do another. My mother went ballistic, came to the temple school, and told them *Moby Dick* was more demanding than the whole list of titles they had and that they better accept my review or there would be big trouble. They gave in and I graduated. Not only did I benefit from mother's willingness to do battle for me, I probably learned to do battle for others.

At a Bar Mitzvah, the ceremony that welcomes 13-year-old Jewish boys into what the religion calls manhood, you have to recite a couple of paragraphs in Hebrew. I didn't have to memorize the paragraphs, just read them. I didn't even have to know what they meant. I just had to pronounce them correctly, out loud, in front of the congregation. Imagine the respect for tradition this inspired. In any event, I couldn't do it. Not knowing what it meant, success depended on rote memory applied to random sounds. It was my worst nightmare. My parents had to pay the temple's cantor to tutor me into marginal competence.

The big day came and I recited my lines, barely, and then the rabbi, a wise and caring person, called me up to chat, much too quietly for the congregation to hear, before the open Torah. So it was Rabbi Schankman, the background audience, the Torah, and me. He did this with each person being processed to manhood. He said, "Michael, congratulations on becoming a man, and I know we are going to see you pursue your religious training in the temple class next semester, aren't we?" The idea was simple—you had to say yes and then if you reneged later it meant you had lied. Or you had to say no, with him staring down at you and urging a yes. I suspect that that moment caused a great many boys to lie and later rationalize it and thereby helped many boys decide that lying was an okay pursuit, which, when you think about it, was quite an achievement for a religious high holy event. In any case, I looked at him and said, "No, I am done." In 1960, I didn't know how to say "I'm outta here," which would have been perfect. I don't think many kids told Rabbi Schankman the truth. Maybe some components of what made me radical later were in place at age thirteen.

I remember one more thing about my Bar Mitzvah. During the party afterward, some friends and I went up on the roof of the club where it was held. Someone had cigarettes and we intended to smoke for the first time. I can't remember how others enjoyed their inaugural cigarette, but I took one puff and broke into a hacking cough, almost losing my lunch. That was the last time I was tempted by a cigarette, which was the best outcome not only of my graduation, but of my entire time spent at any religious functions at all. Given the form-without-content character of my meager Jewish experiences, it was a struggle for me to be anything other than disdainful of religion, particularly Judaism, until I found political reasons for rethinking some of my attitudes.

Blacks and Me

> *The mind of a bigot is like the pupil of the eye*
> *The more light you shine on it, the more it will contract.*
> —*Oliver Wendell Holmes, Jr.*

Part of personal life in America is interactions with people of other races. Furthest back, I remember recountings of what some biographer might decide was a pivotal experience. When I was in grade school my family lived in a large house. In back was a nice large brick patio that we laid down ourselves during one of our few major family undertakings. In the backyard there was also a huge chestnut tree around which our patio sprawled, and in a distant corner was a huge gingko tree producing foul smelling nut-like droppings.

We had a kind of house helper named Chester. He was a large black man who did cleaning, caretaking, chauffeuring, and so on. My mother tells me I was crazy about him and so was everyone else in the family. I don't remember this, as I was just a few years old at the time. Neighbors began to talk. What was this big black guy doing in our house with the kids, and in particular with the young daughter, Anita, who clearly was also crazy about him? Girlfriends of Anita's weren't allowed to come over to spend the night.

In time, I am told, Anita beseeched my parents to give her back her relations to her friends and Chester was fired. My mother tells me she told Chester exactly why he was being fired, and he was very understanding. Incredible, but typical. Perhaps this whole affair, even just hearing about it later, helped spur a hatred of racism in me. Likewise, a biographer might explore what the presence of a maid in our house for my whole young life meant, always black and always treated like a friend or a family member by everyone. It certainly meant that I never did any cleaning up of any kind. It could also have generated racism or it could have generated antiracism; maybe both.

Regarding further experiences of racism in my own life, I went to a typical suburban high school. The town had a mixed population. My side was professional, white, and wealthy. The other side was a small black community plus a larger white working-class area. My grade school was entirely white and my junior high was far more white than the town's other junior high. The high school mixed it all in one institution, but with separate cultures and classes.

As a young boy I never had even one black friend and barely any black acquaintances. No Latinos, no Asians, only white folks. In high school I knew a few white boys on the very popular football and basketball teams, and one black player, at least to say hello. Of course I rooted my lungs out like everyone else, though knowing only a small percentage of the players. My college prep classes were overwhelmingly white. My advanced-placement classes, headed for the Ivy League, were entirely white. This was before the civil rights movement changed society. I was a high school senior in 1964-65.

So my direct personal experience of race was largely nonexistent right through high school, and at MIT, too, the ratios were horrible. In my fraternity there was nothing but whites; all but two or three were Jewish. I lived off campus, later, with whites. The physics department had a handful of black students, probably fewer Latinos, and while there were many Asians, this rarely raised issues of race. Indeed, no one engaged in confronting prejudices or arousing commitments until movement activism made it happen. Nonetheless, I don't know why or how, by the time I was in college I was aggressively antiracist. It probably came in part from my parents, in part from reading, and largely from uncorrupted common sense, or maybe Michael Schwerner's experience.

MIT Blackness

American means white, and Africanist people struggle to make the term
applicable to themselves with ethnicity and hyphen after hyphen after hyphen.
—*Toni Morrison*

O ddly, I remember only one highly race-specific event while at MIT. I was campaigning for student body president and went to the black student union (BSU) seeking support. MIT was so white that the BSU was a lifeline for blacks on campus who had to fight for the slightest space for their views, culture, and dignity.

I gave a typical talk, militant, radical, and highly aggressive, and the audience gave me some trouble. MIT's black students were either the first in their families to attend college, or were from elite families long familiar with college but estranged from the black communities in their cities. It was a difficult mix, typical of many campuses. A number of BSU members told me I was distracting them from advancing in society. I had no right to disrupt campus life. This group, which I should have had as prime supporters, was, in other words, initially put off like many other sectors on campus, worried about implications for their future success.

They said I was out of order. I said, no, they were. Succeeding in science doesn't justify ignoring the war in Vietnam or poverty in Mississippi. It was a heated discussion. But in time we came to mutually respect each other and while I never knew for sure, my guess is I got virtually every black vote on campus. It wasn't only, as I look at it in retrospect, that the black MIT students' weighty responsibility to their families kept them from taking up activist stances, nor the probability that repression might hit them much harder. It was also the character of the movements available. On campuses where blacks attended in much larger numbers, or where they became active early and thus helped define the character of available organizational options, black participation was greater. But at MIT, movement options were so dominated by whites that movements embodied white attitudes and values, which added to the obstacles to black participation.

Halloween Bash

I will say, then, that I am not, nor ever have been in favor of bringing about in
any way, the social and political equality of the white and black races. I as
much as any other man am in favor of having the superior position assigned to
the white race.
—*Abraham Lincoln*

O ne Halloween, living in the South End of Boston at the mid-stage in my history of working at South End Press, I went out to get something from a nearby drugstore. I walked over, got what I needed, and headed home. It was rainy, not pouring but wet, and drifting toward night. There was a gang of young black teens about thirty yards off. They looked at me, I looked at them, and clearly I was in big trouble. They broke into a run, laughing and cursing, menacing me even as they were enjoying themselves, and I ran toward home.

It was sport, I guess. I got hit with a few rocks. One cut my head a bit and, had I fallen, I am not sure how serious it would have gotten. But I didn't fall and as I got near my house the mob turned to other sport, perhaps because neighborhoods in this mixed-race area had a "watch group" to prevent muggings. People from the community would carry a whistle. If they blew it, neighbors would barrel out into the street, sometimes carrying bats in hopes of getting a whack at a mugger or thief, a black one, to be sure.

When I got inside, winded and shaken, I unwound. It was clear how insidiously racism works. The neighborhood was gentrifying. These black kids hated the wealthier white population moving in on their turf. But the kids' thuggishness, however understandable, in turn further fueled white racist fear and aggression. People who would have come out that night had I blown a whistle would have exhibited the same fighting fury as the kids, but from the advantaged position of being in the dominant rather than the subordinate group, defending privilege rather than asserting self-reliance.

On another occasion, Lydia was accosted on the front steps of the same home. A young man grabbed her on the steps up to the front door, seeking to drag her back down. She screamed and I emerged from inside. So did neighbors, on watch. The culprit ran off. Lydia was fine. Like me, she was more distraught over the passions of the neighbors chasing the guy and screaming with vengeance than over the intentions of her mugger.

It's Self-Image, Stupid

> *Segregation is the adultery of an illicit*
> *intercourse between injustice and immorality.*
> —*Martin Luther King Jr.*

Racism, I came to decide, was systemically pretty simple. The privileged group rationalizes a disparity of circumstance, behavior, culture, rights, or other advantage by saying the other is inferior. Racism was generally more about self than about other, even though it affected other more than it affected self. Racism justified advantage, coarse behavior, and dominant culture. Self had more or better income, housing, food, schooling, freedom, influence, or options. Self didn't want to think this was due to something unfair, unjust, or otherwise untoward. The claim that the other was inferior comfortably explained disparity. It was deadly whether in Mississippi cotton fields, Newark ghettos, or MIT labs.

Here's how I understood racism the first time, and to some degree since then, too. I have more wealth than cocker spaniels but it doesn't upset my day. It is okay. It is fair. Cocker spaniels don't deserve and can't appreciate the nice things that I deserve and appreciate. My looking down at them was fine. Racism made people treat other people, who had less, as if they were cocker spaniels. We viewed the other, who had less, as a cocker spaniel, or as a cockroach, a pig, or whatever, and as a result we no longer had to be troubled that we had more.

When the disparity between me and another person or persons was significant, I decided, such as that I lived in a nice home and they prowled the streets or cleaned my house, my wanting a fair and just explanation for my advantage could lead me to seeing them as lesser, causing me to view them more or less like I would view a cocker spaniel, kicking it if I was brutish, being paternal to it if I was kind, but certainly not treating it as an equal. To then make my elitist rationalization survive even against obvious contrary evidence, I realized, I would aggressively defend it. I decided that however anti-racist my upbringing and current habits, to avoid becoming racist I would have to constantly remind myself, uncomfortable as it may be, that my advantages were not due to worthiness and were not mine by right, but instead derived from unjust social relations.

I realized that when there was what seemed like a clear physical distinction between me and others, such as skin color, that difference would provide an easy peg to hang rationalizations on. I could assert that they are black and inferior. I am white and superior. They are female and inferior. I am male and superior. I saw also that when things were less physical, a more subtle formulation might arise. They are working class, I am a professional or owner. They are under-intellectually endowed, I am brilliant. The logic of domination seemed ready to claim me, if I let it.

Thinking about racism in response to the claims of Black Power movements telling me that given my whiteness in America, I too had to be racist, I saw that there were three parts to the process of justifying asymmetrical conditions. The first part was identifying some human quality like race or gender that could be termed systematically different. The second part was using superficial evidence to assert that the systematic difference caused the differential wealth or power that was to be explained. And the third part was deciding that the human difference warranted the social difference. This last link in the chain was often overlooked, I also realized, even in antiracist critiques.

So, over the years, one typical argument against racism, sexism, or classism had been that human differences are not the basis of conditional differences. Men earning more than women, whites having better schools and housing than blacks, and Indians being routed from their land were all caused by social factors that were not outcomes of skin color or anything biological. As this observation was almost always true, it served well to refute racism. But another argument that ought to be highlighted, I realized, even if it wasn't always required to make a convincing case, was that when human differences did provide a foundation for or enforce structural differences, that didn't in and of itself mean those relations were warranted. I thought this took the issues to a deeper level, and I still think so.

For example, I thought—suppose we did live in a meritocracy. This was like supposing Stalin's Russia generated social freedom, but nonetheless, I supposed it was the case to see where it led. In such a society, should those born with more valued talents, and surely some talents would be more valued, eat more and live better? What if it were the case that to some degree, and perhaps even to a considerable degree, one half of the species were hindered as compared to the other half in capacities valuable to society? Suppose men couldn't design or calculate as well as women, across the board. Should the less productive half, the men, for that reason earn less or have less say?

It turned out that it wasn't just the fact that biological claims of inferiority were false for women or blacks, say, that made sexism and racism horrible. It was also the idea that one should link purported productivity to what one was entitled to. This is a point that will resurface later but which subtly connected race, gender, and class in my thinking, even when I was first learning about each. Racism was about ascription of false attributes, most often, for sure. But looking deeper, there was this issue of what society's attitude should be to groups of its citizens who did, in fact, have different attributes.

Racism is partly about interpersonal denigration and denial. As such, it is a matter of words, body language, and daily life behavioral assumptions. Racism is also, however, a matter of institutional denigration and denial. As such, it is a matter of community relationships inscribed in systemic collective behavior patterns, roles, and laws. As important as the first, interpersonal type of racism is, the focus of groups like the Panthers made me realize the bigger and more tenacious problem was the second, systemic one. Self-image and images of others mattered. Words, looks, and assumptions mattered. But what mattered more was huge disparities of income, power, wealth, and position imprinted into social structures over extended periods.

What antiracist struggle really needed, as the Panthers began to assert, was a positive vision of racial and community relations toward which to move by way of interim alterations—not least affirmative action and reparations—as well as by establishing community norms for a new world. But why not just adopt the cultural vision many Marxists offered? Ward Churchill, a Native American activist, brought a book to South End Press about ten years after the Sixties that bore closely on this matter. His collection, *Marxism and Native Americans*, like Batya Weinbaum's book about gender and socialism, contributed to my drift away from

Marxism and toward a more multi-focus approach. Ward's point, made as well by other contributors to his book, was that the reason indigenous communities rebelled sharply against Marxist movements, for example in Nicaragua, was in considerable part a sensible rejection of Marxism's sometimes explicit and other times implicit tendency to homogenize cultures rather than celebrate them. With economics in the driver's seat, the Marxist goal became attaining a good economy and comprehension of what attaining a good culture might mean was lacking.

The Marxist movement, of course, knew that cultural wars, racism, ethnocentrism, and religious bigotry were not good. It knew that all these were utilized in part to divide and conquer people who should have shared agendas. So far as it went, this view was quite correct, but without a deeper comprehension of culture and cultural diversity, Ward argued that Marxism deduced that what was needed was to arrive at one good overarching socialist culture, thereby eliminating the contested differences. This was the worst nightmare of indigenous communities. They knew that the Marxist movement was not going to elevate their culture for everyone, but would instead impose the dominant culture of the dominant elements in the movement on everyone else. This was what they resisted. Ward saw all this, and more, and his book helped solidify lessons from the struggles of the sixties to prod me down the road I later traveled.

Chapter 17

What About Class?

Booking It

Communism, instead of making them leap forward with fire in their hearts to become masters of ideas and life, had frozen them at an even lower level of ignorance than had been theirs before they met Communism.

—Richard Wright

During my time at MIT and throughout the sixties and the seventies, too—the most stalwart activists highlighted class. Capitalism was bad. Profit, oppression, and alienation had to go. Class struggle meant workers against owners, in every leftist's view everywhere. But there was a problem. How come when workers' movements won, the result wasn't an end to all workers' subordination and indignity? Why was Rosa Luxemburg's opposition to Lenin so important to us, young students that we were at MIT? How did I and others understand the AEPi elite, and their view of themselves? What were the positions in society that we were earmarked to fill—lawyers, doctors, engineers, scientists—in class terms? Workers? With what likely attitudes and inclinations? Did it matter?

Questions likes these were on many of our minds, but it was not until a decade after I was expelled from MIT that really powerful answers began emerging. I had helped form a publishing house in the late seventies, South End Press. One of our early books was a collection based on an essay by Barbara Ehrenreich and her then-husband John, titled "The Professional Managerial Class." Their thesis was that between capitalists and workers there was a third class, which the Ehrenreichs called "the professional managerial class" or "PMC," which had interests different from and conflicting with more traditional workers and owners. This wasn't the vague group generally called "middle class" by sociologists and the general public. It wasn't a confused concept that let everyone think they were somewhere in the middle even if they were in the top five or twenty percent, or in the lower forty, thirty, or even twenty percent. No, the Ehrenreichs' professional managerial class was defined by its structural position—as were owners and more traditional workers in standard Left analysis. For the Ehrenreichs, the PMC's position conferred distinct incentives and associated culture, politics, and agendas. Lawyers, managers, doctors, and others weren't like assembly workers, waitresses, clerks, and others. This controversial claim challenged the more typical Left viewpoint, which divided the populace into only two key classes, workers and owners, and made no separate mention of the Ehrenreichs' third group. By pinpointing the third group as a class, the Ehrenreichs raised the issue of its class interests. What did members of this class have as their interests? What kinds of politics and programs might they advocate? The relation of all this to MIT is, of course, that MIT was a school that produced these type of folks. Remember my blurting out to the workers in the Instrumentation Labs that someday they would work for us? The issue lurked there.

The book was called *Between Labor and Capital* and its editor was Pat Walker, one of South End Press's founding members. The respondents to the Ehrenreichs' essay were a diverse group of prominent leftists. I didn't know John Ehrenreich but I did know Barbara. She had studied biology and was a brilliant thinker and major writer, as evidenced repeatedly in subsequent years. A quintessential quality Barbara had then and has retained ever since was the ability to take a very original and unexpected perspective on some event, process, or possibility, and present it clearly and engagingly. Barbara was extremely funny but, even more uniquely, extremely good at injecting new connective insights into readers' minds.

Just this clarity characterized Barbara and John's PMC essay. *Between Labor and Capital* had ten respondents. Seven criticized the Ehrenreichs' lead essay. Three supported the essay, including a good friend of mine, Sandy Carter, with a largely experiential piece called "Class Conflict: The Human Dimension," as well as Robin Hahnel and I with a piece called "A Ticket to Ride: More Locations on the Class Map." The critics included David Noble, Erik Olin Wright, James Weinstein, and Stanley Aronowitz, whose replies bordered on vitriolic. Barbara was distraught, called us, and said she didn't want to continue with the project because she was so depressed by people's hostility. Barbara was put off, I think quite reasonably, that these folks whom she knew quite well would come after her and John with so much anger, having so missed what she was driving at. Barbara was strong, but being reviled by people one thought of as one's allies, being misunderstood, misrepresented, and attacked by folks who ought to be open to serious debate but who weren't, was horribly unsettling. Barbara agreed, however, after some back and forth, to continue with the book's agenda. She and John wrote their reply, very effectively, and the book came out.

My feeling was that *Between Labor and Capital* should have instigated a discussion of class that would overturn existing beliefs and usher in a whole new line of thought and practice. Instead, the book got few reviews, spurred little discussion, and passed into the SEP backlist before its time. A book is published with many of the foremost writers on the Left sharply disagreeing about a pivotal matter and little comes of it. I think the Ehrenreichs' original article, and for that matter the replies by Carter and by me and Hahnel, hold hints to why it happened, as did the pieces by the critics. I would urge that this is still a very timely book for people to read, even twenty-five years later. The book mattered to me not only for the essay that Robin and I did but because writing that essay crystallized our views about class and helped set us off on the journey to what we later called participatory economics.

Antagonizing Aronowitz

> *I can't understand why people are frightened of new ideas.*
> *I'm frightened of the old ones.*
> —*John Cage*

At a Socialist Scholars Conference in New York City the year after *Between Labor and Capital* appeared, Stanley Aronowitz, a very prominent leftist writer/activist, gave a talk on a major panel. I don't remember the stated topic but somehow he got to discussing what he called Left anti-intellectualism and accused Barbara Ehrenreich of it. The idea was that by her arguing that professionals and managers were a class other than workers, urging attention to their tendencies toward elitism, and urging that movements not bias toward PMC agendas instead of working-class agendas, Ehrenreich, in Aronowitz's eyes, was saying that being intellectual was being elitist. This was ridiculous, in my view. After the talk I confronted Stanley in the auditorium's corridor and told him what I thought. He was affronted that I thought he was misrepresenting Barbara, and before long we were shouting at each other with a growing crowd around us. Class issues generate considerable passion, whether they arise from reasoned difference, clashing psychologies, embattled egos, or all three.

Aronowitz, born in 1933 and thus fourteen years my senior, had been a steel worker and an organizer for the Amalgamated Clothing Workers and the Oil, Chemical, and Atomic Workers. He was a full professor, quite brilliant, flamboyant, and aggressive. Most important, he was the author of *False Promises, The Shaping of American Working Class Consciousness*, which was one of the most influential and inspiring books I had read up to that time. In retrospect, I think the vehemence I manifested that day was in part due to my fear that a person I viewed to be more a teacher than an opponent was not in my camp. Most likely, I was also spurred by a defensive fear that I was perhaps wrong. Aronowitz knew working-class life and experience in ways I couldn't begin to approach. So, was Aronowitz right about class, where he was undeniably highly knowledgeable? Were Weinstein, Wright, Noble, and the others right as well when they, too, rejected the Ehrenreichs' thesis of a third class? I didn't think so. It seemed to me then, and it still seems to me now, that it was the Ehrenreichs who were on the valuable path.

Visiting Ehrenreich and a Sad Outcome

America is the only country that went from
barbarism to decadence without civilization in between.
—Oscar Wilde

A few years later, Robin Hahnel and I visited Barbara at her home on Long Island. She was living with a rank-and-file Teamster organizer at the time, not John. We talked animatedly about changing the world and class consciousness. As it got late, spurred by our talk and the passions of the time, a trip was proposed. Robin and I packed into their car at their invitation and went with Barbara and her partner to a truck park not far off. There was a strike going on at the time. We crept in and crazy glued the lock on the plant door and then ran back to our car and drove back to Barbara's house.

Two and a half decades later, I asked Barbara to do an interview with me about participatory economics, a visionary economic system I had helped author and strongly advocate. I had interviewed her, previously, about a new book of hers examining the life conditions of working people and now I hoped that her interviewing me about my book, *Parecon: Life After Capitalism*, would help get the word out. We did the interview by e-mail. Barbara would send a question, I would reply, and again, and so on.

No mainstream periodical wanted to publish the interview. Hostility that lay at the root of opposition to Barbara's original PMC piece has lived on, focused, however, on participatory economics, a vision singularly devoted to eliminating the class difference that Barbara so eloquently excavated. The interview finally ran in *Z Magazine*, a publication I had helped found that was not only open to, but of course, eagerly intent on keeping these issues forefront. Regrettably, Barbara's questions avoided the core topic of class divisions and the third class entirely. Barbara has written powerfully over the years about poverty, work, work conditions, and working-class as well as middle class or PMC consciousness, among many other topics. But Barbara never returned explicitly to the idea of a third class and its relevance to transcending capitalism. It has always seemed a great loss to me that her adroit writing skills haven't honed these issues further.

The Real Deal

A moment's insight is sometimes worth a lifetime's experience.
—Oliver Wendell Holmes, Jr.

The point I took from all of this, as Barbara and John first noted, was about people's role in economic change and how movements seeking to affect economic life should address people and issues. If there were only two primary economic classes, each with interests contrary to the other, then economically focused movements that weren't seeking to preserve or expand the domination of owners over workers had to be seeking to advance workers at the expense of owners. Those would have been the only two sides to take. On the other hand, if there were three centrally important classes—workers, owners, and what Hahnel and I called the coordinator class—a third allegiance would become possible. A movement could claim to be interested in full economic liberation but actually be pursuing something less than that. It might seek elimination of private ownership, but might advance in its place institutions that would guarantee not classlessness, but instead domination by a coordinator class who would continue monopolizing empowering positions in the economy. Anticapitalist leftists could, in other words, be other than what they claimed or even hoped they were. A movement could be hostile to private profiteering and yet also uncongenial to working people. Instead of being a working-class movement it could manifest the aspirations of doctors, lawyers, managers, and engineers. This was the heart of the controversy that the Ehrenreichs' words stirred up in people and what Hahnel and my subsequent efforts have kept forefront. It was why many people have preferred not to deal seriously with the Ehrenreichs' early words, or Hahnel's and my later words. Or that's been my impression, at any rate.

No Nukes and Class

I don't care to belong to a club that accepts people like me as members.
—Groucho Marx

After the sixties, activist movements didn't disappear, of course. One movement that attained great size, great militancy, and considerable success, was oriented around nuclear power. Despite its size and successes, however, the no-nukes uprisings never expanded to stretch into average households and workplaces. It wasn't that ecological concerns, from nuclear meltdown to dumping waste to violating the water supply to fouling the air, weren't relevant to average folks. All these ecological horrors were far more damaging to poor than to wealthy constituencies. So why has ecological activism yet to attain the scale and radical edge needed to really move history?

Eric Sargent, Lydia's youngest son, went with Lydia and me to some no-nuke events. He was quite young but somehow knew he did not much like these people and their environmental concerns. Why not? What was it about the no-nukes movement that put Eric off? Could it have been the same things that put off many unions and labor organizations? That seemed highly implausible, given Eric's young age, yet I came to think it was true. Eric didn't like the mood and manners of this movement. The unions didn't like some of its policies because they threatened jobs. It was the same distaste.

A related talk I had with Noam Chomsky helps clarify. Chomsky told me about having a chat with a bunch of no-nukes advocates and being quite put off by their cavalier rejection of nukes, which seemed to him to be based only on looking at the possible impact of catastrophic meltdowns on consumers and citizens. It was fine to be aware of that—and maybe that danger should outweigh all other considerations—but what troubled Noam was that the movement didn't seem to even notice other considerations. It did not often ask, for example, what the human and social costs of using coal instead of nuclear power are, not only for the environment but also for workers in the mines. It would have been one thing, Noam felt, if the no-nukes movement showed concern in all directions. But Noam's impression was that large parts of the movement were oblivious to the potential impact of their activities on working people. One might predict that this would be a movement with an internal culture dissing workers, and thus a movement that wouldn't appeal to working people, even before they got wind of specific policies, just like and for the same reasons that it didn't appeal to Eric, even without his, at such a young age, having strong opinions about specific policies.

There are those who can read the above and perhaps not feel too concerned about it, but I think that to have that reaction would be a serious mistake, just as I think ignoring insights about the existence of a coordinator class in society is a serious mistake, and for pretty much the same reasons. The following analogy will make this point as aggressively and provocatively as possible.

When Bush and Cheney were deciding to bomb Afghanistan, food aid workers in the area were warning that the implications of that choice could be millions of Afghan corpses due to the disruption of food aid and the long-term impact of bombing on the region. Bush and Cheney went ahead anyhow, and I used to give talks at the time noting that I didn't think they would even understand a question about their actions—"How could you have done that"?—because they would not see the impact on all those Afghans as mattering. I would report in these public talks that I doubted that Bush and Cheney gave ten minutes thought, five minutes thought, even ten seconds thought to the morality of starving millions of Afghan peasants in order to show that the U.S. punished any and all violations of our international agenda mercilessly. I would preach how if bin Laden were going to the first level of hell, and surely he was—however metaphorically—then Bush and Cheney would be on a fast elevator going down even deeper into the flames. But the really disturbing observation is that Bush and Cheney's callousness toward the Afghans, while deeper and more damaging and more cruel and callous, was really not that different in kind than the no-nukes movement's callousness toward working people, even if the cause was entirely different—ignorance for no nukers as compared to willful malice for Bush and Cheney. Like the Afghans for Bush, coal miners for the no-nukers didn't count. Their lives were lived beneath movement radar, unaccounted by movement criteria of justice.

I remember debating the potential of the ecology as a radical focus back when it was first becoming visible. Many early 1970s radicals felt environmentalism would be the next big spur to activism. And those activists were certainly right that the prospect of being fried by ozone depletion or gassed by industrial pollutants could yield important activism. But there were other people at the time, including me, who were skeptical that it would come true. Not only the poor, but also elites, suffer environmental decay, and it might occur to elites to address environmental problems without, however, addressing other social ills. In turn, environmentalists who emphasized ecology but didn't highlight economy, kinship, and polity might try to curry favor with environmentally concerned elites as a road toward changes instead of organizing public militancy. They might even seek cleanup for the rich at the expense of impoverishing or even just not cleaning up for everyone else. They might advocate cleaning up rich people's beaches, rich people's air, rich people's resorts, and rich people's water, while working people not only do the cleaning for pathetic wages, but wallow in toxic effluvium until they suffer asphyxiation. The alternative, of course, would be concerns about ecology that were tied to and augmented by broader concerns about liberated production, consumption, and allocation leading toward classlessness, not to mention transformed gender, race, and political relations. The battles to attain better activism of course continue.

Chapter 18

Sixties People and Books

America's Gandhi

*There are no magic answers, no miraculous methods to overcome the problems
we face, just the familiar ones: honest search for understanding, education,
organization, action that raises the cost of state violence for its perpetrators or
that lays the basis for institutional change—and the kind of commitment that
will persist despite the temptations of disillusionment, despite many failures and
only limited successes, inspired by the hope of a brighter future.*
—Noam Chomsky

I knew Dave Dellinger peripherally in the movements of the sixties but more so
later, as a publisher and coeditor. What was singular about Dave was that
while he completely rejected violence in any form, Dave had no trouble
communicating with, respecting, and even supporting people who were quite
violent. Dave understood the difference between U.S. invasion of a distant land
and Vietnamese defense of their homeland. Dave understood communities trying
to attain the dignity of survival and the integrity of free choices as compared to
other communities and states repressing them. Dave didn't reject police repression
and Black Panther violence equally, but sided with the latter even while criticizing,
quite rightly, its tone and methods.

Two interactions with Dave dominate my memories. The first was not long
after we did a book together called *Beyond Survival*. I urged Dave to write an
autobiography. In time, he agreed. If South End Press would get him a computer to
write on, he said, he would steel himself and write the book. We got him the
computer and he started work. He eventually completed the first volume of a
projected three, but it went to a mainstream publisher instead of South End Press.
Dave needed the money, desperately. Some people at the press were angry. I was
sad. It was depressing to me that Dave was in such need in his later years and that

the movement was so ill-equipped to alleviate his difficulties, and also sad that it would mean that in the long haul his book might disappear from view when it ought to be popular forever. The book didn't cover much beyond the end of the late sixties. Dave never wrote another volume even though he was incredibly active for an additional thirty years. Covering that time would have added many dimensions, not just to recounting his life accurately, but to conveying useful insights to readers. I think it was absent because Doubleday would neither do another volume nor publish a longer initial one.

I remember a fund-raising jaunt Dellinger and I took for South End Press in the 1980s. We were going to talk to folks at a foundation and also to some wealthy individuals. We flew West, and then rented a car, and drove. Riding with Dave and listening to his stories was unforgettable. Also unforgettable was that the wealthy donors we met had no real idea of the history of the person they were with, and failed to ask him anything substantive or to take the slightest advantage of their time with him. To me it was as if Gandhi popped into an office for an hour or two in India, and the functionaries puttered about, pontificating with their usual bluster, never bothering to take advantage of their proximity to Gandhi by learning from his wisdom. We raised no money. SEP was too radical for most donor aid.

On this trip, Dave and I visited Daniel Ellsberg of *Pentagon Papers* fame. We sat in a hot tub with Daniel at his house, my first time in one of those, and listened while Daniel regaled us with an odd theory of how the Cold War could be ended through some kind of letter-writing initiative he was undertaking. Ellsberg kept talking, never trying to induce Dave to instead do the talking. Dave would probably be called arrogant if he thought that perhaps the folks at the foundations, or even Daniel Ellsberg, should have shown some interest in what he had to offer instead of thinking that only they had things worth saying. Heaven forbid that at some point Dave was dismissive or otherwise short with them. The funding bureaucrats, and in this case, Ellsberg, too, would not be deemed arrogant, however, for their part in the dance. This asymmetry seemed perverse and also pervasive, at least in America.

Anyhow, while driving, I asked Dave about his life experiences. I can't relay all he told me and, in any event, for the early parts, there is his autobiography, but what I couldn't forget, even if I tried, were two stories. First, at one point, I asked Dave about threats to his life. Among them all, mostly total nonsense—and I understood that because when I was at MIT I had received some nonsensical death threats myself—he told about one Christmas where he, his family, and some friends were celebrating around a tree in his living room opening gifts. He picked up a nicely wrapped gift addressed to him and opened it. It was a bottle of very fine liquor. Dave was about to open the bottle, he told me, when he saw something odd. It looked like a very thin pencil line down the inside. Dave got suspicious, put the bottle out on the lawn and called the police. It was indeed a bomb and if Dave had opened the bottle, not only would he have died, but his family would have too. He conveyed this story with tears rolling down his face, upset by the memory of what his choices almost brought upon his kids. The story is in his autobiography, but the book lacks the tears.

Later, I asked Dave about his kids. Did he deny them by his choices, either materially or emotionally? Dave was a Yale graduate who could no doubt have earned during his lifetime a hundred times the income he settled for. He chose a different path, though, and I wondered whether he ever regretted that choice—not for himself, but for his children. His kids lost him to jail, often, and when he was not incarcerated he was often on the road, again lost to them.

Dave said he gave his kids what he thought was the best thing he could: a father worth emulating, a life worthy of respect, morals to live by, and feelings to grow by. The fact that he had to withhold much of his time, labors, and even presence was sad, he said, but it was the way of today's world. He couldn't have given them what he did had he not withheld what he did. His kids' lives would be what they made them. He had given his kids what a parent ought to give kids in a world such as ours. I don't know that I agree. I don't know that I disagree. I think in today's world, no one's choices can ever be perfect.

When I go out speaking, I sometimes ask who has heard of Dave Dellinger. Even among leftist audiences, at most a sprinkling of hands creeps up. What a sad commentary on our schools, our historians, and our movements. I tend to have tears in my eyes whenever I see that response, as I do now just thinking about it and about Dave Dellinger. Dave died in May, 2004, but the rippling effects of his life live on. You lose, you lose, you lose, you win. Dave will win.

Mr. SDS

We are people of this generation, bred in at least modest comfort, housed now in universities, looking uncomfortably to the world we inherit.
—Tom Hayden

One afternoon, I think in 1979, out of nowhere Tom Hayden of SDS fame showed up at South End Press's office/home. He wanted to do a book and wanted our help with it. We were flattered and pleased at his interest. I had known Tom peripherally in years past. Lydia knew him a bit more, and also Jane Fonda, because Lydia had worked in the Indochina Peace Campaign with them toward the end of the Vietnam War. The funny thing is, my earlier impression of Tom had been negative. I was almost afraid of him, not personally, but politically. Tom was the only person I had ever encountered in the New Left who I thought might have the potential to be a powerful and highly manipulative leader of way too many followers. Rennie Davis, often operationally coupled with Tom, and more charismatic, set off no such alarm bells. To me I suppose Rennie was Trotsky to Tom as Lenin, but while I knew right off that Rennie was not going to amass the type of power Trotsky had, I wasn't so sure about Tom emulating Lenin.

Tom had been the principal author of the famous SDS Port Huron Statement, which laid down the opening shots for the New Left. He had worked tirelessly in the antiwar and the broader New Left movement, had been part of the Chicago Eight, and had later become an elected official in the California legislature. The book he did with South End Press was called *The New American Future*. What was memorable about the experience, however, was that I spent about a week at Tom's California place, which Jane Fonda shared with him, helping out with elements of the book and hanging out.

Arriving at Tom's place in California was a bit harrowing. I rang the bell, heard some noise, but my calls got no acknowledgment, so I walked in. I was promptly on my back looking up into the face of what at that moment appeared to be a starving wolf ready to have me for dinner. I heard someone yell "heel," and the wolf became a friendly German shepherd. Tom helped me up, and I met the clan and the dog, Geronimo.

Fine-Tuning Music and Capitalism

> *I worry that the person who thought up Muzak*
> *may be thinking up something else.*
> *—Lily Tomlin*

Tom and I had a lot of agreement about his book, though there was friction about the Mideast sections in which he was pro-Israel. More memorably, Tom took me to see a rock singer working on an album, and it was a highly instructive experience. The singer was not so famous or so in accord with my tastes for me to remember his name, but he was more than famous enough to be working in a substantial studio. He was in his own room set off from where I was by a glass wall. My side of the window had the engineers and equipment for recording, and close up, it was incredible. I could talk with the main engineer, compliments of Tom's connections, and he was sitting at a console that looked like the cockpit of a Boeing 737. This sound manipulator had levers upon levers and buttons upon buttons that the engineer pushed and pulled to add and diminish sound levels, tones, bounces, biases, feelings, shadings, or whatever. But here was the thing: in those days I listened to music a lot, and I could identify songs and artists barely hearing a beat. I would swear I heard everything on the tracks. I wasn't educated about it at all. I had no names for most of what I heard. I didn't even know which sounds were which instruments, sometimes. But I could hear what was there, I thought. Still, I watched this guy shove a lever this way and shove another one that way, watched him listen to the results, and then shove them both and some others and listen again, and for the life of me, I couldn't hear any difference after most of the adjustments he made.

Can you really hear a difference when you shift those controls, I asked him? Isn't it so minor as to be imperceptible? No, he said, for him it was clear as cannons. I asked who else could hear the differences and he told me that at this stage of refinement pretty much only other recording engineers could hear the differences. What about people who will listen to the album, I asked? He chuckled and said not a chance. What about the performers? He said some could, but not all of them. I found this fascinating. Here this recording engineer was taking considerable expensive time to, in his view, perfect the sound of the songs for his own especially highly trained hearing. Time is money. But what he was doing at this level would have little bearing, if any, on the success or failure of the record and indeed on anything relating to consumers. Why did the owner of the record company put up with the engineer's silly personal fetish? Why humor the engineer's perfectionism? Why abide the engineer taking expensive time to assuage his concern over how other engineers would regard his efforts? The answer, I realized, was that (at least then) it was the price of employing a good engineer. Recording engineers had sufficient power among the production companies and performers to require time for their perfectionism as a condition of their labor. This occurred even against the profit interests, tastes, and inclinations of those who were more in charge.

That interested me as a sign of the interface between capital, the owners who lost money due to this perfectionism, and what I was at that time beginning to see as a coordinator class, the engineers who gained stature through perfectionism. The coordinator class's agenda was interfering, as I think it often does, with maximizing profits.

It wouldn't surprise me if a quite substantial percentage of the costs of most records, and by analogy of many Hollywood movies, has almost no bearing on their public reception or even on the artistic quality of the products. Consider Bob Dylan's song "Like a Rolling Stone" and its album *Highway 61 Revisited.* It isn't only me that thinks the former is the single best song of popular music in the second half of the twentieth century, and I bet I am also not alone in thinking the latter is the best album during that period. Yet the song was completed in one take, I believe, and certainly not much more. There was no fine tweaking, and ditto for the album. Of course, the Beatles' *Sergeant Pepper*, another masterpiece, was an engineering miracle, and while much of what the engineers did had great impact on the product, one wonders, beyond that, how much imperceptible tweaking there was in that case, too.

To Golden Pond and Fonda on Beauty

Everything has beauty, but not everyone sees it.
—Confucius

Atrip to Squam Lake, New Hampshire (or what was called Golden Pond in the movie of the same name), was one of many perks that came with being a publisher. One memorable part was riding up to New Hampshire. In the car, Lydia and I interviewed Jane Fonda. During the interview, Jane was talking about other actors, and mentioned how much focus there was on beauty. She talked about what this meant, in particular, for the duration and character of women's careers, which was familiar ground. But Jane also spent a few minutes talking about beauty per se, about how beautiful, in fact, many actors were to look at, and in particular about how some of the women were so incredibly beautiful as to almost be painful to view. Was this true? The claim was for many leftists a controversial matter. Many argued that beauty was not objective in any sense, but was entirely in the eye of the beholder, entirely a cultural matter. Whoever Jane found so beautiful as to be hard to look at without lust, she would find ordinary or perhaps even ugly had she grown up among different cultural messages. The reverse view was that while social messages and habits influence taste, humans have wired into their genes certain attributes that make some slopes, shapes, shadows, and segues more attractive, on average, across the species, than others, yielding views like Jane's, not only in her but nearly universally.

This was only one example of a recurring dispute on the Left. Leftists wanted equitable outcomes and circumstances. We saw that wide disparities in widely appreciated or admired productivity or personal attributes were accompanied, in our society and in all others we were familiar with, by wide disparities in power, income, and circumstance. Many leftists concluded that to get equity we had to eliminate differences in attributes. To equilibrate material and social outcomes required, in these people's minds, equilibrating people vis-à-vis mental talents, personal looks, physical reflexes, and the rest. So they looked around and decided that differences of those sorts were artifacts of our way of seeing and ranking attributes, but were not present in our natures.

This was the thinking going on, I believe, when some leftists denied that there were huge disparities among people's looks and physical and mental abilities, and that some of these disparities dramatically affected how pleasant or moving it was to hear someone sing a song, dance, carry a tune, hear the lyrics they conjure, read the prose they present, learn from the insights they uncover, or even just enter a room. The contrary view, which I have, and which I guess Jane had too, was that disparities among people are real. They not only shouldn't be leveled, they should be celebrated for providing tremendous spice and diversity to what would otherwise be a terminally bland regularity. And more, the way to prevent human diversity from generating oppressive hierarchies isn't to imagine or brutalize away the diversity, but to create institutional means by which even while this diversity is celebrated and materially and socially benefits society, it doesn't benefit the people who do art, science, invention, communication, and design wonderfully better than it benefits people who do the same things acceptably, but less well.

This was always in my view a significant matter. The extreme left view irked me. So did rewarding genetics. I thought the disagreements pointed toward what it means to attain classlessness, a point I worked incessantly on later. It might be worth noting, as well, that the leftist leveling mentality isn't confined to things like beauty or mental quickness. There are those who think that the way to avoid racism, ethnocentrism, religious bigotry, nationalism, and other cultural conflict is to homogenize away cultural diversity by seeking one grand culture—generally that of the majority, of course. This is the same mistake in a different set of clothes as the no-beauty recommendation, or the no-brains one, or the no-reflexes one, or the no-gender one. Cultural diversity, I came to realize, like beauty and brains diversity, isn't the problem. Nor is sexual diversity. The problem, I decided, was social structures that rewarded some folks excessively and others insufficiently rather than allowing all to mutually benefit, whatever their various talents.

Tom has remained politically involved throughout his life. First he helped create SDS and the New Left. Later he worked tirelessly to oppose U.S. involvement in Indochina. Still later he was an elected representative in California, and finally, he remains a writer, agitator, and teacher of new generations. On Squam Lake, Golden Pond, in a skiff with a small motor, out on the water on a foggy day, Tom said to me—I think we were talking about the end to the Vietnam war—"Don't snatch defeat from the jaws of victory." It was typical of his insights. What he meant was, when we win small changes, but the government delivers them, we shouldn't let the government taking credit for our changes make us think we weren't responsible and that our victory was a defeat. Tom was more than just clever that way, and is also, by the way, a very funny guy.

Tom wasn't the only Chicago 8 member SEP published during my years there. We published Abbie Hoffman's *Dancing in the Ice Age*, too. I don't remember that book at all, however. And we published a Dave Dellinger book on Vietnam and another book too, which I coedited with Dave, called *Beyond Survival,* about war and militarism and their relations to other dimensions of social life. As you probably discerned from my earlier anecdotes, for me it was a special honor to know Dave. We also had a brief interlude with Bobby Seale, the Panther in the Chicago 8. He wanted SEP to publish a book *Barbecuing With Bobby*. We passed and I never got to know Bobby.

About the Sixties

Those who write clearly have readers;
those who write obscurely have commentators.
—*Albert Camus*

Two other books from my publishing days at South End Press that I greatly liked and that I also thought exemplary were about the New Left. George Katsiaficas, my chutzpah-endowed friend from MIT, wrote *The Imagination of the New Left*, which was largely about the epochal year 1968, but really also about the whole movement and cultural phenomenon of the period. And Dick Cluster, another friend from New Left days, edited a short collection of pieces by people writing about their experiences during that same period. Dick's book was called *They Should Have Served That Cup of Coffee,* a reference to lunch-counter owners not serving blacks, which helped spur the development of the civil rights movement and then the rest of the New Left.

Perhaps the most notable thing about these books was that they were written and published at all. That is, by bucking the typical tide, they highlighted the extent to which my generation's leftists failed to look seriously at our own undertakings. We rarely relayed to others what we had learned and what might best be avoided or emulated from our experiences. It is incredible the extent to which young people in the anticorporate globalization and antiwar and other movements today revisit experiences from the past, replicate mistakes and successes, but don't start off from a more advantageous point due to having imbibed past lessons. The fault isn't within contemporary movements so much as with my generation's abdication of its communicative responsibility. We didn't sufficiently convey worthy lessons.

Partly, our lack of attention to communicating our own history arose because my generation's activists didn't have time to write about their endeavors. Partly, it arose, however, because we didn't have an inclination to do it. I think some sixties leftists were too humble or modest, or too self-deprecating. And I think others feared doing a bad or unworthy job.

It isn't that there are no short works, partial works, or memoirs of merit—though far fewer than one might anticipate given the drama, pathos, and relevance of the times. But where are the really compelling, rich, varied, inspiring, educational histories of the sixties and the decades since? Where are the works that look at the experiences and ideas of the times and extrapolate so that those who follow don't have to reinvent every little activist wheel for themselves, but can instead move forward off a previously established wisdom? I don't know the answers to these questions. My generation did many good things, I think, but we also dropped the ball on many fields of play. Not sufficiently examining ourselves and passing on the lessons we learned from our efforts was one of our big fumbles.

Chapter 19

Still Walking

Incomplete Symphony

You lose, you lose, you lose, you win.
—Rosa Luxemburg

Regrettably, the ringing of revolution of the sixties did not crescendo to lasting victory. On the one hand, we achieved a lot. Minds changed. We won durable gains in race, gender, sex, and authority attitudes, in media and education, and in public policies such as affirmative action and social support. On the other hand, we did not significantly affect society-wide institutions. Families, schools, communities, churches, corporations, the market, and the state maintained their old institutional definitions, and thus continued to emanate essentially the same pressures as in the past. The force fields of these unchanged defining institutions chipped away in subsequent years at the changes in consciousness and policy we had won in the sixties. Our disproportionate affect on ideas that were in people's heads and some policies more than on underlying institutions reflected our out-of-balance emphasis on ideas and not on institutions. In that sense, we got what we sought which was less, much less, than we needed.

We didn't win a fundamentally new world because we didn't inspire enough people, provoke enough tenacity, or generate enough continuity. We understood what was wrong with our society, but we did not understand what to put in its place. We fought fiercely against injustice but we barely fought for new justice. We didn't even know what new justice would entail. We lacked a vision to ground our strategy. We lacked a strategy to guide our actions. We were, in the words of Vice President Agnew quoting William Safire, "nattering nabobs of negativity." I went from the early sixties of SNCC and SDS into the contested conflagrations of the seventies, and then into the rest of the century with undiminished commitment. That wasn't typical, however. Many left the movement, instead.

Where'd We Go?

The intellectual tradition is one of servility to power,
and if I didn't betray it, I'd be ashamed of myself.
—*Noam Chomsky*

The sixties, even just in the U.S., involved three or four million active politically radical participants. If we count the deeply involved hippie movement, not to mention more peripheral participants in both political and cultural dissent, we find many millions more. Yet, by the early eighties, the number of people from my generation who were still deeply involved in dissident politics or even in cultural resistance had horribly dwindled. Was I just a diehard? Or did the rest of my generation wrongly give up its calling?

In either view, undeniably, our movement was not sticky. People could get in the movement's orbit and even enter its central byways, but later drift off. People were rarely lifelong embedded. The movement's gravity was easily escaped. The huge majority of my sixties "fellow travelers" kept elements of their youthful values as they aged, but also drifted into mainstream institutions and habits. They became what we might call typical—rather than dissident— university academics, public school teachers, cooks, cabbies, social workers, nurses, custodians, secretaries, lawyers, factory hands, engineers, day care workers, doctors, policemen, politicians' wives and husbands, parents and grandparents, and even the occasional capitalist employer. Regrettably, in these roles, they acted without conscious dissent, holding on to sixties values peripherally, if at all. The rules of society's roles, unchanged, guaranteed these results. The Left's problem wasn't that people became teachers, cooks, cabbies, and so on. It was that we didn't build up mechanisms of support, involvement, and redefinition so that people could do these things and still be part of the Left.

Some sixties graduates have no connection to their past. Some have tenuous memories. Some donate. Some read. Not many still identify themselves based on revolutionary values. The shared experience that we lived for in the sixties didn't have the staying power in society or in most of our lives that we foresaw it having. It was not the lifetime refuge, school, ally, and social force we claimed it would be when screaming at our parents that our actions were no passing fad. The sad truth is that for most of my generation, so far our parents were more right about our futures than we were. But history isn't finished. And hey, the fact that there were plenty of big-time errors back then is damn lucky. If there weren't big-time errors, what would we improve on next time?

PART 3

Channeling Walking Butterflies

B ut for tweaks of history and chance, I would likely have become a professor of physics exploring quarks, clouds, and cosmos. Where that would have led, in science and socially, I can't guess. Had it not gone well, I might have become an academic economist, with equally unclear results.

In real time, however, I left academia long ago. Still, I did spend a few years attending graduate school and teaching at MIT, Harvard, U Mass Amherst, U Mass Boston, and in a couple of prisons as well. As these institutions are notable, some of the stories may be, too.

Chapter 20

Tech Tooling & Harvard Ed.

MIT Learning

College isn't the place to go for ideas.
—*Helen Keller*

I was at MIT as an undergraduate from 1965 to 1969, though I took a number of graduate-level courses before I dropped out of academics for political involvement. I remember the graduate course in electromagnetic fields, which I didn't much like, and the one in quantum mechanics, which I liked a lot. In the latter we learned not only about quantum field theory, but about how symmetry plays a role in physics, a focus that has grown significantly since. The core of symmetry study in physics is called Noether's Theorem. It links conservation theorems like the conservation of energy or of angular momentum—as well as others that are far more abstruse—with mathematical symmetries in the underlying equations. The theorem is a cornerstone of modern physics. The author was Emmy Noether, a woman. Have you heard of Noether? I bet not. Noether should be revered like Madame Curie, along with the prominent male mathematicians and physicists of the twentieth century. My MIT courses didn't explore Noether's life or her travails pursuing physics in a male-dominated world. That would have been a useful addition to MIT education.

Returning to what did occur, what most struck me about coursework at MIT was the poor teaching. Noted faculty would come in and essentially write a textbook on the board, mechanically, rapidly. One notch up, other faculty would dictate and write on the board something we could more easily read on our own, such as notes they had prepared for a book they had in progress. For these teachers, teaching was a penance that competed with research or in some cases business. Such teachers spent little time thinking about how to convey course content to spark interest and engage imaginations. Better teachers thought hard about communication, but what they were conveying, however cleverly, engagingly, humorously, and passionately, we could readily have read on our own.

The bad faculty were insufferable. I could endure them for one session at most. The good faculty were fine if you weren't willing to read and teach yourself. I was, so they were barely more bearable. These faculty were scientists. We were students. They knew what we needed to know but couldn't learn from books. What was a scientist? What did scientists do? How did scientists do it? What were the ups and downs of it? What were the motives, rewards, and pains? Why didn't these scientists just give us the text and tell us to learn it and then sit with us and convey their experiences, recounting their actual thought processes, motivations, frustrations, failures, and successes. That would have kept me in the room. In fact, that might even have trumped the war's pull on me, though I have no way of knowing.

High School Hijinks

At 18 our convictions are hills from which we look;
At 45 they are caves in which we hide.
—F. Scott Fitzgerald

In junior high school, ninth grade, I had an atrocious English teacher. She had a memory so bad she couldn't coordinate people's names and she taught utterly useless notions in an intensely boring manner. She also had the misfortune of having in her class a once-in-a-generation combination of raucous personalities, each trying to outdo the rest for outrageous acts.

A game emerged that a few of us played and the rest cheered. The idea was you would get out of your seat and move to another and sit down while this ridiculous teacher was turned toward the blackboard. Each time you did that you got a stolen base credited to you. You got ten stolen bases if you got up, ran around a whole row of seats and sat down in a seat other than where you started. You got twenty or thirty stolen bases, I think, if you circumnavigated the whole room before sitting down again in a seat other than your own. If the teacher turned and saw you moving, you didn't get the bases unless you managed to come up with an excuse (such you were sharpening your pencil and got lost on the way) that mollified her.

After a few weeks of this, we graduated to some serious mayhem. These were the days when Maury Wills of the baseball Dodgers was stealing over a hundred bases in a season. That became the Holy Grail. The guy who managed to pull this off in one class session would transcend being a class clown. He would become, at least in this one realm, a mini-god. Yes, it was macho mayhem, and the perpetrators were all male. Well, a guy named Drew actually did it. There were times I encountered this guy running alongside buses out in the real world, barking at them for amusement. He was bored silly by existence, of course, and was deeply troubled, probably just too smart for his own good. Maybe these shenanigans saved me from learning absolute submission that year, which, had I done so, might have lasted for every subsequent year. Thank you, Drew the car-chaser, and Larry Wolfson too, my high school friend, who was base-stealing ringleader.

Not Much Ed. at the Harvard Ed. School

> *To be successful in society it is not enough to be stupid,*
> *one must also be well mannered.*
> *—Voltaire*

Beyond MIT, Harvard is supposed to be the pinnacle of American education. It's School of Education was housed in one building on the outskirts of Harvard Square. I decided to go there to get a masters in education. I was juggling organizing options at the time, but I was thinking that perhaps I would go into social work, or some kind of community activity, to both provide myself an income and have an entré into community organizing. I somehow decided that a Harvard Ed. School degree might facilitate this path. The job notion arose, I think, from noticing the trend of left organizers settling into neighborhoods and working there with local constituencies. A number of my friends had done this, in Dorchester, a part of Boston, and Lynn, a nearby town, with no clear notion of future work and no related skills. I was thinking that maybe I would do it too, with better prospects for durable success.

It was a bit silly, given how divorced it was from anything natural for me. It was not so silly, however, regarding understanding what it would take to enter a neighborhood with a chance at long-term involvement. None of the people who joined the then-emerging "to the community" trend managed to stay more than a few years, at least that I know of.

At any rate, it turned out that at the time I was considering going to the Harvard Ed. School, Herb Gintis and Sam Bowles were teaching economics at Harvard and also, coincidentally, a course about education. I knew Sam peripherally from my friends at Harvard, particularly Robin Hahnel, who had taken Sam's economics classes and liked him. The Harvard Ed. School was a very freewheeling institution. Getting in seemed to require literally nothing, and I found that I could take whatever I wanted. So, I took Herb and Sam's course in political economy and also in political economy of education, and one other economics course. I also took a few reading courses with Herb, for which I did essentially nothing other than play tennis with him, and it turned out that I didn't need to take anything else. I took no education courses. I took no social relations courses. I didn't write a single paper. I took no tests. I got a masters degree in education from Harvard without having learned anything from the Harvard Ed. School itself. It makes one wonder about Harvard's supposedly high standards.

Also that year, I taught a section of Sam and Herb's course on the political economy of education. I became good friends with them both, particularly Herb. Both of these young faculty members were remarkably smart and knowledgeable. In fact, Herb was one of the smartest people I have ever encountered, with all kinds of interests and hobbies, ranging from building his house to writing the word processing software he was then using, to proficiently playing piano, to displaying advanced scientific literacy, to having considerable athletic prowess.

Sam's genius, even beyond the obvious eloquence and creativity that anyone could see, was revealed to me a few years later. We were driving home—which was, at the time, back to Amherst—from a conference where we both spoke. We evaluated each other's presentations. Somehow it came out that Sam had grown up a fierce stutterer. I was incredulous. Sam is a very eloquent speaker, not only in public sessions, but informally as well. I asked how he had gotten rid of such a disruptive speech problem and he said he hadn't. It was still present. I laughed, assuming he was kidding, but he said, no, he wasn't kidding. Sam had learned early on that the only way to defeat the constant interruption of stuttering was to change words before any particular word could become an impediment. He could feel the problem before he uttered a word, and he could switch words on the fly to avoid stuttering over one. He said because he had to be so flexible with so many words at his disposal, he became a good speaker. Was it true? I took it as true then, and I still do, but I have no way of knowing for sure. I never heard Sam stutter, not once in a few years' interactions.

Chapter 21

Becoming an Economist

Off To Amherst

Annual income twenty pounds, annual expenditure nineteen six, result
happiness. Annual income twenty pounds, annual expenditure twenty pound
ought and six, result misery.
—Charles Dickens

While I was filtering through Harvard, or perhaps it was just after I had done so, Bowles and Gintis got an invitation to go to U Mass Amherst to be part of a transformed economics department. These two notable economists, plus a bunch of their peers from elsewhere around the country, were invited to simultaneously join the department. If they all accepted, U Mass would instantly have the premier radical economics department in the U.S. After all kinds of negotiations and machinations, Sam and Herb finally accepted, as did the others. More, Sam and Herb asked me to come as a graduate student, starting in the first year of the new program.

Sam and Herb pushed my joining them, but I hesitated. I had no serious economics background. They said it didn't matter. My math knowledge plus my left political knowledge was excellent preparation. But I wasn't into being a student again. I had taught with Sam and Herb, and also earlier at MIT for Chomsky, and being a student again felt like going backward. Returning to school would interrupt my contemplating what to do for an income while I would be doing politics. Finally, Lydia and I were living together, and leaving entailed considerable time apart, though I could travel into Boston any weekend, or she could come out to Amherst.

Still, this was a special educational opportunity and I told Sam and Herb I would go on one condition. If I was going to do it, presumably to get a Ph.D., I would have to be able to write a dissertation on whatever I wanted without any hassle. It would have to be of my own choosing and not subject to rejection on the grounds of being too radical. They said sure, no problem, what did I think they were doing this whole venture for if not to promote that type of initiative? They said, "if you wrote *What Is To Be Undone* as your thesis, we would accept it." This exceeded my demand, since this book, which I had already published, was about political theory and contained no economics. Even I wouldn't have submitted a doctoral thesis so distant from the discipline. Sam and Herb saying they would take *What Is To Be Undone* clinched the deal.

U Mass Amherst is a very nice rural campus about two hours drive from Boston. I moved there during the week but returned to Boston most weekends to be with Lydia, or sometimes she came to Amherst. The department, the year I went, was populated with a team of radical faculty making it the premier place to learn radical economics. The idea was that the accumulation of radicals at U Mass would provide a basis for serious work that would be impossible with a lesser community. It could not only teach new economists but also be a radical research institute. To succeed, however, it had to attract and admit students of like inclination. The radical faculty, from day one, were excited, but worried. Could they maintain their hold on the school's resources? Would the state—U Mass Amherst is a state school—intervene?

The radical faculty had pulled off a coup creating this department. It occurred partly due to an open-minded administrator, but mostly because the department had recently been losing students and becoming fiscally unviable, so the radicals were able to convincingly claim that shifting the department's orientation would rejuvenate revenues. Irony of ironies, the radicals took charge to reinvigorate the bottom line. And it was true, applications rose.

The radical faculty could have been in a constant war with other faculty, particularly about admissions policies, but this was cleverly avoided. Instead of everyone searching through incoming applications for who they wanted to admit, the radicals proposed that admissions should be based solely on exam scores. Applicants with the highest Graduate Record Exam (GRE) scores would be admitted one by one down to the number of slots available. Nothing but the GRE score would count. No arguments would be possible. As a bonus, the stature of the school would rise as the score level rose.

Everyone agreed to avoid warring over whom to admit by adopting this policy. The radicals had snookered the mainstream staff. You see, a student who had no radical commitments and very high scores was going to apply to Harvard, Chicago, MIT, Columbia, etc. A radical with high scores was going to apply to U Mass Amherst. As a result, the radicals who applied all had much higher scores than the more mainstream students who applied. Every single incoming student, due to being objectively picked based on GRE scores only, was radical. It was a slam dunk procedural strategy. U Mass Amherst, therefore, was unique. Its undergraduates were a mix of students on average quite like students at other schools but with a mixed faculty and therefore much more radical elective content available than at other places. For the graduate program, however, all the students wanted only the radical content, and there were plenty of faculty to provide it. The holdover mainstream faculty was left doing nearly nothing in the graduate program.

From the start, I felt that the U Mass project could only be called a success if it accomplished more via its accumulation of radicals in one place than if each of them was off somewhere else by him- or herself or with maybe one other person of similar orientation. It made no sense to look at U Mass and say it was a great place on grounds that it graduated fifteen or twenty prospective radical economists a year, or that it produced more research and connection with activism then some other school, unless this difference was commensurate to the number of faculty at U Mass. To be successful, the U Mass faculty had to accomplish more being in one place than they would have accomplished were they spread across the country.

The first signs that its assets were being underutilized arose when the radical faculty decided that undergraduates would receive almost the exact same education as they would have gotten if the radicals weren't there. Typical micro and macro courses would be given, with typical texts. Each year, hundreds of students would get no gain from the radicalism of the faculty.

Next up was a debate about the department insinuating itself into ongoing activism on campus, in Massachusetts, and around the country. It happened to a degree, but very little. The rationale was that the department had to toe a fine line to avoid inciting the Massachusetts state government to intervene. Prudent effectiveness was the radical faculty's name for it. Self policing to ward off external policing was my name for it. People built a fine department and then worried more about defending it than about winning more.

I had serious arguments with various faculty, urging that I thought defense of the department should rest not on finessing the government into believing there was no problem worth attacking, but on building massive support to defend the department against any incursions that might come. I argued that if the department was generating revenue, and also won major support from students, off-campus movements, unions, and nonprofits, it could follow a radical path and withstand right-wing criticism.

The cautious road was taken, not the road I favored. There was never serious external pressure to ward off. But the internal fear of external repression drastically curtailed people's agendas. I have no doubt, thirty years later, that the faculty from my time feel the project was a massive success. And I would guess that U Mass Amherst has been the source of more radical thought and perhaps even more radical commitment, and surely more leftist graduates than any other single economics graduate program in the U.S. over the same period. But, I also think the project fell miserably short of its potential. The initiating hope wasn't that the department should be a bit better than other departments. The initial hope was that it should be better than what all of its faculty could have accomplished if spread over six or eight other institutions.

The students in the U Mass graduate program when I was there were highly radical and very activist. Ironically, however, time spent at U Mass Amherst was in many respects a defusing rather than invigorating experience. Per-capita active participation in organizing dropped, rather than increased, with each new year. Requirements of the program never included political activism. Academics crowded out activism.

There was also no positive visionary component to the program. That is, there were no courses on what we radicals want to supersede capitalism. Well, there was one such course that I taught, but it was mostly for undergraduates and it was against the grain of the department rather than central to the department's agenda. My class was an attempt to shift departmental focus toward vision and positive aspirations rather than prioritizing only criticism, but in that larger goal my course failed and I suspect it was the last best chance until now for something commensurate to the department's potential to have occurred along those lines.

We had demonstrations in those early days of the U Mass experiment about the direction of the department. My classmates and I were rooted in the New Left experience. It was to little avail, however, and we all passed on to other places too soon for our dissent to win. The faculty outlasted us.

I arrived at U Mass with Herb and Sam as a somewhat special student. I had published a book about radical theory. I was prominent in activism. I came from a physics and math background that exceeded in technical training not only what the other students had, but what most of the faculty had as well. So I was in an odd position—and my competence was inflated by rumors that circulated before I arrived, rising well beyond what was arguably real.

The truth was that I had taken precisely one course in mainstream economics at MIT prior to arriving at U Mass and I had very nearly failed it. It was an introductory course, using the then-famous Samuelson textbook, but I couldn't make heads or tails of the content. It seemed incoherent and irrational. But the faculty at U Mass, from whatever Sam and Herb had been saying to get me an admission without my even taking the centrally important GREs or even filling out any forms, all thought I was some kind of crackerjack economist already.

In truth, in my view, economics, at least as taught in U.S. universities, is a ridiculous discipline. In undergraduate programs, in those days and for all I know still, students take what is called microeconomics and then macroeconomics. Then students take the same subjects again, and then if they are sure they want to continue into the profession, perhaps even a third time. Those are the courses I missed. The difference each time is that the same conceptual content is conveyed using increasingly sophisticated mathematics. Amazingly, in graduate school, you get it all again, up another mathematical notch. Of course, in grad school there is also history of economic thought, economic history, and specialized focuses.

My main perception was that the field didn't primarily seek to comprehend economics. Departments of economics were primarily oriented to rationalize existing economic relations. Only when it could be done without upsetting that dominant agenda did mainstream economists understand actual economies.

This is why economists' conceptual frameworks failed to seriously address huge swaths of reality. The undergraduate, and even graduate, economics student could know little about the workings of corporations, and yet be considered brilliant in the field. Everyone claimed to know a great deal about markets, yet in fact what they knew about was not markets as they operated in reality, nor even idealized markets as they would operate with real people, but an abstract idealized market as it would operate with an idealized fictitiously simple kind of people.

At any rate, I quickly saw there were two tricks to being impressively economic. First, you demonstrated a math facility by always showing yourself to be a step ahead of the chosen methodology. Second, you developed a knack for telling stories in which you said things like first this causes that, then that causes this, and then over there you get some economic outcome like inflation or rising unemployment or changed interest rates. I had no problem displaying mathematical competence. That wasn't much of an achievement for someone with a math and physics background. But I couldn't tell an economic story for the life of me. And when I heard such a story, even when I sometimes knew what the words people were uttering referred to, I still had little idea why the presenter thought his or her words fit together into a causal pattern.

There were two parts to economics. Microeconomics was about buyer/seller transactions and how they nest together at the level of individual workers and consumers and firms. It was what an economist or mathematician might call an axiomatic system, and in that respect it was a bit like a physical theory. The math was tight, though rudimentary. I knew I could do micro. My only problem was that it seemed devoid of serious purpose and reason. The underlying assumptions diverged incredibly from realism and the deductions were barely better. It was as if physicists assumed items had critical properties they didn't have and then used those assumptions to make predictions that left out what was most important about the items, then also ignored that the predictions bore little relation to real outcomes. But the even bigger problem for me was macroeconomics. That was where stories got told. I didn't get macroeconomics at all.

I remember first meeting Leonard Rapping, the star macroeconomics professor in the group of U Mass radicals. He treated me, an incoming first-year student, like an equal. We went off to talk and play pool. He would spin out story after story about the motion of the macroeconomy. I would nod, occasionally grunt, offer a phrase or two, and say good shot or chuckle at a bad one—and he was so confident of himself and was so sure I was this brilliant wunderkind, that there was no problem. He just took it for granted that I was ratifying his thoughts, or that whenever he had doubts, I was pushing him about those. This persisted my whole time at U Mass, because even after I read about and took courses in macroeconomics, including courses taught by Rapping, while I got so that I was able to mimic the storytelling process pretty well, when it came to keeping up with Leonard outside of class, my comprehension was pure hokum, though he never knew it.

I even think when I did venture to speak, having very little rationale for what I was saying, that didn't matter either. It was a bit like the king who wears no clothes. I knew I was bereft of comprehension, perhaps unlike the king who was deluded about his stature. It was Rapping who imposed knowing on me, injecting comprehension into my words when it really wasn't there. For example, when I sometimes found myself interested but not understanding Rapping and asked questions trying to understand, Leonard always just barreled on, assuming the questions were challenging or trying to provoke him, since it was impossible that I didn't know the answers. If I was brief about a story—leaving openings for inclusions—he would hear me, assume I knew what I was talking about, and easily bend it in his own hearing into something that struck him as compelling. The expectation of wisdom plus the fact that the discipline was so rarified and divorced from reality that reasonable economists could take opposite sides of almost any issue and make typically vague words jump through their own hoops trumped that I had no idea what I was talking about. Rapping filled in my blanks to suit himself. You can perhaps see why I was unimpressed with economics. There were other problems as well.

I took a course in Marxist economics from Rick Wolff, another U Mass star. I had already rejected much of Marxism in my book, *What Is To Be Undone*, so this encounter involved numerous disagreements, but at least there was substance at stake. Wolff didn't read my book, nor did other students, something that at the time, I now realize as I write these words, I never even noticed, which says a great deal, I think, about the lack of mutual exploration and respect that was taken for granted and thus not even worth noting. I was a star for everyone, but not a star you had to read. Academics often read not to learn, much less to teach, but mainly to gather content for their own writings. Students read what they were assigned. Curiosity and broader agendas were rarely operative.

I could barely manage courses in economic history and history of economic thought. The problem was that there were elements of those tiresome and unfathomable macroeconomic stories present. I just couldn't function well in a domain so horribly divorced from real testing, on the one hand, and that seemed so distant from obvious insights, on the other.

I was a teaching assistant for the head of the department, Donald Katzner, who happened to be a nonradical neoclassical economist teaching microeconomics. He was horrible at it, utterly boring and incomprehensible for the students, mostly sophomores, who in any event barely gave a damn. I had a section which I probably butchered too, not least since it is hard to teach what you don't believe in. I have no memory of the section but I do remember that I was tagged to proctor the final exam. I entered this big hall with a couple of hundred students. I handed out the test and blue books for their answers, and I then had to say a few words before letting them begin. Without thinking about it, I said I was there to help and if they had any questions, just ask me.

They were just sitting, slumped, moribund, ignoring me. I repeated the instruction and got the same lack of response. So I said, look, let me give you an example. I picked up the exam, read out a question from it, and said, for example, you might ask me that. Then I gave the answer out loud. I noted that I was doing it out loud because answers are important and so they should all hear what I had to say to any one of them who asked a question. Now they were paying attention, many laughing, everyone incredulous. So I repeated, remember now, feel free to ask me anything. Okay, proceed.

They asked a number of questions during the session. I answered, and by and large, they did a good deal better than expected on the exam. The department head got wind of it and I got called in, but I wasn't removed from the program. It would have been hypocritical to expel me since many of the radical faculty had at various points advocated no grading, all A's, and so on, and since everyone knew Katzner was indeed a horrible teacher. For that matter, everyone knew that the students learned more in that final session than in any other lecture during the semester, which wasn't saying much. So I got reprimanded and was never again assigned to assist any mainstream faculty. If I had only known, I would have done it sooner.

Doctoral Revelation

> *I have never let my schooling interfere with my education.*
> *—Mark Twain*

The second round of violating the norms of U Mass was on a whole different level, and has been broadly unknown ever since. It wasn't just the mainstream faculty who weren't great teachers. Many of the radical faculty left a lot to be desired as well, as did the subject matter. We students felt that being good at taking exams corresponded only to a limited degree to the likelihood that one would pursue an admirable career in the field. As our time for coursework wound down, the time for taking doctoral exams closed in. For some students this was unthreatening. A few hours studying, a few hours taking the exams, and one could move on. But for other students, exam time was traumatic. Even with extensive study they knew they were highly likely to fail.

A couple of my classmates decided this situation was wrong, pretty much the way I had earlier decided that the micro final exam was wrong. Yes, some students might not have aptitude, but others might perform badly due to poor teaching and still others might be bad at taking tests but have fine prospects as future teachers. So my classmates stole the doctoral exams a few days before our class was to take them. They then enlisted folks to provide template answers, including me, and of course I complied. The answers were given to all members of the class in danger of failing. It has to be said that absolutely incredibly, some who took the answers still failed. Perhaps the thieves and coconspirators had been wrong about the only obstacle to some students being effective was lack of good training. Beyond tests, I think a big obstacle for some folks in becoming competent "economists" was integrity. If a field requires phoniness of the sort I displayed with Leonard Rapping, and if some people are just incapable of mustering that kind of behavior, they are doomed.

This phenomenon of an academic discipline being less than it claims to be is not confined to economics. Consider political science. Noam Chomsky told me a story that revealed how the same thing holds there. When Daniel Ellsberg stole highly classified documents detailing decision making in the U.S. government during the war in Vietnam, what was called the *Pentagon Papers*, he wasn't trying to be an ideal academician, of course. But, when you think about it, there was an academic dimension to it.

To convey the insight, Noam asked me to imagine, for example, that some Soviet government employee stole documents detailing decision making in the Politburo during the Stalin purges or the Soviet invasion of Czechoslovakia, Hungary, or Afghanistan. In the USSR, of course, these documents would not be used in political science courses on penalty of losing one's job and being shipped off to Siberia. Courses on political science in Soviet graduate programs would use government public proclamations, reports found in the state newspaper, *Pravda*, etc. Doctoral programs would use specially filtered content consistent with arriving at conclusions acceptable to the Kremlin.

Returning to the U.S., Ellsberg's act was to copy and then to smuggle out of high security offices documents revealing some of the true calculations of U.S./Vietnam policy making. So Noam asked, did our political science departments overwhelmingly use these documents, either then or later, as primary sources for understanding our government? It wouldn't have been a crime to use them, but still, it didn't happen. What should have become virtually universally utilized core material, far more valuable than government pronouncements, public speeches, and *New York Times* reports, essentially disappeared from public and even scholarly attention and certainly never achieved real prominence in the political science discipline.

What the analogy showed me was that political science in the U.S. is not firstly about understanding the operations of the U.S. government. As in the Soviet case, damning data was avoided. Commitment to rationalizing existing institutions precluded full revelation and analysis. My added observation was that this holds for the economics profession, too, so it shouldn't be surprising that you can go through graduate economics training, teach for decades in a university, and still have no serious comprehension of the impact of markets or corporate divisions of labor on human behavior, preferences, or intergroup relations.

A little memoirish sidebar on this history was that one day I got a call from Chomsky. He said he had a friend who needed some help with a project and he wondered if I could perhaps lend a hand. It turned out later it had been Ellsberg. I was busy with my organizing and whatnot, and felt what could possibly be of more consequence, and so passed on the offer. It was the last time I cavalierly passed on a suggestion from Noam.

The above feelings about the economics discipline and its graduate training were solidified in me about fifteen years after I graduated. I had the pleasure of reading a book called *The Making of An Economist* by Arjo Klamer and David Colander. This is an incredible survey of students in elite programs whose interviews and poll results demonstrate that economics bears more in common with astrology than with serious sciences such as biology or physics. If any readers are thinking about pursuing economics, I recommend this book before any other.

Doctoral Denial

If all economists were laid end to end, they would not reach a conclusion.
—George Bernard Shaw

After doctoral exams comes writing a thesis. I had passed the exams with honors, a testimony to the exam's irrelevance as an indicator of serious comprehension since at that time, and ever since, I was pitifully weak at neoclassical macroeconomics, no doubt weaker than some who failed the exams. Nonetheless, next I had to propose a doctoral focus. Remember, I had gone to U Mass on the agreement that doing a thesis would be painless. I would choose something I wanted to do, and, assuming it was of good quality, it would suffice. I

217

wouldn't have to do something unrelated to my own interests or devoid of activist relevance. It would be a productive cakewalk.

I took Sam Bowles and Herb Gintis as my sponsoring faculty since my prior agreement had been reached with them. My first proposal was to examine Marxism's relevance to trying to transcend capitalism. Herb and Sam told me that was acceptable. I went off and wrote quite a lot, submitted it not as a final thesis, but to demonstrate where I was headed, and it was quickly rejected. I was told it wasn't economic or original enough. It covered familiar ground. I was shocked. What had happened to our agreement? This work later morphed into a book I co-wrote with Robin Hahnel called *Unorthodox Marxism*. In Bowles and Gintis' view my first thesis submission was too much "journalism," meaning bringing to a broader public insights that weren't original. In response, I said I thought the work had about as many original insights as any thesis they were likely to get or any essay they had written themselves, but I also told them I didn't want to argue about that because I, in any event, had another idea I wanted to switch to.

What I did care about, however, and what I did spend some time arguing with them about, was different. First, I felt it was wrong to say what I had written was journalism just because I was intent on writing without technical obfuscation—which is why I thought they saw it that way despite what I considered the considerable innovations I had included. But more important, I was upset by Sam and Herb saying that good journalism shouldn't be acceptable as a thesis. That seemed wrong to me. It seemed that if someone demonstrated a capacity for conveying valuable analysis in a popular manner, even with nothing new at all included in the exposition, that was a better indicator of their likely merit as a practitioner of the profession than their doing a thesis that uncovered some new fact or purported to tell a new story in hyper abstruse language. I made no headway with that argument, and to move on we simply adjourned it. That was too bad. It was an important point.

My next idea was to work on economic vision. I had taught about an alternative to capitalism and I had come to think that it was very important for critics of capitalism to offer a positive alternative, so I figured why not do a thesis on that. I went off and worked on it. The results later morphed into two more books, also written with Robin Hahnel, *Looking Forward,* published with South End Press, and *The Political Economy of Participatory Economics,* published with Princeton University Press. Sam and Herb didn't like this effort, either. I honestly can't remember the reasons they gave, probably a combination of insufficient innovation and professionalism (meaning not written in the jargon of the field), plus divorce of my topic from the main byways of the field. At any rate, now there was tension. I had little need for a degree, since by this time I was well into the process of beginning South End Press and I clearly wasn't going to become an economics professional. But I wanted the degree for my father, for whom it would mean a lot, and I couldn't get Sam and Herb to budge.

One day Robin was visiting and we talked with Herb and Sam. Robin needed to do his thesis for American University. He already had a job and only needed to resolve his thesis to solidify his employment. I, in contrast, wanted to be done with all this. Sam and Herb had by this time made clear what the real problem was, at least in my eyes. They talked about how they had mentored other students into the profession. They waxed eloquent about the relation between thesis advisor and student, emphasizing that the thesis process was the key to one's future success. I am sure they believed this for me, though what I heard in their rendition of thesis-learning, despite their sincerity, was a description of hazing, something that I had long since had my fill of. They wanted to mold me into the best economist I could be, like adding another publication to their resume. It wasn't going to happen on my watch, and I was watching closely. So Robin and I next proposed a joint thesis. Sam and Herb said a joint effort would be fine as long as the results were ample for two people.

Robin did the main work. I was a kind of consultant. The thesis elaborated ideas we had discussed for some time, putting them in the profession's technical language. It later became a joint book, *Quiet Revolution in Welfare Economics,* published by Princeton University Press. When we submitted the manuscript to Sam and Herb, they said great, this is a thesis, who wants his name on it. We said it's joint. They said they couldn't do that, it might exacerbate tensions with mainstream faculty and undermine the department's credibility. We asked if the work was sufficient for more than one person. They said yes, of course. Find a way to present it as two separate products and that should work fine. I had no patience for this, but Robin needed his degree and I agreed that he should take it and, with that, hung up my academic hat, without a Ph.D. It was a small loss, not even worth the time to divide the thing up, particularly considering four books had emerged from the craziness. Again, fear of losing the department prevented the department from being what it ought to have been.

Drummed Out

To create a new culture does not only mean to make original discoveries on an individual basis. It also and especially means to critically popularize already discovered truths, make them, so to speak, social.
—Antonio Gramsci

Years later the book version of *Quiet Revolution in Welfare Economics* was used in a graduate level course at U Mass Amherst. That was nice. Not so nice was hearing at about the same time that Herb Gintis had renounced his radical past and had become, in some regards, even rather reactionary, such as supporting the Iraq war. It was hard for me to believe. My guess was that Herb's renunciation of radicalism had much more to do with perception and perhaps even personality, or even political despair, than with personal careerism. A confrontation, a fight, even a harsh debate was difficult for Herb to emotionally abide. So my feeling was that Herb's political trajectory probably owed somewhat to being confronted by leftist students about this or that insight, causing him to become polarized against them, and then against what he took to be their milieu to escape bickering conflict.

To understand this aspect of what I think might have been part of what affected Herb, imagine a ball club. Someone on it conceives a new notion, maybe critical of something the club has been doing, or perhaps proposing something new that others on the team don't like. Teammates respond harshly rather than hearing it out and soberly discussing it. He or she gets riled back. Dispute escalates. To justify its last round of anger, each side digs deeper into its claims. The gap becomes a chasm. The dispute becomes a feud. The party of the first part, who had the deviant notion, renounces the team and its whole philosophy, seeking to be traded.

This dynamic has occurred before my eyes in many variants for political teams and is pretty common in the trajectory of ex-leftists, I think. I never personally knew a fellow named Ron Radosh, but he went to Cuba and had what were plausible and even reasonable doubts about what he saw and experienced. When he came back, he was assaulted for raising them. In reaction, as I saw it, he enlarged his doubts beyond what his own perceptions warranted. The dispute flared further. Indeed, I suspect this kind of thing can probably be found at least partly fueling hostility toward the Left by Todd Gitlin, Chris Hitchens, and even David Horowitz, though in those cases, unlike Herb, I think the allure of mainstream accolades for denouncing elements of the Left or even for leaving it entirely, as with Horowitz, probably also operated. At any rate, it would certainly be useful to discover internal means of defusing bickering before it destroys honest exchange and distorts caring lives.

Returning to Herb, I think he shared another factor with many less prominent ex-leftists that pulled him away from radicalism—doubt. When asked directly, Herb offered, "When the left collapsed, I decided I didn't want to spend my life like the old IWW 'warriors' who went to meeting after meeting thirty years after their movement collapsed. It was not a betrayal of values on my part. I have the same values today as when I knew you." But if taking a stand is right when winning, isn't taking a stand right when times get hard? I tend to think it is not all that exemplary to be part of a growing and even winning surge of dissent. It seems to me both harder and more exemplary to work to pave the way for later success when times are very hard. I doubt Herb would disagree.

Herb is both a thoughtful and a moral guy who doesn't abide inconsistency. So, while I can see his not wanting to be like old 'warriors' endlessly celebrating glory days leading Herb to change tactics and methods—just as it would lead anyone to do in changing contexts—I can't see why the Left declining for a time, even for a long time, should cause Herb to not be radical. I figure, instead, the rocks on which Herb's radicalism broke apart had to be those of a deeper doubt. Questioned further, Herb relayed that he felt the Left had collapsed. The Left had failed. More, he came in time to feel that a democratic economy wouldn't be viable. This is what changed Herb's mind, I would bet, as it has so many others: no future.

Herb acclimated himself, it seems to me, to getting what could be won for people within capitalism. He resigned, however, from seeking to win something beyond capitalism. For me, Herb's story reveals that even the most caring and mentally tough people will rarely, if ever, stick forever with a struggle that lacks worthy and compelling vision and strategy. Few people will endlessly celebrate and participate in a struggle that seems to be Sisyphean. Doubt conquers commitment better than any police truncheon.

Herb relayed that he once went to a pro-Cuba rally on Boston Common, and Pete Seeger sang a Spanish Civil War song. Afterwards Herb reported that Seeger said, "They won the war, but we had all the good songs." Herb told me he never forgot that statement. "I swore that I didn't want to have the good songs," he said, "I just wanted to win the war." I agree halfway with Herb about that. I'd like to have the good songs rather than not. And I even think it is damn important to have the good songs. But along with Herb, I agree that the main point is winning. Herb doesn't believe in economic and social vision as I do, or in a path to attaining it as I do—though, other than the debilitating weight of bad times, I don't know why—but I don't see how he can deny that if we don't try for a better world then we won't attain one, and if we don't attain one, then there will be endless hell to pay.

Chapter 22

The Responsibility of Intellectuals

Teaching for Chomsky

To teach is not to transfer knowledge but to create the possibility for the production or construction of knowledge.
—*Paulo Freire*

Beyond teaching at U Mass Amherst as an assistant for mainstream economics classes, and beyond teaching my own radical courses at U Mass in economic vision, I had earlier taught at MIT in a course on Intellectuals and Social Change set up by Noam Chomsky and Louis Kampf. Having taken that course earlier as a student, I knew its shape and flow. Attendance kept climbing and it needed to be divided into sections. Noam and Louis had me and Nick Egleson, a past president of national SDS, to help out. Noam and Louis taught a main longer session; all four of us taught smaller group sessions, each of which went over the material of the main session and explored its ideas.

Nick was a very effective guy who I quickly lost track of. I wonder what became of him. Louis Kampf was very much into students, as we used to say, as well as into active resistance to injustice. Louis participated with us in many campus events and was even a member of our SDS chapter for a time, as well as of what was called the New University Conference. He hung out with us quite a lot. Louis was, I believe, along with my friend Peter Bohmer, responsible for contributing our local chapter name, Rosa Luxemburg SDS. In fact, this was a runoff choice. We voted among Ho Chi Minh SDS, Sacco and Vanzetti SDS, and Rosa Luxemburg SDS. We went for Rosa for her gender and her anti-Leninism.

Rosa Luxemburg was a tireless libertarian German revolutionary who grew critical of Lenin and the Bolshevik revolution. She said, "You lose, you lose, you

222

lose, you win." The way I understood this was that you engage with power over and over. Along the way you will have repeatedly failed to overcome it. But, there will come a time when you will grow in strength, numbers, commitment, organizational wherewithal, and clarity about what you want and how to get it, and you will win the ultimate desired changes. All the moments, the most decrepit and defeated, as well as the most inspired and victorious, are part of one giant project. Luxemburg gave her life to the cause. We still haven't won. But we will, and when we do, all prior lost battles will find their full meaning.

For me, the main thing about the Chomsky/Kampf course was not the sessions I taught and the new skills and confidence I gained, but that it provided me with another chance to attend classes Noam taught. On the one hand, there was the quality of information he would offer to start each session. Then students would ask questions that ranged far and wide, and it simply didn't matter what was asked, Noam would answer, often with quotations, even page references. His answers would range over wide topics, making connections on the spot. It was like dealing with a vast database that could redesign itself with new linkages on the fly.

Decades later, as Noam slipped into his seventies, he was still providing this same service, with an even larger database, to sessions of our summer school called the Z Media Institute, as well as in his public talks. At ZMI each June Noam would give an evening talk and do two daytime sessions. Everyone would be intent on the actual substance except myself, Lydia, and often Cynthia Peters. The three of us would typically be holding back laughter at the back of the room. This was our odd way of reacting to something extraordinary that we found too incredible to register without the mirth. It is a little like the elation you feel watching a virtuoso in any field when you aren't intent on the content but are instead enjoying the sheer audacity of it.

U Mass Teaching

> *Well, you walk into the room*
> *Like a camel and then you frown.*
> *—Bob Dylan*

In addition to teaching at MIT, Harvard, and then U Mass Amherst as noted earlier, I also spent some time teaching at U Mass Boston. This is when we were first developing South End Press and I taught there largely for income, since I got only room and board from the press in those years. Arthur MacEwan, a long-time Left economist who I had known tenuously, was then or perhaps had just been the head of the economics department at U Mass Boston, so when I asked for a job there teaching a couple of courses as an adjunct—basically a part-time employee—it was fine with Arthur. They were my own courses, again. The first was on broad understanding of current society and the second was on what future vision we want to win. These were night classes and the students were from many backgrounds. Some were young but others were considerably older, as U Mass had many working-class students who had been in the army or had jobs and were trying to get degrees to win better employment. My course description was radical, and my students were aware of what they were getting into. I taught informally. I would talk a while, inviting interaction, followed by discussion and exchange. I would often ask questions to provoke involvement. This has been my approach ever since in classes, lectures, workshops, and often even with large audiences.

As these courses at U Mass were mine in definition and execution, I was supposed to grade people. However, I felt grading as it was generally undertaken, largely due to the associations students and faculty generally brought to it, was a destructive impediment to education. It wasn't evaluation per se I was against. I agreed we shouldn't validate incompetence. Instead, I rejected the competitive dynamics that owed as much to our culture and the habits of students and faculty as it owed to evaluation per se.

At any rate, I announced in the first session that there would be a paper. If you did it and it showed you took the work seriously, you got an A. If not, you got dropped from the course. With few exceptions the students had never encountered this type of environment. They loved it because, though very demanding, the classes were relaxed, provocative, rooted in reality, and without competition. The reading load and intensity of sessions was high. But the students were unafraid, and many reported in conversation and letters both that they had not only learned more—the course content pretty much guaranteed that—and participated more than in any other course they had taken, but that they were more proud of their A than of any grade before, even knowing that it was nearly automatic.

You're Fired!

Nothing in all the world is more dangerous than sincere ignorance...
—Martin Luther King Jr.

There was a premed student in the class who was perpetually openly pissed at me, a tone I probably returned in kind—I wasn't overly careful about my moods with students. He didn't like the course content. For him it was too radical, and he never came to agree with the critiques of capitalism. But the gnawing problem for him was the grading. He felt giving everyone an A, with some not earning it, degraded his well-deserved A and reduced his medical school advantage. He wanted justice. So he went to the administration and complained. Arthur and I chatted and after a bit he informed me that whether I liked it or not, as but an adjunct teacher I had to toe the line. I had to give legitimate grades that demonstrated a sensible curve of accomplishment among my students, some A, B, C, D, and F, or this would be my last class taught at U Mass Boston. This was a shouting confrontation. I couldn't believe Arthur didn't take my side regarding innovative procedures in even a highly radical course. In retrospect, I think Arthur felt that the program might be jeopardized by such a choice and that complaints that might arise. I suspect he thought I was clinging to impractical aims in an environment where compromise was required. The administration won the war and I was out after the course in which the students all got their As.

About twenty-five years later I was speaking at a conference at Brandeis College in Waltham, Massachusetts. Since I lived a couple of hours south of Waltham, I had come up by bus, and I was met by Cynthia Peters at a subway stop on the way to the conference and stayed at her place for the weekend. The conference wasn't particularly unusual, but when Cynthia picked me up at the end of it and we went out for dinner before I caught a bus back home, the conversation did have a feature that transcended the moment. Cynthia was telling me about her work organizing antiwar projects in her neighborhood in Boston and about preparing for the Democratic National Convention leading up to the 2004 election. In the course of her work she had been invited to a house gathering that Arthur MacEwan also attended to talk with a bunch of folks about directions and prospects for the anticorporate globalization movement. It had been a largely liberal discussion, in Cynthia's view, with no radical edge.

After the gathering, Cynthia spent some time interacting with Arthur, striking up a conversation with him about the need for a vision of a better world and the importance of couching even short-run program in terms of how to attain that better world. For Arthur, it seemed to Cynthia, operationally there was nothing but better capitalism to hope for. I doubt that, in fact, Arthur feels that way deep down and for all eternity, but that Cynthia got that strong impression was undeniable. For me, in contrast, there is always quite forefront the possibility of a revolutionary transformation to a whole new system. Was the difference between Arthur and myself over grading twenty-five years before, which in my view was really over whether commitment to a different society had immediate practical implications that should be incorporated in the present, a cause or a symptom of the different impressions we later gave regarding what was possible?

One way of viewing this is that I was too damn wedded to values born of a unique time to mature into adopting relevant new insights, or even just into toning down my positive enthusiasms when compromise was advisable. My thoughts, connected to youthful sixties values, never matured. They lost their real-world relevance. They became ensnared in a youthful dream with no contemporary bearing. Certainly this does happen to people. It is more or less what Herb Gintis indicated to me he was trying to avoid.

Another way of viewing the situation was that many other sixties radicals have been too constrained and pressured by their practical lives to hang on to their prior worthy values. Or maybe they just didn't retain their prior aspirations, letting them slip from being the defining context for daily choices. Did Arthur, for example, evolve a tone that facilitated teaching in today's college, but also consigned his broader thinking to being less relevant to serious change? I don't know, but it would be surprising if not.

Of course, it wasn't just that some people who were revolutionary in the sixties later demoted or jettisoned attention to revolution as naive. Many people who remained broadly progressive and actively and admirably committed gave up at least operational hope of winning anything beyond ameliorated suffering. And on the other side, it wasn't just me who not only retained the hopes of the New Left but developed new insights, not only about what we endure but also about what we can attain.

So here is the thing. In deciding whether I and my ilk were tripping out on hope devoid of rationality, or whether those transcending their past attachments to adopt a more tranquil exterior were accepting and sometimes even extolling contemporary circumstance without hope or rationality, one key piece of evidence for me is my stated arguments for my vision and continued hope, on the one hand, and their stated explanations for why their commitments in the earlier decades were wrong and for why a new system is simply impossible or, at the very least, not a priority that should inform our current public identification and activity. Here is the problem. My visionary case is available. Left arguments for operational hopelessness are not.

To take just the radical economists we have met so far, neither Bowles, Gintis, nor MacEwan have ever to my knowledge written words like, I was wrong to believe in the efficacy and desirability of revolution and its key place in my life and choices. They haven't written their reasons why they think capitalism is forever or even just nearly forever, or even just not going away any time soon. They haven't explained why prioritizing advocating a full-scale institutional alternative to capitalism and using that vision to inform current program and inspire current resistance is no longer worthy of their priority attention.

I think they haven't explained their new stance because they have no reasons for the change, and they may well not even accept that this change has occurred. But I suspect that it has occurred, and that they harbor a hopeless feeling, as do so many others, which is what tempers their pronouncements and constrains them from aggressively talking about visionary alternatives and revolution. I don't mean to ridicule this. Earlier I wrote about my own coping mechanism for dealing with daily life, and I don't even work in capitalist institutions and among people for whom a public commitment to revolution would suggest a deep-going psychosis. At any rate, history will be the judge of these matters, and history takes time.

Dating and Power Relations

> *Don't accept rides from strange men,*
> *and remember that all men are strange.*
> —*Robin Morgan*

There was a socially memorable dating, or rather non-dating, dynamic that occurred around my time teaching at U Mass Boston. In the class I was teaching was a woman, about my age, who thought she fell in love with me. My guess was that she just hadn't been in an environment that was as respectful of her intelligence and hadn't encountered a fellow who was as radical, and the two combined in one situation to jolt her emotions. At any rate, she would bring me apples and ask questions after class, and then she asked me out. She would walk me after class to the parking lot, insisting that we get together. My explaining that I wouldn't ever go out with a student, and even if she weren't a student I was living with someone I loved and had no intention of taking up with anyone else, fell on deaf ears.

This turned out to be more than just a passing event in two respects. First, for whatever reasons, she was horribly caught up in her hopes and saddened by my rebuffs, which I could see and which troubled me. Indeed, her angst was so great that her father at one point came in after class to yell at me for causing his daughter such grief. My protestations that I had done nothing fell on deaf ears. But second, this whole encounter raised hard questions. Should a teacher date a student? I could have easily made a case that my situation was special—I didn't grade these students, giving them all As, instead, so I had no lasting power over them. But even though such a claim would have been structurally true, it would dodge the underlying question. It would have been a kind of special pleading, dodging the fact that if a person in a position of relative authority dates a subordinate or client lower in that hierarchy, there is abuse potential. Abuse wasn't inevitable, but if we asked the odds that such interactions would have a grievous downside, they were high.

On thinking it over, I thought there was a Catch-22 as well. It seemed to me that if an employer, doctor, or teacher thought he (or it could be a she) was above taking advantage of his relative position, then the odds went up he would do so. Being oblivious to the possibility of exploitation would make violations more likely. If the potential abuser was conflicted about proceeding, there was hope for healthy relations. Ironically, the more chance of a good outcome, the less likely dating would commence.

I decided early on I should simply take it for granted in such situations that I was as unlikely as the next guy to escape high probability results. I should not assume I had disproportionately great personal dignity or integrity, and therefore I should not undertake statistically forbidden options. This may explain why I maintain that the structures of a good economy should not assume that people are saints but should instead offer institutional settings that give all people reason to behave well.

My sensitivity to these matters, which has verged sometimes on a kind of quiet fanaticism but at other times dimmed to low embers, arose from other sources as well. My only real battles with my father, for example, were wildly asymmetrical affairs that would always conclude with me harshly accusing him of being an intellectual bigot. For someone I loved to fall short by my standards has never sat well with me, at least in the moment of violation. I wasn't perpetually down on my dad. The heat and fury of these assaults didn't transcend the moments in which we disputed, but I can only regret that these moments may well have been far more debilitating for him than for me. I would not fare well enduring from Eric, Andrea, or Andrew what I threw at my father when, in those moments, I was horribly harsh.

My dad was politically very liberal, highly moral, and extremely good to me. He was, however, also prone to explain social phenomena as outgrowths of the stupidity of the population, which for him meant, by and large, outgrowths of the stupidity of the uneducated masses and whoever managed to sneak into positions of erudition without having donned the accouterments to fit those positions—which condition was evidenced for him by any person's attitudes differing from his in any sharp sense. This became in my eyes a form of degradation of others and elevation of self that was similar to racism and sexism in its ugliness, but I didn't have the words for it then as it was more class- than culture-related. For my dad, people were, overall, dumb and greedy. Human nature produced human ills. It wasn't the abstract oppressive systems that I prattled on about that limited life; it was people's inner beings that produced those oppressive institutions. When Dad and I fought about the war, it wasn't that Dad supported carnage, it was that Dad felt that opposing body counts by appealing to popular sentiment was futile. In his view, protest had a morally admirable motive, but it was strategically idiotic.

I didn't know at the time that Dad's stance was a kind of classism that elevated professionals while also rationalizing relative inaction against injustices by those same professionals. I didn't know, that is, that it was on the one hand a lawyer evincing visceral coordinator-class consciousness, admittedly with dignity and compassion, and on the other hand a relatively empowered and advantaged citizen employing social cynicism to ward off calls for action. But that's what it was, and I suspect finding it so intolerable in my dad had a lot to do with my own nearly messianic persistence in perceiving the importance of that third class above

228

workers but below owners in society, who I call the coordinator class, as well as with my not always successful struggle to avoid seeing myself and others as he had often seen himself and others, and with my working so hard against denying history's potentials.

When I was accepted at MIT, my father was upset that I wasn't going to his alma mater, Cornell, but he was gleeful at another possibility. He knew that I wanted to be a physicist but he thought maybe that desire would wear off. If it did wear off, a technical background followed by law school at Columbia (his legal alma mater) would be a tremendous foundation for fiscal success.

I remember Dad laying out this scenario as a reason for celebrating my MIT admission, and I agreed, thinking to myself, dream on, Dad. But in retrospect the truth is that there was a moment, later, having slid out of physics, not due to aversion to the subject but due to the lure of revolution, when I did, in fact, consider going to law school. One obstacle to doing that, however, was that I knew that law school required tremendous memorization. I might be a good lawyer in the courtroom making compelling arguments, with or without evidentiary basis, a trait that is the currency of success in our legal system due to truth not being the currency of justice, but if I couldn't remember an endless store of precedents, I wouldn't be able to cut it as a lawyer and I especially wouldn't be able to navigate law school to become one. I must have known I could neither have endured nor accomplished it.

My thought, first generated thirty years ago and held ever since, was that each year thousands of students decide to go to law school, just as my father once had, not for money, power, or status, but to improve the world. These law school inductees are deadly serious about intellectual scholarship and religiously righteous about social justice, and they would be horribly offended to be accused of embarking on a career of gluttony plus system maintenance. However, each year law schools graduate their classes and a minuscule proportion of their graduates' ensuing labors go to ameliorate pains within existing structural constraints, much less go to make the world fundamentally better. So what distorted new recruits' righteous motives into graduating lawyers' crass machinations?

As I understood it back then, and as I understand it all the more so now, hazing is what intervenes. Prospective lawyers go through a sustained program of being molded to their profession. It is another variant of hazing in a fraternity, or of the vicious indoctrination of boot camp in the army, or of the physically daunting subordination a fledgling doctor endures, or of the slow climb to stature a journalist navigates. The law student is canned and packaged for delivery. Bludgeoned by forces from without, he or she is worn down until professional priorities replace righteous motives.

The result of fraternity hazing, boot camp, medical training, and covering the beat, among many other hazing processes including law school, is a new mind set, new values, and new priorities. "Get your mind right" is the credo of entry into social life in our society, and for lawyers—like for soldiers, doctors, journalists, politicians, CEOs, economists, or prison guards—getting your mind right means obeying your employer, prioritizing self-gain and system maintenance, eliminating behaviors that violate your position, and becoming emotionally restricted, judicially jaded, hostile about health, ignorant about contrary information, and otherwise matched up to the dictates of one's social role and against the inner beat of one's own idealism.

My father, Melvin Albert, left a flourishing firm to start his own practice, wanting to escape tutelage and subordination as well as assignments that turned his stomach. I don't remember this, but perhaps it rubbed off. Had Dad stayed at the big corporate firm, our family would have been far wealthier but perhaps also more alienated. I might have gone to Yale, not MIT. In any case, to return to where we started above, why did I see an analogy between decisions about law school and decisions about dating a student and how did they contour my choices? I felt if you are thinking about law school and are sure you can attend and graduate and become Bill Kuntsler or Leonard Weinglass (two lawyers who came out the other side and devoted themselves to uncompromisingly seeking justice) there is a very good chance you won't succeed. You are too confident to take the time to struggle against the indoctrination as much as is needed to transcend it. You will slip-slide into a suit, tie, and stock market portfolio, looking down on whoever has less than you and deciding that they deserve less just as you deserve more.

On the other hand, if you think about going through law school and are sufficiently doubtful about coming out the other side humane, you probably won't enter the legal grinder in the first place—but, ironically, you may have been one of the few students who could have passed through positively. My guess is that those who enter the legal profession and become, despite all the indoctrination, serious advocates of justice ironically probably didn't think about that goal before entering law school, but at some point, for whatever odd and remarkable combination of reasons, became radicalized and thereafter grew hostile to the main contours and prominent practitioners of legality. This is, to finally make the connection, the same kind of Catch-22 as governs dating subordinates. And the psychological dynamics of coordinating ourselves and our environments, with or without our values, bears on the processes of dissolution or preservation of revolutionary commitment in hard times, as well.

MIT's injunction against the November Action Coalition.

Commonwealth of Massachusetts

MIDDLESEX, SS.

To Robin Hahnel, Michael Albert, George Katsiaficas, Philip Raup, Stephen Shalom, Peggy Hopper, Stephen Krasner, J. Michael O'Conner, Peter Bohmer, Owen Franken, Michael S. Ansara, Abraham Igelfeld, Jeffrey Mermelstein, Steven M. Soldz, and the November Action Coalition, all of Cambridge, in the County of Middlesex, defendants,

GREETING:

Whereas a suit in equity has been begun against you in our SUPERIOR COURT within and for the County of Middlesex, by Massachusetts Institute of Technology, a charitable corporation organized and existing under the laws of the Commonwealth of Massachusetts, with a principal buildings in Cambridge, plaintiff.

WE COMMAND YOU, if you intend to make any defense, that on the first Monday of December next, which day is the return day of this subpoena, or within such further time as the law allows, you do cause your written appearance

Taking documents from Millikan's desk during the NAC occupation.

Lydia and the *Living Newspaper* troop.

A flyer for the *Living Newspaper*.

Lydia's children: Andrew, Eric, and Andrea
(left to right).

A pensive Lydia in 1971.

Initial promotion for *Z Magazine*.

An issue of *Z Papers*.

Founding members of the South End Press collective.

About

SOUTH END PRESS
Publishing Collective

A brochure circulated to SEP authors.

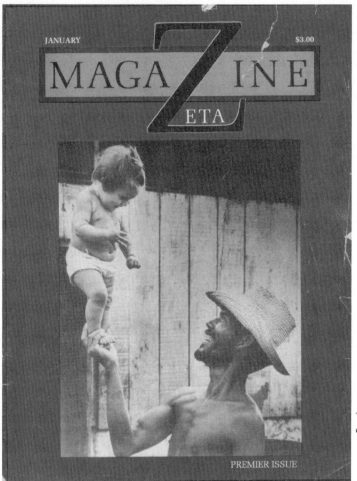

This first *Z Magazir* cover is still my fav

Participants in the Life After Capitalism conference held at the World Social Forum in Porto Alegre, Brazil.

Speaking to an assembly after receiving the Italian Republic Award.

Speaking on a panel at the World Social Forum in Porto Alegre, Brazil.

Lydia and I in 1980.

Chomsky and I at ZMI.

Robin and I in Woods Hole, Massachusetts.

Chapter 23

Prison School?

Threats Work

Is it surprising that prisons resemble factories, schools,
barracks, hospitals, which all resemble prisons?
—*Michel Foucault*

Returning to teaching, in South End Press's early, lean years, I held a simultaneous part-time job teaching in prison. I did it at two centers of incarceration—one low security, the other middle security.

The low security prison was—in those days—like a large suburban home. It had a yard and various common rooms, and the prisoners each had their own bedroom as well as freedom to move around the facility. There were no bars. I would drive up and park in the lot outside, walk to the door, and be admitted. I saw no guns and was never searched. I'd enter a common room to teach, but I could also roam around, eat with folks, and even chat with them in their rooms—although the doors had to be left open. Low security, however, did not mean that the prisoners had committed trivial crimes or were getting out of prison soon. I made friends with people in there for murder who had life sentences. Interestingly, once we established trust—due to the content and style of my classes—many of the inmates would tell me that they were guilty of what they were in for, or, if not for that, then they were guilty of something else. But not all of them. Some, it seemed, were completely innocent.

It was also quite clear that while a few of the inmates might have been at high risk for committing a new crime if released, others were no more likely to commit new crimes than the average person. Their earlier crimes had been committed due to special circumstances, youthful context, bad luck, or economic desperation. I liked the inmates about in the same fashion as I would like a similar-size group of lower-income folks met at a community picnic or ball game, which meant I liked them a whole lot more than I would like a similar group of high-income professionals, much less corporate owners. A particularly eye-opening part of all this for me was that I could have easily taken a prisoner out of there in my car without being stopped. That's what low-security meant, and in this institution it was blatantly true. So I asked the prisoners, what keeps you here? Why don't you just pick up and leave?

I was taken down a hall to a back window. In the distance was another prison, the next one I would teach at, and further off, was still another prison. The third one was high security. The prisoners told me if they were to bolt from their low security home, they would in time get caught and wind up in one of the others—either in horror or in hell. The threat of horror and hell kept them in purgatory. The disgusting web bore considerable resemblance to life outside.

Inmates Teach the Teacher

We don't need no education.
We don't need no thought control.
—Pink Floyd

At the moderate security joint where I taught next, the stick of worse and the carrot of better incarceration both still operated. Inmates endured prison horror. Bad behavior moved them into prison hell. Good behavior might move them into prison purgatory. To get in this prison, I went through gates and bars and searches and saw plenty of guns, not only in holsters but hoisted over guards' shoulders as they stared down from overhanging ramparts. It was like TV, but in the flesh. I never saw hell, but I guess I can imagine. In hell there was no threat of worse. There was only barbarism.

Once inside, I would be escorted to the room for the political economy class I was teaching, but once in that room I would be left alone with the inmates. It was a bigger class with more students than in my low security experience, fifty as compared to thirty. The inmates came to my class to work toward a degree in hopes of getting out someday with better prospects. Most often, the courses inmates took were horribly boring and the arrogance, obscurity, and disinterest of many of the faculty was an additional debit. Expecting the same from me, at the outset my students were barely civil. I taught political economy of capitalism. The prison employer had little idea what was going on in the class and probably wouldn't have cared much anyhow. But it was radicalism 101, 201, 301, all rolled into one. We covered a lot of ground because once we got rolling, the prisoners were hugely motivated and easily talked about everything from sex to sports, employment to war, and people's psychology to institutional pressures, all from an angle denigrating wealth and power and prioritizing change.

During class, at some point, matters of race and gender arose. Battling through many of the prisoners' presuppositions about women was hard, but not impossible. Addressing their views of homosexuality was another matter. These inmates were over half black. As far as I could ever discover, they were extremely homophobic. Guys who were eager for liberty, fraternity, and equality once these terms were given institutional substance, who were highly progressive on issues from war to income to decision making, and who quickly understood and utilized radical values and analyses (often finding in them slightly modified echoes of their own street smarts), were intransigent about homosexuality. Particularly the black prisoners saw homosexuality as a crime against humanity. I had no way of knowing how many of these men were engaging in sexual relations, consensual or otherwise, with other inmates, but I thought it was pretty likely that at least some of the men espousing homophobic views in class were having homosexual affairs in the nooks and crannies of the prison. That was food for thought.

All these years later, it brings to mind one of the oddest political group arrangements I ever heard of. Talking with a Leninist sect member about an article I had recently seen, I asked about the views of its writer. I was told he was the party's chief theoretician. I asked what position he had and was told he wasn't actually a member of the party. Inquiring further, I found out he was gay, and that because he was gay he was not permitted membership. Here was their main party thinker, authoring positions everyone in the party had to make their own, not himself in the party having been banned for practices he had to write against but which he lived by. It isn't only in prisons that people adopt odd stances. In sects such insanity is even commoner currency.

One day after prison class, as a special dispensation, I was eating in the dining room of the mid-security institution. The black prisoners were at their own tables and the whites at theirs. I was sitting at one of the black tables. I looked around and said, "Look, I know that you fully understand how race is used to divide and conquer. So what the hell is going on here? Since you know the prison promotes divisions among you, why do you go along with it? Any of you could go sit at the tables that now have only whites. The divide could be bridged. Why don't you do it?" It wasn't that I thought they were going to do it due to my prodding. I knew better than that, but I wanted to know what they felt about it. Why did they sit separate but equal? Whites and blacks got the same utensils and food, and there was no fence preventing integration. Saying the prison promoted segregation was one thing. In fact, the inmates had to abet the segregation or it would disappear.

One of the prisoners looked at me and said, "Why don't you go sit with them?" His point was immediately clear and the brief phrase was said so precisely and with such an undertone of meaning as to require no further explanation. We returned to other conversation. I never forgot the one-line explanation. It was a matter of the angle from which one looked at the room and its tables. The white prisoners were racist. The black prisoners and even the whites knew that not overcoming racial divisions hurt everyone's ability to bargain with the guards. Yet the blacks also knew that socializing with the whites would be horribly difficult and depressing, and the whites thought doing so would be degrading. They were all saying, look, we see the cost of sitting separately but we have one life to live. Enjoying each other at our own table without having to endure those at that other table is so much better than suffering their racism (or inferiority) and their horrible manners that we opt for segregation. They quite reasonably did the best they could day to day, even at the cost of their own higher potentials.

Walking Butterflies

I do not want the peace which passeth understanding,
I want the understanding which bringeth peace.
—Helen Keller

When I was at U Mass Amherst, Herb Gintis taught me a related lesson by describing an image I will never forget. Herb said to me—and he had written it in a long essay, almost a poem, about aspects of economics—imagine a butterfly on a tabletop. It is at one end of the table and it wants to get to the other end, say for food, or whatever. You pluck the butterfly's wings off. To get where it wants to go, the butterfly walks across the table. Is it rational for the butterfly to walk across the tabletop? Yes. Is it rational for the butterfly to walk across the tabletop? No.

Herb's point was if we think about the butterfly's situation from the angle of what ought to ideally be the case for all butterflies, it is of course irrational for the butterfly to walk where it was going. A walking butterfly is absurd. Butterflies should fly, of course. But if we think about the situation from the angle of the butterfly with its wings plucked, then it is quite rational for this particular butterfly to walk. The alternative is to get nowhere.

In the prison, viewed in terms of advancing the overall bargaining power of prisoners, the segregated seating pattern was irrational. It reduced prisoners' prospects, not to mention the corrosive effects of racism itself. Viewed from the angle of each prisoner enjoying his meal, however, within the limits of the confines they were restricted to and the limits of what the prisoners saw as their realistic options, their seating pattern was rational. It produced a more pleasant day. The same analogy illuminates the irrationality and rationality of the prisoners in the low-security facility not walking out. To find other examples, just look around, or even in the mirror. Yet compromise is often the structurally imposed glue holding us to settings we would much better escape.

PART 4

Tomorrow's Seeds Today

Part of creating changes is, as the famous anarchist Mikhail Bakunin insightfully instructed, nurturing seeds of the future in the present. The future, in other words, can only contain what we put into it today. Often this means having our movements respect and embody the values we favor for a new society. Sometimes it means creating book publishing houses or magazines or institutes or other institutions in the present that operate as we favor for the future. We do this as experiments to learn from. We do it as projects to benefit from. We do it as models to emulate. We do it hoping our efforts will last into the future, providing some of its infrastructure.

Chapter 24

Redefining Publishing

Emulating SEP

I hate the giving of the hand unless the whole man accompanies it.
—Ralph Waldo Emerson

In 1977, a group of new leftists decided to create a U.S.-based publishing house named South End Press. I was one of these book-oriented adventurers who got it going, along with Lydia Sargent, John Schall, Pat Walker, Juliet Schor, Mary Lea, Joe Bowring, Dave Millikan, and a number of other people who played lesser roles. Everyone not involved thought we were nuts. It wouldn't work. More, our friends thought a new publishing house wasn't needed. With a few very supportive exceptions, successful authors said to us, why bother? The mainstream houses will publish radical books that are really good because those books will reach wide audiences and make them money. To me, these people understood the constrained system-legitimating dynamics of mainstream institutions save for the ones they dealt with most often. But how could that be?

Of course, mainstream publishing houses then and now would publish a few books by radicals, when pressure built up around some topic and the books didn't stray too far from mainstream beliefs. Mainstream newspapers did the same for the occasional piece by an activist scholar.

The mainstream publisher would, however, try to bend the writer editorially and, if that failed, often bury the book without promotional support, or later jettison it. But what I saw was that the people who got published could tell themselves they were brilliant and superior writers and that those who failed were simply less deserving. This view of publishing success was so ego boosting and fame enhancing for those few who got published that it tended to offset their general knowledge of capitalist institutions, making publishing an exception that escaped their otherwise insightful critiques.

This self-serving posture of published radicals seeing themselves as superior caused many published authors to enjoy their view from above and not seek to correct injustices toward those left behind. It also made it much easier and more likely that their writing would drift toward mainstream acceptability, to keep the contracts and reviews flowing. The alternative, self-effacing posture required that a successful author see him- or herself as unreasonably and even randomly plucked from the pack, undeserving of fame and therefore responsible to use it to benefit less lucky but no less worthy ideas and activism regardless of the implications for future contracts. This would include needing to look out for other writers who, by virtue of their topics, tone, or depth of passion, were left behind. This is the difference between almost all those who get published and become visible and forget about supporting alternative publishing and unknown writers, and people such as Noam Chomsky, Edward Herman, and John Pilger, who hang in with alternative institutions. Still, those who said we would have a hard time creating a new alternative publishing house weren't entirely wrong. Even naming ourselves was difficult. Full Court Press, Left Press, Heart of the Beast (or HOB) Press, Seventh Wave. Each name had supporters and detractors. Finally we settled on naming our press for our neighborhood, the South End of Boston.

Coming from the sixties, we decided that South End Press (SEP) would have New Left politics and operate democratically. This meant the press would editorially prioritize race, gender, class, and power. Operating democratically meant the majority would rule with attention to minority positions. But in practice people working on promotion had more say about preparing ads and mailings. People working on typesetting set not only type, but also their own schedules. Everyone together decided new titles, pricing, hiring, and firing.

We had to assign ourselves various jobs. No one wanted to do tedious, rote jobs. Why should I only typeset books, or only answer the phone? Why should Mary? Why should any of us? Everyone preferred the positions that guarantee influence as well as a more rewarding workday and a richer and prouder self image. We each cared about the quality of our responsibilities, and the extent of our impact on SEP's books. We realized that a familiar, typical, corporate division of labor would lay waste to our fledgling workplace democracy. If some of us were empowered by our workday while others were exhausted and deadened, the former would dominate the latter.

Suppose, we hypothesized in our mind's eye, we were gathering to decide some policy that would have generally equal effects on everyone and we used one person, one vote, majority rule. Suppose I came to the meeting as "finance minister" with all the relevant budget knowledge and skills. Suppose Pat came to the meeting as "mail carrier" knowing only where the post office was and how to deliver mail. We each would be doing work that must be done, but my work would give me confidence, skills, and information essential to decision-making. It would give me a monopoly over many daily decision levers. Pat's work would give him boredom, provide him no empowering information, and have him not deciding anything. It didn't take genius for us to see the implications of typical work arrangements. All we had to do was imagine this organizational structure, see ourselves in it, and ask what the outcome would be for us.

We described to each other how we would each have one vote. But, we asked, which one of us would set the agenda that was to be voted on? Who would define available options? Who would clarify what was possible and what wasn't? Who would have greater confidence, energy, and belief that he or she should be heard? It wasn't hard to predict the decision-making hierarchy that typical corporate organization would impose. So we realized that we didn't have to endure a disease, much less become so infected that we could never throw it off, to know that we didn't want to drink its germs. We all agreed that if we had a typical corporate division of labor, it wouldn't be long before a few bossed the rest around and sharp hierarchies of pay arose. But if the familiar corporate division of tasks wasn't worthy, we would have to try a different division of tasks.

Since the problem was that some workers could be empowered by their tasks while other workers were disempowered by theirs, we decided that each worker should have a fair mix of tasks. Each worker should be suited to his or her tasks, of course. Tasks for any worker should be compatible with one another and able to be accomplished effectively by that one worker. But we should mix and match so that each job would contain a variety of tasks with different quality of life and empowerment implications, making each job's overall quality of life and empowerment implications like those for all other jobs. As a result, in our little publishing house, we had no janitor, no secretary, no typesetter, no editor, no bookkeeper, no chief financial officer, though between us, we did all those tasks.

All South End Press workers did editorial work, with each member handling a fair share of books during each publishing season, including working with authors, producing the books, and so on. We all did this as one part of our overall responsibility because this was the heart of publishing, and we thought anyone who didn't do this work couldn't possibly hold their own in the overall operation.

We also shared rote tasks; some of us cleaned floors or bathrooms on one day, some did it on another day. One of us took mail or did the phone on Monday, another on Tuesday. The people editing books also carried mail. When you called SEP, the person who answered the phone was never "just" a receptionist. We all answered phones, rotating being the receptionist. Each of us had a key responsibility in a "business" area—finances, promotion, relations with printers, including other ancillary operations, fulfilling orders, and so on.

Between SEP's Covers

The love of learning, the sequestered nooks,
And all the sweet serenity of books.
—*Henry Wadsworth Longfellow*

Within our balanced job complexes, we of course published a great many books. It was particularly hard going in the early years, each book requiring massive labor to produce. After all, we didn't know anything about publishing beyond my and Lydia Sargent having worked on producing my own prior book, *What Is To Be Undone*, for a very small independent Boston publisher. Why would any prospective author think we could succeed when even friends and perhaps even most of those actually involved felt it was, at best, a gigantic long shot? But here we were, going up to writers and saying, okay, let us have your year's writing, or two years' worth, or whatever it might have taken to do your book. You won't be sorry. We will produce it. We will promote it. You'll get royalties. All will be well.

Without Noam Chomsky's willingness to give us books, this whole idea would likely have failed. Even Chomsky's support might not have been enough, without others chipping in submissions in the early years, too. Bertell Ollman, for example, gave us one of our first titles, *Social and Sexual Revolution*. Ollman is a political scientist from New York University. It almost felt, at times, as if Ollman was channeling Marx, as compared to producing his own personal insights, but, in fact, he was doing the latter. His SEP book was a collection of his essays. Most notably, the book had a section dealing with the work of Wilhelm Reich, who had a brilliant period when he investigated how consciousness can prevent awareness of oppression and impede resistance. We accepted Bertell's book, produced it, put it out, and celebrated our great achievement. It was one of our first titles.

Then we got a call from Bertell. He was relaxed, but told us that in addition to all the errors that we had allowed to be published in his book, which was bad enough—we had also put a "no," or maybe it was a "not," in the penultimate sentence of the concluding section, thereby reversing the entire book's meaning and undercutting the logic of Bertell's work. We held the books in the warehouse and inserted a correction page into each one before distribution. Bertell could have told everyone to stay clear of us, but he didn't. Instead, he remained very supportive, and for that Bertell can, I think, take some of the credit for SEP surviving its early days.

Bertell later came up with a board game called Class Struggle, which mimicked the game Monopoly but conveyed the ills of capitalism rather than celebrating buying boardwalks. Ironically, in the early days of his Class Struggle endeavor, there was a strike at a large store in New York that had agreed to stock the game. The strikers wanted Bertell to pull the game from the store, which was its largest outlet, and called him a scab for not doing so. Bertell argued that supporting strikes was critically important, but committing suicide for his multi-year project was too much to ask. Sometimes values conflict. No choice is comfortable. All choices are encumbered with costs.

Many other authors trusted us with their work. Usually a writer approaches a publisher seeking acceptance. If the publisher makes a bid for a book, the writer is pleased. In our case, the situation flip-flopped. We sought books and were judged over and over by writers and for a while our bona fides were a close call.

Manning Marable trusted the early SEP with his exceptionally fine book *How Capitalism Underdeveloped Black America*. Jeremy Brecher brought his best seller *Strike* to SEP for reprinting, and later also brought various books on corporate globalization. Holly Sklar published with SEP her massive and very successful book *Trilateralism*, and then numerous other books as well. Likewise, Ward Churchill came to SEP, also in the very early days, with an idea for a book about why the combination of *Marxism and Native Americans* was oil and water. Ward was unknown among American leftists and had already had numerous rejections regarding his anti-Marxist claims due to a general Left tendency to reject hostility toward Marxism. But SEP was versed in Marxism and had learned from it but wasn't by any means mired in it. Quite the opposite, another of our earliest books was *Unorthodox Marxism* by Robin Hahnel and I, and it was far from laudatory toward traditional Marxism.

To Ward's surprise, everyone at SEP liked his book, and we published it and later published others by Ward as well. Indeed, Ward, like Holly and quite a few other young writers, was "discovered" and made politically visible in wider national circles by his SEP publications. I was Ward's SEP contact and got to know him pretty well. He was an imposing figure, with military experience and bearing, gruff in some respects, and politically very militant. He and I would joke a lot, and he would always leave telling me to keep my head down—below the bullets—something he had a good deal more experience with than I. Ward has been a leading advocate for comprehending and acting on indigenous rights and for challenging narrow economism.

While I was at SEP another unknown writer came along, sending us a book titled *Ain't I A Woman*. This was bell hooks, a pen name she chose, spelling it with a lowercase b and h. She later became SEP's best-selling, and one of its more influential, writers. I never got to know bell very well, though I liked much of her early work. I do remember one exchange, however, that was quite insightful about tangentially connected but nonetheless important matters.

Bell writes much more clearly and succinctly, movingly and energetically, than most scholars. I once asked her about postmodernism and its effects on her writing. She told me that there was tremendous pressure, if she was to be taken seriously in academia and mainstream publishing circles, to make her words more closely match the linguistic habits of intellectuals. She hated these pressures and sought to give only the absolute minimum that she could get away with and still retain her access to reviewers and outlets. Her approach was strategically balanced. Some give in not at all but suffer hostility from academics and invisibility to reviewers. Others give in too much only to extinguish their better selves seeking visibility. Bell found middle ground.

SEP members wanted to publish works that came our way, but also to initiate some ourselves. Could we create a series that explored cutting-edge views from diverse angles? A lead essay would present a controversial position. Then a group of writers would react, with some supporting the position, some critiquing it, and some elaborating on its implications. Then the original author would respond. We'd call it a Controversy Series. We did a few of these, one on class, edited by Pat Walker, called *Between Labor and Capital*, one edited by Lydia Sargent, *Women and Revolution*, and also one edited by Steve Shalom, *Socialist Visions*. It proved, however, nearly impossible to generate more involvement. Plans for books on ecology and capitalism, race and revolution, radical American history, socialism and internationalism, unions and activism, high culture and people's culture all failed. We couldn't get writers to subject themselves to criticism from others or to participate in celebrating and criticizing someone else's work.

Friendly Fascism and Editing Others

I think that there is nothing, not even crime, more opposed to poetry, to philosophy, ay, to life itself, than this incessant business.
—Henry David Thoreau

Another of SEP's early books was by Bertram Gross. Bertram had been published by a mainstream house, but was being dropped from their list. I don't remember what the excuse for dropping Bertram was, but he came to us to keep his book in print. The title was *Friendly Fascism* and the topic was the slip-sliding of America into an authoritarian social condition not via violence, but with a smile. I read *Friendly Fascism* and quite liked it, except that I thought the last chapter contradicted the rest of the book.

I told Bertram and he said come on, it can't be. I said well, I think it is, and I would really appreciate if you would take another look. Rather than being affronted, he took a look and he didn't like what he saw. He had certainly signed off on the last chapter, but now, prodded, he remembered that he had originally written a final chapter and the publisher hadn't liked it. They had gone back and forth, and what had emerged from lots of editing was what I read. At the time

Bertram told himself the result was fine. Good editorial input had made things better. In hindsight he decided that, eager for his thesis to see the light of day, he had compromised a little at a time until the final chapter reflected more the editor's desires than his own. We published *Friendly Fascism*, but with a new last chapter Bertram wrote for the occasion.

For me, this event was editorially formative. South End Press already had very strong author's rights regarding editing and design. But I decided that editing was a very tricky business. A publisher has power. A writer is needy. Even if a publisher honestly wants to help the writer generate the best possible book, which no doubt Bertram Gross's first publisher and editor thought was their intent, and even if the writer sincerely desires assistance in improving his or her words, a likelihood of abuse exists. It isn't just that a publisher can willfully and knowingly bend a book to reflect its preferences above those of the author and to convey ideas the publisher likes even against the author's true intents. It is that this can occur easily, fluidly, and even honestly. Indeed it might have been quite like that with *Friendly Fascism*. Or, of course, it might have been intentional. The key point was, it didn't matter to the final product how Bertram's book turned out to be something different than what he wanted. Malevolent intentions or not, the result was malevolent. So I decided something that virtually no one I know has ever agreed with me about. I decided there was no good reason for a publisher to forcefully impact the content of a submitted book. Maybe suggestions could be offered, but if so, the contract had to be already in place, with the author free to ignore everything that the publisher proposed. Better, it seemed to me, was for the author to seek help not from a powerful publishing house that held a carrot and stick over his or her head, but from friends and critics outside the publishing house.

Folks have repeatedly pointed out to me just how valuable good editing is. Don't I know it, they wonder. Well, sure I know it. I try to get helpful editing for my own writing—I certainly need it—but not with a sword attached, not even a friendly sword. I don't want to give editorial help that way either. Of course this is less of a conundrum for technical books, perhaps even for some novels, than for critical social and political works, but still, even for fiction, power can play a nefarious role. The problem with my take on this, I can easily see, is that in our current world it pretty much reduces editing to a volunteer pursuit. I have to get editing from friends, political allies, and relatives, and none of them get paid for editing. Why not get editing from a professional who does it very carefully for lots of people and who learns from all that work and who is paid for doing it, and who therefore has much more time to give to the task, and who of course works for the publisher? My answer is that everything up to that last qualifier is fine with me, but being employed by the publisher subverts the logic. The publisher's might is more important than the editor's insight. My conclusion is, why not create editorial institutions? Why not have workplaces of people who edit? Either a publisher or an author can go to one of these workplaces and pay to have a book, article, or whatever handled by one or more of the editorial employees. The interaction would then be between the editing operation and the writer, where the former has no power over the book's destiny. Power stays with the author, where it belongs.

The Wharton School's Finest

There are painters who transform the sun to a yellow spot, but there are others who with the help of their art and their intelligence, transform a yellow spot into the sun.
—*Pablo Picasso*

Ed Herman was a renowned economist at the Wharton School of Finance, now retired. Over the years he has been perhaps the most consistent contributor to *Z*'s various projects, both financially, with his royalties, and at times with direct donations too; and, of course, with his writing. Sometimes writing with Chomsky, but much more often writing on his own, Ed has dissected U.S. foreign policy and media relations with essay after essay probing the heart of heartless relations. Indeed, while Chomsky often gets the lion's share of credit for their joint endeavors, not only has Ed been pivotal to those efforts, but for their most central media work, the famous "propaganda model" introduced in their book *Manufacturing Consent*, Ed was the prime mover, the main creator, and the most effective advocate.

Ed's other writings were also important both to the evolution of South End Press, and later to *Z Magazine*, which he has written for more regularly and consistently than any other friend of our efforts. But I have never become really close with Ed, perhaps because he is down in Pennsylvania and I am up in Massachusetts, and he was never one of my teachers. I have known Ed much more as an ally and source of great substance than as a close friend. Things are different with Ed's sometime partner, Noam Chomsky.

Noam Chomsky Published But Not Reviewed

If you're not careful, the newspapers will have you hating the people who are being oppressed, and loving the people who are doing the oppressing.
—*Malcolm X*

That Chomsky was a friend of mine at MIT, and thus of South End Press by extension, that he signed up immediately to publish with South End, told others we had great merit, then stuck with us year after difficult year, and that he donated royalties, made cash donations, and signed appeals was, of course, absolutely necessary for the press's survival and success. Noam published with SEP, not only collections of essays, but many books initiated from scratch, often at our suggestion. Indeed, in addition to being a friend of Noam's all these years, I would guess I have also been the single most annoying thorn in his side, continually getting under his skin with new requests, suggestions, and proposals. He often complains to me that I seem to think I can live my life and instruct him on how to live his, too.

During our years publishing Noam's books, he has been the author most solicitous of our time and well-being, not just by donating to SEP, but by respecting our energies, never using an iota of his effectively infinite bargaining power to impose conditions on us, and complying with our guidelines more than any other writer. The first publication Noam did with SEP began as a monograph that he and Ed Herman had written for Warner Modules, a subdivision of the mainstream publisher, which at about the same time published Richard Nixon's autobiography. Warner, under Simon and Schuster and, above that, Gulf and Western, had accepted and published Noam and Ed's relatively short piece, and then promptly buried it. Literally, that is, they buried it, in a stock room. They refused to promote it or even to fill orders for it. Noam and Ed sued them, trying to get control over the work. Warner lost, since they had clearly violated the contract. But this was a minor setback in Warner's project to bury the book. To get out of their unwanted commitment they sold the rights to another outfit which was not, however, a publisher, and thus had no means of distribution. What had happened, apparently, was that some fair-minded editor had read the monograph and found it compelling, or at least worthy, and had agreed to publish it. Later, when higher authorities saw the product, all hell broke lose, causing the book's internment.

So Ed and Noam asked SEP to publish a new variant of the module. We said yes, of course. Now, instead of working with a confused and unsupportive publisher, they had a publisher, albeit one just getting up and running, that was understanding and eager. Their energies flowed. The short monograph became a two-volume set of nearly 850 pages titled *The Political Economy of Human Rights*. It was SEP's best seller until *No Nukes* came along, plus, the monograph-to-two-book escalation foreshadowed Chomsky's style right to the present day. Indeed, our running joke is, ask Chomsky for a paragraph if you want an article. Ask him for a leaflet if you want a small book. Ask him for an article if you want a tome. Of course, the joke aside, whatever Noam generates, whether an interview, letter, article, or book, you can be sure it will combine detailed information with accurate reasoning. It isn't so much the volume of data Noam offers, however, that is the highlight of his work for me. It is that he always chooses critical data that graphically reveals underlying relations—and every once in awhile he fires off a sarcastic verbal jab that cracks me up.

John Schall was a founding member of SEP. I had known John from the U Mass Amherst grad school that he entered one year after me. We became roommates and close friends. Years later, after SEP had already published a number of Noam's books, John decided to try something new to get broader visibility. None of Noam's SEP books had been reviewed in any mainstream outlet, and understanding why made us no less sick about it. It is one thing to know that mainstream media will ignore serious content that challenges existing relations. It is another thing to be on the blunt end of it. So John decided he would phone the book review editor of *The Boston Globe* and pursue the matter directly.

John had some kind of quality about him that caused his elders to want to adopt him within minutes of meeting him. This occurred once again on the phone with the *Globe*'s reviewer. They chatted a bit and then John asked why the *Globe* hadn't reviewed Chomsky's books. She hemmed and hawed a bit, offering possible reasons: He is not a historian but a linguist, and we review the linguistics. He is anti-American. He has too many footnotes. The books are so long. She tried these ridiculous dodges, but John calmly offered counterevidence and kept on going. What's the real reason, he kept repeating, after each phony reason had been dispatched. Finally she said, look, I am enjoying talking with you, but even so, you should know that you are wasting your time. Even if you were to convince me that Chomsky was the most astute commentator on current events in the country, it wouldn't matter. Even if you convinced me that his most recent book deserved serious review attention, it wouldn't matter. If I solicited a review of Chomsky's work, the review wouldn't run in the *Globe*. The publisher would veto it.

In just so many words, that's what she said. John had torpedoed all the dodges she could offer, so finally she admitted to John what I suspect she had never admitted to anyone else or perhaps even to herself. *The Boston Globe* would not publish a review of Noam Chomsky's political writing under any conditions whatsoever because its owner would forbid it. (Actually, this is a slight exaggeration. One or two Chomsky works have gotten briefly reviewed in the *Globe* over the years, though none from South End Press). John's persistence unearthed an instructive admission of the realities of U.S. mainstream publishing.

No Nukes

Technology—it brings you great gifts with one hand,
and it stabs you in the back with the other.
—C.P. Snow

Probably the biggest-selling book in the ten-plus years I was at SEP was *No Nukes*, edited by Anna Gyorgy. Anna was a very effective activist in the movement against the deployment of nuclear reactors, and she edited a

245

massive book full of all kinds of information, graphical support, evidence, and argument, meant to help organizers make their case and develop their agendas. It was a *tour de force* of information, and by far the most ambitious production project we had undertaken up to that point. The book came out almost simultaneously with the near-catastrophic meltdown at Three Mile Island, an incident that caused the whole country a week of terror and then a longer period of turmoil over what to do about nuclear power.

The no-nukes movement was sponsoring large demonstrations at reactors around the country that included major civil disobedience that, in many respects, foreshadowed the anticorporate globalization movement of later years. The no-nukes movement also overwhelmingly utilized consensus decision making and had decentralized organization. Movement advocates were quite militant, feeling they were battling at the cutting edge of life and death. The demonstrations were very large; a rally in New York had over half a million people.

No major publisher was interested in her book, *No Nukes*, so Anna came to SEP. In fact, I think Anna would have gone with us in any event, given that SEP was so supportive of her ideals and so much better able to place her book in movement hands at high discounts. But, with Three Mile Island and the ensuing cataclysm of worry that the near meltdown generated, major publishing houses smelled big bucks. We got called by a few, each pleading that we should realize that *No Nukes* deserved to be read by a huge audience who we couldn't reach, so we should sell it off to them to handle properly.

We faced a conundrum. Of course, we felt mainstream publishing was a horrible dead end for radicalism. But our interest in the dollars to be easily made was great, and it was also true that mainstream publication could achieve a far wider distribution of the book. We negotiated with two houses, and finally settled on Simon and Schuster. We began talks, which had to be done very quickly. Their production, promotion, and distribution departments were all eager to take the book. Their people were excited that they would get to do a book that mattered as well as at how widely it would sell. We arrived pretty quickly at an agreement that had one unusual wrinkle. They would publish the book, have rights for all kinds of sales and markets, the rate of payment for us was set, and so on. The unusual condition was that we would continue distributing our version of the book to movement groups, including giving them the large discounts we were already offering. That was okay with Simon and Schuster (S&S), so we were ready to go. Then, unexpectedly, with everything moving congenially, we got a phone call telling us the deal was off. We were flabbergasted. Everyone at Simon and Schuster with whom we had negotiated had been eager, but the proposal finally got to the top guns and they summarily rejected it. S&S being a capitalist firm, the top guns were the end of the line.

What happened? My guess is that over lunch some nuke official was chatting with a bigwig at Gulf and Western, the corporate owner of Simon and Schuster, and let drop that so-and-so was concerned about the no-nukes movement, and why was anyone taking it seriously, much less giving it access to a broader public? Once the book had executive attention, the conclusion was inevitable. What happened, in other words, was that Three Mile Island jumbled people's minds, divorcing people from the corporate dictates that spontaneously ruled their choices, and *No Nukes* almost became a mainstream project until saner heads prevailed.

The Toffler Wave

> *And in today already walks tomorrow.*
> *—Samuel Taylor Coleridge*

One of the most surprising episodes of my SEP years was when Alvin Toffler came to SEP and told us he would like to collaborate with us. Toffler was the author of what was at that time a publishing elephant, the multi-million-selling book *Future Shock*. He was one of the most successful nonfiction writers in the country. At the time, Toffler had just completed another book, called *The Third Wave,* that was a chart-topper too. Alvin and his partner Heidi Toffler were a team, very good at meeting heads of state, being on diverse corporate boards, and so on. But, at that moment, what Alvin had come to town for was to publish at South End Press.

I admit, I thought a Toffler book of any kind had the potential to vastly expand our operations. So I was eager to do it, hoping whatever he had in mind wouldn't be politically objectionable. Alvin was indeed, to our surprise, familiar with us and our highly unusual structure, which he said he admired and was why he wanted to work with us. Given Alvin's contractual arrangements with mainstream publishers and agents, he couldn't do a major book with us, but he could do an interview book. Surprisingly, no one else at the press wanted to have much to do with the project. But I liked Toffler and found him interesting, so SEP did the book with him, with me as interviewer.

I read Toffler's prior works, prepared questions, and went to New York a couple of times to tape interviews with him. By initial agreement, Toffler went over the text and put in and took out whatever he wished, but, likewise, I also added questions. We iterated the book to completion. It turned out Toffler had considerable Left background and insight, though he was also quite critical of current radicalism. I tried to get him to relate to a three-class view of society, but this was pretty futile. Still, he took the project seriously and worked hard on the text, smoothing both his words and mine. He was a perfectionist about his writing.

The book came out and, regrettably, the hoped-for windfall never happened. There were no reviews, and sales were quite modest. The publishing world wasn't about to help SEP attain a higher level of visibility even when we unexpectedly published the then-biggest-selling author in the country, and even though the book was a personable but probing exchange that both clarified and in some ways went beyond his other works.

Book Missed: Fat Is Beautiful

Beauty comes in all sizes, not just size 5.
—Roseanne

Some books SEP never published resonated for me as well. One, in particular, was about fatness. This was the most embattled book decision we had in my years at the press. The book argued that the rejection, subordination, and denial of opportunities endured by fat people was a major oppressive dynamic and that fatness was, almost without exception, a genetic physical attribute about which a person should do nothing. It wasn't from eating too much that a person became fat, the book stated, and dieting was irrelevant or outright dangerous. Being seriously fat was like having red hair or brown hair. It could sometimes be detrimental to one's health, to be sure, so perhaps it was more like having 20/20 vision or being very near- or farsighted. But people's attitudes toward fat folks were on a par with racism for the damage wrought and inhumanity imposed.

The SEP staff was evenly divided about this submission, but passions were considerable. I thought the book deserved publication and I also thought the claims were plausible and at least a provocative and useful corrective to public biases. The book was finally rejected after much battling, some of which got very tense and hostile—in my view, a point that validated the book.

There has developed in the U.S over the years since then a movement about disabilities that bears some logic in common with what the authors of this fat book wanted to see develop around fatness. The authors wanted a movement for fat people's rights and liberation, like we now have a movement for disability rights and liberation. Disability is also not, I think, always in all respects an easy issue. It isn't just that people's prejudices and their resistance to even noticing they are prejudiced are strong. That's true and paramount, as with obesity. But it isn't always clear what the most humane or accurate position is regarding disabilities, like for obesity, and I have found myself at times criticized about this point, not regarding obesity since the fat movements the authors hoped for didn't materialize, but around disability, where movements do exist.

The controversial issue has been put to me like this. Is the loss or debit of a disabled person totally a matter of social organization and decisions, or does a disability confer a loss on people regardless of social decisions? Some radical disability activists have claimed the former. They say that to be deaf, blind, wheelchair bound, etc., only diminishes one's life if society makes decisions in a way that cause the disabilities to reduce options. If society provides means that offset absences, or doesn't structure itself in ways that punish absences, then the lives of the so-called disabled are in no sense reduced as compared to the lives of the fully abled. The contrary view, among those also favoring disability rights, says this claim goes too far. To lose sight, hearing, mobility, etc., really is to lose something important. Whatever society may do to redress and soften the consequences, or however much it may try not to be structured to punish these absences, the absences nonetheless have consequences.

It has seemed to me, sometimes under the lash of criticism, that the latter take on the situation is correct, even if it may need some nuanced refinements. I have been, at times, legally blind and have had to use aids to see well, and then have had to have cornea transplants and subsequently use different aids to see well, and often can't see well anyhow due to not being able to use the aids overly long each day. My ears, as well, are now declining, probably with increasing age. That social choices have major impact on the cost of these ailments strikes me as self-evident. What society has invested in discovering and producing contact lenses, cornea transplant methods, earphones, hearing aids, and so on, and how available these are to people, matters tremendously. But I would be even better off if I could see better or hear better without intervention and hassle, and some debits are simply not fully correctable. At any rate, I think the unwillingness to admit that disabilities involve costs that sometimes transcend correction is related to the tendency of many leftists to not admit differences among people in any capacities that we hold dear, which, as noted earlier, seems to me a horrible mistake.

When a very radical disability activist told me that hearing Mozart was no better than only feeling the beat, say, or than even just reading that Mozart exists, I felt it was ridiculous. Hearing matters and is not entirely offset by reducing the dangers or otherwise altering arrangements to alleviate debits that deafness imposes. When another activist told me that a forty year old who had never had hearing didn't want to undergo a new operation that could give her the sense due to her believing that it would only be disruptive and even impossible to cope with, I understood and respected that. But when that activist told me the same forty year old was about to have a child and hoped the child was born deaf, I did not understand or respect that. The presence of people with excess talent increases diversity positively, but I don't think my having bad eyes or declining hearing or a slipped disk, or other people being blind, deaf, or paralyzed, adds to life via increasing diversity commensurately with what it robs from those who suffer the missing qualities. Some shit hurts.

The debate over fat was like the debate over disability. The price people pay should be diminished. People should obviously not be segregated and reviled. But saying that obesity had no debits and should not be diminished made no sense to those who rejected the book and more than offset the book's virtues. Those wanting the book felt, its other virtues offset that debit.

Another story, not about books, but of interest regarding disability, and which clarifies some of the allusions above, involves a disease I have called keratoconus. It is an oddball disease. The cornea in your eye is normally a slice from a sphere. Think of a transparent ball and imagine taking a slim slice of the surface without changing its shape and plopping it into your eye, like a contact lens, but attached. That's the cornea. Light goes through it to the back of your eye to be processed. The disease, keratoconus, causes the cornea's shape to change at some regions to become more like a slice from a cone, or, at any rate, distorted. The cornea's surface distortions in turn distort what you see due to interfering with the light headed for your processing center.

I was having trouble with my eyes, nothing major, and went to an eye doctor around the beginning of college. I looked at the eye chart, seeing not too badly though clearly needing some correction, and then I also looked at some other machines the doctor had, and I remember in particular that the doctor put a picture in front of me and asked what I saw, and then did it with another, and so on. He looked into my eyes, played with lights and probes, and then told me I had this ailment, keratoconus. I said it didn't seem all that bad, couldn't I just have glasses? He said yes, for now, but it would very likely get progressively worse and eventually I would do better with contact lenses and perhaps later would need a cornea transplant, but I shouldn't worry.

Well, I didn't worry. I was young and had no time for worry. He also told me that my condition was already having one very large effect on my vision. I had no depth perception. I told him he was nuts. Of course I had depth perception. I played tennis. I caught fly balls. I could see that the wall to the left was further away then the wall to the right. I would have bet the farm, had I owned one, that I could see depth. But the doctor said, no, you are calculating depths by using various cues that you still see. You aren't seeing depth the way other folks do. I wasn't sure what the hell that meant, or what the difference between me and others was. I guessed it was that I used fewer and more secondary cues than other people used, being insensitive to or unable to distinguish the more effective cues that others relied on. I humorously took this as an explanation for why I wasn't the great athlete I had hoped to be—though there were plenty of other anatomical explanations for that failing—and otherwise paid no attention to the problem, aside from getting glasses, of course. But Dr. Sight had been right and it was only a few years until I needed contact lenses and thus began a tedious saga. I went from your typical lens to a sequence of experimental and otherwise odd lenses. My eyes kept changing and I kept changing the lenses to keep pace. The idea of a lens aiding keratoconus is simple. You put the thing on and there is fluid between it and your misshapen cornea. The outer edge gateway through which light flows to your vision center becomes the outer face of the lens, a properly shaped slice from a sphere rather than a cone. The liquid largely erases the distortions beneath, filling in spaces. The impact of the distorted cornea on the incoming light is dramatically reduced by this trick and, as a result, the patient's sight drastically improves. Without lenses, my sight dipped well below legally blind, which is 20/200, and remained that way for many years. With corrective lenses my sight fluctuated but was always better than 20/40.

The lenses were far less comfortable for me, however, than lenses were, even in those days, for the average user. This was due to their odd fit over my rough corneal terrain and this is what imposed the multiplying experiments in lens types, shapes, and fits. Discomfort and having to take the lenses off due to major pain when anything got under them rather than easily blinking dirt out, and also having them periodically pop off and having to search for them or replace them, was all bad enough, but the unacceptable problem was the steady decline in the number of hours I could wear them.

I had been hugely lucky, however, regarding treatment. A friend of my mother recommended someone who worked at a Boston University clinic who also had his own practice in Lynn, Massachusetts, about forty minutes from Boston. He took care of me for nothing. This was particularly lucky because I had no money or insurance. He prolonged my sighted time by his clever tricks until finally there was no recourse other than a cornea transplant. This whole saga stretched well into my new life as a radical activist. Trips to Lynn for the eye doctor were sometimes by bus, but most often Lydia drove me. I couldn't drive myself because what he did to me while I was in his office precluded having lenses in when I left, and not having lenses precluded driving. Finally, I went to Mass Eye and Ear to get a surgeon, sent by my friend the lens master. I interviewed with the then-head of the cornea department, who was one of the most famous and accomplished eye surgeons of the time. I immediately hated him, even though I rarely have strong reactions to new people. A cornea transplant takes a couple of hours but intense follow-up care continues for a year, with periodic visits to the surgeon to both ward off infections and take out stitches when they surface and cause sharp pain. I knew all this from advance research, and I wasn't interested in dealing with this surgeon repeatedly for a year for one eye, and then again for the other. I said I didn't want him. He was flabbergasted.

Next up was Michael Wagoner, a young hotshot who I immediately liked. He operated on my eyes, quite successfully, and treated me thereafter as well. Michael was probably the only left-wing doctor in the whole eye profession—well not quite—but one of very few for sure. He would charge me a dollar for my visits, each time, the dollar being his way of getting something on the books. He would often give me rides home, ask me about ongoing work, and discuss the medical field or politics. Michael became the head of the department at Mass Eye and Ear, and later went on to head up the eye care program in Saudi Arabia. I still look forward to one day seeing Michael in the Mideast, perhaps for a future transplant, since, regrettably, new corneas often don't ward off keratoconus forever, and mine has resurfaced.

The surgeon I rejected was later fired and I think perhaps even prosecuted for engaging in fraudulent pursuits having to do with some kind of experimental treatments, including what he had tried to talk me into. "Trust your instincts," particularly regarding doctors, is a good rule of thumb, though had I rejected not just the first surgeon, but the transplant itself, I would have been effectively blind for the past twenty years.

The actual surgery was interesting. When talking with Wagoner about it beforehand, I asked if I could do without general anesthesia, that being a very dangerous part of all operations. He said, yes, in fact, it can be done with only local numbing and a head restraint, but he was surprised I wanted to do it that way. He relayed that of all his patients and all those he had heard of, no one under forty had ever even requested to do a cornea transplant without being asleep. Young folks blanched at the thought. On the other hand, many folks in their sixties or older routinely did the operation awake. I was awake well into the operation. At one point, drugged somewhat, I could feel Wagoner in my eye—you do one eye, then when that one is healed a year later and you are confident it is okay you do the other one—and then I noticed the light from the ceiling. Removing the bad cornea caused, I guess, its aberrant effects to go away. I started talking, asking questions, and I vaguely heard the instruction—put him under—which was the last thing I remember. It was one thing to have me lightly sedated and locally unfeeling, it was another thing to have me chatting while they were slicing in my eye.

After the transplants, I swore off contact lenses and used only glasses for two decades. I had okay vision, sometimes nearly 20/20 with the glasses on, but keratoconus slowly returned, messing up my sight again. I now wear lenses as the only effective way of seeing well for about eight hours at a stretch each day, and then for two or three hours more after a three-hour layoff. Luckily, I can also see things that are very near, so even without lenses I can read by holding a book very close.

There is another wrinkle to my eye experience. It turns out that health ailments have diverse ramifications. For a long time I couldn't see people to realize who they were. I could walk right past someone very close to me, even Lydia, say, and not realize who I had snubbed. The same thing is true now, if I don't have lenses on. I would hear people say hello, I would nod back saying hello, and I would never know who they were. Couple bad eyes with horrible recall, you get in a lot of trouble. I had to learn how to finesse not being able to make introductions, which doesn't make you crave social encounters.

Similarly, bright light has, since my college days, been difficult for me. I wear dark sunglasses that wrap around my head, plus hats to keep out glare. This seems affected and odd to many people. I also tilt my head oddly, squinting, appearing to look down my nose at people. I even do this while giving public talks due to overhead lights. It doesn't endear me to people.

Finally, after the transplants I was tremendously defensive of my eyes. I would position myself to protect them, turning myself to avoid not only light but also unexpected jostling. I was very tense in my posture and walking. It was a little like Wild Bill Hickock sitting with his back to the wall and his eyes on the entry door in a saloon, except my defensive activity was largely unconscious. Andrew Sargent, Lydia's older son, was, for a considerable time, a sports massage therapist. When he first started working on me, he uncovered that I had chronic tension in my shoulders and upper back. Now in fact, I would have said that I had no such thing. Where could it have come from? It having been uncovered, I deduced it came from the period after the operations, and later stayed with me even though it no longer served any good end. A natural and desirable cautiousness about my eyes transformed into a physical rigidity that adversely affected not only my physical health, but even my emotions. I thought of children enduring some shock, and the physical ramifications being extensive long past when the child's response no longer had any basis. Sensible choices made in one context often congeal into patterns that persist in other contexts where they impose serious costs.

A related observation is that conservatism—the assumption that patterns that have developed and shown their mettle for a long time should be altered only after meeting a high standard of justification—has much more logic on its side than leftists are often willing to admit. Unwise messing about can make things worse rather than better. A cautionary principle that if it isn't broken, don't fix it makes considerable sense. Even if it is broken, be careful, you may make it worse. But the contrary insight that what has long persisted, even if it seems to get some jobs done well, often carries content that is burdensome or even deadly also makes sense. A radical impetus toward change even just for change's sake also has a certain logic. Between these two inclinations, I finally decided, taught in part by my illness, case-by-case judgment is required.

My other chronic problem has been my back, which first gave me trouble while playing paddle tennis about fifteen years ago and has ever since been a constant nuisance but only occasionally worse than that, when it literally lays me out. Not being able to lift heavy items is bad. A certain amount of pain each day is worse. Not being able to move is worse still, and I have avoided the last debit almost completely. When I was growing up I would hear that health matters most and the truth is, this overused aphorism is largely true. When my back is bad, it trumps all other problems in determining my feelings. When it is fine, my health is taken for granted. When it isn't fine, my health is paramount. And the same goes for my eyes. And even for a bad flu, much less a worse sickness. The truth is, health matters hugely, and a society that makes such a hash of health as ours has a lot to apologize for. I think if there has been a relative hole in the publishing that we did while I was at South End Press, it may have been in paying too little attention to matters of health and politics.

Small Isn't Always Beautiful

Anytime you continue to carry on the same kind of organization you say you are fighting against, you can't prove to me that you have made any change in your thinking.
—Ella Baker

SEP had its share of operational difficulties, but most of the more difficult problems stemmed from the fact that SEP was then (and remains) a small operation. Being small meant that there were fewer overall tasks, making it much harder to define equilibrated and suitable jobs. Worse, being small meant all workers were always together in a small space. It also meant that some positions had an artificially inflated amount of power. If there were twenty-five people and five were involved in finances, the fact that those five held the position together as part of their overall responsibilities, even year in and year out, wouldn't be a serious problem as long as everyone else became sufficiently familiar with finances to have checks and balances and include everyone in decisions. But if there are only five or eight people in the whole operation, and if one person always does all the finances, and if, due to ridiculous demands on time and energy, no one else has time to be attentive to anything beyond their main area of work and everyone is inclined to trust the finance person, year after year, then that person will undoubtedly grow to have undue influence. This prospect is even more harmful if the workers have had very different opportunities and training before their employment, as was the case at SEP, and particularly if the person getting the plum position also had the best training.

Another debit of small size is that having to shift some job assignments after a year's tenure, such as finances, leads to having to periodically shift around everything. So that's what we did, religiously, and doing it had its benefits (people learned all sides of the small operation), but could also be burdensome in its periodic disruption of continuity. Truth be told, our comprehension of job balancing was vague and imprecise in the early days of SEP. Our practice was at times somewhat arbitrary. But mainly, the conditions under which we were trying to do liberated work were horribly restrictive.

We also quickly discovered that when there is no boss, if two people don't like one another but must continually interact due to the small scale of operations, their enmity can become a much bigger problem than it would be in a hierarchical workplace. No one at SEP shut up due to the greater authority of an adversary, since no one had greater authority. There was no boss to intervene, either. In a larger firm, personality clashes could have been easily handled by separating folks who didn't get along. In our tiny firm, however, personality clashes produced a daily headache.

Unfriendly Seas

If you are out to describe the truth, leave elegance to the tailor.
—Albert Einstein

Other problems we encountered had to do with operating with values that were ahead of our times. For example, while many authors admired our commitments, not all liked operating within the conditions these imposed on them. Worse, banks, printers, and others with whom we had to repeatedly deal thought we were irresponsibly utopian. This was even true of much of the world of alternative media. Rarely, for example, did anyone in other Left media come to SEP and ask how we were organized, how we were doing it, or whether we thought it was worth emulating. Rather, while leftists assiduously read our books, other Left projects made believe we didn't exist. This was sad, though at no point did it make us neglect our commitments.

Pressures to operate within markets never let up. We had to sell books. Should we use orange covers that seemed to attract buyers even against their will? Should we hype a lesser book by a known author more than a better book by an unknown author? We had to raise productivity. Should we crush ourselves under a near-impossible workload? Should we impose on everyone the same unbearable load that the most hardy or most crazy member endured, or should we let different members set their own pace? If we did the latter, what should we do about tensions due to workload differences?

Likewise, we had to pay bills. Should we charge more for books, to increase our prospects of surviving, or should we charge less to enhance distribution and political value? Should we suck up to donors and bankers to improve the odds of surviving, or should we risk bankruptcy by letting them know our real values? If we told those with wealth our true incomes, which were essentially zero, they would laugh at us and say we could never persist. If we lied, telling them we earned a whole lot more than we did, how could we juggle the overall budget figures convincingly? More, would lying in one realm infect our behavior in others? Fund-raising for SEP was quite a trick. How many times can you try to get money by touting attributes that you despise and by hiding virtues you are trying to live up to—and not have your values crumble? It's wrong to believe that a Left project that starts strong and then declines is a failure. If establishing justice and equity in one country is problematic, how problematic is it to establish justice and equity in one institution? If establishing worthy norms despite the slings and arrows your enemies launch at you is hard, how much harder is it to establish worthy norms despite slings and arrows launched by your allies?

When SEP began we all worked for no pay, only room and board. We all worked at least fifty hours a week, but each person could work longer and if most of us hadn't done so, some of us to ridiculous extremes, SEP would have failed. There was no overtime pay. We couldn't pay for the duration or the intensity of work, which is the remunerative standard I now favor, because there was really no pay for any work at all. We each had a room to sleep in. We took meals together and SEP bought the food. We lived and worked in the big townhouse. Some of us, including me, liked doing that, because it was so efficient to avoid commuting. Most of SEP's members disliked the situation, however, because they could never get fully away from work. They looked forward to escaping to a place of their own.

At SEP I would typically roll out of bed, go to a meeting, and afterward start typesetting. Someone would take over typesetting later, and I would do some other part of my work, juggling among the rote assignments that I had and my more interesting work such as meeting with an author or assessing a manuscript. I would often wind up typesetting again, however, at some point later in the day, frequently in the dead of night. Typesetting was constant, done on a very large and archaic system. There was no monitor. The system produced film we had to chemically develop. There was no digital memory of our keystrokes. All other SEP work filled in the hours around keying in text and laying out the film, so the typesetting equipment never slept. For the most workaholic of us, or the most driven and committed, depending how you looked at it, typesetting and associated layout might take up four or even as many as six hours a day, worse when we were under pressure of deadlines, with more than a full day's hard work to do on top of that.

None of our work should have been done precisely as it was. For SEP to have been fairly tested as an innovative institution, it should have had at least twice the staff for the amount we published in those early days when typesetting was so onerous and time consuming. And, of course, SEP really should have been doing ten or fifty times as many books, with associated rise in staff. There should not have been constant fear for funds. We should have been able to invest sensibly in promotion and operations. Our minimum work week should have been a sane forty hours, or even less, to be exemplary of a better future. It should not have been that even working like maniacs for endless hours, exploiting ourselves for want of cash to sustain more staff, we were left with time for only the most essential foundational tasks. We should have been able to constantly innovate and diversify.

Successes and Marginalization

> *Nothing succeeds like the appearance of success.*
> —*Christopher Lasch*

T here were many signs of SEP's success. The number and quality of books we published was way out of proportion to our resources. The books' ties to activism were exemplary. Our activist emphasis on getting books to organizations, attending events, and so on, was politically and economically effective. One entertaining sign of SEP's unusual qualities was displayed when we went to book fairs, particularly the international gathering at Frankfurt where publishers from all over the world assembled to sell translation rights for their upcoming titles. Sometimes we would have two or three meetings with people from other publishing houses. At a first meeting we would talk about a title we hoped they would translate, or vice versa. At another meeting we would talk about its possible production, and at a third we would talk about promotion. Of course, each SEP worker was so knowledgeable about SEP's diverse facets that it was no problem for any SEPer to handle all the discussions, whereas for other houses it would first be one person, then another person, and then another, each from a different department.

Our unusual division of labor was not only morally desirable in facilitating real participation and self-management, but also highly productive. Workers at SEP used all their capacities. Even among those whose previous jobs involved only doing creative work, the balanced approach better utilized people's talents and capacities. Thus SEP had remarkable output despite limited assets.

One of the most frustrating things of my time at SEP, and afterwards, too, was the utter absence of interest by people in other Left operations in how SEP operated. Here was a project surviving and thriving despite little capacity for fund-raising and far fewer resources than most other Left operations. It claimed to be classless, without authoritarian features. It could all have all been true, or not, but the point was, no one inquired. SEP, then *Z*, and now ZNet have always been appreciated for their product but largely ignored for their process, and even dismissed as somehow beyond the pale. What this said, I think, is that people who ran other operations didn't want to know about a different approach, and people who didn't run operations had no motive to enquire.

There was an interesting exception to all this. As a result of Internet work I attended a few meetings at *The Nation*, a relatively large progressive weekly periodical in New York City. Once I sat with their business manager, who, incredibly, wanted to know about SEP. He was not all that political but he cared about output and admired ours. Similarly, the two or three times I went to *The Nation*, the interns there wanted to talk about SEP, or *Z*, or whatever. They wanted to know if noncorporate organization could work. But neither Victor Navasky, the chief officer at *The Nation*, or any of the key writers at *The Nation*, had queries. For them, SEP was a priori impossible, and the fact that SEP was historically actual didn't disrupt their perception. Actual or not, SEP was simply impossible.

There was another similar instance. *Publishers Weekly*, the main book-industry periodical, did a feature article on us. They sent a writer and photographer and did a nice spread. It wasn't perfect, but it did explain our structure and policies quite positively. This occurred because the executive editor, John Baker, was sensitive to these issues and, very much against the odds, respected our efforts greatly. He had the clout to escort the piece all the way into publication. What's striking was that this one anomaly in the mainstream gave us more exposure than we ever got from the Left. There was no such article, that I can remember, about SEP as a different and instructive institution in any progressive periodical. *Z* and SEP still endure marginalization by other progressive operations. It is typical, for example, for a media conference to be held and for *Z* to be requested to promote it, while receiving no invitation to attend it, much less to make presentations. Why does that happen? Perhaps it will become evident as we proceed.

Soaring Mice

> *You must be the change you want to see in the world.*
> —*Mohandas Gandhi*

SEP had an employee, at one point, who became disgruntled and finally left. He wanted to clean the toilets, deliver the mail, sweep the floors, and pack books to mail to their buyers, but he did not want to evaluate manuscripts, be involved in SEP's pricing policy, or anything else above the shop floor. The way he put it was that "you all are eagles, but I am a mouse. I want to keep being mouse-like. I don't mind and I am happy to do the more boring and rote work. I am happy that you are being eagles. I respect and admire it. Why won't you respect me? Why can't I do my thing? Why isn't it my decision? I love SEP. I want to contribute, but I want to contribute my way, not your way. I will be happier. I will be more productive. You will have less onerous work to do. Stop imposing your way on me or I will have to leave."

This member's ultimatum precipitated a conundrum. We were saying he had to be an eagle which is to say, he had to do not only his share of the boring and rote work but also his share of the empowering work. He was saying that he would do more of the onerous work and it would make all of our lives easier and his life would be better, too. Since everyone would benefit, Billy wondered, how could it be wrong? "How can you justify telling me, Billy, how I should live?" he asked.

But we weren't saying Billy had to do empowering work for his betterment or enjoyment. And we weren't saying he had to do empowering work because we wanted to do that extra onerous work he would be taking away from us. We were saying that everyone had to do empowering work so there wouldn't be a hierarchy of decision-related knowledge and skill that would destroy everything we were trying to do. We wouldn't accept reimposing class differences. I told Billy, he would likely agree with us that a country is justified to forbid slavery even if someone says he or she would like to be a slave. It ensures that the society as a whole is slave free. The same goes for a society, or a workplace, banning class division.

What became crystal clear through this experience was that societies can't operate according to the idea that anything goes. Societies must have institutions that offer roles that people fill. We choose from what is available. Insofar as SEP was a tiny society, it had work roles, all of which included empowering tasks. You filled one of those jobs or you weren't part of SEP.

Balancing SEP Bias

Prejudices are what fools use for reason.
—Voltaire

From the outset, SEP had men and women staff. Two women provided the start-up finances. Male and female habits, however, weren't absent. Men gravitated more to the finance work and fund-raising. Women gravitated more to design. Cleaning was seriously asymmetrical. Sexual tensions existed as well, at times. Old habits died hard, or not at all. Fights occurred. On the plus side, however, there was no systematic sexual division of labor. Quite the opposite, job assignments were consistently assigned to undo past habits. And the achieved ratios, while never perfect, were never too bad, either.

At SEP, we always wanted to have not only gender balance, but also a culturally diverse staff. But SEP started out with a staff of people who were mostly my friends from the economics program at U Mass Amherst, or friends of friends. With Lydia and me getting the ball rolling, SEP's tone and tenor was white—more or less like the sea is wet. And yes, the difference between black and white habits, cultures, and assumptions, while not quite the difference between submersion in sea and motion in air, was much larger than we easily comprehended. Were white folk to be dropped into a black neighborhood, business, or college, we would have a better, though still very partial, feeling for this difference. It wasn't just that we had different cultures. One culture dominated the other.

When SEP did look to find black staff-members, there was a real dearth of applicants. Two primary factors were at play. Blacks with the background, confidence, and orientation that would leave them interested in working at an operation like SEP, even were it optimally black-friendly, were in a position to choose from a huge number of other options first. Even more important, SEP was intrinsically not optimally black-friendly. It wasn't that SEP was overtly racist—and even calling it covertly or implicitly racist probably obscures the point more than reveals it. SEP was initially overwhelmingly white, rather like something can be overwhelmingly Italian, or, for that matter, overwhelmingly black. The assumptions of its daily interpersonal relations, the way people talked, dressed, carried themselves, played, ate, and did everything, was whiteish and not blackish, and if you were a lone black in SEP, you would be culturally uncomfortable all the time.

At one point, SEP hired a black woman collective member. She had been a physics major, she was vegetarian, and had at least as many white friends as black. She had roomed with whites for the better part of her adult life. It was a virtually seamless fit. But when we later hired a young black man who came directly from a black community environment, his assumptions, mannerisms, and priorities, and his reactions to other people on the staff ignited frequent sparks and even fires, sometimes even with the previously hired black woman. Color in race turns out not to be the only issue. Culture is the heart of it, and, of course, racism. And then alongside those are issues of class and gender as well.

Where to, Whitey?

> *Nobody outside of a baby carriage or a judge's*
> *chamber believes in an unprejudiced point of view.*
> —*Lillian Hellman*

In SEP's early days, diversifying presented a dilemma. On the one hand, what should have happened was pretty obvious. Institutions and their white members should bend and become multiculturally respectful and involved. But what if an institution is tiny, like SEP, and can't grow by more than one person or at most two people at any one time, and can do that only when a member leaves? Such an institution—and this is pretty typical on the Left—can't quickly double in size. Instead, to approach cultural and racial parity would require firing three or four people who don't deserve to be fired. More, suppose people coming on would not only diversify culture, and not only improve SEP's ability and inclination to address matters of race productively, but also change its emphasis on other matters, which those present did not believe it would be desirable to change. What if at SEP it would lead to different editorial decisions, not just benefitting race related choices, but disturbing SEP's focus on imperialism, anticapitalism, or gender issues? Conflicting values contended and a hard situation developed.

Most people at SEP in my years there preferred to try to move toward diversity a small step at a time, rarely proceeding more than one or two steps before encountering problems that twisted and tore the fabric of the organization until the gains were undone. Everyone said they were trying to achieve greater balance consistent with preserving the guiding precepts and aims of the institution. And this was no lie, though it may not have been the only motive that informed our choices. But even if it was entirely the truth, and even if it was entirely warranted, what it felt like to blacks was that the whites were protecting their cultural comforts, not their political or social priorities. In hindsight, I think both these dynamics were probably in play. Indeed, in the American Left it is hard to imagine that dual motives wouldn't operate in cases of this sort. Allegiance to ideals is what makes the Left leftist. And allegiance to communities is endemic to American life. Both had impact, I believe, at SEP.

Regardless, there was overcoming racism to consider. There was building an antiracist movement to consider. In the years since I left, SEP has done much better, over time, at achieving racial and also gender balance. Institutions progress. *Z Magazine* is a smaller project, and while its extended family is quite international and diverse, its local staff isn't. Are we guilty of defending ourselves against hassle or even loss of advantage? Perhaps. Or are we just doing our work, only a few people, in difficult times, as best we can? Maybe.

So why do imbalances persist even on the Left? Surely sometimes imbalance is an accident. But accidents are random and go both ways. If sexual and racial imbalance on the Left is accidental, I reasoned back when I was at SEP, half the time there would be more women than men and more than a representative number of blacks, Latinos, and other "nonwhites." But this hardly ever happened. The "accident" excuse, I realized, mostly displayed either extreme ignorance of what the word "accident" means or an extreme lack of ingenuity at justifying unworthy behavior.

Another possibility was that imbalances in who speaks, writes, and makes decisions derived from habit. But if that was true, how could it be anything other than a crushing condemnation? Whites and men often said that imbalance existed because people reached out to folks they already knew. I agreed that that was true, but then I wondered why publishers, editors, and conference organizers knew mostly white men year after year. It was often regularly asked, why should publishers, editors, and conference sponsors who aggressively seek gender and racial representation but fail to find qualified folks reduce the quality of their product instead of falling back on better trained, more experienced white men who were, after all, experts?

Indeed, this last was the most common explanation for imbalances on the Left. I heard it over and over. I offered it, at times, myself. It was the workhorse, all-purpose answer. But was it really true that there weren't enough available, highly proficient Third World and women writers and speakers to provide excellent contributions on just about any topic any leftist might need?

In my own experience, SEP always had a majority of women in the collective, and there were way more than enough people of color with relevant political literacy, which was actually our main requirement. And in our publications, balance was good, and the quality of women's and minority contributions, even ignoring the domains they brought into priority that would otherwise have been undertreated, was without flaw.

Moreover, wasn't it true, I reasoned, that white men often demonstrated little insight into critical topics—for example, issues of gender, sexuality, and race? Weren't they, then, often underqualified? So why weren't they rejected, I wondered, more often as speakers, writers, and decision makers? Finally, even if racism and sexism had so isolated women, blacks, Latinos, Native Americans, and others from writing and speaking opportunities that relatively few became skilled at these avocations, shouldn't organizers, editors, and publishers still seek racial and sexual balance even though they would have to include less experienced and less polished writers and speakers? What my experiences said to me, however hard of hearing I sometimes was, was that incorporating as speakers, writers, and decision makers those who didn't yet have "exalted skills" was critical both morally and strategically if we were to bring new people into the political circuit.

At SEP, no one who was hired ever had the relevant publishing skills before they arrived. SEP's members all learned on the job. As far as writing books for SEP, first-time authors often excelled for their innovative ideas and with experience their writing got better and better. With a forward-looking timeline, editors, publishers, and organizers choosing speakers could make choices that continually developed new talent and new skills in new people. Yet imbalances persisted.

Many women, blacks, Latinos, Native Americans, and Asians are so suspicious of largely white male-administered progressive institutions that they do not communicate with them or welcome their communications. Women and Third World people often have a style of writing and interacting that publishers, editors, and conference organizers don't understand so that the publishers, editors, and conference organizers exclude whole ranges of insight, not even realizing they are missing. Women, blacks, Latinos, Native Americans, etc., often write and say things that threaten comfortable hierarchical norms that publishers, editors, and conference organizers favor, so that a disproportionate preference for white males is often a conscious choice to preserve favored policies. Overcoming all this hasn't proved simple.

National Averages and Left Averages

> *When all other contingencies fail, whatever*
> *remains, however improbable, must be the truth.*
> *—Arthur Conan Doyle*

Returning to the present, there has certainly been progress, yet, honestly, I think things remain far from perfect. I work at ZNet, a Web site where we put online perhaps 3,000 articles a year. *Z Magazine* publishes in print roughly 300 articles a year. In all this, well under half the articles are written by women and fewer than 10 percent by blacks. Why? Why do I field content, every day, that is less diverse than it ought to be, at a Left site, no less? What makes this record even more disturbing is that if we who post pieces on ZNet or place them in *Z* know that an author is female or black or working class, or young, for that matter, we are far more prone to publish him or her. Likewise, we favor articles on women and race.

If you now look, in contrast, at law schools in America, due to the successes of the women's and civil rights movements, women represent close to fifty percent enrollment and while blacks are probably not so near to matching in law school enrollment their national proportion, they are certainly getting there (though attacks on affirmative action now threaten to slow the progress). Getting into law school depends far more on prior resources, training, and access, than does getting an article selected at ZNet or *Z*. So how can getting into law school be more balanced than getting into *Z*? By what logic and dynamic can the rates of acceptance of women compared to men and of blacks compared to whites be better at law schools, than on the Left?

It is simply not the case that ZNet or *Z* reject a higher proportion of female or black submissions than law schools reject female or black applications. Instead, ZNet and *Z* get a smaller percentage of black and female submissions than do law schools. On the Left, over the past twenty years, women's and black's submissions are proportionately down. Acceptances, as a proportion of submissions, are up. This doesn't mean women and blacks don't want to write Left essays. Perhaps, instead, they see no reason to submit them to white-dominated institutions because they take it for granted that such institutions will not publish their work. But if women and blacks are willing to struggle through the slings and arrows of getting to the point of applying to, and then of going to law school, and then of graduating and entering the law profession, how can the policies of Left institutions regarding publishing women and blacks, policies which are often aggressively congenial, be a major impediment? Has something happened in the past twenty years that has oriented women and minorities to produce relatively fewer people interested in writing about social change? Or, is something causing the leftists these communities produce to be less inclined to write in multiracial, much less in white, venues than were their fathers and mothers during the days of Jim Crow racism and rampant misogyny? Whatever is going on, it needs attention.

Do As I Say Or I Won't Pay

> *We live by the Golden Rule.*
> *Those who have the gold make the rules.*
> *—Buzzie Bavasi*

There is an odd condition in our movements. We know that money matters in society, but we don't seem to realize that money matters on the Left. Where does it come from? How is it handled? Is it empowering a few to the detriment of the many? Is there enough of it? How do we get more without undercutting our ability to put it to good use?

The most egregious instance of large-scale donor control over activists I ever heard of had to do with the largest no-nukes demonstration in U.S. history, which was held in New York in the early 1980s. At this time, Israel, with U.S. blessing, was assaulting Lebanon. On the day of the march a key donor made clear that if Mideast conflicts were brought up from the stage, her donations would not be made and the movement would be unable to pay its bills. She effectively controlled what was said from the podium in front of half a million people, while those people had no idea this was even occurring.

Large donor influence is far more evident, even if still not trumpeted, in smaller scale endeavors. For example, organizations of many types come into existence and then operate beholden to specific donors. Sometimes these donors are part of the operation and invariably run the show, or nearly so. Other times they aren't directly on board, but someone who has access to them is on board, and that person may dictate outcomes. The area I have some experience with, alternative media, is graphically if not universally donor, and donor dynamics, dominated. For example, *The Nation* was begun and financed by large donors who, at most points, occupied the key decision positions in the periodical. The same holds for *Monthly Review, Mother Jones, Utne Reader, In These Times*, and *New Left Review*. In cases where the big donor didn't come aboard, it was generally the best fund-raiser or most financially connected participant who had the corner office. With our activist hats on we decry mainstream media for being owned and thus beholden to big money in its motivations and structural choices, but then, when we don our media hats, we construct operations no less beholden to big-money interests, but now via the largesse of donors rather than direct owners.

When leftists I have known have talked about a major nonprofit—say the Ford Foundation—they have described something marginally better in its structural commitments than, say, the capitalistically owned Ford Motor Company, but they certainly haven't described an institution free of constraint. When leftists have looked in the mirror, however, at our donor-led or fund-raiser-dominated projects, we haven't recoiled and said, hey, we have to improve these, too.

Financing SEP into Existence

I'd like to live as a poor man with lots of money.
—Pablo Picasso

South End Press was saved from bankruptcy when Lydia Sargent received a gift of about $60,000 from her father. This didn't evidence a caring relationship. Rather, Lydia's father was a prominent corporate lawyer who died some years back. Her mother was and remains an old-school, highly active lawyer's wife. Lydia's marriage to Gary Sargent, Jewish, exceeded her parents' tolerance. Lydia was thrown out. Neither of her parents ever acknowledged Lydia's children nor, later, her grandchildren. And while I met Lydia's dad once before he died, and have met her mother on a few occasions, for them I was a nonentity. I am Jewish too. The situation has been a fine advertisement for religion, wealth, and the nuclear family.

In any event, at some point Lydia's dad discovered guilt—perhaps because Lydia and Gary divorced. No one knows why for sure, but he suddenly decided that while he wouldn't welcome Lydia fully back into the fold, he would make some amends—with his checkbook, of course. Thus, there came to Lydia, completely unexpectedly, the aforementioned gift, and thus South End Press was born out of the guilt-ridden patriarchal largesse of a right-wing, bigoted, and callous old agent of ruling-class, racist, sexist elitism. Hooray for guilt!

Another of the initial members of South End Press was Juliet Schor, who I met at U Mass Amherst. Juliet's family also had some money and Juliet helped Lydia finance SEP's start-up. Thus, SEP rested on the funds of these two women. Neither of them felt their largesse entitled them to greater say over SEP's daily operations than anyone else. And since we had equitable job definitions, there just wasn't any way for them to seriously abuse their beneficence even if they wanted to.

Tandler Tango

Charity should be abolished and replaced by justice.
—Norman Bethune

Fundraising for SEP meant writing letters and sometimes calling on people and trying to get them to like us and our operation enough to part with some of their generally not-very-hard-earned money. A fellow named Martin Bunzl, whose source of wealth and position in the whole scheme of things was, I think, largely exaggerated, helped us with a modest donation and at times offered some advice. There was a guy named Martin Tandler, who amassed his money in the textile industry, and who Bunzl told me about. Pat Walker, another founding member of SEP, and Lydia met with Tandler in New York in our very early years and got what was for us a hefty donation, I think it was $5,000 or perhaps $10,000, one of a handful of donations we received that were that large. Three years later, Lydia went back to talk to Tandler again. By then we had a catalog of books and Lydia could argue our worth based on evidence rather than mere promises. It turned out, however, that offering evidence was not wise. Tandler looked at the catalog and said he thought it was crap. When Lydia asked why, Tandler pointed to a number of feminist books and led Lydia into a large room with lots of women working on textiles. He walked up and asked a women laboring away at a demanding machine, "Do I oppress you?" The woman looked up and said, "No, of course not." SEP was a multi-focus press. We did books about everything, and there were bound to be some that any donor wouldn't like. These were usually books addressing the Mideast or corporate power, but sometimes the feminist books scared off support.

Rockefeller Rocks

The love of money as a possession—as distinguished from the love of money as a means to the enjoyments and realities of life—will be recognized for what it is, a somewhat disgusting morbidity.
—John Maynard Keynes

Next came Abby Rockefeller. Lydia and I sought out and became friends with Abby—having a friendship is almost always a big part of successful fund-raising—and over the years Abby gave SEP around $30,000. Abby was quite nice and her heart beat progressively, unlike most donors one encounters. We did some socializing together and had some lunches at Abby's house. Abby was living with a fellow named Lee Halprin. Lee seemed to be involved with Abby's finances, but that may have been our imagination. We went on a canoe outing with them to New Hampshire to ride some modest rapids. During this escapade I tried to experiment, against Lydia's better judgment, with crossing rather than properly riding down the rapids. Lydia and I took a nice spill, riding one section of the river on our backs in the water.

Abby had had problems dealing with the reality of her money. Robin Williams, in skewering the practice of psychiatry, once joked that Freud said, "If it isn't one thing, it's your mother." In Abby's case, it was perhaps more likely her father. David Rockefeller was a very powerful ruling-class figure. But I think for most rich folks who might give money to liberal or progressive, much less radical projects, the cause of difficulty is the mind-bending conundrums associated with having anticapitalist values plus a large stash of cash. Abby thought that to give a thousand dollars here and a thousand dollars there shouldn't be overdone lest her funds dissipate. This denied her true wealth, though it may have accorded with an allowance her financial handlers favored. It made fund-raising from Abby frustrating, even if relatively successful.

Donor Delusions

If you want to know what God thinks of money,
just look at the people he gave it to.
—*Dorothy Parker*

The problem of donors not realizing their own capacity is larger than one might guess. A friend named David Plotke, then editor of *Socialist Review*, coedited a book SEP published called *Eurocommunism*. It was a big collection, and at first David indicated he didn't want to publish with SEP, but I made a pitch to him about the importance of getting SEP legitimated and he came around to our cause. I remember David visiting the press and our going to lunch and having a long conversation about the funding situation of Left projects like SEP and *Socialist Revolution*. During this discussion, we were bemoaning the indignities of fund-raising as well as the complexities of periodicals claiming to be socialist when run by people on the basis of their either having fund-raising ties or of personally providing the funding for the projects. We were also talking about how strange it is that left-wing donors are such tightwads compared to right-wing donors or, even worse, incapable of admitting their own wealth.

David told me about one instance that, if he was correct—and I have no reason to doubt that he was—was perhaps the granddaddy case of all. *Mother Jones* magazine was financed into existence by Adam Hochschild. Adam's money allowed *MJ* to do massive mailings over and over, to build up and maintain a readership. It turns out that Adam's money came from South African mining (done by prior generations of his family, not by Adam, of course). Some would blanch at this, but not me. I like the idea that monies soaked in blood when earned by past generations get passed down and end up in cleaner hands that are willing to put it back into more humane circulation. That's not a problem for me—Hochschild, Rockefeller, Pillsbury—when it happens, good things can follow.

Of course, the fact that Adam not only put his money into *MJ* but put himself into *MJ* too, in the corner office, was less positive, particularly as compared to David Pillsbury, in contrast, who gave away all his funds and did it without ever, to my knowledge, accruing undue power to himself. But the salient point about Adam was the amount of cash he had available versus the amount that he made available. It seemed that Adam was way richer than Adam would admit to himself. What he was giving, which was quite considerable by Left accounts, wasn't even denting his capacity. He was doing a fraction of what he might have done, given

267

his actual resources, had he been willing to comprehend them. Left mental gymnastics to avoid dealing forthrightly with finances afflicted supplicants and providers, too.

Comfortable Anticapitalism

> *Foul cankering rust the hidden treasure frets,*
> *But gold that's put to use more gold begets.*
> —*William Shakespeare*

Regarding the conflicts of having money and anticapitalist values, when Lydia and I moved to Woods Hole we finessed buying a house. Over fifteen years, the value of the house just kept climbing, mostly due to real estate trends, but abetted as well by a refinanced extension that we added. Incredibly, the house would now sell for a small fortune by our standards. This weighs on me. Yet the fact is, we parlayed a little into a lot and now it serves not only as a nice place to live, and for offices for our operations, but also as an insurance policy against disaster. Still, it is incongruous. When people visit, it is hard not to defensively ward off the impression that we must have oodles of money we are hoarding.

At any given moment, while Lydia and I live quite well, between us we will typically have between zero and one full monthly salary check of, after thirty years of raises, a bit over $2,500 in the bank. By each month's end we have essentially no savings. This is roughly opposite the situation of rich people on the Left. Leftists who are very wealthy tend to live vastly below the funds at their disposal due to being unwilling to use even a tiny fraction of their money for their own well-being or for anyone else's, due to not wanting to face the reality of their wealth. Lydia and I, in contrast, manage to live way above our means by repeatedly tapping into what isn't even there to finance both our private and our social agendas.

Still, the house troubles me, so I can only pretend to imagine what a giant hundred- or two hundred- or five hundred-million-dollar portfolio does to rich leftists. On the other hand, I wouldn't turn such a portfolio down. And when Lydia finally inherits what I hope will be something reasonably close to a couple of million dollars, I won't consider it a harsh post-mortem punishment from her right-wing parents, but will instead consider it a delicious irony that once again they will be helping revolutionary ideas that they never remotely perceived, comprehended, or respected. That said, of course I would also vigorously support increasing inheritance taxes to 100 percent, starting tomorrow, as long as it affected everyone.

Hunting Hunter

The Great Humanitarian; the Great Philanthropist.
—*Bob Dylan*

D avid Hunter was the Clint Eastwood of Left funding back during the first decade of SEP. David managed the Stern Foundation as well as the funds of many individuals, and knew pretty much everyone in the progressive funding community. If you were going to make progress with one person in hopes of meeting others who might help financially, David Hunter was the philanthropist to see. My efforts to meet with David failed until one day I met up with an old friend at a party who just happened to know Philip Stern of the Stern Foundation, who just happened also to be at the party. I asked the friend to introduce me and he did. Stern liked me, feeling I was "a nice Jewish boy," and I asked him if I could make a pitch for funding support for SEP. A few days later I got an invitation to see David Hunter in New York City at the Stern Foundation offices. This was not like Wiesner's invitation to Camelot. I wanted Stern's invitation. We needed help and Hunter was the best chance we had for something serious. So I prepared carefully.

The meeting was held over lunch at the Harvard Club. We chatted a bit and Hunter asked to see our financial statements. I had brought along a profit and loss statement, a balance sheet, and monthly cash flow projections. Indeed, I brought a number of projections, some envisioning an abysmal future with no external support, and some envisioning a brighter picture with various levels of outside help. The only thing we never told funders was how little we paid ourselves. We juggled some of the categories so we could show our salaries as being higher than they really were, which in those days was essentially zero. Even with help from Hunter, SEP would remain unable to pay even livable incomes. Funders didn't then, and still don't, believe serious and capable people will work for slave wages or less, and they don't want to fund operations that can't pay employees good incomes. Funders prefer to avoid people who don't earn hefty incomes. Paupers make them uncomfortable. I guess it feels like slumming. This is a Catch-22, however. Those who have money get more. Those who need money get shunned.

In addition to financial documents, I also brought a whole set of arguments for supporting SEP. The main point was that monies given to SEP would not only help us grow, but would lead to more books, royalty payments, and revenues, which we would then put into still more output. A dollar given to us would, over time, pay back far more. We had it all plotted on spreadsheets with nice graphs and convincing data. So as Hunter started to peruse the documents, I prepared to make my oh-so-elaborate and compelling case as soon as he looked up, intending to ask him to look at such-and-such entry in the cash flow, and then walk him through the information. My plan was naive. Before I could even ask his reactions, he folded the documents and, without much interest, put them in his briefcase. I asked if he was done with the documents and he replied that yes, he was. I asked if he would like to go over them and have me explain entries, and he said that no, he wouldn't.

Hypocrisy or Sound Policy?

Wealth, in even the most improbable cases,
manages to convey the aspect of intelligence.
—John Kenneth Galbraith

Since Hunter and I had hit if off very well in the preliminary chatting, I pressed the issue of his ignoring the financials, saying okay, but I would like to go over them because there are important points to raise. He said no, he never did more than glance at such documents. Now you have to realize that while every donor asks for this documentation, many organizations don't really have means to generate it and have to go hire someone to do it, or to invest their own time even though the documents will often be used for no other purpose than fund-raising. So I was a bit incredulous that Hunter was so dismissive, and I asked about it.

Hunter told me, and I don't think he admitted this often, that he paid no attention to the actual numbers in such documents because he took it for granted that everyone asking for donations lied. He required the documents but he looked at them only to see if they were done properly. He, and others in the funding community, believed that being able to generate financial documents was a bottom-line indicator of fiscal savvy. If you couldn't do it, you were so fiscally out of touch that money should not be entrusted to you. It you could do it, you might warrant a closer look. But to base anything on the actual content of such documents would be silly.

Beyond being a fascinating revelation, and a bit gut-wrenching for what it said about Hunter's estimate of people's honesty, and a little more gut-wrenching since we did lie about our salaries, this was a body blow to our funding chances. We had listed honest numbers, except for the pumped up salaries, and our cash flows were as accurate as we could make them and fully substantiated our argument about how money given to us would multiply to benefit many other Left projects. But regarding the implications of that claim too, it turned out I was in the dark.

The idea that donors would like to see their funds multiply made awfully good sense to John Schall and me when we came up with the argument, but John and I were trained as economists, concerned about social change, and had no money. Donors had a different mentality. You got Hunter's aid, and even more, you got aid from other donors, if they liked you, pure and simple. Well, it was that, plus that what you were doing was of such a kind that they could give money to it without being ridiculed or condemned, and, if possible, even proudly taking credit for doing so.

What determined whether donors liked you was mostly personal relations. The more you could talk, sit, walk, and otherwise carry yourself as the donors did, dress as they did, and exude their kind of confidence, the more likely they were to feel comfortable around you and send you checks. But we didn't look, talk, or act like the donors. Being a project they could brag about was out of the question, too. Our publishing was too radical, and, worse, our identification with Chomsky and our so often addressing Mideast politics was particularly off-putting to many donors, like the feminist content had been off-putting to Tandler. Plus, our structural commitments were incomprehensible to most donors, who, if they did understand what we were doing, found our structure threatening or juvenile. Hunter got from us what he needed, the catalog and a couple of hours with me. We got from him a little, but not much.

Zevin, Houses, Packages, Printers, and the IRS

Money is better than poverty, if only for financial reasons.
—Woody Allen

I don't remember precisely how we met Bob Zevin. He was a vice president at U.S. Trust. Zevin became a friend and helped often, particularly with our buying and selling houses. This was generally quite dramatic. We bought a place, worked there for a year or so, and sold it. We made enough to get another place, and to finance operations, too. The downside was that this was part and parcel of gentrification. The upside was that it was us being driven out, and we were taking enough payment with us to benefit our work. Living and working in the same building was initially a part of surviving, and later a good investment strategy, but round about when I left, folks had had more than enough of it.

One of the house sales was another in a list of incredible funding-related events. We were dying of debt. Zevin proposed that we go bankrupt and have the bank auction our house. The proceeds would cover our debts and hopefully leave enough extra cash to keep us operating in a new locale. This was hard to risk, you can imagine, but we went for it. The big day came. There was a public auction, at the house, on the front steps. The high bid got the house. If the high bid was low, too bad. We feared disaster. Imagine the tension waiting for these fat cats to line up, on the sidewalk, outside our house, to spend twenty minutes flicking their hands to note a bid and decide our fate. The bidding got heated. We got a great price. SEP lived on.

Zevin also helped us with a very intricate investment package in which people anonymously put money into SEP, to be paid back somewhere down the road. I don't remember the details of this undertaking, nor what later happened to it. It did help us greatly, however, and thanks go to all involved, whoever they were. There was also a grant from something called The Community Development Finance Corporation. Mel King, friend, mayoral candidate, and later coauthor, gave us some help with getting this one. I remember meeting with the bureau over and over, and finally getting some funds, but not near what we had hoped for. There were hoops to jump through, too, which caused considerable havoc.

For a long time, while hugely short on cash, we would routinely ignore printer bills. The printers would, in time, demand their money. We would say, go ahead, demand all you want, we don't have it. They'd get hostile, refuse to print more for us, threaten legal action, and demand satisfaction, and we'd say, what do you want us to do, we can't do the impossible. We would bully them, rather than the reverse, and we would get them to agree to do more books if we would pay for the new ones and also start paying off overdue debt with modest monthly installments. The deal would be struck, we'd get more books to sell, and in time again we'd stop sending the installment checks and then get behind on the new payments, too. I think at its worst we owed various corporate printers a few hundred thousand dollars.

That was feisty enough, but our biggest bit of bogarting was reserved for the state. The IRS called at one point to notify us that we were, I think it was, $40,000 in debt for payroll taxes. John and I went down to meet with them and they demanded payment. We said no. We can't do it. It would put us out of business. They said, you must be kidding, you will pay or else. We said, okay, let's have or else. Come in and do your worst. Close up a progressive (I don't think we used the word "radical," much less "revolutionary") book publisher here in Boston, Massachusetts, staffed by underpaid young folks, highly praised for our commitment and achievements, and we'll see what the fallout regarding censorship and state bullying leads to.

I don't know if this was pure bluff or not, which is to say I don't know if it would have led to anything other than us being closed down, but the money was minor from their angle, and the danger was not worth risking, and so they reigned in their bluster and said, okay, what can you do? We proposed some low monthly payment we could manage, maybe it was $1,000 a month, and said, take it or leave it. They took it and we walked out shaking.

It is nearing twenty years, as I write this, since I worked at SEP. They have published a few books of mine since I left the press to start *Z Magazine*, and they have rejected quite a few others. I think leaving SEP without maintaining close ties was perhaps one of my and Lydia's greatest and most worthy achievements. We gave a good part of our lives to SEP. We were founding members, there from the start. Hardest times were past. SEP was a successful publishing house. We could stay and produce books forever. We could leave but retain some kind of involvement. We didn't do any of that. I left in 1986, going on a sabbatical for six months and then having another six months off, and then Lydia left, too. Our idea was to do a magazine. We proposed to SEP that we do the new project under the SEP rubric, but the others at SEP feared that a magazine was way too financially risky, and that its failure could drag down the house with it. So Lydia and I left to start Z without involving SEP in any risk, and with it abundantly clear to them and us that if we blew it, we had no ticket back. People thought we were nuts, again.

Why do I say leaving was more meritorious than building the press in the first place? If you look at Left institutions over the past five decades, some have failed and others have succeeded and still persist. Examining them all, you will find that the number of founders who moved on and built another project, retaining nearly no ties to their first creation, is very low. People tend to hang on to their creations until either death or retirement does them part. There is a tendency, if an operation succeeds, to hit a plateau and then take no new risks. The pressure toward stabilization is enormous. Attitudes tend to change from what we all had when we started SEP—which was, "How do we utilize our time and labors to best contribute to social change?"—to "How do we preserve this wonderful project, not to mention our livelihoods, against all dangers?" I understand the change, and it isn't even wrong, per se, but it doesn't lead forward.

To build something and treat it as easily dispensable, engaging in actions that bring it down, is not exemplary. On the other hand, our goal wasn't to create one institution. Our goal was to win changes throughout society. Once I felt SEP had stable finances and would operate fine without me, I saw no reason to stay, and shortly later Lydia concurred.

For good or ill, my preferred mind-set has always been to look into new possibilities rather than preserve good ones already in existence. The minute I can act on that inclination, confident past projects won't suffer, I do so. Lydia's loyalty to SEP was greater than mine, and for her leaving was harder, but she left too, and because it was harder, her decision to do so was that much more exemplary. A similar situation propelled me into ZNet. Now Z is moving toward twenty years old. ZNet is over ten years old. The time to move on is approaching, not even taking into account the no-longer-distant onset of elderliness.

The Open Question: Restauranteering

Life shouldn't be printed on dollar bills.
—Clifford Odets

There is a last SEP-related funding story I'd like to relate even though it is hard for me to write about. One of the founding members of SEP was my close friend John Schall. John understood the extent to which poverty crippled Left prospects and was always trying to do something about it. One day, long after he had left SEP, John was in the Midwest and had a meal in a restaurant called Mongolian Stew. He described the experience: you entered, in the center there was a large cooking area, around the outside there were shelves of items you could select. You picked your ingredients to be cooked on the open stove. You could go back for more, and one price covered as much as you wanted. John felt this type of eating place would be a big hit back east. In a flash he was calculating costs on a napkin, envisioning satisfied diners in his mind, and counting up profits that could be used to fuel political activism. Since then, he founded a very successful restaurant called Fire and Ice in Cambridge, Massachusetts, which spun off other operations as well. But despite having the idea and doing the hard work, John repeatedly got squeezed out of the big bucks by investors. John is still, over a decade later, trying to extricate himself with sufficient funds to repay initial supporters and finance Left operations.

John hasn't done much that is overtly political since he began his money quest, unless it works and then the effort will have been strategic not only in intent, but also in impact. If the quest doesn't work, John's efforts will have been supremely well motivated, and highly dignified, but he will have achieved less than he might have with other life trajectories. Moneymaking in capitalism is hard. John's idea was excellent. Indeed, many people are getting rich off it. John has been too nice to be one of them. In capitalism, garbage rises, and John isn't garbage.

Chapter 25

Monthly *Z*

Z Magazine

> *Listen, Revolution, We're buddies, see*
> *Together, We can take everything.*
> —*Langston Hughes*

L ydia and I loved and were proud of SEP, feeling its creation was a major accomplishment, but we also saw a need for a media project that would have an audience that related to it regularly, with at least the potential to become a kind of community. To create this, we leaned toward creating a monthly magazine with the same editorial priorities as SEP. *Z* would publish articles about the totality of oppression—especially race, gender, class, and power—and would try to offer both vision and strategy, rooting itself in needs and hopes emerging from activism. Even at the outset, however, we hoped to expand beyond a single mode of delivery to video and audio. When we started most people asked us, "Are you nuts? SEP is going great. Don't risk what you have." I have heard that a lot. When I hear it, I wonder, what do people think winning a revolution requires—one victory, one project?

Z Magazine got going when two conditions were met. First, for us to leave SEP it had to be stable. Second, we needed sufficient means to start the periodical we wanted, or at least have a chance at it. This second condition was met when desktop publishing made two people publishing a multipage, monthly magazine viable. The initial money for *Z* was Lydia's cash from her father, paid back by SEP to help us start the new project.

Ordinarily, to start a new national magazine one might want a million dollars, or a few million dollars, in hand. Another campaign was undertaken some years after we started *Z*, for example, to try to create a leftist culture magazine. Interestingly, we had simultaneously thought that doing that would be very good idea and explored doing it as an SEP spin-off with our friend Sandy Carter as key participant. The non-*Z* project assembled various studies, generated a sample issue, and shortly later called it quits. Their start-up funds, just for those preliminary steps, which led to nothing, were about $300,000. In contrast, we began SEP, then *Z*, then ZNet, and then ZMI, with about a fifth of that money, plus some fancy financial footwork along the way.

For *Z*, there was only one avenue to initial stability. We rejected ads. We needed readers' direct payments, as our sole source of steady income. A magazine attracts subscribers by sending out solicitations that people reply to with a check. You mail such solicitations to lists of subscribers to other similar periodicals, or to members of organizations. You buy the lists from brokers—and you in turn sell the addresses that you accrue to others to use for their mailings. So we signed up some writers and produced a description of what we wanted to do and even a mock issue. And with these in place, we prepared a mailing. The trouble was, mailings for magazines tended to return at most a few percent. And we only had enough money for modest mailings. So we sent out our packet to a list of subscribers to another magazine and held our breath, and when the returns came in we opened them and deposited the checks. Now we were committed to filling the orders people had made by providing the year of issues to our first subscribers. But we also needed more subscribers if we were to make a go of it. So instead of using the revenue we had taken in to pay production costs and produce and distribute what people had bought, we put it all into a new mailing to attract more subscribers. And then we did a third mailing with the revenues from the second one. In this way, through repeated mailings to additional lists, we bootstrapped up our base of subscribers. For each new list we mailed to, we sat on a knife edge. One bad reply rate and we were dead in the water. The risks paid off, however, and we parlayed relatively few assets into a whole new institution.

As with SEP, of course, the commitment of thirty to forty initial writers was key to readers signing on. The package we mailed prospective subscribers was actually a kind of mock issue. People we asked about how best to proceed, including people working at other progressive periodicals, advised against the approach we took. If we told people too much about the *Z* we were actually going to deliver, we were warned, the recipients of our mailings wouldn't imagine what they wanted and sign up for it; they would instead judge what we showed them and find fault with something about it and pass on subscribing to it. This wisdom, not entirely false, is apparently what people go to business school to learn, thereby becoming adept at manipulating and deceiving audiences into desired outcomes while having zero faith in the actual worth of what they have to offer. We passed on this time-honored option and instead showed people exactly what we had to offer.

Z was not complicated structurally because it began with just Lydia and I, and even when we shortly later added Eric Sargent, Lydia's son, and considerably later added Andy Dunn, an ex-military man from the West Coast well after I had moved on to ZNet, there just wasn't all that much complexity. Work on *Z* entailed fielding submissions, choosing among them, doing modest editing, laying out the pages, designing the cover, and sending the package to the printer. From there, *Z* would go to stores and also to our subscribers. Indeed, that was the next big piece of the operation—entering new orders and address corrections and renewals for subscribers, and of course inducing new subscribers via mailings. And then there was also dealing with the phone and mail, and handling the finances, bills, and sundry other issues that would arise.

There was one aspect of *Z* that was structurally significant and different, but which ultimately didn't work. When we started, we contracted with a bunch of writers. They would be responsible for some set number of pieces—monthly, quarterly, or biyearly. We engaged these writers in discussions, had a monthly meeting by mail, and tried to make them part of a broader community, which would include having a say in how the periodical proceeded. Indeed, the name was chosen at an early meeting with a bunch of these writers, one of whom suggested it. Policy would go through authors. But our participatory plans never came to fruition. The authors didn't have the time or focus for it. It is one thing to write for a periodical, even for low fees or donating your pay. It is another thing to become fully vested in a periodical as a person who takes responsibility for its well-being.

Z was financially tumultuous for many years. Each summer, we would get down to a few thousand dollars in the bank and make pleas for support. Each time, our readers delivered and we kept going. Each year, it was like starting over from the beginning; one misstep and we would have been gone. When we made such pleas, the project was at stake each time. These were our telethons, and the life we lived and hopes we had rode on every one panning out, year after year. The hardest part of SEP and *Z* was their recurring financial insecurity. I don't think the long hours shortened my life by assaulting my biology, but I suspect the periodic financial tumult probably did.

When *Z* began, each issue was 112 pages. This allowed us to cram in all kinds of content. We could include a few very long essays plus lots of short ones. We could have photo spreads and reports from actions and organizations. We could feature content on war and peace, the economy, families, sexism, racism, gender issues, sexuality, and so on. Lydia and I now wonder how it was that we did that much in the early days, since with more folks and better technology, it now seems quite demanding to do less. At any rate, one of the oddest experiences in the history of *Z* had to do with how long it used to be. We were repeatedly told by people that they didn't want to subscribe because *Z* was too much to read and it made them feel guilty when they neglected articles. They chorused: "Shorten *Z*." We found this infuriating. We were busting ass to publish lesser-known writers, new people, activists, and to deliver more, and readers said, we want less. We replied, do you mean some of it isn't any good? No, they would holler back, "We mean there is just too damn much."

What the hell could that mean? We would get letters saying it with return addresses from university departments. We would hear it from professors face to face. Workers, however, didn't say it to us, nor did activists; it was almost only academics. Of course, contrary to their claims of wanting a shorter product, these people routinely read huge books. They didn't find *The New York Times* too long. They didn't call *Scientific American* too long.

The meaning of their complaints finally penetrated. They were saying, give me my Chomsky and Herman, but don't impose on me essays about racism and sexism, much less revolutionizing the economy inside out. I want to read about the mess the world is in, not about my own society, and especially not about what I can do. The academics didn't want to skip articles they knew were worthy and important, but neither did they want to read beyond their narrow horizon, whatever their particular horizon happened to be. In other words, in our view, the most frequent criticism of us was that we were doing too good a job. We were presenting a multifocus revolutionary perspective and forcing readers to face it all, like it or not. After a few years, we did have to cut back. We couldn't keep paying for so many pages. Too bad.

Sporty Savior?

> *Will the people in the cheap seats clap?*
> *And the rest of you, if you'll just rattle your jewelry.*
> —*John Lennon*

Earlier, I told about our use of buying and selling buildings to help finance SEP. The big funding story regarding *Z* was very different, and infinitely less beneficial. One day about fifteen years ago, a fellow about my age knocked at the door where we then lived in Boston's South End. The home housed *Z Magazine* as well as Lydia and me, and our visitor asked if he could have some of our time. He came in, and we conversed for a couple of hours. Our mystery guest, Jeff Lurie, wanted to help *Z* become more visible. Indeed, he wanted to help us become like "a Left *Newsweek*." He was cogent and sober. He told us about his political identification with *Z* and about his prior trip to Vietnam to see the war's aftermath for himself. He explained that he had the means to help us, being born of a very wealthy family. After Jeff left, with hopes of imminent salvation, I looked into his bona fides. Lo and behold, Jeff Lurie was no joke. His granddad had made a fortune via General Cinema, and the family owned Neiman Marcus, among other holdings. Jeff had juice, not to mention owning his own Hollywood film company, Chestnut Hill Productions, and being an avowed feminist.

Lurie liked us. He also liked the idea of a massive Left media outlet. That's what he told us, anyhow, and what remotely sane reason would there have been for Jeff to be putting us on? The next step, in addition to calls and letters, was a meeting with Jeff's financial advisors in Boston. Jeff explained that before he could put serious money into Z, his advisors had to agree it was an okay thing to do. So I would have to convince them that sending large sums of money our way wouldn't consign Jeff to the investor's hall of shame.

I met Jeff's advisors in their building overlooking Boston Harbor. Their office was opulent, but the meeting was informal, and the main guy I met was young, astute, and open-minded. We talked for quite a while about Z and its hopes and even somewhat about Jeff's means. The interactions verified that the skies themselves weren't a limit. By the end of our discussion, the guy actually said if Jeff decided against helping us and I wanted a job, I should get back in touch with him. I took that as a very positive sign, although I admit that even though it had been my goal to impress this financial advisor, I worried a bit about what it might mean that I had actually carried it off.

Shortly thereafter, conversation with Lurie verified that his handlers had been handled. It was now only a matter of time, Jeff said, and we could get things going—other than, oh yes, managing one little problem. I had already heard all about Jeff's great love of sports. He wanted to propel Z into great visibility for the politics, but for himself, he wanted to become a major player in professional sports. He wanted the fun that would come with that, and he thought maybe he could do it far more progressively than others had, thereby providing a useful model as well. He was a Boston boy and he mostly wanted to own the Celtics, but that possibility wasn't panning out. Football would be great, too, however. He tried for the New England Patriots, and later, I kid you not, he bought the Philadelphia Eagles.

Buying a sports team is a highly vetted process. You have to pass muster to enter the fraternity of sports-team owners. So Jeff told me that while he was being eyeballed as a prospective owner, he couldn't do anything that might rock that boat. Shoveling funds to us would certainly rock the boat. It would make him appear crazy. We thus began a long wait, with intermittent communications and constant wondering, envisioning, and worrying. Sleepless nights wracked by hopes and fears. Every time we communicated, Jeff said there was no problem. Give me a little more time and then we can get on with it.

Fund-raising is a putrid pastime. It involves constant toadying even when you luck out with a relatively healthy relationship with your prospective donor. The

279

intense pain of our Lurie experience persisted for about a year, even though it felt like five. It climaxed with an invitation for Lydia and I to go out to California to see Jeff at his LA movie studio. I had already endured more psychic pain at this guy's hands than anyone else I had ever known, and now we flew across the country, checked into a hotel, and got ready to see him. We paid the fare. The progressive rich can be incredibly cheap. We hoped, or rather I hoped—Lydia was far too astute to have remaining hopes at this point, coming on the trip, I think, mostly to make sure I didn't jump off a bridge—that this would be the beginning of massive financial infusions.

Lydia was right that our flight path to California wouldn't be the yellow brick road. We met Jeff for lunch, along with his "political advisor," who somehow knew me from MIT days. Jeff was still positive, but his advisor, Ira, told us that the problem with *Z* was that it couldn't be read by an "average taxi driver." He suggested *The Economist* as a model magazine that was properly accessible. Of course, if *Z* weren't readable without higher education it would be a serious weakness, particularly if we sought to increase its audience. But *Z* was, of course, already far more readable than *The Economist*. My thought was that Ira probably did have trouble reading *Z*, and not the *The Economist*, but it had nothing to do with style and everything to do with content and the fact that Ira had too much intellectual baggage for radical reading.

We parted for the day, and that evening I called Jeff and suggested readability was key and would be no problem, particularly after he had helped finance massive changes and growth. We met Jeff briefly at his office and then went to a corner food market with him, walking along as he shopped for some items. It was our last few minutes together, and he told us again that he was still positive. He again vaguely apologized for all the delays, and told us he didn't know when things would get better, or even if they would get any better, and we'd see but we shouldn't keep banking on anything—it wasn't fair to us. There went hope. Lydia and I, shattered, went south from LA to Baja for a few days, to kayak there, and then returned home, having given up on Jeff Lurie.

Well, truth be told, having almost given up, I called Lurie's office intermittently for months, but never talked to him again. Barriers up. Lurie bought the Philadelphia Eagles not long thereafter for $195 million. I called to congratulate him and ask if perhaps the time to finance alternative media had come. I didn't get him on the phone. Harcourt General, a Lurie family holding, sold some years later for $4.5 billion. Net cash flow from Jeff Lurie to *Z*: $0.

Did Lurie have any idea how much he gave us hope, and then dashed it? I doubt it. Jeff Lurie floated well above that awareness. Did Jeff's handlers tell him to forget about it, and then he didn't have the integrity to tell us and so stretched it out? Perhaps. But my best guess is that our demise occurred pretty much as Lurie described. The vetting of buying a ball team held off his largesse until the final deliverance of sports ownership changed him from who he had been into a big-time sports owner. I suppose I could be wrong. Maybe Jeff Lurie just needed ownership tenure. Maybe next year, if his Eagles win the Super Bowl, he will be above sanction from co-owners. Maybe he will fulfill his moral destiny. Maybe I should cheer the Eagles. Do you see how wanting financial miracles corrupts reason?

Just to round this out, Jeff Lurie is probably relatively progressive as professional sports-team owners go. In the lobby of the NovaCare Complex, that's the name of the Eagle's offices/stadium/home, Jeff has installed a hall of heroes photo display honoring Martin Luther King Jr., Mother Teresa, and Jonas Salk. I guess that's where his political commitment wound up. Stepping back from his momentary suicidal infatuation with financing Z, he more soberly instead gave a tiny niche of his real estate to a properly balanced and appropriately timid display of social concern. Yay Jeff.

Ostrich Eyes

Follow the money.
—Deep Throat

Of all the questions leftist friends have asked about the experience of Z, or, before, that of SEP, the one you would think would be most frequent—show me the money—has probably been the least asked. Perhaps the reason is best illuminated by a story about another periodical. A friend of mine, David Plotke, decades back, undertook an exemplary task for a magazine named *Socialist Revolution* (later called *Socialist Review*), which was to write about the experience of still another periodical, named *Democracy*. *Democracy* had come into existence a few years earlier, and had already printed its final issue. What was special about what David decided to do was this: for the most part, leftists are not self-critical and evaluative in such ways. We rarely look at our past or present and try to tease out lessons for our future. But David was going to do it. David's journal was broadly Marxist, as was David himself, so you might predict that in addition to looking at the editorial content of *Democracy* and at the views of some if its principal workers and writers and its policy choices, David would follow the money, asking how *Democracy* paid its bills and trying to understand the relations between its finances and its history. In fact, however, there was no mention of such matters in the article.

Democracy began when a large donor provided the start-up funds and pledged continuing support. *Democracy* ended—literally to the issue—when that same donor called up and withdrew from the project. A mental midget, much less an astute fellow like David, looking at that history, would be drawn by self-evident facts to feature the role of money. How could David write about *Democracy* and make no mention of funding? It would be like a Marxist writing about war or poverty or the history of automobile production, and making no mention of private ownership, class relations, or Henry Ford. It couldn't happen, but nonetheless, it did happen. For a fund-raiser to shine a light on the dynamics of movement funding and its implications was simply forbidden and has remained so to the present. Donors won't support those who question their motives or their magnanimity. It is pretty simple. I speak from experience. Even dreams of big donor money are way in our past.

Cocky Cockburn

Reason, or the ratio of all we have already known,
is not the same that it shall be when we know more.
—William Blake

Over the years, publishing articles in *Z Magazine* has been less frothy than publishing books at South End Press. Article authors don't invest nearly as much time and emotion in their work as book authors. A book is not just thirty or fifty times longer, but involves a whole different level of commitment. A person can write and edit an article in a day or two. A person cannot sensibly write a book thirty times as long in a month or two. Likewise, specific articles rarely have the lasting impact of a book, though there are exceptions. A magazine, as compared to just a particular article, affects people by its continuity, which in *Z*'s case is month to month. Each issue is in some respects like a book of essays, but is also more because of that continuity. A magazine develops an audience who are affected and reaffected, supported and resupported, over and over.

Of course, *Z Magazine* has had and now has writers who have had a great cumulative effect. While over the years we had wonderful relations with most *Z* writers, beginning, of course, with Chomsky and Herman, it is controversial events that capture space here. We signed up Alexander Cockburn, for example, to write for *Z* at a time when Alex was arguably the best journalist in the U.S., and certainly a key reason people read *The Nation*. Alex was a brilliant wordsmith, able to engage the reader, turn a phrase, and, without doubt, skewer an opponent or official—whether he or she deserved to be skewered or not. In *The Nation,* Alex could only write short pieces. In *Z*, we had room for a 5,000-word piece, sometimes even more, in each issue. So we asked if Alex would write longer, more in depth, and perhaps even somewhat more personally for *Z*. He agreed, though with some conditions. Alex wanted twice what we were paying other folks. This was still much less than he was paid by other venues, but it was more than we were prepared to pay because all *Z*'s writers get the same and we couldn't afford to double everyone's fee. We fudged, pretty much at my insistence over Lydia's doubts, in what was not one of our most glorious moments.

Chomsky wasn't taking pay for his writing, which at the time was pretty much a long essay for every issue. Noam and Alex were friends, and in fact, if you go back and look you will see that a great many of Alex's best columns for *The Nation* from those days included many passages quite typical of Noam. This was no accident. Alex would call Noam and talk through topics he wanted to address, getting material to use. At any rate, I asked Noam how he would feel about starting to take payment for his articles, but then giving the payment to Alex, to meet Alex's requirement. Noam was game and so Alex got double pay, his and Noam's.

A second odd thing about dealing with Alex was that he refused to use a computer. He would type his articles on an old manual typewriter. He'd then scrawl corrections on the pages and send them in, always after our deadline. I would decipher and then retype his very long essays into our computer, including all the corrections. Once we had that, we would print the article and overnight it back to Alex. Then, invariably at the very last minute, Alex would call us with a new round of extensive corrections that I would have to take verbally over the phone, to then incorporate into a computer file. During the time Alex was writing for *Z*, Lydia worked with all other authors in the magazine and I worked largely with Alex, and this was actually an unequal division of labor, with me the loser in terms of time and hassle. Still, Alex's pieces were awfully good, and so we put up with it. I was more or less supine, over and over, catering like a lackey. I assumed Alex knew, at least to a degree, how difficult he was, but I am not sure that was so. If he didn't know, then of course I blame him less and me more for the situation.

Our relationship with Alex terminated when I entered into a debate with him and the scholar Jim O'Connor about Marxism. This debate ran for a bunch of issues. To read Alex's columns you certainly wouldn't think him a particularly doctrinaire Marxist, much less a Leninist, but in those days Alex did embody a strong streak of Marxism-Leninism. The exchanges were extensive and very interesting, I think, quite unusual in the sense of leftists taking one another's ideas seriously in print, but they ended in a debacle.

Z had discovered Matt Wuerker, a brilliant cartoonist. Matt would do cartoons for articles in *Z*, sometimes at our request, sometimes at his choosing. Matt captured key ideas in beautifully drawn caricatures and/or satiric images. The debate with Cockburn and O'Connor ran from issue to issue, and Matt got into reading it. As the debate was nearing the end, unbidden by us, Matt sent us a bunch of cartoons to go with it, featuring dinosaurs, for some reason, and we put the cartoons in the issue, including using one for the cover. Alex took huge umbrage, feeling that we had misused our power as publisher to graphically stack the deck in the debate. I think he had a point, though it hadn't in fact crossed our minds at the time, and had we thought of it, I suspect it hardly would have seemed egregious, not least in light of the double pay and considerable personal hand-holding Alex received. More, I actually thought Alex would love the cartoons and was surprised that he didn't. Alex had a great sense of humor, loved skewering, and was very much into using art with articles. Indeed, he had as another condition of his writing that he could choose graphics of his own, which were always strikingly unusual, but another unique privilege he had. In any case, Alex didn't like the cartoons and he blew up, thinking, reasonably, that it was he whom Matt had skewered. And after that Alex didn't publish with us anymore, which was a serious loss for our content (though not for our lifestyle). Alex seemed to then get caught up in various pursuits and interests, which also caused him to communicate less and less with Noam. Later, he became involved with a new project, *Counterpunch*, which remains a significant media contribution.

Cockburn and Hitchens, Too

> *Almost everybody is born a genius and buried an idiot.*
> —*Charles Bukowski*

Before all the above, I went to New York to meet Alex at the *Village Voice* where he was then the best regular writer. I went to lunch with Alex, joined by Christopher Hitchens, who then wrote for the *Voice,* too. Chris and Alex, the former a little younger and the latter a little older than me, were educated in Britain, both at Oxford, I believe. That would be a huge contrast even had I gone to Harvard, but having gone to MIT and been schooled in equations and not in prose, history, and culture, our knowledge gap was enormous. And Alex and Chris milked it. The walk from their offices to lunch, the lunch itself, and then the walk back to their offices was a nonstop dialogue between the two of them peppered with literary allusions running from Greece to Russia and back, stopping here and there in the continent, and visiting diverse eras over the centuries. I recognized every fourth or fifth name they dropped (they no doubt thought I was more Harvardish and would at least know who the hell they were quoting) but not the actual references, of course. The funny thing about it all was that I didn't feel dumb, but instead quite bored and irritated at the time I was wasting. I figured there were things to learn from these guys, but certainly not this stuff.

Later Alex and Chris got into a feud. Alex got driven out of the *Voice* for unrelated reasons and Hitchens soon joined him at *The Nation*. Then, as I see it, Hitchens decided that he had had enough of being a leftist literary commentator always looking up at a cement ceiling on income and status, and decided that he could do better being a literary commentator on the right.

One of the very interesting things about Left conversions toward the devil, I think, is that they rarely incorporate a self-critique. Let's suppose Hitchens really believes everything he has been writing since he changed stripes, which I think is probably false. If he does, how come he doesn't tell us why in his earlier years he was so committed to contrary beliefs? Even without mining such oddities as his current support for all kinds of U.S. overseas violence, there is his attitude toward Chomsky to consider. Before his conversion, he regarded Noam as an unparalleled scholar and critic of U.S. international and domestic policies. The only time other than the luncheon date when I spent more than a few moments with Hitchens, he was speaking at an event at MIT. I introduced him to the audience and had some moments to speak with him before and after his talk. He gave a powerful anti-imperialist lecture and during it had reason to bring up Chomsky's work, which he described as seminally and continuously fueling his own views. Since his conversion, however, Hitchens has treated Noam as a demented, careless manipulator of information. One wonders, was the young Christopher dumb and deceived? Or is the old Christopher a liar? Since Chris's conversion, or devolution, or whatever, I haven't had any personal interactions with him.

The other Z author interaction I want to mention was with Joel Kovel, author, green activist, and Green Party candidate. He submitted an article that neither Lydia nor I liked, and we were the whole staff at the time. Kovel was a regular writer. Our approach to authors was if we signed you up for regular submissions, then what you wrote would run unless it was really horribly off base. And if we felt it was horribly off base and we didn't want to run it, the author would have an option to pick three other regular writers to see the piece and if two of them liked it and thought it should run, then it would run even over our objections.

This piece by Kovel was the only time this happened. He petitioned three other writers and they did like the piece, so the piece ran in Z despite the fact that Lydia and I didn't like it. I think it was a good policy to empower regular writers while checking our power. The policy, used formally only that once, faded into operational nonexistence, however, when the relations of writers to Z dropped off from contractual to intermittent.

Z Media Institute

> To teach is not to transfer knowledge but to create the possibility for the
> production or construction of knowledge.
> —Paulo Freire

ZMI began during a discussion between Lydia Sargent and me about the history of another publishing house, Monthly Review Press. Monthly Review was then trying to deal with the aging of its founders. Lydia and I were then far from senility, but we still thought we ought to find a way to pass on lessons from Z's experiences to others. Lydia conceived a fuller proposal for a summer school that would prepare students in the art of creating their own alternative media or of working productively inside media institutions that already existed, in ways consistent with the Z experience. This meant conveying insights into work process, decision making and organization, encompassing politics, and activist skills. And so that's what we set up—or really, what Lydia set up. Lydia is a playwright, director, and actor aside from working on Z Magazine. Through those other activities in our Woods Hole community, and also by working at the Woods Hole Library, Lydia knows what seems like half the local population. This stood her in good stead getting classrooms, making arrangements for housing, etc.

So ZMI began in 1994. Students came for ten days, during which they stayed at a nearby motel, ate at the Woods Hole Oceanographic Institute, and took courses in the community hall downtown, in other town buildings, and at our house. Lydia and I live on Eel Pond. Across Eel Pond a few hundred yards from us is the little town of Woods Hole. Also on the pond, off to the right side from us, is the dining hall of the Oceanographic Institute, which we used for ZMI meals. The setting is idyllic. The pond is a little adjunct of Nantucket Sound, separated by a drawbridge to the ocean. I doubt ZMI could take place in big city. The environment is part of the project, boosting spirits and providing morale without which no one would be able to endure the six hours of courses a day, the additional group session for an hour, a discussion-rich meal three times a day, and a lecture each night, not to mention socializing between classes and, for the students, late into the night.

ZMI houses sixty-five to seventy students for around ten days. At any given time there will be at least four and as many as six or even seven classes held at once. There are four hour-and-a-half slots, and another one-hour slot, between breakfast and dinner daily. Lots of people have come to teach, including Noam Chomsky, Ron Daniels, Cynthia Peters, Stephen Shalom, Barbara Ehrenreich, bell hooks, Danny Schechter, Amy Goodman, David Barsamian, Holly Sklar, Michael Bronski, Chip Berlet, Peter Bohmer, Skip Ascheim, Ezequiel Adamovsky, Andrej Grubacic, and many others. Lydia teaches numerous skills courses and one called Women and Revolution, and I teach sessions on economic vision, political economy, radical theory, revolution, the sixties, participatory society, alternative media, finances, and fund-raising. ZMI doesn't just exhaust the students.

I try to take students through comprehending capitalist economics, the broad dynamics of society and history, an alternative economic vision, and movement strategy. Two of my courses have led to books with the same purpose—*Thinking Forward*, which develops an economic vision from scratch and hopefully conveys the kind of thought entailed in doing so, and *Thought Dreams*, which does the same for radical theory more broadly.

Each session I teach tends to have twenty to thirty-five students. The youngest student might be fifteen; the oldest could be in his or her sixties, or even eighties, one year. Many ZMI students have been in college but some haven't. Many are taking time off from jobs. There have been men and women from the U.S., but also from, in 2005, for example, South Africa, Scotland, Germany, Japan, Canada, Brazil, Turkey, Greece, and Italy, not to mention faculty from Serbia and Argentina. There have been people with tremendous movement experience— ranging from activists from South Africa and Chile, to someone with decades of organizing background in the U.S. There are also new initiates on the Left. What is phenomenal is that everyone operates similarly, attending, talking, and sharing. In my classes, sometimes a new person does better at fielding questions than an old-timer, and other times the reverse happens.

ZMI has graduated over 600 students who are working all over the U.S. and, to a lesser extent, Canada and other places in the world. Of course, the ultimate worth of ZMI resides in the actions of these graduates. But people's time "on campus" conveys a lot. Each summer, when students leave, many relate that they feel they learned more in ten days than they did in their college years. Many cry. ZMI is full of stories of all kinds. Students sometimes perform, showing remarkable talent and creativity. One year, Mark Achbar, as faculty, teamed with some students doing a hilarious skit about participatory economics, the subject of many classes. Songs are written yearly; in some cases life pursuits begin. At any rate, the students arrive and quickly begin to acclimate. Imagine the feelings evoked by a student who had served in Allende's government and reported that after fleeing Chile to Europe, he was horribly depressed both about Chile's condition and about his own exile, and it was only later, by reading Z and finding out about new people with new views, that he gained the spirit and hope to return from despair. Or imagine a student, doing fine, who one day obviously is totally distraught and wants help. In the discussion it comes out that she is a prostitute and her whole world is now upside down. She talks through her experiences and her options in a setting entirely contrary to anything she has known before.

Or, one day, I was walking with a young student who started to cry. He told me he had never experienced anything quite like ZMI. I asked what, in particular, was so special for him. And he told me that while he had already in his young life done a lot of political stuff and met a lot of political folks, he now realized that none of them was really trying to win a new world in the way people he had met at ZMI hoped to. This student was Brian Dominick, who later became closely involved in work on ZNet as well as in pursuing his own many projects, ably applying the lessons he experienced at ZMI. Brian, then very young, explained himself, movingly and cogently. In doing so Brian caused me to adopt ever since as a public-speaking priority rejecting the slogan "fight the good fight." Brian now teaches at ZMI.

I think getting beyond fighting the good fight is actually a very important matter, not just a singular insight of a brilliant young man regarding his own personal perceptions. A social movement that exudes an aura of defeatism cannot win sufficient adherents to change the world. We think we will lose and so, indeed, we will lose. Brian was right that down deep and often even right on the surface, way too many leftists have doubted their own personal efficacy and particularly doubted even the possibility of movements winning new social relations. That's in fact what "fight the good fight" has meant, as I have encountered it, and likewise for the also-prevalent slogan "be on the side of the angels." These slogans say to people, figure out what is morally right and do it and have integrity in the process, so that you "can look at yourself in the mirror." That much is fine, but the slogans also imply we should forget about actually succeeding in our struggles. We are going to get smashed, but hang in there, anyway. The angels will smile on us.

Having been alerted to this attitude by Brian that day at ZMI, I came to think of it as a horrible handicap for leftists. Did Che Guevara think like this? Did anyone who ever helped to change a society think like this? I tried to imagine a sports team or anyone in a struggle having this attitude. The team (or individual) that thinks it is inevitably going to lose has no motivation to develop its struggle-related skills, develop plans, evaluate efforts, and improve them for future undertakings. To hone skills, plan carefully, and assess errors will be a futile waste of time for a team that knows it will lose. When we confront the problem of overcoming racism, sexism, or capitalism, or stopping a war, or winning a strike, or whatever else, if we see the struggle as a monumental mismatch, we won't assess our strengths and weaknesses and the system's, nor continually figure out better ways of struggling. We will have no need for a long view to accompany a short view.

I think this is the mind-set Brian realized he had repeatedly seen and which was replaced at ZMI with an attitude of desire, commitment, and expectation of eventual victory, including a responsibility to bring victory about as quickly and with as little pain as possible. So for Brian and for victory, let's ditch the slogan "fight the good fight" and the associated mind set.

Z Papers, Robin Hahnel, and Me

> *Be true to your work, your word, and your friend.*
> —Henry David Thoreau

In 1994, we produced *Z Papers*, a spinoff from *Z Magazine*. It was a quarterly periodical that would be devoted to longer, movement-oriented pieces. *Z Papers* was designed to emphasize vision and strategy, including debate and accounts of Left practices. *Z Papers* had thirty-two pages per issue, no graphics, and a simple design. We hoped for 5,000 subscribers, but never got beyond 2,500. I think we did some wonderful issues in its near two-year run. I am even inclined to think that we should bring *Z Papers* back, though it was very hard to solicit content. In contrast to *Z Magazine*, where every month we would have three or four times as many articles as we could possibly publish, for *Z Papers* every three months we would have fewer articles than we needed and I would have to write a piece or we would have to solicit one or two at the last minute to fill the issue. This was the difference between having content that was mostly critical of existing relations (as in *Z Magazine*) and having content that focused on vision and strategy (as in *Z Papers*). There was another aspect to *Z Papers*, however, that I would be remiss to ignore.

Lydia, Eric, and I began *Z Papers* with the obvious intention of it being a medium for serious Left explorations beyond what *Z* allowed. It was a journal for the revolutionary Left, not a magazine reaching out more widely. Lydia, Eric, and I were too busy to do it all ourselves. The idea arose to spin off *Z Papers* to Robin Hahnel. I can't remember who had the idea, but, in any case, Robin certainly had the politics and commitments that we wanted and he said he had a graduate student who could do lots of the work with him, and that between the two of them they could solicit content, work with authors, and send us the submissions to prepare as camera-ready copy and to ship to the printers for distribution to subscribers.

This plan ran a bit contrary to our usual notions of organization since it meant Robin and the grad student would initially do almost exclusively editorial work from their base near Washington, DC, and that after they sent the articles up to us, Lydia, Eric, and I would prepare the material for printing, adding a bunch more rote work to our labor. In time, however, we hoped they could do the whole project, taking the whole thing off our hands, not just the editorial aspect. Of course, neither Robin nor the grad student had done anything like this before, both had other responsibilities, and we didn't have money to hire additional people, so the whole picture was problematic.

I went down to visit Robin and when I was there I met with and interviewed the graduate student as well. The session went fine, undertaken in Robin's living room and the project got under way not long thereafter. Robin and the grad student solicited content for an issue, but in the course of working on it, the first stages of hell broke loose. First, Robin didn't like our having a veto over content from Boston. He felt that *Z* was retaining too much control. The key structural point became that Lydia, Eric, and I wrote the checks. Robin would ask us to pay for things, which no doubt felt to Robin subservient, whereas to us, their having complete say over what they were themselves doing, despite having no prior publishing experience of this sort, and despite the fact that it would certainly reflect as much on *Z* as on them, was the major defining feature. Robin felt that unless they had a bank account, they were not empowered. My reaction was that that would be great, if everything worked out, but that for the moment Robin and the grad student didn't have the tools to produce an issue or keep accounts, nor was there any evidence that they had sufficient time, supposing they acquired the means and the skills. It seemed wise to go one step at a time.

While this seemed obvious to Lydia and me, Robin claimed this breached expectations and was a horrible violation of our principles. He felt we were hanging on to the project rather than rightly handing it off completely into their hands. What we saw as their immediately having tremendous say and latitude with a project that rested on our labors for years, including expecting it would in time become entirely theirs, they saw as not giving them enough control fast enough.

I remember Robin getting angry at me over the phone and mainly on a visit down there that was incredibly fraught with conflict of a sort that we had never before had. The *Z Papers* experience became a gigantic and recurring point of pain between Robin and me. Robin and the grad student quit working on the project, and not long thereafter *Z Papers* had to be dumped for want of sufficient readership and writer interest at the level of effort Lydia, I, and Eric could give it.

From my earliest days of meeting and becoming friends with Robin back when I was a senior in high school and he was a freshman roommate to my then-best friend Larry Seidman at Harvard, through our times together as coworkers painting houses, through the tumultuous sixties struggles that we closely shared, through his saving me from LSD, through numerous other dangerous, secretive, and trusting engagements, through our jointly writing book after book and developing shared ideas, through my supporting him in his interpersonal transitions and vice versa, Robin was not only my closest friend, but also a political and intellectual partner of great personal importance.

The last time I spoke with Robin was roughly five years ago in a restaurant in Washington, DC, at the tail end of a visit to try to work things out. Robin claims that his estrangement from me occurred because he decided he could no longer productively work with me. The first link in the chain of dissolution, he said, was the *Z Papers* conflict, noted earlier. He felt at the time that it was about our not fully transferring power. I felt that full transference required demonstrating relevant competence and commitment.

The second link in the chain of dissolution, Robin says, was about our division of labor. When he was arguing this with me he would often say his "comparative advantage" was in writing while my "comparative advantage" was in speaking and creating Left media projects. He said he acceded to my greater talent in speaking and initiating projects, and after thirty years I should accede to his greater skills as a writer. He said our arguing over how something was written was a waste of time for both of us, and he wasn't willing to keep doing it. I should just let him do all our writing. I didn't understand why Robin's thinking he was a better writer would lead him to think I shouldn't write at all, nor why my being a better speaker would lead him to think he shouldn't speak, and Robin's approach to Z Papers hadn't acceded anything. When Robin made his case more aggressively, he would argue that my writing was so horrible it was a debit. Put like that, the logic of his wanting me to completely accede was clearer.

When Robin arrived at this stance, I was writing a draft of the book Parecon: Life After Capitalism. Robin wanted me to stop but I was unwilling to, in part because I thought that while Robin was arguably a technically better writer than I was, I was better at making hard things accessible. Also, whatever the truth on that front might have been, I was without doubt quicker to get things done. I wanted us to do that book like others, which most often meant me doing drafts and Robin editing. Robin didn't want me to write a draft, however, and said his other commitments made it impossible for him to come near the time schedule I preferred. He argued that his doing it more slowly would advance the cause of participatory economics more than getting a book I would write out quickly. I did that book for Verso Press, and Robin did a different one that we had on our joint agenda for Routledge. Each of us worked separately. By the end of this dispute Robin felt my writing anything was selfish and harmful. He claimed it was better that books not exist than that I write them. I didn't agree.

Next, and I think most importantly, Robin claimed that I had become hypocritical and egotistical. Z, and particularly ZNet, wasn't sufficiently pareconish. He felt that under the guise of promoting participatory economics I was promoting myself. While I would angst over these charges to the point of physical discomfort, I couldn't in the end accept them. I tried to be objective, and I hope I was.

My personal feeling that Robin was wrong about my evolving personality, I considered irrelevant. This was because if he was wrong, I would feel that he was wrong, sure. But if he was right, presumably I would feel that he was wrong in that case as well. So my feeling that he was wrong showed nothing.

My long, close friendship made me feel betrayed and hurt, but I thought that was irrelevant to the case, too. That Robin had never constructed anything like a pareconish workplace and had no actual experience with trying to do so amidst market pressures also seemed ultimately irrelevant. Robin was either right or wrong on the substance of his accusations.

Regarding the writing dispute, I agreed that I was a problematic writer. I never needed Robin to tell me that. Writing was never my strong suit. Any gains were hard-won. But my queries of many other folks could never uncover anything like Robin's antipathy. More, I had some amusing evidence to consider. In the ZNet forum system, at its outset, I felt I had to do something to engender participation. People were hesitant to write at all. To prod participation, I logged on with numerous false names, writing messages under each name, giving the system a flow of content that seemed to come from diverse people. I would engage in long debates, not only under my name, but also under four or five other names—including masquerading as two women.

Writing under the false names, I got into debates with all kinds of folks, including with myself. Sometimes these were quite extended and no one ever knew who these prolific posters were. I debated Robin, Stephen Shalom, and other people I knew, using the false personas. I wrote quickly, like for my own posts, though taking significantly different positions for different people. When use began to climb and I was about to stop the practice, I told Robin and others what I was doing. At first they thought I was kidding. When I convinced them it was true and asked them which were my online personas, no one guessed. No one noticed the writing similarity. Yet Robin's claim was that my writing was so idiosyncratically horrible that anyone could easily pick it out, anywhere, anytime, and that my obliviousness to this fact, and my commitment to continued writing despite how harmful my prose was to disseminating our views was no longer tolerable to him.

As to my becoming too hypocritical, egotistical, or intent on my own agendas, I in no way take for granted that this was or is false. It is certainly precisely what one would predict for a person like myself, over time, both with aging and with accruing a steadily growing level of personal visibility and influence. Even in college, I was aware of this danger and trying to prevent it. I had two reactions to Robin saying that I had failed so miserably.

First, if he was right, shouldn't my longtime friend try to help me correct the failings, rather than sever all ties with me? Wasn't that the best choice for him in a personal sense? Wasn't that the best choice for him politically, also? I could not believe that if he did feel as he said, Robin wouldn't have hung in and tried to aid/correct me, rather than jettison me. We had been through too much, with too much shared experience, not to mention the importance of furthering our project of advocating alternative economic vision, for him to throw our ties away. But toss our relationship he did.

The larger structural issue is more or less how do you best incorporate economically desirable structures such as equitable remuneration and work relations and self-managed decision making in operations that must function within markets and with people who have very different backgrounds and commitments? And further, how do you incorporate new people? Do they immediately have the same powers as those who have given years of effort and are lifetime committed? Should they go through a period of partial involvement and empowerment before getting to full equality? How do you have balanced job complexes over long distances, or where there are as yet unlearned skills? How do you cope with differential access to other means of income? How do you protect the long-term integrity of projects even as you pass power over to people who as yet have little background and experience? What do you do about longevity and age considerations?

I think many of these issues arise only because we are talking about an institution seeking to be economically just in a sea of capitalist crap, and not because of desirable workplace priorities per se. I also think these questions don't have one right answer. Rather, in different situations I think different compromises and choices will make sense and will work, or not. For example, I have no doubt that my efforts, alongside others', to help embody worthy norms in SEP, Z, and ZNet have not always been optimal, perhaps at times far from it. But to me, the solution seems to be to try to learn from failings and offer substantive proposals for better ways to function that, in context, aren't personally impossible or institutionally suicidal.

The larger personality issue is more or less how do you exert a lot of influence in the movement at large and garner certain benefits and stature from your efforts as well as your position, and not become elitist? More, if you do show signs of falling down a slippery slope toward becoming elitist, what ought to be done about it?

Again, I don't think there are universal answers. Ironically, many of the choices that guard against the slippery slope to elitism are precisely the attributes others call arrogant and cold. So it goes. My tactics at warding off elitism aren't meant to produce smiles in the manner that crafty paternalism and wily manipulation are wont to do. But how much I have failed or succeeded regarding my own personal trajectory is for others to judge. Indeed, during the dispute with Robin, I asked numerous people to look at e-mail exchanges and to let me know if they felt Robin was on strong grounds. The opposite was repeatedly indicated, with incredulity that the whole thing was occurring.

So what is my take on why Robin and I no longer write together, no longer speak to each other, no longer know that each other exists, in some sense? Confusion. Maybe Robin just did what he had to do. When your best friend sends back all your invitations, what else can you do but understand and move on?

Chapter 26

Going Cyber

Kapor and Bricklin: A Communications Problem

Money is power, freedom, a cushion,
the root of all evil, the sum of blessings.
—Carl Sandburg

It was early in the cyber game that I decided the Internet was clearly going to become a key component of communication. I felt we had to get into it, establish ourselves, and have enough presence so that even if there were an eventual shakeout due to rising costs, we'd be able to stay involved. So in the early 1990s I started, while working at Z, by trying to set up a communications network that lots of folks could relate to. This time I got no negative feedback from friends about the idea. No one knew what I was talking about. They just nodded, there he goes again. This will be a mess for sure.

In those days, creating an online communications network meant establishing our own bulletin board system. I called ours the Left Bulletin Board System, or LBBS. You had to connect by modem. Indeed, LBBS was like a little America On Line, conceptually identical but much smaller, of course. You signed up to join LBBS and you got a disk in the mail. You loaded the software and you could use it to connect to us. After a time, you could also get onto the Internet through LBBS, just like people did through AOL, and you got your e-mail through us, too. Where did the connection software come from? I wrote it. I had no idea what the hell I was doing. I got computer language software called Microsoft Basic, and I got samples of communications connection software. The interface was easy to write and I fiddled about, trial and error, and eventually got the communications part to work.

Providing e-mail was essential to attracting users, but it was torturous for me. Having signed up a few hundred people, I had to keep a computer up and running in the corner of my office or users would lose their e-mail. I was apoplectic when the computer went down. Only about 500 people a week used LBBS, but it was the first stage of *Z* going cyber.

Round one of efforts to fund sustained larger Internet operations was inspired by the way Paul Newman had made an industry out of selling salad dressing. The consumer buys his products and a share of the proceeds goes to social causes. My idea was to do the same thing with software. We would form a company, create programs, and give the revenues from selling them to activist organizations. We would produce games with good educational or political content and tools for organizations and movements.

Many computer programmers in the early 1990s were quite hippie-ish. Once employed in the mainstream, however, they often found themselves creating military, regulatory, or commercial programs of no social merit, or even with a purpose contrary to their hopes. So I thought we could appeal to the country's best programmers and get the more progressive and disgruntled ones to join us. Surely we could then produce good programs, market them, and gain buyers not only because the programs would have value, but because buying the programs would have social benefit.

From my MIT days, I knew a professor named Jerome Weizenbaum who had authored a program called Eliza that mimicked a psychiatrist. It used words you typed in to repeat back to you in question form your own ideas in a "therapeutic session." Eliza was rudimentary but nonetheless made people think they were interacting with something conscious. Some people even preferred Eliza to human therapists. Considering that Eliza was probably a millionth as smart as a pigeon, this was a sad commentary on human therapists. Weizenbaum was very critical of the misuse of expertise in the computer world and I knew he had been moved to the Left by my activities when I was at MIT, so I thought he would listen to our software idea and provide advice. I told him our idea and he put me in touch with MIT graduate students who said they would be happy to work on such a project.

By this time, I had enlisted my friend Michael Ansara into the scheme. He had many more fund-raising contacts than I did. The idea was going to require half a million dollars to set up an operation that would eventually, we thought, earn bushels of cash for the Left. Buoyed by the programmers' reactions, Ansara started looking for money.

The main argument in favor of this project was its multiplier effect. We could ensure donors that the project's programs would be politically and socially valuable, but that was unlikely alone to get them to give us so much money. A sum of hundreds of thousands of dollars, while tiny in the business world, was a lot to seek on the Left. So our primary rationale was different. Give us or just loan us this money, and the operation will not only pay you back with interest, and not only pay all its ongoing costs, more importantly, in in a few years it will yield millions of dollars for progressive causes.

No one would even listen to Ansara about our idea even though, unlike me, Ansara was well known and well liked by rich donors, and could walk their walk and talk their talk. They wanted none of it. I think they ignored our pleas because we were asking donors to fund a machine that could replace them. They liked being donors largely for the stature, power, and control it offered, all of which would decrease by virtue of aiding us since we could eventually provide the funds people were seeking from them.

To call us frustrated doesn't convey how we felt, yet the experiences only got worse. Somehow we got an appointment with Mitch Kapor and Lotus Development Corporation, which Kapor ran and largely owned, and which was, in those days, a notch above the up-and-coming Microsoft. Kapor had been a hippie on a Thursday, and due to programming what became Lotus 123, the dominant spreadsheet in the country, became a multi-hundred millionaire on Friday. Our first meeting was successful. Kapor wore a Hawaiian shirt, shorts, and sandals. Our next session went longer. Kapor liked our plan, and told us that we could create what would become one of the largest computer firms making games and utilities in the country. We asked him to give us some seed money to flesh the idea out for him and others. He hemmed and hawed and hemmed and hawed and finally said, okay, you can have $7,000.

I have no idea how Kapor settled on that figure. Perhaps it was for him the exact equivalent that the price of a hamburger was for me, though by his demeanor you would think he was giving us a king's ransom. Still, Kapor was very interested and he told us about a new program by Dan Bricklin, who had previously authored Visicalc, the main spreadsheet program before 123 and the program that got IBM interested in the desktop computer business. Bricklin's new product let folks easily model their ideas for programs. You could create a shell showing what a program would be like without doing any tedious programming. Mitch made an appointment for us to see Bricklin and try our idea on him, and to get a copy of Bricklin's program to use to bring back software ideas that Kapor could look at.

It seemed we were barreling toward success. Kapor alone could easily fund us, and he was clearly impressed. Bricklin could help, and we were on our way to see him. So we went to Bricklin, told him the idea, and waited for his response. He thought for a bit and told us he thought it was brilliant. Programmers would love to help create socially valuable products. Hell, he himself would love to do so, but, well, he would only join the effort if he could be CEO of the company, including being guaranteed a large percentage of all surpluses plus full control. It was a giant Catch-22. If Bricklin took any part of the profits we couldn't be giving all the profits to the Left, which was the whole sales appeal of our proposal. Likewise, if he were CEO, even if there were some way to generate donation funds beyond his profits, he would oversee their distribution. With him having no radical politics, our priorities would be torpedoed. To our show of incredulity, Bricklin threw up his hands, and said, take it or leave it. He was basically saying, "Yes, it can work. Yes, I like it, but I am too greedy to help you out." We left, unsatisfied, but at least Bricklin gave us his tool for displaying programming ideas and told us that he was sure the idea could fly. For about a week, I took the Bricklin display tool and designed interfaces for about ten possible programs that I dreamed up. All but one were simple games or tools for nonprofits. For the last program, I wanted something more substantial to impress Kapor, so I did a model of a program people could use to generate and evaluate alternative strategies in complex situations. I liked the idea, which I thought had a potentially large audience among athletic teams, businesses, movements, unions, candidates for office, and so on.

So, back to Kapor we went. I demonstrated the various ideas and Kapor was again impressed. He thought they were all doable and could sell. The only idea he had reservations about was the big strategy-creator/tester. That he mulled over for a bit. Then he said, you guys can't do that, it is just too big for you, but it is a good and interesting idea. Maybe someday Lotus will do it. Okay, I was satisfied. He thought the package had the potential to be a large software publishing house. We pushed him to support us. He laughed and said he already had done so: the $7,000. He had gotten us that far, now we'd have to find someone to get us the rest of the way. He didn't have time to be involved and he wouldn't put in a significant sum if he wasn't intimately connected to daily operations. Before long Ansara was off on his own things, I was back to my normal pursuits, and the idea was dead.

LOL and ShareWorld

If you make money your god, it will plague you like the devil.
—Henry Fielding

During the above efforts, LBBS morphed into Left On Line (LOL). It was now a self-contained system on the Internet with a variety of services, including sections of essays, a forum system, and e-mail. You could access it from the Internet or you could dial in. The World Wide Web was just coming into play and it wasn't clear whether the future would belong to the Web, something almost no one believed, or if self-contained systems with their own proprietary content, like AOL and CompuServe, would dominate. I was using some pretty sophisticated packaged software for LOL and had some impressive capabilities on our site, including being able to display graphics and text, and even some audio. It was torturous to maintain, but I was learning and providing useful service even if it was on a quite small scale.

At this point, I guess a year or two had passed, and I went back to Ansara with another idea designed both to get funds for the Left and, this time, also to create something politically positive. We would build a community of networked systems. Each system would cater to a specific constituency, such as all members of an organization or a profession, and would provide all its users a closed online community serving their special needs. A member of a particular constituency would receive our software and have access to their own mini-AOL, created especially for their organization with its look and feel and facilities, but through which they would also be able to connect to the then-fledgling World Wide Web. More, we would link all these many constituency-based systems together so that each user who joined any one of the systems would get access to most of the content that all of the systems provided. This meant Left On Line content would be easily available to all the other constituencies served by the other proprietary systems we would build. Likewise, we would have lots of tools in these systems facilitating discussions, forums, group voting, working together, and open display of information.

Ansara was by now head of a company called The Share Group. The Share Group did primarily phone fund-raising for progressive groups. Indeed, Z had already contracted with Share a couple of times to raise funds by phone. This time I went to Ansara with my idea for a community of Internet systems both because he had the financial foundation from which to back it (the startup costs would be much less than for the earlier project) and even more so, he had the connections to groups that would be needed to make it successful.

Michael did phone fund-raising for Greenpeace, the Democratic Party, and the AFL-CIO, as well as dozens of smaller operations. My idea was a fund-raising scheme for its clients, too. Each organization we built a system for could say to its membership, we want to be your Internet provider. You should not give your money to AOL or CompuServe. You should give it to us—to Greenpeace, *The Nation*, your union, your party, your professional association, or whatever community—because then the funds will enhance your community's ability to serve and/or fight on your behalf. More, the system we provide will be a central tool for communication among all our members. It will facilitate polling and voting, provide information and useful tools, and give users an easy way to meet and share ideas and experiences with other members. Even now, I can't write about this idea without frenzy sweeping over me. It was a good idea. Indeed, here is just how good it was.

After a lot of meetings, as well as a considerable cash outlay by Share Systems, we had an online infrastructure and software package. We were in position to sign on clients. The deal Ansara and I made was simple. He was the CEO. Share would finance the operation. The whole thing would be called Shareworld. Each component would be named for its host, so there would be Nation On Line, Greenpeace On Line, Librarians of America On Line, and so on. Fair Share would own 51 percent and Z would own the rest. For $10 a month the community member would get online access, plus their community system, plus features of the larger Shareworld. Of the $10, after costs, some would go to the sponsoring organization, some would go to Shareworld. For giving up control of the firm that was emerging from my idea and my work on LBBS and then Left On Line, I got, as part of the deal, the right for Z to produce Left On Line, which would be prominently accessible to all users from all communities, and Z would entirely control its contents as well as get 49 percent of the overall surpluses. Ansara and Share Systems, with my help but not my oversight, would do everything else and get 51 percent. This was a very unusual and desirable arrangement. More typically, the fund source would have all but a few percent of a new firm.

Our plan was to sign up a couple of nonprofits in order to test the presentation, create the package and promotional materials, and prepare and test one constituency system, either Nation On Line or Wilderness On Line. Then we would show that established operation to a bigger client—Greenpeace was our plan—and then we would use that deal to go after a megaclient, either Labor On Line for the AFL-CIO or Democrats On Line for the Democratic Party. We reasoned that if we got all this, we would leave AOL and all other providers in our wake. Remember, they were just getting going, and the AFL-CIO was alone a pool of about 12 million people, for whom there was no reason to think that if their unions offered them less expensive and better access than non-union-affiliated corporate operations, plus offered the bonus that their payments would do social good, plus offered special union-designed services, they wouldn't sign up. Shareworld was potentially mammoth.

Well, the bottom line is, after infinite haggling and cajoling, we got the initial systems up and running, built the packages and met with the officials of each organization. While getting big decisions from nonprofits is worse than herding cats, all the targeted first participants were on the verge of saying yes, including Greenpeace, the AFL-CIO, and the Democratic Party. Had things proceeded as they were unfolding, who knows what the result would have been of Shareworld, run by Share Systems and Z Magazine? It could have been bigger than AOL, with LOL prominent, and with the funds shoveled back into the Left. Then, however, the roof cracked a little. Greenpeace announced huge internal cost-cutting due to catastrophic operational problems. They decided they couldn't proceed. That hurt, but wasn't enough to stop us. We just needed either the Democratic Party or the AFL-CIO, both of which Fair Share frequently contracted to do phone fund-raising for and both of which were in negotiations for the system and by all accounts close to signing on. But then the roof collapsed. A news story broke and suddenly Michael Ansara was embroiled in a giant scandal involving violation of the bylaws of a union and breaking various federal finance laws.

Michael had helped fund-raise in a not-so-permissible way for a campaign to beat the young Hoffa in the Teamsters and to elect the more progressive Ron Carey as its president. The ins and outs of what occurred are for his memoirs, not mine. In fact, Ansara refused to even talk to me about the events, afraid that if he did so I could be drawn into the legal actions as well. But the AFL-CIO and Teamsters knew a whole lot, and likewise for the Democratic Party, which was then suffering some scandals of its own. They both jettisoned Shareworld like a hot potato. One day we were contemplating a new world of big money and big communication, the next day we were entirely destroyed. It got far worse for Michael, who was under a kind of house arrest for a long time, fined inordinately, and greatly reduced in his capacity to operate. All this was a horrible shame. Michael had both positive and negative qualities of many sorts, like most people, but in his ill pursuit he was just trying to do some good. Regarding funding, he was one of the few leftists willing to face the difficulties of seeking ways for activists to escape dependence on foundations and big donors. That Michael and I failed to bring Shareworld into being was a horrible setback.

ZNet: Cyber Success

I am always doing that which I can not do,
in order that I may learn how to do it.
—Pablo Picasso

Net's funding was a kind of spinoff of Shareworld in that LOL became ZNet, a free Web site that has grown steadily and is, as I write this, perhaps the largest progressive site in the world and surely the largest site that is so assertively anticapitalist. ZNet often has as many as 300,000 users a week. When I began to travel widely, I discovered that people all over the world not only read ZNet, but downloaded material for local dissemination. My first encounter with this was when a young man approached me at the second World Social Forum in Porto Alegre and told me he lived in a village in the Amazon forest area. He and some friends traveled with difficulty to a larger city each week, downloaded content from ZNet, and then printed it and brought it back to their village for others to read. This gave me quite a new impression of what we were doing and what its reach was.

In the early days of ZNet, we had a page online making a case for why it was important to donate. In our best months we took in perhaps $200. The donors got nothing back except the satisfaction of knowing they were helping build the operation. This wasn't going to pay the bills. We needed more revenue, not only to build the site, but also to underwrite *Z Magazine*, from which the Internet was taking subscribers, and to help finance ZMI and Z Video, too.

I had the fortuitous thought that perhaps we could develop a sustainer program in which people would pledge to donate, on a monthly, quarterly, or yearly basis, to receive access to an online forum where some writers—and, in particular, Chomsky and I, would be accessible for queries and discussion, and also a commentary e-mailed each night. We lined up sufficient writers and announced the program that became a critical foundation for our operations.

Even with that income, however, in 2004, our overall Z operations got into trouble. Our accounts were dwindling fast and we were losing an average of $7,000 a month. We were facing catastrophe in just six months. We met and decided we could cut about $2,000 a month in *Z Magazine* costs and maybe another $1,500 a month in ZNet costs. We also thought we could increase Z Video revenues some, but clearly we had to do something pretty dramatic to the Sustainer Program to avoid returning to constantly recurring crises and perhaps collapse. Indeed, I figured we needed to shift the cash flow in our favor by $12,000 a month to ensure that even if we were underestimating our current shortfalls, or if some of our costs got worse in the next couple of years, we would have at least a modest net surplus each month to help us get back into acceptable shape.

In what we hoped would only be a one-time return to the early days of taking huge risks to win stability against all odds, I made an outlandish proposal. On the one hand, we easily agreed to make a broad and desperate appeal, commensurate to our actual condition, seeking immediate donations. We did that, and over a few weeks it brought in roughly $90,000, which was quite impressive. Second, of course, we would simultaneously aggressively urge people to join as new sustainers. This gained us about 700 new sustainers, which was good for about $5,000 a month.

What "aggressive" meant was that we replaced the ZNet top page for nearly ten days with a call for help, including providing information about our situation, descriptions of how we would use incoming money, instructions for donating, and testimonials from lots of prominent leftists. We also featured this statement from Chomsky, which was sent out to our lists as well, as part of the appeal. I have no doubt that this was the most effective single component, for which we again owed Noam our thanks. Here is some of what he wrote.

Z and ZNet have played a crucial role in serving all of these [movement] functions. I see that every day. I travel and speak constantly, in the U.S. and abroad, and spend many hours a day just responding to inquiries and comments. I constantly discover that the people and organizations I come in contact with are relying very substantially on Z projects for information, discussion, and opportunities for interaction and organizing, to an extent that is quite remarkable. It also is an invaluable resource for me personally, in all of these respects, and also in my case for providing a forum for intense and very constructive discussion, the only one I regularly participate in. And for posting articles, interviews, commentaries, etc., of mine. I know that many others have very much the same experience.

It is of inestimable importance, in my judgment, that Z and ZNet continue to flourish and expand, not to mention their growing video efforts and incomparable media school, arguably the most exciting and instructive I have ever encountered. Again, I do not think it is possible to exaggerate the stakes. I hope that all of us who are committed to resisting and reversing the powerful currents of reaction and oppression and violence, and showing that another world is indeed possible, will contribute as best we can to ensure that the remarkable achievements of Z and ZNet will be carried forward.

Okay, so all that worked well, but we didn't know that it would, so to cover all bases and be sure of success, I controversially suggested that we simply raise the amount that current donors were giving by raising their pledges in our database by 20 percent for most of them and by 30 percent for those at the high end. Someone donating a total of $50 a year would jump to $60 a year. Someone donating $120 a year would jump to $156 a year. My reasoning was that, with the exception of the most recent members, sustainers had been donating for up to four years at one rate. They could choose their own amount. They could change it at any time, either up or down. However, if we were to urge them to go online and access their account page and please raise the donation amount, maybe a few hundred would do it. Five thousand wouldn't, not out of explicit refusal, but because they just weren't inclined to hack their way to their account page and change it. On the other hand, if we did it for them, I argued, few people would mind.

So, we wrote repeatedly to people telling them what we were going to do, and telling them that all they had to do was reply to the e-mail and say they didn't want their donation changed, and their amount would not be touched. A couple hundred did so. Later, we also wrote telling people that they could go to their account page and set new amounts themselves. Chutzpah, call it what you will, I felt that if we didn't do this and the other approaches didn't work, we were risking complete collapse.

If we didn't alter the donation levels, no one would be pissed off, it was true, but in that case, everyone using ZNet would be pissed off when the operations failed. If we did raise amounts, however, some people would certainly fail to see our messages and encounter the change only on their credit report, and call us thieves or whatnot. We had no idea how many would be in this camp. On the other hand, we reasoned, people's money could be refunded and while we would take a hit due to some people getting angry, Z and ZNet would persist. Following this logic, raising the donation levels seemed like a good idea to me—though Lydia, Andy, Daniel, and Eric were dubious. I thought morality was with us due to all our advance communications and because we could easily refund money to those who missed the warnings, and because of the gigantic moral and social costs of ZNet failing. I also thought pragmatics were on our side because I intuitively knew that most people would understand. There would be some hostility, yes, but nothing we couldn't handle.

After a time, we reached a consensus to do it. We sent a few e-mails announcing what we were doing and when, and in response a couple hundred people asked that their rates not be changed. Everyone else's rates were altered, and the money was collected. Later, there were indeed some complaints, but further explanation defused concerns. The upshot of the campaign was that stability and even some room to maneuver returned to Z operations.

ZNet grew in diverse ways. One was through translation into Spanish, Italian, German, Turkish, Arabic, Czech, Bulgarian, Japanese, Norwegian, and Swedish by volunteers. Some of these undertakings have had many more people working on them than work on the English operation. ZNet also has Watch Areas to focus on parts of the world such as Iraq, the Mideast, or Colombia, or on broad areas such as economy, global economy, repression, or race. There are facilities for users to upload quotes and song lyrics. There are two forum systems and a blogging system. We host, also, *Z Magazine* online and a store for Z Videos. And there are sections for debates, interviews, and so on. The work has been done by me, from the start, and by a shifting group of other people including Brian Dominick, May Allen, Daniel Morduchowicz, Justin Podur, Stephen Shalom, and Cynthia Peters. Others have also volunteered by working on particular watch pages, sending materials, and especially doing translations. As I finish this book, we have hired Chris Spannos, as well, to be another staff member.

The structure of ZNet has been very loose. I run the show, I guess I have to admit, in that I do have final say. But all people working on ZNet have pretty much complete autonomy in their area unless they're doing programming that affects the whole site, or perhaps an article that arouses concern among other participants. It is hard to have a fair distribution of tasks with people located in distant cities, giving very different amounts of time, having varying long-term relations to the project, and having different other responsibilities they have to meet beyond ZNet. But we try to get a good balance, not without disagreement and even dispute, so as to apportion decision-making power proportionate to the degree people are affected by the choices made. Actually, truth be told, other then choosing articles to post, there aren't a lot of decisions in ZNet.

Keeping On Keeping On

No pessimist ever discovered the secret of the stars or sailed an uncharted land,
or opened a new doorway for the human spirit.

—Helen Keller

I am often asked how come I am nearly always optimistic, even amidst bad news. I don't know if my approach can serve others, but on the off chance it might, I relate it. Beyond looking on the bright side, I constantly envision highly desirable outcomes. This part is an athlete's trick, I think. Athletes examine the shot, the routine, the climb, the hit, or whatever they are about to do in their mind's eye in advance. They imagine it unfolding to victory. I started envisioning the equivalent of victories, I think, in summer camp when I was about ten years old. If I was getting tired in a canoe or a swimming race, I would focus on just a modest distance ahead, to succeed in reaching it, and would then refocus a little further and succeed again. That had its limits, but later I began envisioning and daydreaming about successful results to motivate continued effort in the face of long odds.

Envisioning winning when I was at MIT regarding the GI sanctuary and, later, the campus presidential election helped me give both undertakings full energy. Envisioning my first book getting published help me to finish writing it. Envisioning South End Press succeeding, and then likewise *Z*, propelled my work on each. Envisioning all kinds of successes that haven't happened, including the computer firm, Shareworld, unions of leftists, and new organizations, propelled work on each in turn.

The second part of my technique is that I typically envision successes that exceed what I can plausibly attain. I saw SEP as being as big as Houghton Mifflin. I saw *Z* attaining audiences like *Time Magazine*. I saw organizations moving masses into world-changing activism. I see this memoir on the best-seller list, transformed into a Hollywood Oscar-winning movie by Damon and Affleck or maybe Redford and Fonda. Sometimes, nearly nothing emerges from my efforts. Other times, something quite desirable comes into being. What emerges, however, rarely lives up to what I saw in my mind's eye. Yet somehow the gap between my imagination and reality never reduces my inclination to move on. Whatever emerges each time I try something creates a new starting point for new daydreams of larger successes to come. I envision victory, but I understand the probability of failure. It keeps my motor churning.

Chapter 27

Alternative Media

Media and Democracy

Our system is one of detachment: to keep silenced people from asking questions, to keep the judged from judging, to keep solitary people from joining together, and the soul from putting together its pieces.
—Eduardo Galeano

South End Press, *Z Magazine*, Z Video, Z Media Institute, and ZNet are all alternative media. But what else? And what defines alternative media? The Second Media and Democracy Congress was held in October 1997. It attracted nearly 1,000 people from media operations around the country. An opening panel on "Money and Institution Building" was sponsored by the conference's grassroots elements. The audience was from small, highly stressed, nonprofit projects. The panelists were Jay Harris, publisher of *Mother Jones*, and Hamilton Fish, past publisher of *The Nation* and current president of The Nation Institute.

At one point, Fish noted that *The Nation*, for various reasons, is not nonprofit. It doesn't matter that *The Nation* has investors, however, Fish told us, because the investors have no impact on the periodical. Five minutes later, he jokingly pointed out that the then-main investor, Victor Navasky, was sitting in the room listening, and also just happened to be both publisher and editorial director of *The Nation*. Everyone chuckled at this tiny little influence of an investor, and Fish continued. But Fish might have also noted that were the structure of *The Nation* (or *MJ*) abstracted out of its masthead and placed alongside a structural map abstracted out of the masthead of *The New York Times* or *Time Magazine*, there would be few consequential differences. No one asked why, if funding played no determinative role, almost all of "our periodicals" are run from the top down by either the primary donor/investor or the key fund-raising person in the institution.

Periodically, folks at the Media and Democracy Congress tried to describe who we are. Their answer—"We are 'independent media'"—meant that "We are media not owned by national or international conglomerates." One analyst explicitly urged that we use this precise term, "independent," rather than such vague concepts as "alternative." Other analysts at least implicitly eliminated all but the "independent media" label by refraining from using other adjectives. And when panelists did use the label "alternative," they were so vague it may as well have meant "independent" anyhow.

"So what?" you might ask. Well, the term "independent media," with its given definition, encompassed Z, the *Village Voice, The Nation, Monthly Review*, micro radio, Pacifica, and NPR—and it also encompassed right-wing newsletters, small corporate Cable companies, and local capitalist consumer guides. In fact, anything fit—right or left, large or small, authoritarian or democratic, racist or multicultural, patriarchal or feminist, statist or anarchist, and corporate or anticorporate—as long as the outfit wasn't owned by Time Warner, et al. So if you were me, sitting there, you felt like most of what matters to you about what you were doing was lost in the stew.

What I was provoked to ask myself was, is *The Nation* an alternative media institution? What about *Dollars and Sense* or *Mother Jones*, or, for that matter, *Z Magazine*? Did these institutions make decisions in an acceptably democratic manner? Did they treat workers properly? Did they have good relations with their audiences? Had *Monthly Review* gone in a good direction in becoming a collectively organized project, or did it make an unwise choice? What had been the problems at Pacifica Radio and did they have anything to do with a contradiction between Pacifica's "alternative" aspects and its lingering (or resurgent) "mainstream" aspects? Were college radio stations alternative? What about micro radio stations? What should an alternative Internet provider look like? What about an alternative video production company?

Within any media institution, a question that drove me was how do we know what is "alternative" and what isn't? How could we judge whether compromises were unavoidable responses to external pressure or reflected a lack of internal commitment? Were the advertisements in *Utne Reader* really alternative to those in *Time Magazine*? To what extent should alternative media institutions work together rather than compete? To what degree could each project be concerned with more than simply preserving itself? To what extent should progressive "media consumers" actively support alternative media? Did getting your critical information for free mean you were an astute alternative media consumer? Were alternative media institutions doing all we could to reach nonelite audiences?

These questions seemed to me to be the strategic ones of substance. Did it make sense that the *Village Voice* called itself alternative but was virtually identical in its structure, finances, and decision-making attributes to typical corporate institutions, and, moreover, had no intention of making any changes in those aspects? It was still "alternative," because the *Voice's* CEO said it was.

What my time at SEP and Z and analyzing mainstream media said to me was that a mainstream media institution most often aims to maximize profit or surpluses. It typically sells elite audience to advertisers for its main source of revenue. It is virtually always structured in accord with, and to help reinforce, society's defining hierarchical social relationships. It is generally controlled by and controlling of other major social institutions, particularly corporations.

In contrast, my experiences told me that an alternative media institution shouldn't try to maximize profits or surpluses, shouldn't primarily sell audience to advertisers for revenues, should be structured to subvert society's defining hierarchical social relationships, and should be structurally as profoundly different from and as independent of other major social institutions, particularly corporations, as it could be. An alternative media institution should see itself as part of a project to establish new ways of organizing media and social activity and should pursue these ends as a whole, and not just for its own preservation.

Of course, I understood that mitigating circumstances could limit how much an institution seeking to be progressive could forgo profits and surplus, avoid commercial advertising, reach beyond elite audiences, remove typical hierarchies, and actively support other similar projects. Social and market pressures might make it hard for people to push in alternative directions on all fronts at all times. But surely trying to make progress on those various fronts should be a condition of being alternative. If the phrase "alternative media" was to have any social implication it must have some substance, was my reply to the panel at the Media and Democracy conference.

Time and Us

> *It is difficult to produce a television documentary that is both*
> *incisive and probing when every twelve minutes one is interrupted*
> *by twelve dancing rabbits singing about toilet paper.*
> *—Rod Serling*

On Saturday night at the Media Conference there was a *Nation*-sponsored thematic panel titled "State of the Media." This has promise, I thought, as I sat waiting for it to get started. Walter Isaacson, the editor of *Time Magazine*, sat on stage with Katha Pollitt, Christopher Hitchens, Farai Chideya, Mark Crispin Miller, and Bill Moyers as moderator. Moyers did his job, trying to provoke interesting exchange, and Isaacson did his job, posturing about his institution. What I found disturbing was "our side" of the affair. Mark Crispin Miller castigated *Time* for running covers that promoted its parent company's movies and there endued an unenlightening exchange about the ills of cross-promotion. Indeed, the only interesting aspect was revealing the extent to which Isaacson's reaction to every point was to first note *Newsweek's* similar policies, saying how could *Time* do otherwise, implicitly acknowledging the power of market competition to limit options.

At one point, Katha Pollitt made the much-needed point that talk about *Time* being owned by a parent conglomerate was really beside the point. *Time* was no better editorially fifty or five years ago, before the intense centralization of media. But no one then asked, okay, what is it about *Time* that makes it despicable, if not media centralization, and, what lessons do we take from that? No one challenged Isaacson with serious documentation regarding *Time's* biases, the relative weight given to certain types of stories, the absence of certain types of content, and so on. There wasn't a single word spoken about the class structure within *Time* or about Isaacson's power within the institution. There was almost nothing about the structural role of advertising; no questions were asked regarding the makeup of the budget or about how important ads are and what advertisers wanted. There was no analysis of ten years of *Time* covers or of a year's worth of its columns. An opportunity to use *Time*, and its editor, to make points more broadly about mainstream media and its role in society was, I felt, squandered.

In some ways, even worse, Isaacson was treated with kid gloves, almost as if the panelists wanted to retain good relations with him. Isaacson is near the top of the media apparatus that sustains, justifies, typifies, obscures, and partakes of crimes against humanity every day of every week. Why was he treated so congenially to the point of avoiding disagreement and contestation? Why wasn't his organization subject to aggressive analysis, to make the points that needed to be made about mainstream media, both for the audience at hand and for those watching C-SPAN or who would hear the exchanges on radio? What was it about a panel like this, or the pressures on its participants, or their circumstances, that yielded such an ineffective outcome? Was it too much cocktail circuit interactions for speakers, as many in the audience said? Had debate become just a game or a job, not a part of movement building? Also disturbing was that the same people who sat in the audience disparaging members of the panel as "performing" would then sidle up to them, praising them, laughing and joking with them, leaving them, of course, feeling that everyone had a grand time, the script had been just fine.

There was much at the Media and Democracy Congress besides these few panels. Some was troubling, some quite productive. For example, there were highly instructive gatherings about radio production and creation, and about telecommunications politics and options. There were informative gatherings about media concentration, about campaigns regarding public media, about building community, about diversifying media staffs, and so on. *Z* did a panel on what makes alternative media alternative that argued that media institutions should be labeled alternative only if they agree that reducing income differentials, disentangling authority from money, developing jobs balanced for empowerment so that all can partake of decision making intelligently, incorporating truly democratic and participatory decision-making structures, steadily diminishing gender and race biases in employment and in on-the-job culture and product, and developing nonelite outreach and mutually supportive relations are worthy goals to inspire our policy making.

Michael Moore gave a sidesplitting but provocative talk arguing that the latent class biases of much of the Left were a horrible obstacle to the growth of progressive activism. The trouble was that after the laughing not much attention was given to the implications of Moore's claims. I wondered what would happen if Moore submitted a piece to *The Nation* that not only said that the antiworking-class cultural preferences of the Left were a problem—how can someone organize in the U.S if they exude condescension toward anyone religious, or anyone who roots for a ball team, or who enjoys Nascar—but went on to say that the more basic problem is the attitude that working people are stupid, manipulated dolts, common to many who are central to defining the Left, and particularly who finance the Left and persist in organizing Left projects that replicate the structure of General Motors.

Suppose I said the *The Nation*'s culture was indistinguishable from the Ku Klux Klan's, or the *The Nation's* gender hierarchy was indistinguishable from the Nation of Islam's. Folks would look at the situation, and if it were true, they would go bonkers. But *The Nation*'s structure was (and is) indistinguishable from *Time Magazine's* and this bothers virtually no one on the Left. Corporate structure is accepted as a given. Anticapitalism doesn't run deep, yet. So, of course, why bother trying to have a truly worker-led and defined Left?

I remember listening to a talk by Pat Scott describing Pacifica Radio. She made reference to the need for our media to learn from mainstream counterparts like *Time* and *Newsweek*, to mimic their structural accomplishments and professional qualities. I sat there infuriated. To me it was as if someone had said we should learn from the gender characteristics of *Playboy* or *Penthouse*, or that we should learn from the racial policies of a Southern slave plantation. Pat Scott was telling us that what alternative media lacked could be found in the structure of CBS, which is to say, in the structure of class-divided corporations. What shocked me wasn't that Scott said it, it was that the audience didn't reject it.

PART 5

Mind Trips

In the sixties, interminable orations often maximized macho debate. Infinite repetition often minimized timely practicality. Everyone hated mental meandering. Nearly all meandered anyway. One alternative was to rush right in, tread foolishly, draw drastic conclusions, act impetuously, and sink like a radical stone. No meandering—but also no victories.

I decided a better technique would emphasize shared concepts that could facilitate quick communication. I started to speak and write and also to organize media projects. I tried to conceive worthy concepts. Writing about mind trips may be even more taxing than writing about events and engagements. Here goes something, I hope.

Chapter 28

Pomo: What Is It Good For?

Postmodern Car Ride

It should be possible to explain the laws of physics to a barmaid.
—*Albert Einstein*

Preparing to ride from Boston to New York to attend a mid-nineties Socialist Scholars Conference, I asked a friend of mine to please explain postmodernism during the five hours we would spend together on the road. He accepted the challenge. Off we went. He lectured. I listened.

When we got to New York, if he had asked me, "What is postmodernism?" I could not have answered. Five hours and I still didn't know what postmodernism was. Was my tutor incapable of explaining one concept in five hours? Was I incapable of understanding one concept in five hours? Was the concept a vague pastiche of mush too tenuous to clarify?

Of these options, I suspected that I didn't get post modernism because there was nothing to get. I thought to myself, suppose you are an English literature teacher and you wanted a high salary, intellectual status, and tenure. How would discussing *Crime and Punishment* or *Ode on a Grecian Urn,* much less Madonna's lyrics, warrant receipt of big salaries, big status, and paid trips to distant conferences?

I decided that to justify these rewards against the claim that the work was commonplace, one good rationale would be that there was a "theory" essential to the work that took years to master and that some people employed better than others. In this view, its incomprehensible "discourse" gave literary theorists defensible stature. Perfectly sensible faculty doing good things had to toe the line, talk the talk, and write the words, to preserve the posture.

Looking at what literary theorists said about novels, movies, MTV, modern architecture, pop songs, and modern literature, I found discourse about

311

postmodern moments, binarisms, pure systematicity, metanarratives, deconstruction, irreducible materiality, and dialogisms. Did pomo's prophets really need such terms to comment on pop music's Talking Heads, TV's *The Young and the Restless*, Hollywood's *Star Wars*, baseball's Dodger Stadium, or literature's Ishmael Reed? And even if "irreducible materiality" and "pure systematicity" were exactly the concepts needed to "theorize" Madonna, couldn't pomo's prophets popularize their results sufficiently for the rest of us to know there was something meaningful going on? Even the most difficult physics is typically described so that nonphysicists can get a good idea of the main results, methods, and questions. If popularization can illuminate theories about quantum decoherence, gluons, big bangs, black holes, and even multidimensional "brane worlds," surely popularization could illuminate theories about everyday culture and communication, couldn't it?

When I wrote about all that in some essays in *Z Magazine*, I got a lot of mail. from people happy that someone was publicly ripping at postmodern allegiances. These messages were not only from young students, but also from full professors. They acknowledged that there was a fog over various professions that people had to call clarity, an obfuscation that people had to call wisdom, an irrelevance that people had to call innovation, a disconnection that people had to call genius—not to mention an obscurantism that people had to call artistry. I became even more convinced that postmodernism included statements that were familiar, long-known truths made linguistically obscure, statements that were trivially false though hard to discern through surrounding verbiage, and statements that were neither true nor false but unintelligible and meaningless. What was wrong with me that I couldn't see pomo's shining light? Was I color blind to pomo's insights?

Close Encounter of the Pomo Kind

The covers of this book are too far apart.
—Ambrose Bierce

I first met postmodernism, cerebellum to cerebellum, in 1992. Stephen Marglin, an economist friend at Harvard, invited me to speak about economic vision to an academic meeting in Amherst, Massachusetts. About thirty faculty from many fields met periodically to explore new ideas and they wanted me to speak. So I drove out and met folks and we chatted and they did some business, and we had some food, and then I began to argue the need for economic vision and why I advocated participatory economics. About ten minutes into the talk I could see I was losing the audience. They weren't walking away, nor were they seriously considering my words. They were drifting. Well, actually, they were past drifting and entirely into another zone.

I stopped speaking, and said, roughly, I can see this isn't working. I am losing you. Is there something causing you to dismiss me? Frederique Marglin, a prominent anthropologist, answered, more or less, yes, you are right, we are drifting off. It is clear you aren't going to convey things we need to hear. Dumbfounded, I asked, how can you know so quickly? I have barely begun making a case for vision in general, much less for participatory economics in particular.

Frederique replied, but we can tell how you think. You are offering evidence. You are using logic. You think you are bringing us truths that we need to address. I bet you are a scientist of some kind. Looking down, I wondered if I was mishearing. I replied, yes, I had a background in physics and economics, but what difference did that make? Yes, of course I was trying to make compelling arguments. Why else would I take their time with my talk?

Frederique said, but there are no truths, only stories, and trying to make a case that you are saying true things tells us that you aren't worth listening to. I felt that I was in wonderland, but Frederique was not kidding. I said, of course there are truths. What about Newton's laws? But before I could list more examples Frederique said, no, they are just another story.

I might as well have given up right then, but after a bit I asked, do you realize you are dismissing me without referring to whether my words are valid or not? "That's Stalinist," I blurted. They laughed and said, no, it was wise. I said, but you use logic all the time. They said, sure, but we know its limits.

I said, I, too, know its limits. I know that I am aware of my feelings of incredulity at your utterances not due to logic but via my emotional reactions. I know that the lawn outside is green by my senses, not by science. I know what love is by my experience of it, not a theory of it. For that matter, I know how to talk and to decipher what other people say not via science, but via my genes and my history. But I also know that in domains where logical argument and evidence can be brought to bear, the logic and evidence have great importance.

They couldn't see that, or at least they claimed not to be able to see it. But of course none of them consulted feelings to decide whether to fly in airplanes, or to decide whether the table in the room was 99.99 percent empty as science said, or was entirely solid as their eyes told them, or whether the sun was a modest-sized smooth orange ball floating about a mile high, as perception suggested, or was a raging tumultuous gargantuan furnace floating 93 million miles away, as science claimed. Rather, when it was available, they believed evidence and logic. But apparently they didn't want me to do likewise.

I was rejected without reason, because reason was rejected. My hosts displayed sectarianism in the name of eliminating sectarianism. They exercised fundamentalism in the name of eliminating fundamentalism.

I spent a lot of time addressing these matters in ensuing years. Postmodernism was not something that welled up inside me as an intellectual curiosity I had to explore or a mental itch I had to scratch. I would never have had a word to say about postmodernism but for the fact that on campuses, postmodernism was attracting many of the most progressive and hardworking potential activists and spitting out something much less beneficial to humanity than ought to have emerged.

The biggest effort I made to curtail people drifting toward pomo was to propose to Lydia and Eric that we devote an issue of *Z Papers* to the topic. They agreed. I asked Steve and Frederique Marglin to recommend others to include as advocates of postmodernism and at their suggestion a number of scholars were included. I asked Noam Chomsky and Barbara Ehrenreich to join me on the anti postmodernism side. We had dueling essays. The issue appeared about eight months after the Amherst meeting. In one sense, it was an exemplary exchange of conflicting views that readers could judge for themselves. In another sense, the whole debate was a bit odd because each side thought the other was blind.

After the exchange, I had some e-mail exchanges with Kate Ellis, one of the pro-postmodernism participants, and I included a query as to how she was doing, and mentioned that I felt the debate so revealed postmodernism's advocates as lacking any serious rationale for their commitments that they might have felt it was a big mistake to participate and might be angry over its having occurred. Kate replied, saying she was feeling fine, thanks, and wondering about me. Did I mind having lost so badly in public? Here we had an extended exchange involving nine people. Six argued for postmodernist views and felt they had annihilated their three critics. Three argued against postmodernism and felt we had barely even had an opposing position to address and felt sorry for them. The communication gap hadn't diminished. It was arguably wider.

I had many more encounters with pomo, but the question arises, having in my own mind established that reason isn't ratty, what did I have to offer regarding social theory? If the meeting with the thirty academics in Amherst had gone on, what truths would I have tried to establish?

Chapter 29

Better Flakes

Theory: What Is It Good For?

*I learned very early the difference between
knowing the name of something and knowing something.*
—*Richard Feynman*

I was once in an auditorium with Victor Weiskopf, who was then chair of the
MIT physics department. We were listening to a renowned practitioner of
physics. Weisskopf confided how he thought only a few people could enjoy
the beauty of nature as we physicists could, comprehending its outer edges and
deepest depths in their most subtle interconnections. I decided this was crap.

There was a time when Pythagoras's theorem was known to a small cabal of
folks on the cutting edge of human thought. Now teenagers make short work of it.
Darwin's theories were once beyond the comprehension of virtually the entire
human community. Now the average college freshman today can better
understand Darwin's work, in some respects, than it was understood by Darwin
himself. There was a joke about general relativity shortly after its public unveiling.
When told that only three people understood the theory, the British physicist
Arthur Eddington wondered who the third person was, beyond Einstein and
himself. Yet relativity is now routinely taught in college.

Some disciplines do operate with a technical language and accumulation of
past understanding so hard to master that only a few people ever get to the heart of
them, even when the knowledge is no longer new. But Weiskopf wasn't saying
that. He thought he was doing what others couldn't do, not what others wouldn't
do. And yes, there are people who do what others can't do, not in understanding
established insights, but in breaking boundaries and conceiving new ideas in the
first place—but they don't often celebrate themselves for their innovations. They
just pursue them.

At MIT, I also once chatted with a renowned pure mathematician, a breed I rarely came across. I asked him how many people could understand his last publication. He said he thought maybe six people in the world. I asked how many people would ever understand it, and he replied probably no more than a couple of dozen. He may well have been exaggerating, but it was true that the path to understanding what he had written was arduous and few people would bother traversing it. The mathematician gloried in that. I found it peculiar.

So what is theory? From Saturdays at Columbia University during my high school days, to four years at MIT, through economics training at U Mass Amherst, and into a lifetime of science and philosophy reading and economic and social theorizing, my answer has been simple. Weisskopf and postmodernists aside, theory is a bunch of words and various special interrelations among them. Each word is a concept. Concepts highlight areas of concern and aid or impede understanding and action.

These thoughts propelled my first book, *What Is To Be Undone,* in 1972. The idea of *What Is To Be Undone* was to discover underlying reasons for problems in Marxist Leninist practice. What was it about how Marxist Leninists labeled the world and how they saw relations among the parts they highlighted that caused their commitments to skew harmfully?

Marxism and Leninism

It is the mark of an educated mind to be
able to entertain a thought without accepting it.
—Aristotle

The beginning of my Left theorizing was my confrontation with Marxism. Of course many people shouldn't bow over with little dignity and nearly no say in their circumstances. Nor should a few people strut with their heads high holding a baton of leadership. But Marxism's deepest concepts let me down as often as they inspired me. Marxism had too much about hours of work and not enough about sex and celebration. Marxism didn't explain the better things in life, nor did it explain rape, lynching, denigration, or sectarianism. People don't solely sleep, eat, and work, as Marxism seemed to assume. On paper, Marxism was too pat, too confident, and too narrow. In practice, it was too centrist, statist, and authoritarian.

When I was first becoming radical, however, Marxism was my guide. Indeed, anyone who was trying to be seriously leftist in the sixties, much less seriously revolutionary, was at least at one time largely Marxist. There wasn't any other accessible and encompassing ideological option. Anyone could ask questions. Questions were blowing in the wind. Answers were scarce. Anarchism was more congenial to young people's preferences, including my own, but anarchism was less popular and had fewer compelling answers. So when young people, I among them, adopted a conceptual toolbox to take us from reflex rejection of the world to reasoned analysis of its prospects, the toolbox that had the most answers was Marxism.

I think I started imagining my first book, *What Is To Be Undone*, the afternoon that Robin Hahnel clarified much about Marxism for me in the MIT Student Center. I never went into Marxism advocacy mode. I studied and used and was made cogently anticapitalist by Marxism's insights, but right from the start I was trying to discern weaknesses. I read books by Marx, but also more recent works clarifying Marxism. I remember an obscure book titled *Human Nature, The Marxian View*, by an obscure fellow named Vernon Venable, for example. I was reflexively inclined by my desire to understand the world in order to change it to try to reveal and even correct Marxism's faults. How could people miss that its conceptual picture of humanity was narrow and restricting?

I had learned regarding physics that a scientist could pursue evidence ratifying an existing framework. She might tease out the implications of a dominant school of thought and refine its predictions in some new situation. She might demonstrate some predicted behavior or verify to greater precision what was already taken for granted. A scientist could also attack a widely-held framework, seeking to demonstrate its inadequacy and find clues to developing something new in its place. She might do a crucially contradictory experiment or reveal conceptual flaws. Even further, a scientist could proactively leap from broad critical feelings amassed via intuition, guesswork, analogies, or any other serviceable means to propose new concepts or connections that provide new explanations and predictions and, finally, a new toolbox. Of these possibilities, critique and innovation were my personal preference when doing physics, and became my preference as an activist, too.

In *What Is To Be Undone (WITBU)*, I sought to unravel Marxism and Leninism, concept by concept. I tried to trace the cause of problems in broad analyses all the way back to errors in core concepts. I didn't think it was misapplication or shoddy use of the Marxist framework at fault, which is what Marxists would claim when accosted with Bolshevik "excesses." I thought, instead, it had to be underlying, defining ways of seeing reality's interconnections. I thought it was not some kind of hijacking by Leninist movements that was the problem, much less stupidity, but the intrinsic implications of Marxism's primary conceptual commitments.

On the road to *WITBU*, I was much influenced by anarchist and also libertarian Marxist literature. Bakunin, Kropotkin, Rudolf Rocker, and Anton Pannekoek were my tutors, among others. I remember being quite affected by lesser-known works, too, such as a couple of essays by Maurice Brinton, "The Bolsheviks and Workers Control" and "The Irrational and Politics." Likewise, an essay by Wilhelm Reich titled "What Is Class Consciousness" affected me greatly, as did Andre Gorz's work on nonreformist reform struggles, some work of Cornelius Castoriadis on values and vision, Stanley Aronowitz's wonderfully enlightening book *False Promises*, Arthur Rosenberg's short *History of Bolshevism,* and Chomsky's work. But what made me write my first book was a movement need. Leninist sect members were all over the place. You looked to the left, you looked to the right, you looked up the block, you looked down the block, you looked anywhere, and there would be some standard-bearer waving his or her bible. Hooray for Mao, Marx, or whoever—jaws clenched and minds rigid. They marched on.

Leninist sects always had answers for everything. In one sect, there was one answer. In another sect, there was another answer. Sometimes the answers overlapped. Sometimes the answers squared off, ready to kill or be killed. Religious devotion made the views of sect members highly suspect even before considering content, but I felt the broader issue was where does such ideological devotion come from? What was it that led good people to holler bad views? What was it about these groups' shared attributes that yielded sectarianism? Maybe some people with stylistically bible-thumping inclinations had gravitated to Leninism, but my sixties impression was that Leninism produced book-thumping inclinations in even the most levelheaded person who joined the fold. In *WITBU,* I tried to unearth a conceptual basis for that. I have to wonder, though, what made me think, at age twenty-five, with no discernable talent for writing, I had enough to say to write a book, much less to feel my book would uproot widespread beliefs.

Beyond its criticisms of Marxism Leninism and its initial formulation of contrary views, *WITBU* had another important attribute. I sent the book to a small publisher in Boston called Porter Sargent. They wanted to publish, but they were horribly short on means, so I volunteered to produce the book using typesetting equipment in a movement center at the edge of Boston's Chinatown. Lydia and I did this together. We went down late at night, night after night, typed, developed film, laid it out, and made endless corrections.

Lydia and I had to keep the typeset pages in our freezer so they weren't ruined by heat. One evening, toward the end of the project, we arrived home and saw that our apartment had been looted and the freezer had been sacked. Typeset pages were all over. Our thief had seen the packages and figured they must contain something valuable. Luckily, only a few pages were seriously damaged. The experience of writing and producing *WITBU* and watching Porter Sargent Publishers do nearly nothing to promote and distribute it helped motivate Lydia and me to create South End Press. On the other hand, *WITBU* did not engender a public discussion leading to widespread dissolution of Marxism Leninism. *WITBU* garnered zero attention and achieved little visible effect.

My next big intellectual step was a book titled *Unorthodox Marxism* (1978), which Robin Hahnel and I wrote together. Many unorthodox Marxist ideas percolated while I was in school at U Mass Amherst as explanations to myself for why I would sit in classes, challenging claims. I would argue with Rick Wolff, for example, about Marxism's denial of the relevance of human nature or its assertion of human nature's infinite plasticity, which I saw as patently absurd. I also argued with Wolff about the pompousness and counterproductive implications of "thinking dialectically." I disputed the Labor Theory of Value's abstractions with Wolff, and also with Bowles and Gintis. After *Unorthodox Marxism,* but continuing the same project, there was *Marxism and Socialist Theory* and *Socialism Today and Tomorrow* (both 1981), which Robin Hahnel and I also wrote together. These books, too, looked at Marxism and Marxism Leninism. Race, gender, and power entered the discussion more explicitly than they had earlier.

WITBU was by a young critic, naive and angry. It had no sense for situating words in context of what anyone else thought or how others might react. *WITBU* gave my views as they were unfolding while I setting them down. *WITBU* unreservedly rejected Marxism Leninism and supported various libertarian and anarchist alternatives. In contrast, when Robin and I wrote *Unorthodox Marxism, Marxism and Socialist Theory,* and *Socialism Today and Tomorrow* we tried to retain ties to Marxism and Marxists. The focus in the first volume was largely economics, though our movement-bred concern for the totality of social factors was evident then, and increasingly with the second two volumes. In the later work, concern for vision escalated.

I quickly went from being a cautious Marxist advocate to being aggressively anti-Marxist, then back to being a congenial critic of Marxism, and finally into full rejection of Marxism—though with nuance. I always knew Marxism wasn't dumb or vacuous. I realized brilliant old frameworks had abiding strengths we always benefit from. I also realized that brilliant old frameworks needed to be transcended. I joked about Marxism's rejection of human nature. Could a baby person become a kangaroo? No? Then of course there is a human nature distinguishing us from kangaroos.

If people and species were infinitely malleable, as Marxists claimed, presumably one could mold a chipmunk into a whale or vice versa by manipulating their environments. Indeed, one could mold Rick Wolff into a chipmunk or a whale. I remember imagining a society that could bend us until we enjoyed being slaves. I imagined another that had us trying to be free, but not enjoying it. In the first case, I saw we would be getting what we wanted though what we wanted

319

would be entirely imposed by our environment. In the second case, I saw we would not get what we wanted and, again, what we wanted would be entirely imposed on us. I realized that the idea that it was unavoidable to mold people, so why not mold people from the top, according to plan, so they would want what they got, was equally serviceable to Leninist and corporate rationalizations of hierarchy. Rejecting this mentality was the stuff of my fraternity days. My morality and personality sought to find a flaw in such beliefs, even before I could muster evidence and logic. I sided with Chomsky, who said we should try "to determine the intrinsic human characteristics that provide the framework for intellectual development, the growth of moral consciousness, cultural achievement, and participation in a free community." Even in *WITBU* I was already trying "to determine the intrinsic human characteristics."

Jean-Paul Sartre once joked that Marxists think of people as eating, sleeping, and working. Robin Hahnel and I ran with that pejorative observation, realizing that our conceptual basis for understanding history had to start with a broader view of human beings. If we wanted to pay close attention to gender, race, sex, and even the human dimensions of class and economics itself, our concepts would have to highlight more than eating, sleeping, working, and ownership. Sartre, by the way, is interesting for many reasons. I once heard that when asked about taking amphetamines to stay awake at night and have more energy while writing his major works, Sartre replied that he knew it would take some years off the end of his life, but that he'd rather have the greater productivity now than a few more doddering years later. Jean-Paul Sartre, in other words, used the same reasoning as my young friends in Somerville who decided they would sniff glue because the gains now outweighed costs in their dead-end futures.

Marxists typically anticipated system collapse. They thought capitalism would unravel and that history's grim reaper circled above society to pounce one day. Since for Marxists people were infinitely malleable, contradictions leading to social change had to owe only to features of society. Marxists think capitalist economies intrinsically push us in contradictory directions, leading to dissolution. Capitalists had to impose obedience and exploit workers. Workers had to seek better conditions and more income. The clash would create a new future.

Robin and I saw society differently. People had intrinsic needs and capacities that couldn't be molded away and that conflicted with restrictive institutions. The clash between people and institutions fueled resistance, including but not confined to class struggle. There was no inevitable grim reaper of societies. The poor and oppressed would have to transcend the present to reach a better future. Robin and I also rejected Marxism's accounting of use and exchange value in its Labor Theory of Value. We prioritized bargaining power as arbiter of relative incomes and emphasized the impact of the economy on consumer preferences as well.

When writing books, Robin and I would talk a lot, most often with Robin sitting and with me pacing around, each of us bouncing ideas off the other. I would write first drafts. Robin would edit them, with me constantly pestering him to pick up the pace. My hectoring wasn't always pleasant for Robin. Then again, his stately pace didn't suit my manic side.

The civil rights and women's movements forced Robin and me to reject economism. Life wasn't exclusively governed by material desires and economic relations. Race/community and culture mattered. Sex/gender and family mattered. But working hard to understand the conceptual myopia of economism forced us to reject the parallel conceptual myopia of cultural nationalism and radical feminism and, indeed, to reject any approach that explained all of society via a single underlying logic. Our critique of economism pointed us toward finding a conceptual tool chest that not only prioritized diverse dimensions of life, but also forced us to see how each dimension affected and altered the rest. We rejected the notion that all society rested only on economic foundations, or only on sex/gender foundations, or only on cultural foundations, or only on political foundations. We asked, how did different realms each exist and evolve, and, more, how did each help determine and even define the rest?

There were other factors and innovations, but I think the driving dynamic determining which ideas took hold of me when I was first becoming thoughtful about social theory was the anarchist tendencies in Robin and me, and around us in the youth movement and also in our elders in Boston such as Howard Zinn and especially Noam Chomsky. All this led Robin and me to a gut level and also to an informed rejection of Leninist party politics and the standard Marxist Leninist visions. I was harsher about all this than Robin, but both of us realized early on that power currupts, or as Bakunin put it, "take the most radical revolutionary and place him on the throne of all the Russias or give him dictatorial power, and before a year is past he'll become worse than the czar himself."

The Marxist Leninists we knew in the sixties did not understand the need to embody the attributes we sought for the future even in our current efforts, much less in our most hopeful aspirations. "We want the world" did not mean to us that we wanted to own it, rule it, or run it. Marxist Leninists did not understand, as Martin Buber put it, that "one cannot in the nature of things expect a little tree that has been turned into a club to put forth leaves." Marxist Leninists did not understand the logic and priority of participation, or, as Rosa Luxemburg put it, that "historically, the errors committed by a truly revolutionary movement are infinitely more fruitful than the infallibility of the cleverest central committee."

Our early opposition to Marxism Leninism was lifted to another level by the Ehrenreichs' essay on class relations. Thereafter our opposition extended into a new attitude to class, economics, and social change. Contesting Marxism led us beyond Marxism, but in the years since those days I have often nonetheless engaged in debates, disputes, and discussions with Marxists. Marxism's heyday in the U.S. provoked Robin and me to write the four books mentioned above, but in subsequent years Marxism's U.S. influence has considerably diminished. My interactions with Marxism Leninism have, since the seventies and eighties, often been with people overseas, and have often felt academic because in many activist movements Marxism now exists only in significantly adapted forms, if at all. But for me, while recent debates have been less urgent than earlier due to Marxism being less ubiquitous, the most basic issues have barely changed. Confronted by Marxism's sixties adherents urging me to embrace their approach, I asked myself how should I decide whether to use Marxism as my guiding intellectual framework. I decided to investigate if Marxism's concepts highlighted what was most important and left out what was most peripheral. Did they reveal the roots of oppression, conceive liberating vision, and inform effective activism?

I knew that Marxism's virtues included that it explained ownership relations, pilloried profit-seeking, revealed market madness, and highlighted class. But I also knew that Marxism misoriented us. I saw Marxist dialectics the way I saw postmodernism years later. I doubted there was anything there, beyond verbiage. I thought that when activists utilized historical materialism's concepts, they systematically undervalued and misunderstood extra-economic social relations.

To my thinking, Marxists needed to admit that Marxism mainly conceptualized economics and needed to admit, as well, that conceptualizations of other realms offered equally central insights. They needed to realize that influences from other domains could centrally contour economic relations, just as economics could centrally contour other domains. But even more, for me the really big issue with Marxism was that it got the economy wrong. As early as *Unorthodox Marxism*, Robin and I felt the Labor Theory of Value misunderstood wages, prices, and profits and turned activists' thoughts away from seeing the importance of bargaining power and social control.

Robin and I also felt, however, that these ills of Marxism could easily be transcended, and we worked to do so by proposing an unorthodox Marxism. But more damningly, we also came to feel that Marxism denied the existence of what we later called the coordinator class and ignored its antagonisms with the working class as well as with capital. For us, it was this failing that most obstructed class analysis of Soviet, Eastern European, and Third World noncapitalist economies and of capitalism itself.

I admired how Marxism revealed that class differences could arise from differences in ownership relations, but wondered why Marxism claimed only property relations could generate class difference. Why couldn't other economic relations divide actors into critically important groups? Once the question arose, it was clear that factors other than ownership could be important. Looking at either a large workplace or the whole economy, Robin and I—following the Ehrenreichs and, before them, Mikhail Bakunin—easily saw that some employees monopolized empowering conditions and had considerable say over their own work situations and over other workers below. Other waged employees endured disempowering conditions and had virtually no say over their own or anyone else's work. Within capitalism we saw not only capitalists and workers, but also a coordinator class of empowered actors who defended their advantages against workers below and who struggled to enlarge their power against owners above. "Class analysis," we thought, needed to better understand the coordinator class and its role in seeking change.

The more attention we gave the issue, the more we felt that this coordinator class could actually become the ruling class of a new economy with capitalists removed and workers still subordinate. My biggest problem with Marxism became that it obscured the existence of a class that not only contended with capitalists and workers within capitalism, but which could become the ruling class of a new economy, most aptly called, we thought, coordinatorism. Indeed, Robin and I saw this new economy as combining public or state ownership of productive assets and corporate divisions of labor. It remunerated power and/or output. It utilized central planning and/or markets. In other words, what we saw as coordinatorism was what its advocates called market socialism or centrally planned socialism. What we saw as coordinatorism was what Marxist Leninists celebrated as the goal of struggle. What we saw as coordinatorism was the system adopted by every Marxist party that had ever redefined a society's economic relations. Thus, what made me feel that Marxism ought to have declining relevance was that Marxism's economic goals amounted to advocating a coordinator mode of production that elevated administrators, intellectual workers, and planners to ruling status.

Marxism used the label "socialism" for this goal, but in my view this was to appeal to people of good will. Marxism did not structurally implement socialist ideals such as equity, justice, and full democracy, nor did Marxism offer a programmatic vision that reflected those values. The situation was ironically analogous—as I thought Marx himself would surely point out were he around to comment—to how bourgeois movements used the label "democratic" to rally support from diverse sectors but did not structurally implement truly democratic ideals. The devastating conclusion of all this reasoning was to see that Leninism was a natural outgrowth of Marxism, and that Marxism Leninism was, due to its focus, concepts, values, goals, and organizational and tactical commitments, the theory and strategy of the coordinator class. My sixties intuitions had matured into a view that Leninism employed coordinator-class organizational and decision-making logic and sought coordinator-class economic aims. If I wanted to help achieve classless relations, and I did, I couldn't be Marxist Leninist—and I wasn't.

Spurred by my critical reactions to Marxism Leninism, it seemed to me that we should emphasize all the material, human, and social inputs and outputs of economic activity. We should emphasize the social and psychological as well as the material dimensions of class division, and particularly the impact of corporate divisions of labor and of market and centrally planned allocation on class hierarchy in capitalism and also in coordinatorism. Doing that would cause us to reject market and centrally planned models of a better economy and to gravitate toward new structures, which seemed to me to include council self-management, remuneration for effort and sacrifice, balanced job complexes, and participatory planning.

For Robin and I, our thinking in this direction was very much propelled by reading about the Soviet experience as understood by its anarchist critics. I thought that council self-management was what the Bolsheviks had destroyed in the Soviet Union. I felt coordinatorism had its roots in various Marxist Leninist concepts and commitments, not least in Lenin and Trotsky's ideas of one-man management, which is why those concepts and commitments had to be jettisoned. My readings of Marx taught me to ask of ideologies or conceptual frameworks, who did they serve? Would their inclusions and exclusions make them suitable or unsuitable for us? I decided Marxism's conceptual framework left out important economic relations to the benefit of the coordinator class. The implication was that Marxism had insights we could borrow, of course. But as to the overall conceptual package—following Marx's advice—we would have to transcend it.

Britain and Marxism

> We don't bother much about dress and manners in England, because as a nation we don't dress well and we've no manners.
> —George Bernard Shaw

I have been to Britain a few times. I have spoken in London, Cambridge, Oxford, and a few less-known towns. Two of my trips have been to speak at a large Marxist conference put on each year by the British Socialist Workers Party (SWP). I am an unrelenting critic of Marxism Leninism and particularly of parties formed according to that rubric. I gave talks in the largest rooms, to large crowds. There was more effort by the SWP to make what I had to say prominent than I often get at talks where what I am saying is congenial to conference sponsors. It struck me that there was no anarchist venue that would feature so prominently a Leninist speaker critical of their efforts. I thought the SWP's willingness to have me criticize their views to their audience was admirable.

An amusing moment occurred while I was sitting outside a hall preparing a talk. It was to be a debate about Leninism with Alex Callinicos, the SWP's most revered theoretician. Someone came up and asked, are you okay? Do you need anything? I said, sure, I'm fine, do I look ill? No, they said, but in just a few minutes you have to go on stage and debate, and Alex will be favored by nearly every person in the room. That's gotta be daunting. Actually, I said, it isn't. Shortly before this event I had spoken at Alex's university and he had introduced me. It was one of the most complimentary introductions I have ever gotten. Alex finds himself wondering why he likes so many essays that I write, given that I am so critical of much that he holds highly important. I think it is because Alex isn't a Leninist because he wants to impose hierarchy throughout society, but out of a sincere belief that only Leninist methods have a chance to win change. Alex doesn't get upset when I talk about coordinatorism, or even when I argue that Marxism is the ideology of the coordinator class. He just says he doesn't like that aspect either, but he thinks, if used well, the Marxist Leninist framework can escape those important problems, and that if we don't use that framework, we lose. It is an honest difference. Nonetheless, I also think under pressure of escalating events, sadly, Alex and I could find ourselves diametrically opposed.

Class or Multitude

> *A map of the world that does not include*
> *Utopia is not worth even glancing at.*
> —*Oscar Wilde*

Antonio Negri and Michael Hardt authored a book that became an international Left bestseller, *Empire,* and then a couple of years later authored a second book called *Multitude.* These books claim to be innovative works seeking to escape old-style Marxist concepts. My own encounter with Hardt and Negri's ideas occurred most forcefully when I was invited to be on a 2005 Left Forum panel with Hardt and some other folks discussing "Class or Multitude." What I had to say shows, I think, how the views I have had on Marxism can have relevance even when dealing with people who say they are seeking to transcend Marxism.

As to the question "Class or Multitude?" my brief reply at the panel was that we need new class concepts, yes, but we don't need the concept "multitude." My reasoning was that class concepts at least focus us on the difference between owning factories and selling one's ability to do work. This difference produces capitalists versus everyone else. The source of this difference has to be eliminated if we are to transcend capitalism. So we must pay attention to it. But further, I stated that I also thought good class concepts should focus us on the fact that some people do work that conveys knowledge, confidence, and control over daily life. The work these people do is empowering. The people doing it give orders. They define tasks and decide who does what, at what pace, and with what distribution of results. Their knowledge increases. Their confidence grows. Other people, in contrast, do work that is overwhelmingly rote, obedient, and disempowering. They follow orders. They do not set schedules or agendas. They do not decide outcomes. Their knowledge decreases. Their confidence erodes. On the one side, I argued to my Left Forum audience, we have people I want to call coordinators—which in the U.S. includes high-level lawyers, engineers, doctors, accountants, architects, and managers—the daily designers and administrators of the economy and its protocols, roughly 20 percent of the workforce. On the other side, we have people we call workers—which in the U.S. includes assemblers, bus drivers, short-order cooks, miners, maids, nurses, and waitresses—the daily implementers of economic dictates, roughly 80 percent of the workforce.

I wanted classlessness, I stated, which meant I wanted all workers to enjoy conditions of comparable empowerment and quality of life at work. I wanted all people in the economy to have a fair say in outcomes. I did not want to transcend capitalist rule only to still have 20 percent coordinators ruling over 80 percent workers. I therefore argued that we needed class concepts not only to perceive the machinations of owners, but to highlight the three-class structure of modern economies and guide our efforts to eliminate not only an ownership basis for class rule, but also a division-of-labor basis for class rule.

What about Hardt and Negri's concept "multitude"? I thought multitude meant those people who, by virtue of their economic position, are very good prospects to become revolutionary in revolutionary times. Taken in that sense, "multitude" would replace the old "proletariat," or even "working class." As Hardt had put it in an earlier interview, "[This] is one way in which you might think of our notion of multitude as being very close to a traditional notion of proletariat, that is, the class of all those who produce, once the notion of production itself has been sufficiently revised and expanded." But wouldn't using a new multitude concept conceived on the basis of production be too much like using the old term proletariat, also meaning revolutionary agent, and also based on people being producers? Despite multitude being defined more broadly than proletariat was defined, like the word proletariat, the word multitude seemed to me to identify a revolutionary agent based only on examining economic foundations. I feared that emphasizing multitude as agents of revolution conceived as economic producers would hide the reality that procreation, sexuality, socialization, celebration, identification, adjudication, legislation, and implementation count as critically as production in people's conditions and consciousnesses, and in potentially igniting or thwarting revolutionary inclinations.

That was one-half of my conceptual case against elevating the concept of multitude. For the other half, I noted that with multitude guiding our thoughts, even just regarding the economy, there would be potential bad guys—maybe multitudinists would call them capitalists, or emperors, or whatever—and there would be potential good guys, the multitude. This would be bipolar, just like when the conceptualization of economic struggle was capitalists versus proletariat or working class. The trouble with a two-class approach, I urged, was that it would exclude perception of the coordinator class and make it seem that beyond bad capitalist economics there could only follow either more of the same or good multitude economics. This was, I suggested, quite like orthodox Marxism Leninism's conviction that there is capitalism and beyond it there is either more capitalism or socialism. But, I told my Left Forum audience, we could also have a bad postcapitalist economy that had institutions that elevated what I called the coordinator class. Trying to shoehorn all social reality, or even just all economic reality, into a narrow class concept like multitude was wildly backward in its implications. Highlighting multitude obscured the independent priority of race, gender, and political structures and papered over the coordinator/worker difference—just as Marxist Leninist concepts had obscured and denied these same central elements.

Maybe I should have stopped at that, but I had a little time left, and I went further. To make a worthy bottom-up revolution in the U.S., I argued, would require at least a hundred million people becoming informed advocates and designers of a better future. This multitude, if you will, of revolutionaries, would have to comprehend historical possibilities. They would have to propose and refine strategies. The tools of revolutionary comprehension would have to be widely shared. To me, it followed that talking about democracy, participation, or self-management in a language that required great privilege to utilize was not conducive to creating democracy, participation, or self-management.

Hardt and Negri's word "multitude" was fine, I therefore suggested, as was the word "empire," as they were usually used. But the fact that I honestly didn't know what either word meant in Hardt and Negri's books seemed to me a damning problem. It could be that I just happened to lack some otherwise widely held capacity needed to read Hardt and Negri and to hear what they said. Or it could be that these books were hugely more obscure than serious activist theory and vision should be, so that they couldn't be understood by more than a tiny fraction of the population. I had two copies of *Empire*, I reported. I had read maybe twenty pages. I understood virtually nothing from doing so. I doubted I was alone. I doubted that it had to be so dense and that, in time, it would be explained. I added that I feared that most often, obscurity in Left communication wasn't a failing of writing and speaking, but instead reflected the implicit view that revolution is to be led by a small sector of professionals who have ample time to learn new languages. That is a Leninist bias, I asserted.

Other panelists gave their presentations. And there was time for panelists to reply to each other and for the audience to ask questions. There was much discussion but none of the panelists had a thing to say about the need for accounting for a third class or the problems posed by the possibility of a coordinator-oriented anticapitalist vision. Not a word. And there was barely a word, either, about a return to economism. I am not saying I was right in everything I argued. I am saying that what I argued wasn't so obviously wrong as to be unworthy of comment. But it got none.

I think the concepts that the other panelists used and the concepts I used illuminated reality differently, and those who used Marxism-based concepts couldn't hear my descriptions of the terrain. It is, after all, the whole point of debates about theory that some theories direct us away from realities we need to perceive, and it is also why the above discussion of multitude appears here. Was I being directed away from what matters, or were others? The second step in my own mental gymnastics, well before debating "multitude" at a NYC Left conference, but well after rejecting Marxism, was to try to help create a new conceptual framework.

Liberating Theory

A child of five would understand this.
Send someone to fetch a child of five.
—Groucho Marx

What kind of concepts, connecting in what patterns, could escape Marxism's tendency to be economically narrow? That was a central question coming out of my sixties experiences of feminism, black power, and antiwar work; writing on Marxism Leninism; getting economics training; and all the rest. How could a viewpoint be simultaneously true to feminism, cultural concerns, anarchistic inclinations, and class concerns? How could a viewpoint see each domain of life in its own right while also seeing how each affects and is affected by the rest? How could concepts combat their user's socially imbued tendencies to exaggerate one side of life at the expense of other sides, yet also inform and support their perfectly reasonable desires to pursue one side of life over others? A black person, woman, gay man, lesbian, worker, or other person with deep and rich experiences of a part (or parts) of social life and a desire to primarily combat one particular part (or parts) of society's totality of oppressions should certainly be aided in doing so. Yet the process should enrich their likelihood of aligning with people prioritizing other parts of social life.

Liberating Theory (1986) was a book that tried hard for conceptual innovation. I enlisted to work on this project not only Robin Hahnel, my regular cowriter, but also Lydia Sargent, Noam Chomsky, Leslie Cagan, Mel King, and Holly Sklar. We were all friends but also had a range of political constituencies we appealed to and different personal backgrounds.

Robin Hahnel and I had already thought through the framework we hoped the book would refine. I wrote a draft, Robin worked it over, and then we sent our work to everyone else, each of whom sent back his or her reactions. Each person predictably had more concerns in the areas closest to his or her experiences, and fewer concerns in what they had experienced less. I incorporated everyone's proposals and requests as best I could. Tensions arose when there were conflicts over different proposals but we finally arrived at a multi-authored text addressing race, gender, class, and power. *Liberating Theory* assessed popular conceptual approaches, proposed improvements, and even set out a new way of thinking about history involving all four angles of analysis at once. *Liberating Theory* wasn't long or abstruse. People could have grabbed, read, and discussed it. Nonetheless, *Liberating Theory* fell on largely deaf ears.

At the time, I wrote that I hoped that our effort could "reinvigorate our desires for and capacities to achieve a better future." Leslie Cagan wanted to "offer activists a nudge in the direction of taking the task of building our theory more seriously." She hoped *Liberating Theory* would "provoke discussion, open up debate, motivate further theoretical work, and play some role in inspiring us all." Robin Hahnel hoped the book would help people "develop a new understanding of society and ourselves suited to human potentials and able to promote solidarity among people with different priorities." Mel King hoped the book would "galvanize antiracists, feminists, disarmament activists, anti-interventionists, gay and lesbian liberationists, and everyone seeking a better world to live and grow in, helping each with their own priorities and to connect to all the others." Holly Sklar wanted the work to "help close the gaps in our movements and serve as a guide for a movement deserving and capable of taking power and creating a new democracy." Noam Chomsky hoped *Liberating Theory* would "stimulate others to undertake a critical analysis of the ideas presented and to develop them further and join in helping to bring the dream of a better world a few important steps closer to reality." Lydia Sargent wrote that she hoped the book would overcome sentiments "that the opposition is too strong or that the Left is too weak, or that political disagreements and sectarianism can never be overcome, or that we lack a vision, solidarity, courage, commitment, analysis, skills, and knowledge" so that "all those involved in Left political practice [would] bring their unique perspectives, personalities, and humor to the process of creating and working for a better society."

The key insights of *Liberating Theory* arose from looking at society as a fourfold product of kinship/gender, culture/community, power/politics, and class/economy relations, with a set of conceptual tools able to reveal how the influences emanating from each of these centrally important parts of society affect the other parts, and vice versa. We realized that if highlighting one center of influence and attention was insufficient, we needed more centers of influence and attention. For that reason, *Liberating Theory* conceptualized fields of social force emanating from core economic, political, cultural, and kinship institutions. But then, having posed the existence of four centers of social influence, we had to describe what kinds of effects each could have on the rest. We quickly realized that one possibility was that a social hierarchy born in one place would be respected, not violated, elsewhere. If the kinship institutions in society put men above women, then the economy would not pay women more than men. We saw, however, that another possibility was that the daily-life features imposed by hierarchies in one sphere would literally force their way into the logic of how things occurred elsewhere. If the community sphere generated various cultural habits and interrelations, these habits and interrelations would not only be respected by the economy, they would influence the actual definition of job roles. Following these lines of thought, *Liberating Theory* showed the key kinds of accommodating or mutually co-reproducing effects the entanglement of influences from one sphere, say polity or gender, could have on another sphere, say race or economy, and vice versa.

We saw that sexist pressure could not only cause men to earn more than women, or men to get some jobs women didn't get, it could change what a secretary or a boss did to incorporate sexist behavior patterns and assumptions that weren't narrowly economic. The same could occur for racism affecting not only pay rates and who does what work, but also how jobs are defined. In reverse, class pressures could affect how mothers, fathers, and children interrelated, not just the funds available—or how cultures were internally structured, and not just which cultural groups earned more income.

Okay, so we realized these four defining parts of society interacted. What about changing over time? Social evolution, we argued, was just where changes occurred without altering defining social relations. Revolution, we argued, wasn't about just economics but was about a change in defining relations in any key sphere of life. A revolutionary change in one sphere existed if its institutions changed and, as a result, the influences it spread through society fundamentally altered. However, if the rest of social life had become so enmeshed with old dynamics such as Jim Crow racism or apartheid, or maybe old class relations such as those of capitalism, the old relations outside the revolutionized sphere might even pull its old dynamics back into existence despite their having been changed for a time. Or, if not, relations elsewhere in society might change modestly to accord with the new relations. Or, more dramatically, they might fundamentally transform as well. We found all these possibilities born out in historical cases. What might induce revolution? What might impede it? *Liberating Theory* had analysis, vision, and strategy. It had critique and innovation. Its new concepts were designed to help generate shared program and goals. I wrote another book, almost twenty years later, called *Thought Dreams* (2004), with Arbeiter Ring Press, in which I tried to develop, as any activist might based on their own experiences and insights, *Liberating Theory*'s conceptual framework, refined due to lessons from more years of experience. *Thought Dreams,* was an adapted transcript of a course I gave at the Z Media Institute. *Liberating Theory* and *Thought Dreams* present a broad way of thinking that still informs my work.

Within *Liberating Theory's* fourfold conceptualization of society and history was an emphasis on the effects of each dimension of social life on the others, a pursuit of a four-focused vision and strategy, and a call to strengthen the concepts applied to kinship/gender, power/politics, community/culture, and class/economy and their interconnections. While we were writing *Liberating Theory*, seeing ourselves as undoing economism, the same agenda was entrancing many people on the Left, even if not in precisely the same terms as we offered in *Liberating Theory*. Robin and I felt, however, that the economic part of Left conceptualizing, unlike the other parts, didn't just need expansion or refinement. It needed full-scale renovation. We thought feminist, antiracist, and anarchist movements were doing well at providing concepts applicable to each of their focused areas. We thought ecological and international activists were usefully renovating ways of thinking about their realms, too. We thought *Liberating Theory* provided worthy tools for synchronizing insights from different orientations. But regarding the economy, we thought that expanding Marxism or even tinkering with its conceptual definitions would not lead to a desirable stance.

Better Economics

> *Ideas are like rabbits. You get a couple and learn*
> *how to handle them, and pretty soon you have a dozen.*
> —*John Steinbeck*

When critiquing Marxism, Robin and I were simultaneously introducing new ways of cutting up economic reality to highlight its important elements. Two books published by Princeton University Press—*Quiet Revolution in Welfare Economics* and *The Political Economy of Participatory Economics* (both 1990)—largely summed up these efforts. The books emerged from our academic and thesis involvements discussed earlier.

331

One of the key ideas explored in these works was how and why people adapt their consumer preferences. Robin and I realized that people's preferences, unlike what mainstream economists tell us, are not formed only beyond economic life, but also arise within the economy's operations. More, we can impact our own preferences. If some item is abundant and cheap, we can develop a taste for it that will be easily fulfilled. If some item is scarce and expensive, we can develop an aversion or an indifference to it, so that we don't feel constantly deprived by being unable to have it. Underpriced items we orient ourselves toward. Overpriced items we orient ourselves away from.

Robin and I noticed, as we talked through these issues, the simple idea that for a kid born in the ghetto, it makes more sense to want to play basketball, which is easily available, than to want to play classical piano, which is barely conceivable. We noticed, also, that if what we could access was beyond our control, then personal adaptation or even personal mutilation could make good sense. If we want our preferences met we shouldn't cultivate desires for yachts that we can't afford or for unalienated labor. We should orient ourselves to gain pleasure from what we can readily have and to avoid wanting what we won't be able to get. Perhaps the key step in understanding this insight was an instructive thought experiment. I imagined I visited a prison commissary while visiting a prisoner. In my mind's eye, I found all the items shoddy and unappealing. A few months later, I was arrested for a long-term stay. A year after that, I was in the same commissary as a prisoner spending limited funds. I now saw items that each had their own distinct features. I liked some and not others. What happened, in this thought experiment, was that whereas economists tell us markets deliver to us what we want, I saw myself coming to want what the commissary readily delivered. To maintain my prior preferences would be to court depression.

In economics, the idea uncovered by these thoughts is called endogenous preferences (the idea that preferences are partly determined by economic situations) rather than exogenous preferences (the idea that preferences are in no sense affected by economic situations). The existence of endogenous preferences was familiar long before Robin and I worried about it, but whereas for other economists the possibility of endogenous preferences was peripheral, it led Robin and me to a powerful critique of market exchange and to a comprehension of what Robin named "snow-balling preferences" wherein the economy underprices (or overprices) some items, such as private goods like basketballs and cell phones or collective goods like parks and clean air, and people then bend their preferences toward (or away) from the items in light of their deflated (or inflated) prices. Availability, in turn, further increases or decreases in accord with our bent preferences. Then prices distort further from accurately reflecting true social costs and benefits and outcomes snowball away from our unbiased inclinations.

Other insights drove our understanding as well. We asked what really gets produced and consumed in an economy and saw that economic activity both uses up and produces not only material goods, services, resources, and labor, but also social relations among people and even people's consciousness and well-being. We also saw that the ways economies affected these social and human inputs and outputs was central to evaluating economic systems.

We next highlighted that markets ignored the effects of transactions that occurred beyond their direct buyers and sellers so egregiously as to misprice all items exchanged. We highlighted as well, based in part on my SEP experience, how markets, due to requiring cost-cutting and surplus maximizing, induce workplace hierarchy even in the absence of private ownership. We realized that markets imposed a need in each workplace for what we called "coordinators" to impose harsh conditions, speedup, and other cost-cutting conditions. More, when we saw how markets had implications for the division of labor inside workplaces, it in turn caused us to highlight that, in capitalism, classes centrally included not only owners of productive property and workers doing rote and obedient labor, but also a third intermediate class between labor and capital which monopolized empowering tasks and daily decision making and which could become the ruling class in a postcapitalist economy.

Roughly speaking, we went from rejecting Marxism's labor prices and values, Marxism's exaggeration of economics in history, Marxism's exaggeration of the material element in the economy, and particularly Marxism's two-class view, to a three-class, social, bargaining-power conception of capitalism that emphasized economic impact on human options and inclinations. It wasn't just "relationships of ownership" that "whispered in the wings," as Dylan put it, but relations of work and consumption, too, especially the division of labor and the methods of allocation. It would be too much to rehearse all the ins and outs of the resulting economic viewpoint here, but we can at least explore the main gain that accrued from the new economic concepts: participatory economic vision.

Chapter 30

Principia Utopia

Thrillers Reveal Popular Consciousness

> *Most everybody I see knows the truth*
> *but they just don't know that they know it.*
> —*Woody Guthrie*

As a kid I read the Hardy Boys, Tom Swift, popular science for young people, and Marvel comics. Now it's thrillers, hard science fiction, and popular science for adults. I used to read political books voraciously, partly submissions at South End Press, but for many years my political reading has been sporadic. Beyond ZNet submissions, I read only the occasional political book that I need for research or that has particular appeal for me.

My appetite for legal thrillers, medical thrillers, financial thrillers, and scientifically sound science fiction, however, is expansive. The interesting aspect of this hobby is that much popular fiction is well to the left of where people think the population resides—as is much TV. I am not talking about how every now and then the top-ten nonfiction book list includes some progressive author's new book. That happens, yes, but what I am talking about are typical entries on the fiction list. You can always find best sellers that take for granted that corporations seek profits above law and humanity. These novels depict characters bent on serving economic and political villainy. Pharmaceutical companies and government agencies, doctors, hospitals, and insurance men and their firms all commit mayhem. Even while avoiding serious social commentary, many typical best-selling novels accurately depict society's institutionally propelled greed and violence. In this respect, popular novels reflect not only contemporary life, but also public consciousness of contemporary life. We all know everything is broken and there is little dignity left in life, and novelists know we know it. However, we and the novelists ignore the broader meaning of what we and the novelists all know.

In public talks, I often use pop culture to demonstrate that people understand problems and even their institutional roots. One of my favorite examples has been the movie *Air America*, which had as its context the CIA's private airline's involvement in heroin trade to fund Indochina violence and to pacify inner cities in the U.S. This 1990 film showed a senator calmly discussing pushing heroin as if it was routine, as, in fact, it was. I remember sitting in the theater and thinking that thirty years earlier, if this same plot was shown to U.S. audiences, viewers would have burned down theaters, outraged at the film's sacrilegious denial of American largesse. When *Air America* came out in 1990, however, after the sixties social movements had transformed people's views, U.S. audiences routinely accepted the story as realistic. CIA drug dealing was put across with a bit of humor, but popular reaction was a serious indicator of viewers' consciousness.

This film and many others, as well as numerous top-ten thriller novels, got me thinking about how much the public already intuitively knew about what leftists were working so tirelessly to convey in incredibly stupefying detail—that society was broken, dignity was nowhere, and the cause of suffering was inhumane social institutions and, in particular, capitalist profit-seeking. This marked a gigantic turnaround from before the sixties.

Vision Problem

> *Those who do not move, do not notice their chains.*
> —*Rosa Luxemburg*

In this chapter's title, the word "principia" refers to logic and principles. The word "utopia" refers to what is vastly better than now. In the sixties I came to believe that if I didn't know what I sought, I couldn't have a very good plan of how I was going to achieve it. If I didn't have compelling vision, I couldn't have good strategy. I didn't see how anyone could justify movements lacking worthy and workable vision over a span of 200 years resisting capitalism. At some point, leftists should have made major progress.

I began to realize that I wanted vision that would be disseminated publicly and subject to continual refinement. What else would promote real participation? I wanted vision about economics, politics, law, families, kinship, culture, ecology, and international relations. What else would respect society's complexity?

I knew leftists had the mental faculties to propose vision. I knew we had experiences from history and from our own lives to ground vision. I knew we had mental and material means to test it. I knew we could, if we wished, invent, evaluate, refine, and, if need be, reinvent vision. More, through our diverse, often revamped phases of activism from 1960 on, not to mention assessing earlier history, surely we had created a store of experiences sufficient to inform credible, inspiring vision. Yet among the many brilliant leftists I have known who had tackled all kinds of problems, virtually none had generated or even tried to generate inspiring, shared vision. Two hundred years of struggle and we had no widely shared institutional vision. I concluded that we lacked vision not because vision can't or shouldn't exist, but because we hadn't brought it into being.

When I gave public talks trying to make my case, I often offered the following thought experiment. I would say, imagine we made a pile from the past forty years of all the public talks, interviews, essays, articles, movies, songs, stories, and books that have been about what is wrong with modern society. How high would that pile climb? To the moon? Only to the top of Mount Everest? Surely it would reach very high. Then I would say, imagine that instead we made a pile from the past forty years of all the public talks, interviews, essays, articles, movies, songs, stories, and books about institutions we want to have in a new society. How high would that climb? Fifty feet? Twenty feet? To my knee? In any case, not very high.

We don't have vision not because vision is impossible, I would conclude, but because we haven't given time to conceiving, sharing, and improving it. For fifteen years I have routinely and repeatedly asserted that huge numbers of people now know that the basics of contemporary society are broken, or, more accurately, that they never worked humanely in the first place, and that, as a result, countless lives are lost and endless souls sundered. Was this true?

During the second World Social Forum (WSF) in Porto Alegre, Brazil, I traveled around with Justin Podur and Cynthia Peters. Each time Justin and Cynthia and I took a taxi ride, they would engage the driver in discussion, later telling me what the driver said, since I only understand English. This was before Lula's election as president of Brazil, and each time Justin and Cynthia would query the cabbies about Lula, and each time the cab driver's answer was essentially the same. One cabbie was particularly eloquent. After explaining how he loved Lula and liked the Workers Party, he reported that he nonetheless wouldn't bother to vote "because we are dust. We float in the wind. Our lives don't get better with changed politicians. We are doomed."

Chomsky had told me earlier about how he had met Lula a few years earlier and asked Lula if he thought he would ever become president and Lula said, no, probably not. "The poor won't vote for me in sufficient numbers. They doubt that one of their own could run the country. They doubt it would lead to benefits. They doubt it would matter."

Later, Lula and the Workers Party came up with a plan for winning anyhow. During the WSF, I got to talk with quite a few folks from Lula's campaign and enjoyed a dinner celebrating Lula where he was sitting a table away. I asked a Lula advisor about Lula's campaign strategy. The strategy was, I was told, to appeal upward to what they called the professional sectors as much as they could. They felt that Brazilian elites were more divided this time, compared to during prior elections that Lula had lost. They thought that if they could keep the media from overly tarring Lula and appeal upward to the consciences of well-off sectors, they could retain most of their present support among the poor and win. When asked why not appeal more aggressively to the poor, bringing out a larger vote, they said they didn't believe they could do it and that trying to do it would cause right-wingers to fight more effectively. It wouldn't sufficiently enlarge support at lower income levels to make up for those debits.

Isn't there a problem, I asked, that if you win in the manner you indicate, you will have so molded your programs to not offend wealthy constituencies that you will lose the ability to do good while in office? Your upward-looking strategy might win the election—though at the time I ignorantly indicated that I doubted it had a prayer—but even if it did win, wouldn't the process distort your project's values? As Kurt Vonnegut put it, "We are what we pretend to be, so we must be careful what we pretend to be." They didn't think so.

There was, it turned out, a sense in which we were both right. They were correct that they could win with their upward-looking approach. I was correct, however, that in winning with that approach they would sunder their radical roots, in turn doing far less good in office than they had hoped. Regrettably, the Brazilian cabbies and those even lower in income may now be even more convinced that they are forever floating in the wind—or maybe there is a festering sore ready to explode.

I had another instructive Brazilian encounter at the same time. I spoke on a panel with a very famous Brazilian journalist for whom the auditorium was packed with crowds overflowing into the halls. Afterward Justin, Cynthia, and I were heading back toward our hotel and a Brazilian friend came up and asked if I would please come with him for a dinner meeting. Justin and Cynthia said go, and I did. It was in a hotel, in a separate dining room, with about ten people. It was to discuss media strategy for the emerging Lula campaign, which Lula later won. The emphasis was that victory depended on keeping a lid on assaults against Lula from elite sectors by keeping a lid on the media. Those present wanted to establish an international committee of media people who would monitor Brazilian media throughout the campaign. The monitor group would criticize lies and manipulations about Lula in Brazilian media, and present accurate accounts. It was felt that if the journalists doing this were internationally prominent, it would put great pressure on the Brazilian media. I didn't know whether it was plausible, and I said so when asked my opinion.

I was beginning to wonder why I was there, when they asked me (a) who should be on the committee from the U.S. and Europe, and (b) would I be willing to put the committee together and chair it? I was flattered, but within seconds I came to the conclusion, wrong for the second time that trip, that Lula didn't stand a chance. If his key advisors thought it made sense to have a highly revered collection of journalists monitoring Brazilian media, that was one thing; but if they thought I was a sensible person to put such a collection of journalists together, they had no idea what they were doing. I told them that I was honored but that no, I didn't think I should do it because I would not be able to enlist the people they wanted and would instead be seen by such people as a good reason to stay away. I gave them names of people who I thought better suited to their task. They were surprised at someone rejecting a plum political position, and that surprised me.

Getting back to people lacking hope due to lacking vision, for a decade and more it has seemed to me that when we keep explaining how bad our society is and how powerful the agents of reaction are, ironically, we are largely telling people what they already know and, worse, we are feeding a main reason for their not lining up on behalf of change—the belief that change is impossible. During the run-up to the U.S. bombing of Afghanistan, the computers we use for Z and ZNet had a major glitch. We had to call in help, and it arrived in the form of a young man who ran his own small computer repair firm. After a time working on our problem, he noticed wall hangings, issues of Z strewn about, and so on, and we began to chat about the work we do, and then about the international situation and the imminent bombing of Afghanistan. I explained, first, Washington doesn't want the UN to handle the matter because that would legitimate international law, and then the U.S. might be subject to its dictates. He understood that argument quite easily. It made sense to him and I had no need to pursue the points further. Second, Washington wants to assault Afghanistan because we need to show the world that no one can behave contrary to our requirements and Afghanistan is, in context of 9/11, the easiest available target to make the case. It is like the Mafia punishing someone who doesn't pay a debt. Even if the Mafia couldn't care less about the individual, the punishment must be meted out lest others in turn fail to pay their debts. More, the Mafia boss doesn't pick the most difficult target to punish, but opts for a target both unable to resist and widely hated. My computer service man understood that argument, too. He was, by the way, a white male, with his own small company, who listens to Rush Limbaugh for entertainment. He had voted for Bush. He was the archetypal recruit of the Reagan revolution. It was just after 9/11. Yet, one on one, talking calmly, it took no time for him to assent to an anti-imperialist analysis.

Next I described how all the aid agencies and UN officials in Afghanistan agreed that bombing might kill literally millions of people from a population that was one-third illiterate, that lived about fifty years on average, and that had, for the most part, never even heard of Osama bin Laden and barely heard of George Bush. Yet, despite and even because of all that, George Bush was going to go ahead and bomb them. For Bush, delegitimizing international law and demonstrating our resolve were paramount, and the lives of Afghan civilians didn't matter. The small businessman not only got it, tears glistened in his eyes. But then he said to me, Michael, you have to understand something. I don't want to hear this, my wife doesn't want to hear this, neither do my parents, my friends, or the people I work with. And when I replied, you don't want to hear this like you don't want to hear about the death and trauma of a hurricane or a tidal wave, he said, yes, that's exactly right. There is nothing I, my wife, my parents, or my workmates can do about war. It is just the way it is. I can work hard and try to live well and help the people around me live well, but I can't do anything beyond that that will matter. And when I said, but surely you can see that the U.S. can bomb or not, and that how the public organizes itself and acts could affect which happens, he said, maybe so, but if we don't bomb Afghanistan we will bomb somewhere else. War is a part of life, he argued, like cancer or aging. You live with it. You die with it. There is no point whining about it, much less railing against it. War isn't like your family's income. Income you can perhaps affect.

This computer businessman was not inhumane. He wasn't enlarging his range of empire. He wasn't cold to human suffering. He wept for the Afghans, just as he might weep for earthquake victims. But he wanted nothing to do with rolling rocks uphill only to get crushed when they slid back down. Without vision, a Left cannot enroll this man, or his family, friends, neighbors, or workers.

What is the bottom line? ZNet has a sustainer program and every once in awhile someone writes in that they wish to discontinue their membership, almost always due to budget problems. One time, however, an interesting note came with a cancellation. "You are doing valuable work. I wish to discontinue my membership because I do not think the 'left' is addressing the most vital issues we will face in the coming years. Given my knowledge of anthropology and human psychology I think it is unlikely that these issues will be adequately addressed by anyone. In the meantime my monthly donation could be better spent assisting the education of impoverished children, or buying beer." Indeed, if nothing significantly better is possible, why not help alleviate the worst pain? If nothing at all is possible, why not drink beer, or for that matter, sniff glue?

Italy and Needing Vision

I'm a pessimist because of intelligence, but an optimist because of will.
—*Antonio Gramsci*

I went to Italy on a book tour for the Italian edition of *Parecon: Life After Capitalism*. The Italian edition was translated by Adele Oliveri, who I had met attending the European Social Forum a couple of years before. A graduate of the London School of Economics, she found *Parecon* immediately congenial to her values and liked the idea of translating it. The Italian publisher, Il Saggitore, wisely accepted her offer. Later, at Il Saggitore's invitation, I went to Italy for about ten days and spoke at many venues in five Italian cities, the largest being Rome and Milan. I also did interviews for mainsteam and alternative print newspapers and magazines, sessions for radio, and even some sessions for TV.

The talks were mostly about parecon—which I'll describe later—with me presenting the model in whatever time was allotted. Follow-up question-and-answer sessions were largely about the vision, but were also about U.S. foreign policy and the then-upcoming 2004 elections. It was striking—as speaking had been in numerous other countries—how similar the questions asked were to those that emerged in talks I have given in U.S. cities such as Chicago, Cleveland, Tallahassee, and Portland.

Aside from the beauty of Florence and Rome—where else would I have the opportunity to give talks in halls off a plaza created by Michelangelo?—and aside from the incredible cuisine, which Italians not only know how to prepare but also how to savor, and especially aside from the incredible hospitality of Il Saggitore, my major impressions of Italy were twofold and typical of my travel experiences elsewhere as well.

First, there was an American's disorientation with the experience of Italian media. I suspect my efforts to convey the reality to my Italian friends were considered courteous exaggeration, but the fact is I did more mainstream media in a week in Italy than I have done in thirty years in the U.S. More, the Italian mainstream interviewers, including TV anchors, asked insightful and informed questions of a sort that not only wouldn't be forthcoming in the unlikely event that I was to appear on comparable U.S. media, but that couldn't even be conceived or understood by U.S. mainstream commentators. U.S. anchors and reporters simply don't have the concepts, knowledge, or, more to the point, the moral compass and openness to conceive, much less ask, such questions. Worse, were they to hear the questions asked by others, the meaning wouldn't even register. The difference is profound. Don't make the mistake of thinking Italian media is magnificent. Berlusconi, a viciously right-wing Italian media magnate, used the media to acquire the Italian prime ministership. It is just that U.S. media is worse.

On the alternative media side of the coin, things are also much different in Italy than in the U.S. Italy has more alternative media, particularly Left daily national newspapers, and also more resources and means than alternative media have in the U.S. On one day in Italy, for example, long interviews with me about parecon, with accompanying photos, appeared very prominently in three Italian Left dailies. The total coverage of parecon in Italian alternative media in just under a week was more than I had seen in the U.S. in the nearly 18 months since the book's release.

It is very disorienting to have people in Italy—who you don't know and who have not previously known you and who have not had a decade to acclimate to a new set of ideas—excited and energetic about exploring for their quite large audiences the nature of parecon, and to know at the same time that in the U.S., progressive periodicals like *In These Times*, *The Progressive*, *Mother Jones*, and *The Nation* not only aren't going out of their way to send people to take photos and do interviews in order to be able to bring this model to their audiences, but are routinely rejecting submissions on the topic, sometimes even by their own regular writers. Of course, international media interest may not persist, once overseas periodicals realize that parecon has implications for them, too.

The second big impression I had from this trip to Italy had to do with the Italian Left. I expected Italy's Left to be overtly and openly anticapitalist, large, militant, and even thriving. My optimism was fueled by reports that during the gigantic international antiwar upsurge of February 15, 2003, not only had two million Italians demonstrated publicly, but activists had staged an effective counter military action whereby they had gone on commuter trains that were on the same tracks as military transport trains and brought the commuter trains to a stop by pulling emergency cords, thereby turning the commuter trains into obstacles blocking the military transports. What amazed me were reports that the commuters delayed this way hadn't pummeled the antiwar activists for bringing their trains to a halt, but had instead applauded them. This suggested a population that was remarkably primed, I hoped, for political upsurge. But I got a rather more complex picture in person, and it was initially quite hard to compare to what I was used to in the U.S.

I found a tremendous volume of self-conscious leftist awareness in Italy, to be sure, not just subterranean and implicit, but on the surface. It extended out into the public, encompassed young activists, but also encompassed all kinds of other people, and even percolated up into mainstream institutions (such as parts of the media), as well as into government branches, such as in Rome, where city officials at high levels, including the mayor, were interested in parecon precisely to understand possible new ways of doing their jobs. Talking with such folks, having them ask insightful questions, hearing stories of their related thoughts, was quite hopeful. Interest in finding new ways of conducting state affairs, for example, is high among certain sectors in Italy where there is a special interest in participatory budgeting, a practical experiment consistent with parecon, pioneered in Porto Alegre.

In private conversation, it seemed to me obvious that most of the most left-leaning elements in Italy would exhibit anticapitalist sentiments. But what was unexpected was a real hesitancy among such people to be publicly and self-consciously anticapitalist, much less openly in favor of an alternative system.

How do I put this? I didn't feel much militancy. I didn't feel much hope of winning fundamental change, nor much inclination to seek to do so. People I encountered had anticapitalist values and interests, but they had no belief that those values could be fully manifested. The difference from the U.S. was that what is more covert in the U.S.—a belief that the system is broken and oppressive—was on the surface in Italy and in most other places I have traveled overseas. But even with the critique of existing circumstances more overtly present, the rest of what typifies U.S. life remained present too: doubt, apathy, and resignation that nothing better was possible.

When I participated on a panel with two other leftists held in a beautiful old church in a small town with a few hundred people attending, while there were many shared opinions between me and the other panelists, there was also a great difference between us. I advocated a long-term full revolutionary transformation of society. The others aggressively asserted that no such transformation was possible. No better world was available. No means of attainment was graspable. They advocated only modest change. For them, and I fear for most of the Italians roused on February 15, the idea of revolution, in any time frame at all, was ridiculous, or worse, dangerous.

What my trip to Italy said to me was that I could expect each country I might visit to have its own unique features arising from different histories, movements, hopes, and fears, but one thing I could anticipate finding in common would be doubt whether any better world existed, and whether it was possible to win fundamental changes from the massive centers of wealth and power now in charge.

Maybe it has been me bending reality to accord with my own expectations, but I have seen this mind-set everywhere. In Brazil, I saw it in the words of the cab drivers. In Italy, I saw it in the words of citizens and Left activists, too. And likewise for Turkey, Australia, France, and India. When I tried to understand how it could be that two million Italians had just demonstrated militantly against the war and that only a blink in historic time later, visible militancy was almost entirely absent, I heard two explanations.

First, I was told that due to the history of Italian civil war, the great prevalence of anticommunist sentiments, and fear of provoking overt repression, people were intent on finding nonconfrontational ways to improve social outcomes. My feeling was that when "nonconfrontational" comes to mean accepting systemic structures as permanently inevitable, this was not a good way forward, yet the viewpoint was conveyed to me repeatedly, including by folks who were bemoaning that it was the common condition.

The second reason offered, in this case primarily by folks who agreed that the situation was a real problem rather than a wise avenue forward, was the absence of a shared, compelling ideology that would distinguish a newly militant Left from the old-style sectarian and authoritarian variants. Quite sensibly, no one wanted to replicate past errors. Not so sensibly, no one felt there was a militant road forward that wouldn't lead to worse results than were now endured.

Seeking Vision

The future belongs to those who prepare for it today.
—Malcolm X

Vision, I know from my days at MIT, does not mean immediate demands for today. It is not even a mid-range program for tomorrow. Vision, I also know, is not just a set of optimal values we aspire to. Vision answers the question "what do you want?" Vision is not a blueprint of every nook and cranny of the future. We can't have that, nor should we want it. Vision has to be a description of key defining institutions in whatever realm of life we wish to discuss. It has to rebut the claim that there is no fundamentally different way of organizing life, neither overdoing or underdoing the task. Many activists rightly believe we should incorporate the seeds of the future in the present. Vision is what tells us what qualifies as a seed of the future.

In my early days at MIT, when I would go around and organize in dorms and fraternities, people would invariably ask, what do you want? What's your alternative? I felt the people asking the question weren't serious. I felt they weren't honestly seeking an answer, but were instead trying to say that I had no right battling against today's system when I offered nothing to take its place. I used to reply, you are right, I don't know what's better, but the slave doesn't need a full alternative to know that slavery needs abolition and I don't need to know how to conduct economic life better to know the war in Indochina is wrong or that adults shouldn't be reduced to wage servility to earn a living. My argument was morally correct. But in time I came to realize that my morally correct stance was strategically bankrupt and if I wasn't so defensive about my early identity, I would likely have noticed sooner that a large percentage of folks asking "What do you want?" really did want to know what I wanted and that giving a good answer would enlarge their attentiveness to calls for action.

When I critiqued Marxism Leninism, I concluded that useful vision for economics, for example, would have to describe the defining institutional features of a new kind of production, consumption, and allocation. It would not only claim that we want to eliminate oppression or exploitation, or that we want to have justice or equity, or even that we want to have classlessness. It would not only reject institutions that prevent such aims, such as private property and also markets and corporate hierarchy, it would describe replacements for what we reject.

The way I realized that only offering fine values was insufficient was by thinking about liberals. After all, JFK, LBJ, and later, Jimmy Carter and Bill Clinton, could movingly say they wanted justice and equity, sometimes more eloquently and passionately than I could. Yet everyone whose ideas I respected dismissed LBJ's, JFK's, Carter's, and Clinton's fine rhetoric on grounds that the institutions they advocated contradicted the claims they made. I asked myself, why shouldn't that standard apply to us, too? Why should I say that I am for justice, equity, solidarity, and people controlling their own lives and expect anyone to believe me if I not only offer no institutions that can do all this, but if I accept institutions in my own movement that produce contrary results?

I have debated the need for shared vision, most often regarding economics, but also regarding kinship, culture, and polity, with many people. Do we need vision, economic and social, as I claimed, or is vision just a luxury, or even an impediment to progress, as those I debated claimed? My case for needing vision has always been simple. I claim you won't wind up where you will be happy if you are aiming nowhere in particular, much less if you are aiming in entirely the wrong direction. I claim that we need a destination if we are to wisely embody features of the future in the present. I claim we need a destination to generate hope and to resist distracting temptations and reactionary influences.

In contrast, a very large number of people who courageously engage in day-to-day activism around poverty, war, violence against women, pollution, globalization, and racism say vision is a luxury or distraction. They say that vision is too far in the future to matter now. Get to work. Stop your sophomoric ruminations. There are wars and diverse injustices and vision isn't going to become actual soon. Isn't that obvious? I have heard this from intellectuals writing books, from activists involved in maintaining projects or in building demonstrations, and from people who do some of both.

An even more dismissive argument says that vision is not only a distraction, it actually impedes social change. People argue that advocating specific institutional aims makes us sectarian even when the aims have merit. Advocating vision closes out options. Most of the time we will be wrong about future goals since we don't know enough to specify them well, and even when we are right about them, having vision will make us narrow and sectarian. Can't we see these trends, the antivision camp urges, in the behavior of past ideologues who bent reality to their dictates rather than correcting their views to fit an ever-changing reality?

In some complex cases, the same person will have all these reactions—we need vision, vision is a luxury, and vision is destructive—and in my view, this more complex person is on the right track, since all of these claims can be simultaneously true. Indeed, Noam Chomsky is the best example I have encountered of being on all sides of the vision issue. His testimonials for visionary efforts undertaken by Robin Hahnel and me have arguably been our greatest boost. Here is a quote by Noam from 1970 I recently came across:

If the present wave of repression can be beaten back, if the left can overcome its more suicidal tendencies and build upon what has been accomplished in the past decade, then the problem of how to organize industrial society on truly democratic lines, with democratic control in the workplace and in the community, should become a dominant intellectual issue for those who are alive to the problems of contemporary society, and, as a mass movement develops, speculation should proceed to action.

The above comment outlined a path I traversed in subsequent decades. The same holds for many things Noam has written on the jackets of books presenting participatory economics. Here is Noam's most recent supportive comment from the jacket of my 2006 Zed Books book about the relationship of participatory economics to the rest of society.

In many earlier studies, Michael Albert has carried out careful in-depth inquiries into systems of participatory economics (parecon), analyzing in detail how they can function justly, equitably, and efficiently, and how they can overcome many of the criminal features of current social and economic arrangements. This new and very ambitious study casts the net far more widely, extending to just about every major domain of human concern and mode of human interaction, and investigating with care and insight how, in these domains, parecon-like principles could lead to a far more desirable society than anything that exists, and also how these goals can be constructively approached. It is another very valuable and provocative contribution to the quest for a world of much greater freedom and justice.

On the other hand, on other occasions, Noam's approach to the issue of vision—an approach shared by many other libertarian leftists and anarchists who worry about elite impositions straitjacketing popular movements—has felt to me like a giant impediment that I continually had to move to do my visionary thing. It isn't easy when a person from whom you have learned so much occupies a bulwark standing between you and where you wish to go. Here is an indicative comment from Noam from 2004 that had this impact:

I think the question for detailed planning for the future isn't so much 'can we do it?' Sure we can do it, but it's whether we know enough about human beings, about society, institutions, the effects of introducing institutional structures into human life. Do we know enough about that to be able to plan in any detail what a society should look like? Or should it be experimental, guided by certain general ideas about liberty, equality, authority, and domination and let people explore different ways of working through this maze and see what comes natural to them?

My own view, and I differ with some of my close friends on this, is that we should be cautious in trying to sketch out the nature of future society in too much detail. It's not that it can't be done. It can be done in interesting and different ways—and it has been done—but I think the real question is to what extent is it important to do it and to what extent is it important to just try out experiments and chip away at existing structures.

Okay, fair enough, but which structures should we chip away at, and with what kind of mallet, shaping what's left in what new ways seeking what ends? More, why experiment if we aren't going to try to draw conclusions? Seeking too many details of a new society before experiencing elements of what we have in mind is obviously overreaching. But how much detail is too much? And how much experience is enough to get us going?

Noam's argument with me is that we don't know enough about people and institutions to have reliable vision beyond general values. But what if, I have often replied to his point, we know some institutions are absolutely contrary to human potentials and needs? Then can't we reasonably say that those shouldn't be a part of our preferred future? And, likewise, what if we can describe an alternative to what we reject that gets needed jobs done, doesn't have the same flaws, and even has lots of highly desirable attributes in accord with our "general ideas about liberty, equality, authority, and domination"? Can't we then advocate and seek those structures?

Noam's frequent reply adds another theme. Institutional vision overextends our insights beyond where we can be confident about them. Institutional vision has to, therefore, emerge in practice and doesn't need in-depth books, articles, essays, and debates. I always wonder, and convey back to Noam on hearing these views, how do we know what's beyond our insights unless we try to enunciate and test them? How can our vision emerge from practice if the lessons of our practice are not written up for people to think about, refine, and assess in books and articles and if we don't debate them? How will people seriously assess any vision's merits, refine it, improve it, and seek to win it, if setting it down in words is a bad idea?

On what I think is a roll, I tend to raise the ante. Since we have a couple of hundred years of highly relevant practice in the modern Left and some people even have all kinds of additional experience in their own lifetimes, including experimental constructions of preferred institutions, both economic and otherwise—if it is not *now* time to advocate shared vision, then *when* will it be time to look at history and our experiences and propose vision that people can publicly adapt, refine, or replace?

There is an interesting parallel to be found to all this in thinking about the physical sciences. For a long time it was thought that what scientists do is look at lots of results from experiments and tease out conceptual insights. In truth, however, while scientists sometimes do that—think of Kepler struggling with astronomical data for decades to discern regularities—they also often use free and imaginative leaps or inventions of mind to propose conceptual insights which then guide experiments—think of Einstein and general relativity. Indeed, the largest and most dramatic changes of approach have often come in the latter way, not the former, or via a mixture, at least.

There is another science analogy, even more instructive. Experiments do not occur without a conceptual framework guiding them. The same experiment undertaken with different concepts and hopes guiding its conception yields different lessons. One person creates an experimental worker's co-op, sees it chaotically torn asunder over a period of a year or two, and decides that corporate organization is necessary lest we all starve from the inevitable inefficiency of equitable institutions. Another person creates the same worker's co-op and sees its dissolution as evidencing the pressures of persistent market forces, or, even better, this second person—having pre-imagined that result stemming from markets, or having seen it somewhere else, or read about it—structures his experimental co-op differently, with different expectations, and does much better.

Here is the claim I keep making to Noam and others: Having a worthy and viable economic vision in mind, even if it is theoretical rather than empirically proven, has the potential to permit activists to both undertake wiser experiments and to perceive their meaning more accurately than does just barreling forward without vision. This claim seems so totally obvious, as does my whole argument about vision, that I can only feel that resistance derives not from logic alone, but, mostly, from fear of bad vision.

I had a typical experience with this kind of dispute when two excellent activists, Hilary Wainwright from England and Judy Rebick from Canada, made a case at a Life After Capitalism meeting at the 2003 WSF in Porto Alegre, Brazil, that everyone should avoid proposing visionary economic structures because thinking about such things and strongly arguing for them would curtail ingenuity, cut off the lessons of practice, exhibit nothing so much as male hubris, and perpetuate an old top-down style of domination politics. I was listening to them as a spectator, not a panelist. They were responding to Stephen Shalom, on their panel, who had outlined a political vision he called parpolity, consistent with parecon, but they were clearly also talking about me and the larger parecon project, and I sat there thinking to myself, what does it mean to insightfully discern and employ the lessons of day-to-day practice if it doesn't include proposing vision that accords with our values based on carefully assessing a few decades of day-to-day practice, including practice at creating visionary institutions? If hundreds of years of collective experience and decades of personal experience in actual visionary structures, plus a widespread hunger from people for vision, plus worldwide movements that say "another world is possible" but don't know how to embody the world they seek in their current practice, plus reactionaries like Margaret Thatcher pointing out that the belief that there is no alternative is a powerful bulwark of oppression aren't together enough to justify trying to publicly propose, debate, and even collectively advocate vision, then when will there be enough basis and incentive to do so?

To say, as Rebick and Wainwright did, that what we want will emerge from examining our experiences and those of the past is a truism. To imply that it will happen without some people taking the steps to actually do it, that it will occur instead in some kind of universal simultaneous osmosis affecting everyone at once, is incredibly odd. Why isn't proposing vision, debating it, rejecting what's not viable or worthy, improving and then advocating what is viable and worthy exactly what is involved in learning the lessons of our day-to-day practice and of history? Will we have to wait 200 years for some people to set down views that others can improve and that can finally coalesce into shared collective commitments? Is it going to occur without anyone setting down and then debating and refining anything?

Similarly, I remember having an extended e-mail debate with Andrej Grubacic, then living in Belgrade, who later became a strong parecon advocate. At the time, I had a difficult uphill battle to overcome his resistance to advocating any economic vision at all. Andrej saw himself as manifesting anarchist attitudes held in common with Noam Chomsky, on the one hand, and with antiauthoritarianism born in the Eastern European rejection of all ideology on grounds that all ideology leads to Stalinism, on the other. Andrej's fears of ideology yielding sectarianism had a powerful basis, but I argued that the solution to fears about bad vision wasn't to advocate no vision. It was to advocate good vision.

I published a book called *Thinking Forward* in 1997, years before my exchange with Andrej and the comments by Wainwright and Rebick. *Thinking Forward* was an outgrowth of classes I taught earlier at ZMI. It attempts to teach how to conceptualize economic vision from scratch. In the introduction, I tried to motivate the need for seeking shared vision against contrary views. It was this formulation that finally broke through with Andrej. I noted the kinds of doubts some people have about vision—we can't know the future sufficiently to formulate vision sensibly, the future must come from everyone's involvement, and for a few people to pose a vision crowds out that involvement. I replied to the concerns, arguing that to move forward wisely, of course we must know something about where we want to wind up. I argued that surely social-change strategies can't only react to what is, but must also seek what we want. I argued that history shows that well-intentioned movements often failed even after defeating opponents because, in victory, they established new structures little better than the old ones, and I rhetorically asked, wasn't this in part because most participants in those movements had nothing better clearly in mind?

But I knew that many critics of vision would say that these are powerful arguments for vision, yes, but they do not tell us how much vision and how detailed a vision we need. Such a critic might point out that developing vision beyond values denies that the future is largely beyond our predictive abilities, and that it would risk cramming history into an inflexible blueprint, leaving little space for flexible experiment and innovation.

In the book's introduction I agreed that these antivisionary corrections are important, but I then added that they don't tell us to do without vision, only not to get too detailed or regimented about what we propose. I argued that we needed a picture of a desired future sufficiently rich and detailed to provide hope and direction, while respecting careful analysis based on real knowledge. I said we should understand our efforts to be cumulative, adaptable, and always the basis for more clarification, refinement, and improvement so that we are not creating blueprints to confine ourselves, but disseminating the skills and knowledge needed for effectively conceptualizing and adapting vision.

I argued that critics of vision couldn't have it both ways. If the world is so complex and the possibility for visionary error is great—which is all too true—than, as with any other human endeavor, some care and thought is in order. And if there is no public effort at creating vision, employing publicly available tools and methods, then a relatively few folks with great intellectual confidence will take these tasks upon themselves privately. Such folks will be, by their training and their position in society, those who are conceptually well-equipped to come up with ideas about new institutions and especially to voice them convincingly, but who are also, due to their elitist academic biases, ill-equipped for doing this humanely. In other words, by arguing against the need to publicly address issues of vision in sufficient detail, critics of vision ironically fostered exactly the ends they wish to avoid: vision created by a self-defined elite, imposed on the many who are excluded from the creative process, and reflecting a narrow set of elite interests. What this meant to me was that the real solution to the conundrum—that people seeking a better society need vision but that having vision can also do us harm—is not to reject vision in public while it is developed privately, but to debate visionary aims and goals publicly, and, more, to disseminate and clarify the methods by which vision is developed so that all people who wish to may partake of the project, confidently bringing to bear their own insights, interests, and experiences.

Brazil and Argentina Conclude the Case

*I never would believe that providence had sent a few rich men into the world,
ready booted and spurred to ride, and millions ready saddled and bridled to be
ridden.*

—Richard Rumbold

Just after the 2003 WSF, I spent a couple of days with Peter Singer, an economist in Brazil, who later worked in Lula's government. In São Paulo, we attended a meeting of people involved in building worker-controlled firms, advocates of what is called Solidarity Economics, a viewpoint Singer helped initiate and that has considerable support in South America and also in parts of Europe and Spain in particular. I was to be the main speaker at the session, but rather than launching into a big talk with fifty worker-control advocates from diverse projects, I instead asked lots of questions about their situations and only provided my input as requested. It quickly became evident, however, as the workers told their stories, that underneath their proud commitment to worker control, there was a layer of grave doubt and vacillation. This was because each time they excitedly and optimistically formed their cooperatives, in case after case, the character of work and the general situation of those who were involved began to look more and more like it had in private firms earlier.

When it was my turn to comment I suggested there were two main problems affecting their efforts. The workers were quick in these projects to change the way people were paid to be equitable and just. That was excellent. Profit was gone and people were remunerated for time worked and for intensity, though at least at the outset, the latter was universally high. But workers in the projects did not change their division of labor and had no explicit understanding of the impact that their division of labor and also market competition had on them. This undermined their projects relative to what they might have been, and led to wrong attitudes about ensuing problems. The experiments, wonderful in motivation, were not sufficiently informed by vision to lead to steadily increasing vision and inspiration.

The workers saw the devolution of their projects as arising from human frailty rather than from the fact that their projects, while disavowing private ownership, profit making, and gross income disparities, still had to compete in the market for surplus, and still incorporated the coordinator/worker division, which was partly held over due to not rejecting its ills and was partly imposed by market logic. In time, I pointed out, old pay methods and alienation would return. New values would dissipate. The point in this account is that the absence of an understanding of what is needed for an environment to be fully suitable for sustained desirable workplace outcomes leads to grave confusions about why workplace experiments are difficult and often fail. This confusion in turn undercuts commitment and hope and distorts experience's lessons. Ignorance of desirable vision obstructs people from taking programmatic steps needed in the present and then learning from what they have done to adapt their vision. It is like the earlier analogy to science. You can't learn from experiments and refine them to gain better outcomes without having a conceptual framework that proposes ideal relations and outcomes.

Another example of the same broad dynamic is the recent experience of Argentina. Cutting to the chase, Argentina enters turmoil. Workers seize firms. Neighborhoods form assemblies to govern consumption and workplace decisions more broadly. It is a perfect maelstrom of learning and doing. Government leaders rise and fall. Experiments abound. But there is no shared vision to replace the market and the corporate division of labor. There is no clarity about rates of remuneration, just desires for equity. There is no shared feeling for a sequence of steps that could be undertaken to move toward a truly just economy or polity. There is massive upsurge, yes, and then there is letdown. And people then think the alternative world let them down, rather than realizing that despite the virtues of their projects, they didn't go far enough for it to be a real test. An alternative world was never tried. Too many key pieces were absent.

But Argentine experiments didn't completely cease in the year or two after their period of great tumult. Rather, through late 2005 when I visited Buenos Aires with Lydia Sargent and Ezequiel Adamovsky, modest residues of the turmoil a few years earlier persisted in the form of Argentina's workers movement to recuperate factories. The recuperation idea was simple. Its implementation, as we saw it on our trip, was profound and inspiring.

Workers confronted disaster when their capitalist workplaces entered bankruptcy. To preserve income and avoid possible starvation, workers decided to recuperate their workplaces back into viable businesses despite the capitalist owners having been unable to make a go of it. Ignoring aggressive competition, old equipment, and failed demand, workers took over.

There were roughly a hundred Argentine worker-occupied factories at the time of our visit. In each case, not only had the capitalist owner left the operation, so, too, had virtually all prior professional and conceptual employees, including managers and engineers. The privileged employees all felt their prospects would be better served if they looked elsewhere rather than clinging to failed operations. The remaining unskilled workers had no such freedom to roam, however. They had to generate success in their failing workplace or suffer unemployment. Thus, the Argentine occupations were not initially an act of ideology, or part of a bigger revolutionary plan. They were initially, instead, acts of self-defense. It was only once the workers fought for and ended up running the firms that the experience became more visionary.

In Argentina, Lydia, Ezequiel, and I visited an occupied hotel, ice cream plant, glass factory, and slaughterhouse, all recuperated by their prior manual, obedient, unskilled, and in most cases barely educated and sometimes even illiterate workforce. In each of these plants, ranging in size from about 80 to about 500 employees—as in all other plants that have been recuperated by worker occupations—the workers quickly established a workers' council as the decision-making body of the plant. In these councils, each worker has one vote and majority rules establish overarching workplace policies. The workers call it self-management.

Almost immediately, in all but a very few of the occupied plants, workers leveled all salaries to the same hourly pay rate. Workplaces that varied from this model tended to allow slightly higher wages for seniority. In a few cases, we were told, there were also small differentials for different types of work, favoring more skilled or intellectual, though these variations appeared generally to be only temporary, yielding quickly to full equality. Workers, in other words, established and then didn't let their firms deviate much from equitable and even equal incomes.

In all the recuperated plants, though, we were told certain tasks having to do specifically with capitalist control proved no longer relevant. We were also told that many other organizational, managerial, and otherwise empowering tasks previously done by professionals—who left at the outset of each workplace occupation—had to be accomplished by remaining workers. A subset of the workers thus took up doing what were for them new tasks, which sometimes entailed having to become literate as a prerequisite.

At the ice cream plant we visited, for example, there were only two women workers. One was the treasurer. Asked what her position was, she at first didn't understand the question, but then said, wasn't it obvious, she was a worker like all others, of course. Beyond feeling like all the rest of the workers, being paid like all the rest of the workers, and having one vote like all the rest of the workers, she also told us she spent only half of each day dealing with finances and records. The other half of each day she worked on the assembly line. But retaining some old tasks while doing some new, more empowering tasks, wasn't the typical job pattern for getting managerial assignments done. We learned there were more often people who did only conceptual tasks without spending any time in assembly or in other rote work, and there were also, in the recuperated workplaces, always many people who continued to do only their old jobs, doing no new empowering aspects at all, and in many cases thus doing only very deadening labor, though admittedly in a very new context.

Asked if she earned different wages than other workers, the treasurer/ assembler said no, she had the same pay rate, why would hers be any different? In further discussion with this woman and with some other employees, we learned that while workers weren't docked for laziness or rewarded greater pay for greater effort, anyone who slacked off would come before the whole council and be set right. Likewise, under the auspices of the whole council, there had been firings for alcoholism, violence, and other misdemeanors. In short, workers had to measure up to their workmates' satisfaction, which seemed to mean people had to do their jobs well and with acceptable effort as understood by the whole council. You carried your weight, in accord with your capacities, or else.

When asked whether she was any different than other workers or whether all others could also do the financial work she was proud of handling, she said sure others could do it. Moreover, everyone else we asked this question also said, yes, of course everyone could do such, or everyone could at least do some tasks of a conceptual sort. But when we asked the treasurer whether it was a failing that only she and two other people in her office did treasury work, and that most workers in the plant still did only rote and repetitive tasks with only about a fifth doing almost entirely empowering tasks, neither the treasurer nor any other worker we queried saw this as a problem, at least before we asked about it. They said they were all workers, after all. They were all friends. As long as they worked hard, gave their all, and shared the rewards, what difference did it make what specific tasks they each did?

In the slaughterhouse, we were told that the five hundred workers elected an eight-person board to handle daily administration. These eight employees were all former rote/repetitive workers now doing conceptual tasks who had been voted to the board by the whole assembly. Their salary was unchanged when they became board members, as it had earlier remained unchanged when they graduated to doing more conceptual and empowering work.

We squeamishly watched the slaughterhouse assembly line dismantling cows, with each worker on the line doing a single cutting motion over and over. The workers' council had changed workplace conditions so assembly workers got ample time off to alleviate the stress and strain of their constant repetitive motions. The council hadn't as yet, however, redesigned the technology to change the actual tasks to be less repetitive and debilitating, nor had they even thought about doing so, as best we could determine.

In the glass factory, again with equal wages, a governing council, and employees who saw themselves as workers even while doing entirely managerial functions, we learned that rote workers carrying hot glass from station to station got a half hour off for each hour they worked scurrying under the burden of the heat to match the speed of assembly. This was a massive change from how the factory functioned in its capitalist past, as was, of course, the equalization of pay rates and the presence of past rote workers doing conceptual tasks.

When I asked in each plant whether the men and women carrying the glass and tending the furnaces could do more conceptual and less onerous work for a part of their day, everyone said of course they could, every effort is made to permit people to change jobs and learn new skills, especially since we know everyone is capable of it. And it was clearly true that this was their intent, up to the limits of the roles imposed by the existing division of labor, that is.

Sitting with board members of the glass factory, I asked what would happen if they went to the whole council and said they wanted higher pay due to their being the board and carrying heavy responsibilities. They laughed and said they would be removed from their positions and would promptly be back on the line. I said, okay, but what if you do more conceptual and skilled work for the next five years, might you not then get higher wages for being more critical to daily operations, more learned, providing more leadership at council meetings, and so on? One board member laughed and said, well, yes, that could happen and would be nice, wouldn't it? In longer interviews we discovered that, indeed, at council meetings, only a subset of workers set agendas, chaired meetings, and provided critical information, and it was of course always these workers who were doing the empowering labor.

Perhaps the most disturbing interchange we had was with the elected president of the glass factory. I asked whether workers in other more successful plants that were still under the auspices of owners would emulate the recuperation movement's accomplishments and seek to take over and run their successful plants, too. With no hesitation, he said no.

He and others explained that workers in successful plants would fear that it would diminish, rather than improve, their conditions if they sought to occupy and run their plants. In addition, they feared being fired or repressed if their uprising failed. They said that prior to actually fighting for and winning control over their work lives, they didn't realize what a difference it would make to their fulfillment to not have profit-seeking bosses. They were quite adamant that their current commitment to the new way of operating their workplace depended for its origin on their having had to fight for the plant, and then their having to run it to survive, but that it didn't exist before that.

I asked the plant president, if I tomorrow opened a plant down the road and offered to hire you to work there at twice the pay you are getting here, but also told you that you would have to work for me and my managers, would you do it? He laughed and told me that I would need to shoot him, literally, to get him to leave their self-managed glass plant to work at a capitalist plant of any kind, for any pay rate. So why couldn't he convey that lesson to his friends working elsewhere and thereby motivate them to act, too, I asked? He shrugged. He didn't see it as likely. Worse, it wasn't on his agenda. Others listening agreed. The defensive posture that birthed their self-managed plants seemed to persist in the sense that their horizon of interest was their own plant and not beyond.

Overall, the most striking and inspiring thing about these factories was the workers' mood. These exceptionally harsh workplaces, having collapsed under capitalist tutelage, and often utilizing outdated or even failed technologies, had been recuperated as successful operations, and the workers were proud of that achievement. They were clearly enjoying not only good wages, but improved conditions and status. Above all, they were operating with dignity, pride, and mutual concern and solidarity unknown in capitalist workplaces. This radical spirit was palpable everywhere we visited.

Finally, the plants had even established collective funds to aid newly-recuperated firms' initial efforts by transferring start-up aid to them. There was also some initial attention to trying to engage one another beyond market competition, based on social values and solidarity rather than narrow self-interest. But even with this intention, workers in these plants admitted that whether they liked it or not, they had to compete for market share. At first this was horribly difficult, they said, as other firms buying their goods shied away. But in time they were able to keep costs down, provide quality output, and get customers. It was clear, however, that market competition had powerful sway over the scope of decisions they could undertake. The workers' councils couldn't initiate too much improvement in their own conditions lest other firms, with managers in place to speed up production and cut costs, out-compete them. This deadening effect of markets hadn't yet reversed workers humane inclinations, but it was clearly a brake on the process that was already slowing down humane innovations.

The upshot of my trip to these workplaces was that I didn't see how anyone, no matter what prior expectations they might bring with them, could look at the Argentine occupied plants and deny the chief lesson they taught. Capitalist society horribly underutilizes most people by providing them only rote and repetitive labor and stifling their confidence, creativity, and initiative until they feel that their repetitive obedient labor is all they should or could be doing. This is called "education," but it is really degradation.

Argentina shows that in a matter of months, even after living their lives being oppressed by others, even when they are illiterate, working people can take up tasks supposedly beyond their ken and accomplish them honorably and effectively. Likewise, Argentina displays the powerful spontaneous desire that drives people who haven't been socialized into elitist mind-sets to want to earn justly and to share power rather than to dominate or be dominated.

Beyond that, however, different people would likely see different things when viewing Argentina's occupied factories. I saw, for example, that without changing the division of labor, without having all workers share conceptual and empowering tasks, even the profoundly egalitarian and participatory impulses of these factories would grow unstable. If a relatively few employees rose to do all the empowering work, in time, the few would come to dominate council discussions, set meeting agendas, impose their policies, and finally enjoy greater salaries as well. In short, despite egalitarian intentions, if some people are set above others through a division of labor that gives them more status, knowledge, skill, and confidence, they will become what they had expected to eliminate: a new dominant class. This time, however, the dominant class wouldn't be comprised of owners, but of empowered employees, but still ruling workers from above.

Argentina's workplace projects, growing in number each month, start with no owners and no coordinator class of empowered workers. They also start with a tremendous desire not only to succeed as businesses, but to share the benefits of success equitably through equal pay rates, improved conditions, democratic decision making, and recallable officials. But, if the old division of labor persists, it seemed clear to me that all the desirable innovations would in time depend on goodwill bucking up against perpetual erosion by the structural difference between the few doing empowering work and the many doing only rote work. On the other hand, it also seemed evident that if the workers became as self-conscious about everyone doing a fair share of the empowering labor as they were about equalizing pay rates, then their aspirations for classlessness would not only be in their hearts, but would also be structurally built into their new division of labor, which would in turn facilitate and advance rather than erode their gains. The problem of the market and broader economy would still remain, even in that case, however. And perhaps the weakest feature of the Argentine movement—its insularity in each firm and the workers' seeming lack of desire to address non recuperated firms by demanding changes in them, too—would, in the presence of market pressures to be individualist and competitive, remain as well.

Finally, it was disturbing to hear workers describe how if they were in successful plants they would not have acted for want of understanding the debits of their position and the possibilities of liberation. This said to us that movements had to figure out how to inspire action in successful firms as well as in collapsing ones, and to do both not from the top down, and not in ways producing class division, but from the bottom sideways and in ways generating classlessness and full self-management.

So how does a vision arise to inform efforts like those in Argentina, to sustain them, to give them direction and intensity, if not by being proposed, probably by a few people at first, but then addressed, adapted, refined, and perhaps replaced with something better that is itself further improved by many people? What the libertarians who get nervous when a book or a talk or a project proclaims that it is offering vision are failing to understand is that ideas need to be set out if they are to be widely addressed, and if they aren't widely addressed, then they either won't exist when needed most, or they will at that point come forth from a very few voices with no time for widespread assessment. Would the Russian, Chinese, and Cuban experiences have been better if millions of participants had clearly in mind guiding institutional goals that accorded with their libertarian values? Might the Argentine upsurge have even overcome capitalism with a new system if the citizens had understood and believed in new institutional structures? Might the occupied Argentine factories have more chance of retaining their virtues and of inspiring others if they were clearer about how what they were doing was part and parcel of new economic ends?

Parecon

The task is not so much to see what no one has yet seen; but to think what no one has yet thought about that which everybody sees.
—Erwin Schrödinger

So have I produced vision myself? Yes, I have done so as a high priority, from the beginning of my political life, but especially over the last twenty years when Robin Hahnel and I percolated our visionary views in endless discussions that became very explicit in the 1980s. Participatory economics, or "parecon," emerged from a multifaceted process. Contributing to its shape was our critique of what are called market socialism and centrally planned socialism, our understanding of class relations including a group between labor and capital who we called coordinators, our emphasis on the full material, personal, and social inputs and outputs of economic activities, our experiential and theoretical rejection of markets as well as central planning, and our critical familiarity with previous libertarian thought and practice and with the South End Press experiment in visionary economic organization.

The parecon vision was built on four central values addressing interpersonal relations, social options, material and social distribution, and decision making. The values are solidarity, diversity, equity, and self-management. Solidarity and diversity meant people caring about rather than violating one another, and options being rich and varied rather than homogenized. But equity and self-management were less clear.

We examined a long tradition of debate about equitable remuneration and appropriate influence over decisions. Economic equity meant people ought to get as remuneration for their labors what they deserve. This led us to a norm. You don't deserve benefit because you are lucky—and therefore not for having highly valued inborn talents, or for being in the right place at the right time, or for having highly productive workmates, or for happening to be producing something in short supply or high demand. You don't even deserve to be rewarded for learned skills and talents, per se. Rather, what we came to believe was that remuneration should be for the duration, intensity, and also the onerousness of the work we do. Of course, making a complete case for this claim, as against rewarding property, power, or output, required more detail, but the essence was intuitively obvious.

Similarly, when thinking about how much say people should have in decisions, we arrived at what we called "self-management," by which we meant that each person should have a say in each decision proportionate to how that person is affected by the decision. If I was going to be more affected by a choice, I should have more say, right up to essentially dictatorial control. If I was going to be less affected, I should have less say, right down to none. The guideline clarified when "one person one vote," or consensus, or other ways of tallying influence made sense.

The key point for us, however, was that the task of filling out a vision meant devising compatible institutions. We had long since realized that private ownership of workplaces and resources (not shirts and PCs) produced class division, violating all our preferred values. We also realized that corporate divisions of labor imposed class rule, and destroyed solidarity and self-management. Remuneration for property and power also obviously violated our notion of equity, and therefore also had to go. And we also decided that market allocation violated our values and we thus became what might be called "market abolitionists." We knew markets would be around for a while. But we thought that somewhere down the road people would look back at markets, incredulous at the incredible damage they wrought.

So the economic visionary question that arose for Robin and I was how could we define production, allocation, and consumption without using any rejected capitalist or coordinatorist structures. We realized owning productive property wasn't needed to determine remuneration or to convey power. It wasn't needed, period. Likewise, the experiences of South End Press, coupled with our priority attention to the institutional roots of coordinator class rule, led us not only to reject corporate divisions of labor, but also pointed us directly toward defining something new in its place: balanced job complexes.

I remember brainstorming these issues with Robin. How can people work together without some people bossing others? It can't be that we all do everything. That's impossible. On the other hand, it would be equally self-defeating to rhetorically reject hierarchy but institutionally retain the conditions that produce it. In that case, our institutional backwardness would subvert our moral innovation.

We also couldn't eliminate expertise, per se. Without expertise we would lose the outputs great talent and training permit and also the personal fulfillment that utilizing talents brings to people. We would have to somehow have people do highly exacting, conceptual, and skilled labors but not have people accrue conditions, inclinations, and means to differentiate themselves from others. To us, the only solution seemed to be to apportion tasks so that everyone had work with an overall average empowerment effect.

Our alternative to a corporate division of labor was that we all would do jobs that we are suited to and that in sum total got the overall agenda fulfilled. But instead of doing only rote or only fulfilling and empowering work, we would each do a mix of tasks—some rote and boring, some fulfilling and empowering—that, on balance, empowered everyone equally.

Beyond the division of labor, considering remuneration, we thought about what was just as well as economically effective. How could people share all the burdens and benefits of labor fairly? We could each do a share of what was onerous, took time, and required intensity, and we could receive for our labors at the same rate per duration, time, and onerousness, as all other folks.

Decision making was similar. How much say should each person have in a worthy economy? Or, more accurately, how much say could each person have consistent with others having the same say and also with each person feeling that his or her input made sense and was fair? Our favoring self-management was a reaction, I think, to both tyranny and to typical democracy as we experienced it.

We first became attached to the remunerative norm and the idea of workers' and consumers' councils and self-management. We could envision, however, that adopting those features but retaining a corporate division of labor would be internally inconsistent. The old division of labor would subvert the new remuneration and council self-management. Thus, we could see that we had to have a new division of labor, which led us to balanced job complexes. But then even having all those attributes, we could see that if the firms were connected to each other and to consumers by central planning or markets, again it would subvert the gains. Our understanding of markets and central planning, and knowledge of their actual history, caused us to feel that these familiar means of allocation would subvert equitable and classless structures and reimpose coordinator-class rule. We needed a new allocation system, which we called "participatory planning" and spent endless time massaging into worthy viability.

The above paragraph indicates some of our thought experiments, and there were many more assuming various structures in proximity to one another, seeing in our mind's eye their implications for each other, and then opting for a choice consistent with our values.

Looking Forward, which first presented parecon, was written for activists and really for anyone who might pick it up to read it. The style was as accessible as we could make it. *The Political Economy of Participatory Economics,* in contrast, was written for professional economists. Its language and math were designed to communicate with professionals in their preferred technical language. Together the pair of books was a double-barreled approach. The second book, done by Princeton University Press, was meant to legitimate the undertaking as a whole, a sad necessity in our eyes. Regarding this, two things were very interesting to me.

Princeton is one of the most prestigious nonfiction publishing houses in the country. As hoped, many people regarded our getting published by them as a sign of the worthiness of our economic vision. In truth, Princeton published us because they accidentally sent the reading copy to folks who would be positive about it, folks who we knew and who liked our work, including Herb Gintis. Had that not occurred—and the odds were very much against it happening—most likely, Princeton would not have published the book. Ir wasn't entirely luck, however, that got the book published. An editor really liked it and cleverly asked us for a list of who they might send it to, and they carried through on one of our suggestions. Getting published at SEP is far more rigorous, not to mention the better company you travel in.

The even bigger and related truth was that the SEP popular book was not a watered-down summary of the Princeton publication. If anything, it had more content. Princeton was parts of SEP written over in a technical manner, with nowhere near the descriptive range. If this reminds you a little of my reaction to postmodernism, you are reading astutely. I don't want to exaggerate. The Princeton book climaxes with a series of "proofs" about parecon and also other economic models, which uses technical language for making very precise the logic of a perspective and testing its steps very carefully. Still, if we had permanently jettisoned clear communication, rather than only very momentarily opting for elements of technical language for very specific ends, it would have been a similar dynamic to postmodern elitism, though having content behind the obscurity.

After *Looking Forward* and *The Political Economy of Participatory Economics*, another book, *Moving Forward,* enlarged the approach to discussing strategy. It emerged from a series of essays trying to apply the logic and aims of parecon to the task of conceiving demands for change and means of winning them. *Thinking Forward,* next, tried to promote and provide tools for conceptualizing economic vision from scratch. It was a print adaptation of courses I taught at ZMI. Next, the book that seems to have propelled participatory economics into greater visibility, published with Verso Books in 2003, was *Parecon: Life After Capitalism.* Finally, and most recently, *Realizing Hope* was published by Zed in London in winter 2005. It is on vision for other parts of society and the implications for parecon and vice versa.

All the books are written as popularly as I could manage. *Parecon: Life After Capitalism* generated translations in numerous countries, trips to many parts of the world presenting the model to often quite large audiences, and a continuing growth of interest. Indeed, as I was first writing this paragraph, I received an e-mail. Check out the site "The Blue Space," the message instructed me. I did so and "The Blue Space" was a travel business, obviously capable in their genre, offering trips to Nepal, Thailand, India, Burma, Spain, Japan, and Austria, modeled on parecon principles. The vision spreads.

Australia, Austria, and Vision Gaining Ground

If the workers took a notion they could stop all speeding trains; every ship upon the ocean they can tie with mighty chains. Every wheel in the creation every mine and every mill; fleets and armies of the nation, will at their command

stand still

—Joe Hill

I went to Australia for over two weeks some years back. There were many talks and interviews. There were, for me, incredibly long periods on television and radio. An afternoon boating in Sydney Harbor with ZNet contributor John Hepburn as host, and a morning at the Sydney zoo. The university in Melbourne was beautiful.

In Australia, I spoke a few times at a large conference of East Asia leftists, almost entirely Marxist Leninist, and at a local social forum in Brisbane, among other venues. At the big conference, which was my first stop, everyone kept calling everyone else comrade. I don't think there were ten sentences without two or more references to comrade so and so and comrade such and such, as well as to comrades, plural. It drove me batty.

In my experience, political groups—the more so, the more sectarian and insular they are—tend to adopt many tightly shared cultural, stylistic, and verbal affectations. I think it isn't hard to understand this insularity as arising from two causes. First, adrift in hostile lands, people in Left groups tend to feel a need to bond. And second, there is often a dominant personality or two from whom others in the group pick up habits.

In the U.S., in the sixties, this was very evident. Even decades later, I bet if I were in a room with five people and one was an ex-Weather person, I could pick the sixties lefty out just by seeing and hearing familiar mannerisms that had hung on for decades. The extreme variants of this are groups whose members try to look like Lenin or Trotsky, suspenders and all. I'd say you gotta wonder about that, but in truth, anarchists, social democrats, republicans, democrats, and, indeed, everyone has their styles. In Australia, then, I quite liked my Leninist hosts save for their "comrade" affectation. But when I asked about it, I got my comeuppance. They said, hey, it isn't leftist, everyone in Australia does it, mate.

Hearing about some of the history of the Australian Left, and particularly about its labor movements and efforts to in some degree control work by what were called "green zones," where workers would use ecological and social criteria to grade job proposals and would refuse to do those that failed to measure up, was highly inspiring. People who had been active in these efforts appreciating parecon as embodying what they had felt was quite promising.

I later was invited to Austria to speak to a large conference of prominent mainstream architects from all over the world. The conference organizers had seen a write-up of parecon in a German mainstream newspaper and looked up the site and decided a talk about parecon would be a great addition to their conference. Given that the trip promised to be a bit different and perhaps engender some ripples on behalf of parecon, I said yes.

In Vienna, my talk went fine, but there wasn't nearly as much opportunity for discussion as I would have liked. A high point was that representatives from the U.S. biosphere project were very excited by parecon. Visiting their room, lo and behold, they had three parecon books they were working through. Since then they have been in touch about working together on a sustainable community project in Texas, just getting underway. But what I found most interesting was that the architect talks I attended all presumed the existing social relations of society and of the institutions their buildings would house. Everyone was concerned about making structures sustainably harmonize with nature. They were aggressive about that goal, but not about better social relations. There was some discussion of how structures could facilitate human participation and desirable behaviors, but this arose only with respect to people eating in restaurants, or visiting a museum, or browsing and buying items in a mall. What wasn't present was concern for the implications of designing workplaces so that all members could be self-managing partners instead of most being merely cogs in a hierarchical corporation. Ecology had become a centrally considered variable. Social relations had not. In all-too-brief conversations, however, it was obvious many of the architects knew why this was so, even if they didn't discuss it. Capitalism delimited their options. Whoever paid their bill determined their tune. I got invited to the conference, but there was a very sturdy wall between my wanting them to address what an architecture of real liberation would be like and their wanting their projects funded.

You had to see the incredible high-tech videos used to punctuate their talks to realize just how wild their imaginations were. They envisioned buildings that could reshape themselves in accord with weather patterns or ecological changes. They envisioned mobile and flexible patterns of buildings and byways in cities—including even mobile mountains. Yet they simply could not envision a workplace that required a horizontal and networked, rather than an up and down, hierarchical flow of information. They could not envision towns or cities whose designs reflected and facilitated self-management. It wasn't, of course, that they lacked imagination to take these steps. It was that they lacked the wherewithal to jump a commercial barrier that walled off another world different from the one they nearly universally assumed to be permanent.

Rimini and Vision Applauded

I once had a sparrow alight upon my shoulder for a moment while I was hoeing in a village garden, and I felt that I was more distinguished by that circumstance that I should have been by any epaulet I could have worn.
—Henry David Thoreau

One day in 2004, a large package arrived for me. Inside were two posters, two large books, and one small one, all expensively printed in full color. The posters announced a yearly conference in Rimini, Italy. It seemed that the package was an invitation to attend and speak at the conference. At that point, since I had been to Italy twice already, I set the whole package aside to get back to it later in the day.

Returning to the pile, I saw that the books were about the past year's convocation. They were full of pictures of people who attended and transcripts of talks. The event was held by the Pio Manzu Institute, an organization that was obviously large and mainstream. I then saw two letters tucked inside the package. The first letter invited me to speak at the gathering, as I had expected, but the included list of names of the officials of the Pio Manzu Institute was incomprehensible. Henry Kissinger and Mikhail Gorbachev were cochairs.

Gorbachev? Kissinger? This had to be a hoax. But how could anyone afford to send me so much stuff as a hoax? Maybe they got the books and poster from the prior year and forged the letter. The second letter said I was not only to speak, but I was to receive the highest award the event offered, which was called—brace yourself—The Award of the President of the Republic of Italy, who was at the time the protofascist Enrico Berlinguer. Yet the letter, signed by Gorbachev, was sober and thoughtful.

Then there was the third and thinnest of the three full-color bound books. It was a draft of this coming year's agenda and I was listed in this volume, as both recipient and speaker. With no lack of chutzpa they had even inserted a title for my talk. The event was divided into panels and I was to both speak on one and chair it. Other speakers on my panel included Gary Becker, a right-wing Nobel Prizewinning economist from the University of Chicago. If I was incredulous about all this, he would be apoplectic to have me chairing his presentation. The

363

whole thing was too outrageous to be credible. But the mailing's contents were way too expensive to be false.

I Googled some, and it turned out Pio Manzu was real. In the past, a few other leftists had attended, including Vandana Shiva and Samir Amin. Many heads of state had received the highest award, as well as Nobel Prize winners and famous artists. In other words, I was being asked to enter far less august company, by Left standards, then I usually considered wise. By mainstream standards, however, this was a big deal.

In Rimini, Italy, parts of the city were closed off each year for the event. The invitation was kind enough to let me know that I did not have to bring my own security people, the hosts would provide safe passage. Imagine my relief. Regrettably, there was no financial award. Worse, I had to buy a suit. But for the publicity that getting the award might generate and to see the events and give the talk, and because I would do just about anything to get parecon debated and more visible, I went to Rimini, and Lydia came, too.

The Rimini events were incredibly boring, as you might expect. They had considerable pomp but little circumstance. The talks I heard were abysmal, I think, particularly Michael Novack arguing that capitalism is humankind's greatest benefactor and André Glucksmann posturing that he himself was humankind's greatest benefactor. Regrettably, while those two awardees attended the session, Gary Becker didn't show up at all. That was too bad, since I had hoped to debate him. But here is what seemed to me to be quite sad about all this. I didn't like being awarded. It was absurd, obviously, and not only given the setting and the benefactors, but because an economic vision emerges from a gigantic process of social change and attention, not from one person. But that said, and it is true of virtually all intellectual awards, it also has to be said that the Pio Manzu award committee at least was doing what it intended.There was no error. With the medals came a statement from Pio Manzu's Mikhail Gorbachev:

> Medal of the President of the Italian Republic Awarded by the International Scientific Committee of the Pio Manzù Centre
>
> The highly prolific American economist Michael Albert is the author of a bold, innovative economic theory aimed at replacing self-serving competition in the economic field with egalitarian cooperation.
>
> Together with his co-author Robin Hahnel, Professor of Economics at American University, Washington D.C., he has developed and popularized a radical economic model, known as Participatory Economics, which constitutes an alternative both to capitalism and to what used to be the Soviet-style model of Real Socialism.

In Participatory Economics, solidarity takes the place of competition and remuneration for duration, intensity, and onerousness of work replaces remuneration for property, power, or output. Likewise, methods of self management replace authoritarian decision making and a new method of allocation called participatory planning replaces markets.

To realize his project of radically changing a private-enterprise production system that generates economic inefficiency, Michael Albert counts on workers and consumers operating in councils according to the principle of participatory self-management.

The Pio Manzù Centre recognizes that this American economist's radical new theory constitutes the most powerful and fully articulated challenge to the current models of socio-economic thought and that Albert's outstanding merit lies in the fact that he has indicated a new major highway in economic organization as a feasible proposition.

Signed
Mikhail Gorbachev, President
Rimini, 17 October 2004

Nothing has ever been published about parecon, at least by leftists in the U.S., that quite matches the above. This isn't because there is no one in the U.S. relating wholeheartedly and equally positively to parecon. There are such people here and around the world. When I went to Greece right after Rimini, I spent about an hour with a Greek war hero, very possibly Greece's next president. He acted as though he were the one being honored by having the chance to sit and talk with me. I've had lengthy television interviews in Greece, Turkey, Italy, Australia, and other countries, sometimes during prime time and with noted interviewers who are quite aware of parecon and prepared to ask good questions. In contrast, the absence of ideologically leftist reactions to parecon, particularly in the U.S., occurs, I think, because the Left literally fears liking new ideas, agreeing about them, celebrating them, or even disagreeing about them, especially those that threaten familiar notions about social change. In the rest of the world, no one knew parecon was threatening. In that context, think how strange it was to see parecon treated so respectfully by the mainstream Pio Manzu Institute, which was not an assemblage of my peers, but much closer to an assemblage of corporate advocates, or by the Greek future presidential candidate, or by mainstream TV interviewers in Turkey and Australia. All this contrasted significantly with parecon's effect in the U.S., where it was off the map at the mainstream level, of course, but was also excluded from broad attention on the Left.

The talk I gave at the Rimini event was titled "Life After Capitalism–And Now Too." It ran about an hour. At the end I said:

Parecon is a vision aimed to replace cynicism with hope and reason. It seeks to clarify that capitalism is not like gravity–we can replace it.

The citation for the Award of the President of the Italian Republic that I was graciously given yesterday, said that parecon is the "the most powerful and fully articulated challenge to the current models of socio-economic thought" providing "a new major highway in economic organization as a feasible proposition."

Anyone who believes that about parecon, it seems to me, ought to fight like the dickens not only to ameliorate the current ills produced by capitalism, but to usher in the benefits of this new type economy.

When we all go to movies and see courageous souls of the past represented on the screen, fighting against slavery, or against the subordination of women, or against colonialism, or for peace and justice and against dictatorships, we rightly feel sympathy and admiration for these acts. The abolitionists, the suffragists, the labor union organizers, the antiapartheid activists, all the seekers of freedom and dignity are heroes for us.

It seems to me we should not admire something and then avoid doing that same thing. If we admire standing up against injustice, we ought to ourselves stand up against injustice. If we admire seeking a better world, we should ourselves seek a better world. If we admire rejecting exploitation, alienation, domination, and its violent maintenance, we should ourselves advocate and fight for an economic model and societal structure that will eliminate these horrors. I believe that participatory economics is such an economy and should be part of such a new society.

When Lydia and I were leaving the Rimini hotel, a young man in a hotel uniform crossed the floor and walked up to me. Lydia and I thought he was going to ask to carry our bags, and I sort of nodded and mumbled, thanks, but we didn't need help. The young man grabbed my arm and said, no, wait. He had a Spanish accent, not Italian, and it turned out he was from Argentina, not Italy. What he wanted was for me to sign a copy of a short Italian collection of articles by me about parecon that didn't even exist in English. He had read this book. He loved the model. This was the high point of the whole Rimini event, from the time I got the invitation at home until leaving Rimini. This young man's interest in parecon was singularly uplifting to me. He was probably the most working-class and least auspicious person we talked to at the Rimini events, and so his taste mattered most, by far. The board of the Pio Manzu Institute voting me the Award of the President of the Republic of Italy mattered only insofar as it might bring parecon into contact with more people like this young Argentinean. The congratulations and admiring-but-largely-ignorant nods from other attendees had for the most part no serious meaning at all, other than to display hypocrisy masquerading as civility. The award itself was not uplifting, but depressing. The young man's interest was uplifting. Who knows what he will do over the course of his life?

Turkey, India, and Relevance

> *Another world is not only possible, she is on her way.*
> *On a quiet day, I can hear her breathing.*
> —*Arundhati Roy*

In September, 2003, I took a trip to Turkey sponsored by my Turkish publisher, Aram, a radical operation not unlike South End Press in the U.S.. I spoke in Istanbul and Diyarbaker. Istanbul is a huge city, beautiful, and, in some respects, quite European. Diyarbaker is in the southeastern part of Turkey, very near Syria and Iraq, and in the midst of Kurdish regions. Diyarbaker's population was greatly inflated by an influx of roughly a million Kurdish people displaced from villages burned and destroyed by Turkish repression.

I found the Kurdish suffering hard to understand in terms.of racial dynamics familiar in the U.S., whether now or in the past. Were a plebiscite held among the Turkish population, I was told, rights would be fully accorded. There was none of the person-to-person racism that we see in the U.S. Instead, the issue seemed primarily national or collective. Turkey was meant to seamlessly have one people, one culture, one population, in the eyes of most non-Kurds, and particularly Turkey's elites. The Kurds resisted losing their modes of celebration, identification, language, and culture—and this pitted national fear of secession against Kurdish resistance to assimilation.

Whatever the deepest causes and continuing basis for the injustices, and whatever their full scope and range, Kurdish pathos was plain to see. Sitting with mothers of disappeared Kurdish youth was like sitting with the survivors of victims of violent repression anywhere. Their strength and solidarity sought to prevent similar pain from afflicting other people's lives. It was inspiring.

The Turkish trip involved a steady flow of media interviews and public talks. The folks from Aram escorted me all over, set up the interviews, took care of the timing, and provided seemingly endless tea. I would be placed in a big meeting area in a hotel, and news correspondents and magazine writers would arrive, one after another. Commentators would arrive early in hopes of extra time, and would stay late, quietly listening in on the next interviewer's session. Commentators had serious and substantive queries about parecon, and, of course, about Bush, the U.S. election, and U.S. empire building.

We would also go to offices of media operations that couldn't come to us. A large alternative radio station, for example, had me on for over an hour. I was on TV for long sessions as well. Print interviews went on from morning to night. Not a single question was asked about the condition of Kurds. Such matters were forbidden. But where threat of repression wasn't in play, for example regarding international relations and also matters of economics, including capitalism and alternative vision, questions were highly informed and asked seemingly without reservation. I was told the resulting articles didn't exclude content either, though I couldn't judge that myself.

Whereas the Kurdish communities in Iraq and other neighboring countries harbor considerable and sometimes almost unlimited illusions about the potential for U.S. largesse to aid their prospects, in Turkey I found this view ridiculed. Turkish Kurds felt their future depended, instead, on their own wherewithal as well as on whether international opinion could be awakened to their plight despite the difficult hurdle of U.S. media opposition.

Turkey, which is generally considered the most repressive Western country, and which was then seeking admission to the European Union, seemed to have media that was way ahead of the U.S. for its comprehension of world affairs and the ins and outs of domestic institutional relations, including capitalism. Judging by my sponsors' descriptions of the contents of newspapers and shows, the Turkish and Kurdish public hears more that is thought-provoking and informative than do their U.S. counterparts—but, of course, the repressive environment constrains what they can do with their understanding. As but one example, I was on CNN Turkey for about an hour. You can imagine my amusement: me on CNN (or the Turkish version of it, anyhow). And what made it really amazing is that I spoke as I would to a leftist audience at a rally in the U.S. The announcer not only had no trouble understanding my words, but asked probing questions, seeking more information and analysis.

On another mainstream TV show, an hour and a half long, a quite famous Turkish interviewer concluded by asking me what they would have to do with their TV station to make it more like the economic vision I described. I did a double take. He noticed and asked why. I have only quite rarely been asked such a question when talking with U.S. or British alternative media people, I told him, and even then never for presentation in some alternative media outlet, but only off the record. In U.S. mainstream media, to be asked such a question would be utterly inconceivable. A star mainstream media commentator in the West would consider it like asking a delusional paranoid maniac how their station should conduct its business. But to one of the most prominent newscasters in Turkey, after an hour and a half together in front of the cameras, it was just an honest question reflecting his sincere interest.

The sense in which I see this differently, perhaps, than other Westerners who have experienced it, is that I think the popular critical consciousness that was more on the surface in Turkey exists as well in the West, and even in the U.S., though it is less visible here. And I also think that what exists in the U.S.—boundless social passivity and doubt—exists as well around the world and diminishes the value of the greater visible consciousness in Turkey, and elsewhere, too. What this says to me is that if we work with tremendous diligence and ingenuity, and if we successfully bring critical consciousness about how the world works more to the surface of people's minds in the U.S., that alone will not ensure that we have more activism, more dissent, and a path to better relations. We would also have to bring to the surface *hope* and *vision*, which are needed as well in Turkey.

In Istanbul, I stayed in a room overlooking the Bosphorus Straits, a very beautiful span running as far as I could see in both directions. Interestingly, police presence was low in Istanbul. It was, at least to my eyes, much less there than, say, in New York or Chicago. More surprisingly, this was also true for Diyarbaker, located in a virtual war zone, though admittedly enjoying a long period of ceasefire. Poorer districts that bordered directly on shopping zones had very little police presence. On the other hand, after one talk in Diyarbaker, an undercover cop came up and started asking questions trying to get me to say something that could be used not to hassle me, but to repress my hosts, the radical Aram publishing operation.

The Left in Istanbul was familiar to me, even though I'd had no prior contact with it. It wasn't just that my hosts from Aram were well versed in parecon and my other writing and therefore were very easy to communicate with because their views were more akin to my own than I might find among the Left in Chicago. It was that we also shared general international knowledge, cultural tastes, and preferences. Particularly familiar was a gathering of leftists in Istanbul assembled for a presentation about economic vision. This audience was, in fact, barely distinguishable from an audience I might speak with in Madison, Wisconsin, say. It had very similar questions. Even the division of this audience into folks with anarchist leanings, Trotskyite leanings, or neophyte views was similar to what I might find in populous U.S. cities. Of course, the history that lurked in people's consciousness was different. And in the Kurdish region of Turkey, both my public talks and the interviews I did went up a notch in their intensity and connection to real practice and aspirations. Audiences were more directly entrenched in struggle, both around the repression and denial of Kurds and other issues as well.

Even though this was a quick trip, it was striking that the Kurdish activists, citizens, and public officials, while congenial, hospitable, smiling, and humorous, were also deadly serious and clearly committed to winning, not merely struggling. Their national and cultural resistance seemed as well to lead them to economic and social desires that were more aggressively radical than for other sectors in the country. It surprised me to find out that the main Kurdish leader, a figure with immense support throughout the Kurdish population of 20 million—a person housed in jail for life and held generally in isolation save from his lawyers, and a person who is in jail due to having been caught in exile in Kenya by the CIA and delivered back to Turkey—was at least at that moment urging a reconstruction of the Kurdish opposition away from their highly nationalist, Leninist, and often violently sectarian and military past, toward a more civil-disobedient, nonviolent, multi-issue, participatory, and antisectarian future by, among other things, urging members of the Kurdish resistance to read the Turkish edition of my book *Trajectory of Change* with every indication that the just-released Turkish edition of *Parecon: Life After Capitalism* would be touted soon.

This revelation was even more dramatic and unexpected than when, a year earlier, a person I met at the World Social Forum in Brazil had explained how in his town in the Amazon area, they would go into the city each week, download materials from ZNet, copy them, and bring them back and distribute them to their agrarian neighbors, or when a young African activist eloquently argued views that I, too, advocate, and touted their relevance as if they had been born in the byways of his continent, which, in fact, in some respects, they were.

It is ironic in the extreme, therefore, to get the occasional e-mail from young white U.S., Canadian, or British activists about how a book written by a white man from inside the beast must by definition be of no consequence for struggles anywhere else in the world and certainly anywhere in the Third World, and then to find that such a book is an important part of a campaign to restructure the Third World revolutionary movement of the Kurds in Turkey, for example, and is helping to inform the thinking of a Left publishing operation in Turkey as well. It is odd also, to have written, as I have, based largely on my own U.S. experiences and mostly for U.S. movements, and to have the results get public visibility more quickly abroad in poor and devastated zones—unemployment in Diyarbaker was 70 percent when I visited—than in the U.S.

In the moments of travel that were more personal and relaxed, even just driving from talks to interviews and back, the architecture was striking and the history palpable. Around Diyarbaker flows a wall, apparently second only to the Great Wall of China for scale and length. To stand on it and stare out over the distant Tigris and into the cradle of civilizations is quite an experience. So, too, was turning in the opposite direction and seeing a McDonald's and other vile and vulgar imprints of multinational growth, largely spurned by the populace, but with a staying power hard to deny.

I should perhaps also say, Turkey is well over 90 percent Moslem but aside from the public calls to prayer and the spires of mosques dotting one's view in nearly all directions, this fact was basically invisible as far as differences in public behavior in Istanbul and was relatively minor in Diyarbaker, too, at least at the superficial level that I could observe while giving interviews, moving from site to site, as well as meeting with mothers of disappeared Kurdish activists. Many of the journalists who interviewed me were women, easily as confident as their male counterparts. I encountered nothing that even implied any religious practices or beliefs—less so than I would have in many places in the U.S.—and the only behavior that seemed slightly different than might have held sway had I been doing interview after interview in LA—other than that the questions in LA would have been so vastly inferior and the idea that I would have been on mainstream media in LA is preposterous—was the ubiquitous serving of tea in Turkey. But again, this was a short visit with very odd limitations in that I was giving talks and interviews on top of talks and interviews. Still, what it suggested was that a liberating theory devised to change social relations in the U.S. could be valuable in Turkey, and vice versa.

Another trip arising from the parecon experience was when Lydia and I attended the fourth WSF in Mumbai, India. Ignoring the forum aspect, India itself was incredible. It wasn't just that the drivers in Mumbai would have been at home in U.S. stockcar races, literally, to the point that Lydia and I were really scared for the first couple of days driving in cabs. Indeed, at one point I was so taken by it that I even asked Arundhati Roy and then later Devinder Sharma, both Indian, both friends from ZNet, whether they themselves drove like their cabbies. They said, sure, of course. Incredible. I can't convey the wild-riding scariness of it.

Likewise, it wasn't just the poverty, shanties, and slums that were striking. To see that was very different than to see poverty in the U.S., only in degree, not in kind. And it wasn't only at the bottom that things were strikingly poorer than we had seen before. Mumbai is more or less India's New York City. There is a major hotel, the Taj Mahal, in Mumbai. This is where rich people stay when they visit. We went into town one day, toured around, and spent a little time, as well, looking at the Taj Mahal hotel. It was barely more impressive than a nice Holiday Inn in Toledo, though markedly bigger.

What seemed different in India was three main things. First, the diversity transcended anything I had ever contemplated. Many places I have been have seemed marginally different from the U.S. A few have seemed quite different, but not shockingly so. But India had nations in neighborhoods. You could see Western ways intruding, but not so much that there wasn't a clear gap. In Turkey, even in east Turkey, far from Europe, I could still understand where I was, and what was what. In India, the range of dress, demeanor, and language, exceeded my ken.

The second thing that struck me was the mindset of the urban poor. If you thought to look closely, you noticed there weren't many police on the streets, and virtually none in the slums. An American could walk among the most extreme poverty with little fear. You could have fancy clothes and a leather bag and not fear it would be stolen away. I don't know the causes of this, but the stark contrast to the typical levels of fear and violence in the U.S. was great. After a time I began to even wonder, why don't these hungry people steal? Why don't they feel intense anger?

Visiting with Arundhati Roy during the forum, Lydia and I asked her about all this and she said she had a similar reaction. She thought it was probably the dynamics of caste, plus colonialism, plus who knows what else. She told me that as large a gap as there was in the violence quotient, we might call it, between what I was finding in India compared to what I knew in the U.S., she felt it even more profoundly when she had been in South Africa. In Johannesburg, she told me, she was always tense, always felt violence in the air, even more than in the U.S. What creates or stifles that tension in the air, and an associated busyness in the hospital wards, seems worth understanding, if someone can penetrate the fog.

The third thing that struck me was the condition of the nonpoor, but also nonrich. Take Arundhati Roy, or any Indian leftist of comfortable means. Such a person must frequently move around the cities and country, of course. He or she will be continually besieged by the poor. People without a limb, or any limbs, constantly ask for aid. From the gutters, they grab at cars. They grab at your ankles. And, to get by, to function, you must become inured to it. You converse with an Indian friend in the midst of this, and for the person from India it is as if these beggars aren't there. If you live in India, you don't notice them, you don't acknowledge them, you don't even ignore them. They don't exist. What does that do to the person who makes him or herself oblivious in that way? I don't know. I think it probably differs from person to person. I have a very hard time with it. It is part of why I no longer live in Boston, much less in Mumbai. Others, however, can be turned off to even noticing such pain most of the time, and can then, when it can accomplish something, be turned incredibly on to the pain and to trying to alleviate it. Humans are diverse.

I don't think anyone knows, other than by experience and experiment, the policies that an intensely poor town in India, in the Amazon, in China, Turkey, or Egypt, or, for that matter, in a well-off or a poor town in Europe or the Americas, should or will choose as its path of development once attaining its freedom. What I think we can say, however, is that the choice ought to rest with those affected, not with pin-striped, callous calculators, floating in high-rises, tremendously far from the effects of their machinations. Parecon, and a participatory society, is about those affected making choices.

Venezuela's Path: Pareconist?

In the discovery of hidden things and the investigation of hidden causes, stronger reasons are obtained from sure experiments and demonstrated arguments than from probable conjectures and the opinions of philosophical speculators of the common sort.

—William Gilbert

In October 2005, I spent a week in Caracas, Venezuela. Having encountered the New Left, Cuba, Poland, and much else, this was new, and in my opinion, quite hopeful. My first and arguably most personally surprising encounter with the Bolivarian Revolution was at the Ministry for Popular Participation, which was created in accord, I was told, with Chavez's desire "that the people should take power." I asked the officials we interviewed, "What does that mean, that the people should take power?" After noting thousands of years of "empires obstructing people from participating in politics," all culminating in "the North American empire," the official said the "U.S. has had 200 years of representative government, but in your system people turn over control to others." Instead, in Venezuela, "we humbly are proposing a system where people hold power in a participatory and protagonist democracy. We want a new kind of democracy to attain a new kind of society."

On the wall was a diagram of their aims. It had lots of little circles, then other larger ones in another layer, and so on. The idea, they said, "was to establish numerous local grassroots assemblies or councils of citizens where people could directly express themselves." These local councils would be the foundational components of "a new system of participatory democracy."

The bottom layer of the diagram focuses on communities with "common habits and customs," the officials said. "We define them as comprising 200 to 400 families, or 1,000 to 2,000 people each." One could of course imagine subunits within each local unit, as well, but that wasn't immediately on their agenda, nor was it in their diagram. The local units would in turn send "elected spokespersons" to units another layer up. Units in this second layer would "encompass a broader geographic region," and from there, "spokespeople would be elected to another layer, and so on," creating a network covering "parishes, municipalities, states, and the whole society."

The participation officials, explaining their diagram and their goal, said the smallest units were meant to become "the decision-making core of the new Venezuelan polity." Chavez and this ministry hoped to have, they said, "three thousand local assemblies in place by the new year." Their goal was to have "enough in place, throughout the country, in four or five years, to account for twenty-six million Venezuelans." They didn't want "a dictatorship of the

373

proletariat or of any other kind," they said. Strikingly, they also said they didn't want "what Che died for, though they wanted to learn from that." They wanted to build something new, from the bottom.

I asked, "What happens if the local assemblies want some new policy, and the ministers, legislature, or Chavez don't want it?" "No matter," they said, "the assemblies, once they are in place and operating, rule."

"But," I said, "you don't want an assembly of 100 families making a decision for the whole country, surely." "Correct," came the answer, "the local assemblies can only make final decisions bearing just on their own area."

"Suppose one assembly decides it wants some change bearing on crime that has to do with federal courts or police or whatever, extending beyond that community?" I asked. "What happens? When does the law or policy change?"

"On every level there should be a response," came the reply. "On the lowest level assemblies would do whatever they can within their community. But crime goes beyond a community, and requires going to the next higher levels where the issues would have to be confronted, too. On the municipal level they might change ordinances, etc., to also respond. And it could go higher, then."

Okay, I asked, "Suppose one local assembly wants a younger voting age. They bring it to the next higher level and members there are excited about it too. Does it go up to a legislature and does the legislature have any choice?"

I was told the local unit would—through its spokespeople—send the proposal to the next layer of the popular democratic structures. "Had they decided something bearing only on their local neighborhood, which is all that is happening now, such as the age required for local votes, it would simply be enacted, under their supervision, for them, without having to be discussed more widely." But if their desire stretched wider, as a general new voting law for national elections would, "their proposal would go up, as far as is relevant. Then the proposal would go back to the base of all assemblies for all to consider."

These Bolivarians, entrusted by Chavez's administration with building a parallel polity, didn't want any more representative decision making than absolutely necessary. They wanted a proposal from one assembly to go up, not so it could be decided by representatives, but so it could be discussed by and then brought back to other local assemblies by their spokespeople, to be decided at large. "If support came," I was told, "then the goal is that it would yield a new voting age, whether Chavez or mayors or the legislature or anyone else wanted the change or not." I said surely there must be many elected or just appointed mayors, governors, or bureaucrats who would obstruct this vision, not wanting their power reduced or that of the populace increased. "Yes," I was told, "many bureaucrats have held positions for twenty or thirty years and about sixty percent of them are putting breaks on the proposal."

"Even among ministers in the Chavez administration," I asked, "do some resent that they would go from having power to just obeying the public? Cuba's *poder popular* began with many of the ideals you express," I noted, "but never got to the point where the national power was participatory. Do you believe that the Chavez government will help the assembly system reach its full development, or that after a while the assembly system will have to push against the government to get full power?"

The answer was, "Only the organized population can decide. We are on a path to invent a new democracy. We have gone forward from what we had before. There are no guarantees, but we are trying to go further." There was no need, the officials said, to remove or forcefully conflict with the old structures. Rather, the new system would be built alongside what now exists and would prove its worth over time, in parallel. Many in the old would come around, others wouldn't. But either way, in time the old forms would be replaced by the impressive reality of the new forms' success, not by fiat or by force.

"How will Chavez's initiative encourage people to create these local assemblies?" I wondered. The whole assembly structure was a project in development, the officials said, and there were diverse ideas about how to make it happen. Here was the most striking and instructive one I heard. "We Bolivarians have a program for citizens in barrios to gain ownership of their current dwellings. They need only petition to do so, but they have to do that in groups of 200 families or more for the petition to be accepted." The dwellers get their homes. The community hopefully becomes a grassroots assembly.

I asked, "Do you find that the government has to prod the people to participate?" The officials replied, "The people are taking initiative, but it is very important that the government support them." People taking power involves "a new way of thinking and a new culture. The president and we are working hard to make participatory democracy happen, but we all have limitations in our heads to overcome, as well as old structures." This was a recurring theme. In Venezuela, while there have been coups and thus struggle against capital and external imperialism, at the moment the struggle seems to be more against the imprint of the past on people's habits and beliefs.

"How many people," I asked, "already support this program?" "The full picture of assemblies is very new, just about to be announced," they said, "but the general goal of people's power maybe about a quarter understand and strongly support, with more soon." They emphasized they didn't want a system "that gives power to another person." They didn't "want representative democracy." The people elect, in the Venezuelan model, "spokespeople, not representatives." What will be proposed in one unit will get to the other units by going up via elected spokespeople, and back down to the base through other spokespeople. What will be decided at lowest levels will be binding. "The country has 335 municipalities. About 255 are with the president."

Discussions about police and courts are also proceeding, I was told, but I didn't get to talk with people working on that dimension of change and apparently it was, as yet, not nearly as far along. These officials told me that the "socialism we are trying to construct incorporates understanding the history of past efforts in Russia, Cuba, etc., but it is not about state-run enterprises or a dictatorship. We have to create our own model to reduce the work week, to defend nature, and to create social justice for both the collective and the individual. If it continues, capitalism will put an end to the planet. We have to find a way for everybody to have a better standard of living but also preserve the planet. A virtuous individual thinks about the community. That is what we are looking for."

On the same trip, regarding health, though I didn't get to talk to any government officials directly involved with the program, or to any doctors dispensing medicine, it was clear that again the government hadn't simply taken over the old structures and, as yet, had no inclination to do so. Instead, in cooperation with Cuba, which sent 20,000 doctors, the government had set up new clinics all over the country, dispensing health care locally in barrios, bringing to the poor their first local health care. We were told these clinics serve people's needs, operate democratically, and have doctors who earn typical worker's pay. The Chavista health officials, I would bet, look for the old structures to bend and break under the competitive pressure of the new ones, but without having been directly sundered.

We visited barrios, which were gigantic stretches of hillside covered with small shack-like homes, and we saw intermittently the newly constructed small but clean medical clinics the Cuban doctors worked from. Compared to nothing, which was the correct comparison, it was a huge improvement and helps explain Chavez's support from the barrio communities. We also heard about a plan for eye care, even offering free eye operations of diverse kinds, 500,000 operations over ten years, to poor U.S. citizens. The Venezuelans would provide the transportation. The Cubans would do the surgery. Having eye problems myself, I listened closely, smiling at the thought.

The same general pattern was true of a project aimed at raising literacy throughout Venezuela. With the same logic and methodology, this project also proceeded by not fighting with the old, but instead existing alongside it. In under two years, Chavez reports and apparently UNESCO verifies, Venezuela has eliminated illiteracy. Indeed, this same pattern is being employed, we saw, even for higher education. The government didn't take over the national universities, private or public. Instead, after the oil industry strike failed during the last coup attempt, when almost a third of the industry's managers and other technical workers were fired for having participated in trying to bring down the government, many of the prior oil administration buildings were no longer needed. Obviously the bureaucratic waste and fraud had been enormous. A group of these liberated buildings was transformed into the new Bolivarian University. Workers' councils ruled the new university. The federal minister of education became its rector. In time, he overrode the council, determining that there would be only meetings of smaller groups, and that he would interact only with representatives from those. This characteristic pattern of a central planner interacting with a workplace and demanding a chain of command in it and in that way interfering with direct self-management was disturbing. The Bolivarian revolution is juggling many tendencies with roots in many aspects of social life. But the pedagogy of the new university is, I learned by interviewing a professor, very innovative, emphasizing serving diverse communities by students having to do projects at the grassroots and in turn relating their studies to social conditions. Also, grading has become a shared task for students, faculty, and community residents.

Bolivarian University has about 7,000 students, we were told, and about 700 staff, of whom 250 are nonfaculty but only 120 are full-time professors. Some faculty resist the new pedagogy as too flexible. Some see it as too community-oriented. In meetings there are radicals and reactionaries. Some faculty resist the trend toward providing classes for nonteaching staff. Some resist having steadily more equitable pay relations among all employees. Some resist the drive to bring the school's resources out into the country, setting up missions beyond Caracas, promoting higher education while reaching out educationally to Venezuela's rural areas for the first time.

Looked at in the large, Bolivarian University competes with the rest of the system of higher education by offering an evolving, but already dramatically different experience. The minister heading Bolivarian University might not be optimal in terms of workers' self-management, but we were told he does talk forcefully about proving that the new approaches are better and replacing the old ways via having people see the benefits of change. The students at Bolivarian University, not surprisingly, are mostly poor, which is the opposite of the old system. Ties between the school and local co-ops, which are, in turn, constructed with uniform wages and council self-management, are continually extended, building a kind of parallel world to what has gone before.

Considering still another key domain of social life, media, the emerging pattern continued as the trip proceeded. A look at the daily newspapers showed that of the first 25 articles, reading from the first page forward, fully 20 were broad attacks on or highly critical of Chavez. The rest were on entirely other topics. And this was typical, day after day, I was told. The papers are privately held corporations, not surprisingly, hostile toward Chavez's inclinations. Chavez doesn't restrict them, however, much less nationalize or otherwise take them over. The same situation holds for key TV stations. Regarding the TV stations, however, and I bet something like this will also happen with print before too long, the government has a strategy.

ViVe TV is a new station created, like Bolivarian University, by the Chavez government. We visited and enjoyed touring its facilities. The widest salary difference, from the head of the company to people who cleaned up, was three to one, but the new payment policy, being steadily if slowly enforced, was to attain equal hourly pay for all by periodically raising wages of those at the bottom until they reached parity.

ViVe has roughly 300 employees. Their equipment isn't like CBS, but it is certainly excellent and far-reaching in its potential. The new ViVe Web site presents their shows, archived, for the world to see. The station's governing body is, of course, a workers' assembly. Workers at ViVe lacking skills are encouraged to take courses, including in film production and other topics, given right on the premises, and those facilities are also used to teach citizens from Caracas and more widely how to film in their own locales. Indeed, the station's mandate is to provide a voice for the people. Its shows, we were told, routinely present citizens speaking their mind, including voices from well outside Caracas, which was a first for Venezuela. To that end, ViVe undertakes lots of community training, distributing cameras to local citizens as well, so people around the country can send in footage and even finished edited material, for national display.

In some respects, ViVe is like a local community cable station in the U.S., except that it is national and the élan is far, far higher, and the desire to incorporate the seeds of the future in the present structure is far, far more explicit and radical, with the employees seeing themselves as presenting to the country and the world a new kind of media that, they hope, will be a model picked up elsewhere as well. ViVe takes no ads, "to avoid being controlled." There is actually, on the shows, much criticism of the government, since the shows convey grassroots opinions. But this criticism, unlike that on mainstream private stations, is honest and heartfelt, not manufactured. Rather than trying to create dissension, it is constructive.

Along with ViVe and a national public station directly under government control, there is also a new federal law that imposes on private stations that 25 percent of their shows must be produced by independent producers, not by the stations themselves. This is a kind of service requirement, but, interestingly, it is ViVe who trains many of these contracting producers. Here again is evidence of a kind of multipronged, legal, almost stealth incursion on old ways. This occurs both within the new institutions which are creating new approaches even against recalcitrant attitudes and habits, and also via the new institutions challenging the old ones by a contrast effect or by outright competition, and injecting ideas into them through the independent producers as well. Venezuela has also embarked on a continental station, to broadcast news and the voices of the poor throughout Latin America.

Regarding the economy, Venezuela starts out with huge advantages compared to other Third World countries. The oil industry is nationalized and is the centerpiece of the society's economy. Moreover, the oil industry provides a gigantic flow of revenues, unlike what any other dissident country has ever enjoyed while trying to chart a new path for itself. Likewise, oil not only provokes great U.S. interest, it also provides considerable defense against U.S. intervention. We were told by an oil industry official, however, that there are still many transnational firms who contract for various aspects of oil business in Venezuela. The government's reaction, he said, was not to challenge them, much less expropriate them, but to form new co-ops doing the same functions, intended to out-compete the transnationals. These new co-ops are worker managed. They usually are seeking equal wages and even in the least egalitarian ones, the ratio is at most three to one. In addition, a minimum social wage is guaranteed. An idea slowly being implemented is to federate the co-ops, facilitating their interacting and exchanging via social rather than market norms. The vision, it seemed to me, is that in time contracts will go almost exclusively to the co-ops so that the transnationals will simply leave, of their own accord, no confrontation needed.

I asked if officials thought using competing on the market as the strategy to drive out transnationals risked entrenching market mentalities, but the question wasn't really understood. Similarly, my asking whether officials were worried that utilizing market competition as a key strategy would impose on self-management old-style aims and means, greatly reducing its latitude for change and perhaps even causing it to give way to new hierarchies, also didn't resonate. There is immense opposition to capitalism and its private ownership. There is major opposition to large disparities in income. There is considerable opposition to disparities in job types imposing passivity versus domination. But only a few people seem to be hostile to markets per se.

One of the few who seems to reject markets, however, is Chavez himself. How else can we explain his approach to international economics which not only predictably rejects the IMF, WTO, World Bank, and particularly the FTAA, but is beginning to hammer out an alternative based on mutual aid and, in effect, violating market exchange rates to instead undertake transactions in light of true and full social costs and benefits, and with a commitment to sharing gains from exchanges not just equally, but more advantageously for the poorer participants. This certainly seems to be the logic of the wide array of agreements into which Venezuela is entering with not only Cuba but many neighboring countries, as well as specific occupied factories throughout Latin America, for example, providing oil at amazingly low rates and beneficial terms, often in exchange for goods, not payments. This is quite like Cuba's historic sending of aid and items to poorer countries at cut rates, but the scale is tremendously increased, and where Cuba primarily offered people, as in doctors, Venezuela is doing this with resources and economic products, more directly subverting specifically market logic.

Returning to my exchange with the oil official, when I asked about CITGO—the oil industry owned by Venezuela operating in the U.S.—moving toward establishing a workers' council to self-manage it, moving toward equal wages, and changing its division of labor not only on behalf of those working at CITGO but as a demonstration inside the U.S. for other U.S. workers of the potential of self-management and equity—the official was very excited, even wanting to immediately call others to talk about this idea. Later discussion of the related possibility of Venezuela making inroads, via CITGO or otherwise, into media and information dispersal in the U.S., instead of information incursions always occurring only in the reverse direction, caused still more excitement.

We were told by the oil ministry officials and also by trade unionists and others how in Venezuela, like in Argentina, there was a movement, just getting up to speed, to "recuperate" failing or failed workplaces. The difference was that while in Argentina this occurs against the inclinations of government, in Venezuela the government welcomes and even propels it. Indeed, the government has now assembled a list of 700 such plants and is urging workers to occupy and operate them on their own. Another difference, however, is that in Venezuela the method of decision-making adopted for the recuperated plants is called "comanagement" and involves both a workers council and government representatives. The upside of this is that the government is often to the left of the local workforce in the affected workplace, helping educate and prod it. The downside is that the centralizing inclination of the government and the participatory inclination of real self-management are in opposition. We saw both these tendencies in the Bolivarian University, with the government minister pushing radical pedagogy on sometimes contrary faculty, but also reducing the influence of the workers' council. In fact, however, it seemed for the moment, in any case, the government was so overstretched that if there were widespread recuperations, government involvement will be slight and workers will in practice be left to self-manage.

Beyond a factory-recuperation movement in Venezuela, the government also creates new co-ops from scratch. These are also co-managed, at least in theory, and also tend to seek equitable remuneration, etc. These co-ops have often been small and local, everything from little dress shops to small construction projects, but plans exist for creating new firms to produce computers, mine resources, run an airline, etc.

As I understood what I heard, the co-ops are expected to out compete old capitalist firms—a very reasonable expectation given that the co-ops have lower overhead (due to reduced management pay rates, reduced numbers of managers, and altered job roles), and that co-op workers have an inclination to produce more consistently and energetically under the new social relations. There are also dangers to the co-op strategy, however. Trying to out compete old firms in market-defined contests may entrench a managerial bureaucracy and a competitive, rather than social, orientation. It may lead more toward what is called market socialism, which in my view is a system that still has a ruling coordinator class instead of toward what the most radical Venezuelans clearly desire, which is a classless, participatory, and self-managing economy. The contrast is to operate by competing and in light of power-based prices and surplus-seeking, where people necessarily adopt a rat race mentality that guarantees some winners and many who lose, versus to operate by way of cooperative negotiation and in light of full social implications with people seeking both personal and collective well-being and in which people are socially motivated and are well-off and efficient.

In capitalist firms, still dominant in economic sectors other than oil, there is a change in mood as well. Workers identify more with the state and feel it is an ally, providing by its initiatives, in the words of a trade-union leader, "a more promising moment for change." This has led to workers in capitalist firms "challenging old union norms and methods" and feeling uncomfortable being "stuck in old relations while others are building new co-ops." This trade union leader estimated that "80 percent of Venezuela's workers firmly support Chavez." She also said that this is why the better unions are thinking about pushing for self-management even against capitalist owners. According to her, "while at first occupying failing firms was just self defense," seeking to protect "jobs and union freedoms," more recently more radical unions are seeking "more consistent strategies to win co-management or self management."

She told us that "five or six years ago the typical Venezuelan worker would not exhibit any class consciousness, but now the Bolivarian revolution was awakening class consciousness not only in workers, but in all people." I asked what would happen if "workers in a successful capitalist firm, knowing friends in co-ops or recuperated firms who enjoyed controlling their conditions and having equitable incomes, struck against their owners and petitioned the government to take over the firm and make it self-managed." She talked about how arrangements would likely be made providing the private owners "credits and investments if they would undertake co-management with the workers." I wondered why businesspeople "would make such a stupid deal when it was clearly just a first step toward their disappearing. Why would they do it, even with short-term benefits?" I

381

also asked again about "workers wanting to take over a really successful firm, not giving the owners anything, but just taking over. Why weren't workers all over Venezuela seeking that? And what would happen if they did?"

The trade union leader replied, "Of course the businesspeople are not stupid, but they believe we are." She talked about unions spreading "the revolutionary virus into the workers" and I asked again, how come it didn't spread quickly, all on its own? She blamed "old union leaders, afraid of taking new steps." But she also said that "just two years ago no one would have believed a worker-managed factory was possible but now there are over twenty, with over 700 under study for occupation to get them back to work." She pointed out the need to do all this "along with raising consciousness of people." She said that, "going too fast, without people wanting it, wouldn't work." And she noted that the businesspeople are "still trying to manipulate and buy off the workers, and especially the leaders." I also asked this trade-union leader, who was explicitly responsible for international relations, about links with movements and unions in the U.S. She reported Chavista unions having links to the "AFL-CIO in California, some grassroots unions, and the antiwar movement," but not with the national AFL-CIO because they are still giving money to those imposing old bureaucracy and fomenting coups."

I asked her what proportion of the paid workforce was female and she replied, "About 50 percent." I asked about women's salaries compared to men's and she said there was no difference for the same jobs, but "women didn't get as good jobs as men." I asked if things were better in the occupied factories, and she said, "as far as I can tell things are somewhat better, yes, but not ideal." She said "the double duty of women is the biggest obstacle to their deeper involvement in union work." I asked if the Bolivarian movement was trying to address this and she said, "The new constitution says domestic work has to be acknowledged as work for social security purposes," but I asked about men and women doing it more equally and she said that that "was progressing very, very slowly. At the grassroots level lots of women participate, despite double or even triple work, but our men are very macho, and regrettably many women spoil them by doing all household work." She said her situation was unusual because she got lots of help at home.

The Venezuelan trip revealed that the Bolivarian movement, and, in particular, President Hugo Chavez, was pushing the population leftward. They are seeking to replace old capitalist forms with new forms that they call "anticapitalist," "participatory," "socialist," and "Bolivarian," among other labels. They were not directly and forcefully challenging and taking over or removing old structures. They were operating legally in the interstices of society to nurture new forms into existence and to then show by contrast and via socially acceptable competition that Venezuela's old forms are inferior, expecting that in time the new forms will legally win out over the old. But as to what these new forms were to be, there was far more clarity concerning political norms and structures than economic ones. I would have liked to have seen provision for a national exploration, debate, and consciousness-raising campaign aimed at clarifying and advocating the ultimate goals of the revolution, and at making knowledge of its goals and continuous critique and enrichment of them a national possession, not a possession only of some leaders.

The trip also revealed that the Bolivarians' unusual transitional approach had as its vanguard aspect that the Bolivarian leadership was ideologically and programmatically far ahead of its populace and trying to get that populace to move further and faster than it was alone inclined to. It had as its anarchist aspect, however, that the movement was being nourished, even if by a national president, mostly from the bottom up. It sought to exist in parallel and to become prevalent without violence and even without confrontation. It sought to embody the seeds of the future in the present to avoid generating a new domination. It was trying to win adherents by evidence, not force.

I felt from what I saw that the centrality of a single leader, at least that it was Hugo Chavez, seemed to be a highly unexpected benefit. Chavez, so far, had not just been congenial and inspiring, audacious and courageous, willing to step outside every box and implement program after program, experimenting and learning, but had also shown remarkable restraint in utilizing the accouterments of central power and has even been a key source of antiauthoritarian influence. At the same time, it seemed also true that the centrality of a single leader, Hugo Chavez, though perhaps unavoidable, was also a debit. The leader could turn bad, or could disappear, and either turn of events would be calamitous. A related problem was the lack of a serious opposition on the Left. Revolution benefits from disagreement, debate, and diversity, but those attributes have trouble arising amidst a siege mentality. I wondered who would succeed Chavez, and how the people would succeed the leaders, unless there was massive popular education in leadership and the revolution's aims.

Finally, to me the idea of out competing the old system with a new one created in parallel was very cleverly beneficial in that it avoided undue premature conflict that might have brought down holy hell on the Bolivarian project even as it also drew on strengths and sidestepped weaknesses. But the idea of out competing the old system with a new one created in parallel seemed also to risk preserving market mentalities that ingrain competitive qualities and methods and buttress bureaucratic and classist structures.

My overall impression was that the Bolivarian revolution was still vague. It didn't have clearly enunciated feminist politics, antiracist politics, or even anticapitalist politics, though in all three cases its inclinations seemed incredibly humane and radical and it was moving rapidly forward toward enunciating full aims and proposing both immediate and long-term program. Chavez, moving leftward at a great pace, appeared to be a remarkable detonator of insights. The Bolivarian revolution seemed most ideologically clear—which was ironic and a powerful testimony on his behalf, given Chavez's military background— regarding political democracy and political participation where it seemed to be already committed to a well-conceived, compelling and innovative institutional vision that outstripped what any other revolutionary project since the Spanish anarchists has held forth.

The future was not certain. The Bolivarian revolution, when I had the good fortune to view it close up, could still stall in social democracy. Comanagement and not self-management could have that outcome. It could still stumble or even rush into typical old-style "socialist" channels. Its market strategies and lack of clarity about class divisions based on divisions of labor pushed that way. There was certainly a danger of authoritarianism when a government was prodding a populace instead of vice versa. But the Bolivarian revolution could also provide a remarkable model, both of a better world and of a very original way to arrive at that better world. Which of these results, or of others, happens is largely going to be up to Chavez, the Bolivarian movements, and the Venezuelan people, though mass external support, not least to restrain U.S. aggressive inclinations before they could corrupt or destroy the experiment, are also profoundly needed.

I left Venezuela inspired and very hopeful. Venezuela looked to me like Uncle Sam's worst nightmare. I was humbled by Bolivarian ingenuity and steadfastness and by my own continued citizenship in the world's most rogue and brutal nation, against which I and other radicals have had such limited organizing success. I felt that hopefully my country could follow Venezuela's lead rather than crushing its aspirations. I felt that hopefully, citizens in the U.S. could make that happen. I knew officials wouldn't, of course.

Parsociety

Those who dream by day are cognizant of many
things which escape those who dream only by night.
—Edgar Allan Poe

Beyond economics, there is participatory society. This would combine parecon with new institutions for politics, kinship, culture, ecology, international exchange, and many other facets of life. Robin Hahnel and I together barely ventured into this domain. We argued broadly over the 1990s for what we called intercommunalist cultural structures, feminist kinship structures, and self-managing political institutions in a few articles and in passing references in books and essays on parecon. We made general pleas for people who had more experience in extra-economic dynamics, and who were more familiar with the relevant history and experiments, to develop vision for each other area, more or less as we had done for economics. Later, I made that general appeal to specific people. I urged Stephen Shalom, a political scientist friend from MIT days to address political vision. He has done it, intermittently, and has called his aims "parpolity." I urged Justin Podur, who contributes mightily to ZNet as a volunteer, to address cultural/community vision. He has done it, intermittently. And I asked Cynthia Peters to address gender vision since she has had great experience not only in visionary institutions through her decades working at South End Press, but also in community organizing in the decade since. She has done it, intermittently.

The lack of consistent effort arises, I think, not only because these people lack time, like all activists who have diverse living and job responsibilities, and not only because it is a bit daunting to think about a better future, but also because there is a constant contrary mood pushing anyone working on vision to feel like he or she must be insane to be focused on what others ignore. This last obstacle could be removed, I think, by concerted calls for attention to vision from movements and media, but, as yet, that hasn't occurred.

My main vision-related efforts after publishing *Parecon: Life After Capitalism* have been partly traveling around speaking about parecon, and partly working on a book about participatory economics and the rest of society titled *Realizing Hope*. That book talks about everything from sports and art to science and journalism by way of not only economics but also culture, kinship, government, and ecology. It was fun to write, going from topic to topic, seeing the implications of participatory economics for some area like technology, schooling, or art, and of those areas back on economic vision. It is very readable and meant largely as a prod to incite others to take up similar topics. I have also made a large number of proposals to periodicals to address vision, but so far, that has met with limited success.

It isn't fun seeking interest from the uninterested. Confidence can lag. More, in my case, it all too often has a personal dimension that makes it even more uncomfortable. For example, imagine sending e-mails back and forth with Matt Rothschild, the publisher of *The Progressive*, a prominent U.S. progressive magazine, with me wondering how come *The Progressive* has over the past decade and more never incorporated any discussion of parecon, never run any article about it, and even recently told two of its primary writers—David Barsamian and Barbara Ehrenreich—that they couldn't interview me about parecon for its pages. Imagine my then asking Howard Zinn, who also writes for *The Progressive*, to be the third person on its masthead to seek to write favorably about *Parecon* and be told to forget it, there is no hope. Howard passed, saying it was a waste of time to try. My entreaties to outfits like *The Progressive, or In These Times* or others feel even to me like special pleading. Hell, when they are viewed as an entreaty by me to pay attention to a book that I have written they are special pleading. But making such requests is also pleading for parecon, and that's why I do it. It is alienating, but if I didn't do it, who would? Ah, maybe that's the question.

People have all sorts of attitudes toward me. I am too pushy, arrogant, cold, demanding, aloof, authoritarian, antiauthoritarian, dismissive. There is some truth to all of it, I am sure, perhaps quite a lot. Oddly, more to the point of this discussion, almost all of those people who are generally positive toward me see my accomplishments as overwhelmingly in the area of organization building. Some even call it, to my distress, an entrepreneurial talent. Almost no one thinks, as I do, that my main contribution has been helping to generate and advocate the theory/vision/strategy package described briefly in this part of *Remembering Tomorrow*. Few, even among friends, even acknowledge that that has happened. Now that could be because they think the package is inconsequential, but if so, why would no one make that case, compellingly and convincingly? Maybe people don't even realize there is a package there, that there could be a package, that packages matter.

If a close friend of mine, or even just an acquaintance, undertook similarly innovative intellectual work and asked me for my support, I'd either enthusiastically support their work or explain why I felt I had to refrain from doing so. If the former occurred, it would be taken in stride. If the latter, it would be deemed dismissive. I wonder why silence is considered better than serious critique?

It seems to me that in the modern Left, while there is room for applying agreed notions to existing relations over and over, innovation is not so welcome. We can write essentially the same books or essays a hundred times, sometimes even write the same article over and over with minor revisions, and that's considered fine, even erudite. Whole careers and reputations are built on it. There is also room for action, of course, and rightly so. But I have to say, in a part of this book on "Mind Trips," it does seem to me that as of yet there is not nearly so much room on the Left for proposing new and original concepts, vision, and strategy, and most especially for undertaking serious debate about such matters, unless, of course, the content is made so abstruse as to be essentially incomprehensible and is somehow anointed in mainstream periodicals by some set of stars as worthy despite that it has few serious implications. If this is true, even to a limited extent, it's a sad situation for the Left that we must certainly transcend.

So, do I think we will do it? All indications are that parecon is already taking root and spreading, albeit slowly, as an economic vision. This makes me think that parsociety, or parsoc, will do likewise, even more broadly, once its branches are better defined and its advocates become more active. This type of participatory, libertarian vision, whether parecon or parsoc, or any other, explicitly calls for everyone on the Left to make vision their own. I have my doubts at times, like everyone else, about how things are going, but in the end, I think we will in time share and utilize valuable vision, even though doing so will require overcoming many large obstacles and bad habits. From there on, don't blink, things will happen rapidly.

Chapter 31

Preconditions

History's Locomotion

Never have the armies of the North brought peace, prosperity, or democracy to the peoples of Asia, Africa, or Latin America.
— *Samir Amin*

In 1999, Lydia and I, Lydia's daughter Andrea, a friend of Andrea's, and my mother all went to Egypt for my mother's 85th birthday. We'd see the great pyramid. We'd see another age-old site. Big deal. We wouldn't meet local activists. We wouldn't see the underside of the city. Happy birthday, let's celebrate. In fact, however, the trip fascinated me more than it did my mother. Egypt's ancient ruins were everywhere. A whole empire inhabited people's contemporary backyards.

In 5000 BC Egypt excelled, but for 4,000 years Egypt stagnated. Reading those words probably didn't shake your world. But to see in the pictures on the walls firsthand signs of culture, religion, industry, and politics staying essentially constant for four millennia shook mine. We saw remnants of 5000 BC and then of 1000 BC. The differences were barely perceptible. Contemporary society changes considerably in a decade, much less in a century or millennium. Not ancient Egypt. Ancient Egyptian life remained constant. Human insight did not continually yield new conditions. Offspring did not advance beyond parents, grandparents, great grandparents, or great, great, great, repeat fifty times, grandparents. The lack of change staggered me. By way of comparison, in 1900 the average life expectancy in the U.S. was about 45 and in 2000 it was about 75. We had journeyed from a few people having barely functional telephones to omnipresent high-tech, labor-saving and sensory-enhancing tools throughout much of society. In contrast, the social relations of Egypt stifled innovation for thousands of years. This is what Marx had in mind when he called capitalism progressive. Capitalism fosters

388

innovation. Walking amid pyramids along the Nile, looking backward in time with other tourists, hammered this home.

Still, for all the innovation that capitalism curries, fundamental social change is never inevitable. Stasis is possible. Nowadays capitalism's accumulation process provokes constant innovation, for sure. But to get structural change down to the logic of how life is lived, we must make it happen. We arrive at strategy.

Chess a Go Go

How many care to seek only for precedents?
—Peter Kropotkin

In high school, I enjoyed tennis a lot. I took lessons and made the high school tennis team, though only for doubles. Tennis included playing with one of the closest friends I ever had, Larry Seidman. I used to call him guppy, to tease him, but, in fact, he was a brilliant fellow, and very hardworking, though a bit indeterminate at times. Larry was a year ahead of me in high school, and in my junior year I spent more time with him and his senior friends than I did with my circle of junior friends. The next year I visited Larry at Harvard a couple of times, which was where I first met Robin Hahnel, Larry's freshman roommate.

I got a lot of pleasure out of rooting for Larry in tennis tournaments and on the high school team, where he was the best our city had to offer. I lost to Larry without pain, happy to appreciate my opponent's better play. Watching Larry I learned how someone could utilize relatively limited physical means with great vigor, to do far better than people with greater means who got less out of them. The Left must do precisely as Larry did: win despite having few assets.

I was pretty good at chess, including being first board on my high school team, but I was certainly not stellar and I was never fanatical. I won often, but Westchester wasn't New York City, where I would have regularly lost. My father taught me to play, and he would always say, look and see what has changed due to your opponent's last move and figure out what your opponent is about to do. Think about your opponent's plan. Refine your plan. Then, make your move. Later, this advice morphed into the insight that when you are in a struggle you should always have an agenda, and if need be you should keep adapting it to ongoing changes. Though this seems obvious, most people, and even most competitors never adequately heed this instruction. If you function with a strategic plan, and you regularly update it, you will do much better than if you operate reflexively, only in the moment. Yet much of the time in life, even in conflict, we operate spontaneously and without a broad plan. Immediate proximate events, not an envisioned path forward, govern our choices. This is apocalyptic behavior.

Like others, I got excited by Bobby Fischer. I once heard that he not only always played with a plan, which all good players do, but also that Fischer almost never had to change his plan. He would conceive what he wanted to do before each game and then during the game he would implement his agenda without alteration. This differed from most players, even at the top level. They would all make a plan before beginning a game, but most would repeatedly alter their expectations and intentions in light of what their opponent did. Fischer so dictated outcomes, I heard, that he rarely had to change his plan. This impressed me greatly, though the story was probably as much myth as reality.

I remember a gathering of first- and second-board players from teams around Westchester County playing simultaneous games against Sammy Reshevsky, a world-class professional. Sammy was born in Poland in 1912, and by the age of eight was winning against adults and even professionals. He later moved to the U.S. and became U.S. champion. Here is how Sammy spoke about the need to have a plan and operate in light of it: "To a chess master, there is no such thing as an 'obvious' move. Experience has shown repeatedly that wins or draws are thrown away by thoughtless play. Careful planning is the essence of chess strategy. Every move must be scrutinized with care. Each must be analyzed in the light of the plan under consideration. Nowhere is waste of time more severely punished than in chess."

Sammy played about twenty Westchester high school hotshot players at once. The boards were laid out on long tables. We students each sat at a board and Sammy moved along, from player to player, table to table, quickly making his moves. What stood out for me was first that the one player who actually beat Reshevsky was, in fact, the best player in the county. This wasn't just poetic justice. Chance plays almost no role in chess. Chance plays a considerable role in social-change events, however. Not just the competing sides make moves, but the board constantly alters unexpectedly. Imagine if the leaky boat that brought Fidel and the other revolutionaries to Cuba sank, as one history-altering possibility.

Second, the rapidity with which Sammy could move from board to board was incredible, especially in light of his attitude about being careful. It wasn't just that his student opponents were not of his caliber, though that was part of it. Sammy possessed a huge store of lessons. He almost instantly knew what was going on and what was broadly appropriate. If Sammy was playing someone of comparable skill, he would have to hone his moves more precisely. But playing us, he could move quickly, knowing that he would be fine. Our plans weren't threatening. Sammy taught me the power of having in one's mind a warehouse of insights, knowledge, experiences, and patterns. Make Sammy a whole movement. The lesson is that beyond being strategic, movements need a shared flexible political framework and associated commitments and vision.

The Megaphone Problem

Tact is the knack of making a point without making an enemy.
—Isaac Newton

When I give public talks people always ask, "How come you leftists always talk only to the choir?" I answer that some activists address only the choir because addressing the choir is easier and less scary than addressing citizens who may disagree with what we say. I might give as an example the radical students at Penn State, Coach Joe Paterno's football home, who, when I visited and gave a talk, denigrated interest in sports and laughed at the idea of trying to talk to folks in the large sports bar off campus. At Penn State, this was the equivalent of being an organizer in Italy and denigrating food, or an organizer in the Vatican and denigrating prayer. I add that folks with such insular attitudes dismissive of all those with different views ought to reassess. Then I add that most leftists talk largely to the choir for a different reason.

From Cleveland to Tallahassee and from Sydney to Istanbul, I have suggested to audiences that they imagine that I have two choices. First, I say, I can look in your direction and can speak to the hundreds of you who are already largely committed to social change, who already are familiar with a good part of any talk I could give, and who are part of our collective choir. Or, second, I can turn around and talk instead to five thousand, or fifty thousand, or five million people who have no prior social change involvement, have never before heard any part of the talk I would give, and have never entered our collective choir. Which way do you think I would turn? (As I ask, I turn my back to them.) Then, turning back toward my actual audience, I add, so how come you ask your question like you think leftists want to be insular? Of course we don't want to be insular. It is just that most of the time we have no better option. We can talk to each other, the choir. Or we can talk to no one. The main explanation I offer for why leftists infrequently reach out to new people is that we don't have a megaphone loud enough to be heard by folks who aren't already searching for our messages. It isn't that we only want to reach the choir. It is that only the choir is reachable. Mainstream media exclude us. Left media invite our participation, but reach only the choir.

During the first Gulf War, in 1990, *Z Magazine* was a prime mover with other Boston-area media projects in forming what we called Boston Media Action. The idea was to not only oppose the war, but to also affect media. In small discussions, and later a big meeting of local media activists, we settled on three themes: trying to aid existing alternative media, trying to "Press the Press" to force it to communicate more dissident content, and trying to create new alternative media to seek mass outreach. The discussions led to a day of alternative media workers collectively displaying their wares and discussing alternative media needs and joint efforts. It also led to an evening event at which Lydia was the moderator and speakers included journalist Alexander Cockburn, the former mayor of Berkeley, Gus Newport, and some others. Lydia's theater group performed sketches. The idea was that this would not only aid the Gulf War opposition buildup for the 500 people attending, but that we would later take a film we did to the local public TV station, WGBH, and demand that they air it. Later, there were related discussions of how to create Left mass media and initiate various media unity projects.

After the anticorporate globalization movement grew following the Seattle events, I traveled around the U.S. urging that we needed to not only expand that movement but build a parallel major international movement aimed at making demands of mainstream media just as our anticorporate globalization movement made demands of the IMF and World Bank. I argued that a media movement could have as targets mainstream newspaper and TV offices all over the world. Danny Schechter, called the news dissector from his days as a radio news personality in Boston in the sixties, who is now impresario of an online operation called Media Channel, has been arguing the same thing, more strongly, for years. After the international February 15 outpouring of antiwar sentiment against initiating a second Gulf War, Lydia Sargent wrote a piece in Z Magazine called "Press the Press" extending the Boston Media Action idea into the present.

Lydia wrote that at the gigantic international demonstrations, many of the people interviewed expressed the feeling: "Now the government has to listen and stop this war." In reaction she wrote:

A similar dynamic occurred during Vietnam antiwar demonstrations. People began to believe, despite all evidence, that one or two or three huge demonstrations would make elites stop pursuing their militaristic agenda and would actually stop the war. What happened, then, when such outpourings failed? Many people's post-demonstration emotional highs turned to resigned fatalism in a matter of weeks. Instead of seeing that progress was being made, people grew despondent over not being at the finish line. The same could happen here: the government rides this out, demonstrations get smaller and more isolated, the media become more contemptuous, and that's that.

Lydia went on to urge, I think quite rightly, that "it is time to direct more of our protests toward the media. What's needed now is a long-term campaign to 'Press the Press.' ...What we want is for mainstream media to include peace and justice programming, prepared by the peace and justice movement, in their daily reports. If they do not agree to this demand, we picket their offices, occupy them if necessary, and shut them down."

But what about creating our own new media? One creative response that emerged from the momentum of the anticorporate globalization movement was

Indymedia. The idea was to create centers of media worldwide. Interestingly, many past graduates of ZMI were involved in this effort. Indymedia outfits each have a Web site, and sometimes audio, print media, and a meeting center. I have met Indy activists not only in many U.S. cities, but also in Melbourne, Rome, London, São Paolo, and many other places. Indy operations are committed efforts, intent upon democracy and participation as well as on conveying truthful and relevant information.

I remember a dinner in Porto Alegre at the second World Social Forum, where I was privileged to attend a dinner with a group of about a dozen Indy staffers from Indy operations around the world. I learned about their concerns and tried to help out with some of their issues. One concern was about a large donation they had received. It had been sitting in a bank, unused, for about a year. There was no mechanism to determine how to apportion it among Indy projects. More, they were afraid spending it would cause a downward spiral to co-optation and hierarchy. Here were young folks, working their asses off, all volunteers, often lacking resources and tools, and sometimes even going hungry. They had money in the bank, but were unwilling to use it for fear that doing so would engender bad dynamics. We talked about how the answer to the ills of money was not to reject money but to utilize it in accord with worthy values. A plan was hatched to disperse funds to local Indy outfits in inverse proportion to the national income of the host country. The Indy activists wanted this type of mechanism rather than having to make subjective case-by-case choices. They had no decision apparatus to undertake the judgments. We talked about that, too, and about how democracy and self-management were not advanced by resisting structures and norms.

Another problem was that Indy on the one hand wanted to promote popular involvement through the public uploading of essays, photos, etc. On the other hand, Indy wanted to offer quality content. They suffered a contradiction between having an open microphone—which is what we used to call it at rallies in the sixties—and having an agenda of speakers chosen for the quality of their delivery. The same issues arose then as now: wanting maximal participation and diversity versus wanting the best possible content. We talked about how having two sections of the Indy sites, one open and one moderated, could enable the provision of both kinds of content. Most users want to have a publisher wade through submissions and select those worth reading because most users have nowhere near enough time to undertake such weeding themselves. Publishing with discernment is good. So is an open approach in which users can post whatever they wish. Why not do both, at least online?

Finally, I remember the Indy's understandable angst over the difficulty of maintaining continuity and growing while using only volunteers. People kept joining and leaving to pursue jobs elsewhere, they reported. It is hard to build up momentum, skills, and lessons. I asked why Indy didn't have some paid staff to promote continuity, and they said they were worried that having paid staff would subvert desires to be fully collective and democratic. The mood was that "money doesn't talk, it swears." We explored how this was a Catch-22. To require that people work for free, I argued, wasn't a model for a new way to conduct media or economic functions more generally. I urged that being remunerated for labor wasn't bad per se, it was being a wage slave that was bad. Why couldn't they be innovative and have paid staff, but with the norms of payment reflecting their equitable inclinations? That would be exemplary.

Another project geared toward expanding alternative media has been the the NewStandard online. This system was to be like ZNet in the sense of presenting information and building community, but different from ZNet in that the NewStandard would try to be a news source rather than a source of analysis. The NewStandard would appeal to people with modest, and even no, political background. It would provide news coverage of an honest and relevant character. It is a bit like Indymedia's agenda, but the NewStandard was self-consciously conceived as a pareconish project, with paid staff. The NewStandard was brought into being by Brian Dominick and Jessica Azulay. Brian had been a first-year ZMI graduate and spent years working very closely with ZNet, helping to build its infrastructure.

Both Indymedia and the NewStandard have had ups and downs. Each project is hard to pursue for want of widespread support. Why is the relatively huge audience that is hungry for better information unable to sufficiently support new and better alternative media projects? The answer is a chicken-and-egg situation. The unity needed to support alternative media is a precondition for the alternative media that can generate audience unity.

At the time of Boston Media Action I began thinking about a number of media possibilities. Ten years later, the ideas haven't yielded material results, but they may nonetheless have merit. I proposed that we needed a network of 150 to 300 radio stations, campus- and community-based, playing their own radical material but also a good portion of simultaneously aired shows, including some national radical call-in talk shows. I thought this could potentially reach millions of listeners. I guessed the start-up cost might be as low as $75,000, about the same money as had started South End Press. I thought the initial staff for a new production company, beyond folks already at work at the hundreds of existing stations across the country, could be as few as three or four people. How it would fund itself to pay its bills month-to-month, however, was unclear.

I also proposed creating a network of twenty to fifty regional weekly newspapers, each with their own local editorial coverage, reviews, and listings, but all with the same national reporting, visionary pieces, national cultural pieces, etc., plus shared nationally coordinated production, bookkeeping, advertising, list-handling, and fund-raising to dramatically reduce local costs by achieving economies of scale. These weekly papers could, I argued, out-compete NY's *Village Voice*, the *LA Weekly*, the *Boston Phoenix*, etc. due to the synergies of sharing costs and talents. Their start-up cost, using economical technology, would be "only" $2 to $3 million. The initial staff requirements would be ten to twelve people in a national office and two to four in each local office, plus lots of writers. The idea, thrown out to movements, elicited little response.

I had in mind, as well, an associated array of national magazines and journals, each gaining readership from the newspaper and radio audiences, and each seeking to advance those projects in turn. Again, there would be modest start-up costs, as the infrastructure already existed. I also envisioned a national distributor for pamphlets, books, and other print materials, and a speakers' bureau that would organize dozens and eventually hundreds of gatherings a week, where speakers with special skills and knowledge would not only give talks and bring useful resources, but would stick around for a couple of days and meet with organizers to create links, help with local problems, and learn from local experiences.

I saw all this entwined. The newspapers should have pages devoted to what's on their local radical radio stations and the radical radio stations should boost the papers. Each should promote speakers and both should promote the more detailed magazine offerings and vice versa, all as a part of an overarching vision of radical media. Moreover, all these institutions should understand the importance of a culture of resistance incorporating humor, love, solidarity, democratic work relations, and means of celebration and collaboration. It didn't happen.

I had another try at media strategic thinking. It was called FAMAS, for Federation of Alternative Media Activists and Supporters. I wrote about it in reaction to the first Media and Democracy Congress in 1996. Readers of progressive media often ask its producers, why not get under one roof? Why not share and cooperate? Why duplicate effort? Of course this sentiment can be taken too far. Magazines have different readerships, resources, agendas, and political aims, and ditto for other media projects. There is no single correct answer on how to do things. There needs to be diverse projects and many efforts rather than few. Still, the question resonates.

Years before, I had tried to impress my peers at *In These Times, The Nation, Mother Jones, Radical America,* and *Science for the People* that we should together form a consortium, seeing each other as partners in broad consciousness raising. Instead of selling each other our mailing lists we should make them freely available to one another. Instead of hoarding names of donors lest others benefit from developing relations with them, we should share the contacts. Instead of charging each other to use pages to make ourselves known to other audiences, each periodical should do it freely for other periodicals. Likewise, we should find ways to mutually reduce costs by sharing resources. And so on.

The effort to act on these ideas got as far as some meetings among the media ventures mentioned above, but eventually foundered and failed. The smaller outfits were eager to proceed, but were pressed for time by their own difficult conditions. The larger outfits could have made solidarity a reality, but they rightly perceived that they had less to gain from the investment of time and energy that attaining solidarity would entail. Left media institutions operated (and still operate) in a market setting that makes us competitors. Emblematic of this was alternative media people hoarding donor names. You can't blame people for doing it. Systemic pressure to survive causes it. But it makes a mockery of solidarity.

Indeed, an explicit instruction of the 1996 Media and Democracy Conference was that participants should go home, distill what they'd heard, and make suggestions for forthcoming sessions. It was that entreaty that led me to propose "creating a Federation of Alternative Media Activists and Supporters (FAMAS)." I suggested that FAMAS might include producing organizations (such as print publishers, radio and recording production projects, film companies, watchdog groups, and media institutes), distributing organizations (such as alternative bookstores, speakers' bureaus, radio stations, activist organizations, and conferences), producing individuals (such as writers, film producers, cartoonists, reporters, researchers, web spinners, public speakers, photographers, folk artists, and comedians), and also progressive media "consumers" (such as readers, listeners, and viewers).

The idea was that the federation could have a decision-making board composed of representatives from a rotating sample of member organizations and communities. Policy could be proposed by this board or by members, voted on by the board and then the membership, and implemented by paid staff. Institutional and individual members might each vote only on the policies that directly affect them. Electronic media could tie all members into an online community for debate, agenda development, and polling. I suggested that FAMAS could seek to enlarge alternative media communication, both within the mainstream and by alternative structures. It could affirm that alternative media institutions (and individuals) should strive not to replicate cultural, economic, and gender dependencies or structural biases common to mainstream institutions and that all members should be committed to acting on behalf of the entire alternative media community.

There was more about specific organizations working toward mutual benefit, new distribution projects that could be collectively undertaken, ways to share and coordinate content, and ways to serve movements and fledgling writers and producers, generate internal funding, and so on. Something like FAMAS, I thought, need not be a coalition around a few shared sentiments. It could promote the mutual support that all its members need, making the whole much greater than just the sum of its parts. Yet it didn't fly.

Apocalyptic Organizing

Then I'll stand on the ocean until I start sinkin'
But I'll know my song well before I start singin'.
—Bob Dylan

In seeking social change, one of the biggest problems I have encountered has been that activists have been insufficiently strategic. Folks creating an antiwar or a no-nukes movement, or embarking on an affirmative action or anticorporate globalization campaign, or creating a new publishing venture or a service group didn't just sometimes enact bad strategy. We often had no strategy at all. We were largely apocalyptic and reactive. The government meets; we disrupt. They bomb; we rally. They propose a law; we seek to overturn it. They arrest; we protest. They act; we respond. They act. We react.

Think of society as a deadly disease. We daily reduce its most outrageous symptoms in a few of the sickest souls we see. But we have no weekly, monthly, or yearly campaign against the underlying pathology. We don't even try to understand what full health would look like. We ironically lack a forward-sweeping time horizon. We oppose the Vietnam and Iraq wars, the IMF and the World Bank, but we don't actively chant and march for replacements for imperialism and international finance. We lack attentiveness to the lessons of the past and the dictates of the future. We choose patterns of action, organization, and personal lifestyle that have failed before and that would lead to ill effects tomorrow if they happened to succeed, merely because they are familiar or feel good today. We rarely establish clear, collectively enunciated and shared norms to assess what we are doing. We rarely learn from gains and setbacks. We don't have collectively agreed upon vision for economic production or exchange or for families, religion, or the structure of legislation and elections, much less for a whole new society. We are too often like a chess player who pushes a piece in reaction to the most immediate move by the opponent. We are too often without a plan for the bigger picture.

Ten million of us demonstrate, worldwide, against war. A year later, relatively few are seriously involved. We don't ask what went wrong. We don't ask why people's commitment and focus didn't grow. We instead ask how come the government persists and what the government will do next, despite that we already know the answers to those questions. We do exactly what my father repeatedly advised against when I was a kid. We play apocalyptically. We could do better.

The Stickiness Problem

*The people will feel no better if the stick with which
they are being beaten is labeled 'the people's stick.'*
—*Mikhail Bakunin*

In my experience from the sixties to today, our movements have repeatedly
urged people: Risk your jobs! Risk your family ties! Risk your friendships!
Risk your career plans! Join us! This was the message people heard during
Vietnam, Nicaragua, and now Iraq. I know that's what my words conveyed, over
and over, to people on the street, in the dorm, at work, and in communities. And
then by our example we showed what we had to offer.

Join us for our long meetings. Join us so you can have your every personal
choice inspected and often rejected. Join us so that every moment you will be as
attuned as possible to all pain in society. Join us so you will no longer be able to
enjoy sports and popular culture. Join us for more loneliness. Join us so you can
say you are part of a movement to change the world, not knowing what new world
you are seeking or how you are going to get it. Ignorance is us. Join us to frown, to
be lonely, to weep. Join us.

Now, in fact, we don't advertise these great benefits and virtues in precisely
this manner, but that's the image we have conveyed. Some people joined and
stuck. Some joined and left. Most ignored our entreaties entirely. Were the last the
smartest ones? Toward the end of one summer about ten years ago, I spoke at a
national Green convention on a plenary panel about movement building. My
initial plan was to discuss the progressive community's outreach problem. We try
to reach out to potential allies in society to "reel them in" to full participation. Not
enough people hear us. My topic was the megaphone problem. But, as I thought
about movement building, I decided another problem was even worse. Waiting to
speak at that conference, I had a kind of epiphany. It just blasted into my mind that
over the prior thirty years, the Left had overwhelmingly squandered its efforts.

I imagined the progressive/Left community as a team fighting against both
apathy and outright support for the status quo. I saw that size wasn't the only
variable affecting the movement's strength, but without numbers we weren't
going far, so we had to reach out more widely. But as we got people's attention, did
they thereafter stay committed? I called this, right there sitting waiting to speak,
the "Stickiness Problem."

To win fundamental change, it wasn't enough to play well. The way I saw it,
our team needed a force field that could draw members steadily leftward ever more
strongly the closer they came. First a person hears about us. There is an attraction,
however slight. As the person is drawn closer, the attraction must increase to offset
counter pressures from society that draw the person away from the movement back

into the mainstream. Once a person joins the movement team, the escalating attraction should sustain permanent membership. Escape velocity should be unattainable.

The question that forcefully struck me was, do we have community stickiness? What was our historical experience with potential recruits in the past? What characteristics of our movement influenced whether its attractive force escalated as people got closer to steady involvement?

Waiting to speak at the Green conference, reconstructing my talk in my mind, I considered the past. How many people had heard about, come into contact with, worked with, or become part of the movement who no longer had anything much to do with it? The number I tallied that day was easily fifteen million or more, and as I write in 2006 it is higher, of course. Remember, this included folks from the civil rights movement, the anti-Vietnam War movement, and the women's movement. It included those who worked with various labor movements or who had been no-nukers or in other green movements, as well as in student movements. It included everyone who had worked in truly progressive local projects, from winning new traffic lights in neighborhoods to keeping McDonald's out of neighborhoods to cleaning up dump sites, as well as in various Left electoral campaigns. It included anyone who had taken a course from a radical faculty person or been part of the antiapartheid movement. It included people who had been in the various Latin American solidarity movements, or the anti-Gulf War movements. It included those who had been in gay and lesbian movements, in pro-choice campaigns, in community and consumer movements, and in union organizing campaigns, labor struggles, and antiracist campaigns, those who had been in strikes and boycotts and disarmament campaigns, and also those who had gone to leftist talks or demonstrations hoping for involvement, and those who had listened attentively to progressive radio, or closely read progressive periodicals. Fifteen million, even just in the U.S., was a conservative estimate of the number of people who had significantly approached the movement, one way or another, from 1960 to 1995. How many were still an active part of our team?

As I faced up to the gap between those we had reached and those who were still actively involved, I was shocked. When I thought in terms of a year or two, Left outreach loomed paramount. How could we get beyond the choir we were preaching to? But from that moment on, whenever I thought about a decade or more, the stickiness problem was even more pressing. Why should someone, once attracted to the logic, behavior, and program of the Left community, stick to it? Conversely, why might people feel steadily less attachment as time passed, only to finally return to the mainstream?

I envisioned a person getting involved with progressive ideas and activity. Did this person merge into a growing community of people who, together, made him or her feel more secure and appreciated? Did this person get a growing sense of personal worth and of contribution to something valuable? Did he or she enjoy a sense of accomplishment? Did this person have his or her needs better met than before? Did this person's life get better? Did it seem that he or she was making a contribution to improving others' lives? Or, conversely, did this person meet a lot of other people who continually questioned his or her motives and behaviors, making him or her feel insecure and constantly criticized? Did this person feel diminished and doubt that his or her actions would make a difference for anyone? Did this person suspect little was accomplished, and see no daily, weekly, or monthly evidence of progress (even when it did exist)? Did this person have needs that were previously met now unmet, and have few new ones addressed? Was this person's life getting more frustrating and less enjoyable? Did it seem this person was only bothering other people and rarely doing anything meaningful on other people's behalf? Did this person find him- or herself steadily less aware of what the Left stood for and repulsed by its vague or bitter attributes, rather than attracted to its clarity, insights, and success?

Later I imagined a baseball, basketball, or soccer team. I presumed it didn't improve its results as time passed. At some point, I saw the coach looking at the choices made up to that point, at the strategies used in prior games, and saying, hold on, we have to make some serious strategic corrections. Okay, I realized that our team has no coach and it needs to be participatory and democratic, so that being self-critical is everyone's responsibility. But I also realized that our team must play to win, not just to be participatory, if it is to exceed mere posturing. This in turn made me realize that we needed to reassess how we organized ourselves, the culture of our movements, how we interrelated, and what benefits and responsibilities we had as a result of our political involvements. The alternative to doing much better regarding "movement stickiness," I realized, would be another long losing season—two or three decades—which, unlike for an inflexible high school, college, or professional sports team that failed to adapt, would mean hundreds of millions of lives unnecessarily squandered for want of greater success and final victory. Are we doing what we are doing seriously, or are we doing it as a kind of hobby, to pass time, look good, be moral, but without impact?

Was I exaggerating our lack of stickiness? That day at the Green convention, my epiphany went further. Suppose, I said to myself, a high percentage of the roughly fifteen million people I counted as having gotten within the orbit of U.S. Left activism over the past thirty-five years had stuck with it. Suppose a high percentage of those who stuck with it had worked hard to attract and retain others over all those years, and to utilize all the resulting collective energies toward winning change. Where would we be now?

The answer seemed to me to be that we would have had forty or fifty million leftists with highly developed commitment and political sensibilities, spread all over the U.S. We might not yet have had a new society, but we would certainly have been on the road toward it. Not being in that position wasn't, in this view, mostly due to the power of the state. The state didn't crush most of us out of our movements, though it was a formidable opponent. It wasn't mostly due to the effectiveness of mass indoctrination and manipulation. Though the media are devastating in their service to power, they didn't trick most of us out of our movements. Instead, millions of folks came into proximity of the Left, participated in various projects, but later left. To join a movement and become lonelier was not inspiring. To join a movement and laugh less was not empowering. I realized we had to prioritize making our movements places where folks from all kinds of backgrounds wanted to spend their time, beyond participating being the moral and socially responsible thing to do. Of course I knew that changing the world couldn't become all play and no work, but my experiences from the sixties to the present said to me that movements should involve more than merely long meetings, obscure lifestyles, and regimenting conformity.

The Umbrella Problem

Never send to know for whom the bell tolls; it tolls for thee.
—John Donne

Part of building movements is having trust among diverse constituencies. Let me take time for one thought experiment I did some years back about how solidarity might have been engendered in the past, but wasn't. Consider the bank accounts of antiwar operations and civil rights operations from the early sixties into the mid-seventies. This period marks the rise, high-level stabilization, and later relative decline of highly radical and effective antiwar and civil rights movements. Imagine each had a master bank account showing a summary of all monies anywhere in the country that were given to or collected or that otherwise helped fund any component operations of these movements. Imagine we could see, that is, the entire sum total financial flows at the heart of civil rights and antiwar activism in the U.S.

What do we see? There are monies coming and going in both cases all the time. Part of the cash flow is from grassroots bake sales, members chipping in to pay for mailings or leaflets, or for a project like voter registration, or a picnic. Part is from selling buttons, from dues payments, or from passing the hat at giant rallies. To pay bills, day-to-day or month-to-month, part of the income also flows in from larger supporters and donors. All of this occurred for both the civil rights and the antiwar movements. The numbers, however, differed. We don't know the totals, even roughly, nor do we know the ratio. But I think we can say with great confidence that the sum total monies across the country that flowed for civil rights and antiracism over that decade and every decade since, have generally been a lot less than the monies that have flowed to antiwar activism, particularly when, of course, a war was in session. The reason for this was not the relative merits of the two broad movement agendas, nor was it the quality of their respective efforts, much less the effectiveness of their utilization of incoming dollars. The reason, rather, was in largest part simply the whiteness of the major donors and the larger cachet of giving toward peace as compared to giving toward racial justice.

Okay, that was the setting. Nothing could have been done at the time to change that donor tendency other than what was being done, which was building the respective movements and trying to improve the country in all respects. But what about the internal distribution of the monies? Why did a movement that could raise more get to spend more? What would have happened to relations among antiracist activists and antiwar activists had the latter movement said to itself, we don't get more because we are working harder or more effectively. We get more because racism impedes their getting more and we lap up that excess. Let's rise above the conditions in which we operate. Let's redistribute some of that incoming money, no strings attached, out of solidarity, respect, and an understanding that antiwar workers sponge up too much money relative to civil rights workers.

The American Left constantly bemoans its internal divisions that arise from persisting racial, gender, and class divides. Its members constantly reiterate their commitment to bridge these divides via personal renovation of residual ill qualities. What I realized from the thought experiment was that this introspection was often largely beside the main point because, in the personal dimension, change is slow and, really, considerable progress had already been made, at least regarding race and gender, if not class. What needed more attention was the structural asymmetries in the conditions of organizing around different focuses. And the basis for these asymmetries was not only racism, sexism, and classism in personal beliefs and habits, but racism, sexism, and classism in the broader society affecting the financing and the outreach done by movements. So why couldn't movements consider their relative funding and redress differentials? I decided that, brotherly rhetoric aside, until that happened, trust would founder. But for money to disperse differently, movements would have to relate differently.

Experiences of women's liberation and civil rights, such as the meeting that the feminist organization Bread and Roses interrupted at MIT, or the formation of Black Power movements that excluded white members, made clear to me that people will form movement projects around specific areas they prioritize. It will occur at least around race, gender, sex, class, power, ecology, and international relations. There was no point in saying, as many have, wouldn't it be better to have one big movement that marches behind one beautiful banner? Life is more complex than oneness. People who dreamt of one banner were blowing into the wind. Yet the solidarity sought by one-banner advocates needed to be accomplished somehow. Movements elevated different priorities, I realized, because people endured different life circumstances depending on race, gender, class, and diverse other factors. This was an inevitable fact of society and history. For decades, I encountered and often interacted closely with such movements. Of course the women's and the Black Power movements were emblematic. But there were also labor, no-nukes, antiwar, gay liberation, and disability movements. The diversity that having many priorities brought to the activist stage was good. Movements not aiding one another was bad. Different agendas certainly needed space to develop, gain confidence, and retain focus. Autonomy had benefits. But to win real and lasting change, different agendas also needed to each benefit from the strength and character of the rest. Solidarity would have benefits too. We needed to solve the problem of respecting diversity and even autonomy while simultaneously having an overarching sense of solidarity that promoted sharing resources, energies, and focus.

What the women's and the black power movements said to me was that one big step in this direction would be for larger movements to voluntarily support smaller ones, and for richer movements to voluntarily help pay the way for poorer ones—unreservedly, with people's bodies and resources, not just cash—due to understanding and respect and not just out of duty.

In the sixties, and this is one of the sixties' true virtues, however often it is forgotten, when people attended events there wasn't one banner, but there was, nevertheless, one movement. The glue holding diverse components together was youth culture and a shared mentality of being under siege. The sign of it all was the upraised two-finger V for peace, and later the upraised fist for resistance. A society certainly has disparate parts and constituencies, but a society is also one big thing. In a worthwhile society, each part understands that differences with other parts are critically important in some regards, but that they have to be subordinated in other regards. Watching the women's and Black Power movements within the broader Left taught me that each part of our movement should have a powerful say where it is most concerned but that it should follow the lead of other elements where they are most concerned.

I first thought about this in context of the antiracist movement, the women's movement, and the anti-war movement. Then there was the anti-imperialist, anticapitalist, gay liberation, no-nukes, ecology, and anticorporate globalization movements. You get the picture. And I have felt the same need regarding smaller entities such as particular labor movements, movements to clean up some ecological niche in one neighborhood and simultaneously across town in another, affirmative action movements, boycotts, fair trade movements, minimum wage movements, and movements to relate to some international events and struggles but not others. Why can't a structure fuel multimovement solidarity?

The aim would be to organize the Left as a bloc composed of a nearly infinite range of projects and movements, all operating together in a giant whole with everyone seeing the bloc as greater than the simple sum of all its parts, rather than operating as only a least common denominator of the whole. This is, I think, what young leftists of the late 1990s and early twenty-first century are seeking when they talk about a "movement of movements" that displays many banners, but also has an overarching solidarity.

Of course complications and difficulties arise. A gay movement says we should punish homophobic speech. Defenders of free speech recoil in horror. An indigenous group calls for a reparation scheme contrary to leading labor/economic principles. An anti-imperialist group calls for taking a position on Palestine that others think oppressively ignores Jewish national rights. A labor union calls for a boycott of Japanese-made cars which anti-imperialists think violates internationalist principles. Incorporating differences is not easy. But letting differences sunder solidarity is disastrous.

The strategic message that struck me most forcefully from my experiences with race and gender, beyond the obvious need to fight racism and sexism, is that finding a way to have elements of the Left enjoy the autonomy of having their own self-managed space is not just essential but positive. It is essential because it is inevitable. It is positive for the diversity, innovation, and development it fosters. Conditions like racism, sexism, and classism will not be properly fought and overcome unless those who suffer their costs lead such struggles. But diverse movements must also relate to one another as parts of a movement of movements, a revolutionary bloc, or a new society in formation.

The Lifestyle Problem

> The only thing we did wrong,
> Stayed in the wilderness a day too long
> But the one thing we did right,
> Was the day we started to fight.
> —"Keep Your Eyes on The Prize," Anonymous

The phrase "the personal is political" first arose from the women's movement of the 1960s. It quickly provided useful insights that have since then been dear to me. But, most recently, the meaning of this phrase has been turned by many activists into its opposite.

In the 1950s to mid-1960s, there was sexism, racism, and poverty, but little public recognition of these oppressions. Folks assumed each individual's plight was of their own making. To improve one's lot meant overcoming one's personal character inadequacies. The civil rights movement then demonstrated that many of the conditions that each black person faced were duplicated in the conditions most other black people faced. From blacks seeking food in restaurants to seats on buses to votes in elections, the public revelations of the era propelled new insights. The enemy was no longer one's own inadequacies. The enemy became systemic and was called "institutional racism" and, later, "white supremacy."

During the same period, a new band of socialists, with Michael Harrington's book *The Other America* in the lead, showed that hunger and poverty were not personal prices that people paid for paltry preferences they harbored, but were systemic outcomes operating against people's higher aspirations. Poverty wasn't personal failure, but systemic failure. The enemy became not self, but capitalism.

The antiwar movement, in turn, revealed the causation and commonality in the patterns of U.S. foreign policy in Southeast Asia and throughout the world. Bombs weren't beneficent. We weren't entangled overseas due to largesse. American foreign policy was greed and power writ large. The enemy became not U.S. errors or overconcern, but imperialism.

The 1960s women's movement came together in part when women in both the antiwar and civil rights movements noticed that their exclusion from leadership and their exploitation doing the most tedious work was not uniquely individual but was, instead, shared. Through consciousness-raising groups in which women told each other their life stories, women discovered that their situations in marriage, child-rearing, sex, work, culture, and even language were not unique but strikingly similar, and that the cause of their suffering was not themselves but something systemic and political. The enemy became not self, but patriarchy.

In each instance, I saw activism uncover that "the personal is political." That is, the experiences, feelings, and possibilities of our lives were not just due to personal preferences but were overwhelmingly limited, molded, and defined by a broader social setting. Our problems felt personal. But their broad texture was systemic. They were imposed on us, not caused by us. In this sense, a central contribution of the New Left I lived through was to say that we suffer a "totality of oppressions" that is systemically based, mutually entwined, and that all needs to be overcome by a revolution in existing institutions and the creation of liberating alternatives. In other words, for me "the personal is political" meant that our personal lives were, in considerable part, politically determined. Improving our personal experiences required collectively addressing political structures. Later, however, a new generation reversed the phrase to mean that our personal choices have political implications. Big deal, you might say. Obviously the personal choice to support an activist project has political implications. What's wrong with saying so? But this redefining of the phrase went further to imply as well that all the choices we make, even the ones that seem totally apolitical, have political implications. You choose to wear makeup or not, to watch TV or not, to eat this or that fish or not, to wear this or that pair of sneakers or not, to use a bank or not. It is personal but it is also political was the new apex of insight.

The idea that personal choices have political implications was and is true and certainly has some explanatory power and informative value. But the reversal of meaning went further. The most telling and instructive meaning of "the personal is political" became, as I encountered such views in the 1990s and since, a feeling that the key thing for each individual to be concerned with in being political was to be personal in the "correct" way. Dress right, eat right, talk right, look right, read right, consume right. That is how to be the best person, politically, that you can hope to be. "The personal is political"—meaning that personal outcomes are largely a product of systemic relations and of impositions on us by structures way beyond reach of each individual acting alone—came to mean, instead, that all political phenomena arise from the accumulated personal choices of individuals acting alone. What needed to be addressed to win better conditions were primarily people's personal choices.

This trend has been partially embodied in many sides of contemporary thought and activism, not least, for example, in elements of what is called "third wave feminism," "identity politics," "food politics," "lifestyle politics," and so on. My reading of my activist history is that it needs reconsideration.

I remember, over the years, young food activists insulting others who ate meat; young anti-imperialists sneering at others who rooted for a football team; young and old anticapitalists putting down others who went to Mass; old feminists, socialists, and all manner of leftists criticizing others who enjoyed elements of popular culture; mighty intellectuals putting themselves above others who read lowbrow materials. It is true that we need to try to live our lives in accord with our values. But it is also true that our values need careful assessment for their own biases and that our own ways of orienting our lives to our values have to be understood not as the only ways to do it, but as our ways to do it, so that we can abide and respect others who find other ways to live out good values, and so we can have patience and even respect for those who are carving out ways of living in less propitious circumstances than we enjoy. More, the impetus to wise, isolated, personal choices cannot replace the need for joining in collective acts and structures. "The personal is political" should mean society largely imposes our personal lives on us. We can change our lives only through collective action against unjust social relations.

The Class Problem

When I rise it will be with the ranks and not from the ranks.
—Eugene Debs

When the women of Bread and Roses said to the antiwar movement, "Clean up your act or you won't succeed," they were right. When the Black Power component of the civil rights struggle said to the movement, "Clean up your own house or you won't succeed," they were right. We are for ending racism and sexism in society. We have learned that we must also persevere to reduce and finally end racial and sexual hierarchies inside our movements. Otherwise we are hypocritical, we are uninspiring, we suffer the ills of these oppressions ourselves, our movements will not attract, much less empower, women and people of color, and we won't retain our broader antiracist and anti-sexist priorities.

However, we are also for ending economic injustice and class hierarchy in society. And we need to learn, I think, that we must patiently, calmly, and constructively restructure our movements so that they no longer replicate corporate divisions of labor, corporate hierarchies of decision making, and market norms of remuneration. This must become a patient but unrelenting priority if we are to avoid class-centered hypocrisy, become economically inspiring, not suffer class alienations ourselves, attract and empower working people in our efforts, and outwardly retain our economic justice foci.

Class, which at various times in history has wrongly crowded race and gender off our agendas, now needs to be reprioritized, but in ways that address not only the ills of capital, but also the ills of decision-monopolizing coordinators, and the positive needs of labor. The dismissive intuition Eric Sargent had about the no-nukes movement being largely coordinatorish is the kernel insight of a large part of the stickiness problem and is at the heart of the Left's class problem. Our movements don't attract and hold working people for the same reason that past movements, disdainful of gender or race, didn't attract and hold women and members of minority cultural communities.

The issue of class and social change was, for many years, just a matter of us versus them. We were on the side of labor and they were on the side of capital. Each side might have members coming from the other side by background (Engels was an owner, cops are workers) but the two sides were the only really important class teams that one could join. If you were a traitor to one class, you were aiding the other. There were two teams, period. Of course, individual people weren't homogenized into precisely two positions. Locations on the class map were much more varied at the personal level. But collectively, when thinking in terms of overall directions, class was bipolar.

From the time the Ehrenreichs wrote their essay in *Between Labor and Capital* to the present, however, I have not believed in a two-class formulation. It isn't just that there is another consequential group. Anyone can see further differentiations among the people labeled capital and the people labeled labor. It is that a movement could advocate on behalf of capital, on behalf of labor, or on behalf of a third class between those two, the coordinator class. There is an economy elaborating the interests of each of three classes as its central logic, not only an economy for two of them. The derivative strategic problem I felt was to develop a movement whose program, structures, and practices led toward a truly classless future rather than toward a coordinator-dominated future. It wasn't enough that many people wanted classlessness. Most of the rank and file in every past revolution wanted classlessness. Activists in KOR in Poland wanted classlessness. Rank-and-file activists in the Soviet Union wanted classlessness. Attaining classlessness, I realized, must be built into the logic of what people do, what they construct, and how they act, not just into their desires. This was a basic movement structural adjustment that had to guide the creation of institutions such as South End Press, for example, but it also had a more personal dimension.

I have polled Left audiences at many talks I have given. I find disdain for religion and for most sports—try asking leftists about NASCAR or bowling, much less about football, and watch the incredulous, dismissive reaction. I find leftists disparage most TV shows and country-and-western music, as well as most restaurants where working people eat and most newspapers that working people read, and even the actual eating and reading. The idea that so many leftists accidentally adopt daily preferences that are not only different from but that routinely denigrate working people, with nary a nod toward comprehension, is not, I think, an accident. There are additional factors, case by case, but overall this derives from our having not yet fully comprehended that coordinator elitism is as vile as capitalist or racist or sexist elitism.

During the 1970s disco era, I remember thinking about consumerism very closely. Watching John Travolta in the movie *Saturday Night Fever,* I began to understand in a new way how people trying to carve out reasonably fulfilling situations in tightly constrained settings can highly value commodities and practices that other people living in other situations utterly disdain. It is partly that sometimes many options are excluded, and partly that sometimes some options are made highly accessible or even essential. Why, for example, do young black boys, and now often girls too, think that playing basketball makes more sense than reading books? Is this genetic? Obviously not. It is structural channeling, and those who are channeled are not doing anything stupid, nor are they simply being tricked. They see reality and they act reasonably in light of what they see. Remember the butterfly? If the wings are off, walking makes sense.

Why did the disco generation spend a week's pay on a shirt for a Saturday night fling? Was it just the shirt itself, or was it because society conspired to make the shirt a uniform without which one could not get friendship, love, and sexual fulfillment? Were they tricked, or were they acting sensibly, given real constraints? Like a butterfly without wings they don't give up, they scrabble along on foot.

Why does a working-class guy spend Sunday afternoon laid out on a couch watching football, I asked myself? Why not play that game or some other? Why not read Chomsky—as I have heard leftists ask about "couch potatoes" with derision? When I ask this question to student audiences some reply, knowing that they better not be denigrating, maybe it's exhaustion. I say, it's a factor, yes, but, how about that playing on Sunday has been essentially precluded by the atomization of neighborhoods, the systematic dissolution of public spaces, and the elevation of associated costs? And how about that this "couch potato," male or female, can watch sports on Sunday and then socialize on Monday as one of the gang, but if he or she doesn't get into sports, isolation awaits? And how about, most of all, because the "couch potato" has to work as a wage slave Monday or suffer incredible losses for self and family, and were he or she to read Chomsky instead of watching sports on Sunday, not only would it be a step away from social engagement with others toward isolation, but it would actually make work all week more painful and less endurable, a luxury working people cannot afford to enjoy. Working people's choices make as much sense, often a good deal more sense, in the constrained world we inhabit, than the choices of those who have the freedom to play ball or to read Chomsky Saturday or Sunday afternoon. The point is, the Left as a whole needs to develop itself, and leftists individually need to revamp their cultural and social insights, in light of a three-class and not a two-class map.

The Electoral Problem

There is a tragic flaw in our precious Constitution, and I don't know what can be done to fix it. This is it: Only nut cases want to be president.
—Kurt Vonnegut

My first memory of an election is of running in ninth grade for class president. I lost. I cared about it somewhat, but I shed no tears. There was nothing political at stake. It involved only ego and social position. I next ran for treasurer of my high school's general assembly. I won. I cared quite a lot and celebrated. Again, there was nothing political at stake. Next, I ran for freshman class president at MIT. I lost. I didn't care about this one at all. There was nothing political at stake. Finally, I ran for president of the MIT student body. I

409

won. I exploited the victory to the hilt. This one was entirely political. What I had learned was that electioneering and winning should contribute to social change. It had no other valid purpose.

In junior high I was in a debate about the upcoming Kennedy/Nixon election. I had to advocate for Kennedy, and I did so, passionately, but I believe my enthusiasm was more about his coolness than his politics. I remember some of Kennedy's speeches, though. I wanted to ask what I could do for my country. I remember being miserable over Kennedy's assassination. But I also remember finding everyone watching his funeral morbid and strange. In fact, Kennedy was the only president I ever cared positively about, and it was only because I had no idea what the hell was going on in the world.

I will never forget Lyndon Johnson, the president who took over after Kennedy. Johnson aroused in me more passionate hate than any other person in my life. When I consider that, regarding domestic issues, LBJ may have been the most progressive politician in my lifetime (of course, largely due to pressures that movements forced on him), my hatred for Johnson is a bit ironic and clearly owes as much to who I was as to who he was. My passion wasn't rooted in LBJ's persona, but arose in light of the times. And it wasn't just that the times were aware, critical, and hostile to authority. I am far more informed now than I was then and my understanding of the crimes of later presidents has been greater than my understanding of Lyndon Johnson's. My fervor had a more subtle foundation.

LBJ was a master of war, but so were Nixon and all presidents since. What reduced my day-to-day anger toward later presidents compared to what I felt for LBJ has been, no doubt, my changing politics, the changing environment, and, I have to admit, perhaps my changing age. I see three broad possible types of reasons that Johnson aroused so much more intense feelings in me than all presidents since. The first explanation is that Johnson was my first hate, with that being the inverse of first love. More, my passion about injustice was then overly personal and not sufficiently institutional, which changed with growing political insight. And perhaps there was also a sense of betrayal fueling my reaction to Johnson replacing Kennedy—from whom I had hoped for more—a mistaken hope that I later transcended.

The second explanation is that in those earliest days of my political awareness there was an outlet for my most honest unrestrained reaction to LBJ and all masters of war, and to the institutions of war and injustice as well. In 1968 and 1969, and for another few years under Nixon, the state of the union was such that to allow oneself to hate the president, and more importantly to allow oneself to unreservedly feel solidarity with those suffering under bombs or under the lash of poverty, segregation, or rape, was not unreasonable. You could not only feel it, you could regularly express it. You could manifest it not just once a year, or once a month, but every day, and you could do so among others doing likewise.

This option or outlet for expressing brutally honest passion began to decline, however, in the mid-seventies. By about 1975, and certainly by 1980, for me to retain remotely the level of constant personal anger about and sensitivity to injustice would have been unbearable, and I didn't do it. Instead, I tethered myself to not feel the same degree of pain on seeing a homeless person, hearing about a rape, or seeing reports of bombs. I could not have constructively survived feeling with the same intensity in 1980 as I felt in 1968 but without the means of manifesting the emotions and expressing them that I had had in 1968. I had to instead navigate daily reality without that much anger, passion, pain, and desire. I had to hang on to the understanding of relations that fueled not only being radical, but being true to oneself. But I had to avoid explosion, and implosion, too.

This is not so easy a condition to maintain. I suspect that many people who have dropped out of revolutionary politics over the past thirty-five years have done so not because they became too greedy to feel continuing anger over injustice, but because they were internally inclined to feel too much anger and couldn't live with that, and defensively, and against their natural and more humane social inclinations, tapered it off past the point of retaining their activist effectiveness, in many cases to nearly nothing.

Living a manageable if tethered life productively for oneself and for loved ones can seem a much better option than living an aroused and passionate existence that is so emotionally draining and hostility-inducing as to be nearly suicidal. This becomes even more true whenever one begins to feel that the passion isn't paying off for yourself, for those far away, or for those close to you. Often radicalism wanes in such cases. I tried to straddle a fence between embodying so much anger and commitment as to burn out, and embodying so little anger as to completely cool off. I'm not entirely sure how successful I have been in this pursuit.

Lydia sometimes questions this choice of mine, saying that I am less passionate, less involved, less driven, and even less me than I was. And I can't deny her point. It is just that, in my mind, the choice isn't being more me in the manner Lydia would perhaps prefer and being less me in the manner I now am. The choice is instead between exploding in bitterness and hate, or being who I now am, even if it isn't exactly who I am naturally inclined to be. My exploding wouldn't advance social change. So if my reading of my motives is right, I have imposed on myself a degree of mellowness (which less charitably you might call a degree of complacency) to be able to get by productively at all.

The third explanation for a decrease in anger and passion is age, called maturity. I like to think there is none of this at play in me. I like to think I haven't mellowed due to synapses becoming rusty, or chemical balances unbalancing my sense of solidarity, or reflexes decaying, all as a result of years unfolding. Similarly, I like to think that whatever mellowing I have undergone to get by hasn't become so imprinted in my personality that if movements exploded tomorrow into a level of sustained activity such that honest, unrestrained anger and passion were again viable and productive, I wouldn't feel almost exactly like I did in 1968, right up on the surface, all the time.

Returning to elections, what about election candidates that progressive people cared about? Within the Democratic Party, I remember Eugene McCarthy and George McGovern and then, after a long hiatus, Dennis Kucinich and Al Sharpton. Those were the only Democratic Party candidates with any semblance of a serious program that come readily to mind. There were also Jesse Jackson and Ralph Nader, of course, treated shortly.

I met Kucinich briefly at a Green conference in Texas in 2004. I was there to speak and he was there giving the major address. I chatted with him briefly. I found his address impressive, especially for a presidential candidate within the Democratic Party. I am sure if I had had the same opportunity to hear Sharpton, my reaction would have been similar. Neither of these 2004 candidates had any chance at all, of course, running within the Democratic Party, because the Democratic Party officialdom considered them naive wingnuts, because they had virtually no money, because the media furthered their isolation and especially their "destined to lose" personas, and, most of all, because, educated by the media, the public assumed these dissident candidates couldn't win and the assumption of imminent failure is tantamount to actual failure, regardless of people's true preferences, in a winner-take-all race.

To me, earlier, Eugene McCarthy was a ridiculous drain on serious activism. In the sixties I felt McCarthy was a phony, and I really see no reason to change my view now. Huge numbers of young people went to New Hampshire to go Clean for Gene—to support him, that is. I went for one day, to see what was happening. I saw good people urging support for McCarthy, and, in the best cases, also talking forthrightly about the war. McCarthy's most active grassroots campaigners cared about the war, cared about injustice and poverty, cared about racism, and thought Clean Gene was going to affect all that. I thought McCarthy was just another politician who smelled an opportunity to take a ride on the back of antiwar opposition. Had McCarthy won, I doubt things would have changed much. Most of his supporters would have been so committed to him personally that they would have left behind their deeper and broader aims simultaneously with McCarthy jettisoning his campaign-induced rhetoric. Of course, if the forces electing McCarthy had congealed into a highly conscious movement, yielding even larger sustained dissent after his election than before it, history could have differed. But I thought McCarthy would defuse and, if need be, dismantle any such trend.

George McGovern, in contrast, impressed me as more honest. I thought he was sincerely against the war. I thought he had no chance to win, however, because he would never go remotely far enough to engender enough grassroots communication with diverse constituencies to overcome the forces arrayed against him. In those respects, the situation wasn't that much different than now. Of course, I saw McCarthy and McGovern through angry eyes.

In all of that, regarding those who won and those who lost, until I reached the age of 53, I never once voted in a U.S. presidential election. I didn't vote for McCarthy, Humphrey, McGovern, or Carter. It wasn't because I didn't care about society, it was because pulling a lever every four years to choose between candidates who are imperceptibly different from one another in their statements, and whose statements bear no necessary connection to their real beliefs, and whose real beliefs bear no necessary connection to the actions they could actually implement in the vortex of social constraints that mold and limit presidents, is barely politics. I aligned with the students who wrote on Paris wall posters in May 1968, "It's painful to submit to our bosses; it's even more stupid to choose them."

If I was in prison and there was an election for a new warden, I figure I might cast a ballot, caring about some meaningful difference in how the two potential wardens would implement prison policies, but I also might not vote, either doubting that the difference was real, or, regardless of small variations, rejecting being a party to my own repression and preferring to go out in the prison yard and shoot hoops rather than vote for a new master. Every four years I was metaphorically shooting hoops on Election Day.

What about nonpresidential politics? I never paid any attention to nonpresidential elections until Mel King ran for mayor of Boston. Mel is black, a coauthor with me of a book called *Liberating Theory*, and a profoundly radical and caring person. Mel was the real initiator of the Rainbow Coalition, which was the name he gave to the wide range of supporters working to elect him. I didn't actually work on Mel's campaign—I can't remember what I was doing instead other than working at South End Press—but I do remember that many of my friends did work for Mel's campaign, including Pat Walker and John Schall, both also from South End Press. Another more distant friend worked as campaign manager for Ray Flynn, a populist who was thought more likely to win the election. Ray was less charismatic, less astute, and less progressive than Mel. But he was white. And in the end, white Ray beat black Mel. Had Ray not run would Mel have won? Maybe; who can say? Flynn in office was nothing special.

I sat with Mel King one day for lunch and asked him why he was running for mayor of what Bostonians affectionately call Bean Town. His effort was progressive, but not aggressively radical. What did Mel actually think he could do, were he to win, particularly were he to win without having forged a massive radical movement able to fight against the vested corporate interests that would limit his options? Mel said he thought there was only one large benefit, beyond the bully pulpit that he could utilize to keep educating and organizing, and which he thought would be very valuable. He said, the mayor turns out to have a lot of unilateral say regarding the disposition of land. Mel felt that if he was elected mayor he could affect public land use and, by doing so, significantly affect housing availabilities, and thereby reduce poverty. Mel didn't run on this platform, however, and maybe it was just a view he tried on me. But the point I heard most clearly was that Mel understood that public officials are overwhelmingly hamstrung. He thought there was one loophole in the net that would enmesh him, just as it enmeshed all other mayors, through which he could propel some humane improvements. I don't know whether Mel was right that he would be organizationally able to do that. And, of course, to succeed, Mel would also have had to remain of a mind to carry through those efforts after having won the election, after tasting higher office's fame and perks, and despite what would appear to be needed to win a second term. But I was sad when Mel lost, though it might have been sadder to see him become mayor and make only piddling changes in the city's possibilities.

There was another, more recent election that greatly affected my view of electoral politics. It was in Brazil, where Lula and the Workers Party, or PT, won the presidency. The result so far has been only modestly beneficial, if even that, much to most people's surprise. Without entering extensively into the history of Brazil, the key fact is that the PT emerged from grassroots coalition struggle and embodied a history of activism, libertarian commitment, and antielitist sensibility as good as could be found beyond the tiniest scales anywhere on the planet. If this array of forces, with this worthy history, with its well-chosen candidates, couldn't convert electoral victory into major social progress, it is doubtful anyone could, or would.

While Lula was gearing up to run in his recent victorious campaign after having lost a couple of other times in the past, I visited Brazil for the first of two World Social Forums that I attended in Porto Alegre. The PT at the time held the mayoralty of Porto Alegre and the governor's post in the encompassing state, Rio Grande de Sul. The PT had or was about to win the mayoralty in other cities as well, most notably in the immense and very important city of São Paulo. I was told that a leftist movement had attained electoral control over the executive branch of various levels of government in a huge country and was contesting to enlarge its grip as well as experimenting to find new ways to operate. It was as if Mel King had run three times, built an ever-larger base of support, and finally won the mayoralty but not all other posts. The PT didn't control the legislatures or judiciaries at any level, city or state, not even in the state where they had the governor's post, nor did the PT control industries or even have a powerful organized presence within workplaces anywhere in the country, though there was a growing number of cooperatives as well as other diverse grassroots projects, including the very powerful movement of landless peasants, for example.

The PT regularly contested nationally, and would do so again after my visit, finally winning the presidential election. It was clear there was tremendous experience and material for learning in Brazil. What does a democratic and diverse Left with unparalleled grassroots credentials that wins limited but important gains do with its newfound offices? In the PT's case, one thing they did was to institute what they called "participatory budgeting." They controlled the state budgets wherever they had the executive branch. So they embarked on making the economic and social investments undertaken by those governments a public matter negotiated by a cooperative give and take with populations organized into assemblies. The new participatory budget intended to replace public government spending decided from the top down or by competitive market dynamics, with bottom-up participation.

On the plus side, the participatory budget and associated experiments, even though very modest in scope, helped make Porto Alegre arguably the best place to live in Brazil. More, the participatory budget began incorporating small but growing circles of the populace into economic planning. The project built infrastructure and explored new methods and interactions.

Negatively, winning executive powers enmeshed the PT in delivering daily operational coherence to the city's and state's activities, taking many of their most talented activists and resources away from direct action and organizing, away from reaching out to broaden the base of grassroots support, and away from winning new gains, and into office buildings and bureaucratic meetings. Gaining back the militant outreach and struggle attributes of their movement, while simultaneously defending, enlarging, and effectively utilizing their new government powers to immediately benefit the populace was the PT task at hand, it seemed, when I was there, as was Lula running for the presidency. The first part of this dual set of priorities, however, took second place to the election and, incredibly, Lula won, attaining the situation that the PT has had in Porto Alegre, but now for all of Brazil. However, in the same election, perhaps even more amazingly, the PT lost in Rio Grande de Sol the governor and the mayor of Porto Alegre.

How could it be, I wondered, that having taken power locally, utilized it as best they could for a considerable span of years, and even with Lula's coattails providing support, these officials lost a new election? The short explanation was

415

that holding the reins of government and mediating the disastrous and unpalatable (including dealing with all the debilitating pressures that imposes, including corruption) led to losing after winning, rather than winning on top of winning.

Beyond handling the budgets in experimental ways and seeking to find means of cooperation and popular power, the governor of Rio Grande de Sol, not too long before I visited, had decided to try to reduce income differentials among classes. The plan was to increase wages at the lowest levels, thereby diminishing the gap up to the higher levels where income would remain unchanged or drop due to the redistribution. The legislature, my hosts told me, promptly passed a law requiring that any generalized wage increases at the bottom imposed by the governor had to be matched by equal increases at the top, imposed by the legislature and courts. That annihilated the governor's plan to narrow the gap, of course. I asked my hosts, okay, why didn't you violate the courts and the legislature? They said that would yield civil war. They were pursuing a nonviolent course. To violate the laws of Brazil would obliterate their legitimacy.

Okay, I said, if the participatory budget is your domain due to the legal realities you confront, why not extend it further? Why not talk about having it operate in the private sector, too? For that matter, if you can't overcome the legislature or the courts with decrees, why can't you at least use the governor's and mayor's offices as what we in the U.S. sometimes call a bully pulpit, educating and arousing the population so that they will, in time, overthrow the legislature and courts? My hosts smiled and said, all in good time. Regrettably, good time seems to have been buried by bad time.

The broad lesson I learned from my encounters with Lula's supporters before his election was that gains in Brazil were unstable. There was tension between delivering better daily administration on the one hand and continuing to actively expand the movement through outreach and struggle on the other hand. An additional and centrally important variant of this tension surfaced in the then-upcoming election. Should the PT utilize as a central logic of the campaign preserving and enlarging existing support, which reached well into the professional levels of Brazil's class structure, or should it try to get out hesitant voters among poorer workers and peasants? The PT was no doubt eminently aware, at least for awhile, that it needed to go to the populace to win legislatures, to topple old judiciaries, and to organize people in workplaces and communities into their own democratic councils to manifest their wills not only regarding a fraction of the state's investment budgets, and then later not only regarding the whole of the state's budgets, but also regarding the whole of the Brazilian economy and society, all its industries and institutions—uprooting old forms and adopting new ones with entirely new values. Whether we are talking about Brazil, the U.S., or anywhere else, we have to understand the logic of building ever more powerful

416

movements, while also constructing the infrastructure of the new society. Many Brazilians certainly understood all this in broad terms, but the main lesson may be that if you are going to run to win gains short of changing society, those who run need to be beholden to movements and movements need to be independent of the pressures of office.

Locally in Rio Grande de Sol, progress was terminated by an angry electorate upset at compromises and corruption. Nationally, Lula won, and then confronted a horrible balancing act. Would he protect his people from U.S. machinations by appealing to international finance capital and keeping local capital from becoming too hostile? Or would he pursue his longtime justice-seeking principles and let the chips fall as they may?

Lula and the PT, at least to the time of my writing this, chose the former path—accommodation—and his principles are rapidly changing in accord with this decision, or so the visible signs suggest. One wonders, or at least I wonder, why Lula didn't manifest the anticapitalist and intensely pro-working-class spirit he showed for decades leading up to his election once he won the post he sought. If I could interview Lula I would ask why, after his electoral victory, he didn't hold a national Brazilian plebiscite, after a period of intense education and discussion, polling the populace as to whether they wanted him to pursue equity and expand democracy and enhance integrity as per his long history of aspirations but at the risk of horrible retribution by international capital and the U.S.—or whether they instead wanted him to accommodate the IMF, the World Bank, the U.S., and local capital, seeking to avoid severe dislocations while making only very modest gains in social relations. Why did Lula paternalistically make the choice between these two broad paths forward for all Brazilians? The answer, I would anticipate, was embedded in the politics of party rule. Given U.S. agendas, Lula's actions have been, at bottom, not solely but largely part and parcel of what rule from above does to leaders themselves, and what rule from above imposes on citizens as well.

Returning to the U.S., Jesse Jackson's Rainbow Coalition campaigns in 1984 and 1988 impressed me primarily for his slogan, "Give Hope a Chance." Jackson is a sophisticated political being. He knows what it takes to mount something truly major. It takes hope fueled by a belief that something better is possible. Jackson's campaigns depressed me, however, in being, in the end, primarily about Jackson himself, and votes for Jackson. At first it seemed that Jackson's own career wasn't going to be the agenda. The Rainbow Coalition, after all, was a movement, an organization, a project, not a person. It was far more than only an electoral campaign for Jesse, though the slogan "Run Jesse Run" foretold things to come. The critical failing wasn't that Jesse ran, but that where Jackson campaigned the priority wasn't building grassroots activism to manifest lasting influence, but was winning votes.

417

I remember urging, in essays at the time, that Jackson should put forth a full and compelling radical program addressing drugs, crime, housing, education, arms dealing, foreign policy, human rights, employment, wages, AIDS, the ERA, affirmative action, agribusiness, income distribution, election reform, and media reform. As history regrettably demonstrated, Jackson didn't pay a whole lot of attention to such entreaties or to anyone who wasn't staring back at him from his own mirror. It was one thing for Jesse not to bend in the breeze. That was okay. It was another thing to be above communication. That was bad. What was even more damning, however, was that when Jackson rolled through Iowa, Maine, Mississippi, Michigan, and California, while hope, momentum, and energy were all undeniably stirred—which was profoundly promising—not enough consciousness and organization were put in place to have lasting effect. Instead of merely getting separate constituencies to each support the candidate, which was what the Jackson campaign did, I and others urged, at the time, that the Jackson campaign should help those constituencies understand each other's priorities so that they could form lasting alliances that would persist beyond election day. That was not done.

I thought the speech that Jackson needed to give was one that said that the enemy was racism, sexism, homophobia, and profit-seeking, and that spelled out how to organize effectively against these and on behalf of justice. It was a speech indicating that justice was something people had to win, not something Jesse Jackson or anyone else could give. Jackson and other Rainbow organizers should have traveled from Miami to Seattle and from San Diego to Boston over and over, patiently and slowly, without media glare, with little fanfare and in a manner minimizing costs, to talk with not only large but also small audiences about how to build organizations for the long haul.

I and others wanted the Rainbow to define itself as an overarching umbrella organization that sought to raise political consciousness in its membership and throughout the country. I wanted it to pressure positive reforms for the poor and oppressed, and to win structural changes that would strengthen the disempowered through electoral victories. I wanted it to seek the transformation of existing institutions and also the grassroots construction of new institutions. This is what Mel King had in mind when he came up with the idea of a broad multirace and multi-issue coalition called the Rainbow, and Mel was right on the mark. I wrote at the time that the proper way to help Jackson was not to give him carte blanche control over Rainbow activity. He must be accountable like everyone else—indeed, because he is a politician, he must be more accountable than most. I worried and urged that it would be a tremendous debit if Jesse Jackson decided that winning the presidency was paramount and that winning required catering to mainstream politicians, the media, and clergy over and above pursuing a clear radical agenda including the use of what Jesse graphically called "street heat."

The trouble with the Jackson campaigns was ultimately that Jackson's feared failings mattered—not the ones the newspapers and pundits pummeled, but the ones that interfered with him carrying through his campaigns into sustained movement opposition. The failings that mattered were the ones that led him to, in time, disband the Rainbow rather than have it achieve power that transcended himself. Jackson was simply unwilling to become accountable to a powerful Rainbow and a broad progressive public.

I remember some conversations with Dave Dellinger and Leslie Cagan at the time. Dave and Leslie were both meeting with Jackson during the period of deciding how to proceed beyond elections into grassroots activism and struggle. This was when Jackson finally disbanded the whole operation. Dave and Leslie described how Jackson totally dominated every meeting. They relayed how what was said, in what order, with what cadence met his approval or, if not, came to an abrupt halt. They described an environment in which cozying up to Jackson meant you had more influence and stature (at least about anything he agreed with), whereas criticizing Jackson or even frequently having contrary views to Jesse's meant dropping in influence and stature, in time right out of the picture.

These are the dynamics of fame and power played out even in a Left that had its deepest roots all the way back in SNCC and in the young SDS, just as the same dynamics ripped at Lula in Brazil in his rise to power. Everyone knows that a movement should not be tied to the will and personality of an individual, yet over and over movements do just this. I still feel that the dissolution of the Rainbow was a horrible loss for people throughout the U.S. and the world. Others on the Left tend to look at periods of great repression, or at international events that turn back progressive attitudes, as our big, bad losses. I look at our failed projects that could have succeeded as our big, bad losses.

Following on Jesse's lead, Ralph Nader ran a very effective campaign in 2000. He was highly visible. He raised good issues. I supported him throughout the campaign, though many leftists did not. The general 2000 anti-Nader argument was simple. To vote/work for Nader meant not voting/working for Gore. In states with close Gore/Bush ratings, Gore could lose enough votes to Nader for Bush to win the state, and ultimately by accumulating states, to win the election. If one thought that Bush had a worse White House agenda than Gore, one should vote for Gore and not for Nader. A vote for Nader, since Nader was not going to win, was a vote for Bush. Most leftists replied that Bush and Gore were Tweedledum and Tweedledee, which was certainly true in the broad sense of both being agents of elite rule, but this ignored some quite important details and especially their appeal to different elite constituencies—Gore to a corporate and coordinator elite, Bush to a religious fundamentalist coterie and a corporate elite.

Other leftists said, yes, perhaps these guys are more different than typical candidates because Bush is so beholden to the far right, but we can't always just vote for the lesser evil, and now makes sense to break that pattern because Nader is mounting a serious effort so we can vote for him and be much truer to our beliefs in doing so. I didn't buy that rationale, either. What does being truer to self matter alongside affecting social outcomes?

I did support Nader, however, quite strongly, but it was because I felt that what mattered wasn't the election itself, but the election's aftermath. My argument was that if Nader ran well and amassed a few percent support and created, in the process, much progressive awareness and infrastructure, the emerging, lasting movement would make the ensuing years better even if Bush was in office. My feeling was that Bush plus a powerful, financially well-off, grassroots, highly-organized, Nader campaign-propelled movement that would restrain Bush was better than Gore plus lesser restraints.

I remember thinking in particular about the cases most often discussed: Supreme Court Justices, taxes, police violence, abortion, and interventionism. The issue for me wasn't whether we could plausibly predict that Bush's preferred agenda for each of these policy areas would be sufficiently worse than Gore's to adversely impact many suffering people. Of course we knew Bush's agenda was worse. Denying that was self-delusion. The issue for me was, instead, if lots of people throughout the country supported and voted for Nader, could that awaken not only hope but also organizational clout and commitment so that neither Gore or Bush, whoever was elected, would be as able to pursue his full agenda? In other words, the real choice in my view was Gore winning without Nader getting lots of support and therefore with a typically unaroused populace that would allow him to pursue his full corporate agenda virtually unopposed, versus Bush (or maybe still Gore) winning but with Nader getting lots of support and translating this support into a highly aroused sector of the populace ready to fight up a postelection storm.

The correct comparison wasn't, I urged, the will of Bush and his constituencies versus the will of Gore and his. The correct comparison was what Bush (or Gore) would do with a 10 percent Nader constituency fighting on, versus what Gore would do with no such ongoing, galvanized, and organized opposition contesting policymaking, plus what the emerging opposition would mean in future elections and movement development.

To my way of thinking, the lesser-evil discussion stacked the deck against third-party politics by simply ruling out the real reason for a third-party campaign, and thus its real value—not only in the long term, but in the short term as well. The lesser-evil discussion most often assumed, that is, that the only thing that mattered about an election is who won it—not the election's impact on constituencies supporting or opposing candidates and on movement organization and commitment. It assumed, in other words, that nothing substantial could ever be accomplished electorally unless it occurred by some kind of overnight miracle that won all things sought in one swoop.

If Nader could win, then it would be okay to vote for him, people felt, but we can't participate in an extended process of work and organizing as a prerequisite to only later winning major gains and even eventual electoral power. The discussion denied that with elections, as with all organizing, you lose, you lose, you lose, and then you win—and thus all those losses weren't really losses at all, but were, instead, part of a process of building eventual definitive support. And, more, the discussion denied that the supposed debit of having pushed some elections in the short-term from Tweedledumb to Tweedledumber (and more vile), were in some cases not such large debits as they might seem, because the electoral swing to the right was offset by the fact that tweedle dumber then had to operate against a far more aroused and organized populace able to constrain his options.

The sad truth is that my scenario didn't work. It wasn't Nader's campaign up to election day that went wrong. It was what happened after the election. Nader went home. He didn't follow through. The movement that supported Nader couldn't persist without the glue of recognition and support that Nader embodied. The project floundered. Instead of getting Bush plus a really powerful opposition movement as opposed to getting Gore plus a weak or no opposition movement, we got Bush plus a weak movement, which was the worst possible outcome. But it didn't happen because Bush won, or rather stole, the election. And it didn't happen because Nader ran. It happened because Nader went home. He tossed in the towel.

Within days of Bush's victory I wrote a piece for ZNet and Z Magazine titled "Why Not Create a Shadow Government?" I noted that of course the new president, Bush, was waiting eagerly to commit domestic and international mayhem on behalf of his favored elite constituencies. I suggested, however, that the big unanswered question was what are Nader and the Greens going to do now that the campaign is concluded? I asked, "Having run an exciting campaign that inspired large audiences all across the U.S., what's next? Having built apparatuses in many states, what is to be done with it?" And then I made a suggestion. I wanted Nader, and his running mate Winona LaDuke, to hold a press conference and announce that they were establishing a shadow government. I wanted them to announce a set of Cabinet members (secretary of state, labor, etc.), a presidential staff (press secretary, etc.), and perhaps even a list of senators across the country. I wanted to see a Web site that included not only the biographies of the shadow officials and a statement by each regarding his or her priorities, but also a forum area for ongoing discussion, a sign-up mechanism to receive future communications, and an extensive, compelling display of ongoing shadow government policy priorities and positions contrasting with those of the actual government.

I foresaw public statements indicating the shadow government's view of every major U.S. government undertaking, and what the shadow government would have done differently, and the estimated difference in impact between the shadow choices and those of Bush and company. I foresaw presentations of what the shadow government would have undertaken each week, explaining why the Washington government was unlikely to embark on similar actions, and what the public gains would have been had the shadow government been able to pursue its aims. I foresaw a tabular summary contrasting the overall impact of the two governments for each week—plus a cumulative summary of major differences for the year. I envisioned the shadow government relating to the economy, polity, cultural issues, family matters, foreign policy, and the environment, for example. I foresaw Web site sections for each Cabinet member, for the president's staff, and even for the Senate, and for a state of the week speech, given by Nader, with a press conference, and broadcast on diverse independent radio stations.

The point of the proposed project would have been to demonstrate as accessibly as we could the philosophical and policy differences between Bush's actual administration and a Green-Nader administration, had it been elected. There could have been a shadow inauguration, a shadow State of the Nation address, shadow press conferences, shadow Senate votes, shadow Supreme Court appointments, shadow budget presentations and hearings, and even shadow White House cultural events.

The shadow government, I urged, could provide a record upon which Greens could run next time around. The site, press conferences, public campaigns, demonstrations, teach-ins, and other events could be a thorn in the side of elite government and, more important, an educational resource and organizing tool in the U.S. and probably around the world as well. The shadow government wasn't proposed to replace getting out and organizing face-to-face. The shadow government, with shadow events, policies, statements, and results that people could judge to determine if they wanted something far more radical than Washington offered, had a democratic, participatory, and engaging aura about it. It could be a tool to facilitate organizing. So what obstructed having a shadow government?

The technology was easy. Effort and creativity were required, and a lot of energy and ingenuity, but the project wouldn't cost much in dollars. More, Nader had three million voters, and, as we knew from the polls, roughly another seven million people who liked him and voted for Gore only as a lesser evil. Think about tapping ten million people for regular monthly sustaining donations for the shadow government. That alone would have been an immense gain for the Left. And since there was no dearth of good people to fill the Cabinet posts, presidential staff, courts, joint chiefs, and even a whole shadow Senate—the only real obstacle to having a shadow government was would Nader and LaDuke do it, or, if not, could others be tapped in their place?

I asked, wasn't it about time the Left managed to generate enough coherence, at least about a short-term critique of events and immediate positive program, to present a united front? Wouldn't creating a shadow government be a plausible, invigorating, and productive way to achieve that? The first step would presumably have been for Nader and LaDuke to sit down and decide they wanted to do it, for them and various Greens to sign on a Cabinet and other central appointments, and for the new shadow Cabinet and as many other appointed officials as possible to together decide how to deal with each week's critical postings and policy and other determinations.

It didn't happen. It wasn't that the idea didn't get traction. The proposal went quickly up the ranks of the Green Party. I heard from many supporters of the idea inside the Greens, including people close to Nader. There was, however, no public debate. The shadow government idea died, rejected by Nader in private. Nader didn't want to have a shadow government that he would be part of. And he wouldn't help anyone else do it. He didn't even join the Greens. Party building wasn't his thing. And as with the situation of Jesse Jackson and the Rainbow earlier, Ralph was the boss, pure and simple. The shadow government idea, and any other idea that might have parlayed the election energies into lasting achievements, was dead on the vine.

The magnitude of this loss is hard to know. Nader got about 3 percent of the vote in 2000. Even more, a fair guess is that 10 percent of the electorate liked him best. If half of these people had agreed to donate just $2 a month, this would have given the Left $10 million a month. If one percent of them had become progressive organizers, this would have multiplied the number of organizers manyfold. When Nader ran for the Green 2004 nomination, I opposed him on grounds that he would largely fail to follow through again, as he did in 2000. In the election, I favored the safe-states approach. In states where the election was close, vote for Kerry and then throw up. In states where either Kerry or Bush was a lock to win, vote for who you like, whether it was Nader or, as I preferred, the Green candidate, David Cobb.

The Jackson and Nader Rainbow and Green campaigns failed, in my view, not for want of possibility, but for want of quality. Jackson could have helped to build and sustain a Rainbow which might have given us a quite different world by now—not one completely revolutionized, but one that was perhaps on the way to fundamental changes, and certainly not one in which empire madness runs amok. Nader, had he built a shadow government, could have saddled Bush in his first term and led toward Bush losing a second term to a Kerry or to someone much better, with whoever it was pushed well to the left of anything we have seen from Democrats, and with Nader getting ten percent or more in 2004, as well. Who knows what level of grassroots organization and consciousness a shadow government might have engendered? These are lost opportunities. We can't get them back. Hopefully we can learn from the mistakes, however, not least regarding whether we engage electorally, with what means, with which candidates, and especially how we view elections and their aftermaths and relate to the latter.

Chapter 32

Actualization

Organization to Liberate Society

I wish that every human life might be pure transparent freedom.
—Simone de Beauvoir

In the sixties we chanted, "The only solution is revolution." Some people meant all you can do that matters is seek a fundamentally transformed world. Seeking less is worthless because less would leave most problems intact, and would in time either fail or be rolled back. Of course, this overlooked that you could win less today as part of a process leading to winning more tomorrow. That was the slogan's flaw. But the truths of the slogan were powerful, too. A world without poverty and indignities required new basic institutions, not just modified versions of those we had.

Between the sixties and the present, I was mostly involved with publishing—South End Press, *Z Magazine*, and finally, ZNet. I wrote about organizing prospects and possibilities, did a lot of public speaking, and tried to form various coalitions of media operations, but I was much less tied into grassroots organizing and movement building than earlier. Still, in 1998, my frustration at the absence of Left organization that could win social change reached a climax. I decided to try to do something about it.

My 1998 idea for an Organization to Liberate Society (OLS) was pretty simple. I didn't know exactly what a good organization should look like. I didn't know exactly what program a good organization should have. No one knew these things, but more, I didn't want these things decided by a small membership, even if that could yield a large membership later. I wanted lots of people involved in deciding the attributes of a worthy organization, both to be sure its structure and program were well-conceived, and to establish democratic participation. So, thinking about that, I figured, okay, maybe we can start an organizational project with a few unifying principles and one priority, to get more and more people to sign on to those unifying principles. When we got a million advocates of the unifying principles, we could democratically establish broader organizational program and structure.

The first step would be to set down the possible principles, and I made a stab at that. A plausible next step would be to get a bunch of other folks to refine the principles and sign on to advocating them. The plan was for the OLS idea to appear with a large group of advocates who had refined the principles, and from then on grow to incorporate many more people. So OLS offered five principles that the first participants believed a truly decent society should respect and asked anyone who agreed with those five principles to sign on as a member and recruit as many other members as they could. Once membership reached a million people (and only then) a specific program and organizational structure could be decided by the entire membership using the Internet for communication. Until OLS got that large, however, the only program of OLS would be "recruit, recruit, recruit." This would avoid a few "founding members" determining the organization's structure and program, and it would ensure that OLS would reflect the interests of people from all over the world. Here are the five principles the initial participants agreed on.

A society is more liberated to the extent that fewer people are denied human rights or opportunities or in any way oppressed due to race, religion, ethnicity, gender, age, sexual preference, property ownership, wealth, income, or statist authoritarianism and exclusion. Reducing and ultimately removing such hierarchies of reward, circumstance, status, or power would improve society.

A society is more liberated to the degree that it fosters solidarity such that its citizens, by the actions they must take to survive and fulfill themselves, come to care about, promote, and benefit from one another's well-being, rather than getting ahead only at one another's expense.

A society is more liberated to the degree that its citizens enjoy comparably rewarding and demanding life experiences and equal incomes, assuming comparable effort and sacrifice on their parts to contribute to the social good.

A society is more liberated to the extent that its citizens are able to democratically influence decisions proportionately as they are affected by those decisions and have the circumstances, knowledge, and information required for this level of participation.

A society is more liberated to the extent that diversity is fostered and nourished in social relations, in relations with nature, and in all dimensions of life.

These five principles, honed over a period of weeks by the initial participants, seemed to capture core feelings that many people advocated. The initial supporters urged people to bear in mind that by joining OLS they were not renouncing any other organization or strategy; they were simply endorsing the five principles and agreeing to enlist other people to endorse them as well.

I felt that, if the effort succeeded, we would have launched a new and very powerful organization that would have great hope of producing progressive social change. If the effort failed, we would at least end up with a publicly accessible e-mail list that any progressive organization could use for outreach. We put up a site with a mechanism people could use to sign up. We included arguments on behalf of the idea and an essay addressing likely concerns. Nonetheless, people didn't get the logic of building something that didn't have an immediate program. People didn't think the transition from lots of people to an organization would occur. People didn't think other people would sign up. I wondered why it was so hard for people to believe a tally of progressives could reach a million. Aren't there way more than a million people who support progressive principles?

An important benefit of the idea, at least in my mind, was that there were no purse strings to maneuver. Likewise, there was no elite position to monopolize. There were no founders to be spokespeople or to otherwise hog the limelight or bend outcomes. When there were a million members and it was time to develop national program and strategy, the process could be truly participatory and democratic.

Looking back, I think OLS was a good idea in the sense that if people signed on in huge numbers, it could have been a great beginning for a new organization. It was a bad idea, however, in the sense that it didn't elicit enough people's participation to take off. The same can be said for various earlier attempts I had made in the same direction. For example, well before OLS there was OTIS, Organization to Instigate Solidarity. That time the idea was to form a group that would work to generate collectivity and solidarity on the Left. The plan was that it would focus on the full range and breadth of goals that were implied by the later five principles. In other words, OTIS had the same basic guiding aim, though it tried a different angle for attaining it.

We Stand for Peace and Justice

Freedom is nothing else but a chance to be better.
—Albert Camus

Nearly five years after OLS, in the aftermath of 9/11, I had another go at helping transcend atomized dissent. I penned a statement called "We Stand" and solicited a bunch of people to refine and adjust it to their liking.

After a time, a group of about ten of us enlisted more signers. We then wrote a multiauthor article to introduce the statement publicly. Finally the project went participatory. We Stand tried to incorporate the range and scope of the prior OLS effort. It had the added appeal, however, of an antiwar, pro-justice statement that began with about eighty very prominent, internationally diverse supporters at a very timely moment. In just a few weeks, We Stand got 90,000 internet signatures and the Zapatistas reported getting another 25,000 signatures in Mexico by hand. Here is what people signed on to:

I stand for peace and justice.

I stand for democracy and autonomy. I don't think the U.S. or any country should ignore the popular will and violate and weaken international law, to bully and bribe votes in the Security Council.

I stand for internationalism. I oppose any nation spreading an ever expanding network of military bases around the world and producing an arsenal unparalleled in the world.

I stand for equity. I don't think the U.S. or any other country should seek empire. I don't think the U.S. ought to control Middle Eastern oil on behalf of U.S. corporations and as a wedge to gain political control over other countries.

I stand for freedom. I oppose brutal regimes in Iraq and elsewhere but I also oppose the new doctrine of "preventive war," which guarantees permanent and very dangerous conflict, and is the reason why the U.S. is now regarded as the major threat to peace in much of the world. I stand for a democratic foreign policy that supports popular opposition to imperialism, dictatorship, and political fundamentalism in all its forms.

I stand for solidarity. I stand for and with all the poor and the excluded. Despite massive disinformation millions oppose unjust, illegal, immoral war, and I want to add my voice to theirs. I stand with moral leaders all over the world, with world labor, and with the huge majority of the populations of countries throughout the world.

I stand for diversity. I stand for an end to racism directed against immigrants and people of color. I stand for an end to repression at home and abroad.

I stand for peace. I stand against this war and against the conditions, mentalities, and institutions that breed and nurture war and injustice.

I stand for sustainability. I stand against the destruction of forests, soil, water, resources, and biodiversity on which all life depends.

I stand for justice. I stand against economic, political, and cultural institutions that promote a rat race mentality, huge economic and power inequalities, corporate domination even unto sweatshop and slave labor, racism, and gender and sexual hierarchies.

I stand for a policy that redirects the money used for war and military spending to provide healthcare, education, housing, and jobs.

I stand for a world whose political, economic, and social institutions foster solidarity, promote equity, maximize participation, celebrate diversity, and encourage full democracy.

I stand for peace and justice and, more, I pledge to work for peace and justice.

The initial signing up of notable supporters had a proviso. We all agreed that neither I nor anyone else would try to turn the list into something more than a protest unless well over half the initial signers agreed with the plan. Once the statement had garnered lots of signatures, all in just a few weeks time, I contacted the original signers. I urged that we should collectively figure out how to move from 100,000 signers to many more, and then establish some kind of international organization based on the agreed principles. Only a handful of the well-known signers replied to this proposal positively, though often without enthusiasm—and it was mostly my good friends, at that. The rest of the statement's initial advocates were either silent, which was almost all of them, or said they wanted nothing to do with such an effort. Reasons for not wanting to move forward from We Stand as a statement to 100,000 signers as a basis for organization and program were basically a conviction that it wouldn't work. The time would be wasted. It would distract from local work. The effort would cost more than it gained. It would become top-down and, in time, lose support. I thought, in contrast, that We Stand was another opportunity lost. I could not fathom what people were waiting for, what they wanted as a basis for constructing lasting structural gains, if not 100,000 supporters garnered in just a few weeks worldwide.

The OLS and We Stand efforts, and other efforts over the years too, have failed. It's a syndrome with an ending. It may require a different approach, different people, even different times, but at some point down the road, people are going to win a truly new world. So I say to myself, okay, let's suppose the new world includes a combination of anarchistic political institutions, feminist kinship institutions, intercommunalist cultural institutions, and pareconist economic institutions. Whatever the details of all that might be, surely we can't move from having none of it to having all of it overnight. I note to myself that it will of course be a long struggle that builds on efforts of the past and heads into new forms for the future. It will construct infrastructure in advance of having a new society, both to learn and to benefit. It will win a trajectory of changes in social relations, income distribution, decision making, electoral rules, family life, and other realms and structures, with each new victory spurring additional efforts and organizational commitments.

My thinking in launching the We Stand statement was that winning all these gains will not be the work of random disjointed activism. It would involve lasting movements and organizations that give the process coherence. It seemed to me that some of these structures would have to form early in the campaigns and last into major victory and even melt into the key institutions of the new society. We Stand, like OLS, was trying to get those structures going. It is going to happen at some point. If not now, when? If not us, who?

Workers and consumers councils, for example, of course tiny at first, would in my view be part of a project undertaken sometime relatively soon but carrying over into a new society. There would also be one or more major political organizations, it seemed to me, that would likely melt into the new political forms of a future society. These structures would come into existence sometime down the road to wage campaigns and struggles for change—so, in my mind, the obvious question was "Why not come into existence sooner rather than later"? Let's get going, was my feeling, and still is, for that matter.

I can't know what the time line will be for actually winning a new world, though I am sure that once things get moving down a path that leads where we will wind up, the pace will quickly accelerate. What OLS and We Stand were about was prodding into existence an organization that could provoke, stimulate, incite, partake of, and help organize and even become central to a long-term, successful revolutionary process. I don't know that I will be around to enjoy a new world that such a process will win. If not, however, I'd like to feel that, at the very least, something that I am part of building will make it all the way into that new world. I find it amazingly frustrating that most other people I know, much less the rest of the population, don't think about social change this way.

Advocate or Overhaul

Isolated individual endeavor, for all its purity of ideals, is of no use, and the desire to sacrifice an entire lifetime to the noblest of ideals serves no purpose if one works alone, solitarily, in some corner of America, fighting against adverse governments and social conditions which prevent progress.
—Che Guevara

I can't deny feelings of relevance, not to mention irrelevance. It has seemed to me, over the years, that arriving at a combination of multi-focus theory, compelling and inspiring vision, and promising strategy is key to creating a sufficiently coherent and capable movement to change the world. It has also seemed to me that for whatever combination of coincidences, configurations, and commitments, I and others have had significant parts of that broad conceptual framework in hand. This has conveyed to us, I think, the responsibility to advocate that package widely, and strongly, or—contrariwise—to discover that my impression about what we have in hand is wrong.

This explains most of what I have been doing since the sixties, including my writing and speaking, my efforts to create media mechanisms, and my forays into movement building. I believe combining race, gender, power, and class into a single flexible and accessible conceptual framework is important. I believe developing and popularizing institutional vision based on values of solidarity, equity, diversity, and self-management is important. I believe adopting strategic ideas incorporating the merging of solidarity and autonomy, the expansion and congenialization of outreach, and the waging of nonreformist reform struggles is important. I believe matching organization and program with initial conditions as well as with ultimate goals is important. And if these commitments are part and parcel of attaining a movement able to win a participatory society, as I believe, then to me it follows that advocating, as well as continually refining and improving the associated theory/vision/strategy package, needs to be a major priority. On the other hand, if there are damning flaws in that package, the task should be to discern the flaws and overhaul the ideas, or perhaps to start over completely.

How does one know whether advocacy, refinement/overhaul, or starting over is warranted? You convince yourself, as best you can, by assessing and especially challenging the package as best you can and seeing if it stands up to your devilish attacks. But what if you feel as a result of that endeavor, as I do, that the package is essential and worthy? Couldn't you be wrong? Well, of course you could.

My experience tells me advocates of Leninism, among others, feel that they have tested and retested their package and that it is irrefutable. Might my allegiance to liberating theory, participatory society (and particularly parecon), and the associated broad range of strategic commitments I advocate be just as out of touch with reality as I think Leninism is? Sure, it might be. If we could look into the future we could see what role ideas like the ones I advocate will play, if any, in the emergence of a better world. Not having that option, our only other choice is to debate and continually test and retest views in light of ongoing experience. Thus, we can cause our ideas to clash with other ideas. Critics can burrow into proposed concepts and try to reveal faulty claims, ill-conceived connections, or outright chasms of inconsistency and ignorance. If critics find flaws that advocates can't remedy, packages can be jettisoned and the search for desirable vision and strategy can be reinitiated. If critics find only correctable problems, then these can be addressed, revisions made, and the package advocated and utilized. If having a package of shared concepts, vision, and strategy is necessary for creating a new world, the above options are a truism. We have to seek such a package. We have to share it. We have to build the associated organizations and movements for winning change interactively in entwined and expanding circles of revision, influence, and impact.

Life After Capitalism

The world is big. Some people are unable to comprehend that simple fact. They want the world on their own terms, its peoples just like them and their friends, its places like the manicured patch on which they live.
—Chinua Achebe

At the third World Social Forum, I worked hard to create a venue for exploring matters of vision and strategy. It seemed the project, called Life After Capitalism (LAC), was welcomed by the forum powers that be. I was put on the international WSF steering committee to ease the effort. (I later left it, or at any rate tried to leave it and stopped participating, on grounds that I was not elected by anyone and wasn't representing any large constituency, though these were reasons no one seemed to understand or acknowledge.)

People in Brazil, on the WSF organizing committee, were assigned to work with me on the Life After Capitalism project. I proposed a slate of workshops and plenaries. We discussed them, I got an excited okay, and I went ahead and invited about ninety people from around the world to participate in the LAC series of interconnected panels, talks, debates, and meetings, to be held as a kind of conference within the forum. The Brazilians wanted me to help organize and bring people from the U.S. I did that. They wanted me to help them get a number of notable people who had balked at coming. I did that. They seemed eager to help with LAC for the months leading toward the events, including connecting us with hotels so we could arrange housing for all our invitees who needed it, which we did. Indeed, at the prior WSF and at the European Social Forum in Florence, the Brazilians urged that we use ZNet to bring their large lists of attendees into mutual contact. They even wanted to give ZNet their e-mail lists, to try to induce everyone who was going to attend the WSF to become ZNet Sustainers, using our sustainer online communications system as the WSF's means of communicating with and trying to tie together attendees at the forums. This was an incredibly enticing political and monetary possibility from our point of view, which, however, would have been politically entirely irresponsible, given that of course the world's supporters of the WSF should not be assumed to be, and even ipso facto made to be, supporters of ZNet by such an approach.

For that reason, we didn't do it, however regretfully. But we did work hard to create LAC, or Life After Capitalism, and to raise U.S. interest in the WSF and help induce particular individuals to come. We invited and arranged an agenda of speakers from all over the world, about forty of whom we got housing for. We set up all kinds of debates, panels, and discussions, with all of the events carefully conceived to flow into one another to permit a serious and sustained debate among different perspectives. We developed and had printed tens of thousands of flyers and posters in English and in Portuguese. All this was done long-distance with the promise that the WSF would provide a massive promotional display for us, put up the materials we did at our expense, give our events very prominent rooms, put the events together in the agenda and highlight them, and so on.

Just before we were to leave for Porto Alegre, thinking all this was in place and proceeding nicely, we were told we would have to cut back to three the nearly forty events we had planned. Perhaps you can imagine the consternation and anger this message induced. Chomsky and Arundhati Roy, this WSF's keynote speakers, were coming, owing to our intervention. A massive number of Americans were coming, in part due to our promotional efforts. We had done what the WSF really wanted us to do, and we could now be jettisoned. That's how it appeared to us, at any rate. Many of our people, coming from all over the planet, would be doing nothing, their events having been cancelled while they were on route. The posters and flyers would be for naught, or worse, they would be misleading. We said no to all that. We were going ahead with all our plans or we were going to go berserk.

There was a standoff and all kinds of long-distance crisis communication. I don't know what would have happened if Noam Chomsky, who was part of LAC, hadn't weighed in that he would be backing out from attending the WSF unless all our panels and events went ahead as planned. This yielded a quick resolution: we would have all our events, yes, but this turned out to be a pyrrhic victory. When we arrived, we saw our promotion was undistributed. Our events were not listed in any schedules. People in our events were scheduled for other events at the same time. And, even worse, if that is possible, without exception, our events were exiled to rooms way off the beaten track that could barely even be found. LAC was, in my view, as a result of all this, a complete fiasco and horrible failure, though others who participated were more reserved and those who came from around the world were incredibly generous in not getting angry at us, their hosts.

Had we been torpedoed? Of course we had. As to why it happened, I am not sure. Could it have been incompetence? Perhaps. Could it have been overt sabotage of events that would, had they gone ahead as planned, been far and away the centerpiece of the WSF, establishing a precedent for the future, as well? It could have been, yes. Maybe someday someone at the top of the decision-making process inside the WSF will tell all. I can't do that. I don't know. But I do know it was one more event in a seamless chain that consistently diminishes rather than enhances the likelihood of serious, sustained, accessible, collective discussion of long-term vision and strategy. We were excisable, exilable, and whether it was intentional or just to make room for others is largely beside the point.

The WSF was born from discussions in France and Brazil. The originators took a great idea, made a courageous leap, and inspired effective work. In time, however, they became a leadership in a tighter, more determinative, and less exemplary manner. Oddly, they began, and for a considerable time remained, largely unknown. They also began, and substantially remained, unaccountable to the wide audience. This was likely caused in part by the difficulties of operating on such an unprecedented scale, partly by the structure and philosophies of some of the NGOs and other organizations involved, such as the French group ATTAC, and probably due to more singular factors as well.

After WSF 2, for example, I was enlisted to help with a variety of forum-related projects. More, to facilitate my doing so, I was asked to join the WSF's international council. I missed a spring and a summer meeting, one in Bangkok and the other in Barcelona. How do people globetrot to all these meetings, I wondered. However, I did attend a meeting in Florence, attached to the European Social Forum held there. My experience was that the council to which I had been appointed wasn't at that time a serious seat of power. It wasn't that the people sitting around the table in Florence weren't an impressive group. They were worldly and wise and a good number of them came from movements and constituencies of importance around the world. And it wasn't that the people at the table didn't want a more democratic and participatory approach. This desire was raised repeatedly. It was that after a short time at that meeting, it became obvious that despite the members' stature and desires, the people on the council were not the locus of WSF power. The true powers had some functionaries present, chairing the meeting, and it was clear that the true powers had decided what the agenda was, what would be made known regarding the overall WSF situation to the people in the room, and what the international council would be permitted to discuss. It was equally clear that those present would have only very limited impact.

During breaks in the meeting, I circled around the room asking many of those present, "Who are the real decision makers of the WSF?" "Who is it that allots limited choices to this group, saving important matters for their own eyes?" "Who is it that makes the bigger decisions that never come before this group?" While a few folks could hesitantly name a leader or two based on knowing the history of the WSF, no one I talked to was confident about a whole list of leaders. It was as if I had been dragged onto a central committee in a country that had a still-higher body that dictated key results, and I had asked my fellow central committee members who those higher authorities were—and no one knew.

The real WSF leadership made many key decisions. Will the event have Lula present, and in what capacity? What about Castro, or Chavez? Will there be exclusions, and if so on what grounds? The Zapatistas? Will being in a party, advocating violent tactics, or even just being from some group that the inner circle finds too radical or otherwise dislikes (such as the Disobedienti from Italy, or the international People's Global Action) preclude prominent participation? What content will be part of the core of the events and what content will be left as periphery? What will get the metaphorical broom, like LAC did? Who will have their way paid, and who will not? Will there be a march, and who will be the key speakers? Will there be a collective statement, with what content? What efforts will or won't be made to achieve gender balance, race balance, geographic balance? How will class differences be addressed? How will press be handled, both mainstream and alternative? Will the WSF start to discuss facilitating an international movement of movements, or will it persist only as a forum? Will there be a change, as there has been, since the early days, away from massive panels and forums? What will be the accommodation between advocating reform of capitalism and advocating a new system entirely?

The decision making of the WSFs I was involved with was not transparent, despite the fact that transparency could be easily attained—just post the relevant names and make public the significant decisions. The decision making was not accountable, which would be far harder to attain, but could at least be approached better, even for so complicated an entity. My own limited experience of the WSF made me think it might be better to emphasize local forums as the foundation of the worldwide forum process. Perhaps each new level of forums, from towns, to cities, to countries, to continents, to the world, could be built largely on those below. Perhaps the decision-making leadership of local events could be locally determined. Perhaps the decision-making leadership at each higher level could be chosen, at least in considerable part, by the local forums within the higher entity. Italy's national forum leadership could be chosen by the smaller local forums in Italy. The European forum's leadership could be chosen by forums within Europe, and similarly elsewhere. Perhaps there could be a mandate that the decision-making leadership at every level should be at least 50 percent women. Perhaps the forums from wealthier parts of the world could charge delegates, organizations, and attendees a tax on their fees to help finance the forums in poorer parts of the world and subsidize delegate attendance at the world forum from poorer locales. Maybe the once-a-year international WSF could become a delegate event. Cities and states in Brazil could have a forum and so could Brazil as a whole, as could other countries in South America, and South America as a whole. And likewise for India and South Asia, South Africa and Africa, and so on. And then the World Event could be be representative.

Perhaps, with this approach, the WSF attendance could be 5,000-10,000 people sent from the major regional forums around the world. The WSF leadership could be selected by regional forums. The WSF could be mandated to share and compare and propose based on all that is emerging worldwide—not to listen again to the same famous speakers who everyone hears worldwide all the time anyhow—and perhaps the WSF's results, like those of all other forums, could be published, and of course reported by delegates back to the regions. Maybe, then, the WSF could feature grassroots activists from movements around the world much more prominently in major events and throughout all forums to counter tendencies toward elitism.

My WSF experiences led me to feel that many of the most insightful individuals on the world stage militantly supported bottom-up organizing, open and transparent methods, broad participation, anti-authoritarianism, multitactical approaches, continual innovation, and considerable spontaneity. And many of these same insightful people, seeing the emergence of large-scale phenomena like the WSF, much less an international "movement of movements," feared that these trends would inevitably be top-down, antidemocratic, and bureaucratically boring and stultifying—and thus aggressively rejected the trends. I think they took a reasonable fear too far.

It was a little like advocates of self-management thinking that institutions per se are horrible because they feared that all institutions would inevitably be as hierarchical as those we now suffer. This throws out the baby (institutions) with the bath water (authoritarianism). What is the point of saying that we are for self-management, participation, creativity, and diversity—and then saying that we don't think these virtues can be incorporated in our institutions, beyond, say, the very smallest? The goal of antiauthoritarianism isn't to be tiny, small, or even medium-sized. The goal is to have world-encompassing, participatory, diverse, and self-managing movements. Self-management won't happen if we cede the field of institution building to people who have no interest or confidence in democracy and variety.

Seeking Serious Intellectual Engagement

> *Sometimes I think the surest sign that intelligent life exists elsewhere in the universe is that none of it has tried to contact us.*
> —*Bill Watterson*

Over the years, I have repeatedly tried to enlist and engage leftists and others in debate about the theory/vision/strategy package I advocate, and about other contrasting packages they advocate. My first book, *What Is To Be Undone* began this process. The controversy series at SEP, *Z Papers,* and most recently, the Life After Capitalism project at the WSF, were just three of many attempts to promote such engagements, as have been numerous debates hosted by ZNet.

Maybe this has been a fool's errand, unnecessary or even ill-conceived. Maybe, as some people would maintain, debate itself, and not just sectarianism, is intrinsically destructive. But I doubt it. Yes, we often mutually attack and disparage one another without serious attention to real and relevant views, dividing almost endlessly from one another over minutiae. But despite that orneriness, we rarely seriously assess one another's words to uncover and resolve real, substantive, meaningful differences and to develop widening unity, or even just indicate unity that already exists. Writers and thinkers, even activists, most often remain intellectually and conceptually separate from one another, acting overwhelmingly as disparate atoms, clashing and jangling, but not trying to congeal into a unified and powerful molecular mesh. In my experience, we tend to backbite and differentiate and pose as better and worse, different and distant, slamming and banging at one another—individually and in groups—over relatively little, even as we claim to be seeking solidarity. We rarely carefully reveal our differences, explore their meanings, and seek resolutions—either conflictually due to disagreements, or congenially when agreeing. We rarely even try to connect one idea to another, and we even resist doing so. Intellectual isolation persists amidst claims of collectivity.

This was my impression when I would look over the last forty years of Left writing, speaking, and organizing and find a gargantuan volume of diverse orientations and choices, each of which often disparaged the rest, but almost none of which very seriously engaged the rest in sustained debate. Rather than each side getting its say, trying to sincerely discern the merits and debits of the other side's view, and to respond to suggestions about itself, for round after round, especially with lots of people paying attention, assessing, and then judging and acting based on the results, such debate was obstructed.

In sciences like physics and biology, there is constant dispute. It can be very pugnacious and get personal. Sometimes feuds erupt and opposing camps develop. But however much all that occurs, scientific debate enunciates differences. It correlates claims to evidence and it conjoins proposals with possibilities. The disputants are serious. People, in time, dispense with perspectives that are proven inconsistent or otherwise faulty and adopt perspectives that prove consistent and worthy. In the lifetimes of individuals and in the epochs of whole intellectual communities, commitments change.

On the Left all this occurs much less coherently and consistently, if at all. Go to a Left conference. There may be dozens, or within the WSF, even hundreds of sessions. In my experience, at most a handful will incorporate widely different and contrary perspectives that challenge one another in a way that advances mutual understanding, much less that changes positions, much less that tallies where everyone assessing the engagement stands. I have rarely seen presenters actually attend another session that they aren't themselves presenting at. I almost never see a prominent presenter actually ask a question honestly seeking to learn something, much less after a session saying publicly that he or she agrees with some other person's innovative formulation, or he or she rejects it, to seriously explore the issues. Too often we travel in ideological herds. We stake out conceptual territories. We don't even want to see the borders, much less cross or remove them. Even inside our own mentally comfortable domains, which are tiny compared to the vast world we intend to affect, new ideas often go unaddressed.

My Case Studies

> *It's a poor sort of memory which only works backward.*
> —*Lewis Carroll*

Let me make this complaint personal, with two broad cases from my own experience. First, I have known probably a few hundred prominent highly active people on the Left, many very well, others only peripherally. The number of these writers, speakers, and influential activists who have said anything to me, much less written anything to me, either overtly indicating that they disagree with the theory/vision/strategy package I advocate, or overtly expressing seriously knowledgeable alliance with it, or even acknowledging that it exists, is probably under thirty. I suspect I have had more communications of that sort, however, than almost anyone else I know.

Maybe fifteen people from this large prominent group have taken up the task of critique or advocacy of that conceptual vision/strategic package, to any serious and public degree. In fact, I suspect only a few more, at most, have done that for any conceptual visionary/strategic package at all.

Now, the particular package that I am mostly talking about and that I myself favor isn't highly specialized, which would be a perfectly fine reason for few people to go public about it. And it is not obscure, either, which would be another good reason for people not taking a stand about it. Instead, it is accessible and actually growing in influence and allegiance. In fact, incredibly, I routinely get letters nowadays from notable folks mentioning that they have noticed parecon is making great strides, people are asking them about it, and other exciting developments, but these same folks never say a substantive word about parecon, even in congratulatory messages.

Think, in contrast, about the kinds of exchanges scientists have with other scientists about the ideas they espouse. They take each other's work seriously.

Leftists, I hate to say it, don't. Moreover, the particular package I propose, if it is relevant and worthy, undeniably bears on everyone on the Left, and certainly on everyone who claims he or she wants to replace existing oppressive institutions and particularly on all those who reject capitalism. You might therefore think that virtually all the people of this sort who I know, and then many other people as well who I don't know, would have substantive pros and cons to point out in public debate or public advocacy about the proposed conceptual package. But that isn't even remotely the case.

If this (or any) conceptual package is unworthy and flawed, then demonstrating that fact, if nothing else, would retrieve me (or whoever else was advocating the package) from wasting time on a flawed effort, escorting us back into doing more worthwhile things, and so you might expect that at least some of the folks in that mass of people I know, who care about my productivity, or who care about Left productivity generally, would offer a serious opinion about it.

Consider by way of contrast the time that I and many other people put into critiquing postmodernism to try to prevent others from wasting time in that domain. Similarly, if I, or anyone else on the Left, were to write something that denied the existence of racism or sexism, or that implied that either phenomenon was unimportant, or that did a dozen other things that don't innovate but that instead deny what is taken to be obvious by most leftists, then despite the fact that everyone would know instantly that the utterances were nonsense, unneeded critiques would fly fast and furious.

In other words, it isn't that there is no energy for saying to someone, I disagree with that. That occurs all the time on the Left when someone says anything that other leftists can easily, safely, confidently, and redundantly dismiss without risking being wrong or appearing ignorant—and lots of leftists say "I disagree" each time. What there isn't much energy for, in contrast, is people saying, "Hey, I disagree with that claim or proposal, and since it is far from obvious what the full truth about this is, here is why I disagree; can we try to resolve the matter?" And something else there isn't much energy for is people saying, "Hey, I agree with that proposal, and since it is unusual, here is why; can we begin to share those insights as part of our agreed perspective?"

How come, to put it in another form, when someone utilizes lots of effort and experience to carefully say something new and challenging, which, if true, would be of general interest and implication and which is not immediately obviously discordant, there is largely silence? People don't think about it and say, "Hey, I agree and if no one has a good rebuttal, let's make this part of our broad views." And people don't think about it and say, "Hey, I disagree, here is how I think the claims can be made better." And people don't think about it and say, "Hey, I disagree, here is why the claims have to be completely jettisoned." Instead, lots of people may read these new claims, think about them, and even change their lives based on them, but few will say anything publicly or seriously engage with others in a sustained exchange. What's more, the prospect that anyone will do that tends to be inversely proportional to their prominence and relevant capacity to spur further discussion.

Returning to reactions to the theory/vision/strategy package that I myself happen to advocate, and in particular to the part of it called parecon, there are now people all over the world relating very strongly to it, changing their views due to it, even giving their full time and energy to building or rebuilding institutions based on it, yet there is still very limited serious public debate of it and what efforts are made in that direction are quite often prevented by editors from appearing. That's what I have seen, at any rate. Is it just that it takes time to notice new utterances? That it takes time to get around to commenting on them? That even once noticed and once having an impact, new perspectives aren't seriously debated because people are too busy? Is it just that people don't want to get sucked into debates that will consume time, and so they wait on others to do it? Or that people don't want to express allegiance to views, lest in time the views prove unworthy? All that is reasonable, but it doesn't explain how little Left meeting of minds there is.

Some of what I am saying is missing on the Left does occur among radical faculty, and even in some radical journals, but it is generally so distant from activist life as to be largely irrelevant to social change. What I am asking is, why doesn't serious, careful debate happen more among the people who are trying to change the world? Why isn't it a priority of our periodicals, Web sites, and conferences? Even more, why isn't debate in general, and especially debate about broad concepts, vision, and strategy, a priority of our organizational agendas?

Of course all the impediments mentioned earlier, particularly time constraints, help prevent this, and are, moreover, unobjectionable case to case. Being too busy to do something worthy is not a sin. Nor is having other priorities that preclude doing something worthy. Nor is thinking others are better suited to doing that worthy thing, and so leaving it for them. But do those reasons alone explain the collective dearth of serious debate among leftists about anything other than long-disputed and intransigent views, or new and obviously silly proposals, or perhaps, for a short time, proximate tactics? Do those reasons alone explain why people waste time repeatedly pursuing redundant content, compared to pursuing serious innovations or trying to generate shared agreements?

Here is a second case study. ZNet has a Sustainer Program. Donors are e-mailed a commentary each night for being part of the program. The nightly essays run from about 1,400 to 2,200 words. About seventy writers provide content, some more often than others. These writers are a cross section of often very notable and always quite influential journalists, scholars, activists, and organizers from about twenty countries. I think a case could be made that no periodical of any kind, online or in print, has a more august and wide-reaching lineup of contributing radical writers than this program has. For the Sustainer Program they generate about 360 essays a year. For the broader ZNet site, we put up about 3,000 essays a year.

Numerous times, sometimes by letters to individuals, at least four times by letters to the whole community, I have tried to induce this troop of commentary writers to become mutually engaged, to address one another's work, to interview one another, and to debate one another. I have tried to set up such interactions among them, even in person at the WSF events. I have urged them to do anything that would cause some of them, any of them, to take serious account of the main themes that others of them propose, all in hopes of getting the writers and readers in the program to arrive at a clearer awareness of commonalities and differences in the community and to try to even resolve differences to create new commonalities. My efforts have failed miserably.

To say these people are busy is true, but I think it begs the question. They all write—why not write sometimes about what each other thinks? Why not take others seriously, and in turn get taken seriously oneself? Time can't explain avoiding this, I think. But we have to get beyond whatever the obstacles are.

IPPS

Everything should be made as simple as possible, but not simpler.
—Albert Einstein

And now for some good news. After concluding this book, and sending it to the publisher, a meeting occurred in Woods Hole, Massachusetts, called the Z Sessions on Vision and Strategy. Amazingly, given the exigencies of schedules, travel, etc., thirty five people from ten countries attended. The sessions ran for five full days. Everyone who presented their views also heard all other presentations of views. People asked questions they wanted answers to. People worked through differences and explored continuities. Amazingly, despite being together such a brief time, sufficient community and connection evolved so that people decided to try to constitute a lasting relationship by establishing the International Project for a Participatory Society (IPPS). How IPPS will evolve is a future matter. But IPPS's intention is to elaborate and advocate vision and strategy for a new world. It is not a party or a vanguard or even a preparty or prevanguard. It hopes, instead to prod new shared commitments and perhaps even help lay groundwork for the kind of revolutionary organization needed for eventual victory. If IPPS doesn't help with that, at any rate, something will.

Chapter 33

Our Generations

In retrospect, from a distance the civil rights movement subtly drove me all during high school. In college, the Vietnam War became my near and far horizon. Experiencing kids sniffing glue and adults dispensing lies, all while witnessing capitalist hypocrisy even within me and my own close friends, helped cement my turn toward a new life. My journey mirrored my generation's best inclinations. For widely varying reasons, we didn't only become irate at particular injustices or staunchly advocate particular changes. We threw off one way of being and tried to develop a confrontational alternative. That choice fueled our rejection of not only society's most oppressive policies, but society's defining institutions as well. I dredged up memories in this book not to revel in glory days, but to provide some inspiration and insights that might fuel new change in years ahead.

Message to My Friends and Myself

And you, are you so forgetful of your past, is there no echo in your soul of your poets' songs, your dreamers' dreams, your rebels' calls?
—Emma Goldman

How many of us in my generation, myself included, have to one degree or another returned to metaphorically sniffing glue? How many are protecting past investments or hoping for future returns? How many are no longer seeking a comprehensive alternative? We all do many things that give us short-term rewards that make good sense within the confines of our circumstances. We partake of life this way each year, month, week, hour, and even minute. We live in the here and now; where else can we live? And to survive in the here and now, we make legions of compromises. If I said what I think all the time, they would probably put my head in a guillotine.

We must use their roads to get around. We must fulfill their wage-slave jobs to earn incomes. We must eat food channeled through their combines to survive. We must use their banks, their newspapers, their police. We must enjoy entertainment, play games, and even sing songs sullied by their commercialism. We must take medicine that profits them. We leftists must work among people who live on a different planet from us, who see a different city, who beat a different drum. But we can not only bang out a bearable and even fulfilling existence amid all this, we can keep our eyes and at least part of our behaviors largely on the prize. Are members of my generation settling for lives not so different from ones we earlier rejected? Or are we still being born?

In the sixties, however young, naive, and unlearned we were, when for whatever complicated mix of reasons and due to whatever special circumstances, many of us came around to calling ourselves revolutionaries, we not only opposed the war, racism, poverty, and sexism; we dreamed of a different way of living that would facilitate all people fulfilling themselves in their work and lives. We sought untarnished equality, universal justice, and preponderant dignity. We saw local fights in a big picture. It was not just the local issues we addressed, or our immediate jobs or student status. It was social, societal, political. What happened to that big-picture aspect of my generation?

When we examined the dead-end lives of the poor—however courageously they made the best of it—or the hypocritical advantages of the rich—however crassly they celebrated it—only resistance made sense. We didn't sacrifice to be leftist. We became leftist to get where we wanted to go.

We imagined our future. No fundamental compromises would pass our lips. No lasting surrenders would gain purchase in our hearts. We sought to invent a new way to be. We sought to achieve circumstances that would allow humans to flourish. Regarding these basic choices, I can't see how 2006 is different from 1968. Is there some compelling new argument against being a revolutionary that I've missed? Is there some new evidence that private ownership, markets, bourgeois democracy, racism, patriarchy, global empire, and ecological suicide offer people good lives? Is there some compelling moral or practical argument against seeking institutions that foster diversity, solidarity, self-management, and equity? Is the degradation of living out of garbage cans below a rock-bottom poverty line less now than 38 years ago? Do we want our kids subordinated to bosses and managers? Do we want them to be lifetime wage slaves?

Does having a single-issue orientation, a short-term time horizon, and an exclusively reformist attitude, or even having no political attitude at all suffice now, where we considered it deathlike in 1968? Is it enough now to wear a Che T-shirt and water the lawn while the world slides to hell under a Hummer? Is that all there is? I think a different task than just getting by beckons us. We must

443

develop an uncompromising critique of our whole society, rather than of just this or that isolated aspect of it, or no part at all. We must show the defining roots of society's defining faults. We must evolve a defining vision of a definable future. We must communicate a compelling analysis and vision as widely as they will reach. We must create, with whatever patience proves necessary, alternative fulfilling and effective ways of being. We must live lives that will help more and more people put distractions and sometimes even their own security aside. We must dare to win.

Bringing the Ship In

And the words that are used
For to get the ship confused
Will not be understood as they're spoken.
—Bob Dylan

In May 1970, Richard Nixon announced the invasion of Cambodia. Unrest escalated. On May 4, four students were killed by National Guard at Kent State University. On May 24 two were killed and twelve wounded at Jackson State. Other shootings occurred and campuses exploded. About 2,000 students were arrested in the first half of May. Campuses were deemed to be in a state of emergency in Kentucky, Ohio, Michigan, and South Carolina. At least a third of the nation's nearly 3,000 colleges had strikes. Over 80 percent of all colleges and universities had protests. Approximately four million students, half the country's total, and 350,000 faculty actively participated in strikes. Buildings were shut down. Highways were blocked. Campuses closed. Nixon's Scranton Commission reported that roughly three-quarters of all students supported the strikes. Pollsters reported that within campuses alone over a million people claimed to favor revolution and called themselves revolutionaries. In early 1971, *The New York Times* reported that four out of ten students, about three million people, thought a revolution was needed in the United States. So as far as my generation is concerned, even if we look in on just a few months and ask where have all the people siding with transformation gone, it is a very good question. This is the stickiness problem, in bold relief, for my classmates. This is what we need to solve.

Imagine a nice spring day years off in the future. There is drizzle in the air. Your eyes are sliding shut. Your memories celebrate you aspiring and constructing, sharing and loving, smiling and fighting. You are leaving knowing that the tools and mechanisms of freedom have been built. Movements retain members. They have clarity. They have focus. The path is clear. The distance is reduced. Battles are being won. There will be no turning back. Ships are coming in. Chimes are tolling.

And imagine another fine day. Another generation has aged. A child of yours is in the bed you left behind. New eyes are slipping peacefully closed. Your sons and your daughters are not beyond your command—they are beyond your universe. Their new memories celebrate enjoyments we only dreamed of, celebrate struggles we never contemplated, celebrate achievements beyond our imaginings. They have enjoyed life and life only, finally. Whatever else we do, shouldn't we contribute to this trajectory of change?

The kids who sniffed glue in Somerville thirty-five years ago on the logic that some calm in the present warranted risking their future health, which was dubious anyhow, are probably, today, war-killed or shell-shocked, vitamin-hungry, or boss-buried in bills. Maybe one or two of them are guiltily trying to be humane even as they impose all those hardships on others. Maybe one or two of them are revolutionaries, somewhere. And what about all my movement friends, with their knowledge and their advantages? And what about all their movement friends with more knowledge and more advantages? We are all butterflies walking. We may wear gold shoes. We may wear no shoes at all. In either case, it doesn't have to be this way. As in 1965, so too now. We can escape the institutions that clip our wings. We can bring the ship in. That's how it seems to me, at any rate, looking forward to tomorrow.

Index

446